FOURTH EDITION

EDITED BY
JAMES F. CASEY
Editor (retired)
Fire Engineering Magazine

a publication of Technical Publishing,
a company of the Dun & Bradstreet Corporation New York

Other Related Fire Service Books

Reprinted 1985
Fourth Edition Copyright, 1978
Technical Publishing Company
Third Edition Copyright, 1967
The Reuben H. Donnelley Corporation
Second Edition Copyright, 1960
The Reuben H. Donnelley Corporation
First Edition Copyright, 1932
Case-Shepperd-Mann Publishing Corporation
Library of Congress Catalog Card No. 78-59985
Printed in the United States of America
ISBN 0-912212-04-7

DEDICATED TO

The chiefs and training officers of every fire department and to those who aspire to such rank.

PREFACE TO THE FOURTH EDITION

We found it most interesting, in researching this fourth edition of The Fire Chief's Handbook, that the first edition was actually the brain child of the Educational Committee of the International Association of Fire Chiefs. The committee felt (in 1929) that there was an urgent need for a textbook that would cover the broad field of fire protection—and in all its ramifications.

In 1930, upon recommendation of the IAFC president, Chief Ralph J. Scott of Los Angeles City, Fred Shepperd, editor of Fire Engineering, was commissioned to write this textbook with the advice and consent of the Educational Committee. It was Shepperd who, quite logically, titled his text, The Fire Chief's Handbook.

In his preface to the first edition, Shepperd noted that it would be practically impossible to include within the covers of one book all the information relating to the subject of fire protection. And as a consequence, he selected those topics that he felt had the highest priority in the fund of knowledge needed by a chief or a training officer—or any fire fighter who aspired to such rank. Shepperd further noted that a portion of the material (in the text) might have seemed too elementary for the experienced officer. He stressed, however, that "elementary instruction is the foundation of the study of fire protection in general."

The field of fire protection has, of course, steadily increased in sophistication since the first edition of this book appeared. And each succeeding edition, including the present, has reflected this sophistication. It seems hard to believe in this age of telemetry that the first edition had very little on the subject of communications. But, nevertheless, much of the information contained in the first edition is still valid today—notably on fire fighting theory and practice—46 years after it was written.

In putting together this fourth edition, we, like Fred Shepperd, selected those topics that we felt had the highest priority "in the fund of knowledge needed by a fire chief or training officer."

The book is organized into 22 chapters, each of which can stand alone but is interrelated with every other chapter in the field called fire service management. As with all other editions, much of the material, including eight new chapters, has been adapted from the pages of Fire Engineering.

Two chapters, Management Principles and The Chemistry and Physics of Combustion, stand exactly as they were in the last edition. The first, which was written by Dr. Joseph Leese, State University of New York, covers what a fire chief should know as a manager and it is still one of the best pieces ever written for the fire service on the subject. The second, written by Dr. Richard L. Tuve of the United States Naval Research Laboratory (now retired), was written specifically with the fire fighter in mind and in layman's language that still carries the depth needed for a fire fighter's understanding of the physical and chemical laws relating to fire.

Fire Apparatus Pumps, written by the late Hugh Walker, also stands, but somewhat shortened. Credit is also acknowledged to Mr. Walker for material used in Chapter 6 that was taken from his many articles in Fire Engineering on apparatus maintenance.

The chapter, Standpipes and Sprinklers, which was written by Thomas Ryan, battalion chief (ret.), New York Fire Department, remains intact. Driver Training, which he originally wrote, has been reorganized and added to. Two of his other chapters in the third edition—Hydrant Operations and Relay Operations—have been incorporated into Chapter 7, Water Supply.

That part of Chapter 17, Advanced Fire Fighting, which covers the extinguishing of natural gas fires and the hazards of liquefied petroleum gas, was written respectively by J. F. Barkley, U. S. Bureau of Mines, and G. F. Prussing, and carried over from the third edition. All other chapters in this edition were either written or rewritten and reorganized by the editor. Heavy stress has been placed on the basics of fire fighting and the everyday fires which account for about 95 percent of all fires.

We are grateful to the American Insurance Association for material drawn from their Special Interest Bulletins which was used in the chapter on Fire Prevention. And to the Insurance Services Office for the information and charts used in Chapter 1 and the various quotes throughout the book taken from the Grading Schedule.

Beyond the above acknowledgements, it would be impractical in these pages to list all the Fire Engineering titles and authors of the material that was researched and adapted, but a few names stand out:

The venerable Roi B. Woolley, former editor Fire Engineering, whose articles on salvage were rewritten and incorporated in the chapter, Ladder Company Operations.

Richard L. Nailen, our Midwest correspondent, for his articles on communications and the emergency medical service.

William J. Clark, author of Fire Fighting Principles and Practices, for material carried over from the third edition and used in Ladder Company Operations, under ventilation.

Then, there is Richard P. Sylvia, associate editor of Fire Engineering. Dick's material, which is read and absorbed as no other fire service author's, was used freely throughout this edition. Particularly noteworthy are those sections of Chapter 6 that treat with apparatus specifications and testing and the section of Chapter 16 which covers the one-room fire.

Finally, there is Dorothy P. Ferguson, managing editor of Fire Engineering, who handled all phases of the production of this fourth edition of The Fire Chief's Handbook, starting with the first manuscript page—a tremendous undertaking.

James F. Casey

New York, N. Y.
April 1978

CONTENTS

THE
FIRE CHIEF'S
HANDBOOK

Introduction

In recent years much has been written about the "mission" of a fire department as if it was something new. But the first fire ordinances were written back in 1647 by the good Dutch burghers of Nieuw Amsterdam under the leadership of Governor Peter Stuyvesant who knew a mission when he saw one. At that time construction was performed on a do-it-yourself basis without regard for zoning. Houses were built with thatched roofs and had wooden (plastered over) chimneys that succumbed to the flames with alarming frequency.

The first ordinance established what was in effect a building department, a three-man group called "the Surveyors of Buildings," who were also the forerunners of today's fire prevention bureaus. The surveyors regulated the erection of new houses within or around the City of Nieuw Amsterdam. Citizens were obliged "to see to the sweeping of their (existing) chimneys," and wooden chimneys and thatched roofs were forbidden for new construction. Four fire wardens were appointed to enforce the ordinance by personal inspections of each house in town.

Failure to sweep one's chimney was considered to be a serious offense, and "as often as any shall be discovered to be foul, they shall condemn them, and the owners shall immediately, without any gainsaying, pay the fine of three guilders for each chimney thus condemned—to be appropriated to the maintenance of fire ladders, hooks and buckets." Further, and in sharp contrast to today's attitude, "in case the houses of any person shall be burned, or be on fire, *either through his own negligence or his own fire,* he shall be mulcted in the penalty of twenty-five guilders, to be appropriated as aforesaid."

Another ordinance passed a few years later took note of the fact that "in all well regulated cities it is customary that fire buckets, ladders and hooks are in readiness at the corners of the streets and in public houses, for time of need, which is the more necessary in this city on account of the small number of stone houses and the many wooden houses here."

Accordingly, the city fathers passed a tax levying "one beaver or eight guilders" on every house for the purchase of 250 leather fire buckets, and also "to have made some fire ladders and fire hooks." And to maintain this equipment, "they may yearly demand for every chimney one guilder." The Dutch burghers, however, did not stop here. They decided that they were going to limit, if not abolish, the hazards of the unfriendly fire and they were not going to turn back.

The first fire company

In addition to the foregoing measures for the common safety in case of fire, a "rattle-watch" of eight men was established. The duties "appertaining to this watch" were imposed upon each of the citizens in turn. Soon, however, most of the citizens were relieved of this duty by the establishment in 1658 of the first fire company. This organization that consisted of eight men was equipped with the buckets, ladders and hooks mentioned above. Each of its members was expected to walk the streets from nine o'clock at night until morning drumbeat, watching for fire while the town slumbered. Despite the fact that they were immediately and disrespectfully dubbed the "Prowlers," this volunteer company soon increased to 50 members. In case of fire, all the citizens who could be aroused from bed assisted in knocking down the flames.

It would appear, then, that early on in the history of our country the citizens were aware of a fire problem, and within the limitations of their times, had the know-how and incentive to do something about it—a mission, if you want to call it that, or an objective to reduce fire losses. That objective hadn't changed much in 312 years when, in 1970, Carl A. Weers of the American Insurance Association agreed with the good burghers to the effect that "the objectives (of a fire department) are to prevent and extinguish fires for the purpose of saving life and property, and that this be done to the satisfaction of those served—meaning at a reasonable cost to the public."[1]

---

[1]*Special Interest Bulletin No. 320,* American Insurance Association, New York, N.Y., January 1970.

It is interesting to note that not all the taxpayers of Nieuw Amsterdam thought that "one beaver or eight guilders" for fire buckets was a reasonable cost—a difference of opinion that still echoes in legislative halls more than three centuries later.

A more sophisticated objective for fire protection can be found in a National Fire Protection Association publication: "Control of the community complex of combustibles should be undertaken by the fire department in furtherance of its fundamental purpose of protecting life and property from fire. The department program should be aimed at keeping the complex of combustibles with which man surrounds himself within reasonable limits."[2]

Please note that the Dutch burghermasters were already aware of the concept of limiting combustibles back in 1658 when they abolished thatched roofs and wooden chimneys. And that the fire prevention recommendations of the 1970s call for the elimination of combustible furnishings in today's high-rise.

Acceptable level of fire

Finally, Harry E. Hickey states that "the perceived mission of public fire safety is to maintain an acceptable destructive fire frequency level and severity level prescribed by the citizens in the area being considered."[3] And there's the rub—acceptable—and the reason that fire protection varies all over the lot.

So, over 350 years ago people in this country recognized the need for an organized group that was set up to protect man from his ancient enemy, fire. And this group eventually evolved into today's fire department, whose basic responsibility is still the same—to protect life and property from fire.

According to the Grading Schedule,[4] "it is necessary that the department have competent leadership; that an adequate number of engine and ladder companies be established and properly located; that these companies be well-manned and suitably equipped; and that members be properly trained so they are able to perform their duties effectively. An inadequacy in one or more of these elements adversely affects efficiency and the department's capability in fire suppression."

A fire department can be a multicompany organization such as the

---

[2]*Organization for Fire Service, Standard 4,* National Fire Protection Association, Boston, Mass., 1971.

[3]Hickey, Harry E., *Public Fire Safety Organization—A Systems Approach,* National Fire Protection Association, Boston, Mass., 1973.

[4]*Grading Schedule for Municipal Fire Protection,* Insurance Services Office, New York, N.Y., 1974.

Chicago Fire Department, but it can also be a one-company unit in a rural area. However, "in order to be recognized for grading purposes"—and in effect to be recognized as a fire department—a department must meet the following minimum requirements:

1. Organization. The department shall be organized on a sound, permanent basis under applicable state and/or local laws. The organization shall include one person (usually with the title of chief) responsible for the operation of the department.

2. Membership. The department shall have an active membership which provides a response of at least four members to alarms.

3. Training. Training shall be conducted for all active members.

4. Apparatus. Response to any alarm of fire shall be with at least one piece of apparatus suitably designed and equipped for fire service. Provisions shall be made for the housing and maintenance of apparatus.

5. Alarm Notification. Means shall be provided for 24-hour receipt of alarms and immediate notification of members.

Any department which cannot meet these minimum requirements shall not be graded, and a deficiency of 1950 points shall be assigned under the schedule.

6. Administration. The department shall be administered by qualified and progressive leadership with adequate authority. Complete rules and regulations, kept up to date and distributed to each member, shall govern administration and operations. Discipline shall be properly maintained.

All appointments and promotions shall be made under requirements which will assure the selection of the best qualified persons. These requirements include medical, oral, and competitive written examinations. Suitable physical standards for appointment, and consideration of seniority, record, and experience for promotions shall be prescribed. Personnel shall be removed from their positions only for cause.

Chief responsible for all operations

The chief, then, is the man responsible for all operations of a fire department, big or small. As such, he is in charge of fire suppression, fire prevention (including code enforcement, inspections, public education), communications, maintenance (of apparatus), training, administration (personnel, finance, accounting, budgeting, purchasing), planning, and investigation—of arson and possibly of internal affairs.

In a one-company department the operations fall upon one man. But as a fire department increases in size because of population and area served, these operations are broken down into separate units such as the fire prevention bureau or division of training with the authority to operate them vested in a senior officer. The chief, however, still carries the burden of responsibility.

And it is to this burden that all the editions of the Fire Chief's Handbook, including the one you have in your hand, have been directed. In general, this Fire Chief's Handbook represents an attempt to cover all aspects of a fire chief's job. Specifically, the chapters follow the suggested requirements of the Grading Schedule for Municipal Fire Departments published by the Insurance Services Office. We must remember, however, that the schedule only spells out *what* is needed, and somewhat cryptically, since it is only 47 pages long. In effect, the schedule provides only an outline of a fire department—the bones so to speak. In the following chapters, we have applied, within space limitations, as much of the muscle and flesh as possible.

ROCKVILLE
FIRE DEPARTMENT

CHAPTER ONE

Grading a fire department

Whenever two or more fire chiefs get together, talk eventually turns to the Grading Schedule and the relative class of municipality that each of their towns has been assigned as a result of a survey based on the schedule and conducted by Insurance Services Office engineers. What the grading does is to classify municipalities according to their fire defenses and physical conditions. The classification that a city carries, however, is only one of several elements used in the development of insurance rates.

This schedule was first published by the National Board of Fire Underwriters in 1916 under the title, "Standard Schedule for Grading Cities and Towns of the United States With Reference to Their Fire Defenses and Physical Conditions." Subsequent editions were published in 1922, 1930, 1942 and 1956, with amendments in 1963 and 1964. The current edition titled simply the "Grading Schedule for Municipal Fire Protection" is published by the Insurance Services Office which has absorbed the grading functions of the American Insurance Association and most state fire rating bureaus.

It is interesting to note that, during the development of the current (1974) edition of the Municipal Grading Schedule, some excellent input was received from such organizations, for example, as the International City Management Association, the National League of Cities, International Association of Fire Chiefs, American Water Works Association and from individual municipal officials.

With this in mind, it is interesting to note a paragraph incorporated into the introduction to the 1974 Grading Schedule which states that "the schedule is not intended to serve as a primary planning guide for local fire protection." The schedule also notes that recommendations made "in connection with insurance classifications can be helpful when they are reviewed in combination with more specific studies of local needs by consultants, staff or local task forces in arriving at fire protection decisions based upon an analysis of local priorities and financial capabilities."

In effect, the Grading Schedule is a reflection of standards that have been developed over many years from a study of "pertinent conditions and performance records." The standards are set forth in the schedule, and the various features of fire defense in a municipality are compared with them. The number of the deficiency points depends upon the importance of the item and the degree of deviation. A municipality's ability to control hazards through laws, codes and their enforcement is graded in the same manner. Additional deficiency points may be assigned because of climate conditions such as bitter cold winters or hot, dry summers that are part of the "pertinent conditions and performance records."

Major items considered

The major items considered in the Grading Schedule are water supply, fire department, fire service communications, fire safety control and additional deficiencies.

Additional deficiencies deal mostly with adverse climatic conditions and the divergence between water supply and the fire department. In the latter, additional deficiency points may be assigned to a city with a top-rated fire department because the water supply is less than can meet the ability of the department to use it—and vice versa.

The surveys are made with the permission and cooperation of municipal officials. One or more field representatives, formerly known as "engineers," survey the water supply, the fire department and its fire alarm system, and obtain data relative to fire prevention and structural conditions.

Municipal fire protection surveys begin in the office of the administrative head of the municipal government. The ISO field reps assigned to the survey meet with the city manager or mayor, as the case may be, to discuss the survey and to make arrangements for working with the municipal departments concerned.

In conducting the field survey, the field reps use records, tests and actual field observations as much as possible. Whenever necessary, this

Elements of a water system are carefully analyzed by study of plans, a review of operations, maintenance records and observation of equipment.

data is supplemented by information obtained in discussing various phases of protection with the city official concerned. The plans of the various elements of the water supply, including dams, reservoirs, pumping stations, purification plants, power supplies and the distribution system are carefully studied and the records of their operation and maintenance are reviewed. The supply works are visited and their operation and maintenance observed. Fire flow tests are made at selected locations on the distribution system and a representative number of valves is inspected.

In the fire department, records of personnel, apparatus, hose appliances, manning of companies, training, and other features of operation are studied. The inspecting team witnesses pumper tests to check on the apparatus condition and competency of the operators. Training sessions at the drill grounds are observed. Each station is visited to check its suitability, including the equipment housed and the manning provided. From a study of the department rules, records of disciplinary action, and observations made during the many contacts with the officers and men during the survey, an evaluation is made of the department administration.

The field reps study the fire alarm system, including headquarters

Grading Schedule Deficiency Points and Subjects

Subject	Points	Percent
Water Supply	1950	39
Fire Department	1950	39
Fire Service Communications	450	9
Fire Safety Control	650	13
	5000	100

Relative Class of Municipality

Deficiency Points	Relative Class
0- 500	First
501-1000	Second
1001-1500	Third
1501-2000	Fourth
2001-2500	Fifth
2501-3000	Sixth
3001-3500	Seventh
3501-4000	Eighth
4001-4500	Ninth #
Over-4500	Tenth *

A ninth class municipality (a) has 4001 to 4500 deficiency points, or (b) has less than 4001 deficiency points but no recognized water supply.

* A tenth class municipality (a) has more than 4500 deficiency points, or (b) has no recognized water supply and has a fire department grading over 1755 deficiency points, or (c) has a water supply but no fire department, or (d) has no fire protection.

equipment, circuits, boxes and receiving devices at fire stations. They carefully check the method of receiving, handling and transmitting alarms. Circuits are tested for grounds and crosses, and a representative number of boxes are operated. In addition to these tests, the field reps evaluate the maintenance of the system on the basis of records of operations and routine tests on file.

The fire prevention code is compared with the applicable standards of the National Fire Protection Association (National Fire Codes) to determine if it contains adequate provisions for the control of fire hazards. To evaluate the enforcement of the code, studies are made of the organization and personnel of the fire prevention bureau, the frequency of inspections, the correction of violations, and the records maintained. In addition, a field representative visits a representative number of plants, mercantile establishments, theaters, and other places in which hazards may exist to observe the actual control being exercised. The building code and building jobs are similarly surveyed with respect to the control being exercised over construction. The National Building

Code, recommended by the American Insurance Association, is used as a standard.

Structural conditions in the principal business district are analyzed, from the standpoint of fire spread, and the conflagration hazard is evaluated, taking into account the effectiveness of the fire department and the water supply available. Similar studies are made in other districts where businesses, industries, shopping centers, apartments and tenements are located.

The field survey closes with a visit to the office of the municipal executive, when a brief oral report is made of the engineers' findings. This report, of course, is tentative.

Upon returning to their home office, the field engineers prepare the report and grading, using the data collected in the field. A group of supervisory engineers in the main office reviews the reports and gradings. This assures uniformity in the reports and in the application of the grading schedule.

A formal report and a grading sheet that shows the classification and total number of deficiency points as well as the points assigned to the water department, the fire department, the fire alarm system, fire prevention program, the building department, structural conditions and climatic conditions (potential for hurricanes, tornadoes, floods and other disasters) are given to the chief municipal officer. The grading sheet is similar to the chart on page 10 and carries basically the same information. The report also indicates to the municipal officer the potential rate-level effect that it will have on his city or town. If the city manager or mayor desires additional information concerning the grading, it can be obtained upon request.

The grading team has frequently been advised at the start of a survey that numerous "improvements" have been made. Such improvements may include an increase in water pumping and purification facilities, considerable extension of the water distribution system, an increase in the number of hydrants. Frequently there are more firemen, several new fire stations housing newly formed companies and new apparatus. Added features might also include more fire alarm boxes and an expanded fire alarm headquarters.

Improvements analyzed

The team soon finds out, however, that the city has annexed a number of areas and that the population has increased considerably. Not only because of the additional territory now included within the city, but also because of development and growth within the former city limits.

Further study reveals that improvements at the water plant have been made to cope with increased water consumption and that the distribution system extension and the new hydrants have been chiefly to supply the newly developed and annexed areas. The engineer may also find that the fire stations, companies and equipment, as well as the new fire alarm facilities, are for these areas. And that although some new firemen have been hired for new companies, the bulk of the increase in fire department membership was due to decreased working hours.

What, then, has been the effect of these improvements which have cost the taxpayers many thousands, and in some cases, several millions of dollars? Not much. The grading of such a city usually shows little, if any, improvement because the various improvements actually are the additions needed to maintain the level of protection enjoyed prior to the annexations and the development of areas. Actually, a city that is able to do this should be commended since it can be accomplished only by a continuous program of municipal planning. Unless such a program is adopted and carried out, a retrogression in protection and grading could occur.

One illustration of what can be done along these lines occurred in a southern city. When the possibility of a large annexation was under consideration, the city officials requested the advice of the rating organization on the additional fire stations that would be needed to properly protect the area to be annexed. Two new stations were recommended and the planning was so well coordinated that at 12:01 a.m. on the day that the area was officially annexed, the two new stations, fully manned and equipped, were placed in service. In other cities, engineers found that the protection in newly annexed areas was often substandard for many months, and in some cases several years, before proper steps were taken to build, equip, and man more fire stations and to provide adequate water supply facilities.

Thruways affect response

Another factor that is frequently called to the attention of the ISO at the start of a survey is the recent construction of a thruway, freeway or limited-access highway of some type. Many city officials believe that such highways improve conditions from a fire protection standpoint because they generally reduce traffic congestion on the city streets, provide good firebreaks, and may have necessitated the demolition of older and poorly constructed buildings. Although these benefits may be quite evident, there are other factors that must be considered in an evaluation of the overall effect on fire protection.

Consider first the effect on fire department response. There is no doubt that improved traffic conditions on the streets of the downtown

Aerial composite of town or county under study is used to check location of units and distance and time involved for adequate alarm response.

area will in general enable fire apparatus to move more easily along the principal streets. It is frequently found, however, that limited-access highways divide communities into two or more sections and provide means of travel between such sections at relatively few locations by bridges or underpasses. Such arrangements can have a considerable effect on the response distances for apparatus.

City planners often make the mistake of determining the response area that a fire station can serve by drawing a circle with a radius equal to the ¾-mile, 1½-mile, or other response distance required. This is not correct because apparatus must respond along streets. In the ISO analysis of fire department response for grading purposes and for rendering advice to city officials, required response distances are actually measured along streets by the shortest possible route, in all directions on an appropriate map. The various points established in this way are joined by a line which will then embrace the response area. In making plots of this type, the response effects of thruways, railroads, parks, rivers, bluffs and other physical features can be readily seen. In recent years, engineers have worked with many cities on these problems with the result that the plans adopted to meet the local situation were on a sound engineering basis.

When a thruway is installed through a city, a great deal of attention is given to the effect that it will have on the general appearance of the areas through which it passes. Although much thought is given to what is being done on the surface, too little thought is given to what effect the thruway may have below the surface. But the subsurface structure that is of most importance to fire fighting is the water distribution system. It is not often realized this system represents about two-thirds of the value of the average municipal water supply.

Water mains crossing embankments

In constructing thruways, the number of water mains crossing through the embankment is kept to a minimum. Very often the mains permitted in the embankment are limited to a few of large size at only a few locations. The routes of thruways are usually determined by factors other than a minimum of interference with the water distribution. As a result, it is not unusual for dead ends to be created at points where the thruway embankment intersects a street. Not only are dead ends formed, but the arterial system or the gridiron of distributors may be broken up in such a way as to lose at least a part of the mutual support which is such an important factor in arterial or gridiron strength. In survey and grading work, a study of the water distribution system is an important feature and adverse effects such as a weakened arterial system, the creation of dead ends, the breakup of the gridiron and any resulting decrease in fire flow test results are given due consideration.

When buildings are torn down for a thruway dividing a business district or separating it from a dangerous exposure, the conflagration hazard is reduced. However, redevelopment projects in and around business districts are usually more effective in reducing the conflagration hazard than thruways. There has also been a trend to remove old buildings in business districts and use the ground for parking lots. Although these changes generally have reduced the possibility of sweeping fires over large portions of business districts, there still remains the possibility of severe fires in single buildings which can extend to group or block fires. It is also true that many large-loss fires in recent years have been in individual buildings or plants.

To effectively fight the possible individual group and block fires, the fire fighting facilities certainly must be equal to those provided before the thruway or redevelopment program began. Generally speaking, redevelopment or thruways has not changed principal business districts to the extent that reductions in fire department response or required water supply can be made.

Another trend still ongoing that is creating fire protection problems in many cities is decentralization. Huge shopping centers are being erected in outlying areas within the old city limits or in newly annexed areas. These centers generally include mercantile occupancies using large, undivided areas. These areas are excessive from a fire protection standpoint and present an extremely difficult fire fighting problem. Very often these centers, particularly if in newly annexed areas, are beyond a reasonable response distance from the nearest fire station. Also, the locations are usually at the extremities of the water supply system where mains are small and hydrants are poorly spaced. A number of large shopping centers have been found to be protected by only a single hydrant. And there are cases where new buildings had automatic sprinklers which proved ineffective because of poor water supplies.

Industry in outlying areas

The trend of decentralization is also apparent in the industrial field. Many plants are locating in outlying areas, where they create the same general type of fire protection problem as shopping centers. High-value areas of both these types are considered in all municipal surveys, and recommendations are made to correct the deficiencies in water supply and fire department response.

In their municipal grading and survey work the field representatives find it most gratifying to make a survey of a city and be able to report considerable improvement in protection with a resulting decrease in the number of deficiency points. However, it must be remembered that it is the function of the Insurance Services Office to evaluate a city's defenses for rate-making purposes only. The field representatives will, however, make recommendations for improving a city's grading, but only if they are asked. In both cases the field representatives render a service to the city in giving it a fire protection evaluation not available elsewhere.

In considering gradings, it should be remembered that the Grading Schedule for Municipal Fire Protection classifies municipalities on a relative basis. This means that a Class 3 city is better than a Class 4 but poorer than a Class 2. The schedule determines relative position only.

The Grading Schedule is periodically revised but any revisions that are made must be of such a nature that the relative classification of a city will not be changed solely as a result of revision. This makes the task difficult because the engineers wish to consider not only all significant changes that are taking place in municipal growth and development patterns, but also those that are taking place in the field of fire protection.

In each past revision of the schedule an attempt was made to recognize modern developments and practices in municipal fire protection. Such recognition can be given, however, only to those developments and practices which are firmly established. As a result of this policy, each edition of the schedule was more effective than the preceding one. Reviews are being constantly made so that the schedule in any future edition will continue to be the best available means of evaluating municipal fire protection.

The water supply accounts for 1950 possible deficiency points out of a total of 5000. It is therefore imperative that the fire department, in the person of the fire chief, take an interest in the water supply problems of its community. Citizens are adverse to spending money, whether through bond issues, by direct taxation or by increasing the water rate. Improvements, however, always involve the expenditure of money, and if the fire department can come out strongly for them because they are needed for fire protection, there will be a greater chance for the money to be appropriated.

Water supply from the standpoint of providing municipal protection is divided into two main sections, adequacy and reliability.

Adequate water supply

The question of adequacy is one which did not receive nearly enough attention in the past. Full appreciation of fire service needs is still not as evident as it should be.

Some years ago, a good fire stream was defined as one of 250 gpm discharge. The basis of this was the experience with hose lines in the mills of New England, where normal pressure on the systems ranged from 60 to 100 pounds and streams were taken directly from hydrants. For inside lines to be handled by one or two men, this stream size is about correct. Actually, in light occupancies, present practice is to use more and smaller streams such as 1½-inch hose wyed from 2½-inch feeders.

A good 1¼-inch stream, such as would be used as an outside line when a large building is involved, runs from 310 gpm at a 45-psi nozzle pressure, which gives a horizontal reach of about 66 feet as a solid stream, to 350 gpm when the nozzle pressure is 60 pounds and the reach is about 75 feet. Fire departments are capable of pumping full capacity continuously and at a good pressure. Therefore it is not unreasonable for the fire department to expect the water system to be able to supply these larger systems.

The value and use of streams too strong to be handled manually is recognized by the Grading Schedule under the heading "Master and

Special Stream Appliances." "Turrets, large spray nozzles, distributing nozzles, foam equipment and siameses shall be provided," the schedule states. In addition, each aerial truck or elevating platform truck shall be provided with elevated stream devices. And where aerial ladders or elevating platforms are not provided, "elevated stream service needed to handle fires in large area buildings shall be provided by special apparatus."

During World War II, the English found in their almost daily contending with conflagrations caused by bombing that ladder pipes were one of the most effective means of preventing the spread of fire from one building to another. These various devices for powerful streams add further to the demands on adequacy. They provide more ready means for the use of the full capacity of fire department pumpers. Through the use of a 3-inch hose and of siamesed lines of 2½-inch hose, 1½-inch and larger nozzles can be used effectively. These give discharges ranging from 500 to over 1000 gpm.

Even where there is not great congestion of buildings, it appears reasonable to expect at least two fixed powerful streams to be used on a fire threatening to spread to other buildings. Pre-fire planning is most helpful in estimating the number of 250-gpm hand lines and the master streams needed for a specific hazard.

Rate of flow

The Grading Schedule has set up requirements for the adequacy of a municipal water system. In a simple statement the schedule defines the required flow as "the rate of flow needed for fire fighting purposes to confine a major fire to the buildings within a block or other group complex. The determination of this flow depends upon the size, construction, occupancy and exposure of buildings within and surrounding the block or group complex; consideration may be given to automatic sprinkler protection."

In order to be recognized for grading purposes, a water supply shall be capable of delivering at least 250 gpm for a period of two hours, or 500 gpm for one hour, for fire protection plus consumption at the maximum daily rate.

The required flow is a calculated value made by a field representative. In his survey the representative gives consideration to the type construction, occupancy, use, and any building congestion for the block or area under consideration. And, understandably, the required flow will vary between downtown and other business sections and the well-kept residential areas in the suburbs.

Key to the field-reps calculated value of what the fire flow for any

REQUIRED DURATION FOR FIRE FLOW

Required Fire Flow gpm	Required Duration Hours
10,000 and greater	10
9,500	9
9,000	9
8,500	8
8,000	8
7,500	7
7,000	7
6,500	6
6,000	6
5,500	5
5,000	5
4,500	4
4,000	4
3,500	3
3,000	3
2,500 and less	2

particular municipality and its specific block and group complex is the "Guide for Determination of Required Fire Flow," published by the Insurance Services Office, Municipal Survey Service. The guide was prepared, according to its introduction, especially for use by "the municipal survey and grading personnel of ISO and other fire insurance rating organizations." It is available to municipal officials, consulting engineers and others interested. ISO cautions, however, that this publication is a 'guide' and "requires knowledge and experience in fire protection engineering for its effective application."

In essence, the guide calls for a determination of the type construction, the ground floor area and the height in stories of the buildings within the block or complex under consideration. Armed with this data, the survey engineer then goes to tables in the guide to determine the "required fire flow to the nearest 250 gpm." There are four separate tables that cover fire-resistive construction, noncombustible construction, ordinary construction and wood frame construction.

Analysis of water supply system is part of grading team's responsibility. Here, engineer prepares to make flow test to determine main capacity.

Other factors taken into consideration are the occupancy—low-hazard or high-hazard—and exposures. The degree of the hazards or exposures can raise (or lower) the required flow.

Lines limited to flow

It is of importance for every fire department to know the ultimate capacity of the water system. Water is most effective when it is thrown on the actual burning material, and to do this a stream must be of good volume and discharged with sufficient velocity to give it a good reach. Fires have been known to get away where a limited supply of water was wasted through the use of too many streams, none of which was effective, rather than a smaller number properly located and used. For example, where a water system can supply a total of 2000 gpm, not more than eight 2½-inch lines should be used. And probably more effective use would be obtained with six lines using 1¼-inch nozzles than the larger number with smaller tips. But certainly these six would be better than 10 or 15 streams with 1¼-inch tips when the discharge from each is 200 gpm or less at a reduced reach.

Adequacy is not just a question of the total supply of water which will be delivered to the district under consideration, but also whether there are enough hydrants to permit the water to be put on the fire without

STANDARD HYDRANT DISTRIBUTION

Fire Flow Required, gpm	Average Area per Hydrant, square feet
1,000 or less	160,000
1,500	150,000
2,000	140,000
2,500	130,000
3,000	120,000
3,500	110,000
4,000	100,000
4,500	95,000
5,000	90,000
5,500	85,000
6,000	80,000
6,500	75,000
7,000	70,000
7,500	65,000
8,000	60,000
8,500	57,500
9,000	55,000
10,000	50,000
11,000	45,000
12,000	40,000

excessively long hose lines. Hydrant spacing in the current Grading Schedule is based on the required fire flow. For a flow of 1000 gpm or less, there should be one hydrant for each 160,000 square feet. As the flow increases, the area per hydrant decreases until at 12,000 gpm, one hydrant is required for each 40,000 square feet (see table).

It is not uncommon in the normal growth of a city for the character of a section to change materially. Often sections that were formerly occupied by well-spaced, single-family dwellings not requiring large quantities of water for domestic or fire service will become closely built with multistoried apartment houses. The result will be lowered pressures and an inadequate fire flow, and generally there will be a deficiency in hydrants.

Other residential areas may change rapidly to heavy industrial districts. Under these conditions, the water needs of these areas will be greatly increased. Many manufacturing plants, because of the size of their buildings and the nature of the contents, require quantities of water in excess of that for the business district. Fire flow requirements of 8000 to 10,000 gpm are not unreasonable if these manufacturing plants are grouped. The need for an adequate number of hydrants is of vital importance in such areas.

Sprinkler demand

In connection with the general study of the adequacy of water supply in any part of a city, the question of pressure may be a vital one. The installation of automatic sprinklers in stores and factories is becoming very common. It is now recognized that the supply to these sprinklers can be taken from the municipal water mains without providing for a secondary supply. On this basis, it is essential that normal pressure be such as to give 15 pounds on the top line of sprinklers when 250 or 500 gallons are flowing, depending upon whether the plant is of light or ordinary hazard. For extra-hazard occupancy a special study must be made to assure adequate supply. If these requirements indicate that pressures of 50 to 75 pounds are desirable, wide hourly fluctuations in pressure should not be allowed. Where a water system is weak and it is obvious there will be a material reduction of pressure during a fire, such that automatic sprinkler supply from the city mains will be inadequate, it will then become necessary for the fire department to pump into the sprinkler system. In fact, it should be standard procedure for the first or second-arriving pumper to be connected to the sprinkler system siamese.

Survey engineers in the past have found fire flow tests to be of great value in determining the adequacy of fire supply in various parts of a water system. These tests can be run by the water or fire department. In some cities, the water department has undertaken a definite plan of running tests in areas thought to be weak and of laying mains to bring the protection up to that considered desirable. Other departments run flow tests to determine whether there will be a good supply for plants equipped with automatic sprinklers.

To have a proper working knowledge of a water system, a fire chief should know the streets with large mains. In fact, he should have a good general knowledge of the entire distribution system. Many cities have their distribution system divided into pressure zones, or high and low services. In such systems it is usually possible to materially increase supply to the lower zone service by opening the valve which separates the two. Knowledge of the location of such closed valves is well worthwhile, but the operation of such valves should be performed by the water department employees.

Reliability of water supply is of vital importance in connection with fire fighting. Great improvement has been made in water works practices in the past generation. But equipment, such as pumps, still have to be overhauled and repaired, and water mains break under certain conditions. Instances are on record of serious interruptions of water supply at times when the fire department was fighting a fire. In addition, it must be remembered that any interruption of supply introduces a probability that even a small fire may not be controlled. And it may become a conflagration as was the case when the earthquake put the San Francisco water supply out of commission.

The reliability factors start with questions as to whether anything can happen to the source of the water supply and extend throughout the system to the actual hydrant in use. This problem is of most interest to the water department. The fire chief should, however, know of any condition that might reduce the quantity of water which is normally available. He should also know whether there is any action the fire department might take to provide some degree of protection during any interruption of water supply.

Broken mains a source of trouble

It is not possible in any one chapter to outline all the adverse conditions which may arise in a water system. However, some of the more important failures which have taken place might well be mentioned to give fire departments some idea of what may happen. This will permit study to be made of the local water system and if shutdowns should occur, just what action should be taken.

The majority of pumping stations are operated by electricity. Experience has indicated that the electrical companies have not in all cases provided the reliability needed for total dependence. As an example, take the blackout which hit the Northeast in 1965.

Broken mains are probably the most common source of trouble. These often leave extensive areas without water and result in a material reduction of pressure and available volume. In some cases the break may be in the single main which supplies the city, or the break may flood the pumping station or may undermine adjoining water mains. The location of pipelines, with respect to side hills, rivers, railroads and like features, have to be considered in studying the probability of interruption of supply. Many pumping stations are not fireproof and others are badly exposed.

Elevated storage, either in reservoirs or in tanks, is of material value in offsetting many of the features of unreliability which may exist in a water system. This storage also provides for greater economy of operation of the supply works.

Companies required

According to the Grading Schedule, "the number of engine and ladder companies shall be sufficient to provide reasonable protection to the municipality." The number is fixed in a table titled "Engine and Ladder Companies Needed Within Travel Distance of Required Fire Flow." Looking at the table, we find that a 12,000-gpm fire flow requires more companies that travel less distance than required by a 6000-gpm flow. In effect, the less flow required, the less the hazard or size of anticipated fire and, consequently, the fewer number of companies needed.

Number of Engine and Ladder Companies Needed within Travel Distance of Required Fire Flow

Fire Flow	First Due				First Alarm				Maximum Multiple Alarm			
	Eng.		Lad.		Eng.		Lad.		Eng.		Lad.	
gpm	No.	Mi.	No.	Mi.	No.	Mi.	No.	Mi.	No.	Mi.	No.	Mi.
less than 2,000	1	1½+	*1	2++	**2	4	*1	2++	**2	4	*1	2++
2,000	1	1½+	*1	2++	2	2½	*1	2++	2	2½	*1	2++
2,500	1	1½	*1	2	2	2½	*1	2	2	2½	*1	2
3,000	1	1½	*1	2	2	2½	*1	2	3	3	*1	2
3,500	1	1½	*1	2	2	2½	*1	2	3	3	*1	2
4,000	1	1½	1	2	2	2½	1	2	4	3½	1	2
4,500	1	1½	1	2	2	2½	1	2	4	3½	1	2
5,000	1	1	1	1½	2	2	1	1½	5	3½	2	2½
5,500	1	1	1	1½	2	2	1	1½	5	3½	2	2½
6,000	1	1	1	1½	2	2	1	1½	6	4	2	2½
6,500	1	1	1	1½	2	2	1	1½	6	4	2	2½
7,000	1	1	1	1½	2	1½	1	1½	7	4	3	3½
7,500	1	1	1	1½	2	1½	1	1½	8	4½	3	3½
8,000	1	1	1	1½	2	1½	1	1½	9	4½	3	3½
8,500	1	1	1	1½	2	1½	1	1½	9	4½	3	3½
9,000	1	¾	1	1	3	1½	2	2	10	4½	4	4
10,000	1	¾	1	1	3	1½	2	2	12	5	5	4½
11,000	1	¾	1	1	3	1½	2	2	14	5	6	5
12,000	1	¾	1	1	3	1½	2	2	15	5	7	5

* Where there are less than 5 buildings of a height corresponding to 3 or more stories, a ladder company may not be needed to provide ladder service.

** Same as first due where only one engine company is required in the municipality.

\+ May be increased to 2 miles for residential districts of 1- and 2-family dwellings, and to 4 miles where such dwellings have an average separation of 100 feet or more.

\++ May be increased to 3 miles for residential districts of 1- and 2-family dwellings, and to 4 miles where such dwellings have an average separation of 100 feet or more.

This table, then, determines the recommended total number of companies required by a municipality. However, structural conditions and hazardous occupancies peculiar to a municipality may call for more companies than are determined by the table since their presence indicates a greater possibility of multiple alarms. Distances, in the table, may also be reduced because of traffic congestion, topographical features, railroad or highway structures or other local conditions that hinder response. There are other considerations given to the required number of companies—protection furnished to areas outside the corporate limits—but they are too numerous to fit in this small chapter and we suggest that each fire chief acquire his own copy of the "Grading Schedule for Municipal Fire Protection."

Apparatus

The apparatus tools and appliances used by the required companies shall meet the criteria contained in the National Fire Protection Association Standard No. 1901, "Automotive Fire Apparatus." And to maintain the required number of companies "there shall be in reserve at least one pumper for every eight pumpers or major fraction thereof required to be in service, but not less than one." Reserve ladder trucks are also called for—one truck for every five, or major portion thereof, required to be in service, but not less than one. The reserve units should be fully equipped, properly distributed and manned by specifically designated off-shift or volunteer members.

Manpower

There are few, if any fire departments, today that can meet the recommended manpower requirements of the Grading Schedule, which calls for six members to be on duty for each of the required engine and ladder companies. But this is still ISO's standard that applies to paid departments. In the call or volunteer departments, three call or volunteer members, "on the basis of the average number responding to alarms," may be considered the equivalent of one full-paid member on duty. Off-shift members of a paid department who respond voluntarily on first alarms may be credited on the same basis as call and volunteer men.

In paid departments where off-duty members are required by regulations to respond to fires, three such members may be considered the equivalent of one on-duty member.

Other factors that enter into the manpower and company requirements include the consideration of automatic aid and outside aid. Both of these "aids" are usually referred to as mutual aid in the fire service. In general, both types of aid, under the schedule, permit some credits for pumpers and ladder trucks that respond from outside the municipality under consideration. Automatic aid specifies that all departments in a mutual aid plan should "operate essentially as one department." The basic difference between automatic aid and outside aid is one of distance. Pumpers responding on automatic aid should be within 5 miles travel distance of the municipality to which they are responding. For outside aid the distance is 15 miles. But any credit for the latter applies only after automatic aid credit has been applied.

Fire service communications

Under the Grading Schedule, fire service communications accounts for 450 deficiency points and represents 9 percent of the total 5000 assigned under the four subjects covered in the table. The schedule does not restrict communications to any particular type (radio, telephone, telegraph) but it does state that the facilities provided "should have the prime requisites of accessibility to the general public, the ability to transmit alarms promptly, and reliably."

The facilities include boxes on the street for use by the public in reporting alarms and the means for the fire department to transmit alarms to fire stations and other locations. A fire department should also have telephone facilities to receive alarms from commercial phones and to carry on its business.

The evaluation of a department's communications system depends upon the degree of compliance with provisions of the National Fire Protection Association Standard No. 73, "Public Fire Service Communications." This should also be in every fire chief's files.

There are other suggested requirements under fire service communications in the schedule, such as the communications center—its equipment and current supply—radio, telephone, fire alarm operators and other items. These items run to about four pages, all amplifying and explaining the basic requirements listed above.

Fire safety control

The Grading Schedule expects that "a reasonable degree of safety to life and protection of property from fire can be provided by state and municipal control of hazards." Such control, of course, can only be attained by adequate laws and ordinances "to properly regulate the manufacture, storage, transportation and use of hazardous liquids, gases and other materials." Building construction, and electrical heating and ventilation installations should also be controlled by laws and ordinances, according to the schedule.

Since there should be laws and ordinances, it follows that there should be enforcement agencies "staffed by sufficient qualified personnel." Within a municipality these agencies, fire department and building department, say, should "cooperate with each other, with utility companies, and with other interested parties." Understandably, lack of enforcement of codes and ordinances is considered the equivalent of not having any. The schedule calls for codes and ordinances to be evaluated by comparing them with applicable standards of the National Fire Protection Association (National Fire Codes).

Fire prevention, which is a subhead under fire safety control, calls for inspections to be made by persons having knowledge of special hazards (noted in the codes). These may be supplemented by inspections of ordinary hazards by fire company members. Inspections are called for as frequently as necessary for enforcement of regulations. But inspections of extra-hazardous occupancies should be made at least four times a year and proper records of all fire prevention activities should be kept.

Fire prevention activities in buildings include inspection of exit facilities, automatic and other alarm systems and fire extinguishing apparatus. Dwellings, of course, are included in any inspection program (on a voluntary basis). Finally, the schedule calls for a continuous education of the public.

Editor's note: Following are the three major organizations with fire protection interests:

American Insurance Association, 85 John Street, New York, N. Y. 10038.

This is a trade association servicing a large number of companies operating in the casualty and insurance fields. The association makes its services available, where appropriate, to non-insurance interests such as government agencies. A service of particular interest to the fire service is the series of bulletins titled "Special Interest Bulletins" that are published by the association's Engineering and Safety Service.

Insurance Services Office, 160 Water Street, New York, N. Y. 10038.

Insurance Services Office (ISO) is a national organization established by the property and liability insurance industry to provide a full range of insurance services, with maximum flexibility and economy, to insurers and other persons and organizations vitally affected by rapid economic and social change.

ISO was formed January 1, 1971, through the consolidation of several organizations: the Fire Insurance Research and Actuarial Association, the Inland Marine Insurance Bureau, the Insurance Rating Board, the

Multi-Line Insurance Bureau and the National Insurance Actuarial and Statistical Association.

ISO is licensed in 52 states and territories and has assumed in those jurisdictions all of the operations of its predecessor organizations. It is licensed as a fire rating organization in most of the jurisdictions and operates as an advisory organization to state fire organizations in the other jurisdictions. Evaluating the fire defenses of every major city in the United States and all smaller municipalities and fire districts in the 42 states in which it is licensed as a fire rating organization is a function of ISO. This vital insurance industry service which dates back to 1889, was transferred to ISO October 1, 1971. Earlier, it had been performed for major cities by the American Insurance Association and its predecessor, the National Board of Fire Underwriters, and for small communities and fire districts by state and regional fire rating bureaus.

The service originally was created as a result of a concern by member companies of the National Board of Fire Underwriters over the frequent conflagrations in cities. Studies demonstrated that conditions conducive to such conflagrations were recognizable and correctable.

A series of major fires in 1904, including the great Baltimore conflagration, gave impetus to the program and led to the development of municipal fire protection standards which were later incorporated into a grading schedule to evaluate fire defenses and physical conditions. The schedule has been revised and improved through the years.

National Fire Protection Association, 470 Atlantic Avenue, Boston, Mass. 02210.

The National Fire Protection Association is a scientific and educational membership organization concerned with the causes, prevention and control of destructive fire. The association's activities may be summarized as follows: (1) fire safety technical standards development, (2) information exchange, (3) technical advisory services, (4) public education, (5) fire safety research, and (6) services to public protection agencies.

U.S. GYPSUM
MAYFAIR
CITY OF MIAMI
FIRE DEPT

CHAPTER TWO

Charting the organization

As mentioned in the introduction, a fire department to be recognized as such shall be organized on a sound permanent basis under applicable state and/or local laws. One person, usually with the title of chief, shall be responsible for the operation of the department. The method of selection of this chief in today's fire service varies widely but in the paid departments he is usually appointed by the mayor or city manager or comes up through the ranks via civil service examinations. In the volunteer fire departments the chief is almost always elected by the membership.

According to the Grading Schedule, then, there is a chief officer in charge of the department, and for a department with more than two companies there should also be an assistant chief or other competent officer (above company rank) who shall be in charge in the absence of the chief. Where there are more than eight companies there shall be, in addition to the chief and assistant chief, sufficient battalion or district chiefs to provide one (on duty in a fire station) at all times for each eight companies or major fraction thereof. And for 12 or less companies, an assistant chief may serve as a battalion chief.

Companies—engine, hose or ladder—should have one officer on duty at all times. For grading purposes, two call officers or two active volunteer officers may be considered equivalent to one fully paid officer up to one half the number of paid officers required.

It should be remembered, however, that in the volunteer service there is no guarantee that an officer will be able to respond to every alarm. Consequently, there should be more officers in each rank of a volunteer department than in a paid department. This is to assure that there will be proper leadership on the fireground at all times.

The above paragraphs actually represent the organization of a fire department in its basic form. But a typical fire department, even a small one, will have many more elements in its organization chart than have been shown so far. There will be someone in charge of, and with at least a few others, looking after maintenance, communications, buildings and other units that make up today's fire departments.

Bureau of fire

The bureau or division of fire is the major element in any fire department and one around which all others revolve. In a small department and naturally in a volunteer one this bureau is the direct responsibility of the fire chief. In larger departments it can be headed by a deputy or assistant chief—one for each platoon. "His responsibilities shall be to see to the operations and capabilities of the line fire fighting force. He shall insure that sufficient resources are available to adequately fight fires that might occur. He shall approve all fire fighting procedures and tactics and shall himself be the officer in charge at fires at which his presence is required. He shall see to the proper support of the bureau by other bureaus and shall himself insure proper communications to other bureaus to assist them in their functions."[1]

There are, of course, grave responsibilities but responsibilities that are shared, somewhat scaled down, by the division, battalion and company commanders who form the balance of this line organization. They are also shared no less by the chief of a volunteer fire department who may have to wear many hats himself.

The fire chief

"The fire chief is the leader of the fire department. His leadership duties include long-range planning, proper allotment of duties to subordinates, delineation of clear lines of authority, inspiration of officers and men and coordination of work within the department and with other departments."[2]

In the larger fire departments the fire chief usually reports to a fire commissioner or director who has the final say in all administration and

---

[1]Fargo, Nicholas C., *"A Plan for the Implementation of a Hudson County Metropolitan Fire Department."*

[2]*"Municipal Fire Administration,"* International City Managers' Association.

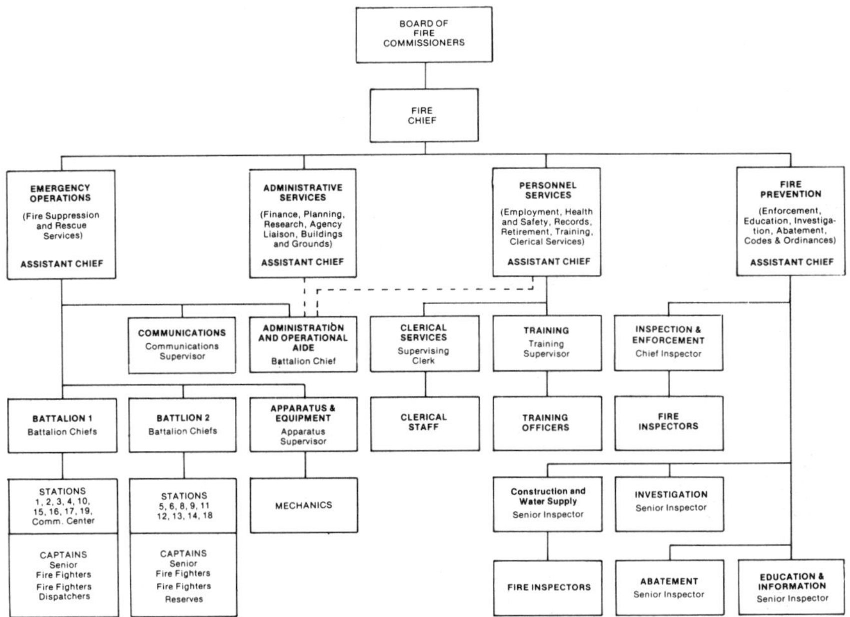

Highly structured organization chart of the Contra Costa County, Calif., Fire Department has four major groupings with an assistant chief in charge of each.

operations matters. However, in the majority of paid fire departments there are only several companies who are under the command of a fire chief who reports only to the city manager or mayor. In these departments, headquarters staff consists of the chief and possibly one or two others. But no matter how small the department the chief will have to take care of all the functions listed in the organization charts shown for the various sized departments. No one chart is the best for every department. The best is probably the one a chief designs himself with the assistance of his senior officers plus some input from the fire fighters.

We can see, then, that depending on its size, a fire department can consist of divisions or commands in charge of a deputy chief, battalions in charge of a battalion chief and companies in command of a captain—or in his absence a lieutenant plus a complement of fire fighters. Each rank reports to and is responsible to the rank immediately above. A division may consist of two or more battalions, a battalion of several companies and a company of six men including a captain or lieutenant. Note, however, that within their capacity, all units have the same responsi-

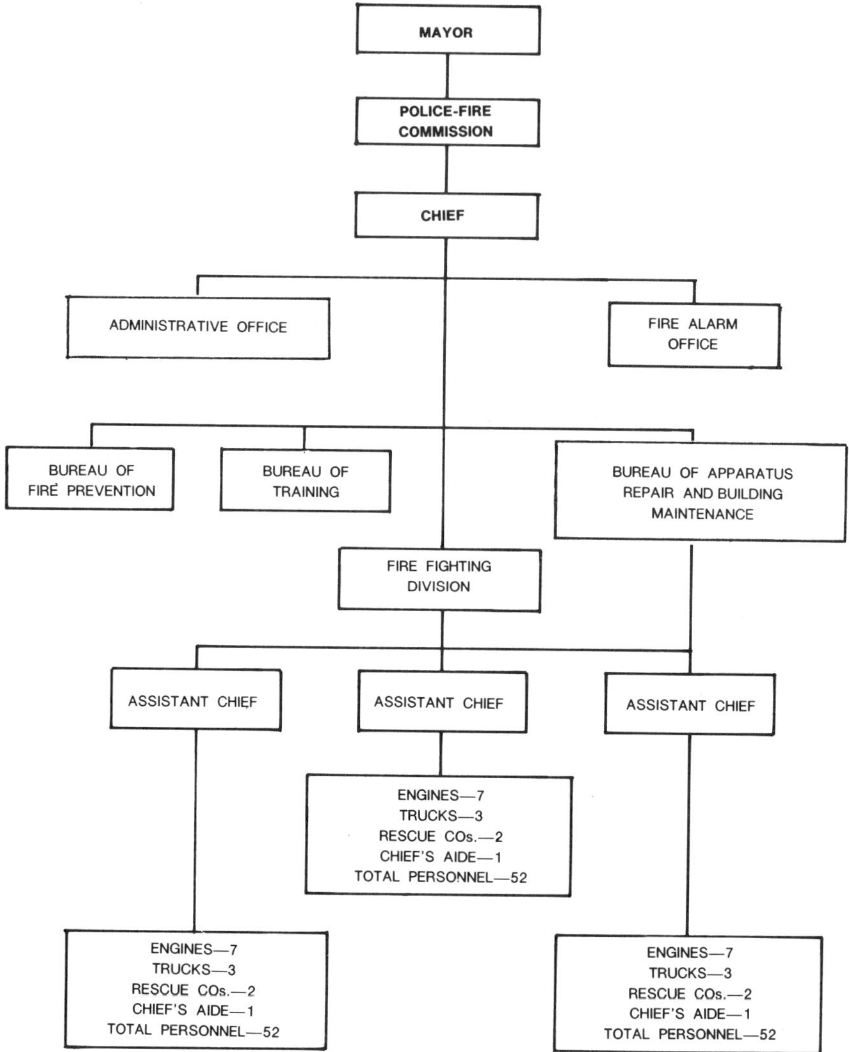

Organization chart of the Racine, Wis., Fire Department is typical of smaller paid department.

bilities quoted above for the chief in charge of the bureau of fire—and ultimately the chief of department.

A company officer, for instance, arriving first at a raging lumber yard fire "shall insure that sufficient resources are available to adequately fight fires . . ." by immediately calling for help. A battalion chief responding to his call, and until relieved by a superior officer, "shall approve (direct) all fire fighting procedures and tactics and shall himself be the officer in charge at fires . . . ."

Bureau of fire prevention

Next in importance to the bureau of fire in any department is the bureau of fire prevention. This bureau is, of course, set up to enforce the laws and ordinances—state and municipal—that have been set up "to provide a reasonable degree of safety to life and protection of property from fire," according to the Grading Schedule. It is also charged with fire safety education.

The schedule states that the "enforcement agencies shall be staffed by sufficient qualified personnel." "Sufficient," therefore, will vary from department to department depending on a department's size and the area and population to be covered. But if there are laws, someone must enforce them—particularly those relating to flammable or compressed gases and flammable or combustible liquids as spelled out in the Grading Schedule.

The schedule also includes special hazards such as repair garages, explosives and hazardous chemicals among others. And finally those miscellaneous hazards that can be found in any town which run a gamut from bonfires to rubbish and trash accumulations. For enforcement purposes, inspections for the most hazardous materials or occupancies should be made by fire inspectors having special knowledge and experience. Ordinary hazards can be handled by fire company members, usually on apparatus field inspection.

Inspections should be made as frequently as necessary, according to the schedule. But in general, "this will require inspections of the more hazardous occupancies at least four times a year."

A fire prevention bureau will of necessity keep records of all its activities which involve inspections, permits, violations and many others. (The activities associated with fire prevention and fire prevention education will be covered in a later chapter.)

Bureau of fire communications

Another highly important unit of any fire department is its fire alarm headquarters or bureau of fire communications. In a large department this unit is generally housed in its own building. In a smaller department, the center is frequently a section within a fire station. Out in a rural area the center may consist of a single telephone in a farm house usually manned by the farmer's wife. But no matter how big or small, a communications center must be manned on a 24-hour basis and shall be responsible for the reception, clearance and dispatch of all fire ap-

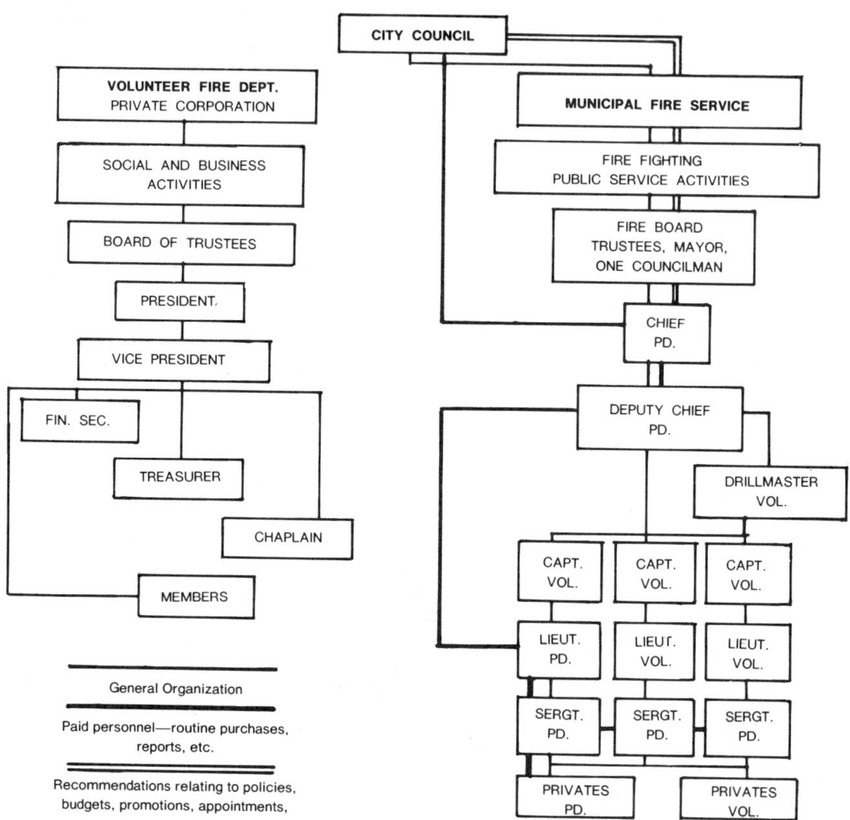

Organization chart for a paid and volunteer department. Note that volunteer members still function under a private corporation.

paratus when a call for assistance is made. In the larger departments the alarm center "shall receive all alarms either by alarm box, 911 telephone or by any other means and according to an established running assignment schedule, order proper combination of apparatus to combat the anticipated fire threat."

Once an alarm has been received, it will be the duty of the dispatchers to monitor any developing situation and be prepared to issue supplementary directions by alerting other units of the circumstances surrounding an alarm. These directions could involve a call for a greater alarm, special units or emergency medical services.

Small departments and particularly volunteer departments cannot afford the luxury of such communications services for a simple first alarm. But every small fire department must be part of a mutual aid group to handle the large fire. And such a group must have a communications center to handle the number of companies involved in a mutual aid call. The center can exist on paper and only be put in effect on an emergency basis. Or it can be a unit, permanently manned and under the command of a regional director or county coordinator. However, in either case, this center will for a time have to operate in the same manner as a big city communications center—dispatching units, moving up covering units, calling for special units, etc. (Communications will be more fully covered in a later chapter.)

Fire department shops

Fire chiefs usually think of maintenance in terms of the care and attention given to apparatus and equipment. But a fire department consists of one or more buildings subject to the same maintenance needs of any other building. Somewhere in an organizational chart this latter need must be taken care of. In many departments the "shops" service the apparatus and the buildings, with one superintendent in charge with as many skilled men as necessary—auto mechanics, plumbers, carpenters among others. A small department might have a committee to handle all functions, with many of them farmed out as necessary to local tradesmen on a contract basis. This could include major repairs to an apparatus, or possibly the installation of a motor-driven apparatus door opener.

Training division

Manpower and equipment are, of course, meaningless unless they are tied together by training. A bureau of training is therefore one of the most important elements in a department.

"Therefore it is the responsibility of the fire chief to develop, maintain and support an effective training program so that all members, whether paid or volunteer, will be able to perform their jobs with the skill and efficiency demanded by modern fire problems," according to the American Insurance Association[3]. The association also calls for adequate training facilities (see chapter 4) with a training center that should be designed "to meet the needs of the fire departments which will use the facilities."

A bureau of training is responsible for the planning and organizing of a department's training program. The overall responsibility for the

[3]*"Special Interest Bulletin No. 234, Fire Department Training,"* American Insurance Association, Engineering and Safety Service.

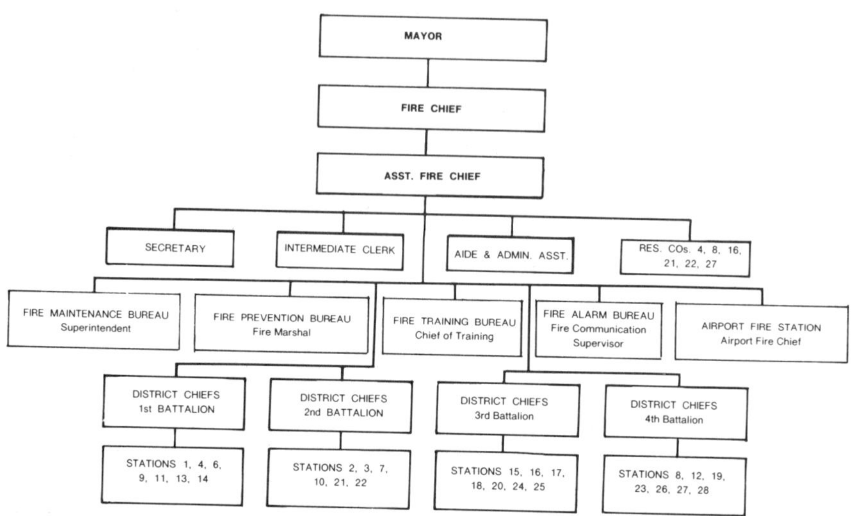

City of Birmingham, Ala., has five major groups under command of an assistant chief who reports to the chief of department.

program rests with the chief. But the actual job is usually performed by a training officer—a key man in every fire department—and a number of instructors that will vary with the size and type of classes.

Every department, large or small, paid or volunteer, has to concern itself with administrative services that fall under the broad headings of personnel, finance, accounting and budget. Purchases must be made and paid for, accounts kept, budgets prepared, and people paid.

Personnel records are necessary for a variety of causes that include insurance, fringe benefits, pensions, among others.

Finally, in our fire department organizational chart there must be someone doing the planning—in a bureau of planning if the department is big enough or in a chief's office if he wears many hats. Someone will have to look down the road and say when new apparatus will have to be purchased, and lay out a plan for getting the money for it, particularly in the vast volunteer service. This same somebody might have to look at a new development on the edge of town and say when and where a new fire station will have to be built. On a smaller scale the planner might have to think of replacements for station furniture or even cups and saucers.

On a much larger scale, and sooner or later, every fire department will have to get in involved in master planning for fire prevention and control. This concept of planning is being fostered and encouraged by the National Fire Prevention and Control Administration, at the state, community and rural levels. It had its roots in the final report, "America Burning," of the National Commission on Fire Prevention and Control. Recommendation no. 10 of that report states:

"The Commission recommends that every local fire jurisdiction prepare a master plan designed to meet the community's present and future needs in fire protection, to serve as a basis for program budgeting and to identify and implement the optimum cost-benefit solutions in fire protection."

PREPARING THE BUDGET

Money to operate a fire department comes from two major sources, taxes and fund raising, from the people who are receiving the fire protection. Other sources would include federal revenue sharing for cities and rural areas.

But no matter what the source, the monies received by a fire department have to be allocated to a formal budget that covers a definite period of time, usually one year. This budget spells out how much is to be spent and for what. It is divided into two parts: the operating budget which includes salaries, maintenance, heat, light, etc., and the capital budget which usually covers high-priced items such as a compressor that is nonrecurring and of enduring value. Often it includes money set aside for future purchases (generally apparatus) which might be five or more years away. Sometimes it includes money for amortization on mortgage or notes. But, a fire department budget whether large or small and no matter what the source of funds should contain at least the following items:

Fire station maintenance: Electricity, telephone, fuel oil, repairs, janitor and insurance (fire and liability).

Fire reporting service: Rental or cost of alerting system whether radio, telephone or telegraph.

Miscellaneous and contingencies

Maintenance of apparatus: Tires, gas, oil, batteries; repairs and improvements; insurance on apparatus (fire, damage, liability).

New equipment: Includes either cost of apparatus, or any equipment carried on apparatus.

Fire fighting supplies: Foam, extinguisher charges, etc.

Radio: Repairs, parts, new units.

Amortization and interest: Mortgage on fire station, notes for apparatus bought on time.

Life insurance: On lives of members; disability and hospitalization also come under this line.

Salaries: Alarm and telephone operators, paid or call men, drivers, etc.

Clothing: Fire, uniforms.

Reserve fund: Money laid aside for future purchases.

This typical budget is a combined operating and capital budget but with variations it is the type used by small departments.

Larger fire departments, of course, have a more complex and sophisticated budget and in such great detail that it would be impractical to cover it in this space. But basically, all budgets are the same and the only difference between a fully paid and a volunteer department is one of salaries. Even at that, many volunteer departments have some paid members—dispatchers, drivers, call men. And then there are such labor costs as life, medical and compensation insurance that are common to both types of service.

A budget begins as a requested budget and one that is almost invariably prepared by the chief of a department with the aid of his senior officers and, in a volunteer department, with the finance committee. This fire department budget is a plan painstakingly prepared in anticipation of what the department will need (in resources) to operate for a definite *future* period of time.

The plan requires that considerable thought and effort be taken well in advance of the date it is to be submitted to the village fathers or city council. And a good part of this planning is derived from an analysis of past budgets. These can show a history of successes or failures and provide a basis for the projection into the future—which is exactly what a budget is designed for.

The budgetary control, which follows the adoption of the budget, compares what is happening to what should be happening. It should be done on a regular and frequent basis during the time span of the budget.

Justifying the budget

When a chief has finished his proposed budget, his job is not necessarily over. He might, and frequently does, have to stand before the city council and justify it, possibly item by item. Recurring items in the annual operating budget generally present no problem and even capital expenditures in this budget may not be questioned.

But for that aerial ladder, that could cost $70 to $90 thousand dollars over a five-year period, a chief must be prepared to have a strong foundation of need—backed up with solid facts and figures. Then there is that new fire station which might cost $250,000 spread out over 10 years. Justification for such an expenditure really calls for a fire chief to do his homework.

Chief suggests funding

As mentioned above, there are two major sources for fire department operating funds: local taxes and fund raising—with fund raising far in the lead for the more than 10,000 fire departments that serve a population of 1000 or less.

A fire chief doesn't have too much to say about where the tax funds shall come from, but he can at least make suggestions. In a large city the chief really has no problem. But in smaller cities and villages, particularly those served by volunteers, he must get involved. For these smaller communities, revenue sharing, pay-as-you-go, leasing, setting up reserve funds and borrowing have all been used, as has straight-out fund raising by the small volunteer department that has no tax resources whatsoever. No matter how the money is to be raised, however, a chief should be able to talk intelligently on the subject and suggest ways and means to acquire the necessary funds.

CHIEF

CHAPTER THREE

Management principles

It is not difficult to convince a community that attention should be given to certain technical aspects of fire extinguishment. It is much more difficult, however, to convince a municipality that increased knowledge and skill in management have now become necessary to insure the most efficient use of resources invested in protecting life and property against fire.

The reason for part of this dilemma is that, until fairly recently, fire protection in most of our communities had been a relatively simple and catch-as-catch-can affair. Few made it a career and, although appalled by the effect when fire raged, few saw the need for a well-organized and responsible agency for its control. Now society is beginning to demand a qualified force obligated to run efficiently.

At the same time, efficient function is becoming more difficult to bring about. The size of fire departments alone has increased the complexity of organization. Chief officers are progressively being separated more and more from the actual fire fighting operation. They are required to relate to men through others and through written communications. Subordinates at the same time have identified more clearly what they want from organizational life—how they want to be fitted in and how they want to be treated. They seek higher pay, fringe benefits, and better working conditions. And they enjoy the support of strong unions.

As higher public expectancy develops and population and community expansion takes place, fire departments are forced to grow, redeploy and adjust to new demands. Esprit de corps needs to be generated in recruits and leadership qualities among those with years in a department must be discovered and employed. The strains that arise from bigness and a hierarchy of levels of operation and command must be understood and eased.

Like any other substantial enterprise, the large fire department needs expert management. The small unit, volunteer or paid, needs it too. Without clear direction, any organization will flounder, spending its energies heedlessly in duplicated efforts, nonproductive conflict and round-about routes to objectives. A fire fighting force can be modeled after a successful unit in the next community and it can even be supplied and equipped with the most modern equipment. But it will flounder, want morale and fail to deliver if it lacks unity, training and the ability to evaluate and improve itself. The goal of good government is on the one hand to avoid the above problems and on the other to develop and employ an agency (men and resources) so effectively that the defined task is done well and at proper cost. At the same time, the doers get rewards and satisfactions from work that maintains and increases their willingness to work.

The function of management then is the creation of a unified, balanced, refined tool which, when applied in the right way, will accomplish the objective desired without undue strain. What managers must do to fashion such a tool has been given greater attention during this century in which we have become essentially a managerial society. With a large part of society's needs turned over to managers, we have been concerned with what managers should do and how they should do it.

There is, despite this concern, no precisely agreed upon set of tasks which a manager should do. Generally, reference is made to planning, organizing, coordinating, directing, delegating, supervising, regulating, obtaining resources, leading and the like. These terms or jobs can be subsumed one under the other, e.g., directing, delegating, and regulating under coordinating; or they can be easily expanded to specify in more detail what is done to regulate, e.g., set standards, communicate, obtain reports, analyze situations, provide suggestions, etc. At a conference, when asked what managing a fire department involved for them, several chiefs said it included:

Getting equipment,
Rating subordinates,
Getting men to drill,
Promoting to officerships,

Pacifying the commissioners,
Writing a rule book,
Recruiting personnel,
Reducing bickering,
Setting up inspection,
Preparing a budget,
Working with union stewardship,
Laying out a district, and many others.

It is easily seen that these tasks can be categorized in a number of ways—under planning, or organizing, and so on. One way of looking at them is to see them in terms of in what direction the effort is moving toward whom.

Directions and roles

Fire chiefs as general managers and often their subordinates, have to work in three directions. First, and most frequently, they do something internally to the organization (people, regulations, internal relationship, patterns for getting work done). Next, they often work with others and negotiate for the good of the organization or in pursuit of its task. And, finally, they report to and work for others transmitting ideas, information and requests in behalf of smooth function, better service, less expense, more happiness, or what you will.

It is obvious that these relationships involve much more than command and giving orders. The chief must know how and when to report, to petition and solicit, to use the resources of others, to suggest, to bargain and compromise, to contend and to give in. All the skills of diplomacy, the qualities of keen perception, experience in decision-making, and patience, as well as courage, are needed to keep the organization poised, ready and on its target. The attributes required of the manager are numerous and the tasks are demanding and complex. His roles are varied: from boss to equal, to subordinate, if not supplicant.

There are those inclined to think that if the department is well organized along military lines, it will run itself. Nothing could be more unrealistic. The management of any organization depends upon the manager, his insight into his tasks and his skill to function in many roles. Good structure, clear specification, and good resources will do much to assure organizational effectiveness, but time and circumstance do not stand still. Constant adjustment is needed to handle new conditions with appropriate action. An organization needs a helmsman or team characterized by brains, flexibility, desire to learn, comprehensive understanding, tact, dedication, energy, stamina and selflessness. With less, an organization will flounder, for there is so much to be done.

PLANNING THE ORGANIZATION

Few fire chiefs are confronted with the responsibility of creating a department. The result of this is that chief officers, more often than not, are concerned with applying, adapting and improving a system already in operation. They observe, consider, and then plan and carry out what can be done. In newly formed districts, the common approach is to adopt appropriate common structures and procedures of other fire districts.

A plan is a series of steps set up in advance for getting a job done, whether it be stating a policy or motivating men. A plan for one activity may differ in specifics from that for another, but planning is essentially a general managerial activity that abounds everywhere, at the lowest level and at the top.

Planning is often done on the spot, but most fire chiefs know it is better to have advance ideas on how to handle a situation. Standard approaches to certain types of fires, predetermined routes, and second-alarm equipment relocations are examples of simple plans established for a nearly automatic implementation.

Such plans have been developed because experience demonstrated the advisability and need for routines, or because forecasts and estimates indicated the existence of conditions requiring a series of steps to avert contingencies. At no time, however, can one rest assured that all the plans have been made or that the existing plans are the best. Most likely than not, in most fire departments there is much less planning than is needed.

Sometimes a chief will have the services of a planning officer who submits suggestions. Ordinarily, however, each chief is his own planning agent and he generally gets substantial help from his subordinates. The benefits of having a number of participants planning for an activity have now become widely recognized. Those who do have a part in making plans, it seems, are much more likely to be willing to help carry them out. Furthermore, the old saw that two heads are better than one is consistently borne out by the elicitation not only of more ideas but better ones from a group.

The advantage of plans themselves are many and diverse, dependent on the situation. Plans have been known to go awry, too, with sorry consequences, but a failure here and there should hardly outweigh the many successes. In fire fighting operations, the saving of time, lives and resources is easily recognized. The profits in well-conceived budgets (spending plans) are not easy to see, but they are there. Systematic recruiting procedures and timetables for property acquisition and building construction provide for protection when it is needed. Good planning secures stability and adaptability; it controls and diminishes emergencies; it gains respect and confidence; it decreases tension and criticism.

Targets for planning

To list all that must be planned for by a department chief and his leadership team would undoubtedly be an endless task. To undertake to establish the order of importance of a few would be asking for trouble, too. At the same time, it seems safe to say some of the more common planning activities should focus on:

Equipment addition and replacement,
Staff development, growth and promotion,
Morale stabilization and improvement,
Public understanding and attitude,
Salary adjustment and increment,
Inspection and reporting, and
Training programs.

Subordinate officers in the service also plan. How to keep equipment in top shape, how to relieve monotony of duty, how to carry out drills, how to proceed with daily routines, how to get cooperation, and so on, confront officers constantly.

In a fire department, as in any organization, there are many ways of doing a job. It is not always necessary to start at the beginning or to use all the steps suggested. Good plans can grow out of some quite unsystematic approaches. It is suggested, though, that better and more useful plans will tend to emerge more quickly if there is

1. Sharp and clear specification of the objective,
2. Exploration of the dimensions of the task, reasons for the planning, etc.,
3. Identification and appraisal of what is likely to be affected and the impact thereon,
4. Delineation of the forces that bear on the outcome,
5. Variety in the possibilities and alternatives proposed,
6. Formulation of alternatives by all those concerned with their implementation,
7. An accumulation of all the data necessary to a plan,
8. Study and assessment for their effectiveness,

9. Testing of ideas by persons with experience and those who will be affected,

10. A set of proposals for assessment or evaluation procedures, and

11. Initiation of planning steps well in advance on the basis of analyzed reports and data, audits, employment of models, etc.

Data

Information about problems, developments, trends and other impacts upon the organization should provide the initiatve and raw material for plans. Manufacturing and marking organizations usually set up more systematic information-gathering machinery than public agencies, and they decide more quickly. Business pressures cause them constantly to ask the hard question: Will it work? And the more data available, the more likely one can tell.

The kinds of data needed for fire department planning are not generally agreed upon. The data appropriate for specific tasks obviously depends upon the tasks. Much work needs to be done by every fire department in deciding what information to obtain regularly. And there is not much help available. One prominent book on fire administration does not mention records and nowhere suggests what information should be available to facilitate planning.

This, of course, raises the question of paper work, the nuisance of interminable reports, and the job of collation and analysis. Information is of no use if it is locked in office files or insufficiently summarized and interpreted. The need, therefore, for personnel with competence and time to develop a useful, comprehensive record and feedback system is obvious. In addition to regular reports, the fire department should collect information on items like the following:

Turnover rate,
Cause of service termination,
Discomfitures and attitudes of personnel,
Effect of training activities,
Impressions of other public services,
Status and condition of equipment,
Deployment of men,
Problems of recruitment,
Types and causes of fires,
Kinds of public negligence,
New type hazards,
Community growth,
Apparatus repair and replacement,
Availability of water supply,

Use made of various tools and equipment.

The sources of data for planning may vary with the activities. Sometimes they are suppliers, the corporation counsel, or inspections over a period of time. But the common, continuing sources are:

Daily reports,
Newspapers,
Periodic surveys and studies,
Fire service journals and trade reports,
Personal experiences recounted,
Analytical conferences,
Regular reports from other municipal agencies.

Problems

Ineffective and unworkable plans evolve in the best of circles. Not every contingency and development can be taken care of, but attention to some built-in difficulties may help. Every person approaches a task in terms of his perception of what he sees as the significant factors. Our inclinations are to maintain our perceptions—even to defend them. The report that morale is bad may not be too meaningful if we see that the problem involves only pay increases or the elimination of two or three articulate spokesmen among fire fighters. Battalion chiefs who want report forms changed may get one reception if they seem constantly to be looking for trouble and another if they just want to cut down paper work.

Changes in ways of doing jobs disturb many people. Something that is working pretty well is often felt to be better if left alone: "There is no use stirring up trouble! Besides, it usually takes time." Seeking to set up a full-scale pre-fire planning program may simply overwhelm subordinates. The work involved may raise more reasons for resistance than compliance.

Similarly, external influences are constantly at work to frustrate. Plans usually affect others who have plans too. The strategy in giving here to get there becomes difficult when someone else "takes here" and "withholds there." Good ideas often fail because others who agree at the outset do not follow through. The administrator must ever be aware that in the making may be the breaking.

Related to this is an administrator's overdrive, which may cause him to push too fast and think that others feel as strongly as he does. The new chief, for instance, may fall victim here, but anybody with a hot idea also is vulnerable. A simple study of five new volunteer chiefs showed that every one of them was determined to get a good training and drill program going. None paid too much attention to the observations from below that things had been "going along pretty good" before. And so, committed to volunteer their own time and energy, they did not even hear it said that not much more could be done. Very often the leader must be ready to put his flashbulbs in his pocket, so to speak, and change his perspective as to what can be done.

Lest the discussion end on a negative note, there needs be a word for those who have the obligations for planning. Some may "rock along" from day to day; others may support reluctantly; and there will always be a few who resist or contend. The responsible officer, however, must constantly diagnose the condition of things, ascertain the effectiveness of present arrangements and procedures, and propose different and better approaches.

Knowing what is best—or could be made better—is not the foremost attribute of all who attain high rank in an organization. Doubtless the grass is not always greener on the other side of the fence, but obviously one does not know if he does not explore to find out. Most of us can have our sights raised by:

Looking at what others can do,
Listening carefully to the dreamers and theoreticians,
Inviting criticism and suggestion,
Understanding more comprehensive objectives.

It is surely not helpful nor useful to feel sorry for oneself. It is worse to do so and not do anything about it. But from time to time there is some advantage to asking, "What is wrong here and what would make it better?" Most fire chiefs could soon identify scores of problems and solutions and thereon hang plan after plan.

It is easy to bring in an outsider, yet not so easy to accept his observations. And it is most difficult to arouse those whose self-expectancy level is at a low ebb. Colleges, extension services, underwriters organizations, private consulting firms, associations of chiefs and fire fighters all can make critical appraisals that will keep a live managerial force busy for long periods. But it takes more than an audit or a survey for the impoverished to appreciate and seek what those with a wealth of ideas have. It takes intention to improve!

DEVELOPING THE ORGANIZATION

The second major principle of management rather generally found in the literature is referred to as organizing. This is the managerial function of marshaling various factors and resources necessary to attain the objectives sought.

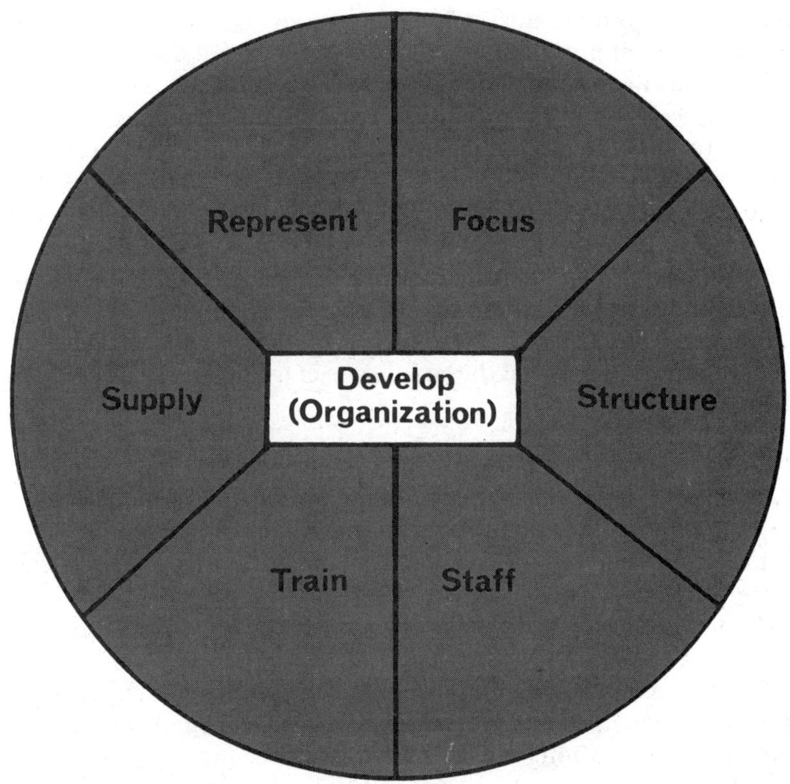

As is indicated above, fire chiefs for the most part inherit a bureaucratic form, familiarly military, which functions through delegation of responsibility with some attendant authority to command. The major job of managing that they have is to develop and strengthen the organization. The tasks identified within this responsibility are found in the chart.

Focus

The purpose of a fire department ought to be obvious to everybody: to save lives and put out fires. But are those alone the objectives? Do we have fire departments to prevent fires, to educate people about fires, to share in encouraging industries to settle in the area by keeping fire losses low and insurance rates down? Some businesses claim their purpose is to provide employment, to supply competition, to give concrete opportunity for skill development and personal growth to people.

Men say they join organizations to earn a living, to obtain a sense of importance, to apply the skills they have, and to get a secure job.

The goals of an organization and those who are in it always must be taken into consideration by those who would develop and strengthen it, get it to function more efficiently and make it more effective. The strains in bureaucratic life grow in large part out of the inconsistency of the bureaucratic form in what needs to be done and what people want.

The manager must organize in terms of what will satisfy as many of the human wants as possible within a priority system that he can get accepted and supported. This is not easy. It needs constant attention to all the possible goals and the adaptation of arrangements for achieving them.

Structure

Most fire departments employ a line organization through which authority and command flow and within which responsibility is distributed in a fairly uniform way. The addition of a staff structure of some consequence follows when departments become larger. On the whole there is reliance upon vertical rather than on horizontal or decentralized patterns. The format is pyramidal rather than flat and it works out well for the most part. It provides direct accountability from units and facilitates decision making. When departments do expand and staff units (personnel, prevention, training, investigation, planning) are added, strains occasionally develop. It is at this point that good training and sound personal development in officer personnel pays off. Of course, the simple line organization more than occasionally fails to serve well too—because there is either inadequate assignment of responsibility or incompetence to perform responsibly by those in the lower ranks. Now and then the chief is weak in determining at what point additional categories or levels in the line structure are needed, e.g., battalions, divisions. Sometimes the organization creaks because bureaus or battalions are not set up when they should be.

The most significant part of structuring a fire department, though, is the setting out clearly and in substantial detail the duties of the various bureaus and divisions and prescribing the relationship between them. Once established, these job descriptions should be periodically reviewed to add duties where enlargement is advantageous and to remove and shift those which tend to increase inefficiency.

All personnel who are employed by the fire service are the staff and there is no argument that no matter how good the structure nor how competent the chief, the department will be no better than the summed ability of its men. The essence of organizational strength is not who is in the tent but who is in the trenches.

The chief, of course, can make up to some extent for fire fighter weakness by wise selection and development of the subordinate officers on whom he must rely. Full success depends, however, upon determination to have at every level capable and devoted personnel, the criteria for whose selection are based on attributes of intelligence, personal integrity, strength and energy, and a sense of obligation to social service.

But it is not easy to get top-notch recruits for the fire department even when the chief is actively improving the image of the department by getting better salaries, better leaders and better equipment. Recruiting the best takes time. It takes energy. It takes imagination. Visits to schools, presentations to groups, pamphlets, glamorous stories, high internal morale, and a number of other steps that invite interest and encourage investment of time on the part of youth.

Training

Practically no recruit can be expected to know much about fighting fires or doing the variety of jobs related to fire fighting. However, a limited number of human beings instinctively possess the knowledge, attitudes, and skills essential to command. Education and training are essential to the development of such persons.

In simple line organizations, immediate superiors carry out training activities. In larger departments, a training division often provides highly detailed plans, gives direct instruction, and provides evaluation for battalion and district officers. Through such a division in a very big city, arrangements may be made for the extensive employment of outside agencies. Extension training services are available throughout the country. Conferences, workshops, officers' schools and others are becoming increasingly available to provide help on technical problems and new developments.

No longer does one get trained once and for all. New products, changing equipment, and improved resources present to the fire service the same challenge of keeping up to date found in other groups. Every fire chief should have a program of training for all the units and types of personnel under his command. He should be able to judge its adequacy for scope and depth and know what evidence he can collect to judge the program's effectiveness. Outlines and suggested courses are available from the state fire agencies, university centers, such organizations as the National Fire Protection Association and more recently from the federal government through a variety of administrations, including Health, Education and Welfare, Housing and Urban Development, and most notably, the National Fire Prevention and Control Administration.

Supply

Fires will not be extinguished quickly without trained men. But trained men are not of much use without proper equipment. It would seem silly to point this out if there were not so many fire departments both undermanned and underequipped. The sad fact is that there are a great many fire companies operating without a full complement of men. It is not difficult to find in community after community outmoded apparatus lumbering forth to battle with only half the equipment they should carry.

Time and time again, to be sure, a tight fist at city hall, or a weak fire commissioner is the cause. But we must remember that management at all levels has its obligation to fill out the organization so it can accomplish its purpose. The officers need to know what equipment, materials and conditions are appropriate for their department. The case presented for any additions or replacements should be simple, argued well, supported authoritatively and comparatively, related to available funds, and tied to ideas that arouse concern and develop understanding. Requests should be reasonable, develop in priority, fit into long-range development, and give promise of an increase in efficiency.

Fire departments usually are not confronted with the consumable resource needs that manufacturing or retail organizations have. From time to time authorized purchases are not made or cleared; specifications and bids may interfere; lax ordering or slow delivery may create gaps. The pressure, however, is there. The need for routines and well-established routes for requisitions and their approval and fulfillment remains. A bureaucracy is often only as good as its paper work and its established rules for initiating action. Fire chiefs long ago learned to write dates on extinguishers and specify times for their inspection. Most departments take inventory on equipment, sometimes after every run, but still there are uneven patterns with respect to preventive maintenance, repair, research, cumulative analysis, and so on.

Represent

Earlier reference was made to the several directions in which officers extend their efforts to establish and fill out an organization. Each of the preceding steps, identified as developmental, depends in substantial part upon the skill of management in relating to, explaining to, and obtaining from those whose province it is to grant or in whom there resides sufficient power to frustrate. Sometimes chiefs may think all they have to do is to ask, or that all they are obligated to do is to give orders to subordinates. When they do this, they either do not last long or the organization deteriorates.

Management is politics, both internally and externally. Organizations grow and strengthen when they have at the helm individuals whose personal warmth attracts, whose knowledge and skills help others satisfy their needs, whose tact and timing set others at ease, and whose purpose is selfless, exceeding any personal return. The able adminstrator does not neglect his subordinates, but he must spend much time face to face with his peers and with his superiors, providing them with insight into his problems and ambitions, sharing theirs, and building the personal interdependence out of which their support comes. The success of a fire department depends as much upon what a chief does for it as it does upon what he does to it or with it.

To relate well, a chief must be able to express his case tactfully in writing as well as orally. He must be available to others while he takes the initiative in seeking them out. Management to him must be seen as filled with chances to work out something better rather than a series of headaches. It should also not be just a confrontation from which to emerge the victor.

COORDINATING THE ORGANIZATION

The central focus and most time-consuming responsibility of management is the coordinating or relating better the parts and pieces of the organization established to do a job. The things one does to put the organization into motion, to lubricate it, and to fit in the units and their functions includes at least those identified in the chart.

Most organizations carry out their activities within the prescriptions of law, in keeping with broad policies established by governing boards, through regulations and rules promulgated by operating officers. When responding to an alarm, an engine company employs all three to get there safely and quickly and to carry out its responsibilities. In some cases the governing conditions are explicit; in others they are open to interpretation. Too many restraints and specifications get in the way of good operation; too few tend to disorganization and poor operation.

In general, managers propose and recommend policies. They make the rules and issue the regulations. The process of good management is how to get them made and how to get them used effectively.

Policies usually supply the broad controls for an organization. They are few in number and generally not too explicit. They also usually do

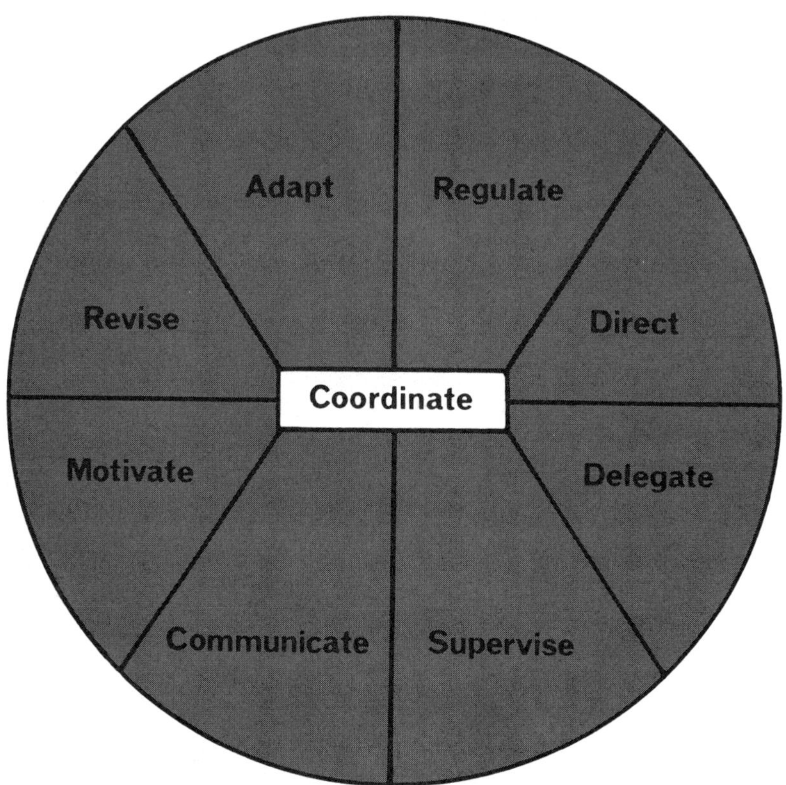

not get written down; and more often than not, they derive from decisions made on the spur of the moment, which linger on in the tradition of the organization. Mutual aid is a policy; it operates under certain legal restraints in many states and is administered and regulated consistent with other policies, and the prerogatives of the chief to make arrangements. But in many places the policy is not written or included in any policy book.

The line between policy and administrative interpretation and rules which are written has been the subject of much discussion among management specialists. No resolution seems to be in sight. Full treatment here is not warranted. One would only invite dispute by asserting what a fire department ought to have as policies—and what it ought not have. It is safe to say that when policies are written down, just as when rules are written, there is more chance a fire department will run smoothly. Through policies, top officers can delegate authority and still retain control.

The development of good regulatory machinery takes time. It should include participation by those who are affected by the rules and good feedback to those who administer them. A fire department is perhaps one of the few organizations where deliberation, time, and participants are available for thorough examination. Widespread involvement ought then to take place.

Good rules, though, have a way of getting lost or violated if they are not thoroughly learned and well reviewed. Too much, of course is too much; and the rule book living would soon take the initiative out of most of us. But well-organized drills, post-fire analysis, pre-fire planning, case study discussion, among other training and development activities, should help make rule review unobtrusive while helpful.

Direct

Rules, standard operating procedures, job descriptions and assigned duties give substantial direction in any organization. There is plenty of leeway left, even guaranteed, for those who have authority to determine tactics, to lay out work for others and to prepare orders and to deliver them in most settings.

Perhaps a fire department, because of its emergency role and its interacting group functions, calls for more personal direction than other services, such as education. Therefore, it might not be guided best by the principle that the less directing an organization needs, the more mature and professional it will be.

Fire fighting is admittedly a team effort. In this effort, certain procedures are governed by the conditions at the moment and follow one upon the other with signals given for the timing of steps. Occasionally the wind shifts, so to speak, and significant alteration is required. One could not do away with direction then if one wanted to.

The nature of directing does, however, have much to do with its success. Imperiousness, failure to provide freedom to operate within latitudes, precise instructions where discretion is necessary, and overzealous monitoring will soon destroy initiative and frustrate the growth and learning opportunities subordinates expect. An officer must learn and must be taught by his chief—through example and counsel—to exercise his prerogatives to order and specify only when absolutely necessary. It is always advisable to test the decision-making powers of subordinates. Needless to say, the giving of orders requires respectful voice and demeanor and constant reference to the feelings and fears of those bound to respond.

Delegate

These comments about directing are naturally implicit for delegating. No chief can be sufficient in himself for all that is required to carry forward the work of even a small organization. There is too much to do if the chief grasps all the dimensions of developing an organization. The jobs must be shared, spread about. Other men must be relied upon. Delegation does not transfer responsibility, but accompanied by enough authority and guided by mature supervision, it can strengthen and provide cohesion for organization. The wise chief selects with care what tasks to delegate. Some men need to be groomed for line operations; others for staff functions. All senior officers should have seasoning under a watchful superior as circumstances and time permit. Executive development requires far more attention than it has received in most departments. It is as critical as training a fire fighter.

Every superior must determine in his own mind what he can delegate. It is normal for any head man to think he alone is judged for the success of an organization. It is normal, therefore, for one to want to keep track of "all the important" matters, to know how major moves have worked out, and to want them done as he would have done them. But fathers free sons and fire chiefs must free subordinates—when they need to have experience, and when they are ready. And generally that's sooner than one would like to admit. Good delegation derives from good preparation, but it also depends on real self-confidence on the part of the superior.

Much writing has been done about two elements of delegation—authority and responsibility. Complete specification of either is impossible. Sharp definition of duties and obligations will never cover all the ground in an emergency operation. Authority conceived as the legal power to tell someone else to do something will always fall short of authority earned out of the essence of leadership. It is the duty of executives to spell out what the subordinate's job is and to explain his prerogatives so the job can be done well.

Most superiors would do well to remember the pull of gravity upon those who move upward into the higher ranks. Unaccustomed as they are to management, faced with the new tasks and frustrated by ideas and people, new chiefs may experience a steady pull to return to do that which they know they can do well. They yearn to show their men they have the old touch, and to get the feel of command where it is simple and direct. The fall back is not necessary, and it will seldom build the maturity and the skills needed.

Supervise

 Contemplate: teach, help, lay out, order, rate, supply, encourage, hire, dismiss, counsel, correct, discipline, reassign. Ask what each involves, how one acts, what one must know, how one can make mistakes, how one learns! This is the concept covered by the word "supervision" which includes nearly the whole of management. The tasks surely are performed in whole or in part at every level.

Jucius[1] has called supervision the "watching-over" process. In it he seems to imply: checking to see if tasks have been performed and how well, ascertaining why standards set have not been accomplished, and undertaking those immediate steps appropriate to satisfactory or better performance. In the background there lies also the obligation to take the next steps, those that require a longer period to experience and which will contribute to better service by satisfied employees.

Most organizations have found it necessary to have supervisors who control activities of small groups within the more general directions provided by higher authority. The engine or truck companies as operating units naturally represent such supervisory groupings. The chief, similarly, although he does in ways supervise the whole department, acts in the same capacity toward a small group of subordinates—assistant, deputy, battalion chiefs—as his organization may require.

Ideas about the essence of good supervision are legion. In recent years the so-called human relations point of view has prevailed. The burden of this theory is that men on the whole are seeking to be mature, self-directing entities. The very nature of modern society, however, has forced these men to work together in groups to get jobs done. So, men have had to give up something of their freedom because a line organization with a chain of command depends upon the power of someone else to get up and run the machinery. But men have become in an industrial, managed world somewhat restive and unhappy at being cogs in the wheel, low on the totem pole. They have, consequently, found ways of relieving the pressures and of regaining some of their independence. The best example is their getting together in unions to protect their rights as humans and to contend with the forces in line-type organizations that tend to dehumanize them.

As a result, management has sought to find the means to provide for all the items previously mentioned (being moved from one job to another, being corrected, being stimulated, being bypassed on promotion, etc.) and still not take from men their sense of importance, self-respect, and control of their lives and surroundings.

In so doing—say those with the human relations point of view—not

[1]Jucius, Michael and William Schlender, *Elements of Managerial Action,* Richard D. Irwin, Inc., Homewood, 1960, page 72.

only will men feel better themselves and give more freely of their knowledge and skill, but organized units will have better morale and will be more efficient. Such supervision will not work overnight or at all in some settings. Nevertheless, attempts to employ it are widespread. The outcomes are consistent with the predications.

Personnel in some fire departments are likely to say, "But we are military-type organizations. We cannot afford to be either democratic or human!" Nothing could be so wrong. Most of the time fire departments are not in emergency status. Their top management certainly ought seldom to be so occupied. The lessons so far learned are simply that human organizations produce greater power and finer discipline in emergencies. Obedience is built neither on fear nor law, but on earned respect and devotion born of identity and concern on a wide and comprehensive basis. Good supervisors are good democrats.

Communicate

Communication is the 20th century bane of existence. Without it, we are lost. With too much of it, we are paralyzed, wondering how to sift it all.

A significant cause of failure in fire departments, here, is the lack of knowledge concerning what information should be known and how to write it, say it, digest it, and explain it. Despite radios, telephones, bulletin boards, newsletters, and reports, "What's up?" gets mangled, muddled, misstated, misunderstood, and misinterpreted. Neither profanity nor volume helps when the transmitter knows not what he wants to say or how to say it. Communication depends upon clarity, consistency and comprehensiveness of information—up and down.

The major cause of breakdown is not lack of skill. It is rather lack of conviction. Information is gold; it is power. With it one can destroy, facilitate, frustrate. Through it one can explain, involve, help and release the interest and ideas of others. Kept to oneself, it can even become a tool for self-destruction!

Why some with information should withhold it, filter it, or contaminate it with inaccuracy or simplification, or why others collect it, send it along, follow up on it is not at all difficult to explain. It lies in both the understandings and in the motives of men. It stems from fear, respect for others, loyalty to purpose, and dependence upon intelligence.

To decide wisely, men must know. That goes for the public, commissioners, deputies, captains and fire fighters. To know whom to tell when and what of how much one has seen, heard, felt or determined bends to no rule of thumb. On the whole, though, the more information made available on a wide basis in an organization the better the organization. Good communication brings a group together, tells them better where others are, explains the situation, invites participation and provides a route for the resolution of problems. It is a critical factor in coordination—requiring freedom of speech, trust in others, many methods and constant attention.

Motivate

Fire fighters know what it takes to get a spark going, and they know what will douse a flame. All are not possessed of the same combustibility, but with either high or low ignition points, they need an environment which motivates them. They need constant stimuli and encouragement from outside to thrive. Like all human beings, they are not self-sufficient.

No organization is likely ever to get all the competent, dedicated, willing men it needs. Neither can an organization dismiss all of those who cannot immediately meet the standards desired or follow the outlines of tasks specified. Mangement is hired to employ methods for holding or encouraging men to task-levels and commitments from which they would prefer to escape.

On the other hand, men do have self-respect. Men can be found who have come to understand in themselves what they can do and thus what they get self-satisfaction from doing. Goads and threats are not needed when a man has a chance to demonstrate competence or fairly test himself.

With those who move quickly up the line there is a tendency to develop an attitude that the less able men do not want to do their best. Sometimes they can't. In every stage of life, there are those who learn that they have come to the end of their rope of competence. These people always have to be helped to adjust at this point and, perhaps, at later periods when they have another burst of ambition. In time and with support, they will improve.

There are those, of course, who are lazy or who lack self-confidence, usually because of something in their background. They need retraining. They must be supported regularly. Patience and good fellowship must pervade. Wherever possible, some task that they can be successful in must be found for these men. Their background has made them immature. They must be treated as such, but always with hope.

On the other hand, consideration must be given to men who are overqualified for the lower ranks. Everything possible then should be done to enlarge the duties of such subordinates. Chiefs should delegate more and more to them and include more and more training, personnel study, fire analyses, inspection, and public relations. Top management then can turn to more complex subjects and more refined study and employment of management.

Revise and adapt

Running an organization teaches one thing quickly: matters could go more smoothly. The invitation, if not the demand then, is ever present. One has but to accept the role.

However, trying to get more smoothness when at idle and more power when under acceleration is often frustrating. Some take the attitude that it could be better, yes, but why tinker until you have to? And if you can get by even when it's tough, why ask for trouble? These are common-sense questions but they do not help. Organizations have to be adjusted. Like a growing boy, the fire department these days cannot wear the same pants year in and year out. New problems in combustion call for better training. Better education insists on enlightened command procedure. Population growth forces expansion, promotion, reorganization, delegation and new policies.

Some changes are wrought quickly and with ease. But others involve people and their feelings, a search for resources, or change in habits—all not submissive to quick change. Every signal that something is not working, every assertion that something could be better, originating from the men, ought to be recorded and considered. The solutions proposed should always be appraised as to who will be affected and how he will respond. This takes communication, time, and involvement as well as intuition. Self-examination or introspection will help a great deal.

But self-search is dangerous too. We are all wishful thinkers, and we have marvelous ways of rationalizing. As we move away from first-hand, immediate experience, we fall heir to nostalgia—yearn for the good old days. Checking present reality is difficult. It needs much attention to getting accurate reports and avoiding delusion.

Most organizations now have built-in means of locating needs for initiating or adjusting action. Suggestion systems, periodic audits, problem-identifying sessions, conferences, staff or self-criticism, etc., provide organizations with ideas on improvement. Some further steps are included in the following discussion of control.

CONTROLLING THE ORGANIZATION

The third major control of the manager is to control his organization. In fact, control and coordination are often hard for the management teacher to separate. A well-coordinated organization does not get out

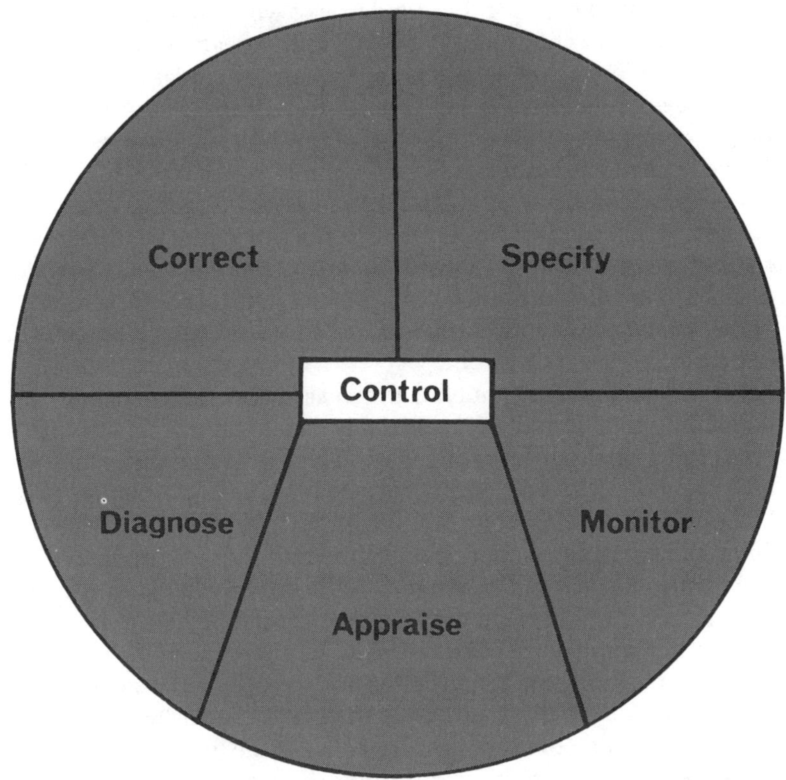

of control. However, control, if not distinct, does constitute a useful third dimension of managing. The chart identifies items commonly thought of in this aspect of function.

Specify

The perfect fire department would soon eliminate its most common activity—extinguishing fires. But it would not put itself out of business. It would be then fully engaged in doing what is required to prevent fires. Realistically, no one expects this to happen soon or ever. Nevertheless, that goal must always be among the chief's aims and the results charted. Such records constitute a measuring stick that will indicate each year how close he is getting to going out of business. And upon such evidence he will plan his steps for the next year. So, too, with all other goals and the measures he applies to attain them.

At every level and in every category of performance there can be, there must be, expectations toward which we are moving and with which we can be satisfied. These are the standards of which we speak so often as we contemplate our children, our wives, ourselves, and those who supply us. When Junior brings home his report card, we must be ready to accept it or reject it if we are to help Junior to do well. When we rant and rave, we engage in one aspect of control. When we order more homework, we engage in another.

The fire chief similarly must determine what he wants—what is sufficient and acceptable. If he can confine the fire loss to $3 million a year without more attention to prevention, he may be satisfied. If he loses six out of 10 new fire fighters a year, he may not worry. A retention of 40 percent may or may not arouse more concern than 40 percent on a report card.

But if it does arouse as much concern as school failure usually does, the chief may well blow his top. He may order exit interviews with uninvolved third parties to ascertain why. He may order tighter inspection and ask for more up-to-date equipment. If so, he is exercising his right and responsibility of control.

Not all aspects of fire department life and function can be perfectly silhouetted against a set of standards. Who knows what is an acceptable fire loss ratio? Some would argue that it should be below the average for districts of similar size or below what another fire department could accomplish in the same type community. Who knows how many grievances and disciplinary actions are normal? Goals to be sought are not always reducible to exact prescriptions. One has to judge on many matters about what is right. And that often results in impossible demands and arbitrary and capricious criteria.

On the other hand, it is possible to set more definite targets for public agencies than "to keep the public happy and to keep out of trouble." We can decide, with the study and advice of top people, how long hose should last on the average, how much inventory loss is acceptable, what items ought to be inspected and how often, what salary increase will hold good men, what complaints will receive action, how many false alarms are normal, how much absenteeism is tolerable, etc.

Indeed the details upon which there must be some standards are appalling, but no organization can efficiently function for long without standards. Someone has to attend to them. The more often they are written down, the more often one can decide to do something about what is happening.

Monitor

Some of what monitoring involves was suggested in the discussion of supervision. It means observing and checking—formally and informally—through records, reports, summaries, surveys, inventories. If there are well thought-out rules, clear directives, loyal subordinates, and competent personnel, things will work out pretty well. But one would be foolhardy to think that neglect of such checking will lead in time to anything but deterioration.

Few fire departments lack regular inspections. They are, in fact, better off in this respect than most organizations. However, a chief officer can get isolated from the daily, local operations pretty quickly. The hierarchial system has a way of "keeping the old man happy." And it also keeps the battalion chief happy and often the captain and now and then the lieutenant. All the information needed to monitor isn't readily apparent. Without being unduly suspicious, the boss in most cases had better recognize the strange and wonderful ways used to keep him uninformed.

Daily and monthly reports are critical, but they are useless if those who receive them do not analyze them, keep track of them, and act on them whether for good or bad. What to look for, of course, is another matter. Experience helps and makes one wise as to what could happen. Management objectives are of the greatest help, however, because they give something more than intuition to go on.

If the objectives of the boss are to eliminate certain weaknesses, employ subordinate time more effectively, expend resources more conservatively, build a better public image, get cleaner equipment, reduce grievances, retain personnel longer, mount more meaningful drills, he can look for the evidence in practices, his own involvements and tasks, his reports, his conferences, his daily feedback, his grievances, his headaches, his public relations.

Appraise and diagnose

Evaluating or judging success against established goals is, of course, a very human and personal matter. Many a manager thinks his organization can achieve miracles—without the help of fairy godmothers. And many another manager thinks his organization is as near perfect as it can be—when its frailties are obvious to everybody.

There are, to be sure, commissioners and the public who can bear down, but it is human for the chief to protect his department as well as himself. Occasionally a chief lays about. He blames his organization for not being up to snuff. He belittles his equipment, his personnel and his staff. Such a critic, however, soon loses his listeners and makes himself quickly the target for replacement.

On the other hand, indefensible and naive championing of a second-rate outfit will not delude folks for long. He who would build must protect his straggling team while they gather strength, but he also has to be objective. That is what a manager is paid for—to develop an organization that will do the job.

A chief can and should engage others to help him make constant appraisal of his department. The internal rating of personnel, practice and performance can be done for the most part by teams of subordinates or individuals. The department as a whole can be best judged by groups of fellow fire chiefs, survey teams, rating boards, etc.

The astute chief not only knows what is awry, but he knows why. Ordinarily, appraisals should be accompanied by explanations, and plans should be initiated for the correction of conditions detected. Good appraisals ought to spark an automatic train of corrections where discrepancies are discovered. At the same time, such appraisal often needs comparative analysis by a person of higher rank to reveal whether one unit or group substantially exceeds, or is beneath, another in some area of performance.

The chief, then, has the alternative of requesting his subordinate to "look into it," e.g., an excessive loss of equipment, or of initiating an inquiry himself. In the latter case, he asks for further information from additional sources.

Correct

When a chief misses the target with his organization, or any part of it, he must adjust. He may add or subtract from the budget, or his plan, for better expenditure of his resources. He may step up his public relations activities. He may discipline through non-promotion or transfer. He may install new forms and new timing for reports. He may set in motion a thorough review of department regulations. The correction steps and devices available to the superior officer are endless. They range from self-discipline to kindly counsel for the faltering.

The problem, of course, is to pick the steps that lead to improvement at the right price. With power, it is simple to lay about. Without conviction and courage one can dissemble. Without imagination and competence one can plead for salvation. "What am I gonna do with an outfit like this?" despairingly crosses too many minds in the fire service.

There is no way to give any manager ready-made answers to all his problems. Experience is perhaps the greatest teacher. At the same time, many, many more organizational strains would yield to a studied and systematic approach. Lieutenants should be given substantial insight into the dynamics of small groups, captains provided with a useful grasp of the psychologist's explanations of variant behavior, battalion chiefs informed about systems of internal communication and the strange ways of the informal structure, and top officers made knowledgeable about social group strategy. All would then be better able to cope with problems.

There are few fire departments that could not have better drills, better running patterns, more thorough evaluation, more efficient command, fewer grievances, less loss, and so on. The answers can be gotten from books, from the procedures in other departments, from trial and error, from subordinates, from the application of theory, from the experience of managers in other type organizations, and from fire service magazines. But no answers will help much if they are used only for the obvious symptoms, or at points so remote from the source that impact is only palliative. The manager must define precisely what is wrong and what lies beneath the malfunction. He must take time, assemble his evidence over time (because hasty conclusion leaves hurt feelings, misuses energy, and lets wrong get a better hold), propose solutions, assemble the resources, and apply them insistently long enough to make a difference.

CHAPTER FOUR

Designing stations and drill grounds

The basic building of a fire department is the fire station, which can house one or several companies—engine, ladder company, rescue ambulance or special unit—fully manned and equipped for instant response 24 hours a day. This station represents a long-term investment by the citizens of a community in their safety and welfare and as such should be constructed of the best possible material in the best possible location with the best design and at reasonable cost.

Too often fire chiefs are not satisfied with a new fire station that they have had constructed, but they will have to live with it (so will their successors) for a long time. Most often, this dissatisfaction stems from their own poor planning and that of the architect which they or the town fathers selected. Few architects specialize in fire station design. Those that do are good. Those that do not often treat the fire station as a garage rather than the highly functional public building it should be. As a result, many fire chiefs find themselves at dedication ceremonies for a new fire station that is badly designed and impractical.

The first decision to be made, therefore, in the construction of a fire station is to hire a good architect and one who is familiar with fire station design and function. We are assuming here that the site of the station has been properly selected and acquired. (This will be covered later.) The architect should know that his building plan must be unique. Unlike most other buildings, the fire station must be manned 24 hours

Four-bay station in New Haven, Conn., houses two engine companies and a ladder company. Two-story-high truck floor is spacious enough to house other apparatus.

a day and all facilities and equipment in the building must be ready for instant use.

The plan of the building must be simple and practical, perhaps spartan would be a better term. It should also be attractive and of a design that fits with and hopefully enhances the architecture of the neighborhood in which it is built. (Too often new fire stations are voted down for failure to consider the taste and, of course, needs of the neighborhood. Most people don't want a firehouse in their or adjacent block under any condition no matter how necessary it is.) For practical reasons, finishes on the building, both inside and out, should require only a minimum of maintenance.

Assuming the site of a new fire station has been pinpointed within a couple of blocks, it should then be placed on a street that is wide enough to permit fire apparatus to swing easily into the street. It should also be on a street that has as little traffic as possible to reduce the accident hazard when pulling out of quarters. The site should be large enough to allow the fire station to be built back at least 40 feet from the property line and with enough room left for parking—if the budget permits. Naturally, there should be sufficient "search" on the property to show

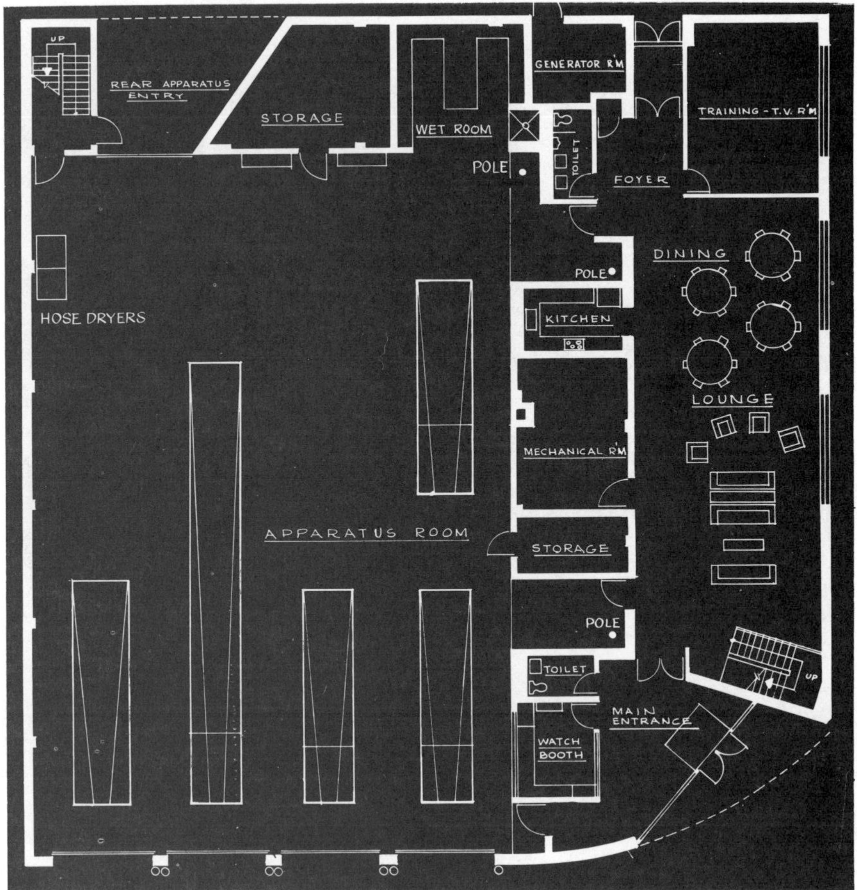

Diagram of four-bay New Haven station shown on opposite page.

that there are no easements or other restrictions that would hinder construction or fire department operations.

A lawyer, of course, is just as important as the architect or the builder and one should be consulted right from the beginning to see that there are no deed restrictions, zoning regulations, or other legal problems that would affect either the design or construction of the station. How the property is to be acquired (purchase or acquisition) also falls under the lawyer's duties.

The architect also figures in the legal aspects of construction since he must be knowledgeable in the state or local codes and laws that cover buildings. Whenever possible, fire chiefs or other officials should ex-

Triangular fire station in Corning, N. Y., measures 200 feet on each side and is clad with fire-engine-red metal panels. Circular windows light interior.

amine fire stations designed by the architect(s) bidding on their new fire station. And talk with the chief who is now living with his design.

Confer with architect

Once the architect has been hired and his contract signed, the fire chief and other officials involved should sit down with him in conference, or a series of conferences on just what the fire department wants. During these conferences, the chief and others should give the architect their views and as much information as possible about the site and the operation and requirements of the fire department. Is a single station or headquarters to be covered by the plan? How many pieces of apparatus are to be housed and what is their length, width, height and weight? Hose tower, horizontal drying, electric hose dryers or no dryer at all? If there is to be a dormitory, how many men will be expected to occupy it at one time? These and dozens of other questions must be brought up in the preliminary conferences.

Alarm systems are another consideration. If the dispatching of apparatus is to be done from the new station, how complex will it be and what systems will be used—siren or air horn on the building? Or radio home alerting?

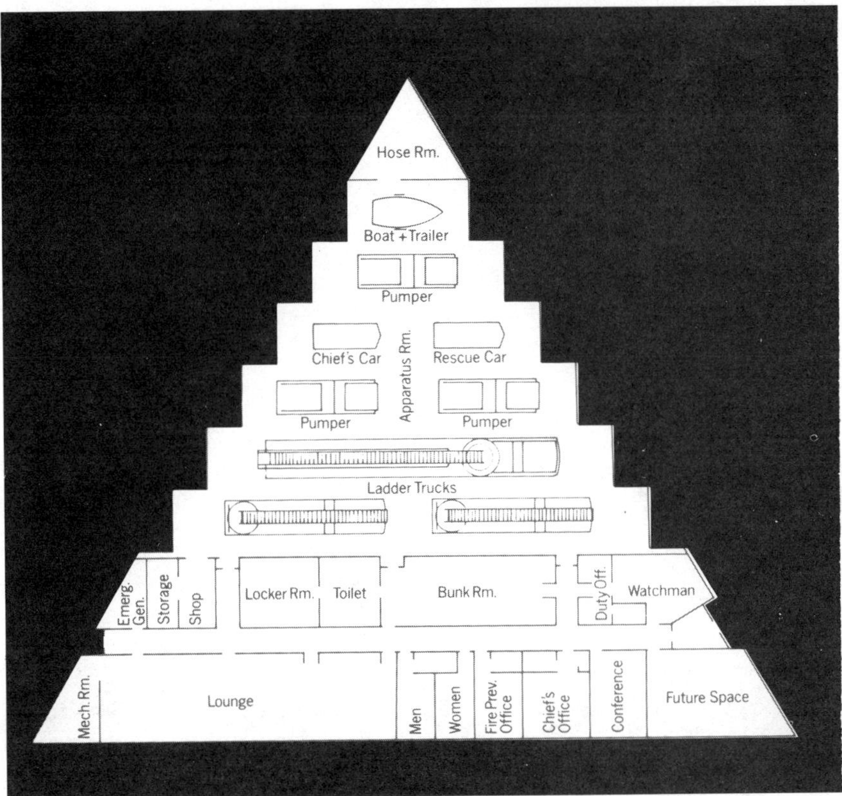

Shape of Corning station reflects traditional fire triangle and provides flexibility.

At the conferences the chief should state what recreation areas he wants in the new station and how much storage space. He should also make known the number and size of meeting and training rooms and the seating space to go with them, particularly in a volunteer department. The chief should look for plenty of storage space, particularly off the apparatus room and the meeting room. Emergency generator space should be given top priority in these discussions. The architect, however, will automatically include janitor's closets, toilet and shower facilities, trophy cases, stairs, boiler room, vestibules and other utility areas. A big decision will have to be made on the height of the building—one or two stories with or without basement?

From the data employed at this preliminary conference or conferences, the architect then proposes preliminary sketches showing his interpretation of the items discussed with the chief. These sketches will show rooms and areas and how they will knit together to give a practical and economic layout. Sizes of areas and their locations in relation to other areas will also be shown.

Sketches revised frequently

The preliminary sketches are generally gone over with a fine tooth comb several times and revised as frequently. They are, however, a tremendous help to the chief's understanding of the architect's interpretation of his needs and desires. Often the chief disagrees with the architect's plans, but further conferences eventually result in agreement and a final plan is adopted.

It is up to the architect to come up with an estimate of the cost for the project. But inflation, building trade wages, some local conditions and their causes rule out the absolute accuracy of such an estimate.

Design features

The architect is usually the one who establishes the exterior design of the building, and unless the fire station must agree with adjacent architecture, let's say Colonial, this selection should be his since he has been educated in this field.

Once money has been authorized for the project, test borings should be made on the lot to determine subsurface conditions. Such borings can eliminate a lot of headache costs should clay or water be found.

Heat and utilities

Following this, the architect proposes working drawings and specifications. In many states there must be separate bids for general construction, plumbing, electricity, heating and ventilation. Again the architect should be familiar with local building codes and laws.

The next items to be considered, again in a conference between the architect and the chief, are the mechanical equipment and the finishes that will be incorporated into the building: the type of heating system, oil, gas or electricity; the type of heat, steam, hot water, forced air and the number of heating zones, or air-conditioned zones required.

Electrical appliances, including the style and type of fixtures—incandescent, fluorescent, surface-mounted or recessed—should be decided at this meeting as well as the location of special appliances such as battery chargers, vehicle exhaust systems, booster fill lines and many others. Particular attention should be given to the selection, location and switch control of night lights, lights for passageways and parking

Control room and dispatching office gives watchmen view of apparatus floor in Bay Village, Ohio, station which has five drive-through bays.

lots. Time switches installed on such lights provide economy and convenience.

Special features

There are hundreds of items that go into the construction of a firehouse and, while an experienced architect will probably come up with them, it would be well for the fire chief or a building committee to have his own list of needs handy at any joint conference.

The apparatus room of a fire station is one of these items that should be given a lot of attention. It must be serviceable and easily maintained. The floor finish can be either concrete with a dustproof hardener or a color-applied terrazzo, ceramic tile or any other durable finish. Guidelines for backing and parking apparatus should be part of the floor's permanent design. Depending on the budget, walls can be glazed block, ceramic tile, plaster or painted block. The ceiling should be perlite plaster if the building code requires fire retarding.

An apparatus room requires easily opened overhead doors which can be either wood, steel or aluminum. However, cheap doors should never

Separate room to hold helmets and turnout gear is found in New Haven fire station.

be considered since the doors must fit properly when closed to prevent heat loss. Insulated doors should be considered for the same reason.

Opening of overhead doors can be done mechanically or electrically. If the doors (under spring tension) are to be opened mechanically, the end of the release rope should be located within easy reach of the driver. Electrically operated doors can have controls at the watch desk, near each apparatus cab (by suspending the control cable from the ceiling) or on a wall. A delayed-action switch can be used for closing the door after the apparatus has left the station. Radio-controlled door openers can also be considered.

Provisions must be included to permit operation of electrically controlled doors from an emergency generator, and manually if both the house electrical supply and the generator should fail. Apparatus doors should be at least 12 feet high and 12 feet wide—wider if possible since no one can tell what future design in fire apparatus will bring. If the property is wide enough, doors at the rear of the apparatus floor should be considered.

Storing turnouts

There should be facilities on or adjacent to the apparatus floor for storing helmets, coats and boots and for drying them. Racks can be

Los Angeles County Station 144 covers 5200 square feet and houses a pumper and patrol truck.

constructed on the floor, or in a room or alcove just off the floor. In paid departments, each man should have a place to hang his gear when he is off duty. Preferably, the racks for turnout gear should be in an area with an electric dryer and an exhaust fan for removing damp air. Some volunteer departments like to have wall space or racks (sometimes on casters) near the apparatus so that men can quickly grab their gear and put it on before riding on the apparatus. Also in volunteer departments, a room or large closet should be provided for storing dress uniforms and turnout gear kept in stock for future assignment.

Means for drying salvage covers should also be provided. Racks or hooks suspended from the ceiling by block and tackle provide a convenient way of hanging up covers to dry.

A toilet and shower room should be provided adjacent to the apparatus room for men to clean up after a working fire. Hose drying and storage facilities should also be close at hand to the apparatus. Hose, of course, means water on the floor which must be pitched to floor drains. These drains can be placed anywhere on the apparatus room floor, but are frequently found just inside the overhead doors.

Locating equipment

An important item on the list of equipment to be stored on the apparatus floor is the battery charger. The chief must decide whether he prefers portable or built-in chargers. If built-in chargers are picked, he must select the location for reels and wires.

The location and type of booster tank fill lines are other items that should be on the chief's list. These can be placed along ceilings or walls, can be manually or electrically operated hose reels, or just a standard hose connection. As with other items, the choice depends on the budget or the chief's wishes. Plenty of hose connections are required in an apparatus room as are plenty of electrical outlets. Hose bibcocks should be recessed for safety and convenience.

Volunteer fire stations need a blackboard on the apparatus floor so the location of an alarm received and the type of fire or emergency can be written down for members arriving after the apparatus has departed. The blackboard's location is important, since it must be readily visible to arriving members and, ideally, it should be so located that it can be read from the cab of each apparatus. It should also be large enough to include notices of hydrants out of service, blocked streets or other unusual conditions that would affect response. Paid departments should also have a similar type board even though the requirement is not as urgent.

In planning the wall space on the apparatus floor, thought should also be given to providing space for a street and hydrant map for the entire municipality or fire district. Paid departments and some volunteer also display all first-alarm response boxes on a wall near the front of the apparatus room.

If a fire department does its own apparatus repair and maintenance, a room should be provided for this purpose. Like the other rooms in the station, it must be serviceable and easily maintained. Its construction is generally the same as other areas. However, ceiling height must be elevated to accommodate a truck lift. There must also be a hoist to move motors or other heavy equipment. Grease racks, oil separators, compressors and almost all other equipment found in any commercial garage are called for.

Other rooms required

In paid departments, dormitories are required, near but not necessarily adjacent to the apparatus floor. Size of the dormitory will be determined by the number of men to be housed. The dormitory should be made as comfortable and quiet as possible and with all conveniences. It should be well heated, ventilated and air-conditioned. A locker is required for each man and adequate shower, toilet and kitchen facilities must be provided nearby. Ceilings for the dormitory will preferably be acoustical tile. Walls are either painted or covered with vinyl.

A bulletin board placed near a well-trafficked location can keep men informed of just what is happening in the company.

If a fire department is manned by volunteers, a dormitory will not be needed. Nevertheless a same sized or larger room should be built for

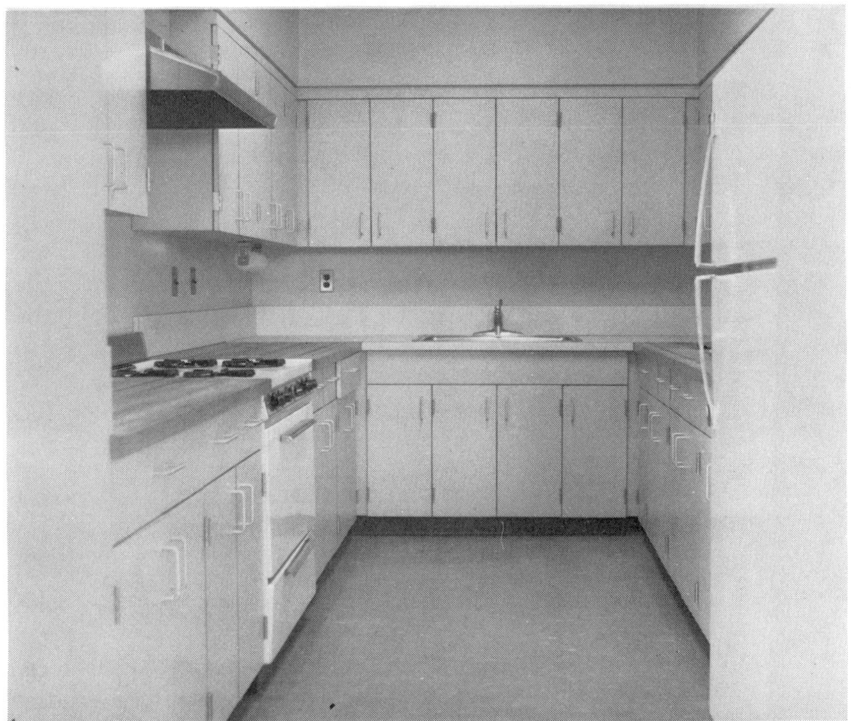

A alcove off dining and lounge hold kitchen facilities for four New Haven companies.

meetings. This room can have either a durable wood or plastic floor, wood or plaster walls and an acoustical tile ceiling. It is best to let the architect have the freedom to design this room since it probably will be used by the public as well as by the fire fighters. Because of the large number of people who will use the meeting room, specifications should call for a good and quiet ventilation system to remove smoke and heat. Microphones and speakers should be provided in several convenient locations so that talks can be heard, say, during the hubbub of dinner.

The meeting room will require a kitchen. Its size and equipment depend on the anticipated number of people to be served and the type of food service—catered or cooked on the premises. Ample refrigeration, ranges, and cabinet space will be necessary, as well as dishwashing units.

Fire fighters on duty need a recreation room preferably near the apparatus room. Again, it should be easily maintained, with vinyl floor,

A two-story addition doubled the size of headquarters of the Syosett, N.Y., Volunteer Fire Department. Three new bays and a recreation room and two meeting rooms were added. Schaardt & Fullan were the architects.

plastic or wood walls and acoustical tile ceiling. Items to be considered for this room would include a clock, radio, television, pool table, a reading area and anything else that would make the men comfortable and relaxed while they are awaiting an alarm. The room should be sturdily and tastefully furnished, well ventilated and air-conditioned.

Versatile rooms

The recreation area or "day room" can and should double as a classroom. To do so, there will be needed a blackboard, preferably 4 by 8 feet and mounted on a wall, and a roll-up projection screen. The screen can be mounted over the blackboard to save space. Electrical outlets should be so spaced that the need for extension cords will be held to a minimum for apparatus used—movie, slide and overhead projectors.

Volunteer fire stations having a meeting hall with kitchen appliances on the second floor, should also have at least limited kitchen facilities on the first floor adjacent to the apparatus or day rooms. Since volunteers frequently respond to the station wearing boots, rooms off the apparatus floor should have scuff-resistant flooring.

Depending on who is to occupy the building, a fire station might have to include offices for the fire commissioner, chief and company officers. Like other rooms in the station, these should be comfortable and air-conditioned since they will be occupied for long periods of time, particularly in a paid department. Considerable thought should be given to the furnishings required for these offices—desks, worktables, files, chairs—and their placement.

After construction starts, the chief should make sure the architect inspects the site regularly (once a week at a minimum) to see that the contractor is supplying what was specified. A good architect will help the contractor to interpret plans and specifications. And if the contractor deviates from the plans, he should stop the work. The architect should also approve requisitions so that the department does not overpay the contractor. Finally, the architect should meet regularly with the fire chief or his representatives to report on the progress of his work.

TRAINING GROUNDS

Experience—learning by doing—is one of the best ways to acquire skills. But, in the fire service, the doing (fighting fires) is hard to come by, except in the largest of cities that have thousands of alarms. There is, however, a substitute for doing and that substitute is training—a training that comes as close as possible to the real thing. This training, unhappily, is almost as hard to come by as field experience, but it can be done. All it requires is planning, money and application that results in drill ground facilities in which live fires and other emergencies can be simulated.

This leads us to the second structure, the building of which a fire chief might become involved in—training tower and associated buildings and facilities. Like the construction of a fire station and perhaps even more so, a training center calls for considerable planning. Large cities can construct a complete training ground, outfitted down to the last thermocouple, and in a relatively short time. But the chief of a small fire department, facing the thought of building a training center, very often surrenders in despair. This need not be be so.

To remove a mountain you begin by picking up the first stone and then keep picking. Eventually the mountain will be moved. The first "stone" for a training ground could be just a hole in the ground used for oil fires. It's a small start, but it might generate enough interest and enthusiasm to add another feature until there is eventually a complete facility.

Where money is scarce, it takes a long time, but no matter how long, it should be done by plan: acquire the land one year, pave it the next, put in main and hydrants the next, and so on. As the training center takes shape, it should be easier to pry more money out of local officials. You have something concrete to show them.

Ogden, Utah, Fire Department's training center, opened in 1975, contains five-story drill tower, burn room and classrooms on a 6-acre plot.

Of course, there are many fire departments that are just too small to ever build a complete training center. But the fact that there are so many is a tipoff of just what action they can take. We are speaking of collective action here in which the fire departments in a region, county or township pool their resources to get a training ground that all can use. In any event, the chief or whatever group in charge should remember that the training ground should provide simulation as real as possible to the fireground.

Assuming that the money is there and a fire chief has the go-ahead to build a reasonably sized drill ground—including tower or buildings, just what does he do? Like the fire station, a training center represents a long-time investment by the citizens of a community in their safety and welfare. Again, buildings in this center should be constructed of the best possible material in the best possible location with the best design and at a reasonable cost. Planning the location is extremely important in a fire department facility that calls for real fires in the Class A and B categories. (There are several fire departments in this country with elaborate training grounds in which live fires were prohibited after the training buildings and grounds were completed. Planning is so important!)

Environmental impact statement

When Chief Charles J. Hansen of the Ogden, Utah, Fire Department undertook to build a training center, he applied for a 6-acre parcel of federal government property that had been declared surplus. With this application he made "a plunge into the pool of bureaucracy that would have drowned a lesser man." Among other items the chief had to provide an environmental impact statement. No mean feat, but he came up with it after two months of research and correspondence.

Chief Hansen's environmental impact statement wound up as a half-inch-thick volume of facts, maps and figures. It contained, among other items, geological studies of the building site, water table statistics, population and traffic studies, emission counts, complete code of air conservation regulations for the county and state, regulations for and control of open burning from the local board of health, plus 11 pages describing the fire department organization, the need for the training facility, and how it would be utilized.

Again, like the construction of a fire station, a contemplated training ground requires the services of a good architect, and a good lawyer to see that the property is "clear" in real estate parlance. Most of the principles applied to the construction of a fire station will apply to the construction of a training tower. In addition, the architect will require the knowledge of just how to construct a room that will have to stand up under repeated training fires.

However, the chief will and should have more input in the original plans. Training buildings, unlike fire stations, are not regularly built, and there are few architects who have designed more than one. The only practical way for a chief to acquire this "input" is by visiting or at least getting the plans of other recently constructed training grounds.

Architectural style

Buildings used for training are usually designed with an eye to function rather than to architectural fitness and style. They need not, however, be an eyesore. Where a drill tower, or fire station, is an adjunct to, or part of, another structure, it should be in architectural harmony with other structures in the compound and, if possible (or necessary), should be in harmony with the buildings in the area. Today's towers, in contrast to the early metal or wooden scaffold-type structures, are built of concrete or brick on steel frames and are closed-in structures. (Windows, real stairs and doors add to the reality of training.) And since in a city there are many types of windows, as many types as possible should be included in the structural fire building.

For instance, the fire buildings in the New York Academy incorporate most of the type windows that can be found in that city—double-hung, casement, pivoting as in the newer high-rises, Florida windows and storms.

Locating the training grounds

It was always preferable that a training ground be located in an isolated area. Remember that some people don't even want a fire station in their neighborhood. Their feelings are even more intense when it comes to a training ground. Add to this the increasing concern with the environment that Chief Hanson of Ogden had to contend with, and you will see that the isolation of a training ground is an absolute must.

Facilities required

The forerunner of the modern municipal fire training grounds was built in Brookline, Mass., in 1939. Built in an isolated section of the city, it was the first municipal fire school in the country that combined a drill tower and fire station (separate buildings) with facilities for actual fire fighting. The fire station and drill tower were of fireproof construction. The plot measured 210 by 178 feet and was completely enclosed by a chain link fence. The buildings skirted the drill yard and the drill tower was so placed that apparatus could maneuver around it.

Training facilities included platforms for cellar pipes and distributors, a 30,000-gallon underground concrete water tank for drafting and testing engines, yard hydrants, a smoke house to demonstrate ventilation, a storage building, a six-story drill tower (with safety net) with all types of connections and fittings and a paved yard for the apparatus. With variations and improvements, today's drill yard follows the pattern set by Brookline.

What to build

Having decided on and acquired a site, just what does the fire chief build? This will, of course, depend on the money he has available. But no matter how much he has, he should make a start. With a low budget he can do as the Brookville, Ohio, Fire Department did. They put four wooden utility poles in the ground for a 40-foot tower, acquired an 18

Each story of the Delaware State Fire School fire building sits on one below, without being tied in, to prevent cracks.

× 30-foot wood garage to use as a smokehouse, constructed a concrete flammable liquid pit and put a tank truck in another burning pit—simple but a highly effective training ground at a total cost of $600 plus many hours of hard work by department members.

On the other end of the financial scale, there is the State Fire School at Dover, Dela. This is a complete training school built at one time in 1968 at a cost of $851,000 that included 13 acres of land. Assuming that a chief has this kind of money available (with the adjustments made for inflation in 1978), the Delaware school incorporates the features that should be included in a training school: administration, classroom and laboratory buildings, drill tower, structural fire buildings, smoke house, forcible entry building, control tower, flammable liquid burning areas, drafting pad, rescue training area (for vehicular extrication, etc.), water main and hydrant system, pump house and a pond.

Structural fire building

Not every fire department can afford a full training tower, but any chief who contemplates building a training ground should give high priority to a structural fire building. This building can be used for fighting interior fires, for drilling in ladder and hose work, can double as a smokehouse for mask drills, incorporate features for drilling in

Low-cost fire building of Bloomfield, Conn., has a cellar, flat and pitched roofs and a fire escape. Built of cement block with complete floors, it is 2½ stories high and about 24 × 30 feet in area.

forcible entry, and for a variety of other drills that cover search and rescue, ventilation and sprinkler and standpipe operations.

Such a building should be made of cement or cement block that can withstand heat that is sufficient to make training realistic as from oil or wood fires. The Bloomfield, Conn., Fire Department constructed a structural fire building in 1965 for $35,000. A 2½-story-high building measuring 24 × 30 feet, it was constructed of cement block with concrete floors. The Dayton, Ohio, Fire Department has a two to five-story fire building which incorporates a six-story drill tower. In Dayton, there is one fire room lined with refractory brick, and this room has thermocouples at three levels to monitor temperatures. At the Houston $1.5 million fire academy complex, the interior walls are made of 3000° refractory brick and the ceilings 2400° refractory cement.

Structural fire buildings can vary in size as seen from the above, but a 2½-story building seems to be the most commonly found. One with a basement is preferable, but if a basement proves impractical or too

Cut-out panel, overhead, permits use of power saws and axes on floor above in the Dayton, Ohio, Fire Department environmental training building.

costly, improvisation can take its place. Designate the first floor as the basement and work down into it from the second. Windows and doors in a fire building should be similar to those found in the fire response area not only for members to become familiar with them, but also to make drills even more realistic.

Whenever possible, structural fire buildings should have a combined pitched and flat roof equipped with scuttles and covers, bulkhead doors and whatever else can be found on a roof to make training more realistic and effective.

Cut-out panels can be installed on the roofs of structural fire buildings (and floors) to provide training in ventilation. Trainees can use power saws, axes and bars such as the claw tool in the same manner that they will be called upon to do on the fireground.

Four stacks take heat and smoke to areas of Dayton Fire Department environmental building, which has six-story training tower. Oil furnace and incinerator provide the realism in training sessions.

As mentioned above, windows and doors should match the windows that will be found in the "field." This calls for a variety of window sizes and shapes: double hung, wood frame, steel casement, etc. They will be found useful in practicing ventilation and entry.

If possible, provisions should be made for movable partitions within a structural fire building to provide a variety of floor layouts. Corrugated iron partitions can be used for this purpose as well as wood set in grooves in the floor. The wood, of course, adds fuel and gases to the fire and should be sufficiently thick to last for a good number of fires.

Training in heat and smoke

In some fire buildings (Dayton and Houston were among the first) there is an oil furnace to build up heat in the various rooms and an incinerator to provide smoke. Parts of the Dayton building can be heated to 2000° which is measured by thermocouples that can be hooked up in various locations within the building. In less elaborate training grounds, fire fighters use damp straw, fuel oil, rags, wood and what have you. But the damp straw, while making a lot of smoke, generates little heat. The other materials, while providing heat and smoke, leave an awful mess to clean up.

Although it was constructed in 1960, the fire building on the training grounds of the Washington, D.C., Fire Department is still considered among the most elaborate and complete of all fire buildings. It offers an excellent model for others to build on. This building (27 × 51 feet) is constructed of fire-resistant concrete and hard fire brick. It is basically divided into two "sides" by both its architectural aspects and movable steel ribbon partitions. The simulated residential side (26 × 27 feet) has a basement, first and second floors. Here again, movable steel partitions divide each floor into four rooms. These steel partitions, while referred to as movable, are floor to ceiling, bolted into place and sectionalized so different doorway arrangements can be made. The basement of the residential side contains four oil pits, one in each room with valving arrangements for fuel intake and water drains. There is an open stairway from the basement to the second floor, and a roof scuttle opening for ventilation problems. At two locations in this area, the roof and the first floor, there are areas approximately 2 by 6 feet, fabricated of wooden 2×6s so they may be chopped through. Slots in the first and second floors under wooden partitions allow the setting and spread of partition fires.

The simulated mercantile area (26 × 27 feet) has three floors and a penthouse. All floors are open areas not divided by partitions and an enclosed stairway leads from the first floor to the roof. A simulated dumbwaiter shaft extends from the first to the third floor. A complete dry sprinkler system is installed on the second floor. Also rising within the enclosed stairway is a standpipe system, which through valving, may be made either a wet or dry system. The roof on this side of the building has a skylight, stack vent, a wood "chop through" area, and a steel ladder leading to a penthouse roof and chimney. In the basement under this side of the building, which is protected from the residential basement by a masonry fire wall, are the control valves for the sprinkler and standpipe systems, a smoke-making machine, and an oil-burning furnace.

The smoke-making machine is one produced for the meat industry, is sawdust burning, and is used for charging the building with smoke. This smoke may be channeled to particular parts or rooms of the building by duct work. The furnace is capable of maintaining a 100° differential temperature within the building at the same time the smoke generator is running. With its highly fire-resistant construction, the building may

Instructor in tower at Montgomery County, Md., $6-million training academy checks readouts for temperature and carbon monoxide in fire building below.

be used to house fires of considerable size for training students in methods of fire attack. There are 18 thermocouples located at strategic points in the building, which are read in the thermocouple dial house. Windows in both the residential and mercantile areas are steel sash, casement, double-hung, and commercial awning and butterfly types, glazed with single-strength glass.

Thermocouple dial house

A two-story building is the control center for outside activities. On the second floor there is a multipoint recorder for 18 thermocouples in the fire training building and a program board for determining sequence of the readings. The programming may consist of reading from all 18 points in consecutive order, or any number of points (with a minimum of two) in any order desired. Also in this location are controls for pumping oil to the basement of the fire training building or the open pits, and a control console for the communication system throughout the outside areas.

The first floor of this building houses a first-aid station, drinking fountain and toilet facilities. In the basement is the fuel oil storage tank

"Christmas tree" at Delaware State training center is a vertical pipe with several short, branched, vertical perforated pipes. Fires are fed by natural or LP gas or fuel oil. The gas line should have a valve that a fire fighter (protected by a fog stream) can reach.

for the pits, the oil pump and a reclamation system whereby the oil and water returning from the pits are separated, with the oil returning to the storage tank and the water running into a disposal sump.

A further refinement to the control building was added by the Dayton Fire Department when they installed recording apparatus for a gas monitoring system. In their separate control building, gases from the fire building are sampled automatically by a monitoring device that has an output in which lines appear on graphs that give the percentages of carbon monoxide and oxygen, as well as the temperature, within the fire building. If readings from the fire building indicate that a dangerous condition is forming, the safety officer in control can ring a bell to alert fire fighters operating within the fire building.

If a fire building is constructed alone (without a training tower) there should be a fire escape for training in the handling of hose lines (in addition to the usual concrete and steel interior stairs).

A sprinkler system should be installed in at least one area of the fire building so that it can be operated under actual fire conditions. A standpipe is another item worth considering even if there is one already in existence in the drill tower.

A unique feature of the Delaware State Fire School fire building is a double-brick interior wall with about a foot of hollow space. This wall extends to one side of the building where there is an interior door at ground level. Instructors place combustible material inside the hollow wall and ignite it to simulate a partition. In the story above, there is a small iron door opening to the hollow space that permits a stream to extinguish the fires.

Drill towers

The first edition of the Fire Chief's Handbook recommended that larger departments have drill towers as high as six stories with basement and roof. It noted that those in large departments did not exceed four stories, and that those in smaller departments were only two or three stories. The point was made, however, that even in the smaller communities "there may be buildings such as schools, institutions, grain elevators and others in excess of five or six stories" and that consequently a small drill tower might not be sufficient for training.

In view of the high-rise hotels and other structures that have been built in small towns in recent years, this advice still holds. Further, since a drill tower offers a reasonable approximation to a high-rise building, it is unquestionably a good practice to enclose the tower on all floors. This is to simulate fire fighting as it can occur on upper floors.

The New York City Fire Academy

Set amidst an array of natural greenery, comprised of shrubs, trees and grass sits the campus of the new New York City Fire Academy. The site consists of a 27-acre fire training center which has been constructed adjacent to 68 acres of parkland which could potentially be available for future expansion. It is situated on Wards Island, which is located among the three boroughs of Manhattan, Queens and the Bronx. The training center, which is partly constructed on landfill, is adjoined on two sides by city parkland, by the East River on a third side, and by a large municipal water pollution control plant on its fourth side. It is primarily flat with the exception of a 10-foot-high berm of raised earth which provides for visual and functional separation of the office and classroom facilities from the demonstration and experimentation elements of the site. A 260-foot-long wharf has been constructed out into the East River as part of the training center.

The overall site consists of nine buildings and several other physical improvements to the 27-acre tract of land. These other improvements include a simulated "subway tunnel," gasoline and diesel fuel pumps, street "mock-up," roadways, a 300-car parking lot, complete site lighting (for 24-hour-a-day operations), a 200,000-gallon water supply tank, a

New York City Fire Academy, opened in 1977, consists of a 27-acre training center constructed adjacent to 68 acres of parkland potentially available for expansion. Administration building (center) equivalent to several stories on one side slopes into a mound of earth on the other.

suction pit for drafting tests, an extra heavy-duty storm draining system (to accommodate large water drain-offs from fire simulations) and a park and picnic area.

The training center is adjoined on its western and northern sides by the Randall's Island City Park. The park consists of tennis courts, baseball and softball fields, walking, jogging and cycling paths and roads. These facilities can be utilized by the academy and its personnel. The location affords the members of the department the opportunity to engage in their physical fitness programs. It also provides a playing site for the various teams and leagues that are associated with "the bravest."

The 22,000-seat Randall's Island Stadium is located just 350 feet west of the site and could be used by the academy for special presentations, gatherings of fire service personnel, public relations programs or athletic events.

Training tower provides instructors and students with a variety of simulated building types, together with working standpipes and sprinkler systems.

The training center consists of two entirely separate sections—an administrative and education building, built of corrugated metal and glass with loudly colored interior spaces, and the actual training buildings, mock-ups of real buildings designed to "burn down" again and again in training sessions. The administrative building is long and narrow, with a roof that is sloped so steeply as to merge into a mound of raised earth on the south side, while rising to the equivalent of several floors on the north side.

The notion of familiar in an unfamiliar context is even more obvious in the training buildings, which are imitations of the sort of real building fire fighters encounter in the line of duty. There is a mock tenement, a frame-type dwelling, a taxpayer and a loft building, all in a row that suggests a city street somehow dropped into the emptiness of Wards Island.

Administration and education building

The main education and administration building is the largest and most important structure on the site. It has 40,000 square feet of space. Included in this building are eight classrooms with a total capacity of 420 students, a multipurpose auditorium capable of seating 550 persons, and a laboratory and lecture room with auditorium-style seating for 75 persons. This lab is equipped with an especially powerful smoke baffle and exhaust system for use in both experiments and demonstrations.

Typical New York tenement. Practically any fire situation found in such buildings can be realistically imitated by instructors for students.

The main education building also boasts a large television studio and control room which are located right in the building with provisions made for the possible future development of videotape programs as well as closed-circuit broadcast to the offices and classrooms located right on the site. A combination of permanently partitioned and flexibly arranged open office spaces are available in this building, accommodating up to 100 persons. Almost all of these desk spaces are already equipped with their own electricity and telephone connections. A large conference room which seats 40 persons is centrally located within the office area. Graphics, reproduction, library annex and photographic areas are also located within the building.

Basic training buildings

The smoke house, the tower and the movie set—a valuable asset for any training center—are primarily designed for teaching and actual practice in the fundamental skills of the fire fighter and the necessary teamwork needed for a given unit to face its daily encounters "in the field."

The basic training building—the smoke house—was designed to allow

Simulated taxpayer (part of a simulated block) makes use of "expandable structural elements"—parts of floors, ceilings and walls made of replaceable wooden pieces for burning during training sessions.

for the construction of high heat and gaseous blazes in both ships and buildings, and is equipped with gas analysis equipment as well as other instrumentation for performing various types of experiments. A measuring sump is also available in this facility so that fire department personnel can assess the most efficient hose streams and suppression techniques.

The simulated city block would rival a movie set as it has the layout and buildings necessary for a feature film on fire fighting.

There are four special buildings on the campus which are equipped to simulate a wide variety of structures and fire fighting problems including tenements, taxpayers (one-story storefronts), and frame dwellings. A training tower provides instructors and students with a variety of simulated building types, together with working standpipe and sprinkler systems.

The training tower is a four-sided, five-story building and is the foundation for the training of the fire fighter in his ladder work.

The exterior of the tower allows ample room for ladder raising to the

Simulated frame dwelling is also part of the typical city block. As with all buildings, interior is constructed or lined with fire brick to resist heat.

ladder wall, achieved by wing walls which increase the area for ground ladder placement. The tower contains a three-window net and a two-window net, permitting two diverse groups to train simultaneously in rope work and scaling ladder work, as well as perform operational exercises from aerial and tower ladders.

The interior of the tower features a standpipe system, a sprinkler system on one floor, complete mock-ups of dumbwaiters and incinerators, classroom space, and storage space. In addition, provisions for creating smoke conditions in the building have been made. A variable floor layout to simulate tenements, high-rise office buildings, etc., has also been provided. The windows on the ladder wall duplicate the various types that are found throughout the city, from double-hung and casement, to modern high-rise keyed to a fire department access panel.

The taxpayer, tenement and frame dwelling structures make use of what has been dubbed "expendable structural components," parts of floors, ceilings and walls which are made of replaceable wooden pieces for the purpose of burning during training sessions, education program simulations, tests and experiments. Most of the partitions and bearing walls are constructed or lined with reinforced concrete with a special admixture, or fire brick, to resist high heat.

Multipurpose auditorium with balcony in administration building is capable of seating 550 persons. Building also has eight classrooms and an auditorium-styled laboratory room for use in both experiments and demonstrations.

Virtually every type of fire hazard situation, ranging from rural bungalows to high-risers can be safely simulated within this group of buildings. Tests of building materials and fire detection and suppression equipment, together with demonstrations of techniques and procedures can be conducted in this controlled environment, where the same experiment can be safely repeated literally hundreds of times.

The diagnostic center

The apparatus repair and development building is ideally suited for assisting in virtually every element of the training center's operations. This building contains lifts and specialized diagnostic and shop equipment which is available to maintain fire apparatus and vehicles used by the center and to assist in the development and evaluation of new fire apparatus and accessories. A calibrated drafting pit has been specially designed to evaluate the capabilities of fire pumping equipment. Provisions have been made for the addition of a variety of other apparatus oriented facilities. It will be the home of the chauffeur training school and will house a unit from repairs and transportation.

The other service building is the breathing apparatus building and is the home of the mask service unit and the radiological unit. Equipment for the repair, testing and the development of breathing apparatus is located in this building's shops, together with compressors for replenishing the air consumed by the academy's staff and students in demonstrations, tests and simulated fire operations.

Land marine facility

The last building in the row of structures as you approach the waters of the East River is the marine facility and the division of training firehouse.

The joint marine building and simulated firehouse complex, together with its adjoining 260-foot wharf and the planned periodic stationing of a New York City fireboat at this location, provides a useful focal point for the development of programs in marine fire protection. The marine building contains two 35-seat classrooms and office space for up to 30 persons who can direct their efforts toward the development of programs in marine fire protection or other areas of interest to the academy. The simulated firehouse contains a mock-up of a typical firehouse and is equipped with large observation windows so that a number of the different elements of firehouse operations can be studied, and potentially improved. It also contains a 25-seat classroom.

VALLEY
METRO

CHAPTER FIVE

Emergency communications

In 1845, New York City was divided into 12 fire alarm districts, each equipped with a bell tower and a 24-hour watchman. When the "watch" discovered a fire in the district he would strike the number of his tower on his bell. This signal would then be passed along by the watchmen in other towers until the entire city and its volunteer fire fighters were alerted. For fires within buildings which hadn't "lit up," the persons discovering the fire ran to the nearest tower to alert the watchman to sound the alarm. Since the entire department could be notified in short order, this was a big step forward in fire department communications.

In this system were two of the three elements needed for efficient communications—discovery of a fire and notification to the fire companies as to where (roughly) it had occurred. The third element, good fireground communications, was still a long way down the road and actually didn't come about until the development of the two-way radio.

The life of the bell tower and watchman, however, was very short. Even before the system was installed, Samuel F. B. Morse, Jr., had demonstrated, in 1842, the first practical means for transmitting electrical impulses. And by 1843, an Englishman, Alexander Baine, established a patent applying the electrical telegraph to the need for sending alarms for fire. But his original model was extremely crude and impractical, and it remained for Dr. W. F. Channing, who had earlier and independently been advocating the use of telegraph for fire alarm, to produce a workable system. This workable street box alarm system was first installed in Boston in 1847. Channing's patents were later bought by John Gamewell, still a familiar name, and under Gamewell and his successors and several inventors the fire alarm box system was constantly improved.

Today's three-fold system provides full noninterference (when two or more boxes are simultaneously pulled on the same circuit), quick succession (of boxes on hold) and automatic grounding which overcomes broken wiring. Associated with proper equipment at the fire alarm central office, the three-fold box when pulled on an open circuit will transmit a full and correct alarm.

The alarm box signals were initially transmitted in Morse code, but soon gave way to the simple number codes still in use. Each box has a number associated with a card that lists the units assigned either to respond to the box or to relocate to cover other units.

Auxiliary systems

A natural outgrowth of the municipal fire alarm system was its adaptation for the protection of public buildings and industrial property. And 1881 saw the development of the first auxiliary fire alarm system which permitted an interior non-code box within a building to actuate a street box. This auxiliary system had a further growth when the automatic sprinkler system made its appearance in 1879. Not only could the sprinkler detect and extinguish a fire but when the sprinkler alarm was developed it could also be connected electrically to the auxiliary fire alarm system to summon the fire fighters, as well as to sound a warning for the occupants of the protected buildings. Still later fire and smoke detectors were built into the auxiliary systems. Such systems were readily accepted by the public and industry and have become increasingly sophisticated and reliable down through the years.

While smaller factories and buildings were installing city-connected auxiliary systems, the larger industrial concerns, with extensive property, were being protected by self-sufficient systems of the "proprietary" type. These were similar to those installed for municipalities except for the more liberal use of automatic detection devices and frequently with combined supervisory and watch facilities. Many such systems were (and still are) user-owned and maintained; others are rented on a maintained-service, annual-payment basis.

Interior alarm systems for private use can be (and the early ones were) extremely simple—no more complicated than the common door bell system. An actuating device (the pull station), an audible alarm (bell or horn), and a power supply are essential components. However, a wide range of variables are offered in the present-day "local" system.

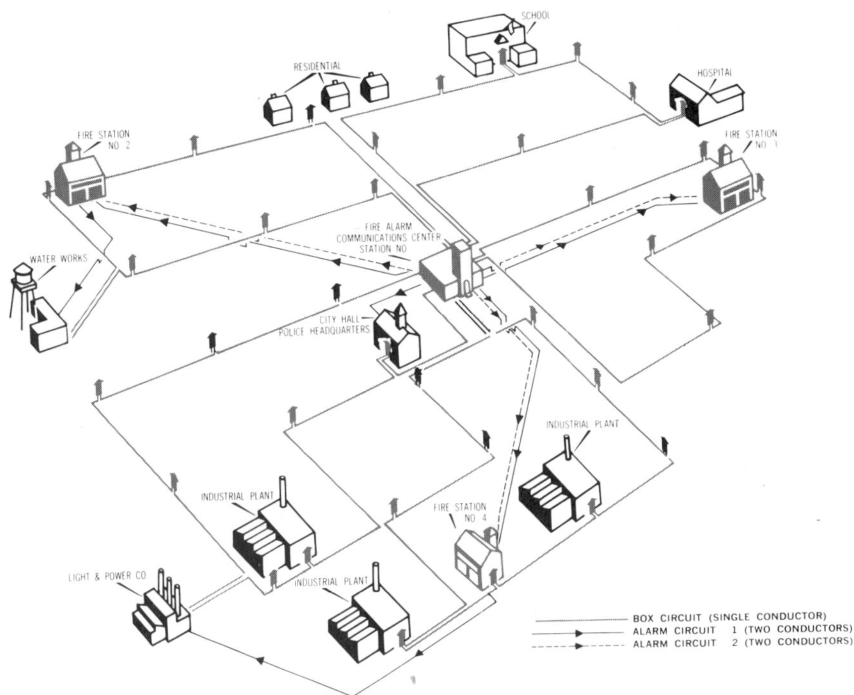

Typical Class A fire alarm telegraph system ties in major buildings in area.

The system can be non-code, sounding only a general alarm, or coded, sounding a distinctive alarm for each station or area. Also there are "pre-signal" systems, providing for an advance alarm at a staff location and requiring a secondary manual action for sounding the general alarm. Except where these local systems are required by law for protection of life or are intended to secure insurance premium reductions, the type and arrangement selected for a particular property depends on the preference of the building owner or, as often, of the seller. By and large, the systems sold today as such adhere closely to the standards set forth by the National Fire Protection Association, thus assuring the buyer of acceptable quality standards. UL-listed components are likewise desirable.

Changes in dispatching

Company dispatching was done by telegraph, using the same principles as the street box circuit. Companies delayed en route for any reason

Emergency voice communications box connects to dispatcher by wire.

First emergency voice communications was a telephone adapted to street box.

could only go to the nearest street alarm box and tap out breakdown signals. By the 1930s, the telephone filled that gap.

After World War II, two developments began to greatly simplify dispatching. One was the vocal alarm system. Bell and register devices were supplemented or replaced by a loudspeaker, over which the alarm information and the responding units were called out for all to hear. More recently, this has gained two-way capability.

The second forward step in station communications was the selective alarm principle, as adopted in Los Angeles a generation ago. Previously every fire station received all alarms. As the number of alarms increased, circuits were modified so that only the stations required to respond were alerted.

The 911 number

Twenty years ago, the International Association of Fire Chiefs recommended a universal three-digit number for reporting fires that would automatically connect the caller (without a coin at a pay phone) with the fire department. In 1967, a national commission on law enforcement urged such a number "preferably over the entire United States" for use in any emergency. The following year, the Bell System made the number 911 available for that purpose providing a single answering point was established for fire, police and other emergency services.

By 1972, more than 500 911 systems had been set up, including those in New York City, Washington, Seattle, Detroit and Denver. The 1973 Emergency Medical Services System Act called for such services to use 911 and a number of states have acted to require 911 statewide.

Equipping street boxes with telephones of some sort was tried or considered in many places early in the 1950s. Minneapolis, which has a municipally owned telephone utility, tried fitting a few dozen boxes with phones in 1955. Pulling the hook both sent a telegraph alarm signal and connected the telephone set to the alarm office operator. The box was locally designed.

By the following year, telephone-type street boxes usable with standard telegraph circuits were on the market. Many problems—proper cabling for voice transmission, vandal-proofing, system voltage, circuit testing—had to be dealt with before today's emergency voice communications systems (EVCS) could be offered. One of the big items in both EVCS installation and maintenance is the cable plant.

This is not needed by the radio box, pilot models of which were on the market between 1954 and 1956. The radio box sends its signal in milliseconds, and it can have push buttons for other emergency services in addition to fire. Typical boxes transmit three tone-coded rounds of three or four-digit numbers with a tape readout. The boxes, which have solar cells that are recharged by the sun, test themselves daily and a central office console circuit can be activated to display the numbers of any boxes that failed to send test signals during the previous 24 hours (as required by NFPA 73). The radio box can be located anywhere, relocated easily, and accidents or storms are never a threat except to individual boxes.

Dispatching paid fire fighters is but one part of the dispatching problem as the majority of the nation's fire fighters are volunteers. The alerting of volunteers by a watchman's cry or a fire bell was replaced in the mid-1800s by factory steam whistles in mill or railroad shop towns. Later electric sirens and air horns were used. The air horn allowed the use of coded signals to indicate actual or phantom box locations.

In smaller communities, the telephone operator became in essence a fire alarm dispatcher. She received fire calls from people who merely took the receiver off the hook and she either activated a fire siren atop the firehouse or called volunteers—or sometimes did both.

As dial telephone systems expanded, local operators disappeared, forcing volunteer fire departments to hire dispatchers or to have the local police answer the fire phone and operate the dispatching system. Still others used the 24-hour guard office of a local factory, and some hired a commercial answering service to receive fire calls.

Special phone circuits

The second major postwar development was the wide availability of special phone circuits whereby a person calling the fire department number would ring each phone on the circuit simultaneously. The first person to answer could operate switches to cut off the microphones of the other phones, but everyone at the other phones could listen. Another switch at each phone could start the fire siren or air horn to summon the volunteer fire fighters.

An adaptation of this type circuit was installed in December 1958 in Garden City, N. Y., to alert volunteers. The dispatcher could cause a distinctive ringing signal on 70 home phones simultaneously by dialing a single digit. He dictated the alarm information into a transcriber which repeated the message for three minutes as volunteers picked up their telephones.

The problem of a busy phone in a home was solved by technology. If a phone is in use in the system installed for the Glenbrook Fire Department in Stamford, Conn., the alarm transmission signal produces a distinctive tone. The fire fighter asks his caller to hang up and so does he. Then he picks up the receiver to hear the transcribed dispatch message. This variation was first developed in the early '50s by the Mountain States Telephone Company in Colorado.

Radio alerting systems

The third major development in alerting volunteers was radio. In 1946, four Maryland communities asked FCC permission to use experimental "power-casting," or carrier, radio. This couples audio signals directly into normal power lines. Messages are received by a properly adapted home radio receiver plugged into these power lines. Carrier transmission also was used without voice in 1950 in Rockville Centre, N. Y. Through the municipal power plant, box alarms were transmitted to volunteers' homes via a 3800-cycle tone signal and a receiver plugged into any home receptacle.

Direct radio transmission, without power line connections, began appearing in alerting systems 25 years ago. In Prince Georges County, Md., and Erie County, N. Y., a central dispatcher activated public alarm sirens by radio.

Currently, the most widely used form of volunteer dispatching is the home alerting receiver. To avoid confusion and garbled messages, home receivers were activated by sending out tone codes.

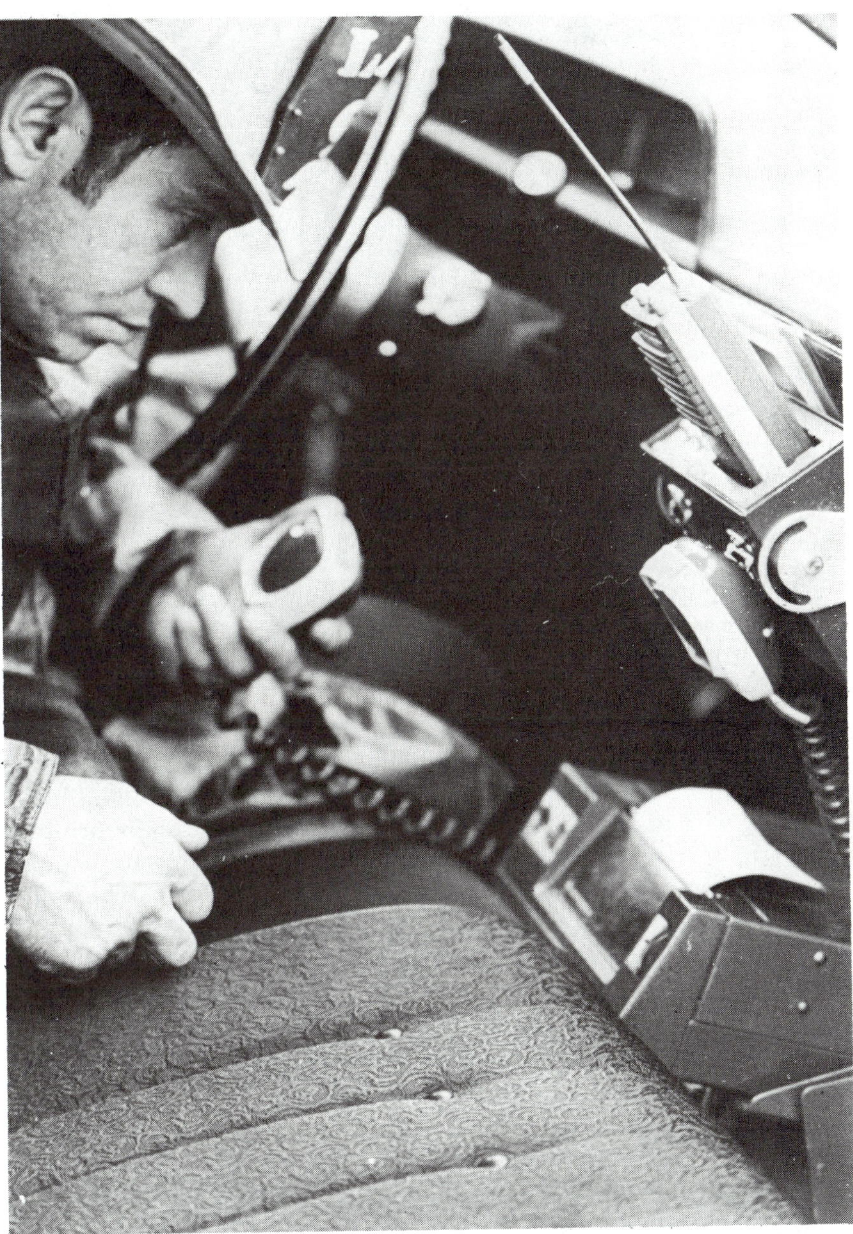

Mobile radio teleprinter gives chief officer printout of information about location of alarm and the companies dispatched. Same unit is installed in fire stations.

Status board and map are prominent features of San Francisco's $2-million computerized dispatch system set up in 1976.

The last decade has brought growing use of the pager or beeper, a pocket receiver a man can take with him almost anywhere. The next step was the hard copy transmission of maps, messages and even building plans by wire or radio. Electronic voicewriters or facsimile printers began fire service use about 1961. Later, the fire station teletypewriter became a common communications medium for both dispatching and routine departmental messages.

Teleprinters may operate via land line or radio. In Worcester, Mass., teleprinters are in chief officers' cars. Both Denver and Los Angeles have experimented with the transmission of map data on hazards, hydrants, etc., from microfilm central office copies to receivers in vehicles.

Computerized dispatching

The ultimate is now computerized dispatching. Radio and wire links between central office, fire station and apparatus can be tied in with computer files.

San Francisco, the latest city to go on computer, launched its $2 million system in 1976. The dispatcher is at the heart of all such systems. He must be able to decide quickly and accurately what equipment the emergency requires, where such equipment should come from, and how best to cover areas vacated when that equipment is sent elsewhere. The computer can process information so fast that, if properly programmed, it can make these basic decisions for the dispatcher, leaving him free to deal with the unexpected. In simple terms, the system uses computer files of all streets and blocks in the city, all box alarm assignments, service status of every fire fighting unit, a "quarters listing" of every unit location, a "common place" file on all major public buildings, street hydrant data, and response route descriptions.

When an alarm comes in, the dispatcher keys the location into his console. A screen at once displays a suggested assignment of companies. If the dispatcher wishes to make changes, he enters them on his keyboard, then presses the dispatch button. Station lights are turned on, teletypewriter messages sent, the public address system activated and the apparatus rolls.

As wireless telegraphy, mobile radio first entered the fire service when a set was installed aboard the New York fireboat James Duane in 1913. However, the expense of round-the-clock operators soon ended the experiment and all of New York City's fireboats did not carry radio telephones until 1937.

Before mobile radio could become useful on land, size, weight and reliability problems had to be solved. Plagued by serious interference, fading or distortion, radios of those days were simply not worth while for emergency communications. The superheterodyne receiver was an improvement, along with more rugged tubes using less power. However, the transmitter took much more power than the receiver, and automobile electrical systems were inadequate for the higher power demand. So it's not surprising that the first emergency service radios were one-way police receivers. By 1940, most large police departments and a few fire rescue units had two-way radios, which were often the size of a footlocker.

A 1940 Fire Engineering survey showed that most or all the chief officers' cars in major cities such as Boston, Baltimore and Washington carried one-way radios and in a few cases, two-way radios. The latter were more common on fireboats, which had room for the bulky transmitter.

Universal practice at the time was for the fire department to use the police radio system and dispatchers. No independent fire service radio systems existed because the FCC was not issuing licenses to fire departments. Direct telephone lines linked fire alarm dispatchers to police radio equipment.

World War II brought about reliable, lightweight sets and FM (fre-

Two-way radio mike and controls at rear of elevating platform are supplemented by walkie-talkies. Two intercom mikes permit conversation from ground to basket.

quency modulation) radios with their superior transmission and reception qualities began to supplant AM (amplitude modulation) sets, a trend that accelerated during the 1950s.

By 1946, the Los Angeles City Fire Department had two-way FM radios on all land and marine units, and the department's three 250-watt base stations were augmented by a fourth.

Detroit completed its fire radio installation, separate from police communications in 1949, and a survey that year indicated that nearly 70 percent of the communities with more than 5000 population had fire radio.

On July 1, 1949, the FCC designated three bands for the fire service: the low band, 25 to 50 MHz; the high, or VHF band, 150 to 174 MHz; and the UHF band, 450 to 470 MHz.

The FCC in June 1958 created the local government radio service to allow local governments to set up radio communications for any official function. This was a firm basis for separate fire radio operations. At the same time, it was announced that further use of police channels for fire radio traffic would not be allowed after October 1963.

Band widths split

Also in 1958, the FCC ordered transmitter band widths reduced in five years. This band-splitting doubled the low-band channels and tripled the 152 to 162-MHz channels.

The licensing of mobile repeaters was approved by the FCC in 1972. A mobile repeater, carried in a vehicle, retransmits a walkie-talkie transmission through the vehicle's more powerful mobile radio. Base station repeaters, available for years, permit mobile units to broadcast areawide by causing the higher power base transmitter to simultaneously rebroadcast the mobile message.

The already heavy radio traffic worsened during the 1970s because of the rapid growth in emergency medical services. Clear-channel transmission of vital medical information such as electrocardiograms had never been anticipated by the FCC or the fire service. In August 1974, the FCC made 12 pairs of channels available in the 450-474 MHz band for this new purpose with the caution that interagency cooperation was essential because the channels would have to be used on an areawide basis.

Although many fire departments use one frequency, two are common—one for the base station and general use and the other for fireground communications. From four to a dozen channels may be needed by metropolitan departments.

Statewide radio links

Some states are almost totally blanketed by individual radio systems that are interconnected through county and statewide frequencies. This has been true for a decade of Connecticut's eight counties served by more than 300 departments.

Mobile radio equipment has gone through four generations of technology. First came the tube/vibrator/dynamotor sets using wide band FM. Second were the narrow band or split-channel FM sets, which sometimes used switching transistors in the power supply. The third generation, quite common today, uses solid-state circuitry and printed circuits. Tubes are used only in some high-power base stations. In the fourth generation, now making its debut, integrated circuit (IC) chips permit extreme miniaturization.

It was the third and fourth generations which made possible the growth of walkie-talkies. Through joint recommendation by the IAFC and the International Municipal Signal Association, separate frequencies

Telegraph headquarters in Stamford, Conn., provides readout of messages.

in the low and UHF bands were set aside for portables with up to 3 watts of power.

Advent of walkie-talkies

In the early 1950s, the transistor was just coming into commercial use, so the backpack or shoulder strap portable radio with a telephone handset was the normal equipment. Small rechargeable batteries were also being introduced at that time, the forerunner of today's power supplies with their compact solid-state chargers. The greatly reduced power required by solid-state transceivers had a great effect in reducing battery size, so that miniaturization has compounded itself.

But as late as 1958, the portable walkie-talkie was still not used in many fire departments. The small belt-carried set had only recently been introduced. The next step was a set for each chief officer. It was another 15 years before a walkie-talkie was in the hands of many company officers.

There has been some attempt to bring the individual fire fighter into the communications network via radio-equipped masks. However, it has not caught on.

The next improvement was the mobile communications center, a field base station that frees the normal base station dispatcher for other operations. In some cities, the mobile center may simply be a designated car which links fireground units to the main base. Or it may be a fully equipped mobile radio or TV studio. Chicago's van carries closed-circuit television equipment plus radios to communicate with all city utilities, transportation authorities, and city and suburban police. Several major cities have similar rigs.

In between these extremes are the more modest vehicles like the Anne Arundel County, Md., communications van converted in 1972 from a former police vehicle at a cost of only $1100. It contains map desk space, four sets of radio equipment with seven channels, spare portables and batteries, plus running cards and data on all county fire departments.

The first FCC licenses for mobile fire dispatch centers, suitable for any fire frequency in the state, were issued in 1960 for five California units intended for statewide use in mutual aid work at major disasters.

Understanding the message

There is more to communications than the hardware listed above—much more. Communications is the "transmitting and understanding of words" which underlies all fire service operations. And in this transmission, clarity is all important. To obtain this clarity the "10 codes" were introduced about 30 years ago. Since then about half the nation's fire departments have adopted them in some form or other. However, the IAFC Radio Committee in 1955 recommended that they not be used because of the lack of completely standard meanings.

"Actually there is good sound reasoning for using the codes," according to Chief W. Varnedoe, Jr., of the Green Mountain, Ala., Fire Department[1].

"Experts in information transfer have come up with a general principle: the smaller the selection of possible messages, the higher the probability of the receipt of the intended message by a given means in a given time or, with the same probability of receipt, the fewer the possible messages, the shorter the time to get the message through.

"In a simple example, if only two messages are permitted—yes or no—versus a system of five possible messages—yes, no, probably, maybe and improbably—then the number of times the listener will ask for a repeat will be greater in the second system.

"In the real world using radio voice, the number of possible messages

[1]*Clarity Should Be Goal of Radio Codes,* Fire Engineering, September 1975.

is almost infinite. We are helped somewhat because we expect the text on the fire frequency to pertain to fires or the fire service. The word 'booster' conjures up an image of a hose, not a club supporter or a high chair. This is a message-limiting of a sort. But even the English of the fire service has a great number of words at its disposal."

Making improvements

Varnedoe felt that we can greatly improve our transmissions by doing nothing more than limiting the words and phrases permitted in the most used messages. Instead of letting the man on the radio phone choose whether to say "on the scene," "we're here," "at the site," "have arrived," etc., we tell him always to say, "We've arrived," for example. The dispatcher is expected to hear arrived, so if only . . .ived is received, he still understands.

The techniques of limiting the message pool, according to Varnedoe is carried to a practical limit on the numerical code system. It forces a limit on the normal vocabulary without totally restricting possible messages "because one can always revert to words to say anything." It is also clear when the speaker is stating a message from the limited pool (using numerals) or is stating something out of the ordinary (using words).

The most effective codes seldom use more than 40 to 60 signals. But when fewer signals are used, the resort to words becomes too frequent. For years each department has devised its own code or at best has joined with surrounding departments in developing a code. Some use "Signal

Darien, Conn., Fire Service Radio Signals
51—Apparatus responding to alarm
52—Back in quarters
53—Reduce response to ordinary road speed
54—Return to quarters
55—Going on drill
56—Apparatus on the air

RADIO CODE SIGNALS

INSTRUCTIONS

10-1 Call your quarters
10-2 Return to your quarters
10-3 Call dispatcher by phone
10-4 Acknowledgement
10-5 Repeat message
10-6 Stand by
10-7 Verify address
10-8 In service by radio
10-9 Off the air
10-10 What is your location
10-11 Request radio test count
10-12 1st arriving unit, give preliminary
10-14 Breakdown of apparatus
10-18 Return all units except Engine Co., Ladder Co. required at scene
10-19 Return all units except unit required at scene
10-20 Proceed to box location at reduced speed

PRELIMINARY REPORTS, FIRE

10-21 Brush fire
10-22 Outside rubbish fire
10-23 Abandoned Derelict Vehicle fire
10-24 Auto fire
10-25 Manhole fire, condition
RED: (a) Fire extended to building
(b) Gas main leaking area
(c) Gas leak in structure
ORANGE: One or more manhole covers blown
YELLOW: Smoke seeping from manhole
WHITE: Fire in building (main fuse box affected)
10-26 Food on stove
10-30 Request for 2 Eng., 2 Ladders and a B.C. response

PRELIMINARY REPORTS, EMERGENCIES

10-31 Clogged incinerator
10-32 Defective oil burner
10-33 Odor of smoke
10-34 Sprinkler malfunction
10-35 Defective alarm system
10-36 Auto accident
10-37 Assist civilian
10-38 Steam leak
10-39 Broken water main

Code signals of the New York City Fire Department that relate to fires and emergencies. Additional signals (not shown) less frequently used cover requests for ambulance and police among others.

XX," others use the 10-XX codes. The purpose of the word "signal" or "10" preceding the significant numeral is to be sure that the squelch has opened the receiver so the main messages get through. It also alerts the receiver that a code rather than words will follow. Mutual aid agreements and common dispatching have forced a certain standardization in limited areas, but at the time of this writing, there is still no standard fire service code in the United States.

As Varnedoe put it when he called for a standard code, "I would propose the ubiquitous 10 codes as the base for a standard. Many use it already. Unfortunately there are no real standard 10 codes upon which to draw. Solely by popular usage, there has jelled a more or less standard meaning for many of the '10' signals in most areas of communications. Many fire departments have used this list, changing those not applicable to their use and adding others.

3 4
OPEN
1 2
REAR DISCHARGE
CLOSE
DRAIN
CONN.

CHAPTER SIX

Apparatus specification and maintenance

Under the heading "Design, Maintenance and Condition of Apparatus," the Grading Schedule states that "apparatus shall be of suitable design and shall be maintained in good condition," and "that repair facilities, preferably departmental shall be adequate to properly service all apparatus." It also calls for a sufficient number of personnel who are trained in fire apparatus maintenance. Beyond these simple statements, the schedule suggests that spare parts be on hand or readily available and suitable test facilities (for apparatus) be provided. With such parts and facilities a preventive maintenance schedule should be maintained. This schedule includes service tests of pumpers and an inspection and test of aerial ladders and elevating platforms annually and after major repairs. Finally, "the age and obsolescence of apparatus shall be considered in determining condition and reliability."

This last statement brings up the question: When should an apparatus be replaced? What should a fire department buy? And how does a department go about buying it? The decision to buy comes first, of course, and "in general, apparatus 15 to 20 years old should be considered for replacement," according to Special Interest Bulletin No. 39 of the American Insurance Association, Engineering and Safety Service. And to carry out this recommendation, municipal officials "should institute a program that would allow for purchase of new apparatus, as that in service reaches the age for replacement."

Smaller departments and in particular those just starting up occa-

Traveling crane in the Milwaukee Fire Department shops takes repaired motor back to pumper. Mezzanine is used, among other things, for ladder repair and hose work.

sionally look into the purchase of a second-hand apparatus which is being discarded by another community. The AIA advises against such practice because a city, in discarding such apparatus, usually does so because the piece "has outlived its usefulness." It could also be expected to be unreliable and costly to maintain.

The AIA in Special Interest Bulletin 250 recommends that when purchasing apparatus, fire departments should use the National Fire Protection Association Standard No. 1901, "Automotive Fire Apparatus." It is desirable, the bulletin states, to require the Underwriters Laboratories test "to insure strict compliance with pumping standards."

Maintenance facilities

The degree or extent of maintenance facilities provided in a fire department is determined usually by the number of vehicles in service. Every department would prefer to do its own maintenance, but there is no way that a department with three or four pieces of apparatus could justify or afford the cost of separate maintenance facility shops, such as are found in large cities. The extent of apparatus maintenance and particularly major mechanical repairs depends, therefore, on the size of the fire department as well as on the availability of commercial services for apparatus. Even in a fair-size department, it would be impossible to justify, on a cost benefit analysis, installation of wheel alignment equipment, tire changing machines and other items such as the latest electronic motor testing units. However, a department located a couple of hundred miles from a city where specialized service is available will have to depend more on its own facilities than a department more favorably located. Some fire departments are fortunate in having available for major repairs and overhaul the use of municipal service facilities provided for other departments such as police, sanitation and public works.

According to the late Hubert Walker, there are three classes of maintenance: (1) preventive maintenance, (2) minor mechanical maintenance, and (3) major mechanical maintenance[1]. He felt that the first two classes could be performed in nearly all fire departments regardless of size. They cover work that can be performed without placing an apparatus out of service except for short periods. Under these two classes we find such items as oil changes, tire changes and rotation, flushing the cooling system and battery changes.

Special tools required

In addition to the usual mechanic's tools, preventive maintenance and minor mechanical maintenance require the following: heavy-duty jacks (10 to 20-ton), wheeled-type hydraulic lift not less than 15-ton capacity and torque wrenches in at least two sizes. Maintenance manuals provided by manufacturers give definite torque values and they should be rigidly adhered to. All engine manufacturers, for instance, give definite torque values for cylinder head screws or stud nuts. Tightening them too much can distort the cylinder head and block. Such distortion can deform the cylinder (out of round) and lead to cylinder or piston scuffing, rapid cylinder wear and increased engine-oil consumption.

Insufficient tightness of studs invites a burned or blown cylinder head gasket that can produce leaks into the cooling system and loss of compression and power. In addition to employing the correct torque values, mechanics should know the definite sequence that must be followed in tightening cylinder head screws and stud nuts. And only a torque wrench should be used to tighten wheel stud nuts and chassis spring-clip nuts.

[1] Apparatus Maintenance Facilities, Fire Engineering, January 1970.

Ladder truck is parked over 60-foot grease pit that is in one of the bays of the Tucson maintenance facility. Overhead system supplies lubricants.

An air compressor is a necessary component of any maintenance program, as is an accurate hand gage for testing tire air pressure. Battery maintenance requires a heavy-duty battery charger, a hydrometer and voltage tester, and in cold climate a tester for the reliability of antifreeze solution.

Minor mechanical and preventive maintenance for ignition and combustion systems call for a reliable vacuum gage, a timing light and instrument for checking ignition performance.

Selecting a mechanic

In a single-station fire department, housing one or more pieces of apparatus, all preventive and minor mechanical maintenance should be done in quarters. It is usually performed by one of the firemen, particularly a driver, with skill and experience in motor mechanics. The maintenance may also be supplemented by a service contract with a fire apparatus manufacturer that calls for a six-month or annual inspection schedule. A typical volunteer fireman-mechanic would be paid for this work, putting in six or seven hours a week when his regular job permits, but usually on a Saturday. He would be responsible for regular maintenance, engine oil changes, chassis lubrication, battery changing and testing, repairs to lights, replacement of gaskets and other minor repairs.

At some point the number of fire stations and the consequent number of pieces of apparatus dictate that the department should have a shop facility. Attached to this facility would be a service truck or trucks manned by a mechanic who would visit each fire station on a regular basis to perform the lighter maintenance jobs such as engine oil change, hydraulic oil change and chassis lubrication. The major mechanical maintenance will be performed in the shops but, except in the very largest, even some of this will have to be farmed out.

Selecting outside facilities

Locating local or area sources of supply for repair or replacement parts, or units, and selecting reliable specialty facilities with a reputation for good work is essential for any maintenance scheduled to get the quickest possible satisfactory service. At one time fire departments made it a practice to stock quite a supply of items that were a recurring requirement. This eventually led to costly obsolescence due to design changes by manufacturers, and the practice has been largely discontinued. Only electric lamps, fuses, ignition distributor points, condensers, spark plugs and items of this type are now stocked. In a larger fire department, 20 or more vehicles, the list will be much longer due to the increased frequency of need.

If the department has several vehicles with the same power plant and specialized facilities are some distance away, then oil filters, spare carburetor, fuel pump, fan belts and air cleaner filter (if the cleaner has a replacement type filter) may also be stocked.

The two outside facilities most frequently used are for brake work and electric systems. Brake jobs that may be required (other than an exchange of shoes for brake shoes with new linings) are reworking or replacement of a wheel cylinder, reworking the master cylinder, or exchanging the Hydrovac unit for one that is factory rebuilt. For an air brake system, in addition to an exchange of brake shoes, the brake chambers may require new diaphragms (diaphragms should be replaced every two year) and repair or replacement of system units such as the foot brake valve, quick release valve or governor. New linings may need to be ground to correctly fit the drums. Brake drums may need turning to correct out-of-round or bell mouth, or to remove scoring or checking.

Relining clutch disks is a job for specialists. The department may remove the transmission (manual shift type) and clutch assembly to disassemble the clutch disk(s). The replacement disk(s) with new lining is then reassembled by the department mechanic. After assembly of the universal joints of the drive line and all control linkages, the clutch

Two bays in the 5000-square-foot shop area of the Tucson Fire Department maintenance and supply facility have three-point hydraulic lifts that can handle largest apparatus.

can be adjusted for proper engagement and pedal travel. This procedure facilitates the replacement and keeps the cost to a minimum.

Manual shift-type transmissions may be rebuilt in the department shop if the required facilities and replacement parts are available. Otherwise, rebuilding should be done in a specialty shop.

Automatic transmissions are a bit too sophisticated for the average fire department shop. While the number in service is large, most fire departments do not have the special tools, parts or facilities. The overhaul is best done by an authorized shop specializing in automatic transmissions.

In the electrical system, most malfunctioning parts or units are replaced without repair. The two major exceptions are the distributor and the alternator. An alternator in need of major overhauling is best serviced by a shop authorized by the alternator manufacturer to ensure proper testing, competent workmanship and use of proper replacement parts.

Major maintenance a problem

Minor mechanical maintenance of the engine is not a problem in most fire departments. The cost of tools and instruments is not excessive and is an actual economy for the fire department. Major mechanical

Welding area has metal screens and other safeguards to maintain safe working conditions in the shop area of the Tucson Fire Department's maintenance and supply facility.

maintenance for the engine is another problem, which the larger fire departments are usually equipped to handle. To the smaller department, it can be a problem, but there are ways to stall off such a time if they are put in practice soon enough by proper maintenance.

Judged by engine mileage obtained by the trucking service, it is 50,000 to 100,000 miles before overhaul is necessary. The limited mileage in fire service might be expected to eliminate a need for engine overhaul during the active service life of the apparatus before obsolescence retires it to a reserve status. But it doesn't work out that way.

A number of factors affect the service life before overhaul is necessary. These are how conscientiously attention is given to the recommended preventive maintenance schedule and minor mechanical maintenance, vehicle driving practices, type of operating terrain, and frequency of alarm response.

The very nature of fire service use—a fast response with cold engine and extended idling periods—causes increased rates of wear in cylinders, bearings, valves, etc., and a relatively high rate of dilution of crankcase oil. The diesel engine has entered the fire service with a good record of dependable service and long life. But, in fire service use, the picture can change unless more attention is paid to the engine manufacturer's recommendations and driving practices are improved. Some departments have had trouble with fuel flooding due to lugging the engine on a grade or attempting to accelerate in too high a transmission gear.

Washed cylinder walls and crankcase oil dilution are inevitable consequences, and the remedy is for the driver to learn to keep the engine speed at proper level.

For major mechanical overhaul, the first operation is removal of the engine from the chassis. Departments without a chain hoist usually rent a portable hoist or use a hoist on a wrecker.

The subsequent amount of tear-down of the engine will depend on the availability of other facilities, such as equipment for grinding and honing the cylinders or replacement of cylinder sleeves. The crankshaft may require regrinding of the main bearings and the crank pins. Such work is usually done in a specialty shop except in the larger departments.

In the smaller departments, it may be advantageous to truck the engine to a facility that specializes in engine overhaul. In such a shop, the engine receives a complete overhaul with every part inspected and worn parts replaced. Many such facilities have a dynamometer for testing the engine after reassembly, assuring the fire department of a properly working engine.

To have a maximum of maintenance facilities available for fire service vehicles, the maintenance for all municipally owned vehicles is done in the municipal garage in some cities. Such an operation is successful only when specially trained mechanics service fire department vehicles. Not only are the maintenance needs different than they are for other services, but emergency service requires a degree of proficiency and assumption of responsibility for the quality of work performed by the mechanics not demanded for other services.

In those states requiring annual or semiannual inspection as a public safety measure, most fire departments use local garages licensed to perform the required inspection.

Finally, each fire department, according to size, location, and interest in fire apparatus maintenance, operates along the lines that suit the local conditions best. A strong man in the department, either fire chief or maintenance supervisor, determines to a great extent the maintenance facilities provided in that fire department.

Repair facilities in the big city

In the larger departments, repair shops can vary considerably in size and design, but the equipment needed for major mechanical maintenance is almost the same. The repair facility of the San Diego Fire Department, which was opened in 1971, is a prime example.

 The department's 132 vehicles are serviced in a 162 × 80-foot Butler

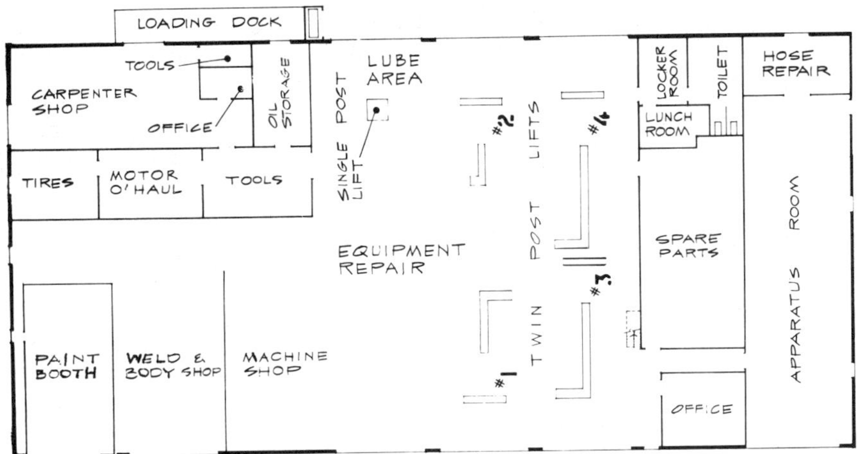

San Diego's 132 vehicles are serviced in a 162 × 80-foot Butler prefab steel structure that also includes quarters of Ladder 3, not shown on diagram.

prefab steel structure that, in addition to various shops, includes the quarters of Ladder 3. The building cost $281,000 and is two stories high. Designed by Fred A. Johnson and Associates, the structure has on the main floor the apparatus repair shop as well as machine, carpenter and paint shops. On this ground floor there are areas for lubrication, engine overhaul, brake relining, wheel balancing and aligning, welding and fabrication, and body and fender work. Besides an extensive parts section on the main floor, there are two storage areas on mezzanines.

In the repair shop, there are five hydraulic vehicle lifts, three of which are adjustable for lifting fire apparatus as large as 100-foot aerial ladder trucks. A 5-ton bridge crane can travel both the length and breadth of the building. It has a maximum clearance of 20 feet between its hook and the floor so that loads can be carried over apparatus on the floor.

In designing the facility, one of the objectives was to build a rigid steel frame structure with metal siding and an insulated roof that would provide as much resistance as possible to fire and earthquakes. Translucent fiber glass is used over five large metal doors in the front of the shops and the three in the rear.

The building has concrete floors and concrete block partitions. The carpenter shop is like a separate concrete block building with a mezzanine for storage above it. This shop is protected by a sprinkler system.

The entire building is heated by gas-fired radiant heaters, and fluorescent lighting is used throughout the building. Forced ventilation is provided for all areas. This ensures the removal of exhaust gases from vehicle engines. The layout of the shop areas was designed to provide a safe, uninterrupted flow of maintenance, adjustment and repair work. Also, consideration was given to the safe movement of vehicles entering or leaving the shops. The entire interior of the repair facility is white and the exterior is buff.

There is adequate mechanical equipment for all the jobs that must be done in the shops. With this equipment, the department shops have built a command vehicle, a light and power truck, and a chemical unit. In addition, several tankers, buses, utility trucks and other vehicles have been converted or reconstructed.

In the smaller departments

Some smaller departments do have a "maintenance room" but they are few and far between. However, any department planning to build a new fire station should try to include such a room in the design. The ceiling height of this room will, of course, have to be increased (compared to other rooms) to provide for a truck lift. And there should also be a hoist for motors and other heavy equipment.

The equipment in this miniature shops should include all the equipment found in a garage: grease racks, oil separators, compressor etc.

PUMPER TESTING

In the large fire departments with their elaborate shops and sophisticated equipment, pumpers can be tested indoors or at least outdoors in an area adjacent to the shops. But for the smaller departments, particularly volunteer, testing a pump requires considerable time and effort, and frequently considerable ingenuity. Suitable test sites, such as lakes, ponds and other sources of water must be located. And often the specialized equipment required for the test must be borrowed or bought. Testing a pumper, then, is no easy job. However, it is a job that must be done not only on delivery of a new pumper but during its entire service life.

Testing fire pumps has two objectives: to determine the present capability of the pump and engine and to provide statistics for comparison with previous and future test figures.

The first test of a pumper—the acceptance test—should be made when the apparatus is delivered to a fire department. During the service life of the apparatus, the pump should be tested every year and after every pump or engine overhaul.

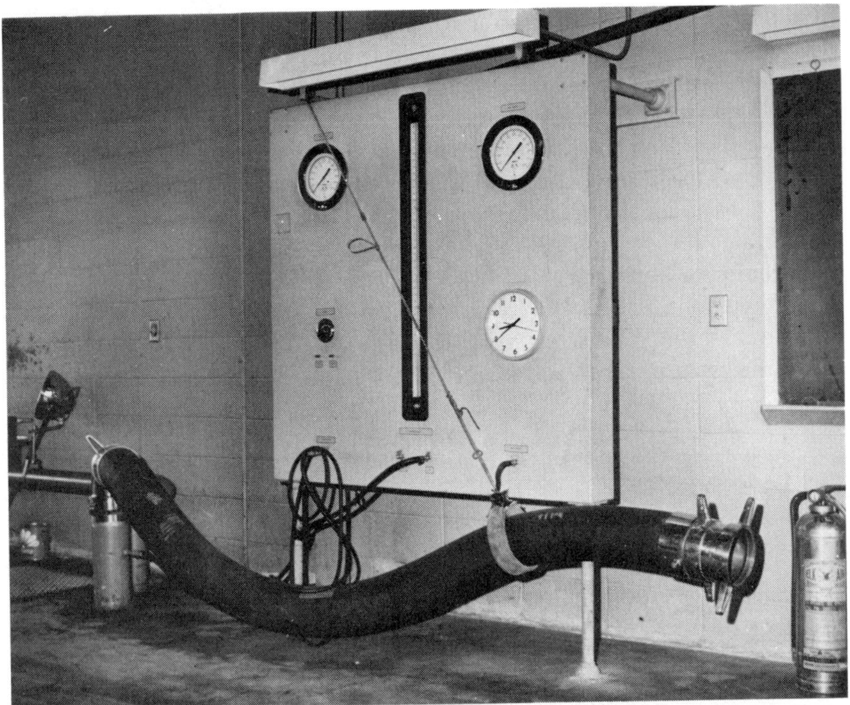

Instrument panel for testing pumpers indoors at Kansas City training center has a manometer, tachometer, engine and nozzle pressure gates and an electric clock.

Some may question the necessity for an acceptance test when the pumper has received an Underwriters Laboratories, Inc. certificate of inspection as a result of a test made by a UL representative at the factory where the pumper was made. We do not downgrade the UL test, which is made for a fee included in the final cost of the pumper, but there is a period of time between the UL test and the delivery of the pumper. In many cases, delivery is made over the road, when both pump and engine are subjected to the ordinary wear and tear—and even hazards—of travel.

It seems only right that when a fire chief signs acceptance papers for a pumper that he should be certain that the apparatus meets the pumping requirements specified in NFPA 1901, "Standards for Automotive Fire Apparatus," *after arrival in his department.* Inasmuch as apparatus remains the property of the manufacturer until the fire department has accepted it, the specifications should include a statement that the pumper will be given an acceptance test upon delivery. This also permits the manufacturer to make arrangements for the delivery engineer's time while participating in the test.

The delivery engineer may wish to operate the pump or he may let one of the department's pump operators take over the controls. "Personally, I'm happier when the delivery engineer operates the pump," Dick Sylvia says, "because if anything goes wrong, there is no doubt—however tenuous—of the local pump operator's capability."

It is also handy to have the delivery engineer present if a minor mechanical problem arises. He can tighten, adjust and possibly replace a part without any undue loss of test time.

The difference between acceptance tests and service tests is only in the time required for each part of these tests, as the table shows.

Volume	Acceptance Test	Service Test
Rated Capacity (150 PSI)	2 Hr	20 Min
70 Pct. Capacity	30 Min	10 Min
50 Pct. Capacity	30 Min	10 Min
Excess Power*	10 Min	5 Min

Rated capacity of pump at 165 psi.

Thus, the required pumping time for an acceptance test is 3 hours and 10 minutes, while for a service test, the time is 45 minutes. However, the Insurance Services Office pamphlet, "Fire Department Pumper Tests and Fire Stream Tables," does not specify an excess power, or spurt, test in its service test requirements. Nevertheless, a spurt test is advisable to see if a pumper, as it grows older, retains its margin of extra power. The excess power test is a required part of an acceptance test.

The total time for testing a pumper will vary for both acceptance and service tests. The shortest overall times are in a very few fire departments that have pump test facilities with permanently installed gages and preconnected suction and discharge hose. Without these facilities a department has to include in its overall time driving the pumper to the test site, making the hose layout for the capacity test and then changing it for the other tests. That's why it makes sense to test as many pumpers as possible during a day so that time can be saved by leaving hose and deluge sets in place until the last test has been completed.

Pitot gage reading is taken at deluge set to obtain nozzle pressure during test.

The equipment needed includes 2½-inch hose, a deluge set (two for 1500-gpm and larger pumpers unless 2¼, 2½, and 3-inch tips are available), an assortment of straight tips (see table for nozzle sizes and pressures) and a variety of other equipment. Foremost among the latter are a pitot gage, pressure gage, vacuum gage, hand counter, stopwatch and gate valves if your deluge set doesn't have one. Other equipment needed includes a steel tape to measure the draft height, a wrench to remove the plugs from the test gage connections on the pump panel, cord to tie the test gages in place, a clipboard, a form (printed, typed, or handwritten) for recording the test data, paper for notes and pens or pencils.

The pressure and vacuum gages should have pressure hoses, about 3 feet long, so the gages can be hung on the pump panel for convenient reading. When testing a pumper, carry an adjustable wrench because the size of the plugs that have to be removed can vary. Also, if the plug size is different from that of the test gage hose couplings, one wrench will handle both jobs.

Now that NFPA 1901 offers an option for a pumper to carry either hard or soft suction hose of adequate diameter for capacity flows, you have to make certain that hard suction is available to conduct a test. A single hard suction line consisting of two lengths (a total of 20 feet) is needed for 500 to 1500-gpm pumps. Two 20-foot suction lines are necessary for 1750 and 2000-gpm pumps. The minimum suction hose

Nozzle Sizes and Pressures for Pump Tests

Desired GPM	Nozzle Diam. (In.)	Tip Pres. (PSI)	Actual Flow (GPM)
250	1	72	251
350	1¼	58	351
375	1¼	66	375
500	1⅜	80	500
	1½	56	499
525	1½	62	525
625	1½	88	626
	1⅝	64	627
700	1⅝	80	700
	1¾	60	704
750	1¾	68	750
875	1¾	94	881
	2	54	873
1000	2	72	1008
1050	2	78	1050
1225	2¼	66	1224
1250	2¼	70	1260
1400	2¼	88	1412
1500	2¼	100	1506
	2½	66	1508
1750	1¾ & 2	68 & 72	1758
	2 & 2	52 & 58	1762
	3	44	1773
2000	2 & 2	72	2016
	3	56	2000

diameters are 4-inch for 500-gpm pumps, 4½-inch for 750-gpm pumps, 5-inch for 1000-gpm pumps and 6-inch for 1250 and greater volume pumps at a maximum lift of 10 feet. At 8-foot and lower lifts, dual 5-inch suction lines are sufficient for 1750 gpm.

With a little foresight, the operator can make certain that all the equipment needed is taken to the test site. The amount of 2½-inch hose needed depends on the capacity of the pump to be tested. However, there should be two extra lengths on hand in case a length blows or a bad coupling turns up.

In testing pumps, only 2½-inch hose is used. This size provides both the volume and friction loss needed. For 500-gpm pumps, a single length of hose to a deluge set is sufficient. Two 100-foot lines are siamesed into a deluge set for 750-gpm pump tests. For 1000-gpm pumps, "Fire Department Pumper Tests and Fire Stream Tables" recommends using three 100-foot lines into a deluge set.

Pumps with rated capacities above 1000 gpm can be tested with hose layouts designed to meet the limitations of the nozzle sizes and deluge

Friction Loss Allowances for 20 Feet of Suction Hose

Rated Capacity Of Pump	Hose Diameter (Inches)	Allowance in Feet
500	4	7
	4½	4
750	4½	8½
	5	5½
1000	4½	15
	5	9½
	6	4½
1250	5	14½
	6	7
1500	6	10
	4½ dual	8½
	5 dual	5½
	6 dual	2½
1750	4½ dual	11½
	5 dual	7½
	6 dual	3½
2000	4½ dual	14½
	5 dual	9½
	6 dual	4½

sets available in a fire department. If 2-inch tips are the largest available, two deluge sets are used when testing larger than 1000-gpm pumps. See the accompanying table for nozzle sizes and pressures for the combination suggested for each flow desired. For example, if there is no 2¼-inch tip for a 1250-gpm test, the operator can obtain the same flow with a 1¾-inch tip at 68 psi (750 gpm) and a 1⅜-inch tip at 80 psi (500 gpm). The hose layouts are the same as those suggested for the same flows in the second paragraph above.

If there are 2¼, 2½ and 3-inch tips, then a single deluge set can be used with four lines feeding it for flows to 2000 gpm. If friction loss is excessive, shorten one or two lines to 50 feet. Remember, the friction loss should be less than actually needed to operate the pump at the required pressure and have the proper nozzle pressure. The additional friction loss is achieved by partially closing one of the pump gates or a gate valve at the deluge set.

After the pumper is in position for drafting, measure the vertical distance from the surface of the water to the center of the pump suction inlet. This drafting height should be no more than 10 feet for testing pumps.

Now connect the pressure and vacuum test gages and hang them as close as possible to the level of the pump gages. After measuring the vertical height of the test gages from the water surface, compute the suction pressure and deduct it from 150 psi to determine the net pump pressure for the capacity test. The table on the preceding page gives friction loss allowances for 20 feet of suction hose.

From this table, figure the suction pressure according to the formula:

$$\text{Suction Pressure} = \frac{\text{Lift} + \text{Hose FL}}{2.3}$$

Let's look at the acceptance test of a 1000-gpm pumper that was made for the Glenbrook, Conn., Fire Department to see how net pump pressure is determined with the use of the formula for suction pressure. The lift to the pump, measured to the center of a side suction inlet, was 6 feet, but it was 3 more feet to the height of the test gages. Therefore, for computing the suction pressure, 9 feet was used for lift in the formula. The suction line was 20 feet of 5-inch hose, so from the table above, 9½ feet was determined to be the suction hose friction loss allowance. Therefore, substituting in the formula:

$$\text{Suction Pressure} = \frac{9 + 9\frac{1}{2}}{2.3} = \frac{18.5}{2.3} = 8 \text{ psi}$$

By dividing the lift and the suction hose friction loss allowance in feet by 2.3, we convert the total to pounds per square inch. In the test we are considering, 8 psi is deducted from 150 psi, the capacity test pressure, to get the new pump pressure, 142 psi.

For the 70 percent of capacity test at 200 psi, you deduct 1 psi from the suction pressure to obtain the net pump pressure, and for the 50 percent of capacity test at 250 psi, you deduct 2 psi from the suction pressure to determine the net pump pressure. In the Glenbrook test, therefore, the net pump pressure for the 200 psi test was 200 − 7, or 193 psi, and for the 250 psi test, it was 250 − 6, or 244 psi. These net pump pressures are the pressures that should appear on your pressure test gage. Any gage errors should be corrected in making calculations.

To start an acceptance or service test, you first must prime the pump. Use your stopwatch and check the time it takes to obtain a prime. It will vary with the size of the pump, piping and valves, but it should not take more than about 30 seconds.

Master stream is pumped by Glenbrook, Conn., pumper during acceptance test.

Then flow water through the pump to discharge through the nozzle, or nozzles, in the test setup at about 100 psi engine pressure for about five minutes to allow the engine, apparatus transmission and pump gear train to warm up. During this time, check the engine speed from the tachometer, oil pressure and engine temperature. With an automatic transmission, check the transmission oil temperature if there is a gage for this.

If everything is satisfactory, throttle up the engine until the test gage shows the net pump pressure desired. Now you begin taking pitot gage readings to attain the right nozzle pressure to provide flow at the rated capacity of the pump. As indicated before, you may have to use two deluge sets (or deck pipes) when testing 1500 gpm and larger pumps, but the procedure is the same as for handling one master stream. With two streams, you have to do a little more coordinating.

During the adjustment of valves controlling water flow, the pump operator must maintain the net pump pressure required for the specific test being conducted. It is more convenient to have a gate valve or valves at the deluge set to control the nozzle pressure. One man operates the gate valve under the direction of another who takes pitot gage readings.

The nozzle pressure may be 76 psi when 72 psi is needed on a 2-inch tip for 1000 gpm. If so, the first man closes the gate valve slightly. This has the effect of increasing friction loss, which in turn will drop the nozzle pressure and the volume of flow. The result will be a slight change in engine pressure, which the pump operator will have to correct by changing the engine speed with the micrometer throttle control to bring the pump pressure back to the required psi.

If there is no gate valve for the deluge set, flow control can be accomplished by operating one of the discharge valves being used on the pump. The net effect is the same, but you have to signal to the pump operator instead of talking to a man at the deluge set gate valve as you keep your pitot gage in operation during the adjustment. Another trick is to have a man at the deluge set signal the pump operator, or use a walkie-talkie to tell him what is wanted.

When you have the proper nozzle and pump pressures, you are ready to start the capacity test, which lasts two hours, without interruption for an acceptance test and 20 minutes for a service test. Note the time the test starts from a watch that will be used throughout the testing. Record the time in military style so that if a test continues past noon, subtraction to determine elapsed time is simplified. If you start a test at 11:19, you know that the capacity test will end at 13:19, or later. In looking at the test data, it is easy to see that a reading at 12:29 was taken 1 hour and 10 minutes after the test started.

Test Pressures and GPM

Rated Capacity (GPM at 150 PSI)	70 Pct. of Capacity (GPM at 200 PSI)	50 Pct. of Capacity (GPM at 250 PSI)
500	350	250
750	525	375
1000	700	500
1250	875	625
1500	1050	750
1750	1225	875
2000	1400	1000

Immediately after taking the first pitot gage reading and recording it for the test start, record the pump pressures indicated on your test gage and the apparatus gage. Then take a hand counter reading for engine speed and note the rpm reading on the apparatus tachometer. Alongside the engine speed cable head where you place your hand counter on the pump panel, there is a plate reading 1/10 or 1/2, indicating that the cable is turning at 1/10 or 1/2 engine speed. If your hand counter records 165 revolutions in a minute with a 1/10 speed cable, the engine speed is 1650 rpm. If the engine is operated at the same speed with a 1/2 speed cable, the counter would show 825 revolutions in a minute.

SERVICE (or ACCEPTANCE) TEST

_______________ Fire Department Date _______________, 19___

Pumper No. ____ Make ______________ Year ____ Model ________ Ser. No. ________
Engine: Make ______________ Model ______________ BHP ______ at ______ Governed RPM
Pump: Make ______________ Model ______________ Rated Capacity: ______ GPM at ______ PSI
Gear Ratio, Engine to Pump: 150 PSI ________; 200 PSI ________; 250 PSI ________
Transmission Gear Used for: 150 PSI ________; 200 PSI ________; 250 PSI ________
Test Requirements: ______ GPM at 150 PSI; ______ GPM at 200 PSI; ______ GPM at 250 PSI
(Net Pump Pressure) Excess Power Test: ______ GPM at 165 PSI
Tested at: ______________; Temp. ______ F°; Elev. ______ Ft.; Bar. ______ In.
Suction Hose: Diameter ______ Inches; Length ______ Feet; No. Lines ______. Lift ______ Feet
Hand Counter Speed Check Readings Taken From: ______________ Ratio to Engine: 1:___

150 PSI TEST Nozzle(s):
Hose Layout:

Time	Counter	RPM	Tach	Pump Pressure Appar. Gage	Pump Pressure Test Gage	Pitot Gage

200 PSI TEST Nozzle(s):
Hose Layout:

Time	Counter	RPM	Tach	Pump Pressure Appar. Gage	Pump Pressure Test Gage	Pitot Gage

250 PSI TEST Nozzle(s):
Hose Layout:

Time	Counter	RPM	Tach	Pump Pressure Appar. Gage	Pump Pressure Test Gage	Pitot Gage

FINAL RESULTS

	150 PSI	200 PSI	250 PSI
Duration			
Av. Noz. Press.			
Correction			
Corrected Press.			
GPM			
Pump Stg.(Par-Ser)			
Av. Pump Press.(a)			
Gage Correction			
Suction Press.(b)			
Net Pump Press.			
Engine RPM			
Pump RPM			

(a) Test gage
(b) See "Fire Department Pumper Tests & Fire Stream Tables," AIA

Excess Power (Spurt) Test:
______ GPM at 165 PSI Net Pump Pressure
Speed: Engine ______ RPM; Pump ______ RPM

REMARKS:

These results are certified to be correct.

____
(Signature)

____
(Rank)

Data form for service and acceptance tests can be typed on $8\frac{1}{2} \times 11$ paper, leaving $\frac{3}{8}$ inch margins at side and three lines of space at top, by using a typewriter with elite (smaller size) type. This form is an adaptation of the "service test results" form of the American Insurance Association and the certificate form of Underwriters Laboratories.

From this, you can see that any error in using the hand counter is magnified. For greater accuracy, it is best to start the stopwatch after placing a clutch-type counter in position on the speed cable head. When the stopwatch hand reaches an easily identified point like 10, 15 or 20 seconds, allow the counter to turn and stop it exactly 60 seconds later. Taking the counter reading for half a minute doubles the margin of error and should not be done.

For the first hour of the capacity test, take pitot gage, apparatus gage, test gage, tachometer and hand counter readings every 10 minutes. Minor adjustment of the nozzle pressure may be necessary—it shouldn't be more than a couple of psi. If the readings are steady during the first hour, then you can increase the time between readings to 15 minutes during the second hour.

During the capacity test and the other tests, constantly check the oil pressure and temperature gages on both the pump panel and the cab instrument panel, as well as the ammeter and the engine hour meter or engine mileage recorder (some pumpers have both). This is a good time to see if they are working properly and to spot any engine oil pressure or heating problem.

While you are waiting between taking gage readings, keep your eyes and ears open for malfunctions of any type. Check the pump packing to see that a few drops of water per minute pass through it. Look at the engine and listen to its sound.

Because the same hose layout is used for the capacity and excess power tests, make the latter test at 165 psi immediately after the capacity test. This will show if the engine has a reasonable amount of reserve power.

No stops during tests

Then you can conduct the 200 psi test for 70 percent of capacity. You establish the proper nozzle and pump pressures in the same way as you do for the capacity test. For this 30-minute test, all the readings previously mentioned are taken at the start of the test and then at 10-minute intervals. As a precaution, take these readings five minutes after starting the test to make sure that everything is going smoothly. If necessary, adjustments can be made immediately. If major adjustments are needed, start the test over again. If no adjustments are needed, don't bother to record the readings but wait for the 10-minute interval, when readings are taken and recorded.

This same procedure is followed for the 250-psi 50 percent of capacity test. There should be no stop during an acceptance or service test except for the time necessary to change nozzles and hose between test segments.

At the conclusion of the pumping tests, test the relief valve or pressure governor. NFPA No. 1901 calls for testing the pressure control device while pumping capacity at 150 psi and while pumping 50 percent of capacity at 250 psi. NFPA No. 1901 also requires a pressure control test at 90 psi after first pumping rated capacity at 150 psi and then throttling down to the lower pump pressure. At each pressure mentioned, close all the discharge valves and observe the pressure test gage and apparatus pressure gage. The pump pressure should not rise more than 30 psi. Although NFPA No. 1901 does not require it, open the pump discharges that were closed for each test and note how close the pressure returns to the starting figure. Some pressure controls are extremely good. In applying a relief valve test to the Glenbrook pumper, the pump pressure varied no more than 2 psi as the discharge gages were closed and reopened slowly.

The final check made during a service or acceptance test is a vacuum test. Attach two lengths of suction hose (20 feet) to a pump suction inlet and cap the end of the hose. Remove the caps from all discharge outlets and develop a vacuum of 22 inches of mercury. The vacuum should be developed in less than 30 seconds. In any event, don't operate the priming device for more than a minute. If you can't get sufficient vacuum in that time, stop and check for leaks. Once your test vacuum gage shows 22 inches of mercury, stop the priming device and if the pump is turning, disengage it. The gage should show a drop of no more than 10 inches of mercury in 10 minutes. If the test is conducted at high elevations, the required 22 inches of mercury is reduced 1 inch for every 1000 feet of elevation.

With the completion of this test, go to a quiet spot with a desk and work out the averages for the nozzle pressure, pump pressure, engine rpm and pump rpm for 150, 200 and 250 psi tests. For the latter, multiply the engine rpm by the pump ratio figure supplied by the apparatus manufacturer.

Fill in the rest of the data called for in the "final results" box in the test form. Under remarks, note the results of the vacuum and pressure control tests and any other pertinent information.

Signing the form completes the responsibilities in conducting an acceptance test. By following the procedures described, tests made later during the service life of the pumper can be compared with previous tests to indicate how well the engine and pump are maintaining their original efficiency as a pumping combination.

SPECIFICATIONS FOR APPARATUS

Next to planning a fire station, writing specifications for a new apparatus is probably the most important duty of a fire chief and his associates. Like the new station, a new apparatus is something the fire department will have to live with for a long time—at least 15 to 20 years. The specifications, therefore, must be prepared with care and skill.

The purpose of the specifications is, of course, to inform the bidders (manufacturers) of the exact requirements of the fire department and to protect the purchaser (fire department) from substandard deliveries.

Those who write specifications should have an understanding of a department's needs and a good knowledge of what equipment is available to meet these needs. Fire records of a community and a knowledge of its hazards help to determine what is needed. Shop records, when properly kept, will show whether or not present equipment has given good service. If the service record is poor, let's say, for batteries, then specifications for the new apparatus should call for heavier-duty batteries or a larger-capacity alternator. The chief mechanic or the committee that is writing the specifications should also talk with company officers and particularly the apparatus operators. This probing will give him a good understanding of how the various types of apparatus and equipment are performing.

Bids invited

If a department is to get the most for its money, then the specifications must be written so that the bids will be truly competitive. With this in mind, specifications should be written to require the standard of performance desired. Unless you intend to write all but one manufacturer out of your specifications, don't get too technical on some of the mechanical details.

This does not mean, however, that certain items cannot be specified in detail—even by trade names. If you wish to get a specific flashing light, radio transceiver or siren, such an item may be specified by trade name and model number with the words "or equivalent" after the reference. There is little difficulty here because such items are usually available to every apparatus manufacturer.

It is when you specify a particular major component, such as an engine, a transmission or axle, that you stir the ire of an apparatus manufacturer who does not normally supply or have access to that particular item. If you are willing to consider an alternative, then you write "or equivalent" after the description of the item. But if you are determined to get a specific major item, then you may find that you are writing one or more prospective bidders out of the specifications.

Purchasing agents are likely to feel that if your reasons are logical and at least three firms can bid on your specifications, then the specs are not unduly restrictive. On the other hand, if a volunteer fire department wishes to buy a specific make of apparatus with its own funds, then the specifications can be written so that only one manufacturer can submit a satisfactory bid.

In the opening paragraph of specifications, you state that bids are invited from manufacturers to supply a specific type of apparatus, which is described in general terms as a certain size pumper, aerial ladder, elevating platform, rescue truck, or whatever it may be. The name of the fire department and the municipality in which the apparatus will be used also should be mentioned. In the volunteer service, the name of the department is not always the same as that of the municipality. Whether the purchase is actually going to be made by the municipality or the department, if a volunteer one, also should be stated.

The specifications should then be divided into sections to cover the following areas:

1. Chassis
2. Body
3. Pumps
4. Aerial ladder or elevating platform
5. Electrical system
6. Equipment
7. General conditions

Under these general headings, there are numerous specific items that should be considered when preparing specifications. All of them need not be included in specs for a particular apparatus, but the purchaser should be just as much aware of what he leaves out as he is of what he puts in specs. When a desired item is standard with most manufacturers, include it in the specifications anyway. You might get a successful bidder who does not regard this item as standard.

Some of the things that should be mentioned in discussing features to be included in specifications are as fundamental as the engine and axles. Other items are generally desirable, like a divided hose bed, and you will probably wish to include them in your specs. Then there are features that might be useful in your department or nice to have if you wish to spend the money for them. You should at least be aware of the many features that can be built into a piece of fire apparatus. Then you will have an opportunity to make decisions and enjoy the feeling of forgetting nothing that should be part of your apparatus.

Engine most important

The most important decision that you will make concerning the chassis is the engine to be used. This is so because the torque and horsepower of the engine will influence the choice of transmission and rear axle and

Hose bed can be divided in any number of ways to suit requirements of operating procedures. Preconnected large suction is at lower right, and wye for preconnected 1-½-inch lines is at lower left.

the resultant road performance of the apparatus. By the time you begin to write specs, you undoubtedly will have decided what model diesel or gasoline engine you would like to get. Although in some municipalities you cannot specify an engine by name, you can state the minimum cubic inches of displacement, the minimum brake horsepower at a specific revolutions per minute and the minimum torque acceptable.

In some cases, these figures can limit the choice to one engine model. Where two or more engines can meet the minimum figures, talking with sales representatives before the bids are received—usually before the specifications are written—can lead to the engine you want being offered by two or more manufacturers. It is possible for many apparatus manufacturers to supply certain engines.

The specifications should demand the engine manufacturer's latest model diesel or gasoline engine that meets your requirements, and it should be the type that the manufacturer offers for fire service use. Practically all apparatus today are ordered with diesel engines, but if you select a gasoline engine, you should note whether you require dual ignition and two sets of spark plugs. With diesels, unless you have narrowed your choice sufficiently, you may wish to specify a naturally aspirated or turbocharged engine. If your community is at an elevation of over 2000 feet, this should be noted because the power of naturally aspirated internal combustion engines decreases at higher altitudes.

For the comfort of the pump operator, the engine exhaust should be discharged on the right side of a pumper. It doesn't make much difference on an aerial ladder or an elevating platform without a pump. Also, there should be a heat shield over the end of the tail pipe where it passes under a compartment or the running board. A heavy-duty truck muffler should be required, and if you desire a specific type of air cleaner, then that should be mentioned.

The cooling system must have the thermal capacity to maintain cooling water at normal operating temperatures under all operating conditions. On pumpers, there must be an auxiliary cooling system of the heat exchanger type, and there should be a radiator-fill valve in the engine compartment. Where severe winter weather is encountered, you may need fail-safe radiator shutters. And as a safety measure, the fan should have a shroud over it.

A minimum fuel tank capacity should be specified. NFPA Standard No. 1901, "Automotive Fire Apparatus," recommends that the minimum capacity be 20 gallons and for pumpers enough fuel for at least two hours of pumping at the rated capacity. If it is necessary to install two tanks on a commercial chassis, there should be a free flow between the tanks, and the fuel gage should be designed so that the operator does not have to do any mental calculations to determine the amount of fuel in the tanks.

Two or more fuel pumps should be installed so that the failure of one pump will not affect the other pump's ability to supply the engine.

On the instrument panel in the cab there should be a speedometer, an odometer, a trip mileage recorder, an ammeter, a tachometer, an engine cumulative revolutions counter, mileage or hour meter, an engine temperature gage, an engine oil pressure gage, a fuel gage and a plate showing the gear shift pattern. Also, the gages should be properly illuminated. You also may wish to have a light on the panel to read notes or maps.

What type transmission?

The engine will, of course, influence the choice of transmissions. The major decision is whether to call for an automatic or a stick-shift transmission. Also, if a power take-off is required, this must be specified. The gear ratio should be left up to the manufacturer, who must build an apparatus that will meet your road and pumping performance requirements. If you wish, you can express a preference for a specific manufacturer's transmission and designate a model number if apparatus manufacturers interested in bidding on your specs indicate that they recommend that model.

Like the transmission, axle engineering details should be left up to the manufacturers, although you may wish to indicate a preference by brand name. But with their advice, minimum capacities for front and rear axles should be specified. Many fire departments have a policy of specifying axles with capacities greater than those required by the weight distribution of the apparatus. The specifications should state whether a single or two-speed or a positive traction rear axle is required.

Minimum weight capacities for front and rear springs may be specified along with a requirement for front shock absorbers. It should be noted that the suspension system must be adequate for the load to be carried, including personnel.

Brake system wanted

You have to decide whether you want full air or vacuum-hydraulic brakes. With either system, you can have a brake-locking device that will retain the pressure against the brake drums. This is not to be confused with a parking brake, although it is used while the vehicle is parked. If a vacuum-hydraulic system is desired, then you should specify that the master hydraulic cylinder be installed so that it is readily available for inspection of the hydraulic fluid level. This might require a removable plate in the cab floor.

For fire service, a quick buildup air brake system should be specified as including a 12-cfm compressor and two reservoirs properly check-valved so that from zero psi, air pressure can be built up to 90 psi in at leas one reservoir within 15 seconds. There should be a front axle brake limiting valve with a switch on the cab instrument panel, a quick-release valve for the front axle brakes and a quick-release or relay valve for the rear brakes. Your specs should call for both an audible and a red light low-pressure warning signal and an air gage on or next to the instrument panel.

The manufacturer should be required to state the sizes of the front and rear brakes he proposes to supply. If you wish the service and parking brakes to be capable of holding the loaded apparatus on a grade steeper than 20 percent (the grade specified in NFPA 1901), then you must say so in your specs.

The frame, which is the subject of innumerable firehouse debates, needs but brief treatment in specifications. You should ask for the measurements of the rails and you may wish to know what kind of steel

Permanently installed bed ladder pipe should have at the base a two or three-way siamese, a gate valve, a pressure gage and a drain valve at right.

will be used. If the apparatus will have a water tank, the rails should extend to the end of the tank. As for the rest, let the manufacturer provide the frame that he has found to be best.

Steering and the wheels

The steering mechanism raises only the question of whether you want power assistance. If so, it is recommended that you specify "power-assist" steering. This means that a hydraulic ram will be installed between the steering box and the front axle, and the steering box gear ratio will be the same as it would be for non-power steering. Then, if your power fails, the apparatus will be no more difficult to steer than it would be without power-assist steering. The steering mechanism and the hydraulic pump and ram to be used may be specified by trade name if you have a preference. To comply with NFPA 1901, the front wheels must be able to turn 30 degrees to the right and left.

Wheels come in two types for fire apparatus, so you should specify either 10-stud steel disk or steel spoke wheels if you have a preference. Some departments specify that the wheels on all axles be the same model so that they may be interchanged. Here again, you can call for a specific manufacturer's product.

If you use chains, then specify that the dual wheels be spaced so that skid chains can be used on the outside tires. You also should state that there must be adequate clearance from the fenders or other body structures for the use of chains.

Tire specifications should include the minimum size and ply rating acceptable, the minimum capacity in pounds and whether tube or tubeless tires are desired. No truck tire should bear a loader greater than that recommended by the Tire and Rim Association, Inc., Akron, Ohio, for intermittent operation. If you require mud-and-snow treads, this should be stated. Steel cord tires sometimes are specified for the front wheels of elevating platform apparatus. If snow treads are not used, you may wish to specify that all tires be the same size. Some manufacturers use larger tires on the front axles of cab-forward apparatus. Although they may not be necessary, the larger tires can be used on all axles for convenience in stocking spare tires or to allow full rotation of tires.

If you specify a tire by brand name, you may have to pay a premium because the apparatus manufacturer may not normally buy that tire. Questioning of sales representatives can determine the brand usually supplied by each manufacturer, and you may be willing to accept any of these. Some manufacturers offer a choice of two or more brands.

Two towing hooks or eyes should be on the front of the apparatus, and you may want them also on the rear. You must state whether you want hooks or eyes, and you should specify that they be attached directly to the frame and be forged.

The front bumper, made of heavy-duty channel steel, should be properly braced and attached directly to the frame. The bumper should wrap around the front edge of the fenders. You must specify whether the bumper shall be painted or chromed. A heavy tread plate should be over the area between the bumper and the cab of cab-forward or cab-over apparatus.

Selecting the chassis

The type of chassis—standard, cab-forward, cab-over or tilt-cab—must be specified, and for aerial ladder trucks, there is a choice of a single chassis or a tractor and semi-trailer. If dual axles are necessary, such as for elevating platforms and big tankers, they must be specified.

Undercoating is not standard and must be in the specs if you want it.

Protective plates can be placed beneath the entrances to the cab and on the front and rear of fenders of cab-forward apparatus to eliminate scuffing paint in those areas. The plates can be ordinary steel diamond plate under the cab entrances and stainless steel on the fenders.

In cabs, you have a choice of a semi-closed cab with a windshield and doors but no roof and a closed cab with a roof. The specifications must state which is desired. Whether you wish a two, three, five or seven-man cab also must be specified.

In the cabs that seat two men alongside the driver, you can call for a bench-type seat for the two riders and a separate driver's seat that is adjustable up and down and fore and aft. If you like luxury, you can call for bucket seats. A bench seat is used for the four men in the rear of a seven-man cab. Foam rubber cushioning and a preference in upholstery material also can be specified. Required safety belts can be of the roll-up type.

Compartments in the cab may include one on the right-hand side of the instrument panel and one under the front bench seat, which can be designated for the installation of a mobile radio. The panel compartment should have a spring-hinged door, and it can have a light inside.

The United States Department of Transportation requires a heater and a defroster in every cab and separate controls for the temperature and the fan. The DOT also requires a windshield washer as well as wipers.

There must be two outside windshield wipers for closed cabs, and for the semi-closed cabs, you should specify two additional wipers on the inside of the windshield. These wipers should be installed so that each inside and outside pair moves in unison. Electric wipers should be the two-speed type, and if the apparatus has air brakes, you may wish to specify adjustable speed, air-operated wipers.

On major fire apparatus, West Coast type mirrors and minimum width and height should be specified. Sun visors should be on closed cabs.

All glass in cabs should be approved automotive safety glass, and in closed cabs, there should be sliding glass between the driver's compartment and the rear passenger area. You also may wish to require dome lights in both the driver's and rear passenger areas of closed cabs with a separate switch in each area.

Hose to be carried

The hose bed can be divided according to your desires, but in describing the sections for various hose sizes, you should state the amount of hose that is to be carried in each section. In addition to longitudinal hose bed divisions, you may wish to call for a transverse bed for 1½-inch hose forward of the regular hose bed of a pumper. Sometimes a compartment at the rear step is specified for soft suction hose. All hose beds should have removable hardwood floor gratings, painted or varnished.

Hose bed sections for preconnected lines should be designated and the location of hose connections must be described.

Compartments can be built in any number of sizes, but you will save money by generalizing your specifications to accept sizes standard with each apparatus manufacturer. Because of the difference in layouts, you can express your preferences by writing, "at least one compartment forward of the rear axle on each side" or adding "and as many others as are standard with the bidder." Or you can call for a compartment over each rear wheel by adding "if available as a standard option." Sizes should be given as approximate so that the nearest standard size can be offered each bidder. Compartments built to special dimensions are seldom worth the extra cost.

Piano hinges (stainless steel, chrome or painted) for compartment doors should be specified. Latches can be spring-loaded or positive locking, and the latter come with T handles or D-ring handles. Again, you should indicate your choice and whether there must be one or two latches on the doors.

All cabinets must be waterproof with rain gutters made of stainless steel or aluminum. Cabinets that are intended for the storage of rope, clothing and equipment with gasoline engines require louvers for ventilation. You may wish to specify that louvers be on the inside wall of some compartments. Any compartment shelves or dividers must be indicated in your specs. Also, you may wish to have removable hardwood floor gratings in some compartments. Indicate whether they should be painted or varnished.

Specify size of booster tank

The size of the booster tank should be specified in gallons and the configuration should be left to the manufacturer. The specs should call for adequate baffling an an overflow pipe of not less than 3 inches inside. The booster tank valve and the piping from the tank to the pump should allow a flow meeting or exceeding the minimum standards in NFPA 1901.

There should be a tank fill line from the pump, or a bypass line, with a valve controlled at the pump operator's position.

The tank should be made of corrosion-resistant steel, preferably not less than 10 gage, and coated inside and out with an epoxy, or equal protective coating. There should be a convenient cleanout drain, not less than 2½ inches in diameter, at the bottom of a sediment sump at least 12 inches square and 7 inches deep. The top of the tank should have removable covers, at least 24 inches square, for access to all compartments for inspection and cleaning. These covers should have gas-

Operator's position on this pumper has individual gages for each of the hose gates and two 2-½-inch gated suction inlets. The panel is stainless steel.

kets to prevent leaking and the bolts should be corrosion-resistant or insulated from the water. If nuts are used, they should be welded to the tank.

The capacity and material should be specified for any auxiliary tanks desired for foam concentrate, wet water or other additives. If stainless steel is used, then heliarc welding must be required for long service.

Handrails should be chrome or stainless steel, and the locations have to be specified. They are needed at cab entrances and above the hose bed at pumper rear steps. Safety belts or subway-type hand grips can be used on this rear handrail. Because hose beds are often quite high, you might consider an additional handrail just above the rear compartment door of a pumper. This rail can be covered with rubber, such as is used on aerial ladder rungs, to provide a good grip as a man swings onto the rear step. Walkways over the lower compartments of aerial ladder trucks also need handrails, and there are other suitable locations, depending on apparatus design.

If coats and boots are to be carried on a pumper for volunteers, then trip rails atop each side of the hose bed should be specified.

Steps to reach the hose bed of a pumper, the rear of the walkway on an aerial ladder truck and other apparatus areas not easily accessible can be either the rigid or folding type. The rigid type can be made of diamond plate or expanded steel. Their locations on the apparatus must be spelled out in the specs.

Diamond plate, regular or stainless steel or aluminum, can be specified for the vertical panels, compartment doors and inside the wings at the rear of pumpers. On cab-forward apparatus, you might consider calling for diamond plate on top of the engine compartment, or even for the entire engine compartment.

Paint shade used

The color the apparatus is to be painted can be described by the code number used by a paint manufacturer, or the general color may be specified with the qualification that it will be one of the shades generally used by the successful bidder that will be selected by the fire department. If the color desired is white, a non-yellowing white should be specified. All metal to be painted should be properly prepared and primed.

The amount of lettering and seals, if any, should be specified by size in inches and by general location. "Center of each cab door" is sufficient for general areas. Specific locations can be agreed upon with the successful bidder. To look best, all "gold" lettering and striping should be specified as gold leaf, and any municipal seals should be handpainted in oil colors.

Pump type and capacity

The main pump is generally described as single or two-stage centrifugal with a rated capacity of 500, 750, 1000, 1250. 1500 and 1750 or 2000 gpm at 150 psi. You may also require the delivery of 60 gpm or less at up to 600 psi. If you frequently pump salt or other corrosive water, the pump should be made of bronze. Nonferrous piping and valves also may be specified for these conditions. If the pump is to be used at over 1000-foot elevations, this should be stated in the specifications, as this will affect the performance.

The type of priming system will vary with different pumps. But if a gear type priming pump is used, then the options include a mechanically driven pump, an electric pump and an electric pump with a mechanical override. With any priming pump, there should be mechanical override, controls for the pump and priming valve.

High-pressure pumps, operated by power take-off, can be either centrifugal or piston. The capacity, normally at a working pressure of 850 psi, should be specified. Incidentally, midship pumps also can be powered by power take-off.

Your specs should require a pressure control system for all pumps, and to avoid writing anyone out of the specs, you can ask for the pressure control systems to be described.

The size of the suction inlets, their locations and whether any must be gated have to be specified in detail, including the thread required. In addition to the big inlets, two 2½-inch gated inlets are recommended. If you want a gated front suction for preconnected soft suction hose, you also should describe how the hose is to be carried, such as in a well between the bumper and the cab or atop the tread plate at that location and secured by straps. The control for the gate can be at the pump operator's position or at the suction inlet.

Discharge gates also have to be specified by size—2½ or 1½-inch. You may wish to have 2½-inch gates equipped with 2½ to 1½-inch reducers. All gates should have caps with chains secured to the apparatus. If you do not use national standard hose thread, you must specify your local thread. Gates should be numbered.

Drains should be provided for all piping. The pump should have a master drain valve, and each hose gate should have a drain valve on the discharge side of the gate.

Gages for the operator

The pump operator's position should have gages for pump pressure and suction. The suction gage, of course, must be the compound type, but both may be compound gages if you wish. You can call for separate gages (2½-inch is big enough) for each hose gate. The range of these gages should be specified to accent the highest pressure developed by the pump. You also need oil and temperature gages and an engine tachometer. A gage or indicator for booster tank water also may be specified.

Controls at the pump operator's position should include those for the pump master drain, the relief valve or pressure governor, and the heat exchanger. The tank to pump, pump to tank and booster reel valves also should be controlled at the operator's position. The engine throttle should be the micro-adjustment type. Swing-type hose gate handles should be the type that will lock in any position by being twisted to the right. Push-pull hose gage controls should have a fixed-type stop.

Aerial ladder and its equipment

In writing specifications for an aerial ladder, the height of the ladder when fully extended at maximum elevation and the number of sections must be stated. You can ask that each bidder supply structural and operating details of the ladder offered. An inclinometer and load guide should be on the side of the ladder next to the operator. A solid-state intercom system between the ladder tip and the turntable can be specified with an open microphone-speaker on the fly and a press-to-talk intercom station on the turntable pedestal. The top fly should have a pair of folding steps and, according to your desires, have mounts for an ax, a pike pole and a hand lantern.

If a permanently mounted bed ladder pipe is specified, then you spell out the installation components: a ladder pipe with a model number, a 3-inch aluminum pipe conected to the ladder pipe with a short (about 3-foot) section of 3-inch, 100 percent polyester, 600-pound test hose, a two or three-way aluminum alloy siamese with clappers and 2½-inch intakes, a gate valve between the siamese and the aluminum pipe, and a pressure gage mounted at the side of the ladder to show water pressure at the siamese outlet.

To avoid possible damage when the bed ladder is placed near a cornice, the bed ladder pipe can be protected by a steel structure that extends below the ladder on both sides of the ladder pipe.

A hose tray can be built at the ladder bed level to hold 1000 feet of 3-inch hose and a siamese so that the fly ladder pipe can be set up quickly.

Turntable area

The turntable area has several items that should be considered. A stainless steel or chrome guard rail at the pedestal is a must for safety of the operator. The pedestal should have a pressure gage for the hydraulic system and an engine starter button. Any gages should be illuminated. Some manufacturers offer a load indicator on the pedestal or the bed ladder.

There should be provision for lighting the turntable area. Usually three lights, with hoods to keep the illumination downward will be sufficient. Two spot lights should be mounted on universal swivel brackets near the rail at the base of the bed ladder. Each light should have a switch.

The turntable itself should have a nonskid surface. Diamond plate is standard with some manufacturers, or you may prefer a surface coated with a special thick, nonskid surfacing that can be brushed or troweled onto the steel plate.

There is a choice in the type of ground jacks you prefer, and your preference for mechanical or hydraulic jacks should be specified after you have considered the types offered by various apparatus manufacturers. It may be necessary to allow variance from your primary choice to avoid writing a manufacturer out of the specifications. Rear-mounted

Electrical receptacles, with waterproof hinged caps, can be installed for the quick use of portable lights and power tools. Note the handrails.

aerials are built with A-frame hydraulic jacks. It is advisable to have a red warning light on the cab instrument panel to indicate when one or more jacks are down.

The booms of elevating platforms (articulated and telescoping), like aerial ladders, are built according to each manufacturer's specifications, and you accept them along with the hydraulic jack system. However, there are options that you should consider. You can have a breathing air system piped to the basket from one or two large cylinders near the turntable. Storage space can be built in the basket for two air masks and hose. A roof ladder can be carried on the upper boom, as well as a pike pole. An ax and a claw tool can be mounted in the basket.

Depending on the manufacturers you are considering, you may have a choice in the size of the water pipe to the monitor nozzle. In specifying a monitor nozzle on the platform, you should state the size and type of tip or tips you require. You also can call for one or two spray nozzles under the platform with a valve control in the basket. A foot control is often used. There should be an intercom system, such as has been mentioned for aerial ladders, between the basket and the rear step. Also, a heat shield around the basket is desirable.

The electrical system for any apparatus should be specified as 12-volt with a master switch to cut all supply from the battery system. You should require color-coded wiring to simplify checking out any troubles that may rise in later years. NFPA 1901 calls for an alternator with minimum capacity of 100 amperes, but because of the electrical load most new apparatus now carry, a minimum capacity of 125 amperes seems preferable.

There should be two banks of batteries, and you should specify whether you wish one 12-volt battery in each bank or two 6-volt batteries in series in each bank. The batteries should be the heavy-duty, truck type, and you should specify a minimum ampere-hour rating. There must be a switch for changing from one bank of batteries to the other, and the supply to all electrical equipment, including the siren and radio, should be affected by this switch.

The battery compartments should be weatherproof and accessible with swing-out or roll-out battery trays if necessary. There must be an appropriate securing device for the batteries.

Transformers

If receptacles for lights and power tools are desired, they should be of the two-wire, twist lock type with hinged, watertight covers, and you should designate their location. A 110-volt transformer, 1200 watts, is required and you can specify an engine-mounted solenoid control with a transformer switch in the cab for increasing the engine speed to provide the maximum amperage output. Because an alternator produces 3-phase current, the power consumed must be balanced on the phases within the alternator manufacturer's recommended limits. No more than one transformer on a single phase or a 3-phase transformer must be specified.

A T-type, polarized weatherproof double receptacle should be provided at the rear of the apparatus for connecting a line from a battery charger. The specs should require that the polarity of the receptacle slots agree with that of the prongs of the battery charger line. This may prevent damaging the alternator the first time you charge batteries on the new apparatus.

The ignition switches should be keyless, but if a keyed switch must be accepted on a commercial chassis, then the key should be secured to the instrument panel by a light chain.

You can specify that an auxiliary generator be started by use of the vehicle batteries, or you can have a permanently installed auxiliary generator or alternator operated by power take-off.

 There should be a light in each cargo compartment and two lights with individual switches in the engine compartment. Except for the engine compartment lights, all compartment lights should have automatic switches operated by the doors and a master control switch on the instrument panel in the cab. There should be a red jewel light on the instrument panel to indicate an open compartment door.

Pumpers should have two hose bed lights on universal swivel brackets.

There must be clearance, identification and backup lights to comply with Department of Transportation regulations.

The emergency lights you want must be specified, and this can be done by naming the model of each type of light desired. You can have rotating, pulsating and flashing lights on the front and rear of the apparatus. Smaller units are usually used on the rear corners of apparatus. Large rotating lights can have two-color domes so that, for example, a flashing white light used for fire apparatus in some states shows forward and a flashing red light shows to the rear. In open cabs, this can eliminate interference with the driver's vision, which a white light might cause.

The type of turn signals, front and rear, should be specified. Some departments like the large, bus-type signals on the front. There must be a switch for flashing all four turn signals simultaneously, a DOT requirement.

The electric siren you wish can be specified by model number. The siren should have a floor switch on each side of the cab. Or you may wish to specify an electronic siren by model number. The public address feature of an electronic siren can be connected to the mobile radio so that messages received go through the PA system when the switch is activated.

If you wish to have air horns, the type and location should be specified. If they are mounted where they can be seen, you will probably wish to ask for chrome horns. When an electrical horn is required, that should be noted in the specs.

The specs should state the size of the bell and type of mounting required and note the location if there is a preference. All apparatus will not accommodate a bell in some locations.

Radio model number

The radio you prefer can be specified by model number. If your frequency is in the 30-50 MHz range, you may wish to call for a loaded antenna to keep it shorter and avoid hitting overhead doors. The number of speakers and their locations should be specified, and they should be weatherproof if necessary. A phone-type microphone may be desired for the cab and a weatherproof, field-type microphone for other locations. On cab-forward or tilt-cab pumpers, it is advisable to have a microphone and speaker at the pump operator's position. On elevating platforms, this equipment should be at the rear step. On aerial ladder trucks, a speaker and a microphone can be mounted in a box built near the turntable. The microphone should have a coiled wire cord long enough to reach the pedestal, and there can be a mike clip on the outside of the box. The operator can then reach the mike with little difficulty.

Flexible conduit can be installed at the factory so wires for the radio can be installed easily. You can specify that the radio be installed by a local radio man.

Booster reels

In specifying booster reels, you should designate their hose capacity and location. The size of the reel will depend on whether you specify ¾ or 1-inch hose. Reels are available for 1½-inch hose. You have a choice of manual or electric rewind reels. If you choose electric rewind, you should say whether you require a pushbutton switch at the operator's position or a foot switch mounted under the running board. The latter leaves a man's hands free to guide the hose. The reel assembly should include horizontal and vertical rollers, a brake on the reel, and nozzle holders. If you require hose and nozzles with the apparatus, you should specify the types desired. Pistol-grip nozzles may handle better with a swivel connection, which should be specified.

For apparatus with a pump, you should specify the size, number of lengths and type of suction hose to be supplied by the manufacturer. In addition, you must provide the dimensions of your local hydrant steamer thread so that the manufacturer can supply one swivel connection with the pump suction thread on one end and the large hydrant thread on the other. You have to write special instructions for installing the suction hose trays and brackets if they vary from normal installations.

Ladders required

Ground ladders can be made of wood or aluminum, according to your wishes. Most apparatus manufacturers buy ground ladders from ladder manufacturers, so you can specify ladders by trade name and model or series numbers. Standard equipment for pumpers is a 14-foot roof ladder and a 24-foot extension ladder. You may wish to require a longer extension ladder. NFPA 1901 lists the suggested number and sizes of ladders to be carried on ladder trucks. Local conditions may demand changes in this list, so ladders should be specified by type, length and number.

Four wheel chocks are a necessity for aerial ladder trucks and elevating platforms and two are highly desirable for pumpers. They should be specified.

If a foam system is desired, then you first should confer with representatives of manufacturers of this equipment so that the specifications can be written with a detailed knowledge of what is available and what will be most suitable for your needs. The specs should also call for all accessories associated with the foam system.

Recommended equipment

Before putting the equipment section of your specifications into final form, you should review NFPA 1901, which has three equipment lists for each type of apparatus. One list contains "basic equipment which should be provided by the manufacturer," the second notes equipment "recommended to be carried," and the third lists equipment "which might be desirable to be carried." You will pay for what you get, so you should determine what equipment the apparatus will carry and what equipment should be shifted from the old to the new apparatus. Then you should write a detailed list of equipment to be supplied by the apparatus manufacturer.

You should also note in your specifications whether loose equipment like extinguishers and axes are to be mounted at the factory or are to be mounted after delivery by either the delivery engineer or department personnel.

Sometimes equipment is included in specifications on an optional basis. This equipment should be included in the total bid price, but each item should be priced separately. This is done so that if the total bid is above the budget allotment, enough optional items can sometimes be eliminated to bring the final price within the allotment. Also, it may be possible to arrange to buy some of the eliminated equipment with other available funds at the old prices and save money.

Drawings necessary

Preliminary drawings of the proposed apparatus should be required to be submitted with the bids. These drawings should show the configuration of the apparatus, location of major equipment and detailed measurements of overall length, maximum height and width, wheelbase, front and rear overhang, cab size and any other important features.

Detailed drawings should be required to be submitted within 60 or 90 days of the award of the contract. Depending on your requirements and engineering capability, these can include chassis and body drawings, layout and flow diagrams of all piping and control valves for the pump(s),

Overhead clearance must be considered in relation to the upward tilt created by rear axle's higher elevation as apparatus passes through doorway.

and a wiring diagram for all electrical equipment. Many departments will not need more than body and chassis drawings to show the general design of the apparatus, hose bed details, compartments and sizes, and the location of major equipment and accessories.

The specifications should inform bidders that the apparatus will be required to pass the road test detailed in NFPA 1901 upon delivery. If any other road test will be given, that should be described in the specs.

If you wish to have a pump test supervised at the factory by Underwriters Laboratories, you must include that requirement in your specs so that the cost, which is modest, can be figured in the bid. Also, a pump acceptance test (see above) should be run in accordance with NFPA 1901 upon delivery of the apparatus. This shows the capabiity of the pump at the time of acceptance by the purchaser and provides a chief with the assurance he should have before signing for the apparatus (see following section).

Height limitations important

Upon delivery and before being accepted, aerial ladders and elevating platforms both should be tested according to the applicable provisions of NFPA 1901.

The minimum angle of departure (made by a line from the bottom of the rear tire to the end of the body) recommended in NFPA 1901 is 8°, measured below any equipment mounted under the apparatus. If the entrance to your firehouse or local road condition requires a greater number of degrees, this should be specified. If there are height limitations imposed by firehouse doors or bridges over roads, the specifications should note them and require that the apparatus be built to pass under these obstructions. The department should be prepared to submit an elevation profile to the manufacturer if asked. The maximum height of the apparatus may be less than any overhead obstructions, but the rise of an aerial ladder or the boom of an elevating platform as the leading axle rises may cause trouble. If apprised of these conditions, manufacturers can lower the standard height by a few inches.

Another safeguard to include in specifications is a requirement that the apparatus when delivered conform to all rules and regulations of the U. S. Department of Transportation and the motor vehicle laws of the state where it is to be used.

The specs also should require that the apparatus meet or exceed all specifications and requirements set forth in applicable chapters of NFPA 1901, which should be cited for each type of apparatus. You should state that your specifications shall be interpreted as minimum and that when the manufacturer's standard exceeds these, the apparatus and equipment shall be furnished in accord with the manufacturer's standard.

Furthermore, the specs should require that the apparatus, components and accessories be of the latest design and production and be unused.

Warranty and replacement parts

The warranty asked for depends on your desires. One way is to ask each bidder to state the conditions of the normal warranty on the apparatus and components. Normal warranties may or may not include free labor for installing parts supplied without cost. On the other hand, you may demand a warranty for one to five years or more that includes the replacement of defective parts and the correction of any defective workmanship or design at no cost whatsoever to the purchaser. Whether you get what you ask will depend on a number of things. Tires and batteries generally are subject to the guarantees of their manufacturers.

You also should ask for an assurance that replacement parts will be available for up to 25 years, depending on whether a custom or commercial chassis is desired. The interchangeability of parts as a result of the use of modern manufacturing methods also should be assured.

The technical data that should be supplied with the bids varies with the needs of various fire departments. Literature describing the apparatus and a certified brake horsepower curve for the engine, indicating gross and net horsepower and gross and net torque and the governed rpm, certainly should be required to be submitted with each bid. Other departments may require detailed engineering figures, such as a summary of computations for determining the grade ability and the equivalent acceleration rate of the proposed apparatus. Full information on the drive line components also may be demanded.

The specs should include the number of maintenance and operating manuals, parts catalogs and price lists that must be delivered with the apparatus. You will want to include manuals for engines and other components that the apparatus manufacturer does not publish but should supply.

Stated delivery time

There must be a requirement for each bidder to estimate the time it will take to build the apparatus. This may be stated in working days, weeks or months after the signing of the contract by both the purchaser and the manufacturer.

You also should state in your specifications how long you will require the services of a delivery engineer to indoctrinate a sufficient number of men in the operation of the new apparatus. In volunteer departments, it may be desirable to specify that the number of days the delivery engineer stays shall include a weekend because it is on Saturdays and Sundays that most volunteers have more time for training. However, the manufacturers should know this in advance because of the salary problem.

If it makes any difference, you can specify whether delivery is to be made over the road or by rail.

There should be a provision in the specifications for exceptions, and you should require that exceptions to any part, or parts, of the specifications be made in writing and included in the proposal of the bidder. You also may wish to state that if a manufacturer is unable to supply a component specified by trade name, equal consideration will be given to an alternate specified by the bidder in writing as an exception to the specifications.

Generally in the last paragraph of specifications there is a statement that any or all bids may be rejected. And sometimes added to this is the explanation that because of the special requirements of the fire service, the proposal judged to be in the best interests of the fire department may be accepted.

Ask for what you want

In preparing to write specifications, keep your attitude flexible. Ask for whatever you desire—no matter how unusual you think it is—when talking with apparatus manufacturers' sales reresentatives. But then listen to the feedback from the manufacturers. A particular request may not be as unusual as you think, and its cost may be nominal for the effectiveness obtained.

On the other hand, you may not be asking for a rare engineering project, but the cost estimate may price it right out of your specifications. Then there are the proposals that are not only rare and costly, but also will scare away manufacturers. For example, the demands for pump outlets and inlets can be so numerous and the piping so complicated that a manufacturer may decide there is no sense in asking for that kind of a headache.

Listen to the manufacturers' representatives. You can tell by talking with several of them whether your more exotic ideas are practical or idiotic. Sometimes discussions with manufacturers can lead to a modification that will transform the idiotic into the ideal. Then you wind up with something that is practical to make and desirable to use.

As you can see, a great many things can be considered in writing specifications. A few departments go into greater detail than we have indicated while others find it unnecessary to include in their specifications all the items discussed. However, it is best to be aware of what can be covered so that anything you leave out is done by decision and not by chance.

The advertising for bids must contain a date, time and place for the opening of bids. There should be enough time between the advertising, when the specifications become available, and the opening of bids for apparatus manufacturers to study the specs and prepare their proposals. Sometimes this requires a good many hours of engineering work.

Sales representatives can tell you how much time their manufacturers need, and you can set the date for opening bids accordingly. This time may range from three weeks to a month or more.

23
MECHANICSVILLE
VOL. FIRE DEPT.

CHAPTER SEVEN

Water supply for fire fighting

Water for fire fighting can be taken at draft from a stream or a pond, or even a swimming pool. It can also be carried to a fire in a tanker. But most frequently it is taken from a hydrant which is part of a public water supply system.

Public water supply systems have two principal functions: to provide water for domestic, commercial, and industrial use, and to provide water for fire protection. Most of the water used for fire protection is delivered from water distribution mains through fire hydrants to fire department pumpers. These in turn increase the pressure to develop fire streams. In addition to providing water for hose streams, pumpers can augment the water supply to sprinkler and standpipe systems in buildings through fire department connections installed on such systems.

This public supply system is fed by a supply works. The works include the sources of water such as lakes, rivers, springs and wells, and also the facilities necessary to take the water from the source, treat and purify it as necessary and then deliver it to the distribution system. These facilities include impounding reservoirs, intakes, pumping systems, treatment and purification plants and supply mains.

A chief's, and for that matter all fire fighters', knowledge should extend to all elements of a water supply system which is used for fire suppression. But their first consideration should be directed to the distribution system.

The distribution system consists of a network of pipes usually provided with elevated storage tanks at various points within the system. The mains of the distribution system are of three general types called arteries, secondary feeders and minor distributors. The largest of these mains are the arterial which extend from supply mains or supply works to all portions of the system. They are generally "looped" and supply the secondary feeders. The secondary feeders are usually smaller than the arteries. And in turn, they supply the minor distributors. The three terms are relative, however, since there is not always a sharp line of demarcation between them. Obviously, an arterial main may range from a 12-inch one in a small community to 60-inch or more in a big city. Similar variation in size holds for secondary feeders.

Nevertheless, minor distribution will generally be 6 or 8-inch except where there is a high required flow or high consumption that may require 12 to 16-inch. Sizes smaller than 6-inch are not recommended to provide fire protection.

The minor distributors generally form a pattern which is called a gridiron. From the gridiron there are service connections that provide water to individual buildings for domestic use and occasionally for fire protection systems (sprinklers and standpipes). The gridiron is also equipped with hydrants for fire suppression. Shut-off valves are regularly placed in the grid, usually near street intersections to control any breaks in the mains, or to make necessary repairs. Good practice also calls for the installation of a gate valve in the branch connection between the hydrant and main for servicing or replacing the hydrant.

Main capacity

Assuming that an adequate supply of good pressure is available from the supply works, the amount of water available for fire protection and general consumption depends on the carrying capacity of the mains—those extending to the distribution system and those that comprise the distribution system. The carrying capacity of the mains, in turn, depends on a loss of pressure or head.

This loss is attributed to what is commonly called pipe friction, a misnomer actually, because the resistance to flow is not due to friction in the true sense of the word. Studies have shown that the resistance to flow is due to the shearing forces between particles or layers of water. Turbulence in the flow caused by roughness of pipe walls or high velocities causes an increase in the effects of the shearing forces and consequently a greater resistance to flow. The greater the resistance to flow, the larger will be the friction loss in a main and consequently the larger the head (H) or pressure loss. This loss of head is:

1. Directly proportional to the length (l) of the main.

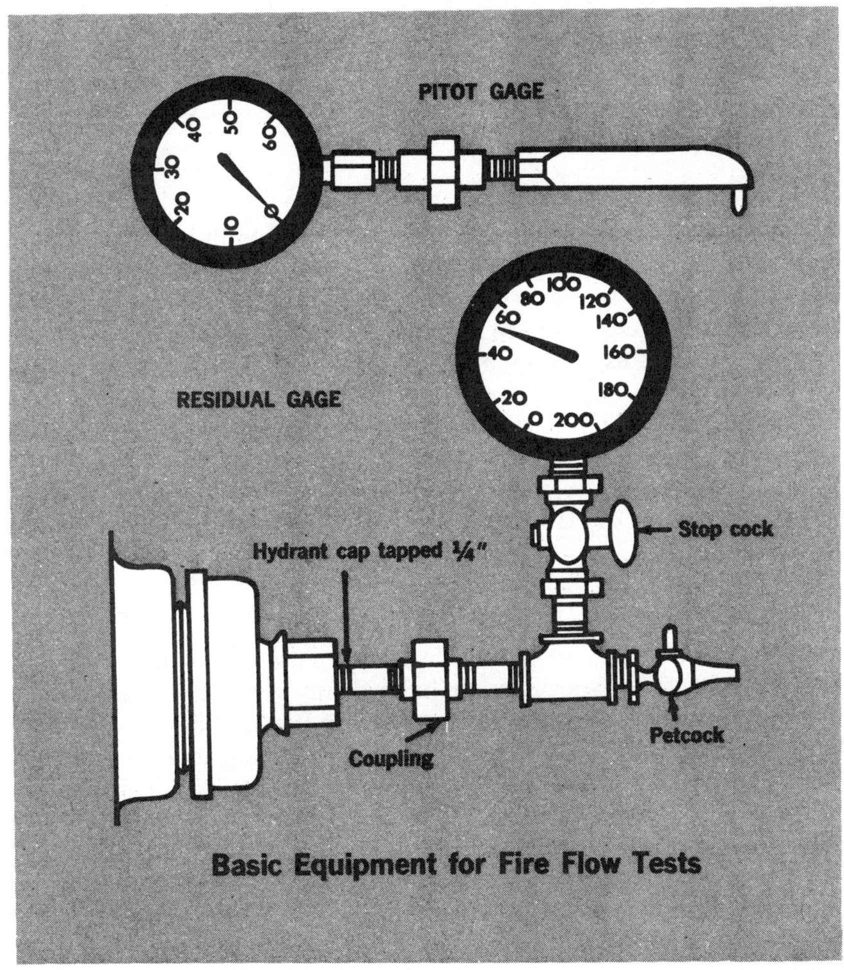

Basic Equipment for Fire Flow Tests

2. Variable with some power (n) of the velocity (V) of the water flowing.

3. Variable with the roughness of the pipe.

4. Inversely proportional to some power (x) of the pipe diameter (d).

It is written as an equation:

$$H = K\frac{lV^n}{d^x}$$

K is a constant of proportionality which takes into account the roughness of the pipe. This formula is difficult to use because n varies with the roughness of the pipe and x varies with the velocity. More convenient formulas have been devised which are modifications of the above formula and are based on actual flow studies. They are rather involved and lengthy and can be found in Fire Service Hydraulics, Second Edition.

Pipe materials

Supply mains extending from reservoirs or pumping stations are of large size and may be made of reinforced concrete, steel, cast iron, or asbestos cement. In recent years ductile iron has also been used. Although mains of any of these materials extend into and form parts of distribution systems, the majority of the distributing mains are cast iron or cement.

Standards for cast iron, steel, asbestos cement, plastic and reinforced concrete pipe have been developed by the American Water Works Association, and most pipe manufactured and installed in municipal water supply systems in the United States conforms to these standards as a minimum.

Hydrants

There are two principal types of hydrants in use today—the dry-barrel and the wet-barrel. The latter can be used only in milder climates where there is no freezing weather. The American Water Works Association has prepared standards for both types of hydrants, and a good fire department always has a set on file. AWWA Standard 0502 covers "Fire Hydrants for Ordinary Water Works Service" and AWWA Standard 0503, "Wet Barrel Fire Hydrants for Ordinary Water Works Service."

These standards cover hydrants designed for a working pressure of 150 psi and provide for a hydrostatic shop test of each hydrant at 300 psi. The use of these standards enables a municipality to purchase hydrants that are well designed and constructed and well adapted to regular municipal service.

Dry-barrel hydrants

The dry-barrel hydrant consists esentially of a footpiece, a barrel, a bonnet, an operating stem, a main valve and a drain. The footpiece, sometimes called the elbow or shoe, provides the inlet for the hydrant from the branch connection that extends from the main. It also contains the seat for the main valve and the drain outlet.

The barrel or riser, which may have more than one section, extends vertically from the footpiece and continues above the ground surface. It contains the outlet nozzles and houses the operating stem.

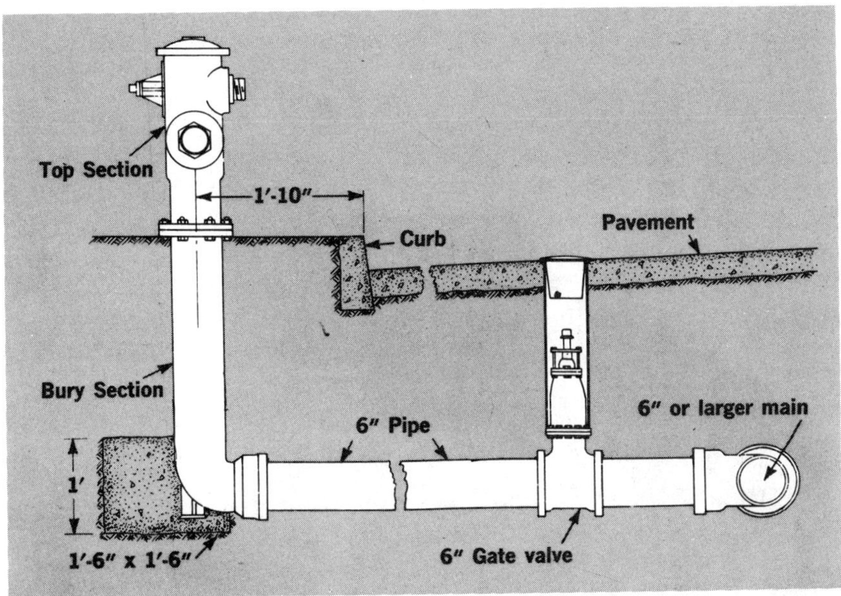

Typical hydrant installation shows the underground, including bury section, connection to main and service gate valve.

The bonnet, or top, is fastened to the barrel at the upper end to form a protecting cover. The mechanism for turning the stem is housed in the bonnet and is controlled by the operating nut which extends out of the top.

The operating stem extends through the length of the barrel and usually carries the valve at its lower end. Its upper end is connected to the mechanism in the bonnet.

The main valve, which is attached to the stem, moves away from the seat in the footpiece as the hydrant is opened and moves against the seat as the hydrant is closed. The valves on most hydrants manufactured today are arranged to open against the pressure and to close with the pressure. An obvious advantage of this arrangement is that if the stem should be broken, the pressure in the footpiece on the supply side of the valve would hold it in the closed position.

Draining the hydrant

Dry-barrel hydrants require a means by which the water remaining in the barrel after use can be removed. Drain holes, together with a suitable drain mechanism, are provided in the footpiece for this purpose.

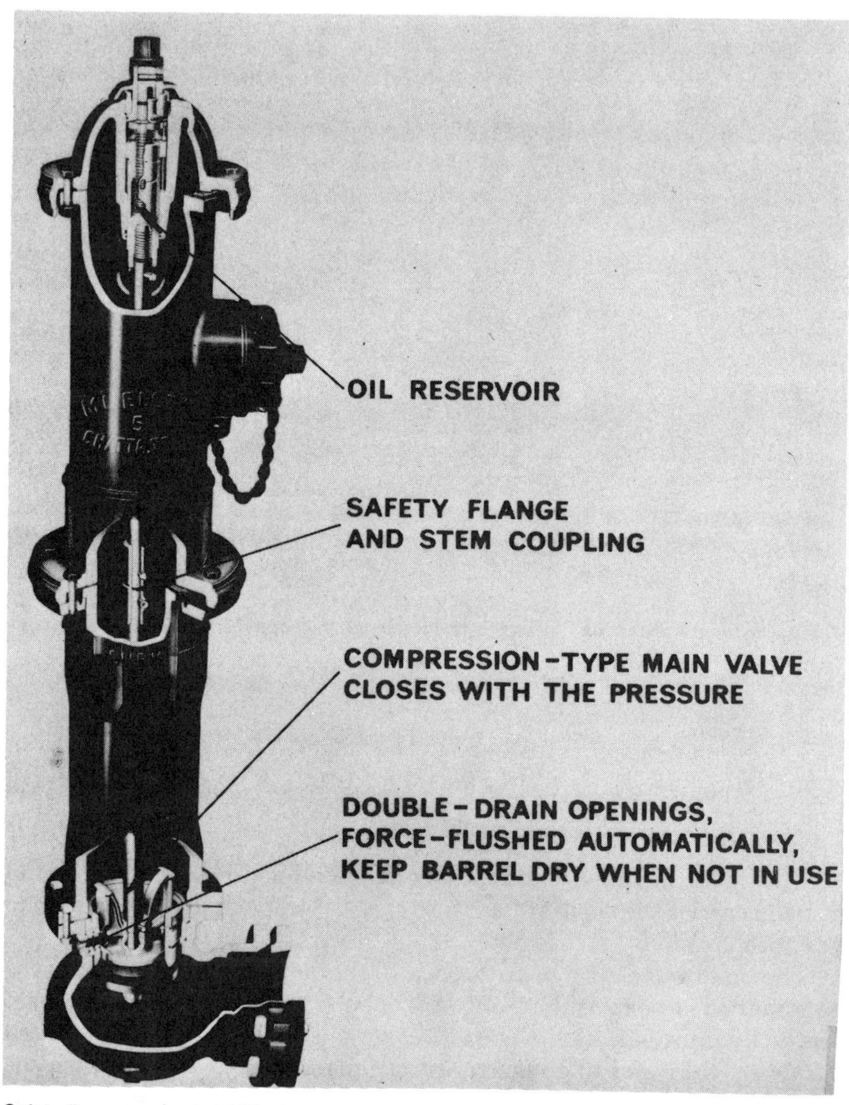

Safety flange on dry-barrel hydrant permits the upper portions of barrel and operating stem to be broken off (accidentally) at ground level without damaging buried parts which would otherwise discharge water.

When a hydrant is closed, the drain opens. As the hydrant is opened, the drain closes (during the first few turns) and remains closed while the hydrant discharges. As the hydrant is shut down, the drain opens

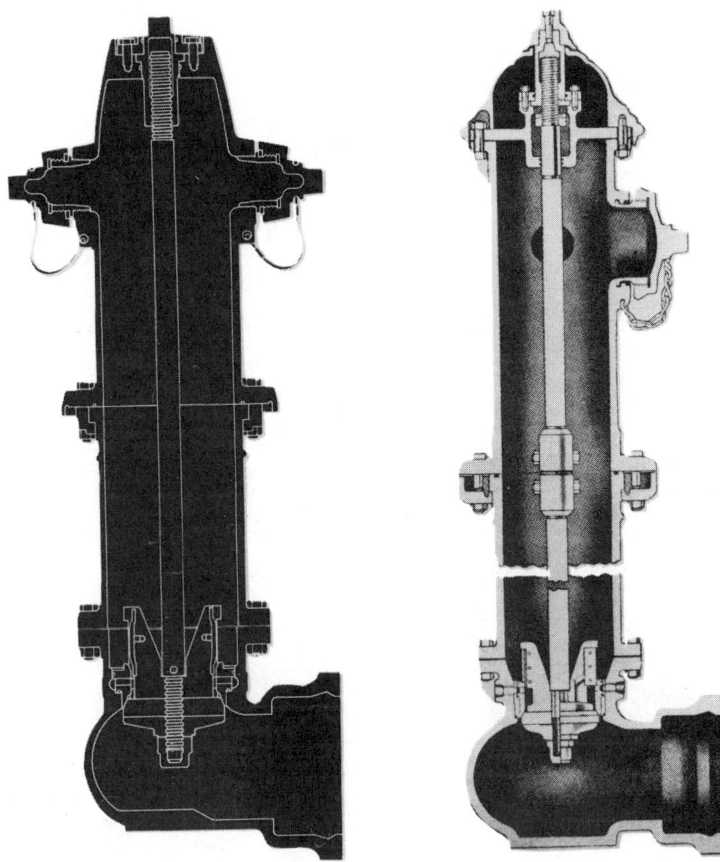

Main valve on dry hydrant moves away from seat in footpiece as hydrant is opened. Valves on most hydrants close with the pressure.

(during the last few turns) and remains open until the hydrant is operated again.

At the time a dry-barrel hydrant is installed, it is necessary to make certain that it will drain properly into the ground. For this purpose a sufficient quantity of clean stone or coarse gravel is placed around the lower portion of the footpiece and extended up to several inches above the drain holes. This practice will usually enable hydrants to drain properly even where soils may have a low permeability. It also helps to prevent the clogging of drain holes with dirt or sand.

In some locations the ground water level may normally be higher than

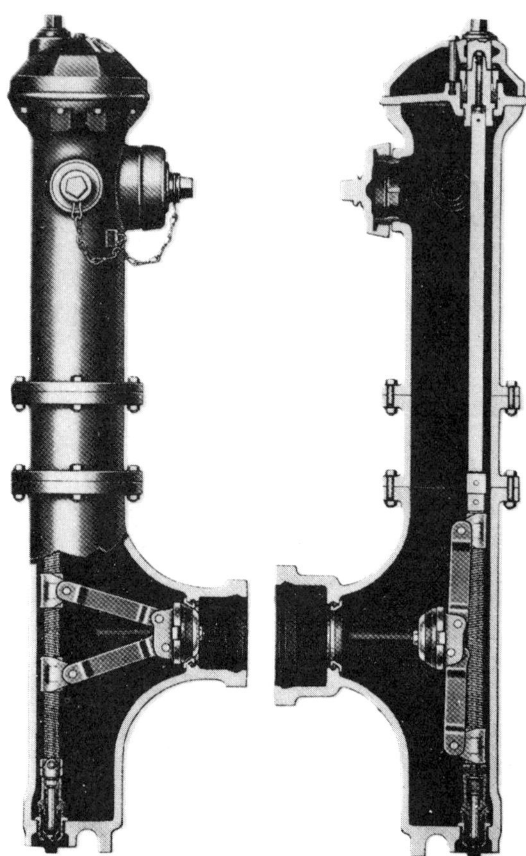

Knuckle-jointed main valve on this hydrant opens with pressure in the main and closes against pressure.

the hydrant drain holes. When this happens, water enters the hydrant barrel and rises to the level of the ground water on the outside. The water is then subject to freezing in winter, which could render the hydrant inoperable. It is common practice, therefore, to plug the drains of hydrants installed in areas where the ground water table is high. Plugging the drain makes it necessary to pump out the water remaining in the barrel after each use. In some business districts where normal drainage from hydrants has leaked into basements, it has also been found necessary to plug the drains to prevent damage. It is essential that hydrants with plugged drains be properly identified so that fire department and water department personnel will be on notice to pump them out after use.

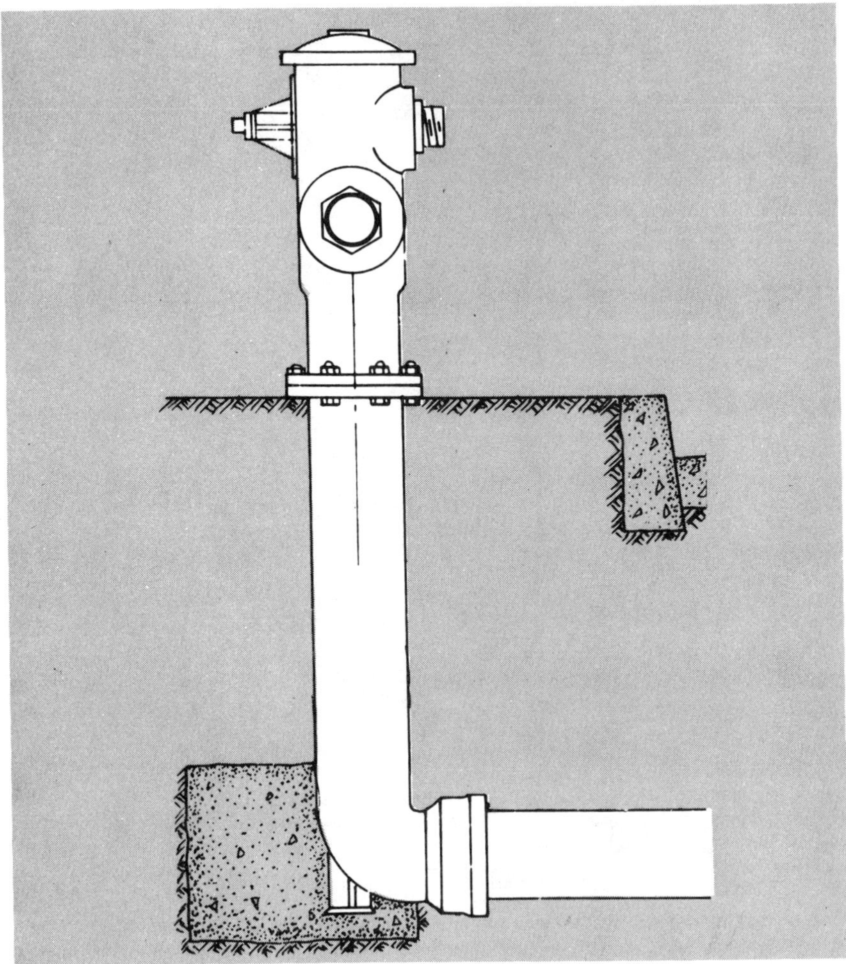

Wet-barrel hydrant consists essentially of a bury section and a top section. It has fewer parts than a dry-barrel hydrant.

A wet-barrel hydrant consists essentially of a bury section and a top section, and has fewer parts than a dry-barrel hydrant. The bury section provides the inlet for the hydrant from the branch connection that extends from the main. It has a 50-degree bend just like the footpiece of a dry-barrel hydrant but extends vertically to a point above the ground surface. It is a piece of cast iron pipe with a 90-degree bend on one end and there are no moving parts within it.

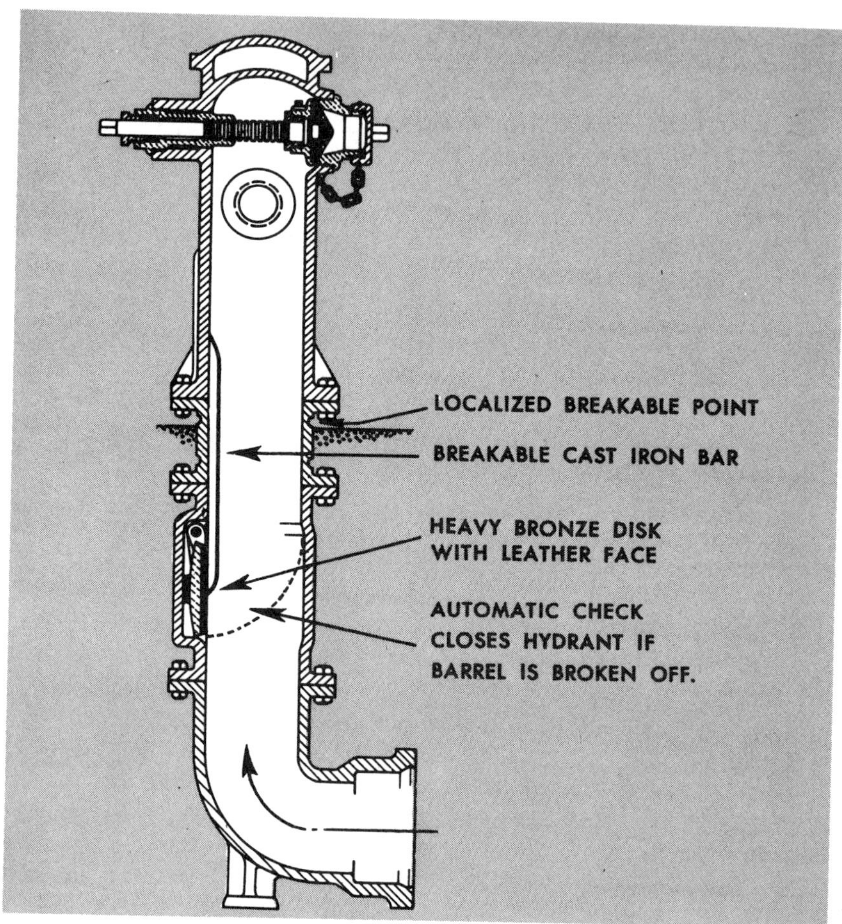

This type of breakaway hydrant was designed to give a "dry break" for wet-barrel hydrants. Check valve is released when breakable units fail as when struck by an automobile.

The top section, also called the body, extends vertically from the bury section and contains the outlet nozzles and the independent valves that control the flow from each nozzle. Each valve is mounted on a threaded stem which is supported by a housing on the opposite side of the body, 180 degrees apart. This housing contains the threads that enable the stem to move the valve on and off its seat which is on the inside end of the outlet nozzle. The operating nut is on the exterior end of the stem that protrudes from its housing.

Another type commonly used in connection with high-pressure systems, as well as in some low-pressure systems, is the hydrant with an independent gate on each outlet, in addition to a main valve. The advantage of this type is that the stream from each nozzle is under independent control so that any line may be shut down without interfering with the other lines. In the hydrants previously described, opening the main valve immediately charges the hydrant barrel, and hose lines must be attached before this valve is opened.

Outlet nozzles

Every hydrant should have at least two outlet nozzles so that a damaged outlet nozzle will not prevent the hydrant from being used. Further, because pumpers are needed to provide satisfactory fire streams in most municipalities, one of these outlet nozzles should be a pumper outlet nozzle (steamer connection). An exception to this can be made in areas in which the fire flow needed can be obtained from the water distribution system at residual pressures (not less than 75 psi) suitable for the use of direct hydrant hose streams in which hydrants are spaced 250 to 300 feet apart. This is to insure short hose lines.

For most municipalities, hydrants with a pumper outlet nozzle and one or two 2½-inch outlet nozzles will provide satisfactory service. In some large cities hydrants with two pumper outlet nozzles are installed in districts where large flows are needed. In order for such hydrants to be used effectively, the distribution system should be capable of supplying 2000 gpm at each hydrant. Fire department standard operating procedures should include appropriate methods for connecting two pumpers to a single hydrant.

The threads on outlet nozzles should conform to American National Standard B 26, "National (American) Standard Fire Hose Coupling Screw Threads," except where the threads in use in the municipality installing the hydrant are of different dimensions.

The outlet nozzles for both dry and wet-barrel hydrants are provided with caps. In the case of the dry-barrel type, the caps are needed to protect the threads from damage, to prevent foreign material from entering the barrel, and to prevent discharge from the outlet nozzles not in use during hydrant operation. In the wet-barrel type the caps protect the nozzle threads and also the portion of the valve that would otherwise be exposed. Outlet nozzle caps are often provided with chains connected to the hydrant barrel to prevent the caps from being stolen or lost at a fire. The installation of chains is optional with the municipality or utility purchasing the equipment.

When water flows from the main through the branch connection and through the hydrant there will be a loss of head or pressure between the main and the hydrant outlet nozzles. This loss of head will be small for

Maximum Permissible Loss of Head for Hydrants

No. of Outlet Nozzles	Nom. Diameter of Outlet Nozzles (in.)	Total Flow From Outlet Nozzles (gpm)	Max. Permissible Head Loss (psi)
1	2½	250	1.0
2	2½	500*	2.0
3	2½	750*	3.0
4	2½	1000*	4.0
1	4½	1000	5.0†

* 250 gpm, approximately from each outlet nozzle.
† Also to apply to pumper outlet nozzles of other sizes.

small flows, but may increase to excessive amounts for large flows in a poorly designed hydrant.

The loss of head in the hydrant itself is limited by AWWA standards as shown in table, "Maximum Permissible Loss of Head for Hydrants." A study of this table will show that for a 1000-gpm delivery through the pumper outlet nozzle (irrespective of size), the loss cannot exceed 5 psi. The standards also specify that if a hydrant (such as those with two pumper outlets) is designed to deliver more than 1000 gpm, the total loss of head cannot exceed 5 psi no matter how large the discharge. Therefore, it is quite evident that hydrants purchased under AWWA standards should not present any problems arising out of excessive head loss. Although a great many heads installed at present conform to AWWA standards, there are hydrants in service in many municipalities that do not meet the standards and in which there will be excessive head losses with large flows. In some of these hydrants the loss may be so high that an adequate discharge cannot be obtained. Many such hydrants are old or of makes no longer available. They are gradually being replaced.

Branch connection

Part of the loss of head between the main and the outlet nozzle takes place in the branch connection. The minimum size considered satisfactory for this connection is 6 inches, and this size or larger should be installed. Hydrants which have two pumper outlets and may be required to deliver 2000 gpm or more, need an 8-inch branch connection.

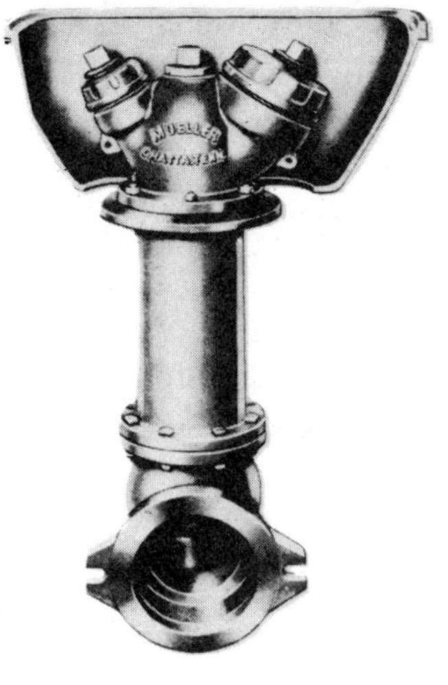

Flush (with the ground) type hydrants are used for airport runways, loading areas and similar installations. They are made with wet or dry barrels and are enclosed in a special cast iron box or manhole.

There are, however, many water distribution systems in which supply to hydrants is restricted by 4-inch branch connections. And in some cases the originally inadequate size has been further reduced in capacity by tuberculation (deposits).

It is good practice to install a gate valve in the branch connection so that a hydrant can be replaced or repaired without shutting down a portion of the distribution system. The gate valve is of special importance for wet-barrel hydrants because if the barrel is broken off due to an accident, the water will discharge geyser like until a shutoff can be made. The gate valve has also been found to be very helpful when after a long period of use at a fire, a hydrant cannot be closed because of a defect.

Flush hydrants

Post-type hydrants are, of course, not suitable for all installations. Airport runways and loading areas, for example, call for a hydrant that is flush with the ground. These flush-type hydrants are also made in wet and dry-barrel configurations. The outlet nozzles of a flush hydrant are located just below the surface of the ground and are inclosed in a special cast iron box or manhole. The cover for the box must be strong enough to carry the weight of vehicles and at the same time be light enough to be easily removed for fire use. It should also be clearly marked so that it can be readily identified.

It is obvious that there are a number of disadvantages to the use of flush hydrants. They are difficult to locate particularly in a street which may have other manhole or box covers. Motor vehicles may be parked directly over them. And in winter they may be covered with ice or snow. There is also a greater delay involved in getting a fire stream into operation compared with a post-type hydrant. This delay is greater where it is necessary to use a portable chuck such as found in the City of Baltimore.

Private yard hydrants

Many industrial plants maintain a private yard main system for fire protection purposes only. These systems are supplied by a special fire pump and are usually designed to supply the yard hydrants at pressures suitable for direct hose streams. The hydrants generally have from two to four hose outlets, each provided with an independent gate. Such hydrants may be located in hose houses and have hose connected to one of the outlets for immediate use.

In some of the larger cities special high-pressure fire systems are provided to augment the supply available for fire fighting from the regular public water supply system. These special systems were designed to operate at pressures ranging from 150 to 300 psi. The hydrants are of the post type, with the exception of Baltimore, and are of extra-heavy construction. They are usually provided with three or four outlet nozzles each with an independent gate.

Flow tests essential

One of the most important factors in a community's fire protection is the water supply in any given area, as indicated by the fire flow available from one or more hydrants at various residual pressures. This information is needed by fire departments, fire insurance engineers, and personnel responsible for plant fire protection.

It is good practice to test the water supply from a group of hydrants simultaneously. The performance of one hydrant may not be indicative of the water system's ability to supply the desired flow at a satisfactory pressure throughout the rest of the area.

The data obtained in these tests provide information on available pressures throughout the entire area or distribution system. Furthermore, if a marked change in residual pressure is observed at a given hydrant, it may indicate that a nearby control valve in the water main has

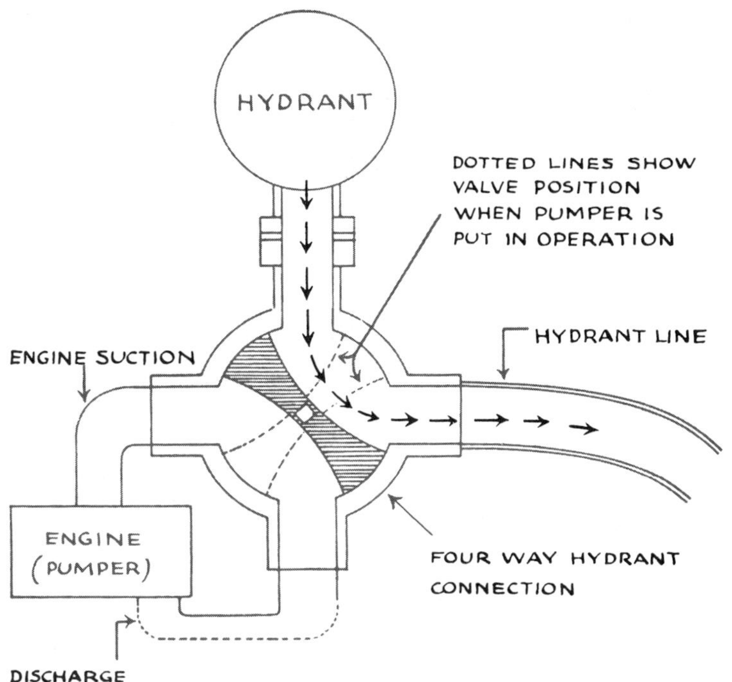

Four-way hydrant connection provides a means for changing from a direct hydrant stream to an engine stream without shutting off flow of water.

been fully or partially closed; or that the industrial or domestic water consumption in the vicinity has increased considerably since the last inspection. Any marked change in static or residual pressures should be reported to the water utility for investigation. Such may reveal the need for changes in underground piping, closed valves, heavily encrustated piping, defective hydrant, a change in designation of the hydrant for fire flow or a flaw in the maintenance procedure.

Another acknowledged benefit to be derived from a knowledge of fire flow is that such information promotes efficiency in positioning pumpers at hydrants in fire areas. These tests also show whether there is an adequate supply of water for fires of the magnitude which might occur in an area, particularly near schools, hospitals, shopping centers, warehouses and industrial plants.

In running a flow test it is usually advisable to start with one hydrant. Open it up and measure the flow. Then open a second hydrant. With both flowing, take readings. Then open a third hydrant and take

Discharge From Hydrant Outlets at Various Pressures

Hydrant Outlet Pressure in Lbs. PSI	Discharge from $2\frac{1}{2}$-In. Outlet in GPM	Discharge from $4\frac{1}{2}$-In. Outlet in GPM
1	170	550
2	240	770
3	290	940
4	340	1,090
5	380	1,220
6	410	1,330
7	440	1,440
8	480	1,540
9	500	1,630
10	530	1,720
12	580	1,890
14	630	2,040
16	670	2,180
18	710	2,310
20	750	2,440
22	790	2,560
24	820	2,670
26	860	2,780
28	890	2,880
30	920	2,990
32	950	3,080
34	980	3,190
36	1,010	3,270
38	1,025	3,334
40	1,055	3,420
45	1,120	3,627
50	1,182	3,827
55	1,240	4,014
60	1,294	4,290

readings on all three, and so on until it is definitely determined what the average flow in the particular area might be.

An understanding of the difference between the terms static and residual pressure is necessary to appreciate what test figures on a hydrant truly indicate. Although there is nearly always some leakage or domestic flow from the water main, static (nonflowing) pressure is accepted to mean the pressure at the hydrant with its main valve opened but all the independent valves closed or the outlets capped. To obtain this figure, the most common method is to tap a pressure gage into a hydrant cap which is then placed over one of the outlets. With the main valve and any necessary independent valves opened, air is released from the barrel and a reading taken.

This figure means little insofar as fire protection and the ability of the hydrant to deliver water are concerned. The pressure shown under the setup for a static test may drop off considerably when nearby hydrants are opened or as water is discharged from the test hydrant.

Residual (or flowing) pressure is shown on the same gage as the one used on the main and any necessary independent valves are opened to discharge water from an outlet.

From the residual pressure, we can calculate the actual discharge at this figure and predict in approximate terms the available water which can be expected from a particular hydrant as more outlets are opened or as pumpers connected to it supply additional lines.

Using the pitot

Pitot gages are used not only to check flowing pressures and discharges from nozzles and playpipes but also constitute a practical means of performing the same function on the outlets of hydrants. In usage, most accurate results are achieved by inserting the knife edge of the gage into the stream so that the water opening of the tube is in the center of the stream and about one-half the diameter away from the end of the nozzle.

The formula for determining the amount of water issuing from a fire hydrant is as follows:

$$\text{Discharge (gpm)} = 29.7 \times D^2 \times \sqrt{p} \times 0.90$$

"D" is the diameter of the hydrant outlet in inches and "p" the pressure at the hydrant outlet in psi. The coefficient 0.90 represents hydrant losses and was derived empirically.

Combining the constant (29.7), the D^2 and the coefficient (0.90), the hydrant formula may be reduced for different outlet diameters as indicated below:

For 2½-inch outlet:	$\text{Discharge} = 167 \times \sqrt{p}$
For 3-inch outlet:	$\text{Discharge} = 240 \times \sqrt{p}$
For 4-inch outlet:	$\text{Discharge} = 428 \times \sqrt{p}$
For 4½-inch outlet:	$\text{Discharge} = 541 \times \sqrt{p}$
For 5-inch outlet:	$\text{Discharge} = 668 \times \sqrt{p}$
For 6-inch outlet:	$\text{Discharge} = 962 \times \sqrt{p}$

In connection with fire flow tests it is well to bear in mind that extreme accuracy is not a factor. The purpose is not to determine exact gallonage but the number of fire streams which can be obtained from a hydrant or group of hydrants.

Since the so-called standard fire stream discharges 250 to 300 gpm, fire flow test results are usually given to the nearest 50 gpm for quantities of less than 1000 gpm and to the nearest 100 gpm for quantities above 1000 gpm.

Once the capability of a hydrant has been determined, it should be painted a specific color to indicate the relative available fire flow. It must be understood that the colors signify only the individual capacity of the hydrant as tested and not group hydrant effect. Naturally, the pressures and discharges from hydrants drop off as other hydrants in the vicinity are opened.

The plan commonly employed to indicate individual hydrant capacity is as follows:

Class	Flow	Color of Tops and Nozzle Caps
A	1000 gpm or greater	Green
B	500–1000 gpm	Orange
C	Less than 500 gpm	Red

Capacities are rated by flow measurements and tests of individual hydrants at a period of ordinary demand. Rating is to be based on 20-psi residual pressure when initial pressure is over 40 psi. When initial pressure is less than 40 psi, residual pressure should be at least half of the initial.

To supply hose streams directly from a hydrant, the residual pressure should be at least 50 psi. This figure is considered minimum to overcome friction losses in the hose line and provide sufficient throw at the nozzle. Therefore, as a rule, this operation is impractical, particularly if the stretch is long and/or a large nozzle is used. In most cases, it is more practicable to provide necessary nozzle pressures through fire department pumpers rather than streams direct from hydrants, even if it is possible to raise hydrant pressures from a pumping station.

Estimating hydrant performance

As previously explained, the color scheme signifies only the capacity of a hydrant and not the results which may be expected from it as other nearby hydrants are opened. It should be understood that each separate hydrant has a performance characteristic of its own that is the sum of many factors, such as hydrant design, size of its waterway, size of the connection to the main, etc.

A high static, or nonflowing, pressure is no guarantee of the number of lines which a hydrant may be expected to supply. It is the changes in residual pressure as water is discharged that indicate the volume available.

The difference between the static and the residual pressures is the sum

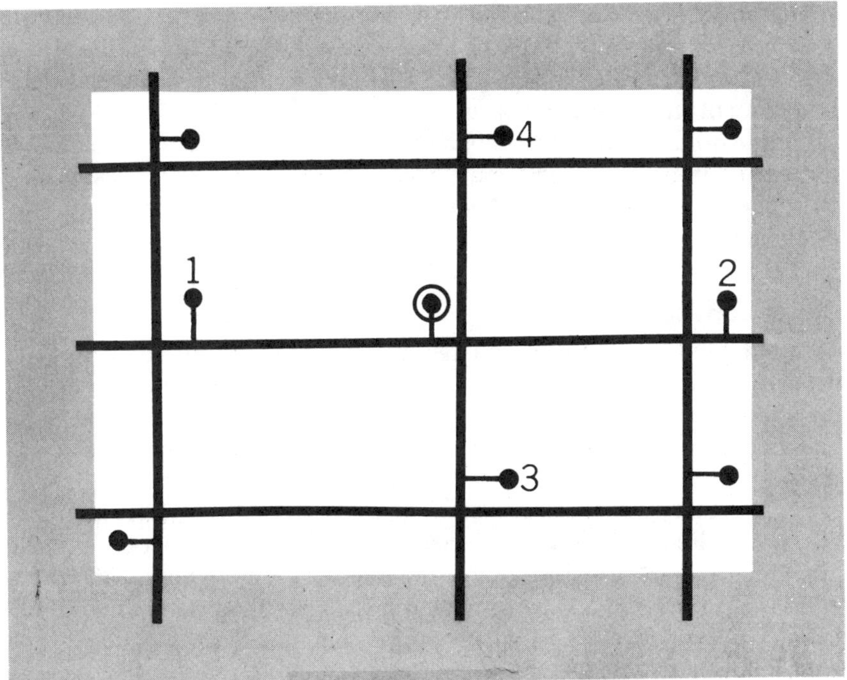

Sample flow test layout. Hydrants 1, 2, 3 and 4 on the grid are flowed. Residual pressure is observed at hydrant in center of grid.

of the resultant losses in the connection from the hydrant to the pumper, as well as the losses in the hydrant and in the main leading to it. At the same flow, losses in the connection to the pumper will vary according to the length and cross-sectional area of the carrier; in the hydrant they vary according to its design; in the main they depend on the size, length and condition of the supply main and whether it is cross-connected.

At working flows these losses increase approximately as to the square of the proportionate increase in discharge. From the drop in pressures one can roughly estimate the water that can be expected from a hydrant at a remaining residual pressure. Suppose, for example, there is a static reading of 60 psi when the pumper is first charged from the hydrant and that this figure drops to 50 psi as a single line is supplied. The 10-psi difference, representing the sum of all the losses, may be used in approximating additional water available.

If a second similar line is now charged from the same source (doubling the discharge), we may expect an additional 40-psi loss (four times as great) and the reading should drop to roughly 10-psi or less residual pressure. No attempt should be made to supply additional lines from this hydrant below this figure and this fact should be brought to the attention of the officer in charge.

On the other hand, even though the initial static pressure is relatively low, if a hydrant is on a large main, well looped or gridded, the losses may not increase to any extent as lines are supplied. Thus the hydrant may easily supply all the water that a pumper can use.

Utilize capacity

A fault common to many fire departments is the failure to utilize the capacity of fire hydrants, particularly at large fires and where hydrants are spaced relatively far apart.

Where a hydrant is connected to a large main and good pressure is maintained, it may satisfactorily supply two pumpers. In the high-value section of a city where mains are cross-connected at relatively short intervals, a single hydrant may supply even three pumpers. Off the gravity-fed, high-pressure system in New York City, where static pressures range from 100-120 psi and the residual pressures are not materially less, four pumpers can easily be supplied from one hydrant using 3-inch supply lines that are relatively short.

At a department test, 40 pumpers operated at capacity (total discharge of 30,000 gpm) within an area two blocks wide and three blocks long without reducing the residual pressure below 57 psi within 100 feet of the boundaries of the area.

A guide for hooking up additional pumpers is the residual pressure as read on the pumper intake gage as each pumper is connected and discharges its capacity. A figure of 10-20 psi is considered the safe minimum to be maintained. No additional pumpers should be placed at the hydrant when this figure is reached and the fact should be reported to the chief officer in charge of the fire operation.

Dual pumper operations possess several advantages:

1. The speed with which the second or third pumper can stretch hand lines or supply heavy-duty equipment.
2. The conservation of hose used at large fires. The same amount of water can be put on the fire with fewer lengths of hose. Remaining hose on the apparatus can be used for additional lines. With fewer lengths of hose stretched, taking up operations are facilitated.
3. Closer grouping of apparatus. This provides for more efficient operation. Since fewer streets are blocked, there is less traffic stopped and less inconvenience to the public.

4. A more efficient use of pump pressure which is normally wasted in friction loss when hose stretches are lengthy.

5 Shorter hose lines make possible quicker water on the fire from deck guns, monitor nozzles, deluge sets, etc., and increase the potential discharge since pump pressures can be more efficiently used. This may spell the difference between prompt extinguishment and a defensive operation.

Placement of pumpers at hydrants

There are a variety of methods in which more than one pumper can get its water from the same hydrant. No single method can be endorsed above all the others, as the width of the street, the number of outlets and the direction they face (i.e. roadway or sidewalk) and other factors have a bearing on the choice.

For example, two pumpers may take their water from a single hydrant if one is connected to the 4½-inch connection and the second pumper to the other connection or connections.

Or one pumper may be connected to the 4½-inch connection of the hydrant and the second pumper to the unused suction connection of the first pumper.

Since in most cases one pumper is supplying lines before the second attempts to get water from the same source, the advantages of putting a hydrant gate or gated wye on the hydrant before opening the main valve are obvious unless the hydrant is independently gated. In the second layout (suction to suction) the use of a Keystone valve on the suction inlet of pumper No. 1 (which will be used by pumper No. 2) obviates the need for shutting down the hydrant. These large gate valves on pumper intakes serve other purposes such as making possible the use of the booster tank water while connecting to a hydrant.

Combinations of the two methods may be used if three pumpers are to operate from one hydrant. For example, the first pumper could be attached to the steamer outlet of the hydrant, the second pumper would be connected to the other suction connection of the first pumper and the third pumper would be connected by parallel lines of hose to the other outlet or outlets of the hydrants.

If the hydrant has but one other outlet, a single line may be stretched to pumper No. 2; or two lines from a gated wye connection with suitable fittings.

Pumping in tandem

A less recommended method is known as tandem pumping. The first pumper hooks up and supplies its own hand lines plus a short length of large-diameter hose connected to the intake of the second pumper. In this operation (in reality a relay) the second pumper receives its water under high pressure and can take advantage of this assist in pressure when discharging.

Consider friction loss

If a large connection is not used when hooking up a pumper to a hydrant, much of the pressure available at the hydrant is wasted in overcoming friction losses in small-diameter supply lines to the pumper. This friction loss can be reduced by using larger-diameter hose or parallel lines.

The shortcoming of excessive friction losses in the supply line is even more pronounced in in-line pumping. A hose line is stretched from the hydrant (with gate on unused outlet) to the pumper, which is spotted as close to the fire as is practicable. Booster tank water is used on the fire while the supply line is being stretched and charged. It frequently happens that this limited supply in the tank is more effective when immediately applied to the fire than several thousand gallons applied later.

HYDRANT MAINTENANCE

Hydrants are installed principally for fire department use in emergency situations involving fire control and extinguishment. Unlike other parts of a water system, such as pumps, filters, flow meters and recording devices, whose functioning is under more or less constant surveillance, hydrants receive little attention. In fact, some hydrants may not be used for a fire for years at a time.

For this reason, some procedure must be followed to assure satisfactory hydrant performance, if and when they are needed for fire service. Experience has shown that the most practical procedure for providing this when-needed availability is by a regular hydrant inspection program.

The frequency of inspections may vary from community to community, and from area to area in any one community, depending on variable factors. Inspections twice a year, if properly conducted, have proven to be satisfactory in most cases. It is relatively unimportant whether the fire department or the water department assumes this responsibility. The main consideration is to see that this work is done regularly and properly.

The actual time of the year for inspections will depend on the climate. Where the year-round weather is mild, semiannual inspections can be made at any time. In areas subject to freezing weather, it is advisable to make one in the fall and another in the spring. Needed repairs can be made before cold weather sets in; the spring inspection will reveal any damage that has occurred as a result of freezing weather or other factors. An individual hydrant record card should be available for this purpose.

The following hydrant inspection procedure is suggested:

1. On approaching the hydrant, check the hydrant record card or other form for accuracy of its information. A notation of any changes (e.g. location, type, other data) should be made at the scene and later transferred to some permanent record. A visual external inspection should be made for possible damage, such as cracked barrel, which may have resulted from the hydrant having been struck by a motor vehicle; unauthorized usage that has damaged the operating nut; or vandalism which results in missing caps or chains or foreign objects being placed in the barrel.

2. Conduct a pressure test. This is done by removing one of the hydrant caps and replacing it with a special cap provided with a pressure gage. Check all caps for tightness and open the air cock.

After water is discharged, indicating that the air has been exhausted, close bleeder cock and record the static pressure reading. Inspect the bonnet, packing, and caulking around the nozzle outlets for leaks. Observe the ground around the hydrant to detect any underground leaks in the hydrant or a defective drain valve which has not closed. The bleeder cock should then be opened or the outlet cap loosened, and the main valve closed.

3. Remove an outlet cap (or two caps, if more than a single outlet) and open the main valve to flush the hydrant and check its operation. The hydrant should be opened wide if this can be done without damage to streets and nearby property. Distributing the flow over more than one outlet nozzle reduces the possibility of damage by decreasing the discharge velocity and throw of the stream.

If the water is discolored by sediment, the hydrant should be flowed until the discharge is reasonably clear. In opening and closing the main valve any unusual stiffness in operation should be noted and reported.

4. After closing, hydrant drainage should be checked by observing the water receding in the barrel. After it has dropped out of sight, drainage can he checked by placing the palm of the hand over the outlet to see if air is being sucked in as water recedes.

If there is any doubt as to whether or not all the water has drained, a small weight on a cord or a lightweight chain may be lowered into the barrel to sound the presence of water.

5. Freezing in hydrants may be detected by:

(a) Sounding by striking the palm of the hand over an open outlet. Water or ice shortens the length of the "organ tube" and raises the note.

(b) Attempting to turn the hydrant stem and encountering difficulty. The stem will not turn if frozen solidly. If only slightly bound by ice, a hydrant wrench should be placed on the operating nut and smartly tapped. This may release the stem. Blows should be moderate to avoid breaking the valve rod.

(c) Lowering a weighted object on a string into the barrel. Such may strike ice or come up wet indicating the presence of water.

6. Steam is the most satisfactory medium for thawing a frozen hydrant. The use of sodium chloride, or gasoline or other flammable liquids is not recommended for thawing.

Antifreeze fluid is commonly used for preventing frozen hydrants in much the same manner as it is used in automobile radiators. Although common salt (sodium chloride) has been used, it is not recommended. Calcium chloride is more suitable, because it creates a solution with a lower freezing point, and has little or no corrosive action on iron and brass.

7. Where hydrant drain valves are in ground water, they should be plugged. Care should be taken to see that these hydrants are pumped out immediately after each test or usage during freezing weather.

8. A female hose coupling should be screwed on each outlet to determine if a connection can be made. Chains should be free of excess paint and should be straightened to insure free movement of the hydrant cap.

Gaskets in the caps should be examined and replaced if necessary. All cap and outlet threads should be swabbed with a mixture of lubricating oil and graphite, using a small brush. The caps should then be replaced and drawn hand tight.

9. If the hydrant requires the oiling of certain parts, this should be done during each inspection.

In addition to their regularly scheduled inspections, hydrants should be thoroughly inspected after use at fires. To make sure that this is done, many communities have an established procedure whereby the water utility inspection crew must be notified each time a hydrant is used by the fire department.

Moreover, during freezing weather certain hydrants which are known to give trouble should be checked as often as weekly or even daily. The schedule for such inspections will have to be determined on the basis of local conditions and experience. These situations include hydrants with poor drainage or those in areas where rising ground water may fill the barrel and freeze. In such instances it is usually not necessary to make a full inspection; free movement of the main and drip valves is usually sufficient without actually discharging water from the hydrant.

A definite procedure should be established to make certain that all defects found on inspections are reported and corrected as quickly as possible. If the hydrant cannot be used for fire fighting purposes, an out-of-service disk or other device should be placed on it so that the hydrant will not be connected in the event of a fire.

In cities where both hydrant inspection work and maintenance work are done by either the water utility or the fire department, the same crews should handle inspections and repairs so that the defect can be corrected immediately.

When inspections are made by the fire department and repairs are handled by the water utility, a daily written report of hydrant defects should be sent to the utility, and the fire department should be notified when the repairs have been completed. For quicker action, where hydrants are out of service, a telephone call should precede the written reports of the fire department.

The results of hydrant inspections should be recorded on an individual card or sheet. Information should include the date of each inspection, pressure observed, defects noted, and repairs made as a result of the inspection. This card can also be used for recording additional data, such as make, type or model, date of installation, dates painted, size of the water main, whether hydrant is on a dead end main or a main not cross-connected, pressures normally maintained and any other information necessary for proper maintenance.

CHAPTER EIGHT

Hose design and care

Back in Colonial Days fire fighters had to struggle with leather hose to get water on the fire. This hose was made by forming stitched leather hides into a tube and fastening them together with copper rivets. It was stiff, extremely heavy when wet, was difficult to couple and in cold and freezing weather was as hard to handle as iron pipe.

Later, rubber hose evolved in answer to the challenge for an easier, safer, more reliable and more efficient means of getting a large volume of water on a fire. The first hose was delivered in 1871 to the Cincinnati Fire Department by the B. F. Goodrich Company. It was made by plying alternate layers of heavy, square-woven, cotton duck and thin rubber over a rubber tube, with a final layer of rubber covering the fabric.

By modern standards, this rubber fabric hose was stiff and unwieldy, but it was gratefully received by firemen who previously had to struggle with leather hose. The new hose was lighter, waterproof, much easier to couple and much easier to handle in all types of weather and thereby saved a vital element in fire fighting—time.

Rubber-covered, rubber-lined hose was used until the circular woven seamless cotton jacket we know today was adopted. This new method eliminated the heavy duck plies and rubber cover and although not as resistant to abrasion or the elements permitted equal or greater strength with a marked saving in weight and greatly increased flexibility. This meant hose could be stored easily, compactly and in greater quantity. Also, more hose could be carried on industrial and municipal apparatus with fewer men required for handling it. Since the introduction of the woven jacket rubber-lined hose, no other type of construction has been devised which does the job as well.

This does not mean, however, that there have not been great advances in design, weaving and manufacturing techniques, rubber compounding, synthetic fibers and rubbers, and treating jackets against attack by the elements. Refinements and developments include lighter, higher tensile yarns designed for decreased weight with increased flexibility at no sacrifice in strength; flat cure for easier storage; end protection for increased flex life at the couplings; constructions utilizing loose folds reinforced at the edges for improving racking characteristics and performance; improved tubes for better aging and longer life; mildewcides and water-repellent dips for the jackets.

Tube stands long storage

Rubber-lined fire hose, in general. consists of one or more woven fabric seamless jackets into which a rubber tube has been inserted and vulcanized.

The tube is that member which retains the water within the hose. Essential characteristics of fire hose tubes are the absence of defects and pinhole leaks, good aging, and surface smoothness. Desirable aging characteristics are required to prevent fold or edge cracking and subsequent failure in service. Since the hose is stored during the greater part of its life, this feature is most important.

The compounding of fire hose tubes involves the selection of ingredients to assure a satisfactory balance of all desired properties. The first and most important of these selections is that of the basic rubber itself. Twenty-five years ago natural rubber was the only choice possible. However, several man-made rubbers have become commercially available in the years since then. So great has been the acceptance of these man-made rubbers that their nationwide use now exceeds that of natural rubber. Man-made rubbers, whose resistance to ozone, weather, oil and fuels is far superior to that of natural rubber, are now readily available and have found their rightful place in the manufacture of fire hose.

Starting with the basic rubber, loading pigments, processing oils, antioxidants, antiozonants, accelerators, and curative ingredients are added to provide the desired physical properties in the finished hose.

Tubes are manufactured by two basic processes—extrusion and calendering. In the first process, the compounded rubber is extruded from a tube machine in a seamless form to produce a tube. A calandered tube is made from a flat sheet which is hand-lapped to form a tube.

After the tube is formed, it is semi-cured to facilitate handling and

Single-jacket hose (left) consists of a synthetic rubber liner combined with a closely woven textile jacket. Double-jacket hose (right) uses a second closely woven jacket to provide extra durability and higher test pressure. Hose in center is single-jacket, all-polyester, that is wrapped with synthetic rubber outer covering.

to provide the smoothest surface in the finished hose. This reduces friction loss caused by the passage of water through the hose. To adhere the semi-cured tube to the jacket requires the use of a soft, uncured backing, which is a layer of calendered sheet stock. The backing is applied to the semi-cured tube before its insertion into the jacket. The backing also tends to keep the waterway smooth while the hose is under pressure.

The textile jackets have two basic elements—the warp yarns and the filler yarns. Warp yarn is the term given to those ends or yarns that run lengthwise through the jacket; filler yarn is the term applied to the cords running circumferentially around the jacket. During the weaving operation on circular looms, these two yarns are interwoven, with the warp yarns covering the filler yarns. The warp yarns accept the lengthwise component of the internal pressure stresses and the filler yarns accept the circumferential stresses.

Fibers used

Although cotton is still used, polyester fibers rank first; other manmade fibers, such as nylon, are used in smaller amounts.

Each fiber has its particular advantages and disadvantages. Cotton has good abrasion resistance; however, it is susceptible to mildew. Mildewcide-treated jackets are available, but the hose still must be thoroughly dried after use. The polyester fibers have good chemical resistance, good abrasion resistance, do not mildew even when stored wet, and possess high unit strength. Nylon is used primarily in industrial hose for rack use in factories, mills and offices.

Jackets may be woven with the same fiber for both the warp and filler or they may be woven with one fiber in the warp and another in the filler. A hose construction that uses two fibers is "cotton-polyester filled" jackets. The cotton's bulk in the warp provides excellent abrasion resistance and the polyester filling gives a high burst strength.

Pressure distortion controlled

The most important quality characteristic of any fire hose is its pressure behavior as a finished hose. The elongation, warping, twisting, circumferential expansion or any distortion under pressure must be reasonably low to effect desirable performance. Quite naturally, the ultimate strength of the jacket is a fundamental requirement of any finished hose.

In weaving, the interlacing of the warp through the filling ends results in a crimp in the warp yarn. The crimp, or bending as the yarns go over and under the filling yarn, detracts both from the pressure behavior and the strength of the hose. It is, therefore, desirable to keep the crimp at a minimum. Also, the filling yarns must be placed in the jackets under uniform tension to be sure that each carries its full share of the load and keeps its circumferential expansion to a minimum.

A basic pressure behavior of a woven jacket is a tendency to twist. This twisting tendency results from the effort of the circular-woven construction to unwind. Therefore, the direction of twist of the finished hose depends directly on the direction in which the jacket is woven. It is a prime requirement of all fire hose that its twist be in the direction to tighten the hose couplings rather than to loosen them. All single and double-jacket hose is designed to meet that requirement.

In double jackets, inasmuch as the two jackets are made completely independently, the direction of weaving the outer jacket is reversed so that the tendency of the inner jacket to twist will be counteracted to a great degree by the outer jacket. Therefore, the importance of fit between the inner and outer jackets becomes quite obvious. After the jackets are woven and before usage, the inner jacket is inserted into the outer jacket.

If hose is to be treated with an anti-mildew and water-repellent solution, the jackets are run through dipping tanks where each fiber be-

Loom platform at hose factory produces jackets with filler yarns completely covered.

comes saturated with the solution. The jackets are then dried at controlled temperatures and are ready for further processing.

After the component parts are assembled, the semi-cured tube, covered with backing, is inserted into the jackets. Vulcanization is effected by internal steam within the hose tube, forcing it out against the woven jacket. This is accomplished in a multiple-length curing unit. Careful attention is given to keeping the temperature and pressure at specified levels. During the curing, each length is under individually controlled tension to obtain a low level of elongation in a finished hose when under pressure.

Fire hose can be cured "round" or "flat." Round cures are produced by introducing internal steam pressure and letting the jackets assume a natural round shape. Flat cures are produced by an initial round cure cycle to ensure even flow of the backing into the interstices of the jackets, followed by a final cure cycle with the hose confined in a flattened position between metal plates. The flat cure molds the edges, leaving the rubber stress relieved in the flat position in which the hose is normally stored and produces a hose with excellent racking characteristics.

Inserting the couplings

After the final cure, the finished hose is transported to machines for coupling prior to hydrostatic testing. The most common coupling for fire hose is the expansion-ring type. The female end has a bowl into which the hose is inserted, but the threads are cut into a free-swiveling, heavy, brass ring. This swiveling thread section provides easy joining of the male and female couplings without twisting the hose. The hose end is anchored in the bowl by a metal expansion ring which forces the hose wall against the inner surface of the bowl under controlled hydraulic or mechanical pressure. The inner surface of each bowl is corrugated to make a more secure attachment to the hose.

Expansion-ring couplings and expansion rings are generally made of a brass composition. Its corrosive characteristics, appearance, and ductibility are all desirable for this application. There are several types of lugs used on the fittings by which the couplings are tightened—pin lugs, rocker lugs, guard lugs, forestry or slotted lugs. Other methods for tightening couplings are spanner holes, long handles and the Jones Snap.

There are three basic types of manufacture: casting, forging and extruding. The forging and extruding processes result in a coupling with a higher tensile strength designed for heavy-duty service but with less ductibility than a cast coupling. The finish of couplings can be either a rough case finish, satin finish, a highly polished finish, or chrome-

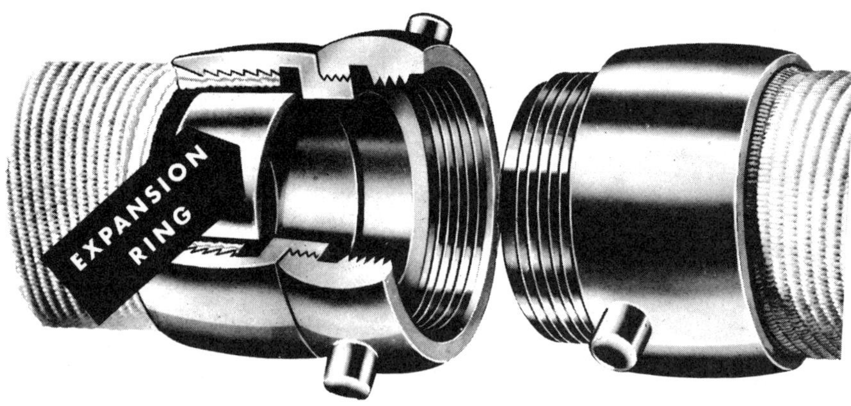

Hose end is anchored into bowl of coupling by a metal expansion ring. Typical power expanders (see opposite page) that use hydraulic power, force the hose wall against the surface of bowl.

plated. Practically all industrial couplings are of the cast type as the service is not too severe. Forged and extruded couplings are used for the heavier-duty municipal service. There are many different fire hose threads in service, but in municipal applications, the National Standard Thread is by far the most prevalent.

Expansion ring couplings are reusable; only the expansion ring itself and that part of the hose within the coupling need be replaced when the coupling is reapplied.

Hydrostatic testing

Before shipment, each length of fire hose receives a hydrostatic hold test at the designated test pressure, depending upon the construction or specification. While the hose is under this straight pressure test, it

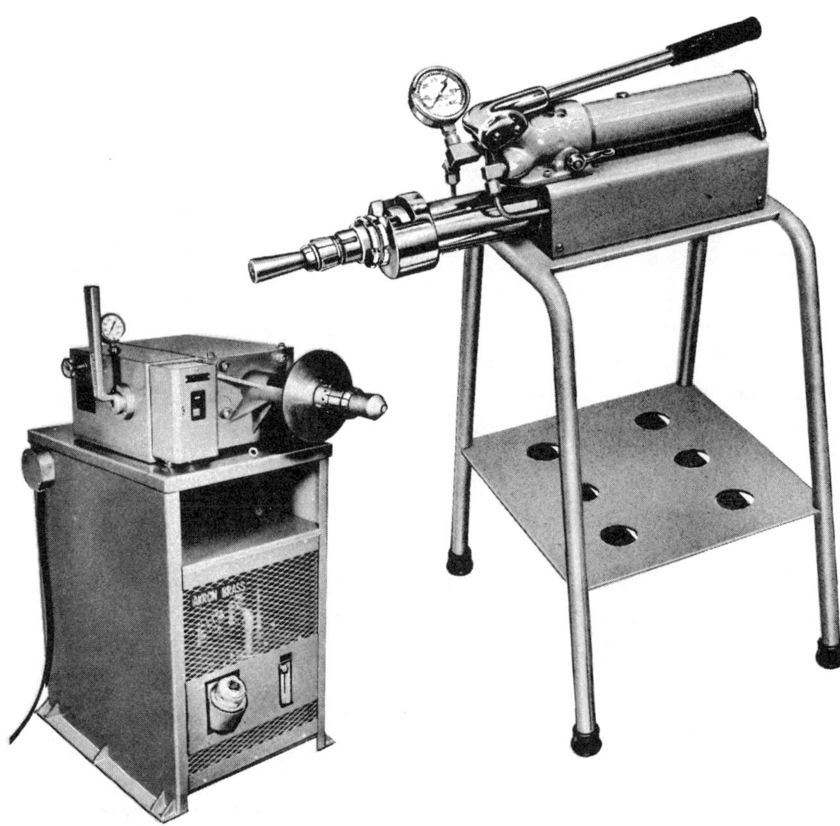

is inspected for any signs of leakage or coupling slippage. The inspectors also check twist, elongation, warp and rise. The twist is determined by how many turns the free end of the hose rotates under pressure from 10 psi to the test pressure. All twists must be in the direction to tighten the couplings. Warp is the amount the hose deviates from a straight line under the test pressure. Rise is the measure of how far the hose lifts from the test table at the test pressure.

When required, or at specified intervals for regular productions, a "kink" test is performed to determine the ability of a hose to withstand sudden kinks or bends in service.

Burst control tests are usually run on 3-foot samples. Control tests are also conducted to measure the adhesion of the tube to the jacket and to measure the physical properties of the rubber tube, both aged and unaged.

Annual testing

Proper care of fire hose is important from the standpoint of safety, effectiveness in use, and economy. Since fire hose spends much of its life doing nothing, constant effort must be made to keep it ready for instant use. As new hose is received, it should be unpacked immediately and checked for any damage during shipment. It should be recoiled loosely. It should also be tested upon receipt to see if it meets the specifications.

Again, going back to the Grading Schedule, under "Hose" we find that it should be "maintained in good condition and tested annually to at least 250 psi pressure." The schedule also calls for suitable facilities for washing, drying and storing hose. A service life of 10 years for 2½-inch hose and larger should be expected under normal conditions of use and five years for 1½-inch hose. Hose older than one-half its service, if not annually tested to a pressure of 250 psi, shall be considered in unreliable condition. Deficiency points, under the schedule, will be given for hose coupling threads of 2½-inch (and 3-inch if provided) if they are not uniform with 2½-inch outlet threads.

The total amount of hose in a department, exclusive of suction hose and that provided for elevated equipment, shall provide at least 2400 feet of 2½-inch hose (or larger), 600 feet of 1½-inch and 200 feet of booster hose (or equivalent preconnected larger hose) for each existing engine company.

The above figures, of course, include spare hose for replacement when hose on an apparatus is used or regularly changed as suggested above. Each engine company should carry at least 1200 feet of 2½-inch hose or larger, 400 feet of 1½-inch and 200 feet of booster hose (or equivalent

Air-driven pump for hydraulic tests of fire hose was developed by the National Aeronautical and Space Administration.

larger hose). The booster hose shall be preconnected to the pump.

Fire hose, like any other rubber product, requires care in use and storage. Injuries to hose may be classed under three headings: mechanical injury in service, injury by heat, injury by chemicals.

Mechanical injury in service might be classified in the following subdivisions:

Cuts from sharp edges of cornices, glass, nails, etc. If the cut is large, it is likely the lining will give way when the hose is tested.

Abrasions from vibration of hose against (a) curbstones, (b) paving, (c) window sills, (d) cornices, (e) cinders, (f) frozen ground.

Chafing

Vibration of hose is greatest near the engine, for at this point the engine impulses are transmitted with very little diminution to the first section of hose. This hose, therefore, vibrates severely and it is this vibration that causes the wearing or chafing of the jacket against the above-listed objects.

Farther away from the engine, the vibration is gradually absorbed by the elasticity of the hose, which gradually smoothes out vibrations throughout its length and helps deliver a comparatively vibrationless stream at the nozzle. Thus the greatest attention must be given to chafing near the engine.

If hose is found to be rubbing on any rough surface, it should immediately be protected by wrapping around it a piece of burlap, a piece of rope, or a chafing block made for this purpose. Any of these will protect the hose against chafing.

Chafing blocks on all suction lines to prevent chafing against the ground offer the best protection. Some departments also use chafing blocks on the first section of discharge hose. These chafing blocks can be easily made or purchased and afford excellent protection against abrasion.

It should be remembered that the vibration of the hose may not be perceptible except on close observation, but the damage is occurring just the same. It may take but an hour or so for the outer jacket of good-quality hose to wear through if permitted to chafe on a curbstone without protection.

If the chafing has gone through the outer jacket and partly through the jacket adjacent to the lining (of multiple-jacket hose), then the hose is materially weakened. On the other hand, if only the outer hose jacket is damaged, with the proper care the hose may still be serviceable for years.

Running over hose with apparatus

One of the most common causes of injury to hose is the crossing of lines by heavy apparatus. This should be avoided whenever possible. When the hose is charged and under good pressure, there is not apt to be any serious damage done, but where it lies flat or under low pressure, the damage may be severe.

A piece of hose may not appear to be damaged after having been crossed by a heavy piece of apparatus, even though the hose was flat. But if this section were opened up, the lining would probably show separation from the jacket and might even be torn apart.

Under no condition should heavy apparatus cross dry hose without bridges. These bridges should be carried on every apparatus.

A lot of unnecessary crossing of hose lines may be avoided if a department follows a uniform method of placing lines at fires. Where

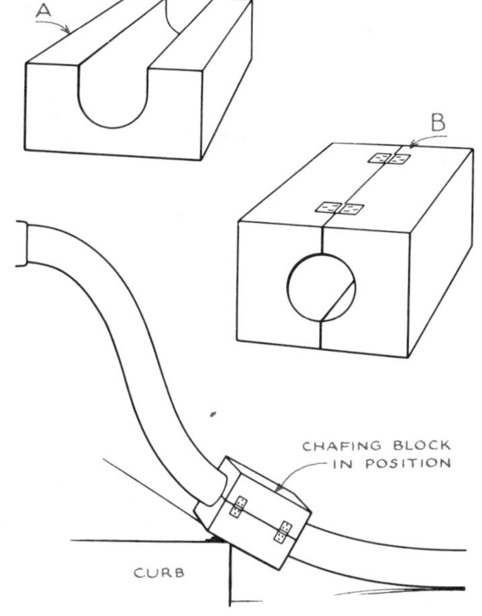

Chafing blocks prevent wear on hose caused by vibration of hose near pumper. Hose is laid in open block (A), then lashed. Jacket type block (B) encloses hose.

possible, an engine company stretching the first line should take a hydrant on the same side of the street as the fire. Lines can be stretched alongside the curb. Any apparatus crossing in front of the fire building will not have to run over these lines.

If a hydrant on the opposite side of the street from a fire building must be taken, the line should again be stretched parallel to the curb on the same side of the street as the hydrant. The only point where a line should cross is approximately opposite the fire building. In this way, apparatus pulling in from either end of the fire street after lines are placed, will not have to ride over them.

Handling frozen hose

Another common cause of injury to hose in winter weather is the handling of frozen hose. When the jacket is saturated with water and frozen, the fibers are weakened. If the hose is treated roughly, the warp threads (running lengthwise) are apt to be broken and the hose seriously damaged.

Removing hose frozen to the street is an exceedingly difficult task. No attempt should be made to pull the hose out of the ice, but rather it should be chopped clear by using an ax to free the ice beneath it. Any ice still attached to the hose should be permitted to remain and the hose

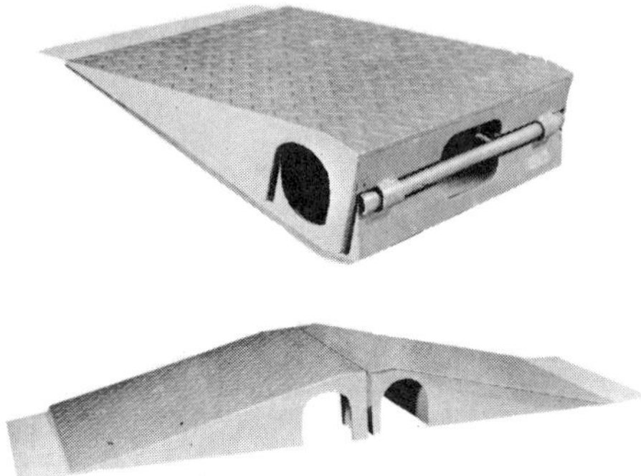

Injury to hose caused by vehicles running over it can be avoided by using crossing blocks. This type can be folded and stored. Blocks are of steel, aluminum, rubber or wood.

should be placed on the apparatus in any manner requiring the least bending or forcing. Once frozen hose is in a station, it should be permitted to completely thaw. Only then can it be properly cleaned and prepared for drying.

The advantage of double-jacket, triple-jacket or quadruple-jacket hose over single-jacket hose lies in the ability of such hose to withstand a great amount of chafing and even the total destruction of the outer jacket without going out of service. In the case of single-jacket hose, if the single jacket is worn through, the hose is no longer serviceable. The lining of the hose possesses no appreciable strength and serves only as a watertight passageway for the water. All the strain is taken up by the jacket, and as soon as the jacket is ruptured, the lining instantly follows suit. Where multiple-jacket hose is being used and where the jacket next to the lining is carrying the pressure required in the stream, the outer jacket, or jackets, may be considered as buffing plates, protecting the inner jacket against injury.

Injury by heat

Rubber is not a stable article. The fire hose line, which is made of rubber, will not stay in its original state indefinitely, no matter how much care and attention is given to it. As stated previously, proper care of fire hose merely delays the ultimate "going bad" of the lining.

The higher temperature to which hose is exposed, the more rapidly the lining hardens and loses its life. At very high temperatures, such as are encountered next to steam pipes or radiators, vulcanization takes place so rapidly that the hose is readily put out of commission. Even though it may not actually come in contact with a radiator or steam pipe, it may be near enough to absorb a great deal of heat radiated by the pipe.

As a result, portions of the hose lining become hardened and, on being used, the lining cracks and leaks.

Care must also be used in regulating the temperature of storerooms or drying towers so that the hose will not be subjected to injurious heat.

Damage is occasionally done to hose by dragging it over burning embers and cinders at fires. In this case, the jacket is damaged, but the lining usually remains uninjured.

Fibers lose their strength when scorched, and a scorched piece of hose (particularly where the discoloration has penetrated the jacket to its full depth) is unfit for use. A scorch cannot be removed from a piece of hose, and the only recourse is to cut off the scorched piece and recouple it if there is a portion sufficiently long enough to use.

Hot oils and greases will produce the same effect on the lining of hose as does heat from any other source. These materials, however, have an additional damaging effect which is described below under the heading, "injury by chemicals." If the oils are hot, they will expedite vulcanization.

Hot water acts in the same manner and care should be exercised to see that hose lines are not permitted to pass through vats or other containers filled with hot water. A momentary submersion of a line of hose in a vat of hot water will do no appreciable harm, for it requires some time for vulcanization to progress to a point where it will injure the lining.

Injury by chemicals

Injury by chemicals is hard to guard against. For example, where there is a large amount of water flowing from a burning building, it is impossible to tell whether the water is charged with chemicals. The result is that frequently hose is found to be discolored from exposure to chemicals and the department doesn't know where the exposure occurred.

Chemical injury to hose does not make itself evident until quite a while after the contact, and at that time a department may be at a loss to know where to look for the source of the trouble.

In treating this phase of injury to hose, injuries by chemicals, gases, oils, greases, paints and acid will be considered.

Gasoline: Gasoline, which is a solvent for rubber, has been found responsible for a very large amount of the damage to fire hose. If gasoline gets on the hose jacket, it can work its way through and separate the lining from the jacket. Then, when the hose is used, the lining may tear apart and cause either a partial or a full stoppage. Not only does gasoline dissolve the cement in the hose and permit the separation of jacket and lining, but it also acts on the rubber lining directly and causes its rapid deterioration.

Oils and greases: These substances have varying effects on fire hose, depending upon their composition and fluidity. Thin oils and greases which go readily through the jacket are more serious than the thicker oils and greases which are apt to stay on the outside. Almost any of the oils soaking through and coming in contact with the rubber lining tend to destroy the lining. And once they get through the jacket and reach the lining, they tend to remain there and continue their damaging work.

If there are signs of oil or grease on hose after returning to the station, the hose should be thoroughly scrubbed with a stiff brush and warm (not hot) water. This will remove a portion of the grease on the surface and will prevent its working in.

Paints: These are chiefly troublesome to fire hose because of oils in their composition. The same care should be used in keeping fire hose away from paint as is exercised in keeping it away from grease and oil.

This warning may be added: Never use paint in any form for marking fire hose. The oil is almost certain to soak through and separate the lining from the jacket and also do serious injury to the lining. If it is necessary to mark hose, stencil it with indelible ink and use only enough ink to color the jacket surface.

Where hose lines are used in paint or varnish plant fires, damage from greases and oils may not be entirely avoided, but care should be exercised by not letting the hose rest in paint, grease or similar materials, unless absolutely necessary.

Acids: A very weak solution of sulfuric acid, as well as many other acids, will do irreparable damage to fire hose. Those who have had any experience in working around storage batteries and have found how quickly a drop of the solution from one of the batteries will make a hole through a garment can well appreciate how serious a matter it is to permit acid, even though in very dilute form, to come in contact with hose.

Manufacturers continually complain of the number of lengths of hose sent back for replacement as being defective but which have been damaged in service by contact with acid.

It is difficult to determine damage immediately after exposure to acid. This applies in all cases except where a concentrated acid is encountered. Where there is a damaged spot on the surface of the jacket, it is a very simple matter to determine positively whether or not acid is responsible for it.

Some acids will brown the hose jacket instantly, while others cause the fiber in the jacket to turn to powder. It is sometimes not possible to visually determine which acid has injured the hose, but there should be no question as to whether or not it is acid which has done the damage. The acid itself will destroy the jacket, but not the lining, as in the case of gasoline or oils.

If spots are found on hose which, on being rubbed, turn to powder form and which show actually no strength of fiber, it is safe to assume that acid has been present. A simple test to determine whether acid has done the damage is to taste a bit of the powder rubbed off the hose. If this has a sour or tart taste, it is acid. Of course, no attempt should be made at such a test until after the hose has stood for some time and the acid has used its energy in eating away the jacket.

The hose may be exposed to acids at fires in places like automobile repair shops, battery stations, etc. Then there are a variety of industrial establishments in which acids are used. Where suspicion exists that hose has been subjected to acid, each length under suspicion should be noted, and inspected regularly to check if deterioration is under way. It is very essential that hose be washed off thoroughly after exposure to acid or acid fumes.

Clean and inspect after use

After each fire, every section of hose should be thoroughly inspected for damage. This inspection should cover such items as scorched spots, frozen strands, cuts, chafed or worn spots, or indication of damage done by oil, grease or acid. Any damage should be noted in the hose record.

The washing, draining and drying of fire hose immediately after use, as well as the periodic washing and drying of hose, are essential if maximum service is to be obtained.

Even where drying towers and storage space are lacking or limited, hose can be given proper care. A drying rack is readily made and can give almost as satisfactory service as an expensive tower. Further, electric hose dryers are available that simplify the proper drying of hose. Because of the compactness of these units, they may be installed in even the smallest fire station.

To a fire department, the care of hose when not in use is of greater importance than when the hose is actually in service. Hose stored in the station must have additional care over that which is given to hose on the apparatus and which is used frequently at fires.

Most hose "ages out" rather than wears out in service. This is due to the nature of the materials in it. Cotton-jacket (no longer in general use) hose deteriorates due to mildew. If such hose is stowed away with a wet jacket and permitted to remain in this manner, mildew soon forms unless the hose is well ventilated. Mildew, which is a form of fungus, weakens the strength of the material on which it forms. The only way to prevent mildew is to thoroughly dry the hose and keep it in that condition when stored. A moist atmosphere calls for adequate ventilation of the storage area.

Changing hose

Another condition which arises in the storage of hose around stations or on apparatus is the formation of "sets" at the point where the hose is sharply bent. If hose is folded sharply, the rubber lining is under great stress at the bend. If it remains in this position for a long period on a pumper, the rubber eventually loses its elasticity through fatigue, and on straightening, does not respond and resume its original shape. Instead, it may have lost its resilience and crack on being straightened out under pressure. The only way to avoid these sets is to so arrange the placing of hose so that it will not remain in one position for a long time.

Various methods have been followed, such as periodically changing all hose in storage and on the apparatus. This is particularly necessary for apparatus that have few runs and consequently few working fires. An ideal arrangement is to have the hose changed at least once a month both on the apparatus and in storage in such a manner that bends fall at different points.

Suction hose

A fire department occasionally has the experience of suction hose between the hydrant and engine bursting when a nozzle is suddenly shut off. While this is not a common occurrence, it is, nevertheless, one which should be guarded against in the same manner as guarding against bursting hose between the engine and the nozzle.

Although not generally known, the shock produced by instantly shutting off a nozzle, particularly where the line is short, is transmitted directly to the pumper and, in certain types of pumpers, through the pumping mechanism to the suction hose and even into the main.

Just what the water hammer, or water ram, may amount to in a line of hose depends upon the flexibility of the hose and the rapidity with which the shut-off is closed. The greatest pressure is created if the valve is shut off instantly. However, closing the valve instantly is not possible, for no matter how quickly it is closed, it takes a certain amount of time for the valve to go from full opening to the closed position. In any event, to avoid the water hammer and the shock which it produces on the fire pump and the suction hose, the nozzle should always be shut down slowly.

Hose size increases

While fire hose customarily used was becoming lighter and stronger, some rural fire departments began to seek a way to obtain more water through pumper relays.

At first, 3½-inch hose was tried and its initial success led to the trial of 4-inch and even 5-inch hose. This polymer—man-made rubber—hose is extremely light and has a single jacket of polyester yarn between the waterway and the outer covering. The elastomers used in the waterway and outer covering vary with the different manufacturers, but the final results vary only in competitive quality.

This large diameter hose increased in popularity in the '60s and can now be regarded as standard hose in both rural and large municipal fire departments. Rural departments going to large diameter hose are buying mostly 4-inch hose. With a pumper relay, one demonstration supplied 1000 gpm through a mile of 4-inch hose. A single pumper at the water source can deliver 500 gpm to the fireground through as much as 2600 feet of 4-inch hose and still provide 20 psi intake pressure at the fireground pumper.

One manufacturer reported selling more 5-inch than 4-inch hose to fire departments in large cities. By carrying 200 to 300 feet of 5-inch hose, the first-in pumper can stretch a "water main" from a hydrant on a corner to the middle of the block and then become a pumping manifold for attack lines (see Engine Company Operations).

Another manufacturer introduced double jacket 4-inch hose at the International Association of Fire Chiefs conference in Denver in 1977. A 100-foot length weighs 70 pounds uncoupled, and the two couplings add another 8 pounds. The outer jacket is impregnated with Hypalon and the thin, smooth waterway is applied to become the inside coating of the inner polyester jacket. This new entry in the hose market maintains the American tradition of double jacket hose while competing with single jacket hose, traditional in Europe, on a weight basis.

Use of 1¾-inch hose

The '70s have seen two developments that have resulted in a growing demand for a new size hose—1¾-inch. The introduction of a friction-reducing agent, first in the New York Fire Department, made it possible to deliver 2½-inch attack line volumes of 200 to 250 gpm through smaller hose. New York decided that 1¾-inch was the right size and this size has become increasingly popular.

A 1250-gpm pumper with 6-inch hose was designed at Texas A&M University, Fireman's School, to supply master streams quicker and with less manpower and apparatus.

The other development was the automatic nozzle. More and more fire departments are combining an automatic nozzle with 1¾-inch (in a few cases 2-inch) polyester double-jacket, rubber-lined hose to replace both 1½ and 2½-inch hand lines.

With plain water, friction losses in 1¾-inch hose have been found to be 12 psi for 100 gpm, 26 psi for 150 gpm, 45 psi for 200 gpm and 70 psi for 250 gpm. With a 150-foot preconnected line, an engine pressure of 168 psi will provide 200 gpm to an automatic nozzle working at 100 psi.

For a smaller fire, 1¾-inch hose, 150 feet long, can deliver 100 gpm to the nozzle at 118 psi engine pressure to provide 100 psi nozzle pressure.

A look to the future

Indications in the field are that the trend to 1¾-inch hose will gain speed. Whether 2-inch hose now being tried by a few departments will fall by the wayside or take over from 1¾-inch hose remains to be seen, but all indications are that 1½ and 2½-inch hose will be used less and less.

In the last few years, more and more fire departments have replaced 2½-inch hose with 3, 3½ and 4-inch hose for supply lines, and some of the suburban and rural departments that have adopted 1¾ or 2-inch hose have adopted 4-inch hose as their larger hose for supplying both master stream equipment and pumpers.

These trends in fire hose sizes respond to the problems of reduced manning of paid companies and the daytime lack of manpower in volunteer companies. Fewer men can apply the necessary rate of water application to extinguish most fires.

CHAPTER NINE

Fire service pumps

It is now only of historical interest, but the first piston pump for fire fighting use was invented by Ctesibius of Alexandria sometime around 200 B.C. And this piston pump, with improvements, of course, was still in use up until the present era. Operated manually for centuries, the pump was eventually adapted for the steam fire engine in the 1850s. It went out of use with the introduction in 1906 of the gasoline-powered fire engine equipped with the rotary gear pump. But the rotary gear pump itself became obsolete when the centrifugal pump was adapted for the gasoline-powered fire engine in 1911.

The piston pump is still with us but is now produced only in a small size for high-pressure, low-volume use. The rotary gear pump, so popular in the early 1900s, is now used only as a booster pump, generally with capacities to 200 gpm, and as a priming pump for the major centrifugal pumps.

There are several reasons why the centrifugal pump made the other two obsolete, but the principal one was the ability of the centrifugal pump to fully utilize the positive pressure of water supplied from a hydrant. Secondary factors were freedom from the pulsation found in positive-displacement pumps, lower unit weight and reduced cost.

The fire apparatus centrifugal pump consists basically of one or more impellers mounted on a shaft which is supported in a housing equipped with one or more suction inlets, plus two or more 2½-inch discharge outlets and a pump transmission. This transmission provides the necessary increase in impeller speed above the engine speed (see illustrations).

In the operation of the centrifugal pump the water is directed from the suction or supply hose to the eye of the impeller. The water is picked up by the vanes of the rapidly rotating impeller, which produce an increase in pressure and velocity of the water in an outward radial direction. The water discharging from the impeller produces a partial vacuum at the eye or entrance to the impeller. In this way, water is forced up through the suction hose by atmospheric pressure to replace the water discharged by the impeller. The water leaving the impeller enters a spiral chamber, called a volute, which forms a progressively expanding channel that produces equal velocity flow and gradually converts most of the velocity energy to pressure energy.

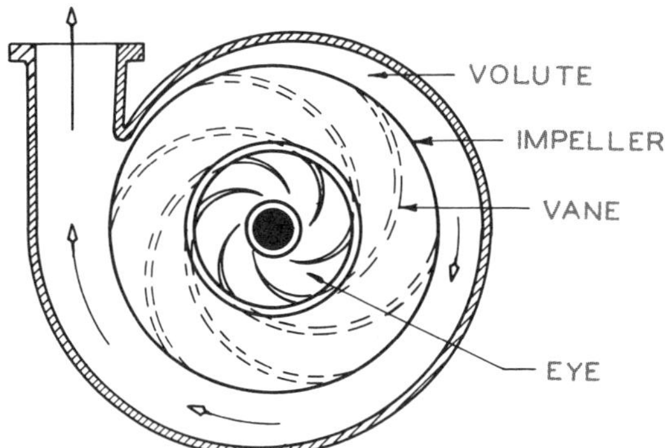

Principal parts of centrifugal pump (single stage) showing direction of water flow.

The centrifugal pump, unlike the piston or rotary pump, is not a positive-displacement pump. It does not discharge a definite quantity of water per revolution or cycle. It is not self-priming. An auxiliary priming device must be used to exhaust the air from the pump and suction lines when the pump is operated at draft. When the pump is used from a source of supply having a positive pressure, as from a hydrant, the priming system is not needed.

Centrifugal pumps for fire service use are built in six major capacities to meet the standard rating requirements for Class A performance: 500, 750, 1000, 1250, 1500, and 2000 gpm, each at 150 psi pressure at draft with not more than a 10-foot vertical lift. The test requirements are given in National Fire Protection Association Standard 1901.

The major centrifugal fire pumps are built today in two designs: single-stage and parallel-series. The single-stage and parallel-series

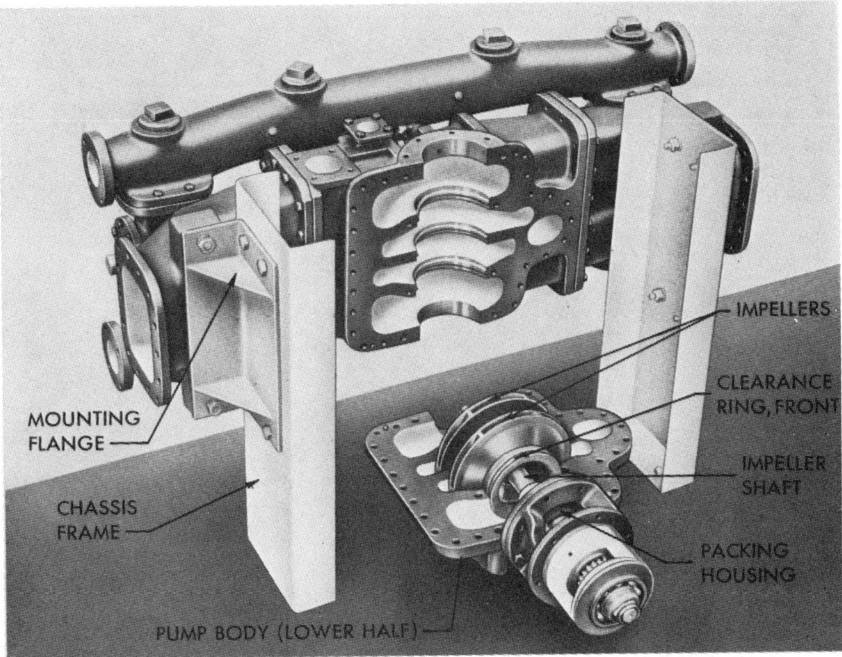

Inside view of two-stage pump from underside shows impellers and waterways.

2-stage designs constitute most of the major fire pumps in fire service use, and have been for some time.

Single-stage centrifugal pump

The single-stage pump has one impeller. For rated capacities through 750 gpm, the impeller is usually the single-suction type. The single-suction impeller is also used almost universally in the parallel-series design of fire pumps.

When capacities greater than 750 gpm are required, the double-suction impeller is used to preserve the high-lift characteristics required for the fire service. The double-suction impeller is sometimes used in the parallel-series centrifugal pump as the first-stage impeller when operating in series to meet the 70 percent capacity requirement at 200 psi with increased reserve.

The output of the single-stage pump, both volume and pressure, is controlled directly by the engine throttle setting, making it the simplest type of centrifugal pump to control.

Each centrifugal pump will have a point of maximum volume which

Parallel-series two-stage centrifugal pump is built in all standard rated capacities—1250 gpm unit is shown.

is determined by the pump design, power available and suction or supply conditions. There is also a "cutoff" or maximum pressure which the pump is capable of producing, which is determined by the pump design. For fire service centrifugal pumps, this pressure is approximately 450 psi, although the maximum service test specifications are 250 psi.

Any centrifugal pump will have some point where a maximum efficiency for water flow will be obtained. This point of maximum efficiency for fire service pumps is usually at a flow rate approximating the capacity rating in gallons per minute.

The single-stage centrifugal pump is used for front mounting on apparatus with capacity ratings of 500 or 750 gpm and for midship mounting in all the standard rated capacities.

Parallel-series 2-stage centrifugal pump

The parallel-series 2-stage centrifugal pump is built with two impellers of the same diameter mounted on a single shaft. Unlike the single-stage pump, the engine throttle for this pump is not the only control for the pump discharge.

A valve, called a transfer valve, controls the direction of water flow through the pump. There are two positions for the valve control setting. One is the capacity setting with each impeller taking suction supply from a common source and each discharging in parallel into a common outlet manifold. In the capacity setting each impeller discharges approximately one-half of the total volume being discharged.

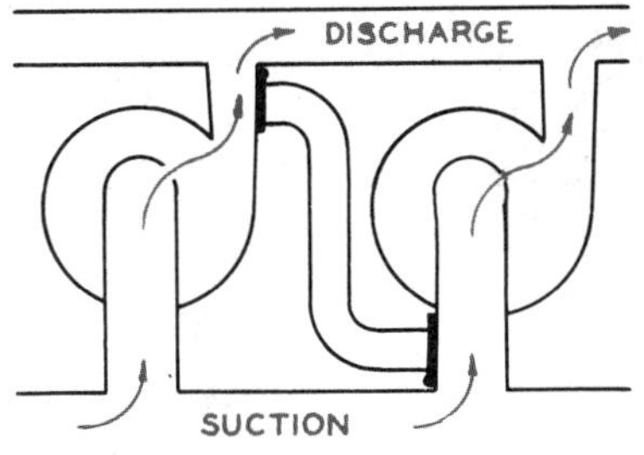

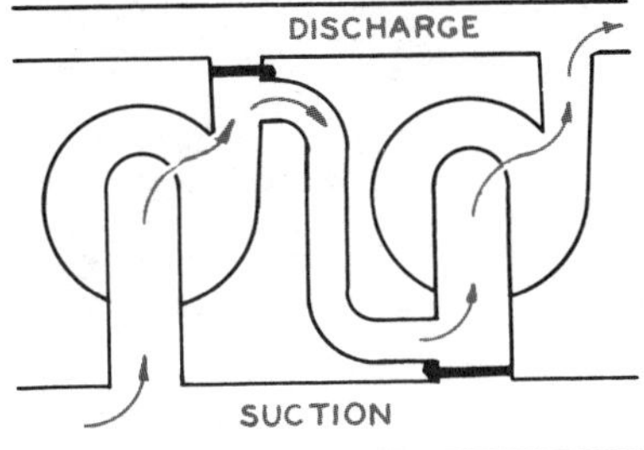

Flow schematic for parallel–series, two-stage centrifugal pump. Position of valves at left is for capacity. Those at right are in pressure or series setting.

The second is the pressure or series setting, which permits water to enter only one impeller from the external supply. This impeller discharges into the suction inlet of the second impeller, which discharges into the outlet manifold.

The advantage of this arrangement for fire service use is that in the series or pressure arrangement, the second impeller adds the same pressure to the water as the first impeller added to the incoming supply. For example, if a discharge pressure of 160 psi is required, each impeller need develop only 80 psi if operated at draft. If working on a hydrant that has a 40-psi residual pressure, then each impeller need develop only 60 psi. This arrangement permits very low engine speeds and is practical since a great percentage of all fires are extinguished with booster or 1½-inch lines.

The transfer valve is operated either manually, electrically or by hydraulic pressure from the pump. The location of the transfer valve in the pump varies with different manufacturers. It may be in a suction inlet passage or in a discharge passage, but the purpose and action are unchanged by location.

The pump design permits use in the pressure or series arrangement for discharge to at least 70 percent of rated capacity. A simplified recommended rule for pumps of 750-gpm capacity, and larger, is to use the pressure setting for all pumping requirements up to and including two 2½-inch lines (250 gpm for each). For larger-capacity pumpers, 1250 and 1500 gpm, it would be entirely safe and practical to operate with three 2½-inch lines. Pumping requirements greater than these limits require the capacity setting to obtain the increased discharge.

The parallel-series 2-stage centrifugal pump is built in all the standard rated capacities and is midship mounted. An important feature is the

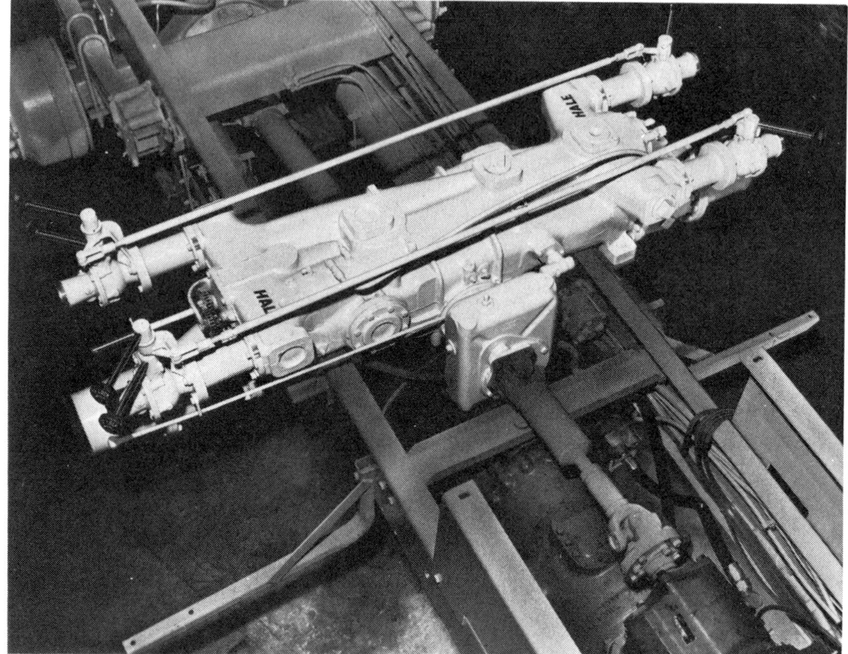

Pump mounted on apparatus frame showing drive shaft connection to pump transmission. Low profile leaves space above pump for equipment.

low profile, only high enough above the chassis frame to accommodate the suction passages, providing a maximum of space above the pump for other required equipment. Most midship-mounted pumps are powered by a gear drive and clutch mounted in the drive line at the rear of the road transmission. Manufacturers can also provide a pump drive at the rear of the flywheel, ahead of the road transmission, permitting operation of the pump while the vehicle is moving.

The reserve, or "runaway" point, above rated capacity is limited by the engine power available and suction conditions. The maximum pressure at the "cutoff" point is usually about 450 psi. However, special impeller and volute designs have permitted pressures of 600 psi. This high-pressure performance does require some sacrifice of the reserve capacity.

The uniformly high efficiency over the entire operating range, coupled with the lower engine speeds at the higher pressures, has made this pump popular with the fire service.

Parallel-series 3-stage centrifugal pump

The parallel-series 3-stage centrifugal pump, built for fire apparatus mounting, is a parallel-series 2-stage pump plus a single stage for use only when high pressures are required.

The parallel-series 2-stage part of the pump assembly has all the performance characteristics and features previously described for this type of pump.

When high pressure is required, the main pump is operated in the pressure setting for series 2-stage discharge to the third stage. In this arrangement each impeller develops approximately one-third of the final outlet pressure, and permits a range to 800 psi.

Parallel-series 4-stage centrifugal pump

The parallel-series 4-stage centrifugal pump is another pump not commonly used in the fire service. It is a special-service pump designed for volume flow at high pressures to protect very high buildings through standpipe connections, and not too many have been built.

The pump is built with four impellers mounted on a single shaft. Three transfer valves permit operation with the impellers discharging in parallel to provide the capacity rating; two sets of impellers, each set operating as a 2-stage unit, and discharging in parallel; all impellers discharging in series for the high-pressure requirements.

In operation, this pump with a capacity rating for 1000 gpm at 160 psi, in parallel setting, would produce 250 gpm at 160 psi from each impeller for a total discharge of 1000 gpm at 160 psi. In the series-parallel arrangement, the first impeller in each pair discharges 250 gpm at 150 psi into the second impeller in each pair. The second impeller adds 150 psi to discharge 250 gpm at 300 psi into the manifold for a total discharge of both pairs of 500 gpm at 300 psi. With the 4-stage series setting, each impeller discharges 250 gpm, adding 150 psi pressure to provide 250 gpm at 600 psi at the outlet manifold.

2-Stage centrifugal, front-mount pump

The 2-stage centrifugal, front-mount pump with a major capacity rating, 500 gpm, is a special-purpose pump used by the fire service in a region where a relatively large volume discharge at medium high pressures is required while the vehicle is in motion.

The pump is mounted at the front of the apparatus and is driven from the front end of the engine crankshaft. The pump is built with two impellers mounted on a single shaft. Water flow is in series at all times.

As the vehicle operates at low speeds off the highway, the engine speeds are controlled for vehicle movement rather than pump requirements. Under these conditions the series pump meets the needs with a minimum variation in volume and pressure.

Auxiliary pumps

Pumps used on fire apparatus having a capacity rating less than the minimum standard rated capacity of 500 gpm at 150 psi are classed as auxiliary pumps. Such pumps may be used in combination with major fire pumps, mounted with a major fire pump but separate from and operated independently of the major fire pump, or mounted on a fire truck as the only pump. The latter mounting is usually on a light, all-wheel-drive truck for brush, grass and forest fire fighting.

In the auxiliary classification there are two subclasses—booster pumps with discharge capacities to 250 gpm at 120 psi and high-pressure pumps developing 600 to 850 psi or more with a maximum volume of about 100 gpm.

Most of the auxiliary pumps are driven by a power takeoff mounted on the side of the road transmission. This drive is usually limited to 40 hp. Therefore, pumps requiring more power or having certain characteristics may use a different type of drive. The power takeoff drive does permit pumping simultaneously with vehicle movement, which is advantageous when fighting certain types of fires.

Booster pumps

The booster pump with the longest record of service to fire departments is the rotary. The rotors are gear type for positive displacement and the pump is self-priming. The pump is available in two capacities, 100 and 200 gpm, each rated at 120 psi. A relief valve is provided to protect against excessive pressure rise in the hose line or damage to the pump.

The pump suction supply and discharge piping are usually provided in one of two arrangements: In the first, the suction supply piping runs from the water tank on the apparatus, and discharge piping runs only to the booster line reel or reels. In the second arrangement, the pump has two suction inlets (one 2½-inch each side of the body) in addition to the suction piping to the apparatus water tank. The discharge piping includes one 1½ or one 2½-inch gated outlet on each side of the apparatus in addition to discharge piping to booster line reel or reels or to preconnected 1½-inch lines.

The single-stage centrifugal booster pump is available with higher capacity ratings than are produced by the rotary booster pumps. These

High-pressure, four-stage centrifugal pump can deliver 60 gpm at 1000 psi.

pumps have ratings up to 450 gpm at 150 psi, with the rating dependent on several factors: pump design, type of drive (front-mount, crankshaft or power takeoff) and suction conditions. One of these pumps is power takeoff driven and rated 250 gpm at 150 psi when operating at a 10-foot lift with 20 feet of 3-inch suction hose. It is also rated for 450 gpm at 150 psi, with supply through 3-inch piping from the water tank on the apparatus.

With such capacities available, the pump can easily supply two 1½-inch hose lines or one 2½-inch line. The maximum pressure is 350 psi, with discharge at this pressure from 50 to 150 gpm, depending on the torque capacity of the drive being used.

The pump is not self-priming. A priming system should be provided even if the pump is not to be operated at draft from an outside source. To depend on the water tank head for priming is not recommended. It is not a reliable means of exhausting air from the pump.

The pump is usually equipped with one 3-inch suction inlet on each side of the apparatus, in addition to the 3-inch suction piping to the water tank. Two 1½ or 2½-inch gated discharge outlets are provided, one of the preferred size on each side of the apparatus.

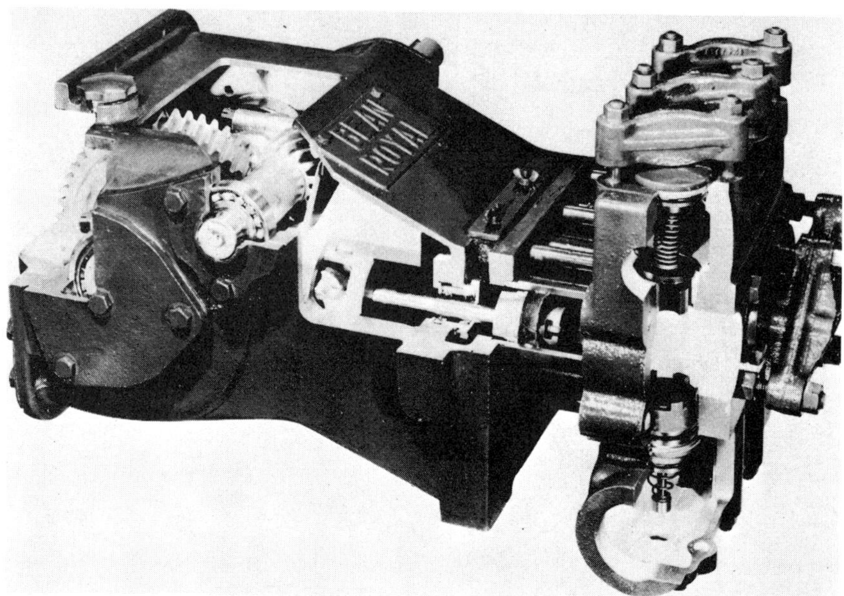

Positive displacement high-pressure piston pump is self-priming and single-acting. With three cylinders, it is rated at 75 gpm at 850 psi.

A set-pressure type of relief valve is provided for discharge pressure control.

High-pressure pumps

High-pressure pumps for fire service use are designed for working pressures up to 850 psi. The pumps are of two types—centrifugal and piston.

The centrifugal pumps are built in 2-stage and 4-stage designs. The 2-stage pump will deliver with standard power takeoff drive 60 gpm at 600 psi and 30 gpm at 800 psi. The pump is capable of greater volume at higher pressures when increased torque is available.

The 4-stage centrifugal pump will deliver 60 gpm at 800 psi and 40 gpm at 1000 psi. The high-pressure centrifugal pumps are not self-priming and require a priming device.

The piston-type high-pressure pump is a three-cylinder, single-acting pump. It is a positive-displacement type and is self-priming. The pump is driven by a power takeoff mounted on the side of the road transmission, with V belts providing final drive to the pump.

The pump has a rated capacity of 70 gpm at 850 psi. It can be operated at draft as well as from a water tank on the apparatus. It is equipped with a preset relief valve to protect against excessive pressure.

Priming systems

Centrifugal pumps on fire apparatus require a priming system to exhaust the air from the pump and suction line. NFPA Standard 1901 requires the priming system to be capable of developing not less than 22 inches (mercury) of vacuum at altitudes up to 1000 feet above sea level. For each additional 1000 feet of altitude, the vacuum requirement is reduced 1 inch (mercury). The priming systems are required to have a capacity to prime all major centrifugal fire pumps, except those of 1500-gpm capacity, in 30 seconds when taking draft at a lift of 10 feet with two lengths (20 feet) of suction hose. The priming time limit for a 1500-gpm rated capacity pump is 45 seconds. Actually, most priming systems will prime a major fire pump in 15 seconds.

There are four priming systems in use for priming fire apparatus

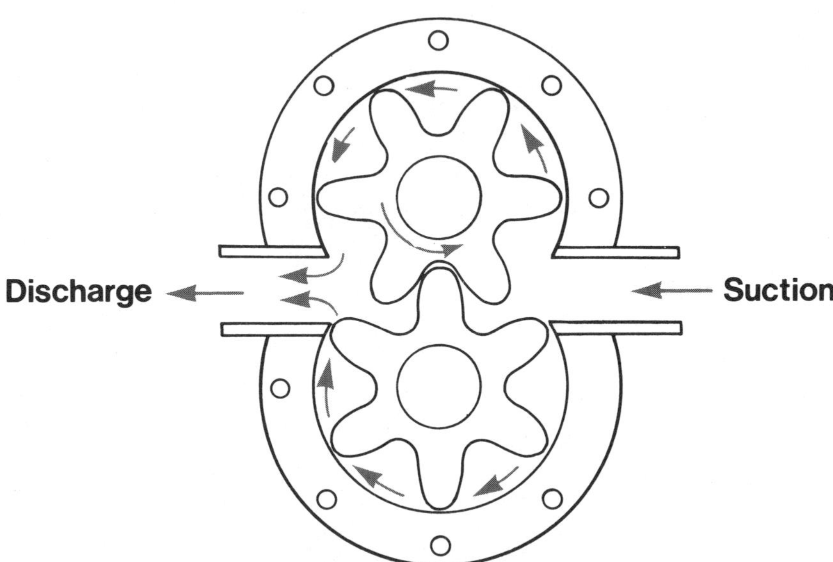

Rotary gear priming pump may be gear-driven at the pump transmission, or coupled to an electric drive motor. It varies in size and displacement according to the type of drive which governs the speed of rotation.

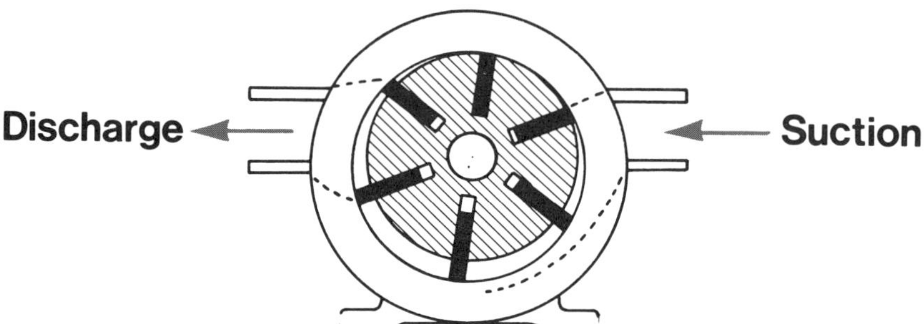

Rotary vane priming pump is an eccentric vane positive displacement pump. Rotor is mounted on a shaft which is off center, or eccentric within the housing.

centrifugal pumps. These are: (1) rotary gear; (2) rotary vane; (3) exhaust ejector; and (4) engine intake manifold.

Rotary gear primer

The rotary gear priming pump is a positive-displacement pump and is driven by one of two methods. With one method, the priming pump is driven by gearing in the pump transmission, with the drive controlled by a vacuum-operated clutch. The second method uses an electric motor connected directly to the priming pump.

The pump operates by picking up air in the spaces between the teeth from the inlet or suction side of the pump. As the rotors move, the air is carried to the discharge side of the pump where the meshing action of the teeth, as they roll to engagement in the center, forces or displaces the air to the outlet. The same action continues when water enters the pump after the major pump is fully primed.

Rotary vane primer

The rotary vane priming pump is an eccentric vane, positive-displacement pump. The rotor is mounted on a shaft which is off-center, or eccentric, within the housing. The rotor is driven either by gearing or an electric motor, the same as the drive described for the rotary gear priming pump.

The rotor has four slots in which vanes are inserted. As the rotor turns, the vanes move in and out, keeping contact with the housing due to centrifugal force. Automatic lubrication is provided to seal and lubricate the vanes and housing.

The rotor, which is eccentric in the housing, has a close clearance with the housing at one point with a wide space on the opposite side. As the rotor turns, the space between the vanes increases to draw air from the fire pump and suction line. As the rotation continues, the space between the rotor and housing decreases, and as the outlet opening is cleared by the vane ahead, the air is forced out of the space between the two rotor vanes. This displacement of air occurs four times during each revolution of the rotor.

Exhaust ejector priming system

The exhaust ejector priming system uses the vacuum created by a high-velocity gas flow through a venturi to prime the fire pump. The system requires a butterfly valve in the exhaust line to divert the flow of exhaust gas through the venturi outlet. The venturi is in a housing to which is connected the piping to the pump.

In operation, the butterfly valve is closed, diverting exhaust gas from the engine through the venturi outlet. The whistle-type valve in the priming line between the fire pump and venturi housing is opened to permit air flow from the fire pump and suction line. The engine throttle is then opened to obtain an engine speed of approximately 2000 rpm. At this speed, due to the relatively small orifice in the venturi, the exhaust gas pressure increases to 15 to 18 psi, which produces a high-velocity flow through the venturi. This creates a vacuum at the venturi outlet which is used to prime the fire pump.

Engine intake manifold priming system

The engine intake manifold primer utilizes the vacuum in the engine intake manifold, when the engine is running, to prime the fire pump. To use this vacuum, it is necessary to use a valve or trap to prevent the entrance of water into the engine during the priming operation. This valve or trap is installed in the priming line between the fire pump and the engine intake manifold.

To operate this priming system, the engine speed should not exceed 1000 rpm, as the highest vacuum—and this means, too, the fastest rate of prime—is with the engine operating at a medium speed when the throttle is nearly closed.

Pulling out a handle marked prime opens simultaneously two valves, one in the line from the trap to the engine intake manifold, and one in the line from the trap to the fire pump. As priming continues, water enters the wet chamber, causing the main float to rise and close the lower valve (ball) and open the upper valve (ball), venting the trap to atmospheric pressure and stopping the priming action.

An added safety valve is provided in the upper or dry chamber. If the

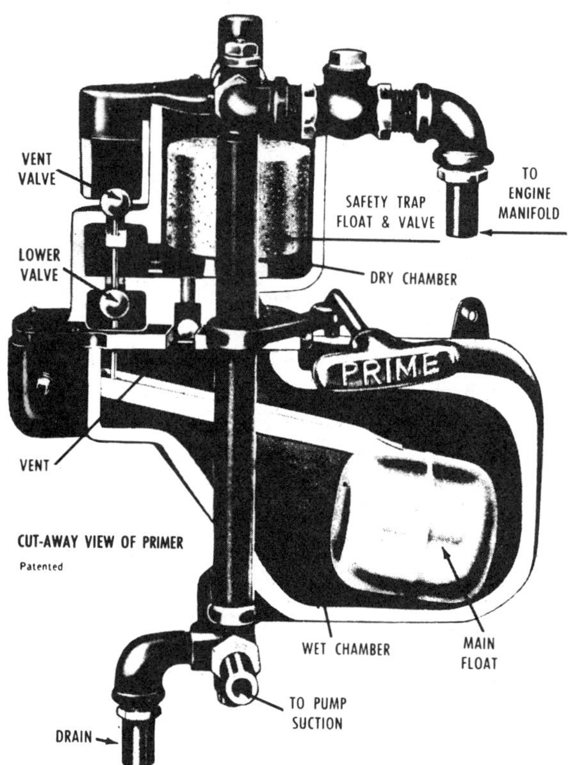

Engine intake manifold primer uses the vacuum in the engine intake manifold to prime the fire pump while engine is running.

water does get by the other valves, the upper float rises to close off the priming outlet and protect the engine.

Relief valves and pressure governors

A pressure control device is required for all major fire pumps to protect against an undue pressure rise in the other lines when one or more lines are shut down. The pressure control devices for pumps mounted on fire apparatus are one of two types: relief valve or pressure governor.

NFPA Standard 1901 requires that the relief valve or pressure governor limit the net pressure rise to 20 psi and provide pressure control over an operating range of 90 to 300 psi net pump pressure.

The two devices operate with a basic difference. The relief valve bypasses water from discharge to suction to maintain a preset pressure without a change in the engine throttle setting. The pressure governor acts automatically to close the engine throttle, reducing the engine power output to maintain the preset pressure for the hose lines still open.

Relief valves: The relief valve assembly is actually two valves which are separate, the pilot valve and the relief, or bypass, valve. There are many other possible arrangements, but this one has worked out well in fire service use.

With these valves it will be noted that water at discharge pressure is acting against the relief valve to open it and, at the same time, the same water pressure is acting against the top of the piston. The piston being larger, the greater area provides a greater total force against the top of the piston to keep the valve closed. If the discharge pressure exceeds the pressure of the setting of the spring on the pilot valve, the pilot valve will open and water will flow back to suction. The important factor that makes this a successful design is the restriction in the passage from the discharge to the chamber above the piston. This restricted flow is essential. Otherwise the pressure above the piston could not be relieved when the pilot valve opens, permitting water to flow back to suction.

Pressure governors: The pump pressure governor, like the relief valve, has one basic purpose: to automatically protect men handling the remaining open lines from an excessive pressure rise if one or more lines are shut down. The governor controls the pressure rise by acting on the engine throttle.

The governors designed to provide this control vary considerably with the different manufacturers. One design is a spring-loaded diaphragm type with a hydraulic fluid remote control.

To place the governor in operation, the pump pressure is increased about 10 psi above the desired operating pressure. The handle on the control panel is turned until the dial reads well above the desired pump operating pressure. Then open the governor valve that admits discharge water to the governor. Now turn the governor control handle until the governor reduces the pressure to the desired figure. This action causes the throttle to reduce the engine speed—and therefore the pump pressure.

The hydraulic master cylinder mounted behind the pump control panel has a reservoir for hydraulic oil with a small passage to keep the slave cylinder on the engine and the line full of oil at all times. As the handle on the panel is turned clockwise, the dial rotates to indicate the approximate pressure being transmitted to the spring in the governor housing. As the handle is turned, moving the piston to the right, it closes the oil passage from the master cylinder reservoir and transmits the pressure to the slave cylinder spring. This pressure is then applied by the spring to the diaphragm. When water under pressure enters the water chamber in the slave cylinder, no movement occurs unless the water pressure exceeds the spring pressure. The diaphragm end of the spring is carried in a special cup which moves in the cylinder as the diaphragm moves from water pressure. The cup is connected to the throttle by gears which act to close or open the throttle as the cup moves.

In another governor control system, when the governor is to be placed in operation, the control handle on the pump control panel is pulled out, which makes the governor inoperative. The water supply valve is opened to admit water under pressure to the governor. The throttle is advanced to increase the pump pressure about 5 psi above the desired operating pressure. The handle is pushed in. This sets the governor. The throttle is now moved to return to the desired operating pressures.

Pump pressure gages

Two gages to indicate pressure are provided for all major capacity fire pumps and many of the smaller ones. One or both gages may be of the compound type designed to register both positive pressure and vacuum. A compound gage is connected to the pump suction inlet to indicate positive flow pressure from a hydrant or vacuum when operating at draft. The second gage is connected to the pump discharge manifold to indicate the discharge pressure.

The compound pressure gage is calibrated to indicate positive pressure ranging from 0 to 400 or 600 psi, and the vacuum from 0 to 30 inches of mercury (hg).

An atmospheric pressure of 14.7 psi at sea level is the accepted standard; so is the corresponding value of 29.92 inches of mercury (hg). The common instrument to measure the atmospheric pressure is the barometer. A perfect vacuum permits the atmospheric pressure to raise a column of water 33.9 feet, which is the equivalent of 29.92 inches of mercury. Thus each foot of lift when operating at draft requires .88 inches of mercury vacuum. In the fire service, a sufficiently accurate figure would be .9 inch per foot of lift. On a 10-foot lift, the primer would need to produce 9 inches of mercury vacuum to prime the pump.

The priming requirement of 22 inches of mercury, as given in NFPA 1901, will actually provide the ability to prime on a lift of 24.9 feet.

Vapor pressure

Evaporation of water from an open surface is a continuing process, the rate depending on the temperature above 32°F. When water is confined, as in a pump, the vapor builds up a pressure which may reduce the capacity of the pump. When the water temperature exceeds 95°F, the pump will no longer deliver its rated capacity on a 10-foot lift. As the water temperature increases, the ability of the pump to operate at draft decreases rapidly. At 212°F, the vapor pressure equals atmospheric pressure, so it is impossible, theoretically, to even prime at draft. Actually, the pump cannot be primed at a temperature considerably below 212°F.

In the temperate zone a water temperature of 95°F is seldom reached except in ponds, creeks and small pools during midsummer in some of the southwestern states.

The water temperature, with the corresponding vapor pressure, is a factor in producing pump cavitation and should be considered when choosing a source of water supply during high-temperature periods.

Cavitation

Cavitation is a condition occurring within any pump; the type is not a factor. The condition producing cavitation may be caused by one or more of the following: restriction in the suction (plugged strainer), lift too high for the volume of water being pumped, suction hose too small, or pulling a high vacuum reading on a small water main.

Cavitation makes the pump sound like there are many small rocks inside and causes vibration and a high vacuum reading on the suction gage. Cavitation occurs at the eye of the impeller, where the pressure is lowest. As the pressure decreases to the vapor pressure, the water liberates many vapor bubbles and some air bubbles which move with the water into the impeller. As these bubbles move outward in the impeller into the high-pressure zone, the bubbles collapse, producing noise and vibration. The larger the pump, the greater will be the sound and vibration. This action causes pitting and erosion of the impeller and if continued, the impeller will fail.

When cavitation is observed, the pump discharge volume should be reduced as a practical measure. The height or lift or suction size cannot usually be changed during the urgency of a fire.

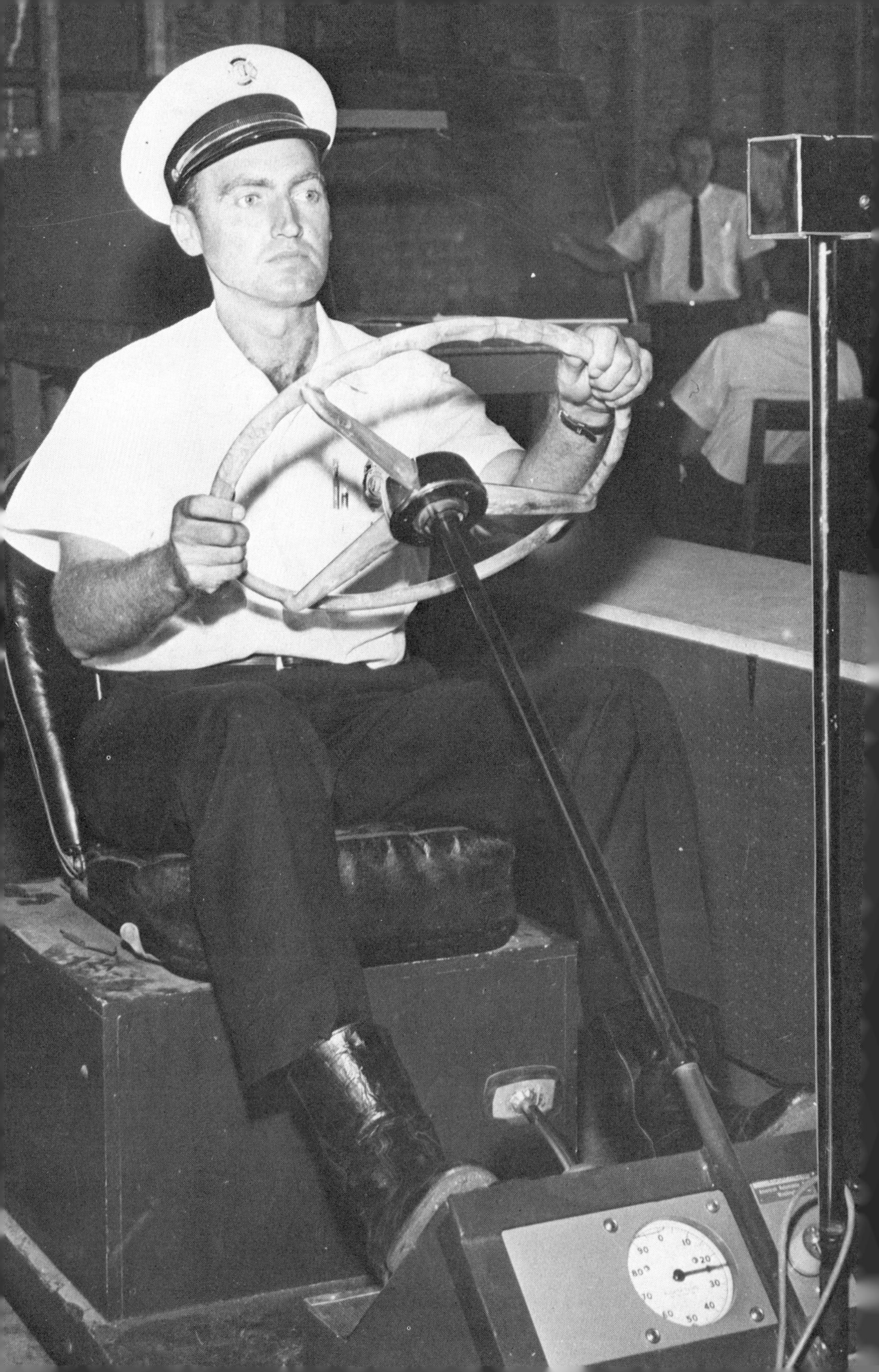

CHAPTER TEN

Driver training

A driver of an emergency fire vehicle carries heavy responsibilities for the safety of his vehicle, his comrades and other vehicles and pedestrians along his route. He must be constantly aware of these responsibilities and have his vehicle under control at all times. He must be familiar with traffic laws, particularly those which apply to him in his specialized driving capacity.

He must recognize his limitations and those of other drivers on the road and realize that, while he may know what he is doing, the other driver or pedestrian may not. Therefore, he must always be prepared for the unexpected to happen.

The emergency driver must possess fine coordination in controlling his vehicle and reacting to traffic problems. He cannot drive faster than traffic permits, nor should he drive faster than he can stop in an emergency.

The right of way given to an emergency driver does not relieve him of his responsibility for the safety of all other users of the streets. The law allows certain exemptions to emergency drivers when responding with flashing lights and sirens, whistles, air horns or similar devices. But it does not overlook any arbitrary use of these rights when such use endangers life or property.

Excessive speed, reckless driving, failing to slow down or obey traffic signals, disregarding traffic rules and regulations, and failing to heed warning signals are often prime factors in fire apparatus accidents.

Psychophysical tests measure field of vision, glare acuity and night vision, reaction time and depth perception (shown above), all on compact portable unit.

Surveys show that in accidents caused by excessive speed of the fire vehicle, the apparatus was very often on the straightaway, entering through streets or other intersections, or rounding corners on curves.

Selecting drivers

A responsibility that is just as heavy as the driver's rests on the shoulders of the man who selects the driver. This selection generally falls on the commander of a fire fighting unit, but the ultimate responsibility rests on the chief of department, who should set up a program for this purpose. Before a man is selected to drive he should be closely screened as to his habits, aptitudes, limitations, and what is most important, his attitudes.

Only then should he be permitted to enter a candidate's course in driving. And only then should he be tested and trained for the job.

Psychophysical tests

A variety of testing devices are used for the selection and training of drivers. They are widely used by driver training specialists in the armed forces as well as in the commercial field, and many fire departments have adopted them for training courses as well as in accident investigations.

If these tests are properly administered, they serve several important uses:

1. They vividly impress upon the driving candidate the many personal characteristics involved in driving so that he will appreciate the importance of the job.

2. The candidate is made to realize that other drivers are likely to have deficiencies for which allowance must be made; he is encouraged to drive (defensively) in a manner that will compensate for the faults of others.

3. Many deficiencies unearthed by the tests are unknown to the candidate, but pointing them out to him permits him either to correct them or make allowances for them. In addition, certain tests indicate where additional training is needed. It must be remembered, however, that even though a man has a good or perfect score on these tests, he is not to assume expertness as a driver. Proper driver training and experience, plus correct driving habits and attitudes, are also essential.

The psychophysical tests measure:

1. Field of vision (peripheral): This is an important consideration in approaching or driving through intersections as well as passing other vehicles or being passed. People who have only a narrow visual field are said to be afflicted with tunnel vision. By forming a habit of turning his head from side to side while approaching intersections and slowing down, a driver may compensate for this shortcoming.

2. Depth perception: This device measures in a limited way a man's ability to judge space, distance and relative positions of objects. This judgment is important in making turns in traffic, parking in small spaces, following another vehicle closely or cutting in sharply when passing. Below-average ability in this area indicates the driver should not follow other cars too closely and, before attempting to pass, he should wait until there is more clear space than appears to be ample.

3. Glare acuity and night vision: These measure how well a driver can see with limited illumination at night and how he is affected by glaring headlights of approaching vehicles. These factors are of particular importance since the fatal accident rate is three times as high at night as during the day.

4. Reaction time: This measures the interval which elapses between a driver's sight of the need for stopping and the movement of his foot from the gas to the brake pedal. This figure can be correlated with various vehicle speeds to show the distance traveled.

5. Other psychophysical devices measure eye dominance, as well as strength and steadiness. Audiometers and jerk recorders are also widely used. Portable units are available containing all these devices.

Driver-instructor team in San Jose completes a controlled-stop test at designated traffic stanchion during field portion of training.

Men who are candidates for assignments as drivers should have the benefits of classroom instruction and a chance to break in in an area of perfect safety. Later, they should drive back from alarms, in addition to gaining experience at company drills. Until qualified, they should not drive at night or while responding.

There are two phases of driver training: One for candidates in a formal program that includes class work and driving and another that constitutes a refresher course to check or retrain those men already assigned to drive. In smaller departments, it may be advisable to combine the two phases at company level due to limited facilities.

Apparatus road-e-o

Based on and patterned after the National Truck Road-e-o of the American Trucking Association, fire apparatus road-e-os have come to play an important part in adding interest and making definite contributions to courses of instruction for those who are beginners and for those regularly assigned to drive. The trucking industry has recognized the event itself as a significant morale builder and road-e-o drivers as true champions. Complete details of layouts for each event of the road-e-o are available from Director of Safety, American Trucking Association, Inc., Washington, D.C.

As a teaching aid, the road-e-o is invaluable in developing skills under conditions which simulate those likely to be encountered on the road. Several of the larger American cities have made extensive use of apparatus road-e-os in training drivers. Admittedly, it is not always physically possible nor practical to establish a setup as extensive or detailed as might be desired. Departments must lay out and pattern their courses in accordance with physical facilities at their disposal.

Make scale drawing

In addition to the skill tests in driving, the following are also used: Smooth stopping, space gaging, spotting front and rear limits of wheels and bumpers, judging position of vehicle in depth and to left or right, gaging limited space backward and forward, angle parking, stall parking, and figure eight driving (forward and backward).

Other tests may be included which take advantage of facilities near, or on, the course. In training chauffeurs of aerial trucks, for example, the problems might well include spotting the truck and raising the ladder against a nearby building. This maneuver should be on a proficiency and time basis. Furthermore, drivers of ladder trucks with tiller wheels should be given ample opportunity to become familiar with the tiller to properly understand its specialized problems.

It is suggested that after selecting the tests to be used, a scaled diagram of the course be made prior to attempting to lay it out. Extra allowances must be made on the tests for parallel parking, offset alley, serpentine course and alley dock parking for vehicles with a limited turning radius or vehicles of unusual length.

Since it is the aim of the road-e-o to instruct as well as to test, candidates are first given a considerable warm-up period under the guidance of an instructor. Each skill test should be gone over repeatedly, and all instruction should be on an individual basis. During this period the instructor explains and demonstrates desirable practices for each problem, pointing out what will be looked for on the official score sheet. When he has practiced sufficiently (and such time varies considerably with individuals), the candidate is given an official run over the course with one examiner at his side and another on the ground to mark his faults. A trial run over the course, with demerits to be given in accordance with items listed on the score sheet, would be as follows:

Starting and shifting: Starting the motor in approved fashion, the candidate circles the field, shifting gears through the entire range, up and down, as he traverses each half. If the field is not long enough, he may be required to drive around twice to complete this operation. Perfection in shifting means perfect coordination between handling the gear shift lever, the clutch and the accelerator incidental to setting the vehicle in motion and passing from one gear to another smoothly and at the proper time. The net result of such perfection from a maintenance standpoint is less wear on the clutch and prevention of undue strain and shock transmission from the engine back throughout the entire power train.

Practice in shifting may sound somewhat anachronistic in an era when most new apparatus is delivered with automatic transmissions. But there are thousands of apparatus in service that still have the conventional clutch (some are still ordered) and this must not be ignored in any driver-training program.

Offset alley: This problem is designed to develop and test a candidate's ability to gage space in maneuvering a vehicle within a limited area. He is required to halt the vehicle in front of a narrow alley and back through it safely. Then, from a limited depth, he must cross over into another alley and drive through it without knocking down or touching any of the markers (stanchions or traffic cones) for a perfect score.

Serpentine test: Vehicle is driven forward, weaving between stanchions placed on a straight line. The truck is then backed through the course, passing on opposite sides of the stanchions to those of the forward movement. Such a test simulates weaving in and out of traffic and develops judgment and accuracy for tight squeezes. Operation should be smooth, without stops and without slipping the clutch or excessive use of brakes.

Parallel parking: Driver is required to pull up and stop beside another parked vehicle. Then he must back into a parking area between two parked vehicles on the blind side. Among other benefits, such skill would be invaluable in getting unused fire apparatus out of the roadway to permit access for other apparatus (ladder companies or units with deck pipes) to the front of a fire building. A perfect score means parking within 12 inches of the curb without unnecessary maneuvering and without striking any of the markers.

Alley dock parking: The problem simulates that of entering and leaving quarters and familiarizes drivers with the proper turning radii for such maneuvers. Movement forward or backward must be continuous, with necessary stops and realignment costing a driver points. Widths of the doorway and street approximate those of average quarters and areas in front of them.

Whenever possible, the course should include grade parking and driving practice.

 Grade parking: Grade parking constitutes a valuable training aid in developing proper habits for hill parking. The driver must stop the vehicle smoothly, cut the wheels to the curb and start without stalling the motor or rolling backward

Driving practices: Drivers must properly approach and safely negotiate three intersections, the most common location of serious smashups. As he nears each intersection he must drop gears and slow down to a controlled speed, awaiting the command of the examiner to stop or go ahead. Throughout this problem, shifting must be smooth and with proper timing. Coming back over a crest, he must drop to low gear to show the braking effects of the gears in assisting a vehicle to slow down or stop on a downgrade.

Hydrant hookup: Driver must bring pumper to a stop with suction opening in alignment with hydrant for hookup with hard suction. The clear space in front of hydrant and between parked vehicles is in conformity with that legal requirement. The test is eliminated when using apparatus other than pumpers.

Straight line driving: The left front wheel (driver's side) must be kept on a 4-inch-wide line, while traveling a total distance of 100 feet, with each 25-foot section marked. The apparatus is then realigned with the opposite front wheel on the painted line and backed the full distance. The line is straight, but at an angle to any fence or roadway, so that these may not be used as a guide. Points are added or subtracted for each 25-foot section completed without leaving the line, racing or stalling the motor or sinuous motion of vehicle.

On-the-nose finish: This problem is designed to develop and test a candidate's ability to judge the position of the vehicle in depth and to the right or left. He approaches the problem at a speed of about 15 mph, in high gear, and is not permitted to ease apparatus into position. He gradually reduces speed and stops on the nose, i.e., with front wheels on painted lines or between stanchions and with front bumper 12 inches or less from front line or stanchions. He then blows the horn to signify he is satisfied with his position and the official run is over.

As an example of what can be done to teach fire apparatus driver training, let us look at the program initiated at the Texas Firemen's Training School in its eight-week recruit course. The program is set up to improve the driving habits of the trainee and to teach him what his vehicle is capable of doing and not doing.

The program starts out with an eight-hour classroom defensive driving course that was developed by the National Safety Council. It is taught by Texas Department of Safety officers. Included in the course are discussions of state laws applying to the driving of emergency vehicles and case histories of accidents involving fire apparatus.

From the classroom the students move to the performance testing area where each student gets an opportunity to test his capability to drive a fire apparatus. To add realism, most of the maneuvers are performed with sirens and warning lights operating. Each student has an opportunity to operate a variety of apparatus each day for one hour under the supervision of an instructor. And each time the student drives, the instructor fills out a check list on those areas in which the student needs improvement.

The areas covered by this check list of driver performance are graded, excellent, fair, poor or not applicable, and are as follows:

I. Outside check
  A. Tires
  B. Secure apparatus
  C. Personnel clearance
  D. Apparatus lighting
II. Personal adjustments
  A. Seat (driver's)
  B. Seat belts
  C. Mirrors
III. Knowledge of controls
  A. Emergency light switches
  B. Starting procedure (transmission in neutral, warm engine)
  C. Parking brakes
  D. Check all gages—temperature, oil pressure, etc.
  E. Signal lights
  F. Shift pattern
IV. Backing safety
  A. Sound warning (horn)
  B. Use mirrors
  C. Alertness
V. Vehicle control
  A. Smooth starts
  B. Smooth clutching
  C. Safe speeds
  D. Lane safety
  E. Cornering ability
  F. Intersection safety
  G. Braking smoothness
  H. Following other vehicles at safe distances
  I. Parking ability
  J. Avoid "tights" or "blind spots"

In conducting the five skill tests, each of the operations checked in a test is judged either satisfactory of unsatisfactory. The skill tests are as follows:

A. Test 1—straight line

1. Objective: To determine a driver's ability to drive both forward and backward 200 feet in a straight line.

2. Markings necessary: Painted line 200 feet long and 4 feet wide.

3. Procedure
   a. Have driver place vehicle with the front left wheel just touching the painted line. Then drive forward, keeping the left wheels on the line, stopping when the left rear wheel reaches the end of the line.
   b. Have the driver keep the left wheel on the line for 200 feet while driving the vehicle backward.
   c. Repeat both operations but keep the right wheel on the line each time.

4. Check list and score sheet
   a. Forward—left wheel
      1. operates apparatus smoothly
      2. Keeps wheel touching line
      3. Even speed
      4. No stops
      5. Stops smoothly at end
      6. Shifts gears smoothly
      7. Does not race engine
      8. Does not lug engine
   b. Backward—left wheel
      1. Operates apparatus smoothly
      2. Keeps wheel touching line
      3. Even speed
      4. No stops
      5. Stops smoothly at end
      6. Shifts gears smoothly
      7. Does not race engine
      8. Does not lug engine
   c. Forward—right wheel
      1. Operates apparatus smoothly
      2. Keeps wheel touching line
      3. Even speed
      4. No stops
      5. Stops smoothly at end
      6. Shifts gears smoothly

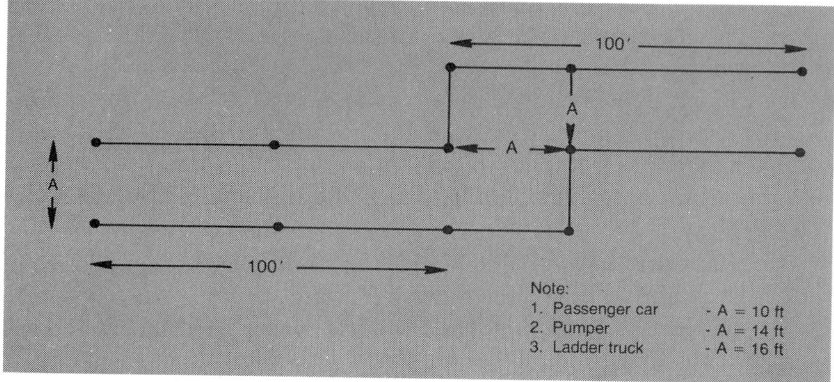

Test 2: Steering in close quarters

7. Does not race engine
8. Does not lug engine

d. Backward—right wheel
1. Operates apparatus smoothly
2. Keeps wheel touching line
3. Even speed
4. No stops
5. Stops smoothly at end
6. Shifts gears smoothly
7. Does not race engine
8. Does not lug engine

B. Test 2—Steering in closing quarters
1. Objective: To test the ability of a driver to steer and maneuver an apparatus quickly and accurately in a limited area.
2. Materials and markings necessary: Painted lines as indicated and traffic cones.
3. Procedures
a. Have driver line up the apparatus with the front bumper at the left limit line; he is to drive in the right lane and turn into the left lane through the spaced marked out by the painted lines and traffic cones. He is not to touch any of the cones or lines.
b. After going through forward, have the driver back through the same path, shifting from the left to the right lane.
4. Check list and score sheet
a. Forward
1. Operates vehicle smoothly

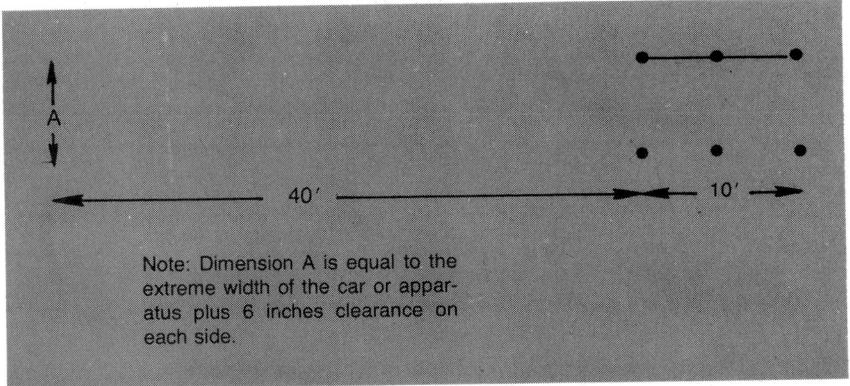

Test 3: Smooth stopping

2. Does not touch lines
3. Even speed
4. No stops
5. No cones touched

b. Backward
1. Operates vehicle smoothly
2. Does not touch lines
3. Even speed
4. No stops
5. No cones touched

C. Test 3—smooth stopping
1. Objective: To determine the ability of a driver to make a smooth stop, traveling at 20 mph, within a distance of 40 feet.
2. Materials and markings needed: Painted lines as indicated and traffic cones.
3. Procedure: The driver will drive the apparatus in high gear at 20 mph between the three cones, entering from the right. The driver should apply the brakes when the front wheels pass the last cone before entering the 40-foot area. Have the driver stop the vehicle as close to the last line as he can.
4. Check list and score sheet
   a. Keeps even speed
   b. Smooth stops
   c. No jerky steering movements
   d. Does not hit cones
   e. Shifts smoothly

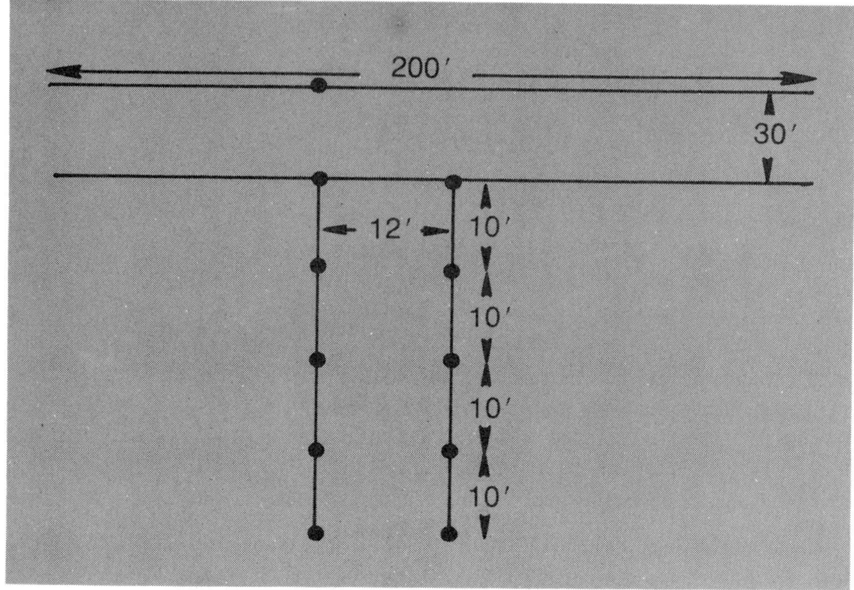

Test 4: Backing into alley

D. Test 4—backing into alley
   1. Objective: To determine if the driver is capable of backing an apparatus into an alley.
   2. Materials and markings needed: Painted lines as indicated and traffic cones.
   3. Procedure: The driver will drive the apparatus past the alley and stop. The driver will then back his apparatus down the alley to the end, stopping with the rear running board even with the last cones.
   4. Check list and score sheet
      a. Right approach
         1. Smooth operation vehicle
         2. Smooth stops
         3. Does not hit cones
         4. Shifts smoothly
      b. Left approach
         1. Smooth operation vehicle
         2. Smooth stops
         3. Does not hit cones
         4. Shifts smoothly

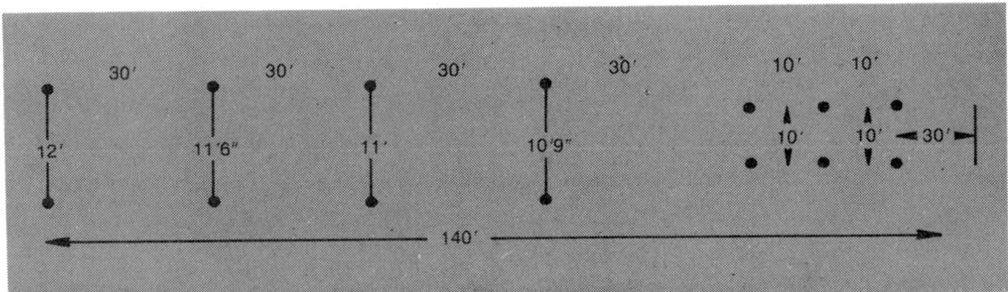

Test 5: Close clearance

E. Test 5—close clearance
1. Objective: To test the ability of an apparatus driver to judge the position of his vehicle in a diminishing roadway.
2. Materials and markings necessary: Painted lines and traffic cones as indicated.
3. Procedure
   a. Driver should enter marked roadway at a speed of 20 mph. Speed should remain the same until the end of the course. Stop at the marked line with the apparatus front wheels on the line.
4. Check list and score sheet
   a. Does not hit cones
   b. Even speed
   c. Gets the big picture
   d. Stops on line

Selective-gear transmissions

Despite the policy of many departments of including automatic transmissions in specifications for apparatus, the fact remains as mentioned previously that a lot of the current rolling stock has selective transmissions and conventional clutches. This presents a training problem because many new firemen have operated only vehicles equipped with automatic transmissions. Improper selection of the current gear position, jamming the gears into mesh, or rough treatment of the clutch may damage the entire power train, including the crankshaft, clutch, transmission, drive shaft, and rear axle.

The rotative force developed by the engine is called the *torque*. The motor speed range (in rpm) is called the *torque range* and is often indicated on the tachometer. This range varies for individual motors and is the chauffeur's guide to when he should shift to a higher or a lower gear.

When the engine speed approaches the top part of the torque range, the driver should shift to a higher gear; and when the engine speed drops markedly below the bottom figure of the range, he should downshift. The speed of the propeller shaft, driving the rear wheels, is proportional to the motor speed depending on which set of transmission gears is engaged. Various ratios are used between these gears, since with gradual engine acceleration, the vehicle moves through its lower speeds until it reaches direct or overdrive position.

Many times it may be advisable or necessary to slow down because of traffic conditions or to make a turn or ascend a hill. Here the chauffeur drops into a lower gear that will enable the engine to run in the desired operating range and pick up or retain its speed without laboring or lugging. It is generally recommended that the downshift be made before starting a turn, so that both hands can be used on the steering wheel.

A capable chauffeur should never approach a hill at high speed in order to have enough momentum to climb without having to drop to a lower gear. Instead, a safe speed should be maintained on the approach and a shift to a lower gear should be made before starting to climb, thereby retaining the vehicle's momentum as it ascends the hill. Again, the use of a lower gear is frequently advisable before descending a hill for better vehicle control. With foot off the accelerator, the motor has a tendency to revert to idling speed and thus has a braking effect on the drive shaft and the rear wheels.

Using the clutch

The term *slipping the clutch* is used to describe the highly undesirable practice of racing the engine with the clutch not completely engaged (clutch pedal partially depressed). This action heats the clutch disk and wears or damages other parts of the clutch assembly, including the throwout bearing.

An inexperienced or improperly trained chauffeur often slips the clutch:

1. Trying to maintain speed without downshifting while moving up an incline,
2. Backing into quarters (to avoid stalling at low speeds),
3. When there is difficulty in meshing gears,
4. Trying to warm up the engine quickly before leaving quarters.

Double clutching: This action is recommended in order to synchronize, approximately, the rotative speed of the engine-driven countershaft with the gear-driving main shaft of the transmission, a necessary move before shifting gears in a heavy-duty transmission which is not fully synchromesh. The engine is used to slow down the gear train by engaging the clutch with foot off the accelerator (upshift) and to speed up

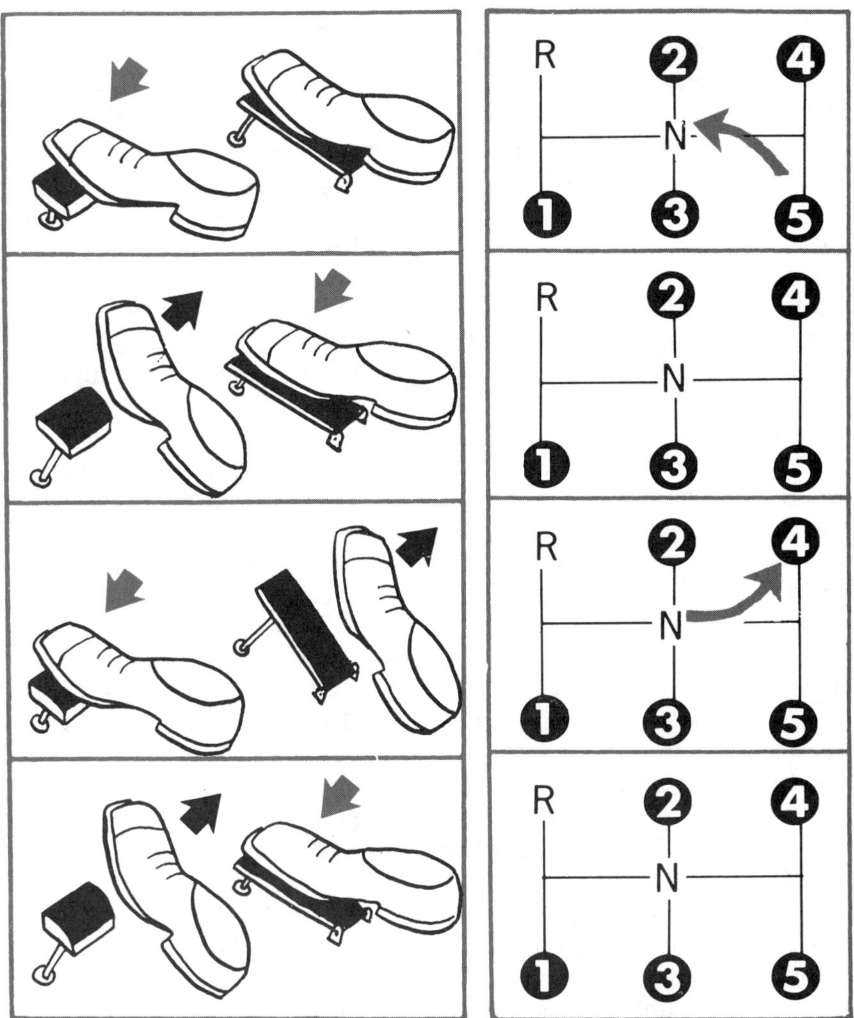

Double clutching, as indicated in the above four steps, synchronizes the rotative speed of the engine-driven countershaft with the gear-driving main shaft of the transmission.

the gear train by engaging the clutch with the foot on the accelerator (downshift), as follows:

1. Depress the clutch pedal and move transmission stick to neutral position.
2. Release the clutch pedal and depress the accelerator (when making

a downshift) or allow engine to slow down (upshifting) until the motor speed approximates the road speed of gear to be selected.

3. Depress the clutch pedal, move the shift lever to the selected speed.

4. Release the clutch pedal and accelerate the engine.

Normally, double clutching is not necessary when upshifting, but it is recommended for the sake of time. In the interval of double clutching, the motor speed usually drops to a point where gears can be meshed readily. If in upshifting, the gear shift lever is held in neutral too long before placing in higher gear, the motor speed (and transmission countershaft speed) drops below the point at which gear shaft speeds are approximate. Therefore, the gears cannot be meshed smoothly. In these instances, the proper procedure is as described under the recommendations for downshifting.

Avoid coasting! When under way on the road, and the gas throttle is closed, the momentum acquired by the apparatus is driving the engine instead of the engine driving the apparatus. If the clutch is disengaged at such times, the engine idles, slows down or may come to a dead stop. Then, if the clutch is let in without first accelerating the speed of the engine, serious damage may result. Broken timing gears, cam shafts and crankshafts, as well as twisted drive shafts and ruptured transmissions, are more directly chargeable to shocks imparted by the force stored up in a moving vehicle than by any force which can be developed directly in the engine itself.

If the engine should stall while free wheeling in the neutral position, any attempt to mesh the transmission gears while the vehicle is moving can easily result in chipping the teeth of the gears or doing other damage to the power train.

A stumbling block in attempting to curb accidents involving emergency vehicles is a lack of understanding and appreciation of the actual stopping distances necessary at various speeds and under unusual conditions. The total distance a vehicle travels before it can be brought to an emergency stop (stopping distance) depends mainly on two factors. The first of these, reaction distance, is determined by the driver's reaction time and the speed at which he is driving. The second factor is called the braking distance. Authorities in this field are in agreement that to the sum of the reaction and braking distances (the stopping distance) must be added a third factor called the perception time or distance.

1. Driver reaction time or distance is the time elapsed, or the distance traveled, between the instant the driver perceives a demand for braking and the point at which he starts to depress the brake pedal. Drivers with

well-practiced habits are able to make correct decisions more quickly than those who have not consistently followed good driving practices. It is commonly accepted that a reaction time of three-quarters of a second for thinking plus muscular reaction is fairly representative. The reaction time-distance varies directly as the speed. Therefore, if the speed is doubled (say from 20 mph to 40 mph), the reaction distance is doubled (from 22 to 44 feet).

2. Braking distance is the distance traveled between the point of first retardation by the brakes and the point where the vehicle actually stops. Under the same conditions, braking distance increases as to the square. If road speed is doubled, braking distance becomes four times as great.

New apparatus on road tests generally show excellent braking efficiencies, but it must be borne in mind that these tests embody several advantages, among them power brakes, new tires, dry concrete road surfaces and the driver's anticipation of the stop signal. We cannot count on such optimum braking efficiency after a unit has been in service for some time or under less than ideal weather or road conditions.

The braking force a vehicle is able to exert depends not only on the speed at which it is traveling, but also on the friction between the brake shoes and brake drums, as well as between tires and road surfaces. The actual braking force is determined by the weakest source of friction among the brakes, tires and road (at the same speed). Studies have shown that stopping distances may increase two and a half times on a wet road, particularly if tires are worn. Also, without tire chains, it may take as much as ten times the distance to stop on an icy pavement as it does on the same road when it is dry.

Ice, even with good chains, may triple the required braking distance. Wet leaves, sand or gravel, oil slicks, mud and wet steel rails also lengthen this distance.

3. Stopping distance is the sum of the reaction distance plus the braking distance.

4. Perception distance is the distance traveled between the time the driver could have perceived a dangerous situation and the time he actually does notice it. It varies with the alertness of the driver, his experience, and his attention to street and highway conditions. There is no average for this factor for all drivers in all driving situations. It may vary from one-tenth of a second to as much as two or three minutes. On account of its variability, it is not included in published charts on stopping distances.

Another prime consideration in accident control efforts is the adamant attitude displayed by some emergency drivers in constantly demanding and expecting to be given the right of way under all circumstances and conditions. Traffic regulations grant fire apparatus the right of way, but the courts have often noted in accident suits that this right does not relieve the chauffeur from driving with due regard for the safety of other vehicles and all pedestrians. A fire vehicle should never be driven at such excessive speed that, if the need arises, it cannot be quickly and safely stopped at intersections, when turning corners, or in other similar driving situations.

If, in responding to an alarm or returning to quarters, two or more pieces of apparatus are on the same thoroughfare, they should proceed in single file, and should not attempt to pass each other unless authorized by the commanding officer of the leading unit. Units should not travel less than 200 feet apart in responding to alarms. Headlights should be on at all times.

Requisite signals (sirens, air horns, whistles or bells) should be sounded in a fluctuating instead of a steady manner to indicate an emergency response. This provides an opportunity to hear signaling devices of other responding vehicles. Accidents have occurred between two emergency vehicles sounding sirens and approaching an intersection at right angles. Neither driver was aware of the approach of the other, as he could hear only his own siren. The use of radio-controlled signal lights has effectively reduced incidents of accidents between apparatus approaching intersections from converging directions. Their installation is highly recommended for any community.

Flooded areas

To avoid soaking the brake linings with oily or dirty water, flooded areas over 2 feet deep should not be traversed by fire vehicles. If the road is flooded, drive on its crown and proceed slowly in low gear. In a flooded area where it is necessary to negotiate deep water, the fan belt should be removed to prevent blowing water on spark plugs, distributor coil, etc. Replace before pumping or operating aerial to avoid overheating engine.

When parking a fire vehicle on a grade, the front wheels should be cut to the curb, all brakes set and the wheels chocked.

To negotiate long stretches of sand, approach slowly to avoid skidding (front wheels do not always respond to the action of the steering wheel when in loose sand). Proceed in low or second gear, but keep on going! Do not stop, for it may prove impossible to get under way again.

Do not slip the clutch in order to keep the apparatus from rolling backwards while waiting on a grade for a chance to proceed. Use the brakes.

Proceed slowly over bumpy or rutted roads to avoid damage to front wheels, front end assembly and steering mechanism.

Always start the apparatus in low gear from a standstill. Generally, it is not advisable to shift into second gear until the vehicle is clear of the fire station and the driver has an unobstructed view of street and road conditions.

Don't race the engine and then turn the ignition switch off. This charges the cylinders with raw gasoline, which seeps into the crankcase and dilutes the oil.

Care of engine

The engine of the apparatus should never be started except when that vehicle is to respond to an alarm, is to be tested, or is to be used in performance of a routine duty. The practice of turning over the motor on change of shifts has no value and is harmful. It does not show that the engine will start the next time it is needed to respond to a call. Besides diluting the lubricating oil, frequent starting of a cold motor and running it for only a brief period results in excessive wear, deposits gum and carbon on valves, and puts an unnecessary drain on the battery. The water vapor from burning gasoline condenses in the crankcase and tends to emulsify the oil. It also causes corrosion of valves, valve stems and other parts of the motor. Avoid getting raw gasoline into the cylinders by using the choke only when necessary.

Remember that dusk is the most hazardous time (especially when it is raining). Visibility is not only poor but also deceptive, and it is at this time that traffic commonly reaches its peak with many civilian drivers fatigued after their day's work. Nighttime is only slightly less dangerous than dusk with blinding lights and drinking drivers providing many dangerous situations which worsen as the night wears on.

Avoid skids

Clean or new concrete presents a surface much like coarse sandpaper with a high coefficient of friction between the road and the wheels of an apparatus. In time, the pores of this surface become filled with oil, grease or dirt, or the rough edges are worn off—lowering the friction coefficient and reducing the gripping power of the tires. A light rain, particularly, can float this oil, grease and dirt from the pores of the road surface, making increased braking distances necessary and increasing the possibility of skidding.

If a vehicle starts to skid to either side, take foot off gas and turn the steering wheel in the direction in which the rear end is sliding. In bringing a vehicle to a halt, the driver should decelerate gradually instead

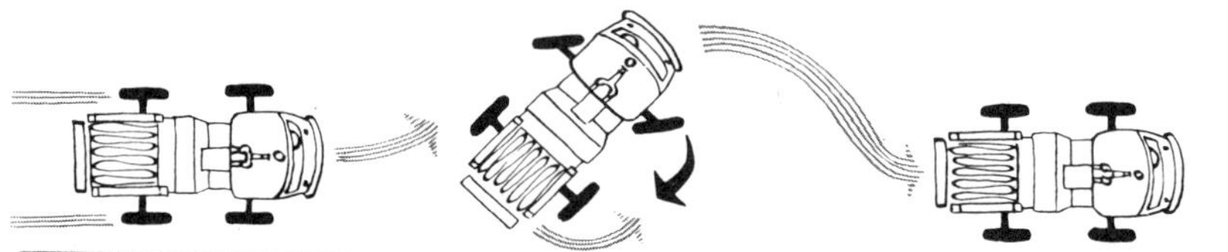

To stop a skid take foot off gas and turn front wheels in the direction that the rear end is sliding, as indicated above.

of jamming the brake pedal in such a way as to cause the wheels to lock and slide along the pavement, resulting in a skid. Researchers have found, through years of testing that the safest way to slow down or stop on ice or other slippery surfaces, is to rapidly pump the brake pedal, thereby applying the brakes quickly and then momentarily releasing them.

When two pieces of fire apparatus are about to turn into a thoroughfare, only one shall turn at a time, and the one which turns to the right shall have the right of way.

Whenever it is necessary to back apparatus, the driver should do so only after receiving a safe signal from firemen at the rear of the apparatus. If no lookout is available, the driver should first make certain it is safe to proceed. In backing into quarters, a very slow rate of speed should be maintained while other members of the unit are stationed in the street to control traffic from both directions. Street traffic should be similarly controlled while a fire vehicle leaves its quarters for any reason.

Drivers and officers should at all times keep themselves posted on the condition of roads and thoroughfares, as well as other unusual matters affecting the route the apparatus may have to travel. Where indicated, alternate routes should be plotted well in advance of a response to an alarm.

Major contributing factors in accidents

1. Carelessness on the part of the "other driver."
2. Carelessness on the part of the apparatus driver.
3. Placing full reliance on understanding the signals of policemen, crossing guards or well-intentioned citizens when crossing an intersection.
4. Apparatus, especially aerial trucks, contacting other vehicles or

objects while turning corners, going through narrow streets or congested traffic, entering or leaving quarters. To insure clearance in these situations, full cooperation is required of all members, particularly the officer.

5. Other vehicles coming up an inside lane, out of sight and shielded by a line of stopped vehicles.
6. Conditions of road or weather (night, fog, wet, snow, ice).
7. Inexperienced apparatus drivers.
8. Inadequate warning signs or signals.
9. Mechanical defects or failures.
10. Disregarding traffic or signals and warning signs.
11. Leaving apparatus improperly secured on an incline (no wheel chocks, parking brake or air-park brake applied).
12. Lack of proper precautions toward oncoming vehicles, particularly at night or under adverse weather conditions.

5
HIGGINS AV

CHAPTER ELEVEN

Handling utility fires

The expansion and development of industry and the ever-increasing drive toward man's greater comfort involves the use of an ever-increasing number of appliances and equipment that use electricity, gas and oil as a source of energy. Of the three, electricity is probably the most versatile, ranging in its most ordinary uses for lighting and heating through a variety of industrial purposes. Gas and oil is used mainly to provide heat, a good part of which provides electricity indirectly through the generating of steam.

Despite their unquestioned blessings, the increased use of these three main sources of energy in conjunction with overloaded lines and pipes, deterioration due to age and wear and malfunctioning of equipment, has brought about a situation wherein the three blessings have become one of the country's foremost causes of fires. And it must be recognized that, as the future entails even greater uses of energy, its hazards and costs in lives and property will in all probability increase proportionately unless adequate preventive measures are taken and suitable knowledge is disseminated to fire prevention and fire suppression personnel.

To insure operating efficiency and safety at fires and emergencies involving the three power sources, it is not necessary that members of the fire service be utilities engineers or qualified servicemen. But it is necessary that the special hazards involving these sources be recognized, and that efficient and safe actions be taken in fire or emergencies involving these dangers. Such recognition and actions can only be developed at a school for safety provided by the training division of a fire department or by cooperating utility companies who are generally only too glad to provide such schooling.

HANDLING ELECTRICAL HAZARDS

The efficient handling of electrical hazards on the fireground comes from good inspection practices, pre-fire planning, and effective training. The location of electrical equipment, fuses, switches, and other shutoffs, the type of equipment, voltages carried and the location of the circuits within and approaching a building should be noted during routine inspections. This information should then become the subject of discussion and be carefully analyzed during planning sessions, with special emphasis placed on the development of ways and means of shutting down power supplies in the event of an emergency.

Elements of electricity

The flow of water from a pumping station through mains or hose lines has often been used as an analogy in an understanding of the flow of electricity through conductors with the resultant effects. The three important factors involved in the two flows is shown by the following:

Factor	Electricity	Water
Pressure	Voltage	Pounds per square inch
Rate of flow	Amperage	Discharge in gpm
Resistance	Ohms	Pressure drop per length of carrier due to friction loss

The size of the electrical conductor and the type of insulating covering have a direct bearing on the maximum safe current which may be carried. This without overloading and consequent overheating of the wiring which, in turn, may cause deterioration of the insulation and ignition of nearby materials. Heat is generated in an electrical conductor and varies as the square of the current.

By itself, the voltage of a circuit is not necessarily a measure of its fire or life hazard. Certain types of circuits may have very high voltages but of such low capacity (amperage) as to be incapable of passing sufficient current, even though a shock may be experienced. A common example of this would be the high voltage of the secondary circuit of an automotive ignition system. It is the amperage which actually kills or injures a person. But, if the resistance remains the same, the higher the voltage,

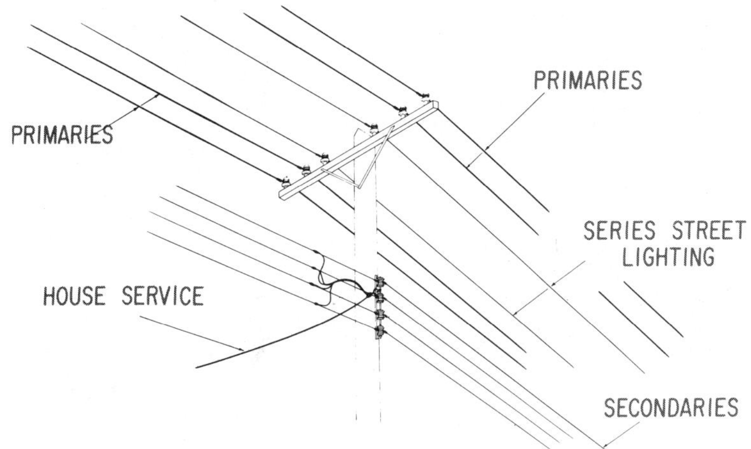

A local distribution system that is fed by "high line" power transmission. Primary lines, with few exceptions, are located on cross arms at top of pole. "Foreign" attachments, such as telephone and fire alarm wires, are placed beneath secondaries.

the higher the amperage. Hence, special precautions should be taken in occupancies where posted signs indicate high voltages.

Transmission and distribution of electricity

Again, the comparison of an electrical and a water distribution system can be used to advantage in understanding the transmission of current, generated at a power plant, to distant distribution points by means of overhead or underground conductors and use of high voltages. From such distribution points the current—also high voltage—is carried to the transformers servicing the consumers. From the low-voltage side of the transformer, service connections are made to the establishments wherein current is used. In connection with step-down transformers in which current is reduced, the term "primary" is used to designate the high-voltage side and "secondary" to indicate the low-voltage side of the transformer.

Static electricity as a fire cause

Until comparatively recent years static electricity was not generally recognized as a serious fire hazard. But experiments and experiences have shown that static electric sparks can and do ignite flammable gases, vapors, dust clouds, cotton in the process of manufacture, and other easily ignitable fibrous materials. Originally believed to be generated only by friction between different substances, static electricity has also

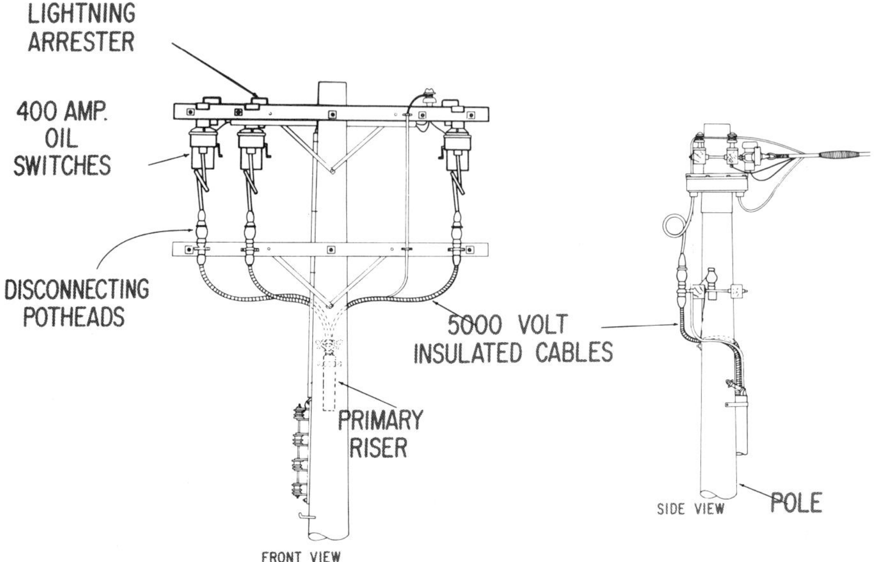

Overhead systems can also be fed by risers leading from underground cable.

been shown to be generated by contact and separation of two unlike substances, regardless of friction.

Static charges are undoubtedly generated in nearly all industrial and manufacturing operations, but in most cases they are dissipated or neutralized without becoming a fire hazard. However, if a spark does occur, it may not be of sufficient intensity to ignite combustible material or there may be nothing combustible in the immediate vicinity. Sometimes small static charges, which are not a fire hazard in themselves, may indirectly result in fire by causing finely divided stock to adhere to parts of a machine to such an extent that clogging and mechanical friction result. Such a situation and effect are commonly found in cotton gins. In flat-bed printing press work, unless means are provided to prevent it, static electricity can cause the sheets of paper to adhere to parts of the press or to cling together.

Static electricity is also generated when liquids flow through pipes and when the liquids are broken up into drops. Unless the liquids have a very high electrical resistance, the charges are usually neutralized or conducted to earth as fast as they are generated. Some so-called dry liquids, such as gasoline, benzol, ether and carbon disulfide, have very high electrical resistances and frequently create dangerous accumulations of static charges in processes and on machines in which they are used.

If a liquid having a high electrical resistance is discharged in the form of drops or spray into a closed metal tank insulated from the ground, the entire tank can be charged. For this reason, there is a real hazard in discharging flammable liquids, particularly those of high electrical resistance and low flash points, into the tops of tanks. Under such conditions the filling pipe should always be carried down close to the bottom of the tank. On days when the relative humidity is low, high static voltages can collect on the surface of a liquid and be discharged to the tank itself, unless means are provided to dissipate the charges. Even gases in motion may generate static electricity but ordinarily appreciable charges are not apparent unless there are solid particles or drops of liquid in the gas.

Neutralizing the charge

It is impossible to prevent the generation of static electricity in industrial operations, but it can be neutralized or conducted to ground harmlessly as fast as it is generated. If the objects on which the charges collect are good electrical conductors, they can be kept at earth potential by means of ground wires connected to water pipes, rods driven into the ground, etc., but if the charges collect on nonconducting materials, ordinary methods of grounding are ineffective and they cannot be completely discharged unless contact is made with the entire surface by the grounding medium.

Charges of static electricity are not always confined to machines, fabrics, belts, etc., but are frequently found on the human body, especially at times of low humidity. Such charges may be generated by the clothes, by rubbing of the soles of shoes on nonconducting floor coverings, or by various industrial operations. For these reasons, special footwear and floor surfaces are recommended for special occupancies such as hospitals, in which anesthetic gases are used.

It has been found that most fires that are caused by static electricity occur during the winter months when artificial heating is required and the indoor humidity is low. Under normal conditions of humidity a thin film of moisture exists on most substances, which greatly reduces the electrical resistance and allows the charges to be neutralized or conducted to earth as fast as generated. However, abnormally dry conditions may produce static electricity in dangerous quantities.

The surface conductivity of most materials changes through wide limits when the humidity is varied; an increase in conductivity being noted when moisture condenses on the surface of the material. Artificial

Overhead, line oil switches are connected to the uppermost primary lines. Open wire used on the overhead is normally bare and where wire has weatherproof coating such coating has no insulating qualities.

humidification of hazardous locations is, therefore, an excellent method of preventing dangerous accumulations of static electricity. Humidity has another effect in the prevention of fires in the textile industry. In addition to preventing accumulations of static electricity, the amount of moisture in combustible materials is an important factor in determining whether or not they will be ignited by static sparks.

Air is ordinarily a nonconductor of electricity, but when ionized it has sufficient conductivity to prevent the accumulation of static charges. For this reason, ionization by gas flames has been employed for many years in the printing industry; but this method is limited in application as it cannot be used in any hazardous location or where flammable inks are employed. Another method of ionization uses silent high potential electric discharges produced by "static neutralizers." A high-voltage transformer of small capacity is used to supply a high alternating potential to discharge units which may be mounted on printing presses or other machinery. The silent discharges ionize the air and increase its electrical conductivity so that the static charges are dissipated or conducted to the grounded framework of the machine.

Although dangerous accumulations of flammable gases, vapors and dusts should be prevented by the use of proper ventilation and exhaust systems, it is advisable to make tests for static electricity in places where such flammable materials exist, particularly at times of low humidity.

In view of the number of industrial operations in which volatile flammable liquids are used and the myriad ways in which static electricity can be generated, with its high potential hazards, this topic well merits due consideration in any fire prevention, fire investigative or fire training program.

High voltages

As previously stated, under normal conditions, the degree of life and fire hazard increases with the magnitude of the voltage. Therefore, firemen as well as officers should be familiar with the various conductors and their voltages. Circuits carrying electricity from the power plant of the utility company are divided into the following general groups according to the voltage carried.

1. Transmission Circuits: Wiring from generating plants to substations. Line voltages in some localities are about 15,000 volts, whereas in other areas voltages above 8000 are so classed (phase-to-phase voltage).
2. Distribution Circuits: Wiring from distribution points to transformers servicing consumers. Line voltages vary from 601 volts to the minimum for transmission voltage, although in some locales line voltages in this class may be as high as 24,000 volts.
3. Service Circuits: Wiring from the low-voltage (secondary) side of the transformer to the consumer's home or place of business. Line voltages are 600 volts or less. These low voltages should not be interpreted to mean "safe" voltages, for a voltage as low as 120 can be fatal to a well-grounded person.

OVERHEAD TRANSMISSION LINES

Overhead lines are most commonly used for power transmission in rural and residential areas. The so-called "high line" (meaning ultrahigh voltage) is normally suspended by long string-type insulators from galvanized steel towers whose current-carrying phase wires are usually protected from a direct hit by lightning by stretching one or two grounded wires from tower to tower above the phase wires to furnish a path to ground. In some parts of the country, high-voltage transmission lines are carried on A frames or H frames built up from wood poles.

Despite the fact that these overhead wires are not always insulated, as are underground cables, they normally present no special hazards until some unusual condition is set up. When there is a severe wind or ice storm, these overhead conductors may be broken somewhere in a community. Also, temperature changes over a long period of time can cause a bad connection which, in turn, can result in enough heat being generated to burn a line apart and permit it to fall to the ground or on a building or other structure.

Lightning can cause immediate and obvious damage, or it may damage an insulator sufficiently for it to break down some time later in good weather, thereby burning a conductor apart.

Overloaded circuits, caused by excessive consumption of current during certain periods of time, the accidental grounding of conductors with some object such as a tree, and heavy cranes or motor vehicles smashing into poles are only a few of the many conditions which cause wires to be contacted from the ground and thereby set up an emergency condition. When they fall, they may land on and energize cars, pools of water, metal fences and aluminum-siding homes. When lying on the ground, these wires create a hazard to the public and to fire fighting personnel operating nearby.

General precautions

Of particular danger to firemen operating where overhead high-tension wires are present are the possibilities of contact between exposed wires and aerial or extension ladders; of contact between metal ladders and charged wires; and the forcing together of wires of different potentials by careless manipulation when raising or lowering ladders. Again, careless use of roof ropes, especially when hoisting hose or ladders, may draw high-tension wires of different potential together, and cause injury to the man handling the rope.

Using metal aerials

The conductivity of metal aerial and portable ladders in contact with lives wires is apparent. But even wooden ladders should be used with care in their vicinity. While the wood itself is nonconductive, the fact exists that components of such ladders are in many cases made of metal. These items would include, among others, wire extension cables, beam bolts, turnbuckles, reinforcing plates on beams, heel plates, tie-rods, and locks, pawls, or dogs.

If an aerial ladder should contact a live overhead wire, the entire apparatus could become charged without the man on the truck being aware of it. But death or injury could result immediately if some person on the ground were to touch any part of the truck. Until this occurs, the truck in contact with the live wire poses no appreciable danger to the men on the ladder or the truck, unless they become grounded as in stepping off or mounting the apparatus. Therefore, if an aerial ladder appears to be in contact with overhead wires or if doubt exists as to this fact, men should *jump free* when leaving the truck and should not touch any part of the apparatus while standing on the ground.

Firemen should use extra care when climbing into windows of buildings under construction. Live wires are sometimes laid across the sills and, if the insulation is burned or worn, a metal ladder in contact with such wires could provide a path for the current through a man's body on or in contact with the ladder. Likewise, a sagging or fallen wire could turn a metal fire escape into a dangerous conductor.

Insofar as operating conditions will permit, the placing of ladders, apparatus, etc., under overhead wires, whose integrity is in doubt, should be avoided. Another common cause of injury and damage is the practice of leaving ladders, especially the light metal type, unattended so that high winds may blow them into electrical overhead or lead-in wires. Finally, if it is expedient in overhauling operations to throw any burnt material out of a window of an upper story, make sure this material does not fall on or damage any wires in its descent.

Determination of voltage of a conductor

Generally speaking, approximate voltages may be judged from the locations of the wires on the various crossarms. It is the common practice to place the higher voltage wires above those of lower voltages but at times a high-voltage cable (twisted wires) is mounted below low-voltage wires on a pole. The position of the wire on the insulator, the size and shape of the insulator, and its position on the pole may assist in identifying the wires but these cannot be used *with definite certainty* in determining voltages. Therefore, if voltage cannot be positively identified and no qualified utility company representative is present to give positive information, the safest procedure is to *consider it as high voltage and act accordingly.*

Wires down or sagging

In most cases of downed electric wires, efforts should be immediately concentrated on keeping the public, particularly children, at a safe distance from the danger zone (at least one span each way from the break or sagging wire). These adjacent wires may have been weakened by the break and any movement, caused by the wind or rescue work, may burn down nearby wires.

The power company, railroad or other organization involved should be notified immediately. While awaiting the arrival of their qualified

Transformer installation (3-phase) is used to step down line voltages.

representative and until definite assurance to the contrary is received from this individual, all overhead wires should be treated as high voltage and "hot."

Whenever possible, have utility men do any necessary cutting of electric wires, especially those running from pole to pole or from pole to building.

Particularly in a fire or emergency operation wherein electric hazards exist, members should not operate unless wearing protective clothing and using properly insulated tools.

Extra care should be used when hoisting or lowering hose lines, tools, ladders, etc., in the vicinity of overhead wires or cables. Bringing two energized lines together may cause them to arc intensely, burn apart and fall to the ground.

Take special precautions if a tingling sensation is felt in the soles of the feet when approaching an area where a wire is down. The ground itself may be charged and the intensity of the current will increase as the wire is approached.

Apparatus should be kept at a safe distance to avoid coming in contact with wires. If fallen or sagging wires come into contact with the apparatus and the men thereon, the fire truck should be removed to safety.

In dismounting, before the truck is free from the wires, men should not step to the ground so that the feet are in contact simultaneously with the truck and the ground, as this would eliminate the insulating effect of the rubber tires. If the apparatus is in contact with other vehicles on which wires have fallen, pull away from such vehicles and get off the apparatus by *jumping clear*.

Avoid touching any metal ladder, fire truck, iron fence, building with aluminum siding, etc., which is in contact with a downed electric wire. The body may become an electric "bridge" for the current to cross to the ground.

In many installations (overhead and underground lines, railroad lines, and even in television sets) for a time after the current is shut off at or near the source, a residual charge remains in the line. This charge is, of course, capable of causing injuries or damage, if it is ignored.

In many cases, the utility company provides an alternate feeder system to their distribution circuits in order to maintain service. For this reason, a break in an an overhead wire can be "hot" at both ends. Therefore, service at a building should not be cut in a manner which allows wires to rest on the ground. If more than one wire is down, the wires may be equally dangerous, even though one is arcing and the other is not.

Vigilance should not be relaxed for even a moment. Mistakes can be costly!

Where life is in danger

Occasionally, to save human life it is necessary for firemen to cut or remove live wires. In these situations it should be recognized that these operations can be extremely hazardous and should be carried out with utmost caution, considering all wires as energized. Depending on conditions found, it must be decided whether it would be more expedient to remove the victim from the live wire or the energized wire from the victim. The utility company should be notified and medical aid summoned immediately. A dry pike pole or dry length of wood can be hooked into the victim's clothing to drag him clear of the wire, if he is lying on the wire and it is not entangled with his body. Stay as far away from the wire and the victim as is possible while doing this.

Another dry pike pole, a dry length of wood, or a "hot stick" should be used in this operation to hold down the live wire, while the victim is being dragged clear. A less recommended procedure to follow, if the foregoing tools should not be available, would be to loop a long dry rope under the victim to drag him clear. Do not, under any circumstances, allow your clothing or any part of your body to touch the wire or the victim until he is definitely clear.

High-voltage tongs: These tongs (also known as a "hot stick") can be used to pick up or drag anything in the way of wire, from heavy-duty cable to a telephone wire, without adjustment. The body of the tongs is made of fiber glass or wood impregnated with paraffin to protect against moisture, sap and acid. A coating of lacquer over the wooden type renders the tool immune to atmosphere moisture.

To operate, the tongs in their open position are forced across the wire and a hand piece on the shaft of the tool is drawn backward, locking the wire in the grip of the device. In removing a live wire from a victim, it is best to drag the wire toward the rescuer, as he walks backwards, lifting it clear but keeping it in contact with the ground, thereby reducing its voltage. Pulling the wire in this fashion is recommended, as there is less danger in case the wire unhooks from the tool.

Cut wires at nearest support

Wire cutters: At times it may be necessary to cut wires on live electrical circuits for rescue purposes or because the wires are handicapping or endangering fire personnel. If power cannot be shut off at a nearby or distant source, and live wires must be cut, this should be done at the nearest support on the side of the source of supply. In other words, if wires must be cut within a building, they should be cut at the support nearest the front of the building, so that the end which drops will be "dead."

After being cut at one support, the other end of the wire at the next support should also be cut, so that the wire will not hang from the ceiling and endanger the men. Even though it is certain that the wire has been cut at a point nearest the source of supply, there is always the possibility of cross connections that could still make the wires live. For this reason the wire should be cut at both ends and the section taken out of the way of the men working at the fire.

Live wires of up to 8000 volts may be cut by firemen in outdoor operations, where utility company representatives are not present and fallen live circuits must be cut. **These men should be adequately trained, wear proper protective clothing (linemen's gloves, etc.) and use the tool which is specifically designed for this purpose.** (Electric utilities send linemen's gloves to a laboratory for testing every two weeks.) The hook on the end of the Steck wire cutter provides a means for grasping the wire while cutting. Another design, the Boston wire cutter works somewhat on the same principle, having a double hook attached to the side of the blade to hold the wire while it is being cut. Only one wire must be cut at a time, for if both wires are cut at once, an arc may be created and men injured by molten metal produced thereby.

Unlike a bolt cutter, which should never be used for this purpose, this tool has properly insulated handles and is termed a "hot wire cutter."

The wire should first be held securely so that the loose ends will not snake around. This can be done by placing an all-wooden ladder over it or pinning it to the ground by the use of pike poles. Even though disconnected, the pinned ends must not be released until the utility men arrive.

First, cut the wire on the side nearer the source of supply at a point close to the ladder or pike poles, to prevent it from curling up and making contact with anyone. When cut, separate the ends of the wire by means of the wire cutters or high-voltage tongs. Where a victim is trapped, the same procedure should be employed in cutting the wire on his other side, unless it is certain that there can be no source of electricity leading to the wire (dead end with no electrical connection thereto). Remember, there is always the possibility that the supposedly "dead" end of the wire may be backfed.

Remember above all, that seconds count here. If the victim is not breathing, do not move him after the wire is cut but start resuscitation immediately.

There is another recommended method for removing a disentangled wire from a victim lying on the ground or trapped in a car. He is safe in the car as long as he does not form contact with the ground. A dry rope about 100 feet long, with a small coil for weight at each end, is used in this rescue procedure. First, all persons are cleared out of the danger area and the rescuer dons linemen's rubber gloves. Standing at a point opposite to that to which the wire is to be moved, and approximately 30 feet from the wire, he tosses one end of the rope under the wire a distance nearly equal to his distance from the wire. He then tosses his end over the wire so as to land near the first end thrown. The ends are then picked up by another man, similarly protected, or by the thrower and the wire is dragged out of the way.

Lineman's rubber gloves

When working in the vicinity of known or suspected energized electrical conductors—particularly if it is necessary to cut or handle live circuits—properly tested linemen's rubber gloves, with leather protective gloves over them, should always be used. The rubberized canvas gloves used by firemen for general purposes do not give the protection necessary for such operations. Leather gloves are worn over the rubber gloves to protect them from being torn or coming into direct contact with substances which could cause the rubber to deteriorate. These leather gloves should not be used for other purposes, as in such usage they may become oily or greasy or pick up small metal shavings or splinters which upon contact could damage or penetrate the rubber gloves.

Because of their importance in protecting against injuries in situations in which electrical hazards exist, it is extremely important that these gloves be kept in good condition at all times. They should be stored and used with great care, tested in accordance with a set procedure, and used only for the purposes for which they were intended.

When not in use, linemen's rubber gloves must be protected from conditions or substances which might cause the rubber to deteriorate, such as heat, moisture, oil and grease, sunlight, acids; and from objects which create holes and bring the wearer into direct contact with the electric current, such as puncture, tearing, rubbing (abrasion), and creasing. After usage, or when tested, they should be washed with soap, both inside and out, rinsed with clear water and then dried thoroughly. To prevent the rubber from sticking, they should be well chalked.

It is important that rubber gloves are stored or worn rightside out since this puts less strain on the rubber. If both are dry, place the rubber glove inside the leather protector glove. If either is wet, separate and put them in a safe place to dry.

Care of gloves

For reasons of safety and to promote their service life, rubber gloves should be kept in an approved, ventilated and protected carrying case on the apparatus. Spare sets of gloves, to be interchanged at intervals, should be similarly stored and protected in the fire station. Rubber gloves should not be left in storage (unused and untested) for longer than 60 days to prevent deterioration of the rubber. On the apparatus, they should never be placed in compartments with tools or equipment, oil, grease, or other foreign substances.

Because rubber tends to deteriorate under certain conditions, the gloves should be inspected and tested at intervals of 90 days maximum. Many manufacturers of rubber gloves test their products at 14,000 volts and recommend them for use up to 10,000 volts. However, utility companies do not normally depend on rubber gloves on voltages above 5000 volts, or 8000 volts if the combined rubber and leather gloves are worn. To provide a margin of safety, a laboratory test (over the maximum recommended usage figure) should be performed at stated intervals on the rubber gloves. This should be done by a technician in the laboratory of the city government, or a private testing laboratory, or a local electrical utility company which may extend this courtesy.

In addition, a field test (both visual and air) should be done at frequent intervals by the members of the fire department in accordance with the procedure outlined. Inspections and tests should be made both inside and outside of gloves: (1) Examine inside of cuff for tears, punctures, etc. (2) Squeeze air into parts to be examined. Careful attention should be given to palm and fingers. (3) By listening or feeling, punctures and tears will be detected by escaping air. (4) By stretching cuff slightly, abrasions and weak spots will become more evident. (5) Examine entire outer surface for burns, cuts, cracks, punctures and weak spots. (6) Roll cuff of glove to trap air. Hold tightly in this manner to compress air for test.

Fires on poles or pole-mounted equipment

Grass fires frequently spread to and involve utility poles. Fires may also originate on the poles themselves due to malfunction of equipment, or the pole may become involved by a fire in a nearby building, or the cause may be due to a motor vehicle accidentally smashing into it and knocking it down.

It is usually the best procedure to let the fire burn itself out, if it is confined to metal-enclosed equipment, such as a transformer, regulator switch, or pothead. Notify the power company and stand by until the arrival of their representative. Search nearby buildings to ascertain if any emergency exists due to the shutdown of power.

If fire is consuming the pole or its crossarms so that the equipment (including wires) may fall, constitute a hazard, or actually cause damage, extinguish the fire by means of a nonconducting agent and protect adjacent property. If it necessary to use water, employ a fog nozzle or "whip" the stream from a distance, but bear in mind that, because of the possibility of electrical conductivity, power company men prefer not to climb wet or ice-coated poles.

In all cases, keep the public, as well as fire apparatus and nonoperating personnel, at a safe distance from endangered areas.

Underground lines

For the installation and maintenance of underground primary and secondary power lines in the congested sections of large cities, concrete vaults or "manholes" are located several hundred feet apart. They also serve as junctions for branch lines and for services into customers' premises. Transformer vaults, cables, switches, and a large variety of heavy-duty equipment are normally installed in these manholes, which may also provide access to tunnels through which the conduits run.

Because of their location, these installations are normally safer than those aboveground, but at times emergencies do arise due to overload, breakdown of equipment with severe arcing or explosions. When ex-

Vault transformer is usually installed under sidewalks or inside a building in the basement or on an upper floor. A nonflammable insulating fluid is used in many transformers, particularly in buildings.

plosions of accumulated gases and vapors do occur in these manholes, their heavy covers are often blown into the air and carried considerable distances. This ignition of flammable gases may be due to a spark resulting from the blowing of a fuse, or a short circuit in the electrical conductors themselves, or it may occur when a manhole is unseated, thus permitting air to mix with the gases in proper proportion for rapid oxidation. It commonly happens that the initial explosion is followed by a series of explosions and fires in other manholes in the same or nearby areas.

Notify the utility company immediately, giving the exact location of the incident and the number of manholes involved at the scene. To prevent additional explosions, do not pull covers from adjacent manholes, unless requested to do so by a qualified representative of the power company.

All fire fighting personnel and the public should be kept clear of the involved and nearby manholes and a check made to make sure that no fire apparatus is parked over one. All vehicular traffic should be stopped. It is good practice to have fire personnel examine the cellars and basements of buildings in the block, paying particular attention to the locations of electrical service entrance to these buildings. A thorough check should be made to determine if the burning of a street cable has affected the electrical service equipment in the building, or vice versa.

Under no condition should a manhole be entered unless it is absolutely necessary to perform rescue work. Remember, the fire or explosion has usually done its maximum damage when the failure first occurred, and it is not imperative that further action be taken until the conditions are checked by the utility company. If entrance is necessary, only approved self-contained masks should be used. If lighting equipment is used, it should be explosionproof.

If the insulation in a street manhole appears to be smouldering or burning, one or more dry chemical or carbon dioxide extinguishers may be discharged into it, the cover reinstalled, and a wet blanket or salvage cover placed over it. These steps will starve the fire of necessary oxygen, resulting in extinguishment, provided the cables have been deenergized by the utility men or by the fire itself.

Do not use water, even in the form of fog, to arrest a fire in a manhole or vault, unless such a request is made by a power company representative. If water in large quantities is used, it could remain in depressions, pits or low spots and become a dangerous conductor of electricity.

In addition, the use of water, foam, or soda-acid extinguishers in manholes or underground transformer vaults may permanently damage the cables and/or equipment and provide an electrical path to the man at the nozzle or operating the device. Exhaust fans may be used to advantage to remove any remaining explosive or poisonous fumes or gases from these underground locations.

Electric power plants and substations

The generation, transmission, and distribution of electric energy by private utility companies and by publicly owned and operated commissions present many fire prevention and fire protection problems. The power is produced at the generating station, sent out over transmission feeders to substations, and thence over distribution feeders or cables to the consumer.

Electric generating stations are mainly hydroelectric or steam-electric types, although atomic power is now also being used commercially. Among the problems connected with steam turbo-generators is the fact that they cannot be stopped quickly, nor can the lubricating oil supply to bearings be shut off while the unit is rotating. Therefore, in the event of escaping oil being ignited by contact with hot surfaces, the fire will likely be fed for a considerable length of time. Fire problems are also presented by the large supplies of bituminous coal, natural gas and bunker C oil which are commonly used as fuels at steam-electric generating stations.

Substations are of several types: The bulk power switching station; the older-style indoor substation; and more modern outdoor substation; the small unit substation consisting of transformers and control cabinets surrounded by a chain-link fence; or, for a large industrial plant, the transformer vault located under the sidewalk or in a manhole of a city street.

Large quantities of insulating oil may be found in all such premises as it is used to cool transformers and circuit breakers. A fire in such oil should be handled the same as any other oil fire.

For fires or emergencies in such premises, the initial step would be to find and cooperate with the plant superintendent or substation operator. His advice should be asked as to the best point or entrance and what special areas to avoid. This representative will know how to shut off the electricity to stop the arc which may be sustaining the fire and he will be familiar with the entrances, exits, special hazarrds, and the voltage ratings of the equipment.

A line of sufficient length to cover the entire area should be stretched, but the nozzleman should stop at the point of entrance. Do not stretch in until water is needed and employ only a high-velocity fog nozzle, preferably of the nonadjustable type.

All fire department and plant first-aid extinguishers suitable for electrical fires should be assembled at point of operation and all metal tools, such as lock breakers, claw tools, etc., should be left outside the working area.

If, as is becoming more common, the plant or substation is protected by a fog-spray type of sprinkler system, stretch a line or lines to its siamese but do not start water until so ordered.

A built-in carbon dioxide extinguishing system may be found in such an occupancy. As this gas in high concentrations can be hazardous to operating personnel, do not enter these areas after CO_2 systems have been discharged unless self-contained masks are worn.

Customer high-voltage (primary) installations

These primary (high-voltage, over 600 volts) installations may be found feeding office buildings, large apartment houses or large industrial plants. They are usually in a fire-resistive enclosure, itself located in a separate building. They may be recognized by a sign reading "HIGH VOLTAGE" or "DANGER 5000 VOLTS" on the door of the fire-re-

Cable manhole carries primary and secondary feeders. In the event of fire in such an installation, no water should be used until cables have been isolated in all directions.

sistant room or vault housing the transformers, high-voltage motors, etc.

Firemen should be familiar with all high-voltage installations in their territories. On pre-fire inspection tours, a check should be made to see that oil drains in and around high-voltage installations are clear and marked with some identification for ease of finding them under darkened conditions.

In case of fire in a transformer room or vault, call the power company and get a qualified building or plant employee as a guide.

Do not be misled by the presence of a great deal of smoke. It may be coming from an electrical installation which does not require the immediate use of fire extinguishing agents. Pulling a switch or removing a fuse may solve the problem. However, pull no switch and remove no fuse unless absolutely certain of the effect. This act or improper ventilation of these areas may touch off explosive gases which were only waiting for the proper air mixture or source of ignition. Some vaults are equipped with ventilator shutters which close when thermal links melt due to fire. Prematurely letting in fresh air is undesirable as it may provide mixture for the gas to be within its explosive range.

Because of the toxic gases usually formed in fires in electrical trans-

Underground secondary service boxes are similar to cable manhole, but smaller. They are used for splicing secondary wires, including customer's house service.

formers and other equipment, firemen should not enter a high-voltage installation until conditions are checked out by a utility representative. This admonition, of course, does not apply if rescue work is necessary. If entry is necessary, only masks of the self-contained type should be worn.

When groping in such dark or smoky areas, the hands should be extended in front, *palms turned toward the face.* This inhibits the natural reaction to grab any live equipment which may be accidentally contacted.

Customer low-voltage installations

Despite the fact that low-voltage (under 600 volts) installations present less hazards, all safety precautions should be observed, especially when working in an area with water on the floor. Guard against brushing against exposed wiring, especially if wearing a metal helmet or carrying a metal tool.

The possibility of explosion of gases or flammable liquid fumes must also be considered in these installations.

If a building is damaged by fire to the extent that electrical service is no longer required, the power should be shut off by the utility company man, if possible. This could be accomplished by opening the main switch or by cutting the wires in the drip loop leading into the building.

Power and light should be left on as long as is practicable from the standpoint of safety. Light may be needed as a help in overhauling operations, and power required to operate fire pumps, elevators (for tenant evacuation) and other vital equipment. There are cases on record where relatively minor fires were allowed to spread and destroy buildings because of water failure resulting from unnecessary shutting down of the fire pumps.

In removing fuses, pulling control switches, etc., only that section or building affected by fire or water should be isolated if possible. When a switch is pulled or a fuse removed, a recommended procedure is to attach a fire department red tag to the box indicating that the power has been cut off. This tag should be removed only by the utility company representative or by an electrical inspector when service is resumed.

In removing a cartridge-type fuse from its prongs, a dry object such as a piece of wood should be used instead of the bare hand to eliminate the danger of shock. If it is necessary to operate an electric switch while standing in water or when the switch is wet, do not grab the switch handle barehanded. Use a rope, pike pole, wooden handle of a tool, or other safety device to open the switch.

Water in its natural state contains a variety of impurities which, like wires, can conduct current from an electrical source to the nozzle and subject the nozzleman to an electrical shock. Therefore, it is not generally good practice to apply water to fires involving "live" electrical equipment, particularly if high voltages are present. Actually, it is the amount of current (amperage) which kills or injures. But if the resistance remains the same, the higher the voltage, the higher the amperage. In the usual fire fighting operations, there is ordinarily little danger to firemen directing hose streams on wires of less than 600 volts to ground from any distance likely to be encountered.

A number of studies have been made by investigative agencies to establish the safe distances between hose nozzles and live high-voltage conductors for the various extinguishing mediums (foam, wet water, fog, solid stream, etc.). **The results of these studies should be used with caution, as the factors involved vary considerably with conditions encountered; and exact knowledge of the factors is not available at many fire or emergency operations.** The findings however, do provide a basic understanding of the factors involved and their extent.

Naturally, an increase in voltage or the amount of current flowing results in a greater hazard to the nozzleman. Among the other principal variables in stream conductivity are the following:

1. The length (or reach) of the stream and its cross-sectional area.
2. The purity of the water and its corresponding resistivity.
3. The resistivity of the nozzleman.
4. The resistance to ground through the hose.

Length and cross-sectional area of the fire stream

Under certain conditions dangerous amounts of current can be carried through a solid hose stream. The analogy of electrical conductivity through wires of various sizes and lengths can be used in understanding this phenomenon. Briefly, the closer the nozzleman is to the electrical source and the larger and more intact the stream, the greater is the likelihood of conductivity. Pressure has no bearing on the conductivity of the stream except as it affects its solidarity.

In one investigation with solid streams, the current readings were quite steady for short distances from conductor to nozzle; but as the distance was increased, the ammeter would fluctuate more and more until at the greatest distance of about 36 feet the meter pointer would read zero most of the time, with only an occasional indication of current flow. These fluctuations were, of course, due to changes in the continuity of the stream when it began to break up at some distance from the nozzle.

Because it eliminates stream solidarity, a fog nozzle, particularly of the nonadjustable type, definitely decreases the hazards of stream conductivity when working in the vicinity of live electrical apparatus. This is due to the fact that water particles in the finely divided state don't provide a continuous path for the flow of current the way a straight stream does. **Fog nozzles of the combination or adjustable type are not recommended for use on electrical equipment or sources, because of the danger of hitting the energy source in the straight stream position.**

To eliminate this possibility, the fog nozzle should be of the type which can only discharge a fog pattern. **A fog applicator should not be used on electrical fires for water application because of the danger of accidentally touching the live equipment with the metal applicator.** Where only a combination or adjustable type of fog nozzle is available, it is important that the nozzle be opened and turned to the fog pattern only when pointed away from the electrical equipment.

Some years ago, the Chicago Fire Department, in cooperation with the Commonwealth Edison Co., conducted tests and established recommended safe distances to be maintained between spray nozzles and live electrical apparatus of varying voltages. Tests had shown that

Chicago hydrant water normally had a resistance of about 3800 ohms per cubic centimeter, while river water ranged from 1671 to 2393 ohms per cubic centimeter.

Electrical Conductivity of Fog Streams

Phase to Phase Voltage	Corresponding Phase to Ground Voltage	Minimum Safe Span–Feet
33,000 and below	19,000	4
66,000	38,000	6
132,000	76,000	8
220,000	127,000	14

(The minimum safe spans are to be observed with proper precautions. Furthermore, even after the current has been shut off, a high electrical potential may remain in the apparatus)

For lower voltages and different size nozzles, the American Insurance Association (Special Interest Bulletin No. 91) recommends certain procedures to minimize hazards when working in the vicinity of live electric circuits. For ordinary lighting wires, with voltage of 120 volts to ground, any type of nozzle can be held within a few inches of the charged wire without endangering the fireman. The distance at which a straight stream nozzle can be held without discomfort is 3 to 4 feet from a wire carrying 550 volts.

Below are the minimum distances between straight stream nozzles and electrical wire or equipment carrying voltages higher than 600 volts to avoid danger of fatal shock to firemen at the nozzle or on the hose line.

Straight Stream (Fresh Water)

Voltage	Minimum Safe Distance $1\frac{1}{8}$-inch Tip Nozzle Feet	Minimum Safe Distance $1\frac{1}{2}$-inch Tip Nozzle Feet
1,100	6	9
2,200	11	16
3,300	15	22
5,500	18	27
6,600	19	29
11,000	20	30
22,000	25	33
33,000	30	40

This table applies to solid fire streams of fresh water. Dirty water, salt water, or the discharge from a soda-acid extinguisher may have such high conductivity that no rule can be applied as to the safe distance for a solid stream.

The conductivity and consequently the safe distances from the energy source to be maintained by the nozzleman vary considerably with the mineral content of the water. Some fresh waters are better conductors of electricity than others. Well waters, because of the greater quantity of dissolved mineral salts, are, in general, better conductors of current than surface waters such as streams, lakes or other bodies.

Electrical resistivities of waters in one state (Indiana) were measured some years ago by C. S. Sprague and C. F. Harding of Purdue University. These tests of the resistivities of public water supplies showed results ranging from 710 to 5400 ohms per cubic centimeter, the lowest values being found in supplies from deep wells. These supplies generally had a resistivity ranging from 1000 to 2000 ohms per cubic centimeter, while that of lake and river water approximated 4000 ohms per cubic centimeter.

Even the season of the year is a factor which comes into play in the determination of water resistivity. In real dry weather water from rivers goes up very noticeably in conductivity. Filtered (pure) water is only slightly conductive because of its lack of minerals and salts in solution.

Individual resistivity

The resistance to ground through a person's body may be influenced by his location (whether on wet ground or not), his skin moisture, the amount of current his body can endure, the length of exposure to the current and other factors.

Research by Underwriters Laboratories, Inc. indicates that the maximum continuous (uninterrupted) current to which an individual may be safely subjected is 5 milliamperes and that there is a definite relationship between the length of exposure to electric shock and the effect of the shock. A momentary exposure has much less serious effects than a continuous one.

The susceptibility of different individuals to electric shock varies widely, and some are unusually sensitive. Many authorities consider that a current of 50 milliamperes passing through the human body is the approximate lower limit of current likely to cause fatalities. However, it must be borne in mind that some men wince or recoil from the slighest electric shock. This characteristic presents a hazard, particularly where men are operating in a precarious position. Even a mild sensation of electric shock, coupled with natural apprehension, can cause a fireman to let go of the nozzle, which action can then result in injuries.

In the Indiana (Purdue) tests it was assumed that the resistance of the human body is 5000 ohms. Based on this, it is estimated that at a frequency of 60 cycles per second, which is that usually supplied by utility companies, a current of 1 milliampere will just be felt. Currents of 4 to 10 milliamperes, depending on the individual, cause a sense of pain; a current of 30 milliamperes may cause unconsciousness; and a current of 100 milliamperes is dangerous and may be fatal. The statements involving currents up to 30 milliamperes are based upon tests using human subjects, with the duration of the current at least long enough for the subject to analyze and register the sensation.

From their observations, the Purdue experimentors established an upper safe limit of 3 milliamperes for the current which may flow down the fire stream (an ultraconservative limit). This assumption practically eliminates the possibility of any injury from the current itself, as it is well below the maximum current that can be endured by the average person. (Tests made by the National Bureau of Standards show that the resistance of the human body may be as low as 300 ohms under favorable conditions, such as encountered on naval vessels, because of the presence of water and perspiration.)

Based on the 3-milliampere limitation, the following table of safe distances from high potential lines was developed by the Purdue investigators.

Minimum Safe Distances (Feet) from High Potential Lines

Volts	500 Ohms	1000 Ohms	1500 Ohms	2000 Ohms	3000 Ohms	4000 Ohms	5000 Ohms	6000 Ohms
440	11	7	5.5	4.5	3	3	3	3
1,100	30	18	14	12	8.5	6.5	5.5	5
2,200	*	30	23	20	15	12	9	8
4,400	*	35	31	28	23	19	16	15
6,600	*	*	34	33	30	26	23	22
13,200	*	*	*	*	33	31	29	28
22,000	*	*	*	*	*	*	*	*

Nozzle pressure, 50 psi. Nozzle size, 1¼ inches

* At these resistivities, for the respective voltages, and for all voltages above 13,200 volts, the fire stream should not be allowed to strike the line.

The safe distance values as given in the preceding table include a generous factor of safety for the following reasons:

1. In the experimental work the currents measured were the maximum possible currents.
2. A current of 3 milliamperes should not injure any normal person.
3. With the nozzle handled by two men, the probability is that the current will be divided between the two men.

4. Fire streams should not be allowed to strike high-tension lines of phase voltages above 13,200 volts.

5. The safe distances, as given in the table, will limit the current flowing down the fire stream to a maximum value of 3 milliamperes.

6. It is suggested that firemen become familiar with the sensation produced by a current, say, of 3 milliamperes at 60 cycles. Familiarity with this sensation and the direct knowledge that no injury will result may very well minimize the fear of electricity. Also, such a procedure would indicate to those in charge any particular individuals whose reactions to such small currents might be excessive.

It is noted in this connection that salt water streams, foam streams and streams from soda and acid extinguishers should not be used on high-voltage electrical equipment, due to their good conductivity of electricity.

As was explained previously, fog provides a very poor conductor of electric current, and may be used safely on fires of any voltage commonly encountered, since the detached particles of water do not afford a continuous path for the electricity to flow back to the nozzle.

Hose resistance to ground

Where voltages and amperages are high and other conditions are in order, a limited amount of current can be conducted along normally dry ground, since there is always a certain moisture content in it. But this possibility is magnified when the ground is soaked and a wet hose line rests on it or in a puddle of water. Under these conditions the hose line becomes part of a path of current flow to the fireman holding the metal nozzle.

Conclusions

Any or all of the variables listed in the preceding paragraphs may become telling factors in any particular situation. Therefore, where it is necessary to apply water to electrical apparatus, the nozzleman should stay at a safe distance from the energy source, employ only high-velocity fog and beware of water flowing toward him. Rubber boots cannot be relied upon for protection, as they do not supply the necessary resistance to ground, since the rubber commonly contains carbon black which will permit the passage of electric current.

GAS EMERGENCIES

Gas-fired appliances were in existence almost 50 years before electricity was introduced in this country. Like electricity, gas required a manufacturing center which was also a distribution center from which

Pressure-reduction valves and associated piping are explained to fire fighters.

gas mains (pipes) fanned out through a grid system similar to the electrical cables. And similarly, the mains were tapped for customer service. Originally, the gas was manufactured from coal and coke and had a high carbon monoxide content when inhaled. It was, of course, highly flammable and explosive unless controlled through a burner which was used for cooking and heating.

Pressure within the street mains, except for feeder lines, was usually quite low, and measured in inches of water. However, some 25 years back, natural gas was discovered in tremendous quantities (mostly in the Southwest) and since then has been carried in big "pipelines" to all parts of the country.

This natural gas, while still as flammable and explosive as the old manufactured gas, contains practically no carbon monoxide. And its introduction has the side benefit of reducing death by "gas asphyxiation" to almost zero.

The pipelines created a tremendous potential hazard to the areas in which they pass through. And as they got older the hazard of leaks increased—corrosion, ground settling, etc. There have been incidents

Long-handled gas key is used to shut off a street cock on a service line.

around the country in which leaks from a pipeline, that were eventually ignited, brought death and destruction to large areas. Even the bigger, low-pressure mains have this potential. The most recent example occurred in New York City in 1967.

Natural gas pipeline fires and explosions present almost a hopeless problem to fire fighters particularly those in rural and exurban areas. The best they can do when a leak is discovered—and before ignition—is to evacuate the area and summon experienced help from the pipeline owners. Should a leak ignite—and this is usually a violent happening—the best they can do is to try to protect exposed property. However, pipeline incidents are happily few and far between. Most incidents involving escaping, or the potential for escaping, gas take place in a residential building; less frequently in a factory or commercial building. And such incidents are usually brought on by a fire unrelated to the gas supply or appliances.

It is sufficient, therefore, for a fire chief and his men to have a good idea of just how a gas company distributes from its plants for local consumption. Fire fighters are usually the first to arrive at a fire or gas emergency and it is important that they know how to eliminate or control hazards. This, of course, requires specialized training which is fre-

Gas meter should be the most familiar part of a gas supply system to a fire fighter.

quently not available at fire department training grounds. When not available it can often be gotten from the local gas company.

A good example of this cooperation can be found in Philadelphia, where all members of the fire department attend a safety course given by the Philadelphia Gas Works on a school site developed by the P.G.W. At this training field fire fighters are instructed in and given the opportunity to become familiar with gas piping installations, meters, regulators, shutoffs, etc.

The course stresses that a fire department should turn off the gas supply in a burning building, even though the fire may be in a part of the building remote from the meter.

The gas meter is, or should be, the most familiar part of a gas supply system to a fire fighter and the component of the system most quickly and frequently used at an emergency. It has a shutoff (in Philadelphia always on the left when facing the meter). When this shutoff lever is parallel to the supply pipe the gas is flowing. When turned at right angles to the supply line, the gas is off.

Usually, this is all that a fire department has to do at a fire to eliminate the gas hazard. But at times the meter may be inaccessible because of heat, smoke, or other reasons. When this happens, the instructor ex-

Vivid consequences of a natural gas fire and explosion in a San Francisco dwelling.

plains, the fire fighter should go outside the building and look for a small covered box, called a curb box, usually at the edge of the sidewalk. This box extends down until it meets a valve in the service main supplying the premises. When the cover of the box is removed, a "gas key" is inserted into the box and the valve is shut off. This key has a long shaft, a "tee" handle for turning and a socket fitted into one end that conforms to the shape of the valve stem.

Parallel meters

During the course the instructor shows all types of meters, including the parallel installation of meters. In this type of installation, the instructor warns, never close both inlet and outlet valves because this will trap gas inside a meter which, under fire conditions, can expand and rupture the meter.

The instructor emphasizes, "Shut off only one valve—the inlet valve. That is safe."

In sections of the city fed by medium pressure systems of 3 to 5 psi, fire fighters must be able to identify three things in a building: the meter, regulator valve and shutoff valve.

On industrial meters, the large valves have indicators that show the on or off positions. On this type installation, there is usually a bypass valve. This valve always has a padlock on it and is in the off position. Fire fighters are cautioned never to touch it.

In the outdoor demonstration, gas is released in high-pressure piping, 15 psi, and set on fire at a flange and at a split weld in an elevated pipe to familiarize fire fighters with the sight and sound.

Should fire or trouble arise in a district regulatory station, which is below ground, the advice is, "Keep people away, and keep fire department personnel out, pending arrival of the PGW crew. This type of installation can be recognized by a painted post with a 4-inch vent aboveground.

OIL BURNER FIRES

Safe and efficient operations at oil burner fires and emergencies are dependent on a fire fighter's understanding of oil burners. The various types of burners all vaporize or atomize oil before it enters the combustion chamber where it is mixed with air in predetermined proportions. Oil burners require approximately 2000 cubic feet of air per gallon of oil consumed. An insufficient air supply is one cause of dense, black smoke and soot; an excessive air supply can blow out the flame.

The oil spray entering a combustion chamber burns in suspension. Any part of the spray that impinges on the combustion chamber will cause a smoky fire. In time, carbon deposits may build up in the chamber and cause a burner failure.

It is essential that refractory material in the chamber be close to the flame and that the oil be burned by reflected heat. Insulating firebrick is a lightweight firebrick that will become cherry red 15 seconds after a burner starts. It is used in small installations or residential buildings.

Reflected heat, which increases combustion efficiency, is the heat that is reflected back into the combustion chamber to complete the combustion triangle and maintain fire after the ignition is turned off.

Exterior view of typical oil burner assembly.

Major causes of trouble

1. Defective pressure regulator on fuel unit. The pressure required to atomize oil in a high-pressure burner is 90 to 120 psi. If pressure falls below 90 psi, the oil will not be atomized properly.

2. Defective oil cutoff valve (afterdrip). Afterdrip is one of the most common faults. If fuel oil drips into the combustion chamber when the burner is off, excessive oil will be absorbed by the combustion chamber. At first it will cause a burner to be unusually noisy when it starts or shuts down. If this condition continues, a carbon deposit may eventually be built up. This type of defect is also responsible for fires in oil pits if the leak is serious. This defect can also cause a fire on the floor in front of heating units.

3. Leaking seal on oil pump shaft bearing at burner. Oil leaks from a defective oil seal and the air fan throws it into the combustion chamber. Oil may leak on the floor in front of the heating unit and may become ignited.

4. Dirty or damaged nozzle or rotary cup. This causes improper atomization and a carbon deposit forms in the combustion chamber.

5. Blockage in chimney or flue passages. This causes cellar or boiler room to fill with smoke.

6. Water in fuel oil or wrong grade of oil. Either condition can cause improper atomization.

7. Protective relay failure. This control is supposed to shut down a unit if a flame is not established in approximately 90 seconds or less when the firing rate exceeds 7½ gallons per hour. Delayed ignition is the most common cause for burner puffback, which causes boiler doors to blow open and the smoke pipe to fall down.

There are many causes for improper operation of an oil burner, but the ones mentioned are those most frequently encountered.

The white ghost

We will now consider the most dangerous condition encountered at oil burner fires and emergencies—the so-called white ghost.

The temperature of a combustion chamber can be as high as 2600°F, and if an oil burner goes into operation while the chamber is hot and the source of ignition fails, the oil may be ignited by the heat of the chamber.

If the chamber has not been preheated, the combustion chamber, flue and chimney can become filled with vaporized oil fumes that may find another source of ignition and cause a puffback. This condition occurs only when the protective relay does not shut the unit down first. If ignition does not take place, the only evidence of the flame failure will be a strong odor of fuel oil in the area.

If delayed ignition occurs, it can violently blow the door off the furnace or boiler, knock down the smoke stack and in extreme instances cause windows and walls in buildings to be blown out.

In some instances where there is delayed ignition, the vapor can form quickly and cause a minor puffback, which will merely blow open the furnace doors.

While making a diagnosis, an experienced oil burner repairman will always have the boiler or furnace fire door open and will crouch below the door when starting the burner in case there is a short delay in ignition lightoff. Crouching below the fire door is a safety measure which will protect the person in front of the unit in case flue doors should blow open or fire should come out of the fire door.

Opening the fire door will relieve any excessive pressure in a unit if

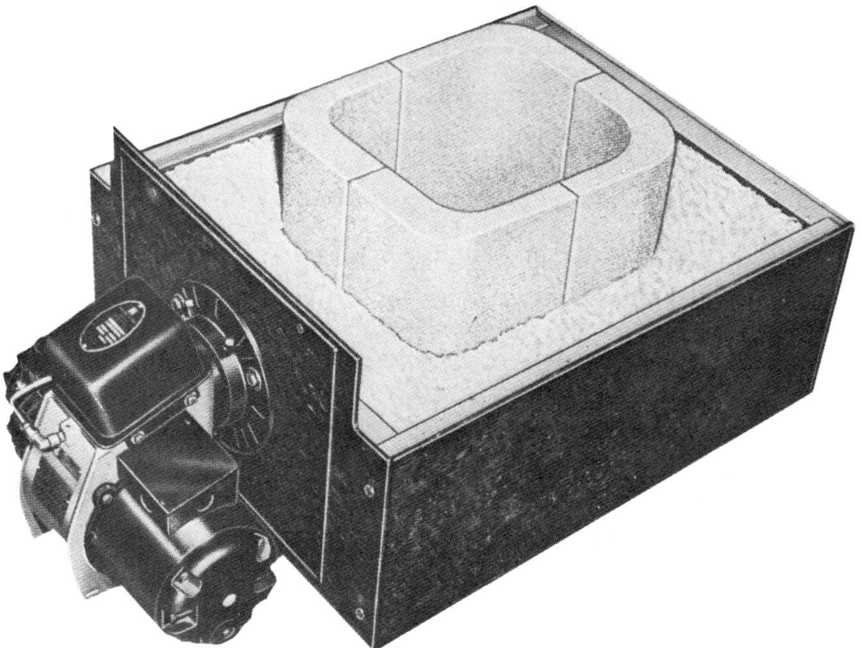

Boiler base with high pressure gun-type oil burner and prefabricated combustion chamber surrounded by insulation.

the burner does not ignite properly. Delayed ignition is responsible for many injuries because of the carelessness of experienced repairmen or do-it-yourselfers.

Vaporized oil looks like condensed steam (a regular steam leak). It is pure white but tastes and smells like fuel oil. It is sometimes irritable to the eyes.

When this condition is encountered, it should be handled as a gas leak by quickly shutting off the burner, venting the area and eliminating any possible source of ignition.

Limit men in room

As few men as possible should enter the oil burner area with a hand line and fog nozzle set for a wide pattern. This will serve two purposes: (1) it will protect the men if the vaporized oil ignites and (2) it will help ventilate the area. Before entering the room the remote control switch should be turned off and/or the oil supply valve shut off as quickly as possible.

The remote control switch is usually installed at the top of the stairs leading to the cellar. If not, it should be placed outside the burner room entrance and as close to the entrance as practical. When an outside location is impractical, the switch may be located immediately inside the boiler room. If the remote control switch and/or the oil supply valve must be shut off inside the boiler room, it should be done under the protection of a fog nozzle.

The locations of remote control switches are usually specified in state and local oil burner, fire safety or building codes.

The boiler room should be vented as soon as possible, preferably in a direction remote from where the fog line is being advanced so that oil vapor will be forced out of the area.

It must be remembered, however, that it is not always the white ghost which causes doors to be blown off a unit. Some other causes are as follows:

1. **Excessive oil in the combustion chamber.** This results in severe pulsation which causes doors to open. The area becomes filled with thick black smoke, but the fire is usually contained in the combustion chamber. If a fire continues to burn after the remote control is turned off, there is excess oil in the combustion chamber.
2. **Delayed ignition.**
3. **Defective ignition system**

Fire department operations

When there is excessive oil in a combustion chamber, turn off the remote control switch, turn off the oil valve at the tank and/or burner, ventilate the area, replace the smoke pipe if it was dislodged, and do not close the fire door if it is open.

If water is needlessly applied to a combustion chamber, it can cause fire to spread outside the boiler area.

No attempt should be made to put out a fire in the combustion chamber unless structural parts or contents of the building are exposed to flame. Remember that the combustion chamber is made to withstand extremely high temperatures. The chamber fire will rapidly diminish in size and ultimately go out once the remote control switch is turned off and/or the oil shutoff valve is closed.

If for any reason the fire has to be extinguished in the combustion chamber, it is better to use a fog stream to cool the chamber down below the ignition temperature of the fuel oil. If the chamber is hot and the fog stream is applied only long enough to extinguish the fire, the fumes in the chamber will reignite with explosive violence as soon as the nozzle is shut down, causing fire to blow out of the fire door and severely burn

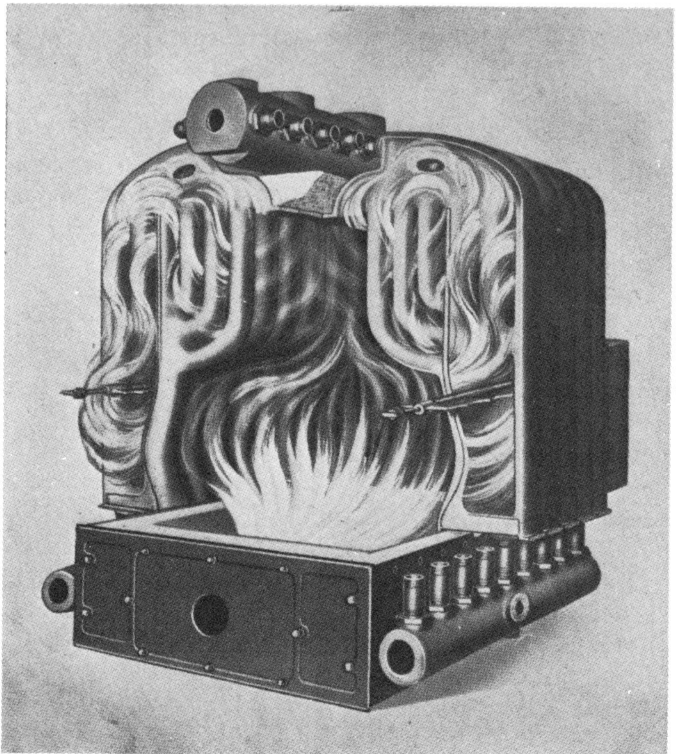

Cutaway of interior showing flue passages and tubes.

anyone standing in front of the unit. The flue doors might also be blown open.

You should keep in mind that if water is applied to a red-hot chamber, it can cause a steam explosion, which may blow firebrick out of the heating unit and injure anyone standing in front of it.

In most instances where water is used in a combustion chamber, the chamber will have to be rebuilt. In those few cases where the chamber is not badly damaged, the chamber must be subjected to a slow drying process. If the burner is ignited before the chamber walls are completely dry, there is a possibility of the chamber being blown apart by the remaining moisture expanding to steam. Replacing a combustion chamber can be very costly, especially in large units.

If the officer in command is concerned about oil seeping out of the chamber onto the floor or into the pit, he can have a thick blanket of foam applied to the floor around the chamber or in the oil pit. Foam should be applied to the floor or pit if there is oil on the floor or in the pit.

If foam is put into the pit of a large horizontal rotary burner, it will enter the combustion chamber through the secondary air door. This type burner is found in larger apartment houses and commercial and industrial buildings.

All large burners are supplied with both primary and secondary air so that the large amounts of residual (heavy) oil has sufficient air to assure proper combustion. Primary air is not adequate.

Primary and secondary air

Sometimes bricks from the front of the wall beneath the burner are removed. Or an open checkerboard design is constructed in the chamber floor near the front of the boiler and a swinging door is installed in this space to regulate the amount of secondary air needed. With some industrial burners, a chain is attached and regulated by a steam pressure regulator.

If foam enters the secondary air door, no harm will be done even if the chamber is extremely hot. The fumes that might come through the foam blanket will be ignited by the hot walls of the chamber or the fire on the walls.

Foam is not recommended for extinguishing a fire in a hot chamber due to its poor cooling effect. A fog nozzle is much more effective.

If foam is applied to a hot chamber with excess oil burning in it and the foam is shut down as soon as the fire is extinguished, the oil may ignite and flash out the fire door.

Gas pilot

In addition to shutting off the remote control switch and closing the oil valves, turn off the gas pilot if there is one. This type of ignition is found in larger apartment houses and commercial and industrial buildings.

The gas pipe and pilot light are usually to the left of a horizontal rotary oil burner. The gas shutoff valve is similar to the gas cock at a meter or range.

Closing the gas cock is especially important when an oil burner has been exposed to direct fire. Some of the electric (magnetic) gas control valves are made of plastic and they may be cracked or damaged by the heat of the fire. Occasionally the pilot on the burner is connected to the gas pipe with a piece of tubing. If exposed to fire, this tubing may melt, creating an explosive atmosphere—especially if the gas flame is extinguished when a foam or fog nozzle is used to extinguish an oil fire in front of the unit.

When operating a fog or foam nozzle on a fire in front of a boiler, look to the left of the burner for a blue flame. The blue gas flame can be easily distinguished from the orange flame of the fuel oil. It is better to shut off the gas supply than extinguish it. If the gas cock cannot be quickly located or the unit cannot be approached because of the heat, the gas should be shut off at the meter.

Burner pulsation

Never close a fire door on a unit if it is found open upon arrival due to a malfunction of the burner and fire is still burning in the chamber. Closing the door can cause severe pulsation, which can blow flue and fire doors open or dislodge the smoke pipe. If a unit is pulsating, it can be relieved by opening the fire door slightly. Use a 6-foot pike pole to open the fire door while standing off to the side of the unit on the hinge side of the door to avoid the possibility of being hit by flame.

Some heating units have 1 to 2-inch-diameter peepholes instead of fire doors. They might have a fire door bolted or welded in place with a peephole. Never direct water or foam into this opening if there is fire in the chamber. There is no way for the pressure created to be relieved other than by the blowing apart of the unit or the smoke pipe.

When closing oil and gas valves at the burner while there is fire in the chamber, crouch in front of the unit, keeping below the fire door opening in case the fire or flue doors should blow open. If fire comes out, it will go up toward the ceiling. This is an important safety measure.

Safety precautions

Here are some other safety rules:

Always stay away from the front of a boiler whenever possible.

Stay out of a boiler room if you are not needed there.

Do not crowd the boiler room doorway.

Do not direct a fog or foam line into a fire door unless is is absolutely necessary.

When visibility is poor, keep operating a foam line low around the front of a unit to avoid extinguishing a possible gas leak on burners equipped with gas pilots.

If soot is burning in flue passages and smoke pipe and the boiler is excessively hot, this is generally a sign that there is no water in the boiler. No attempt should be made to add water to a boiler and a hose line should never be used to cool the boiler. Shut off the water supply to the boiler and let it cool by itself.

Also, remember that soot burning in a smoke pipe and flue passages can also be caused by a dirty heating unit.

The electric switch is the type of remote control fire fighters almost always encounter. But the control can be a hand-operated shutoff valve on an oil line in some municipalities as long as it is labeled. This type of remote control might possibly be found in a large industrial installation.

Turning the remote control off does not always stop the oil supply to the burner. It shuts off the electric motor and oil pump, and in some cases it shuts off the electrically operated magnetic valve. If the magnetic valve is defective, or if the oil pump seal or the oil line is leaking, we may still have an oil leak at the burner or elsewhere.

The fire department should always shut off the oil valve at the burner or tank when a unit is on fire or defective. If the valve does not shut off the oil supply because the shutoff valve is defective or the oil line is leaking, a copper tubing oil line can be flattened with the back of a flat ax. This will stop the oil flow. Most oil lines in private dwellings and smaller installations are copper tubing.

In conclusion, we suggest that every officer and fire fighter familiarize himself with oil burners so that they can recognize the different types of installations.

CHAPTER TWELVE

Respiratory protection

Annual studies conducted by the International Association of Fire Fighters indicate that firemen have the highest death and injury rates of any occupation. More significantly, the study for one year showed that of 233 fire service deaths, 222 (95 percent) were from heart and lung related diseases. And further, of 463 fire fighters who left the service because of occupational diseases, 390 (84 percent) had heart and lung related diseases.

Should anyone question these statistics, there is a report "Chronic Effect of Fire Fighting on Pulmonary Function," published by Dr. J. M. Peters of the Harvard Medical School after a three-year study of Boston fire fighters. Peters' conclusion was that the lungs of these men were aging much faster than those of the general population.

These "old lungs" are unquestionably attributable to the repeated exposure to toxic gases produced at fires. The most treacherous (and ever-present) is carbon monoxide. In what began as an experiment, and is now an ongoing program, the Milwaukee Fire Department analyzes the breath of every fire fighter exposed to smoke on the fireground for evidences of carbon monoxide.

The heart of the program is an Ecolyzer, a 9-pound portable instrument developed for air pollution monitoring, whose operating principle is based on the electrochemical oxidation of CO. It proved ideal for measuring CO levels in breath. From the amount of blood, COHb (carboxyhemoglobin) could be estimated similarly to the use of breath alcohol measurements to detect intoxicated drivers.

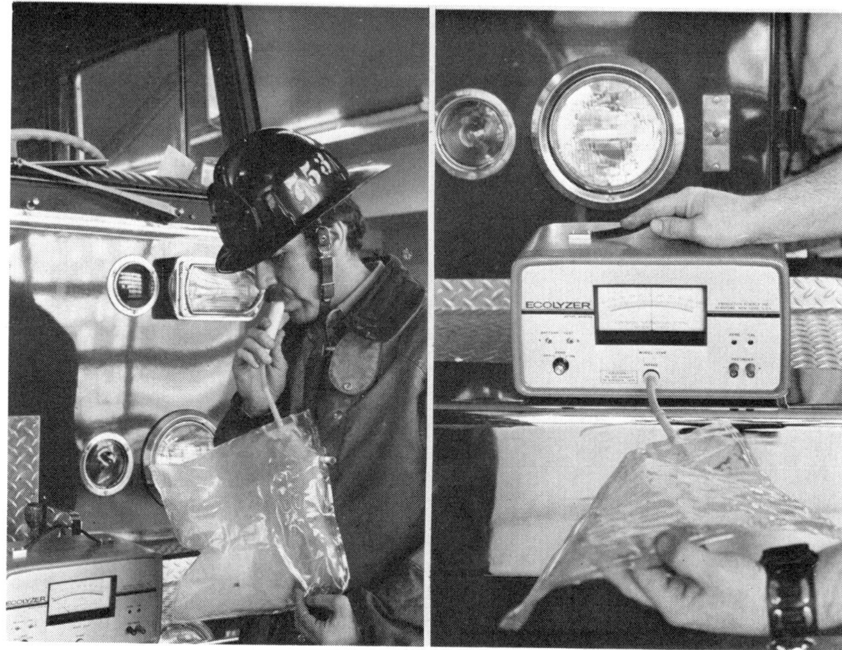

Milwaukee Fire Department health surveillance program for fire fighters includes breath analysis shown here. Breath sample is collected in plastic bag and then fed into "Ecolyzer" which indicates amount of carbon monoxide in blood.

To collect the breath samples, the fire fighters are instructed to hold their breath for 20 seconds, then discard the first portion of their expired breath, and collect the last portion in a plastic Saran bag. The bagged breath is then immediately analyzed in the Ecolyzer.

The amount of CO in the breath, which is directly related to the amount of COHb in blood, is read directly from the dial of the Ecolyzer.

The amount of COHb detected determines the course of action. Fire fighters who have no symptoms of illness but have an estimated COHb level between 11 and 12 percent are given oxygen by face mask to hasten the elimination of CO and lessen the stress on their hearts. If no symptoms develop, the oxygen is discontinued when the estimated COHb is acceptable, according to an established formula. The fireman is then returned to active service. Fire fighters with unacceptable COHb levels are immediately given oxygen by face mask and referred to a physician.

The accuracy with which the blood COHb could be estimated was determined by actually obtaining blood samples for COHb analysis at the time breath samples were obtained for CO analysis. The Ecolyzer breath method proved extremely good and had an error of only 1 percent COHb. The developer of this screening technique was Dr. Richard Stewart of the department of environmental medicines, Medical College of Wisconsin.

How the program began

During the spring of 1975, all MFD members were tested on this equipment, company by company, on a voluntary basis. Most of the work was supervised by Stewart's son Scot, a college student. As each group was assembled, he explained the pilot program briefly, assured the men the medical data would remain confidential and had each man fill out an initial screening questionnaire. This covered smoking habits, some past medical history, any breathing problems, etc., with space at the bottom for entry of the screening results.

For the 1st and 2nd Battalions only, this "base data" (including copies of EKG strips) was then filed alphabetically in a binder carried on Squad 1. The squadmen would then be able to recheck any man in those two battalions in the field and compare the results with the original data. Although one set of portable equipment couldn't cover the entire city, men from other districts could still be tested when on duty at fires in Squad 1's response area.

Gases and the human body

Hundreds of firemen died through the years primarily because of a lack of adequate respiratory protective equipment. They also died because of ignorance of the limitations of breathing equipment when provided and because of their ignorance of the effects of gases on the human body. The man in charge of a fire department should therefore see to it that his men are adequately equipped with masks and well trained in their use and limitations. They should also have a good knowledge of the biological processes that make a mask necessary.

Normal air consists of 21 percent oxygen and a remainder of 79 percent that is mostly nitrogen and traces of rare gases. Without oxygen there can be no life. This wonderful substance is drawn into the lungs and then distributed to all the cells in the body. Any interference with this process, if prolonged, can result in a condition called asphyxia (lack of oxygen or excess of carbon dioxide in the body) and eventually death. Human life ceases when the oxygen in the air drops below 16 percent.

Asphyxiation can be brought on by an inert gas, otherwise harmless, that displaces the air in the atmosphere or dilutes the oxygen to a point

Many fire departments have their own compressor and purifying system tied into a cascade system located in a fire station.

where there is not enough to support life. Carbon monoxide, probably the greatest killer of firemen, is more readily taken in by the oxygen-carrying agents of the blood than oxygen itself. It causes human tissue to die, particularly the brain cells. This is known as anoxia, another form of asphyxia.

The fumes from corrosive acids and irritant gases, such as ammonia, attack the delicate membranes of throat and airways, causing swelling

Breathing apparatus technician at Maryland Fire and Rescue Institute draws monthly air sample for analysis by independent testing lab.

or edema that prevents air from reaching the lungs. Finally, there are gases that paralyze the nerves that control breathing. The end result with all such gases is oxygen starvation that brings on asphyxia and eventually death.

Carbon dioxide and carbon monoxide are the two most common gases met at fires. Carbon monoxide (CO) is a colorless and odorless gas that is produced by the incomplete oxidation of ordinary combustible ma-

Covered facepiece takes the place of a smoke-filled atmosphere in training.

terial such as wood, furniture, textiles and paper. Carbon dioxide is also odorless and colorless but it is produced by complete oxidation of carbon. It is not poisonous but can deplete the oxygen in air to a point where asphyxia results. In concentrations up to 10 percent, this gas stimulates breathing and if mixed with toxic gases can increase the effects of such gases by increasing the volume taken into the lungs per unit of time. Also, carbon dioxide under ordinary conditions is heavier than air and can collect in pockets that will exclude all air and, hence, oxygen.

Carbon monoxide is met mainly in those fires where sufficient air cannot reach the burning material—in cellars and basements or in any closed-up building or part of a building, where fire has burned for a considerable time before discovery. Fires in piled materials, rugs, rags, newsprint, and fires in oils or oiled substances are also great producers of carbon monoxide. Fire conditions conducive to the liberation of great quantities of CO often give off heavy volumes of black smoke, which warn that masks are a must. However, charcoal and manufactured gas, when burning in an atmosphere deficient in oxygen, can produce large amounts of carbon monoxide with little smoke.

Other gases produced by a fire depend upon the material involved. Burning rubber can release carbon dioxide, carbon monoxide, hydrocarbons, hydrogen sulfide and sulfur dioxide. Woolen fabric, in addition to the ever-present CO, gives off hydrogen sulfide, hydrocyanic acid and ammonia gas in varying amounts. Silks release prussic acid. And finally, there is the giant plastics industry turning out materials that were unknown 30 years ago and which under fire conditions can produce almost anything and everything. Notable among these materials is the polyvinyl chloride plastic that gives off hydrogen chloride and other toxic gases. These gases affect not only the fire fighter's lungs, but his heart as well.

Masks needed

In view of the gases that can be produced by even the ordinary dwelling fire, it is mandatory that a fire department provide its members with complete respiratory protection. Ideally, every man responding to a fire should have a mask available. But failing this, there should be a supply for at least 50 percent of them. Even in the poorest departments there should be two masks—always two since in no other activity is the "buddy system" so important.

However, the mere possession of masks does not guarantee the health or efficient performance of a fire fighter. A man untrained in the use and limitations of a given type of breathing apparatus is probably less useful than a man without one. And more dangerous to himself and others!

According to Dr. Edward P. Radford of the Johns Hopkins University School of Hygiene and Public Health:

"Blood samples taken from Baltimore City fire fighters, while still on the fireground, indicated that the amount of carbon monoxide in the blood—carboxyhemoglobin—was not much different for those who wore breathing apparatus *intermittently* and those who did not wear breathing apparatus at all.

"However," he said, "the carboxyhemoglobin was substantially less for men who wore breathing apparatus *continuously* at a fire."

This indicated to Redford that fire fighters may be unaware of the presence of carbon monoxide after knocking down a fire. And that they still may be seriously exposed to this gas.

Training in the use of masks, therefore, should be a continuing process beginning the day a man enters the department and ending only when he retires. It is not something the fire fighter should be taught for a few days and then dropped. He should put it on and take it off, over and over again, until the act of donning a mask becomes as automatic and natural as putting on an overcoat. Practice with the mask should include handling hose lines, climbing ladders, chopping, and any other simulated

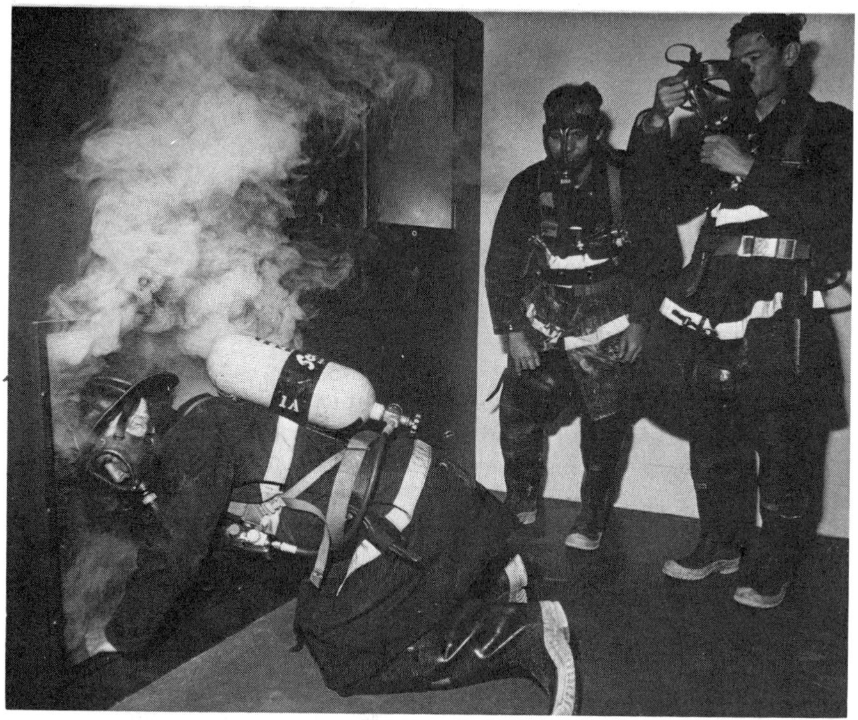

Breathing apparatus training at the Toronto Fire Department academy. Fireman shown entering the start of a smoke chamber maze.

rescue or fire condition. Only in this way will men acquire the skill and confidence needed for mask operations.

Such training calls for the mask to be properly donned, facepiece snugly adjusted, and hose connected to the demand valve. Dry runs, in which the hose is not connected, certainly saves the cost of a refilled tank, but it is not training. Understandably, the man in the mask should not be dressed in a tee shirt and work pants, but in full fire fighting clothing, including the helmet, turnout coat, and boots he will wear at an alarm.

A fire building, such as found in the more elaborate training grounds, provides the best training in masks. Here two—always two or more—trainees enter a smoke-filled room or rooms and stretch a line to the seat of the fire, find and shut off a gas meter, or rescue a dummy concealed by an instructor.

For those departments not blessed with a drill ground, the same effect can be simulated by covering the lenses of the facepiece with an opaque material and turning the trainee loose in any building.

In addition to training in its use, a fire fighter should have a good knowledge of the construction of his mask and how to maintain it. The company officer, who is ultimately responsible for the care of masks, should make a record card for each mask. Information on this card should include the date or receipt, manufacturer's name, weekly inspections, time in use at fires, time in use at drills, and pressure readings on air cylinders if so equipped. All entries, of course, should have a notation on the overall condition of the mask assembly, including the carrying case, plus any repairs or other maintenance performed.

A wet rag placed over mouth and nose has persisted so long in man's folklore that it was probably his first attempt at protecting himself from the effects of smoke and heat. But it was not until 1825, when the Aldini apparatus was introduced, that a scientific attempt was made to protect fire fighters from smoke and heat. The apparatus consisted of a thick mask of asbestos surrounded by woven iron wire and slits for eyes, nose and mouth. The cooling effect of the iron mesh gave some protection from heat, but the mask gave little or no protection from gas and smoke.

The hundred years that followed produced many versions of supplied air respirators, filter masks and self-contained equipment. Air line respirators, or breathing tubes, received the greatest amount of attention because of their obvious simplicity and ease of manufacture. Unhappily, they were limited for fire fighting to the length of the trailing hose and they created a heavy drag on the pulling power of a man's lungs.

Air pumps and reinforced hose were introduced in the late 1800s but were never well received in the fire service. With the introduction of the elevating platform, supplied-air respirators have made a comeback. Air is piped from high-pressure cylinders to outlets on the platform. Men working on the platform are assured an adequate supply of clean air simply by plugging in their facepiece hose to the outlets.

Crude filter masks were employed in the fire service as early as the 1870s, but most were discarded almost as soon as they were invented. Not until 1920, when the chemical catalyst Hopcalite was developed, did a filter mask, if properly maintained and used, offer respiratory protection to fire fighters. But this, too, was outlawed for fire fighter use in 1971.

Since the wearer could carry his own air, independent of outside sources, self-contained breathing apparatus always appealed to inventors. The first attempt at such an apparatus produced a large goatskin bag filled with air from a bellows and strapped to the wearer's back. Two tubes connected to a mouthpiece were supposed to cycle the air, which was under considerable pressure. Such an unwieldly apparatus was quickly discarded by the firemen called upon to use it.

The first practical self-contained apparatus appeared in the 1880s. These were oxygen-cylinder rebreathing devices developed in England and Germany and were used mainly for mine rescues. The first American self-contained appratus was brought out in 1918 by W. E. Gibbs. It was the first to use a completely lung-governed principle of operation, but the cost was high and beyond the reach of most fire departments. This mine rescue apparatus was also relatively complicated and heavy, and consequently not well suited for fire fighting.

The self-contained breathing apparatus most popular in the fire service today is the demand-type, which uses compressed air and a demand regulator to supply air at the required rate to a facepiece. Such apparatus was an offshoot of the oxygen masks developed for high-altitude flying in World War II.

Self-contained demand-type apparatus

The self-contained demand mask has proven to be the breathing protection most preferred by firemen. It consists of a compressed air cylinder connected to a facepiece by a hose which incorporates a regulator. The regulator consists of a pressure reducer that lowers the pressure of air coming from the cylinder (generally 2000 to 2300 psi when filled), a demand valve that provides air at normal pressure as the user's lungs "demand" it, and a bypass valve that bypasses the other two if either fails. An exhalation valve in the facepiece permits used air to be exhausted to the atmosphere.

Every mask assembly contains two gages—one connected to the cylinder, and the other to the demand regulator. Both give the pressure in the cylinder. Newer models of the self-contained demand masks have been equipped with speaking diaphragms and amplifiers that permit conversation and a warning device connected to the cylinder that either buzzes, whistles or rings to indicate that the pressure is getting low or provides a momentary restriction of air flow for the same indication. These devices operate at a preset pressure reading which provides the wearer with enough air to reach safety. Cylinders come in various sizes, but the one rated at 30 minutes has become the standard in the fire service. The 30-minute rating, however, does not mean that the user would get 30 minutes of use under fire conditions.

Except for minor refinements, the standard self-contained demand mask looks much the same as the prototype developed some 30 years ago,

Some departments have installed a cascade system in vans that can service several companies in quarters and at fires.

and it weighs the same. However, the National Aeronautics and Space Administration recently developed a prototype self-contained breathing apparatus that weighs less than comparable units now in use and is designed to last 30 minutes under fireground working conditions. This NASA mask is, at the time of this writing, being field-tested in several fire departments around the country. One of these departments, New York, describes the mask as follows:

"It is a self-contained (compressed air), open-circuit, demand-type breathing apparatus. The backplate is made of solid plastic and is designed to accommodate either a 40 or 60-cubic-foot cylinder.

"The cylinders are constructed of an aluminum liner and are fully overwrapped with resin-impregnated fiber glass, providing a lighter and stronger cylinder than that used on our present masks. The cylinders are charged to 4000 psi. (see picture page 284)

"Using the 40-cubic-foot cylinder, the mask weighs 20 pounds and provides at least 20 minutes of operating time. With the 60-cubic-foot cylinder, the masks weighs 26 pounds and provides at least 30 minutes of operating time. The backplate and harness assembly is unique in that most of the weight is carried on the hips instead of the shoulders, making it less fatiguing to the wearer. This is accomplished by employing a curved backplate and a wide waist belt.

"This new mask is not as bulky as our present model because it uses a smaller cylinder, and one of the design features has moved the regulator which was formerly worn on the chest. The pressure reducer assembly, which reduces the high cylinder pressure, is mounted on the backplate and supplies a lightweight demand regulator now attached to the bub-

Demands of the New York Fire Department calls for extra large cascade system using extra large tanks.

ble-type facepiece. As compared to our present mask, the demand regulator on the NASA mask can provide a much higher flow of air to the wearer with less breathing resistance."

Novel demand mask

A new type of demand mask has been introduced fairly recently that uses for its air supply an air module consisting of coiled stainless steel tubing that contains air pressurized to 5500 psi that is controlled by a flow regulation unit.

It comes equipped with the conventional mask, or facepiece, and hose to carry the air from the supply. Available as optional equipment are two additional facepieces:

One is designed around a type of crash helmet that can be used with a proximity suit. Made of fiber glass, it is built to withstand temperatures up to 1500°F for several minutes.

The other facepiece is made of a clear polyurethane material in the shape of a hood that seals around the user's neck. This latter facepiece starts to fail at relatively low temperatures and other than as an escape mask (which the Navy uses them for) they offer little protection to the structural fire fighter.

Refilling the air module is accomplished by a booster changing station that is attached to a cascade system.

Filling the cylinders

The introduction of the demand mask also introduced the problem of refilling. The standard 40-cubic-foot cylinder was rated for 30 minutes duration of use—but under ideal conditions. Body weight, respiratory rate and a number of other factors varied from man to man to a degree that no average use duration could be arrived at. The answer to this problem was to have more than enough reserve cylinders on hand at all times. Refilling, then, became a maintenance job.

In the beginning, most fire departments had to send their bottles out to local concerns to get this job done. Most still do it today. But about 20 years ago the "cascade" system for refilling the "bottles" was introduced and almost immediately adopted by the larger fire departments.

In the cascade system the cylinders for the demand mask are filled from a manifold connected to a bank of larger cylinders, usually four or five, with a capacity of 300 or more cubic feet. These large cylinders, like the small ones, can be refilled by an outside supplier. But many fire departments have their own compressor tied into a cascade system and are therefore completely self-sufficient. The cascade systems are usually stationary installations located in a fire station. But several departments have installed such a system in vans that can service several companies in a department and, more importantly, respond and service cylinders at fires where mask use is high.

Self-generating oxygen breathing equipment

The self-generating equipment consists of a facepiece, breathing bag and a canister that generates oxygen. The reaction of the moisture in the wearer's breath with the chemical contained in the canister generates the oxygen. Standard canisters are rated for up to 60 minutes, but no matter how briefly used, the canister must be discarded once its seal has been opened. Such disposal must be carefully accomplished by puncturing the canister and placing it in a pail of water. This action causes a vigorous bubbling of the water until the materials in the canister are neutralized. Only then can it finally be disposed of. Care should be exercised not to expose the canister to oil until it is completely inerted, as an explosion might occur. The caustic solution formed during the bubbling period can cause burns and should be carefully handled.

The introduction of the self-contained breathing equipment practically phased out the hose mask in the fire service. However, the intro-

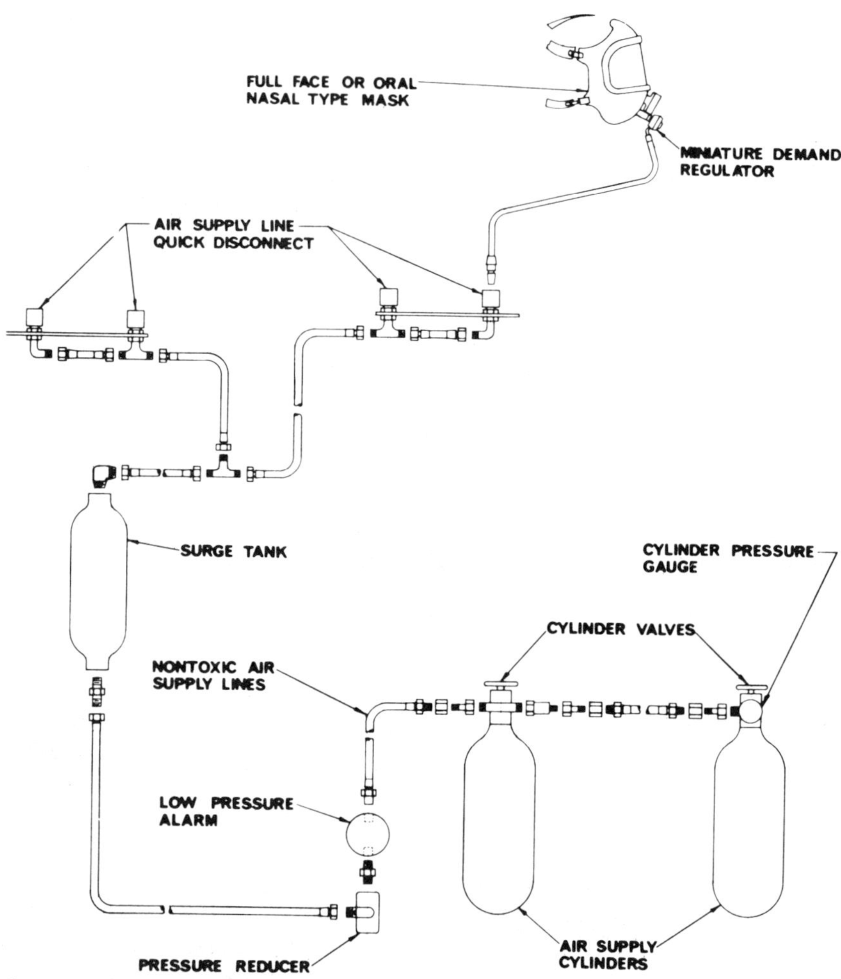

Schematic for supplied-air respirator for elevating platforms. Heavy supply cylinders are placed on bed of truck. Tubing is threaded through booms.

duction of the aerial platform has reintroduced the air-hose mask—but in a more sophisticated form. The platform, with its ability to maneuver in, around and over a fire area, posed a problem of clean air supply for fire fighters working in the basket. Lowering the boom to replenish air cylinders reduced fire fighting efficiency. On the other hand, the installation of large-capacity tanks in the basket posed a critical weight problem.

The problem was solved by installing one or two 220-cubic-foot cylinders mounted on the turntable or the lower boom structure. In a typical installation, a pressure reducer was installed on the supply side of the cylinders and air reduced to 100 psi was routed up the boom structure through flexible hose to a storage or surge tank. In the illustration shown, two air lines continue up from the surge tank, each of which terminates in outlets fitted with two quick-connect couplings on the side of the basket. Two are used for normal operations and two for reserve or remote supply. Mask facepieces are fitted with a miniature demand regulator and a length of air hose which plugs into the couplings.

Since the ability to operate off the ladder and into a building is often necessary—particularly in rescue work—an air hose measuring 75 to 100 feet is provided. However, a man so operating should carry a small emergency hip cylinder to plug into, should the hose be pinched or cut.

All such equipment should be equipped with safety check valves, pressure relief valves and pressure reducers. These will vary in design among manufacturers of both the breathing equipment and aerial platforms.

Scuba diving

In recent years, self-contained underwater breathing apparatus which gives a diver complete independence of a surface air supply, has been adopted by an increasing number of fire departments. It was used first for search and rescue in drownings, later by departments with fireboats for propeller and hull inspection and equipment recovery. Finally, scuba was recognized as a tool for fire fighting that enabled firemen to float hose and nozzle in and around previously inaccessible locations under piers and other waterfront installations. This latter operation is not in a true sense diving since the fire fighter remains on or just below the surface.

There are two general types of scuba equipment—the closed-circuit and the open-circuit systems. The closed-circuit type utilizes oxygen as a rebreather. It is used only in military operations and then only by highly trained personnel. In open-circuit scuba, which is the type used by fire fighters, ordinary air is breathed. The system is called open-circuit because exhaled air is exhausted to the water and not recirculated as in the closed type.

Open-circuit scuba is constructed generally of the following basic components: cylinders, air reserve mechanism, check valves, breathing tubes, mask or mouthpiece or both, and an exhaust valve.

The cylinders contain compressed air and are constructed of galvan-

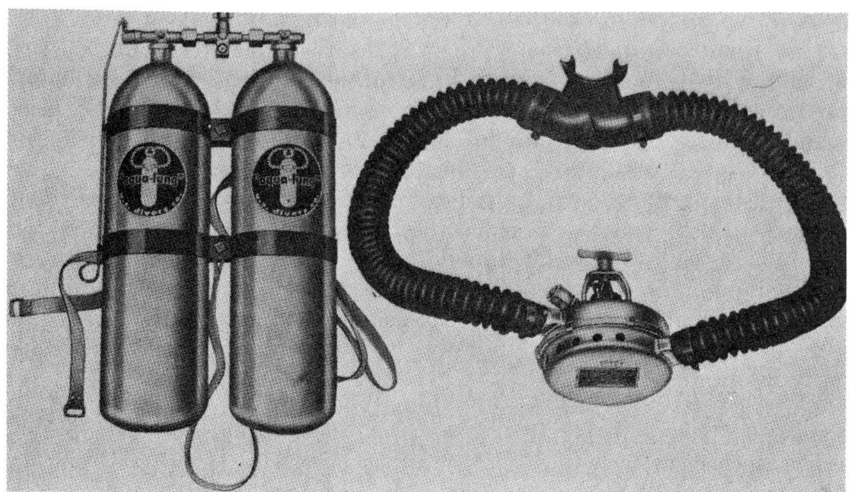

Open-circuit scuba system consists of cylinders, air reserve mechanism, check valves, breathing tubes, mask (not shown) or mouthpiece and exhaust valve.

ized steel and sometimes aluminum. They are constructed to withstand high pressure—usually 3000 psi. Steel cylinders must be inspected and stamped in accordance with Interstate Commerce Commission rulings. The capacity of cylinders varies with use. They are usually worn on the back and fastened to the diver by a harness which has a quick release for emergency ditching. Safety practices for the handling, storage and use of scuba cylinders are the same as for all other high-compression cylinders. It must be remembered that a broken valve can convert a cylinder into a jet-propelled missile or an exploding bomb.

Open-circuit scuba must have an air-reserve mechanism to warn the diver when his air supply is critically low. This is accomplished usually by an air-reserve valve which permits normal supply of air to the regulator until the cylinder pressure drops to about 500 psi. Then the valve restricts the volume of air, which causes increased breathing resistance. The diver then opens the air-reserve mechanism which restores the full flow of air and permits him to resurface.

The demand regulator is the heart of any open-circuit scuba. The first satisfactory one was patented in 1866 by Benoist Rouquarol of France. But because of a lack of a suitable supply of high-compression air, this regulator was developed into a surface-supplied apparatus. Another open-circuit scuba was introduced by a French naval officer in 1925 that had the advantage of using compressed air. This unit also proved unsatisfactory since the supply of air was regulated manually by the diver.

Then, in 1943, Commander Cousteau, another French naval officer, introduced the Cousteau-Gagnan Aqua Lung. This apparatus also used compressed air, but the air was supplied to the diver through a demand regulator that adjusted the pressure automatically and supplied air as needed. Since then, several American manufacturers have developed their own equipment.

Regulators vary somewhat, but basically the demand regulator incorporates two chambers separated by an air and watertight diaphragm, one side of which is exposed to the water. The other side is an air chamber containing a lever and valve mechanism connected to an air supply. An inhalation hose with a mouthpiece leads from this chamber and supplies air to the diver. Air pressure inside the chamber is always exactly equal to the water pressure on the opposite side of the diaphragm. This pressure equalizes automatically—no matter what the depth.

Breathing tubes in open-circuit scuba are made of nonkinking corrugated or bellows-type rubber or neoprene hose. Mask pieces may use a full face mask or a mouthpiece, or a combination of both, to supply air to the diver. Full masks generally incorporate the regulator. Mouthpieces and mouthpiece-mask combinations are usually used with breathing tubes and cylinder-mounted demand regulators.

An open-circuit scuba has at least one check valve—the exhaust valve that allows exhaled air to leave the system. There may also be an inhalation check valve that prevents exhaled air from entering the inhalation tube and which also prevents water from entering the demand regulator. An exhalation check valve is another that is not necessary for the scuba operation, but it prevents water in the exhalation tube from flooding the mouthpiece.

The arrangement of the components varies considerably among manufacturers, from whom a more detailed description can be had. As with masks, scuba calls for thorough training in the use and care of equipment.

STATION
89
90

CHAPTER THIRTEEN

Engine company operations

For the purposes of this chapter an engine company is a unit consisting of five men, one an officer, a pumper usually of 1000-gpm capacity that carries sufficient hose, nozzles and fittings to properly utilize available water resources to extinguish a fire. This engine company can be expected to stretch a 2½-inch line for some distance and advance it into and if necessary, up the stairs of a building. Within reason, they can handle simultaneous operations such as laying a hand line while attaching a second line to a siamese connection.

Understandably, if these five men had enough time they could stretch other hand lines and supply a deluge gun or two. But the first lines on a fire are the ones that usually make for a quick knockdown. Attack must be mounted quickly or else. And there is only so much that an engine company can do within the short time frame permitted by an expanding fire.

The main function of an engine company, therefore, is to extinguish fire as quickly as possible with a stream of water discharged from a fire hose nozzle. This stream of water, however, has to be adequate for the task. An 1½-inch line, for example, can easily handle a fire in a bedroom of a dwelling or an apartment. But an 1½-inch line is worse than useless at a supermarket or a factory fire when flame is boiling out the windows like an angry surf. What is needed at such extensive fires is the heaviest stream or streams possible that can carry enough water to pass through the superheated gases and reach the material that is actually burning.

Under such heavy fire an 1½-inch stream from an 1½-inch line would probably turn into steam 10 feet inside a supermarket show window which distance would probably be 40 or 50 feet short of the stream's target—the burning material. Actually the amount of water required depends on the amount of material burning (the fuel loading of a structure). And at heavily involved supermarket fires, as at lumber yards, warehouses, shopping centers and other large-area and heavily loaded occupancies, it is outright foolishness for any engine company to stretch a line smaller than 2½ inches.

The fire stream, then, is the key to the successful handling of almost all fires. And since this is so, it is important that all engine men—in fact all firefighters and particularly the pump operator—have a thorough knowledge of what constitutes a proper fire stream (for the job on hand) and how to achieve it.

Freeman's experiments

The most complete and reliable series of experiments on the hydraulics of fire streams were conducted in 1888 and 1890 by John R. Freeman, C.E. Later experiments were conducted by Marston and Fleming and the associated Factory Mutual Fire Insurance Company. These experiments and Freeman's, although extensive, covered only nozzle pressures up to 100 psi and tips up to 3½ inches in diameter.

Additional tests that extended the pressure range were made in 1942 by the National Board of Fire Underwriters in conjunction with the Chicago Fire Department. Freeman's findings, however, were reinforced by these later experiments with but minor changes.

Freeman conducted his experiments in Lawrence, Mass., on the premises of the Washington Mills Company which had recently installed a new hydrant system. Foremost among his findings was that an effective solid fire stream is one that:

1. At the limit named has not lost continuity of stream by breaking into showers of spray;
2. Up to the limit named appears to discharge nine-tenths of its volume of water inside a circle 15 inches in diameter and three-quarters of it inside a 10-inch circle;
3. Is stiff enough to attain in a fair condition the height or distance named even though a fresh breeze is blowing;
4. At a limit named will, with no wind, enter a room through a window opening and just barely strike the ceiling with force enough to spatter well.

Freeman's choice of these conditions was arbitrary, but the choice in general was good and it established a standard by means of which streams can be compared and tied in to his experiments. Later experimenters tended to modify Freeman's statements as to what constitutes a good stream and accept in its place the distance from the tip where the stream appears to break into slugs of water which are still closely grouped and effective for fighting fires. This effective reach apparently is what Freeman and Marston took as the reach of a *fair* stream.

In a paper published in Fire Engineering, H. A. Musham adjusted Freeman's data with other experiments and plotted them on logarithm paper. He extended them with a degree of accuracy within 2 to 3 percent of the original experiments to cover all ranges and tips in common use, or which might be used in the future.

Air resistance

Very little is known about the resistance encountered by a fire stream as it passes through air. However, the analytical work that has been done indicates that resistance increases at an accelerated rate as the pressure is raised *with the same tip.* And at a high, though probably lower rate, if the pressure is kept constant while the tip size is increased. This rapid increase in resistance accounts for the decelerating increase in horizontal effective reach attained by raising the pressure and increasing the tip. It is probable that resistance can be broken down into three components: that due to friction; that caused by the piling up of air in front of the stream which eventually breaks it up into spray; and that caused by the displacement of surrounding air necessary to permit the passage of the water. This third component probably causes some form of wave disturbance in the air which is accentuated by the pulsations of the stream itself.

Because of the numerous elements which enter into air resistance, it is not likely that such resistance will ever be accurately known. These elements include the temperatures of both air and water, atmospheric pressure, density of the air and its relative humidity, viscosity and surface tension of both air and water.

Local air currents set up by the stream between it and the ground also play an important part as can be deduced from the fact that the greatest horizontal effective reach occurs at elevations of from 30 to 34 degrees for the tips and pressures in common use, instead of 45 degrees as would normally be expected. The length of the curved path of the stream itself remains approximately the same regardless of the elevation of the nozzle.

If the nozzle were placed but a few feet off the ground, then the stream would strike the ground a short distance from the tip. As the elevation is increased, the distance is increased until all the effective length of the

Table 1—Effective Reach of Fire Streams

Showing the distance in feet from the nozzle at which streams will do effective work with a moderate wind blowing. With a strong wind, the reach is greatly reduced.

Pressure at Nozzle	Size of Nozzle									
	1-Inch		1⅛-Inch		1¼-Inch		1⅜-Inch		1½-Inch	
	Vertical Distance, Feet	Horizontal Distance, Feet	Vertical Distance, Feet	Horizontal Distance, Feet	Vertical Distance, Feet	Horizontal Distance, Feet	Vertical Distance, Feet	Horizontal Distance, Feet	Vertical Distance, Feet	Horizontal Distance, Feet
20	35	37	36	38	36	39	36	40	37	42
25	43	42	44	44	45	46	45	47	46	49
30	51	47	52	50	52	52	53	54	54	56
35	58	51	59	54	59	58	60	59	62	62
40	64	55	65	59	65	62	66	64	69	66
45	69	58	70	63	70	66	72	68	74	71
50	73	61	75	66	75	69	77	72	79	75
55	76	64	79	69	80	72	81	75	83	78
60	79	67	83	72	84	75	85	77	87	80
65	82	70	86	75	87	78	88	79	90	82
70	85	72	88	77	90	80	91	82	92	84
75	87	74	90	79	92	82	93	84	94	86
80	89	76	92	81	94	84	95	86	96	88
85	91	78	94	83	96	87	97	88	98	90
90	92	80	96	85	98	89	99	90	100	91

Note.—Nozzle pressures are as indicated by Pitot tube. The horizontal and vertical distances are based on experiments by Mr. John R. Freeman, Transactions, Am. Soc. C. E., Vol. XXI.

stream is clear of the ground. Nearness of the stream to the ground drags the air away from over the ground. This creates a decrease in air pressure under the stream, and air above it presses down and reduces reach.

As the elevation increases, the reach increases until the maximum is reached at 30 to 34 degrees. Beyond 34 degrees, the horizontal *effective* reach decreases as the length of the curve's path remains the same or approximately so.

Effect of wind

Little experimental work has been done to determine the effect of the wind on fire streams. Such experiments as have been performed indicate that a faint tail breeze may increase horizontal distances by 10 percent. A moderate tail breeze may lower effective vertical reach from 10 to 15 percent. Head breeze will raise the vertical reach and shorten the horizontal. A high-velocity head wind will destroy the stream at the tip by turning it into spray that is then driven to the base of the nozzle or pipe. Similarly, a strong tail wind will, while carrying the water forward, break it up into spray.

The wind also has a serious effect on the air resistance. Tail winds reduce it and head winds increase it. In both cases the stream wastage is increased.

Limits of reach

Any given tip has a pressure limit, beyond which its effective reach decreases. As an example, small tips at high pressure have very little reach. Increase of pressure beyond proper limits increases wastage and such increase will progressively destroy the stream until its reach is nil. In general, increase of pressure increases reach, but the reach progressively decreases at a rapid rate as excessive pressure builds up. This is due to the acceleration of air resistance, and the *coning* of the stream at the nozzle.

As the water leaves the tip, gravity takes hold and it begins to drop. The stream takes on a curved conical form, increasing the surface area exposed to friction. The water shreds off in wisps of mist which with drops of water form a water curtain under the stream. If the coning becomes excessive, it is probably because of a defect in the nozzle's interior shape, or a roughness of the interior due to lack of proper maintenance.

The interior of nozzle barrels should be kept highly polished to insure good streams. Excessive coning also indicates that the pressure is too high and the discharge too much for the nozzle to handle.

NOZZLE PERFORMANCE

The source of water supply, the operating rate of the apparatus, the length of hose lay, system losses, the size of nozzle and its elevation all contribute to the performance of a nozzle. With the exception of water supply, which is here considered adequate, nozzle performance is directly controlled by the pump operator and the company officer or nozzleman.

Range of streams

In considering the range of fire streams and the proper size of stream to be employed, many points have to be taken into consideration. For

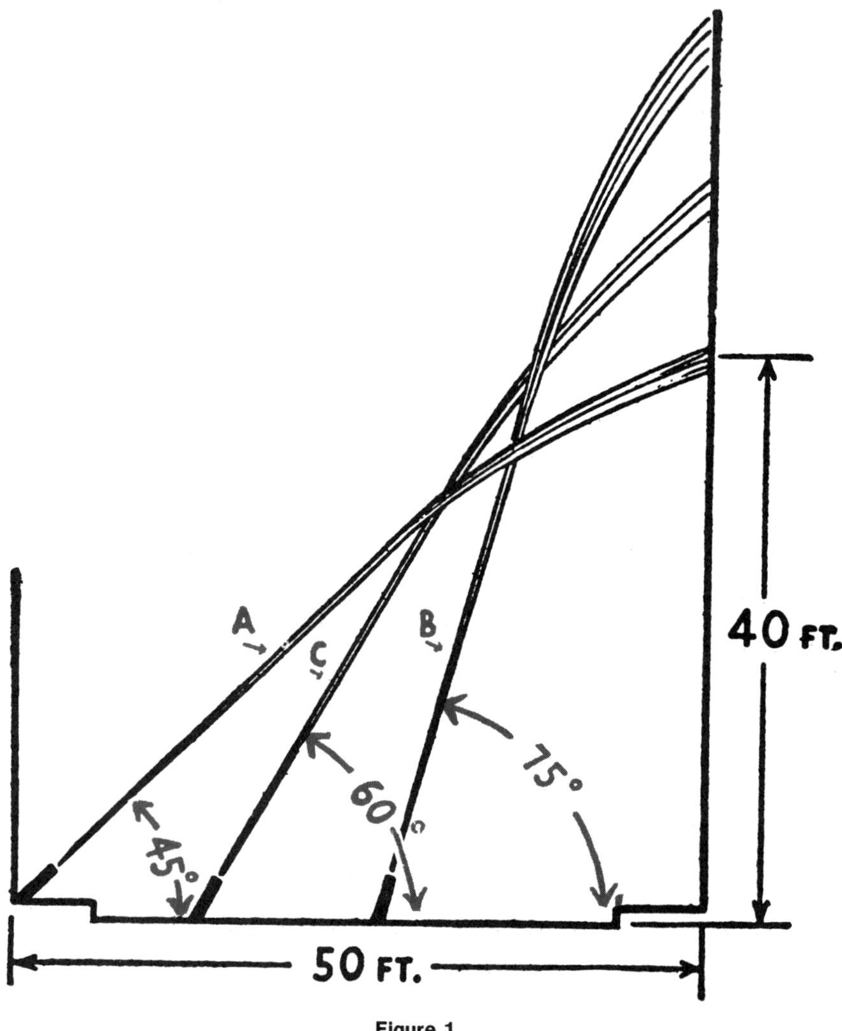

Figure 1

instance, a stream that has broken into a spray may be quite effective and satisfactory on small fires, but when directed at a hot blaze may be useless. Again a stream which would be ideal in calm weather could be absolutely worthless in a gale.

Horizontal range

Knowledge of the horizontal range of fire streams is particularly valuable when streams are to be thrown from one building to another across the street, or from pier to pier at waterfront fires, or from fireboats to waterfront property. For instance, knowing that the distance required to span a street and hit in on a floor is 60 feet can make for efficient fire stream operation right from the start.

Theoretically, a fire stream has its greatest horizontal range when the center of the stream as it leaves the nozzle makes a 45-degree angle from the horizontal. However, Freeman found that an angle of 32 degrees gave the greatest actual horizontal range. The formula derived empirically from his experiments was therefore based on this 32-degree angle.

The formula, $S = \frac{1}{2}NP + 26$, is applicable to nozzle pressures over 30 psi and for a ¾-inch nozzle where:

S = horizontal distance in feet

NP = nozzle pressure in pounds per square inch

For nozzle diameters in excess of ¾-inch, add 5 to the 26 for each ⅛-inch increase in nozzle diameter. This formula gives satisfactory results within usual working pressures and nozzle sizes.

Vertical reach

The maximum vertical reach is attained when the nozzle is placed perpendicular to the ground. However, such a nozzle position is rarely found in actual fire fighting.

The angle of stream commonly used for maximum effective reach varies between 60 and 75 degrees (figure 1). Stream A making a 45-degree angle does not require calculations to determine the maximum range. It would be difficult in an ordinary street to get the nozzle sufficiently far from the building while at an angle of 45 degrees to make the vertical height the important factor. An ordinary stream at 45 degrees and 50 feet from a building strikes the building only 40 feet from street level.

Streams B and C are directed at an angle of 75 degrees and 65 degrees, respectively, and the determination of their effective reach requires a different formula. This formula was worked out (also empirically) to give values of vertical distances of fire streams when nozzles are inclined at or around an angle of 70 degrees.

The formula gives the height of an effective stream using a 1-inch tip and is applicable up to a nozzle pressure of 100 pounds:

$$H = \sqrt{240p - p^2 - 1900} - 15, \text{ where}$$

H = effective height in feet

p = nozzle pressure in pounds per square inch

For pressures of 50 psi or less, subtract 1 from the 15 for each ⅛-inch

Table 2—Friction Loss in Fire Hose
Based on tests of best quality rubber lined fire hose*

Flow, Gallons per Minute	Pressure Loss in Each 100 Feet of Hose, Pounds per Sq. Inch				Flow, Gallons per Minute	Pressure Loss in Each 100 Feet of Hose, Pounds per Sq. Inch		
	2½" Hose	3" Hose	3½" Hose	2 Lines of 2½" Siamesed		3" Hose	3½" Hose	2 Lines of 2½" Siamesed
140	5.2	2.0	0.9	1.4	525	23.2	10.5	16.6
160	6.6	2.6	1.2	1.9	550	25.2	11.4	18.1
180	8.3	3.2	1.5	2.3	575	27.5	12.4	19.0
200	10.1	3.9	1.8	2.8	600	29.9	13.4	21.2
220	12.0	4.2	2.1	3.3	625	32.0	14.4	23.0
240	14.1	5.4	2.5	3.9	650	34.5	15.5	24.8
260	16.4	6.3	2.9	4.5	675	37.0	16.6	26.5
280	18.7	7.2	3.3	5.2	700	39.5	17.7	28.3
300	21.2	8.2	3.7	5.9	725	42.3	18.9	30.2
320	23.8	9.3	4.2	6.6	750	45.0	20.1	32.2
340	26.9	10.5	4.7	7.4	775	47.8	21.4	34.2
360	30.0	11.5	5.2	8.3	800	50.5	22.7	36.2
380	33.0	12.8	5.8	9.2	825	53.5	24.0	38.4
400	36.2	14.1	6.3	10.1	850	56.5	25.4	40.7
425	40.8	15.7	7.0	11.3	875	59.7	26.8	43.1
450	45.2	17.5	7.9	12.5	900	63.0	28.2	45.2
475	50.0	19.3	8.7	13.8	1,000	76.5	34.3	55.0
500	55.0	21.2	9.5	15.2	1,100	91.5	41.0	65.5

* Rough rubber lining is liable to increase the losses given in the table as much as 50 percent.

increase in nozzle diameter. Above 50 psi, subtract 2 from the 15 for each ⅛-inch diameter increase.

Both formulas give approximate agreement with the table drawn by Freeman (table 1). And from a practical standpoint they are satisfactory since in fire fighting an exact measure of reach cannot be determined.

Approximate calculation

For quick calculation, but with less accuracy, fire fighters in the field can allow a pound of pressure for each foot of effective range of stream either vertically or horizontally. This rule is most accurate at low pressures, but for high-pressure streams where effective reach is a problem, it is still fairly accurate.

Furthermore, this rough rule gives results which in most cases are too large, but which can be desirable.

The ranges usually given in tables for fire streams are for those operating in comparatively still air. With an appreciable wind blowing, this range is materially reduced. Therefore, greater pressure than that actually needed provides a margin of safety.

Friction loss

Working back from the nozzle, one finds that the next factor entering into effective streams is friction loss. Friction loss is mainly governed by the quantity of water flowing (gpm), the diameter of the hose and the length of the line. In addition, there is a coefficient which must be determined experimentally from the material of the hose, its interior roughness, the viscosity of the water and its density. Friction loss is measured in pounds per square inch.

Friction losses given in table 2 published by the Insurance Service Office (Fire Stream Tables) were based on tests of best-quality rubber-lined hose and were for 100-foot lengths measured without pressure applied. The underwriters also established an approximate formula for friction loss in 2½-inch hose. The formula states: Friction Loss $= 2Q^2 + Q$ for each 100 feet of hose, in pounds per square inch, where Q is the quantity in gallons divided by 100.

For less than 100 gallons, Friction Loss $= 2Q^2 + \frac{1}{2}Q$. Factors are given that convert losses in 2½-inch hose to other sizes.

Supplying the nozzle

Assuming that water supply is adequate, the final factor contributing to an effective stream is the pump (or more likely the pump operator). The hydraulic gradient runs in a straight, descending line from the pump to the nozzle. Losses are represented as friction loss. In addition, the pump must supply sufficient pressure to overcome head loss, if any, and provide proper nozzle pressure for adequate reach and effectiveness. Pump operators should therefore have a good knowledge of what constitutes an effective fire stream and how to achieve it.

For interior fire fighting, shutoff nozzles in sizes up to 1¼-inch with pressures ranging from 40 to 60 psi will supply lines that are considered good. Apartment houses, dwellings and small interior fires call for smaller nozzles ranging from 1⅛-inch downward. In fact, today's fire fighters generally carry a combination straight stream and fog nozzle to fit either 1½-inch or 2½-inch hose for interior fire fighting.

As a rule, nozzle diameter should not exceed one-half the diameter of the hose used and should be reduced depending upon the length of stretch. A short stretch is considered to be about six lengths; a medium stretch about 12 lengths; and a long stretch, 18 lengths or over.

A nozzle which is too large for a particular diameter hose gives a weak, ineffective stream. A large nozzle results in a large flow of water and a large flow of water produces large friction loss. With a long hose stretch and a large flow of water, the nozzle pressure may be weak because of excessive friction loss. In such case, an increase of nozzle pressure requires the use of a smaller nozzle, assuming engine pressure, hose diameter and length of stretch remain constant. Since the velocity of flow remains the same in the hose, the water must flow faster through the smaller nozzle, thereby increasing pressure and reach at the tip.

If the nozzle is too small and the engine pressure high, the stream will form a spray pattern on leaving the nozzle and its effectiveness is lost.

It is difficult to specify the precise nozzle used on any one stretch. However, empirical rules have been advanced which give adequate approximations for combinations of stretch and nozzle size:

Hose Layout	Hose Diameter (inches)	Nozzle Diameter (inches)
Long stretch	2½	1
Long stretch	3	1¼
Long stretch	3½	1½
Medium stretch	2½	1⅛
Medium stretch	3	1⅜
Medium stretch	3½	1⅝
Short stretch	2½	1¼
Short stretch	3	1½
Short stretch	3½	1¾

Master streams

One-line fires rarely present any problems to a fire department. However, the multiple-alarm fire raging fiercely in a warehouse or lumber yard is another matter. Heavy streams, also called master streams, are in order for the big fires, where reach and penetration of great quantities of water are required.

Heavy streams range in size from a 1¼-inch nozzle up to 2 inches. Fireboats and some special land apparatus may have nozzles up to 4 inches. Nozzle pressures required for such streams range from 60 to 90 psi. Delivery from such streams runs from 400 gpm on an 1¼-inch nozzle to over 1000 gpm on a 2-inch tip such as may be found on an elevating platform.

Such tremendous streams require a fixed appliance for operation. A

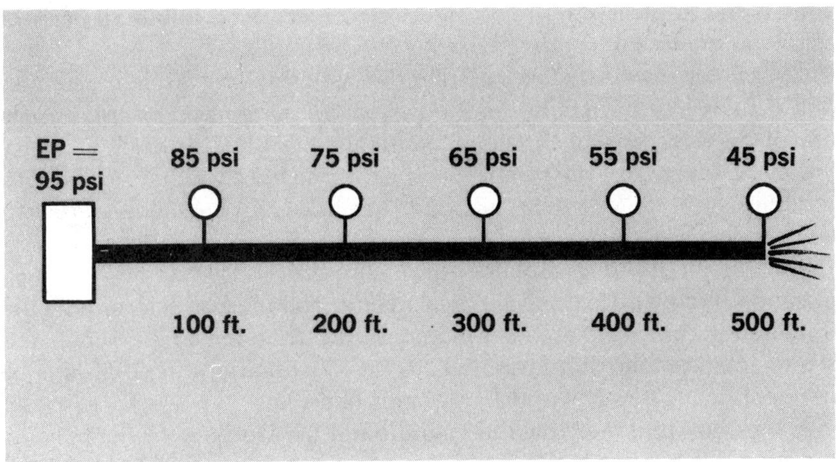

Simplified schematic of the hydraulic gradient shows what happens to the water pressure from the time it leaves the pumper until it reaches the nozzle.

2½-inch hose line flowing 400 gpm is too dangerous for men to hold and a pipe holder of some sort is indicated. Flow beyond this requires appliances such as portable turrets, turrets mounted on apparatus, or nozzle assemblies rigidly fixed to an apparatus as are found on aerial ladders and platforms.

Multiple lines

The large quantity of water required by heavy streams produces a problem in overcoming friction loss that can be solved only by the use of multiple lines.

Referring to the friction loss table (table 2), one finds that 500 gallons of water flowing through 100 feet of 2½-inch hose produces a friction loss of 55 psi. Six hundred feet produces 330 psi friction loss. This is only 12 lengths! Such excessive friction loss can be overcome only by using larger size hose or, for the average department that carries only 2½-inch hose, by using multiple lines.

Friction loss in multiple 2½-inch lines can be figured by reducing the multiple stretch to a single line of 2½-inch by using appropriate factors. However, a pump operator on the fire scene has no time for arithmetic and must have a simple and quick method of determining his losses.

Referring to the tables, we find that two siamesed lines of 2½-inch hose have only 15.2-psi friction loss as compared to 55.0 for the single line. Dividing the conversion factor 3.6 for two 2½-inch lines into the 55 pounds given for the single 2½-inch, the answer comes out at 15.2 psi.

This is the same as the table's figure and represents about 28 percent of the 55-psi loss in the single line of 2½-inch hose.

A pump operator at a fire can therefore assume that two siamesed lines of 2½-inch hose have only about one-quarter the friction loss of a single line of 2½-inch hose of the same length and carrying the same quantity (gpm) of water. By the same reasoning, three lines will have one-ninth the friction loss of a single line; and four lines will have one-sixteenth the friction loss.

The same reasoning applies to other size hose. Two siamesed 3-inch lines will have approximately one-quarter the friction loss of a single 3-inch line; three siamesed 3-inch, one-ninth that of a single 3-inch and so on. Remember that larger size hose, if available, should always be used for heavy streams and siamesed if possible.

Hand lines and multiple lines should not be stretched from the same pumper. Two lines supplying a turret can produce a discharge at the tip of 600 gpm or better, which is close to the capacity of a 750-gpm pump. Putting a hand line into the same pump can reduce the efficiency of the turret while producing only another ineffective stream. At the same time, it complicates the job of the pump operator who will have to make frequent adjustments of his controls, particularly if the hand line supplies a shutoff nozzle that is used intermittently.

DIRECTING THE STREAM

As mentioned previously, the curvature of the stream causes it to drop so as to strike the building at a point lower than that at which the nozzle is pointed. This is due to gravity, which pulls it downward so that the water takes a curved path from the instant it leaves the nozzle until it strikes the building.

Figure 2 shows diagrammatically a calculated stream, based on the assumption that the stream travels in a straight line, and also an actual path of a stream.

The dotted line indicates the straight line path of a stream, while the solid line gives the actual path.

The curvature of the stream is an advantage in one respect. A stream from the nozzle to an upper floor of a building, instead of going straight on over the sill and striking the ceiling at a point directly in a straight line from the nozzle, curves as it crosses the sill and tends to strike farther in on the ceiling than calculated. Not only does it strike farther in on the ceiling, but the deflection of water is also at a smaller angle, which means that the water will spread much farther than it would if it traveled in a straight line.

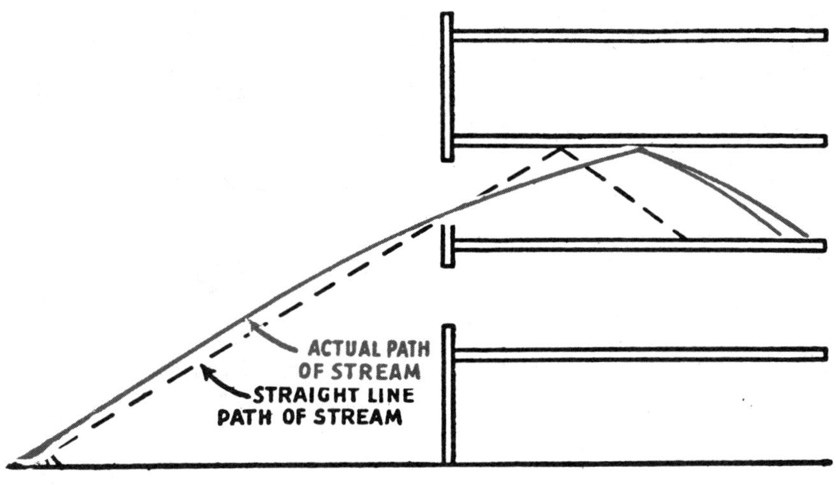

Figure 2

Where it has been mentioned that the 50-degree angle is the maximum angle at which to direct a stream, the 50 degrees refers to the angle of the stream where it leaves the nozzle and not the angle of the stream where it crosses the sill or after it enters the building.

Thus while a sketch drawn with straight lines showing the probable penetration of the stream might lead one to believe that penetration was really ineffective or useless, an actual stream might prove to be effective. This is, as noted above, accounted for by the tendency of the stream to curve or take a curved path due to the action of gravity.

The third floor may be said to be the highest floor to which streams may be thrown effectively from the street level.

Theoretically, it might be possible to reach a higher floor than the third, but this would necessitate moving the nozzle farther away from the building to keep the angle of the stream small. But moving the nozzle away from the building means that the stream will have to travel farther, and the possibility of its breaking into spray is thereby increased. Then, too, increasing the range of the stream necessitates a higher nozzle pressure to do effective work.

Street streams are ordinarily directed with full effectiveness into the second floor of a building. But they may, as noted above, be used into the third floor. In this case, it is good practice to place the nozzle at least as far from the building as the point where it enters the building is above the street level.

Refer to figure 3. While the greatest effective range is secured by

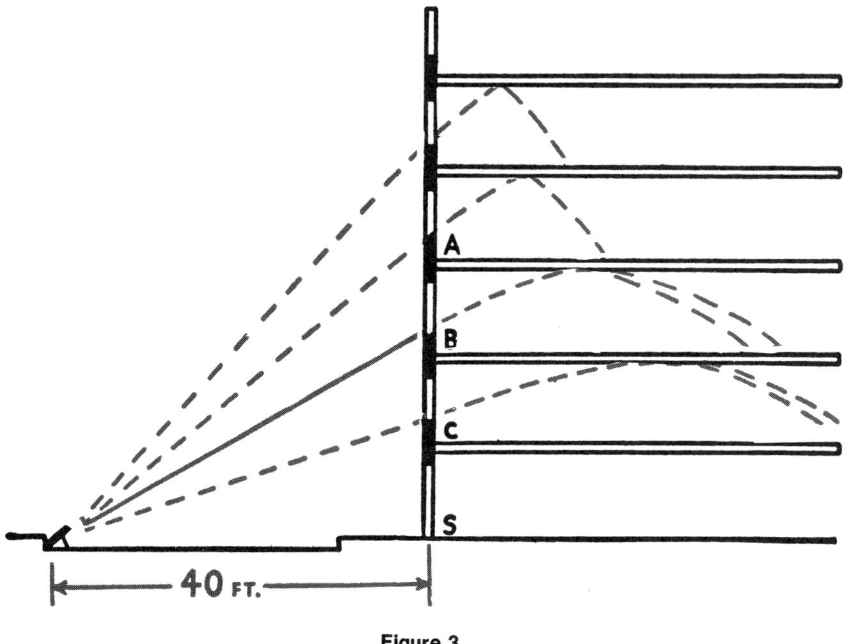

Figure 3

sending the stream from the position as placed through the second-floor window (at C), still satisfactory penetration can be secured at the third-floor window (at point B). A stream crossing the sill at point B passes into the building quite a distance before it strikes the ceiling, and the water is deflected downward almost as far again, increasing the penetration to double that which is represented by the distance from the window sill to the point where the stream strikes the ceiling.

The distance B-S in the diagram should not be greater than the distance from S out to the nozzle. This means that an angle of 45 degrees is the maximum which can be considered effective for any street stream or other stream use.

A lesser angle than this is, of course, much more effective.

The diagram shows the nozzle placed 40 feet from the building. This is a little more than should actually be used in practice, unless apparatus is between the nozzle and the building.

When the stream is thrown through the third-floor window, as shown in figure 3, the angle it makes with the ground is 30 degrees. This angle is the one which gives the greatest effective horizontal reach to fire streams.

To sum up, the third-floor window should be considered the maximum height to which a stream can be operated successfully from the street.

Under no conditions should the angle of the stream be greater than 50 degrees at the point where it leaves the nozzle. Allowing for the natural and unavoidable sag of the stream from the nozzle to where it strikes the building, the stream would likely pass, under these conditions, through the third-floor window instead of through the fourth-floor window as might be assumed from theoretical calculation and straight line path of stream travel.

Master streams

The turret pipe, or monitor, mounted on a pumper or hose wagon possesses two advantages over the street stream. First, the nozzle is up to 9 feet above the street, and second, the heavy-caliber stream is easily manipulated.

The logical position for such a pipe is at the opposite curb from the fire (figure 4). This gives the maximum distance away from the building, which in turn means a maximum vertical reach, provided the stream is not broken up before it strikes the building. But in this case again, the stream is not considered effective above the third floor.

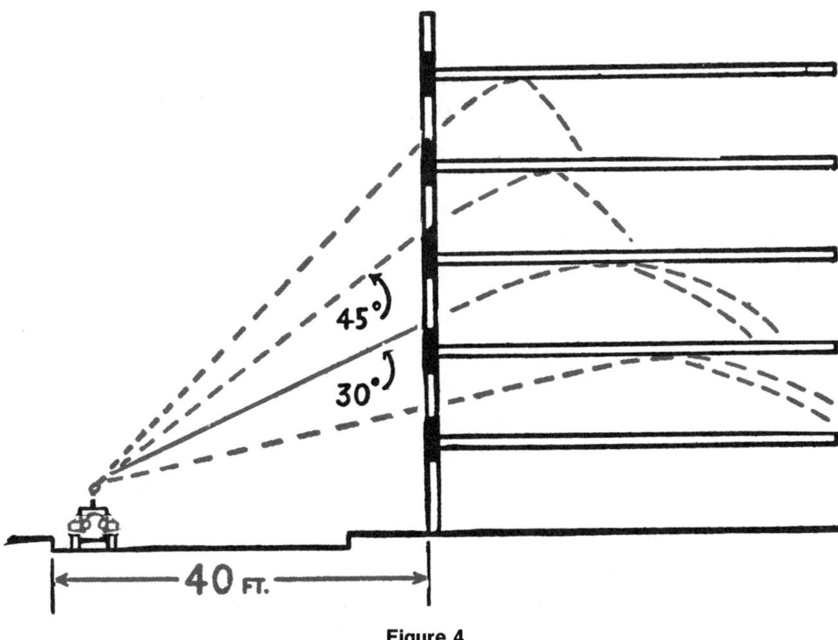

Figure 4

As in the street line,a 30-degree angle for throwing water to the third floor gives the most effective results, and above the third floor the effectiveness decreases. This decrease in effectiveness is directly due to the decrease in penetration of the stream, or in other words, the decrease in distance from the front wall to the point at which the stream strikes the ceiling. The higher the angle at which the stream is directed, the nearer to the window it strikes the ceiling.

Also, as in the case of the street line, when the stream leaves the nozzle at a 50-degree angle, the natural curvature of the stream brings the point at which the stream might be calculated to strike the building down considerably on the building and instead of the stream passing through the fourth-floor window to the building, the stream strikes into the window of the floor below. This is the case unless unusually high pressures and large-diameter tips are used on the pipe.

To sum up the case of the turret pipe, the third floor is considered the highest floor at which effective work can be done.

Heavy streams and their uses

Heavy streams have definite uses which are as marked from small streams as are aerial ladders from portable ladders. And heavy streams are not confined entirely to outside use. A brief summary of the uses of heavy streams follows:

1. For fires involving large floor areas.
2. Fires in buildings which have involved entire floors and made it necessary for lines to operate from fire escapes.
3. Fires on second, third, or even fourth floors which have to be handled by street lines.
4. For operating across streets, air shafts, alleys.
5. For operating in buildings of large area and height such as sheds, armories, churches, railroad stations, etc.

It is not only the quantity of water which the large stream discharges that makes it more effective, but also its greater range.

An example of increased range by using a large nozzle may be seen from table 1, which gives the vertical reach of streams from nozzles 1 inch to 1½ inches in diameter at pressures of 20 to 90 psi.

Defective streams

The chief causes of defective streams might be listed as follows:

1. Insufficient pressure. This may be caused by too little pressure at the engine or hydrant, or it may be caused by too lengthy hose stretches and consequent heavy friction loss. It may also be due to using

tips that are too large on lines of excessive length. The latter practice increases the friction loss in the hose.

2. Too much pressure. High pressure can be used on large nozzles without excess spraying, whereas with small tips high pressures often cause the stream to break up within a few feet of the tip, with immediate loss of effectiveness.

3. Defective tip (nozzle). This is occasionally the cause of a poor stream. It results from a burred or dented waterway brought on by rough handling. A nozzle with a small burr at the edge where the water leaves will break up the stream and cut its range down greatly.

4. Air in the line. This is usually caused by operating pumps under negative pressure. Air leaks into the line and is carried along with the water to the nozzle. It can be detected by the sputtering sound and broken condition of the stream. Air, when imprisoned in a line under high pressure, is compressed and on reaching the nozzle is free to expand in all directions, with the result that it breaks the stream.

5. Twist in hose near pipe. A double twist in the line near the nozzle causes a rotary motion of the water in the line, which in turn, results in a sprayed stream as it leaves the nozzle. The remedy is to make sure that the line of hose leading up to the nozzle has but one bend in it: the bend which leads from the horizontal stretch up to the nozzle.

Master stream devices

Both electrical and hydraulic power are employed in several master stream devices now being used in the fire service. The electrical application has been limited to ladder pipes and some fixed monitor nozzles. Hydraulic applications include both fixed and portable heavy-duty, or master stream, devices.

One design of a hydraulically operated giant deluge gun has an effective range of better than 320 feet, and elevated to 75 degrees, its stream will reach a height of 165 feet. At 30 percent elevation, the nozzle will deliver 3000 gpm at an overall distance of 425 feet. Notwithstanding this volume and reach, and the fact that pressures may vary from 30 to 300 psi, the hydraulic controls are positive and rapid. Only one man is needed to manipulate the stream.

The giant deluge gun (permanently mounted) is supplied by multiple intakes servicing either 2½ or 3½-inch hose. All pipe turns are gradual, with no sharp turns or flanges to increase friction loss. The length of this gun measured from the horizontal supply line to the extreme of the stacked tips is 71 inches. Tips employed range from 1½ to 3-inch.

The deluge gun itself is constructed with a helical barrel from 3 to 6 inches in diameter, with a 270-degree loop which is maintained to balance

Electric ladder pipe that attaches to fly section of aerial is controlled from panel on turntable.

all vector forces. This loop eliminates the need for splitting and subsequently uniting the stream. The gun is hydraulically operated through vertical and self-contained power joints. The motion of the device can be speeded or retarded by hand valves on the power unit. If desired, with slight modification the control levers can be made portable, permitting the operator to manipulate the gun by remote control from a safe area.

Hydraulically operated ladder pipe

The hydraulically operated ladder pipe has a 3½-inch waterway throughout with a ball joint which permits vertical directional control of the stream without any gooseneck or yoke restriction.

Hydraulic controls operated from the ladder turntable enable the operator, by means of a small box with two simple levers, to control both elevation of stream and pattern from straight stream to wide fog. A

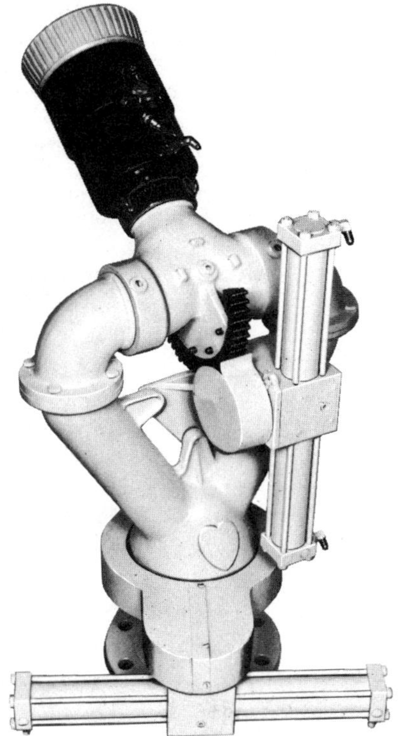

Hydraulically actuated monitor is remotely controlled and can be moved horizontally and vertically. It delivers fog or straight stream.

movement of one lever one way raises or lowers the pipe; the other lever governs the nozzle pattern. To meet underwriters' requirements, all operations can also be controlled manually. The pipe itself can efficiently handle flows through a 2-inch tip with no appreciable loss.

Electrically controlled ladder pipe

An electrically operated ladder pipe makes available push-button operation of ladder pipes to the fire service. A control panel is mounted on the aerial turntable pedestal within reach of the fireman operating the ladder. A heavy-duty cable connects the panel to the ladder pipe assembly on which are mounted two weatherproof motors. One controls the elevation of the nozzle through a worm and gear drive and the other varies the setting of the 500-gpm fog nozzle with which the ladder pipe is equipped. By means of the push buttons, the operator can quickly control the stream elevation and the shape of the nozzle pattern from 90-degree fog to straight stream.

Hand lines may be described as those lines stretched to the seat of a

Bresnan or similar type distributor is used for small cellar areas. In operation it is dropped through hole cut in floor.

fire and operated or manipulated by fire fighters at this point. A hand line may be used through a shutoff nozzle, a cellar pipe or a fog nozzle, which may be a combination fog and straight-stream nozzle.

A shutoff nozzle should be used at all times when working in a building or at other locations where it is apparent that there will be considerable shifting of the line. On entering the floor of a commercial or loft building, store, tenement or an apartment, fire fighters should understand that the nozzle should be opened and closed judiciously. Where there is a great deal of smoke, but no great amount of heat, water should not be used until the fire is located. By waiting until fire shows, a considerable amount of unnecessary water damage may be avoided.

A delay of a few seconds may give the smoke time enough to break and disclose the seat of the fire. Shut off the line as quickly as possible when not needed. Do not keep it playing after the fire no longer requires it. Minimize the use of water as much as possible and thereby minimize water damage. Use reducing tips as early as conditions permit.

In cellars of large open area, cellar pipes of the Hart or Baker pattern, or the old bent cellar pipe should be used. The Hart or Baker types are more flexible in operation than the plain bent pipe and can be used in closer quarters. The newest types of these pipes have shutoffs and, of course, the nozzle can be manipulated vertically or horizontally by the operator. The proper use of the Baker or Hart type calls for the nozzle to be directed upward so that the ceiling of the cellar will be covered by the stream. When shifting it from point to point, a very slight change in the position of the handle is all that is necessary.

The bent pipe also requires changing the direction of the stream to get effective coverage. Horizontal sweep of the stream is secured by shifting the hose from side to side, while vertical sweep can be produced by raising the hose up and down.

Distributor

For covering fires in smaller cellar areas, a Bresnan or similar type distributor is used. In operation, this distributor is dropped through a hole cut in a floor. When the distributor hits the floor below, it is raised to approximately two-thirds the distance from floor to ceiling or adjusted, if stock intervenes, to a midpoint between stock and ceiling. It has a much smaller range than the cellar pipes mentioned above and provides a spherical spray rather than a solid stream. To cover any great area, it must be shifted from point to point.

The bent nozzle (New York Nozzle) is particularly efficient in handling floor, ceiling, cornice and other fires that are hard to get at with straight nozzles. The bent nozzle, as its name implies, has a right-angle tip and can be placed in a small opening and turned in any direction.

Fog nozzle

Fog or spray nozzles also come under the heading of shutoff nozzles in that the stream can be shut off at will by the operator. There are two general types: one that distributes fog only and one that can be manipulated by the operator to discharge either fog or solid stream. The latter is probably the most popular nozzle in the fire service today for inside fire fighting.

Depending on the manufacturer of the nozzle, fog or spray nozzles can discharge in a variety of adjustable patterns.

Since there is no one formula for determining the discharge of fog nozzles, performance data must be obtained from the manufacturers. Tests, however, have indicated that nozzle pressures below 50 psi are ineffective for reach and penetration. In general, 100 psi is accepted as the most effective fog nozzle pressure.

The range of fog streams as commonly used is limited, although with a certain type of fog nozzle under high pressure coarse fog can be projected well over 100 feet. Fog nozzles are well suited for confined fires such as are found in the rooms of ordinary dwellings, apartments and tenements. Ventilation is important at such fires to provide an opening for gases, smoke and steam to leave. In this way, heat and gases are driven ahead of the fire fighter, making prompt extinguishment possible. If no forward ventilation is provided, there is danger of pressure being built up ahead of the fog blast, with the possibility of a sudden flash-around enveloping the nozzlemen.

STRETCHING THE HOSE

Armed with the knowledge of what constitutes a good fire stream a company officer must then address himself to the problem of getting water from a source of supply to the seat of the fire. The solution, of course, will be based on the officer's experience, knowledge and judgment, applied to what might be called a mini-sizeup of the situation on hand:

Amount of fire showing: A heavy volume of flame, pouring out of a warehouse's windows or through the roof might immediately call for master streams and forget the hand lines. Conversely, flame showing from a second-story bedroom window in a dwelling calls for a quick, interior and aggressive attack with a hand line since there may be lives endangered.

Type of occupancy and structural condition of building: An officer should never connect a pumper to a hydrant in front of the wall of a 100-year-old factory building that could conceivably collapse, or a chemical plant that might be subject to explosions. Further, a pumper placed in front of a building can inhibit the use of other equipment, particularly aerials and elevating platforms.

Exposures present: The first line might have to be stretched to protect a hospital or school.

Length of the stretch: Usually the shorter the stretch the better, but for reasons given above, among others, this is not always possible.

Number of lines and size hose needed: Size of hose depends on the type of streams needed, and the distance from the water source to the fire. As mentioned elsewhere, a booster line would be useless at a lumber yard fire in the initial stages. Reasonably long stretches can be overcome by using siamesed lines that can reduce friction loss. For long stretches large-size hose—3 to 6-inch—is a must, particularly in "relay" operations.

Available water supply: Every engine company officer and pump operator should be familiar with the main sizes and hydrant pressures available in his and adjoining districts. Where there are no hydrants he should be familiar with every drafting site available to his department either for stretching a line to a fire or for tanker-shuttle operations. Then there are other sources of water available such as roof tanks and swimming pools.

Once a plan of attack is made by the engine company officer (based on his mini-sizeup) he must then decide how to stretch his hose. There are really only two options available to him: stretch from the source of water to the fire or stretch from the fire to the source of water. The first is called a "forward lay" or a "running stretch" and the second is called a "reverse lay" or a "back stretch."

Forward lay

In the forward lay, the pumper stops at a hydrant, drops off one man who pulls an end of the connected hose from the hose bed and secures it around the hydrant. The pumper then "runs" to the fire "laying" out hose as it proceeds. When the pumper stops, the hydrant man connects the hose to a hydrant outlet. (More likely he will have first connected a switch valve to the outlet before applying the hose.) Meanwhile the men with the pumper will have pulled sufficient house out of the bed—to maneuver in and around the fire—and capped the hose with a nozzle.

If the hydrant pressure is sufficient they can attack the fire. If not, the pumper can return to the hydrant, connect to another outlet on the switch valve and provide the necessary pressure without having to shut the line down. This action can also be performed by a second pumper which in addition to supplying the original line can pump lines in a simple relay into the first pumper from which additional lines can be taken if needed.

This forward lay has the advantage of placing the pumper and all its additional equipment, including masks, at or near the fire, ready for instant use. However, should the pumper have to return to the hydrant, at least the most necessary equipment should be dropped off.

The reverse lay

As its name implies, the reverse lay simply means that the hose is stretched from the fire to the source of water—the opposite of the forward lay. Here, sufficient hose is dropped at the fire and the pumper runs to the hydrant or other source of water, laying out hose as it goes. This has to be done in a reasonable hurry but again care should be taken that sufficient, and immediately necessary, equipment is dropped at the fire scene.

The reverse lay has the advantage of placing the pumper at the hydrant where the full capacity of the hydrant and the pumper can be used without taking any additional steps.

In actual practice the decision to make either a forward or reverse lay is frequently determined by which location—the fire or the hydrant—a company arrives at first.

In-line pumping

Actually, in-line pumping is a form of the forward lay. The pumper, however, is placed much nearer to the hydrant than to the fire. The effect sought here is to move the capacity of the hydrant from its location to a point nearer the fire (the pumper). In theory, the pumper can utilize the full capacity of the hydrant and consequently supply a longer line or multiple lines for fighting the fire. Another advantage is to move tools and equipment nearer to the fire.

In-line pumping has the big disadvantage of being risky. For one thing, the flowing pressure at the hydrant my be too low to supply the pumper with an adequate intake. Consequently, the pumper cannot supply any more water than it receives. So great care should be used in selecting a hydrant for in-line pumping. And, as mentioned previously, it calls for a familiarity with the water system.

The "blitz" attack

Several years back, the "blitz" attack was introduced at the Fire Department Instructors Conference and it has been growing in acceptance ever since. In this extinguishment concept, an "attack pumper" that has a 500-gallon tank and is set up with preconnected 2½-inch hose goes directly to the fire building where an attack can be made instantly—without the delay of hooking up and stretching lines to or from a source of water.

The advantage of this method of attack is that it catches the fire in its early stages before it roars out of control. The disadvantage is that if the blitz doesn't work, precious minutes will have been lost in getting to a positive source of water.

The officer employing the blitz attack will have to demonstrate considerable judgment—and courage. But once the attack has been initiated, it should be carried through to the last drop of water. There is no point in saving water just to wet down the ruins.

Hose manifolds

The concept of the hose manifold began with the simple wye in which two lines were taken from one supply line. The gated wye—double or

Portable hydrant (manifold) with four outlets can be fed by 4-inch hose.

triple—extended the concept. And finally, in recent years there was introduced the manifold, a large-diameter pipe sealed at each end and into which four or more 2½-inch gated outlets were tapped, plus one large-diameter inlet. Inlet size can be any size and depends on the size hose to be used. More recently, nozzle manufacturers have introduced a simpler and more sophisticated manifold in a variety of configurations.

In practice the manifold is placed in a spot near the fire building and lines are stretched from it when and where needed. The large-diameter hose, 3½ and 4-inch, supplying the manifold must be, of course, supplied from a pumper connected to a hydrant or at draft where a large and reliable supply of water is available.

A 1000-gpm pumper can therefore supply four 2½-inch, 250-gpm lines at a considerable distance and with friction loss considerably reduced (by use of the large-diameter hose). Manifolds also help to eliminate the clutter of apparatus and hose frequently found in front of a fire building at large fires. They are also useful at ship and pier fires.

The only real disadvantage of the manifold is that three or four lines would be knocked out of service should the large-diameter supply line burst, or the pumper fail.

How much hose?

The length of hose needed for outside streams should be readily apparent. But most fires call for hand lines operated within the interior of a building. Sufficient hose, therefore, should be pulled off the apparatus to cover all parts of the interior of a building. Since buildings can differ in interior dimensions, the amount of hose used will depend on the officer's judgment, experience and observation. However, according to Clark[1], "A long-standing rule of thumb has been that from the front door of the building there should be one 50-foot length of hose for each floor up to the fire floor, plus one extra. For example, if the fire is on the fourth floor, it would call for five lengths from the entrance. This usually gives enough hose to reach all parts of the fire floor, but if the building is large (over 100 feet in either width or length), it would be well to add another length." Clark also recommends that hose lines, other than the first, be taken up on the exterior of a building by fire escape, aerial ladder or rope. Many departments, however, insist that the first line be backed up by a second just in case the first line fails for any reason.

Another rule of thumb—this one for lines taken up the exterior of a building—calls for one 50-foot length for each three stories plus one for the fire floor. But again, this calls for judgment from observation. In any event, it is better to stretch too much hose rather than have too little. But "too much" should not be carried to an extreme that would clutter the inside of a building with hose.

Maneuvering the hose

In general, hose stretched within a building should be stretched uncharged to the point of operation and water then called for. However, care must be taken to see that the empty hose is not snagged, kinked and particularly pinched—as under a door. When these cautions are overlooked, there can be difficulty in further advancing the line. And, in the case of the pinched or kinked hose, not having any water—with a consequent delay in the fire attack. These cautions apply particularly to hose stretched up the stairs of a building.

Inside attack calls for the use of a shut-off nozzle at all times and this nozzle today invariably combines a straight stream and fog position. The nozzle should be brought as near to the fire as possible and in enclosed rooms be directed "over your head and all around" as some instructors put it.

A stream directed at a ceiling will have a heavy sprinkler (almost a deluge) effect and cover a greater area more quickly than if directed at

---

[1]Clark, William E., *Fire Fighting Principles and Practices,* Dun-Donnelley Publishing Corporation, New York, N.Y., 1974.

the seat of a fire. It will also reduce the intense heat that collects at the ceiling over a fire, particularly when alternated with the fog.

In large-area rooms, the stream should be shut off as soon as the fire has been darkened down in the immediate area of operations. It should then be advanced. As Clark puts it, "An adequate hose stream will put out all the fire it can reach in (within) a few seconds. If it is not moved, any additional water used from that position is being wasted."[2]

RELAY PUMPING

In the spring of 1977, and as a publicity stunt for a fund drive, 61 fire companies in the Philadelphia area participated in what has got to be the longest relay pumping operation in history. The relay stretched for 12 miles from the source of water to the nozzle which discharged 341 gpm. In between the source (the Delaware River) and the nozzle there were stretched 64,900 feet of hose connected to 64 pumpers. The elapsed time from the moment the water left the first pumper (at draft) until it gushed out the nozzle was 2 hours and 48 minutes.

It would seem then that the only limitation to relay pumping is the amount of hose and the number of pumpers available. At the test described above, 5, 4, 3½ and 3-inch hose was used for the first 6 miles, 2½-inch for the remainder. While this 12-mile relay was only a stunt, it dramatized the capability and importance of relay pumping—actually an extension of the straight or running lay described above.

Pumpers are considered to be in relay when two or more are placed in a hose stretch with the discharge of one pumper supplying the next in line. This operation becomes necessary when the distance from the source of water supply to the fireground is too great for a single pumper to provide adequate pressure and volume at a nozzle.

Friction loss determines need

Basically, the necessity for relaying rests on the amount of friction loss in the lines. This in turn depends on the size and length of the lines, the diameter of the nozzle, and the required nozzle pressure. In the same stretch, friction loss can be reduced by using larger size hose, running parallel lines between pumpers, reducing the nozzle pressure, using a smaller size nozzle at the same nozzle pressure, or any combination of the foregoing. Therefore, if at maximum recommended engine pressure a layout of hose does not provide adequate pressure and volume at the

---

[2]Ibid.

Company officers in the Philadelphia area plot 12 mile relay. A publicity stunt for a fund drive, the relay involved 61 companies who stretched 65,900 feet of hose connected to 64 pumpers.

nozzle, the condition can possibly be improved by a change in the previously mentioned items, or by inserting additional pumpers in the stretch and relaying water.

In a relay, the desired flow, the resultant friction loss, and the pressure

Parallel lines of 4-inch hose can be laid by the twin-reel pumper of of Wheeling, Ill. Fire Department. Rear outlets are an added convenience.

which the hose can stand—with a margin of safety—must be taken into account.

Laying out hose in a relay

At a fire there are usually so many imponderables which must be taken into consideration that a generalized procedure should be followed, even though it may not result in all pumpers operating at or near the same engine pressure. From a practical standpoint, there is no reason why equalization of pressures should be attempted, particularly in view of the variables such as the time element, topographical conditions, difficulty of estimating distances, pumpers out of touch with another, etc.

The minimum recommended incoming (or residual) pressure to all except the source pumper is 20 psi.

Most departments relay with 2½-inch hose with a flow goal of 200 gpm. The simplest procedure for each pumper, except the one at the water source, is to stretch its full hose load. Then all pumpers, except the one at the fire, pump at 200 psi. Allowing for 20-psi residual pressure at each pumper in the line, 180 psi is available for friction loss.

Tractor-trailer tanker which holds 5000 gallons is used by the Huntley, Ill. Fire Protection District. Once used to haul milk, it was converted for fire use.

At 200 gpm, the friction loss is 10 psi per 100 feet, so there can be 1800 feet of hose between pumpers in the relay, if the stretch is reasonably level and back pressure does not have to be considered. The engine pumping the hand lines for the fire must supply sufficient pressure to take care of the friction loss, nozzle pressure and any back pressure. The engine pressure problem of this pumper is the same as that for any pumper at a hydrant. Any variety of hose layouts may be taken off the pumper at the fire as long as the total gallonage required by all nozzles does not exceed the 200 gpm in this example. Therefore, the engine pressure of the pumper at the fire may be above or below 200 psi, but it should not exceed the pressure at which the department tests hose.

This method of laying hose and standardizing engine pressures may not result in ideal engine pressures, but it gets a relay into operation quickly. Without a standardized relay procedure, confusion often reigns with a resultant loss of time and inadequate water. Any adjustments can be made after water has been started on the fire.

Based primarily on the operating principles of an ordinary pumper relief valve, relay relief, or "dump," valves discharge water to the ground when pressures reach a setting. These portable valves are coupled to the suction inlet. A length of hose is usually coupled to the valve bypass to carry the water away from the immediate area of the pumper. Fixed mounted types are also used.

Relieving excess pressure

Dump valves prevent an excessive pressure buildup throughout a relay each time a nozzle is closed and the flow of water stops. Unless controlled, these increases can burst hose and injure firemen. They also control excessive pressure received in a line from another pumper.

Centrifugal pumpers take full advantage of the pressure at which water is delivered to them and, with no increase of motor speed, their discharge pressures are increased accordingly.

Before a properly balanced relay operation is achieved, pump pressures and relief valves have to be adjusted. It has been found that many relief valves have their settings affected by variations in intake pressures. The result is that even with all relief valves in the stretch properly set, a marked increase of pressure is inevitable when the nozzle is closed.

Under this condition, the pumper at the source delivers its discharge pressure without reduction to the next pumper. With its relief valve set to open at a certain figure, this second pumper now attempts to control pressures by opening a path for the discharge to return to the suction side of the pumps. However, the inlet pressure may now be at or above the former discharge pressure and the energy created by the rapidly turning pump impellers results in a discharge pressure buildup beyond the setting of the regular relief valve.

This serious condition is multiplied when there are more than two pumpers in a relay. A dump valve on the pumper nearest the nozzle minimizes this problem. The discharge pressure on the lead pumper cannot be directly controlled by a dump valve placed on the suction side of the pump. The relief valve or governor should, therefore, be properly set.

Although not strictly necessary in most relay operations, the pump relief valves and pressure governors on other pumpers in the relay should also be set. With such protection, an interrupted or reduced flow of water, caused by a heavy vehicle passing over the hose line at any point behind the lead pumper, will not result in excessive pressures between the hose and the source pumper. In this setup, the dump valve on the lead pumper will not afford protection, but protective devices on the other pumpers will.

Pressure governors reduce but do not eliminate this problem in relays. The best a governor can do is to throttle an engine down to idling speed. Even at this speed, however, pressures can be multiplied particularly if the discharge is small and the pumps are in series position.

Fundamentals of relaying

The following rules should be used as a general guide to relaying water:

1. Place the pumper with the largest capacity rating at the source of supply. Use the largest size hose available.

Water Pressure Conversion Table

psi	ft.	psi	ft.	psi	ft.	psi	ft.	psi	ft.
1	2.31	53	122.43	105	242.55	157	362.67	209	482.79
2	4.62	54	124.74	106	244.86	158	364.98	210	485.10
3	6.93	55	127.05	107	247.17	159	367.29	211	487.41
4	9.23	56	129.36	108	249.48	160	369.60	212	489.72
5	11.55	57	131.67	109	251.79	161	371.91	213	492.03
6	13.86	58	133.98	110	254.10	162	374.22	214	494.34
7	16.17	59	136.29	111	256.41	163	375.53	215	496.65
8	18.48	60	138.60	112	258.72	164	378.84	216	498.96
9	20.79	61	140.91	113	261.03	165	381.15	217	501.27
10	23.10	62	143.22	114	263.34	166	383.46	218	503.58
11	25.41	63	145.53	115	265.65	167	385.77	219	505.89
12	27.72	64	147.84	116	267.96	168	388.08	220	508.20
13	30.03	65	150.15	117	270.27	169	390.39	221	510.51
14	32.34	66	152.46	118	272.58	170	392.70	222	512.82
15	34.65	67	154.77	119	274.89	171	395.01	223	515.13
16	36.96	68	157.08	120	277.20	172	397.32	224	517.44
17	39.27	69	159.39	121	279.51	173	399.63	225	519.75
18	41.58	70	161.70	122	281.82	174	401.94	226	522.06
19	43.89	71	164.01	123	284.13	175	404.25	227	524.37
20	46.20	72	166.32	124	286.44	176	406.56	228	526.68
21	48.51	73	168.63	125	288.75	177	408.87	229	528.99
22	50.82	74	170.94	126	291.06	178	411.18	230	531.30
23	53.13	75	173.25	127	293.37	179	413.49	231	533.61
24	55.44	76	175.56	128	295.68	180	415.80	232	535.92
25	57.75	77	177.87	129	297.99	181	418.11	233	538.23
26	60.06	78	180.18	130	300.30	182	420.42	234	540.54
27	62.37	79	182.49	131	302.61	183	422.73	235	542.85
28	64.68	80	184.80	132	304.92	184	425.04	236	545.16
29	66.99	81	187.11	133	307.23	185	427.35	237	547.47
30	69.30	82	189.42	134	309.54	186	429.66	238	549.78
31	71.61	83	191.73	135	311.85	187	431.97	239	552.09
32	73.92	84	194.04	136	314.16	188	434.28	240	554.40
33	76.23	85	196.35	137	316.47	189	436.59	241	556.71
34	78.54	86	198.66	138	318.78	190	438.90	242	559.02
35	80.85	87	200.97	139	321.09	191	441.21	243	561.33
36	83.16	88	203.28	140	323.40	192	443.52	244	563.64
37	85.47	89	205.59	141	325.71	193	445.83	245	565.95
38	87.78	90	207.90	142	328.02	194	448.14	246	568.26
39	90.09	91	210.21	143	330.33	195	450.45	247	570.57
40	92.40	92	212.52	144	332.64	196	452.76	248	572.88
41	94.71	93	214.83	145	334.95	197	455.07	249	575.19
42	97.02	94	217.14	146	337.26	198	457.38	250	577.50
43	99.33	95	219.45	147	339.57	199	459.69	251	579.81
44	101.64	96	221.76	148	341.88	200	462.00	252	582.12
45	103.95	97	224.07	149	344.19	201	464.31	253	584.43
46	106.26	98	226.38	150	346.50	202	466.62	254	586.74
47	108.57	99	228.69	151	348.81	203	468.93	255	589.05
48	110.88	100	231.00	152	351.12	204	471.24	256	591.36
49	113.19	101	233.31	153	353.43	205	473.55	257	593.67
50	115.50	102	235.62	154	355.74	206	475.86	258	595.98
51	117.81	103	237.93	155	358.05	207	478.17	259	598.29
52	120.12	104	240.24	156	360.36	208	480.48	260	600.60

2. The discharge pressure of any pumper should not exceed 200 psi.

3. The residual pressure at each pumper, except for the source pumper, should be 20 psi.

4. Relief valves (including dump valves) or pressure governors should be properly set on each pumper.

5. Charge lines with the throttle at about one-half motor speed until a sudden buildup of pressure indicates water has reached the next pumper. Then adjust the throttle to meet the requirements.

6. Until water reaches a pumper, the bleeder valve on an unused discharge gate, or the gate itself, should be open to vent the air in the line. Close the valve or gate when water is received.

7. Open and shut nozzles slowly, or better still, keep them partly open, if it is practicable. This precaution will prevent burst lines due to water hammer.

8. Monitor radio communications to keep abreast of conditions and regulate pressures accordingly.

CHAPTER FOURTEEN

Portable ladders, aerials and platforms

Every ladder truck and elevating platform designated as a truck company should carry at least 163 feet of various sized ladders. But some units carry more, depending on the size of the truck and the needs of the department. Pumpers should carry at least one 14-foot roof ladder and a metal truss, 24-foot extension ladder.

Today's portable ladders evolved from the basic design first developed by cave dwellers, using short and long tree branches tied together with vines. The design has changed very little since then. The long branches evolved into solid rectangular beams, sanded smooth. The short ones are now round for better conformity to man's foot, and are fitted to the beams in sockets after the manner of dowels. Metal reinforcing rods were later added to hold the assembly together more tightly, and steel hardware was placed at the top and bottom of each beam to protect the wood from mechanical injury and to dig into the supporting surface.

As man tried to reacher higher with ladders, he discovered that a longer ladder required progressively thicker and heavier beams that ultimately made the ladder too heavy to carry and manipulate. To get around this problem, he employed trussed beams instead of solid wood. These gave him practically the same strength with considerable less weight, since a truss consists largely of empty spaces.

Now, metal ladders have all but replaced the wooden ladders on new apparatus coming into the fire service. These ladders use a lightweight metal, generally an alloy of aluminum, to replace wood. Coming in all sizes and styles, metal ladders are considerably lighter than wooden ones. They have almost replaced fire service wooden ground ladders, since they can be manufactured more cheaply and easily than wooden ones which require increasingly expensive lumber, considerable handcrafting and greater care.

Both solid-beam and trussed-beam ladders are still in use—metal and wood—but in the fire service trussed ladders are the more popular, particularly in sizes above 20 feet. Not only are trussed ladders lighter to handle, but they add less weight to the apparatus that must carry a number of them.

A continuing problem with ladders is length. For one thing, a long ladder is difficult to store, either in a building or on an apparatus where the length of the longest portable ladder is determined by the length of the apparatus itself. For another, it was realized long ago that ladders often were needed within buildings, but because of the limitations in size and shape of doors and stairs, often could not be taken inside.

The invention of the extension and folding ladders solved this problem.

Sizes and types

Ground ladders can be classified as straight or wall ladders, extension ladders, hook or roof ladders and attic (also called folding) ladders. They range in size from 10 up to 55 feet.

The function of the ground ladder at fires is to facilitate rescue, stretch lines, and ventilate whether directly (smashing windows) or indirectly by permitting men to reach roofs or other difficult-to-reach places. Ladders also serve admirably at emergencies or disasters such as train wrecks, building or shoring collapses, drownings, accidents on utility poles and many others. It is at such occurrences that the smaller ladders with their variety and flexibility come into play. Most fire departments serve these functions by sending a combination of ladders to each alarm, generally on one or more ladder trucks.

Placing the ladder

The selection of the right ladder for a job at a fire depends on the training, experience and on-the-spot judgment of the fire fighter. A 35-foot wall ladder that stretches 10 feet above the top of a window is surely not the proper ladder for a rescue from this window. Neither is a 12-footer the proper one for stretching a line into a building when the tip is 10 feet below the sill.

When properly placed, a ladder should rest against a building at a 75° angle. This is the ideal and such an inclination provides stability for

Six steps to be taken for four man ladder raise. Fourth man (not shown in lower right) has stepped aside to guide the three-man carry.

climbing, and utilizes the maximum strength of the ladder. A ready rule for attaining this ideal is to divide the used length of the ladder by 4. The result gives the distance the butt of the ladder should be placed from the side of a building or from a point vertically beneath any overhang. Such placement, while the ideal, is often the exception rather than the rule at fires, where much improvisation must take place. Fortunately, fire service ladders are well made and even when placed at too acute an angle are generally strong enough to carry the load.

Over the years there has been much discussion about the placing of a straight ladder with relation of the truss to the building. Truss in or truss out? No complete agreement has ever been reached on this subject among fire fighters or manufacturers. However, specifications for truss ladders always state that they must give non-fail performance whether the truss is in or out. Such specifications take into consideration that men on the fireground sometimes don't have either the time or the space to place the truss in either this or that position.

No matter what the position of the truss, or the butt of the ladder, the most important point of focus should be the tip of the ladder. It is here that a person will be rescued or a line stretched into a building. There is general agreement that the tip of the ladder when raised to a window should be placed at either side and somewhat above the sill. Such placement leaves the window opening free of obstructions and permits easy access or egress in the event a person has to be removed or a line stretched in. The exception to this is where rescue is involved. Some rescue officers prefer that the ladder tip reach only to the window sill or slightly lower. They believe it facilitates removal of persons.

Ladders stretched to a roof should be long enough so that three or more rungs extend over the edge. This position not only makes for easy access to the roof, but in the event of a hasty retreat, makes the position of the ladder readily visible. When ladders are in use, they should always be butted by at least one man. For safety's sake, ladders placed in general use should be located away from exits, passageways, hose lines, etc., and lashed or dogged if they are to be left unattended.

Extension ladders follow the general rules given for the placement of straight ladders, but again there is disagreement on the over or under position of the truss. However, with extension ladders, the various manufacturers make specific recommendations on the positioning of the truss, and it would be well for the fire fighters to know the name of the manufacturer of the ladders carried on his apparatus. Manufacturers of metal extension ladders generally don't indicate which side should be out, and apparently they feel that the ladder is at full strength either way.

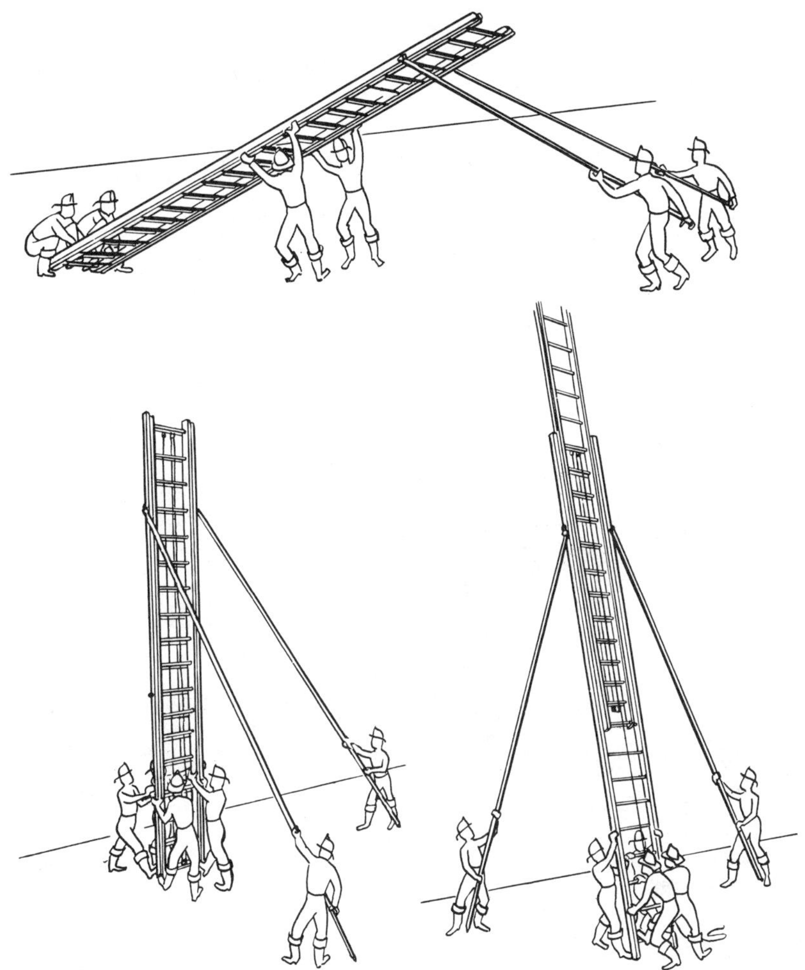

Raising pole ladders requires six men. At start ladder is placed parallel to building with butt end in line with center of window to be reached.

A note on the raising of the fly: It is easier to hoist when the ladder is in vertical position, with the halyard held as parallel to the beam as possible. The fly on a small extension presents no problem and can be raised by hand or with a pike if no halyard is provided. Extension ladders in larger sizes, 35 feet or longer, come equipped with stay poles (tormentors) that are used for beam support and stability in raising or lowering.

Roof ladders may be either solid-beam or truss and are provided with

Beam raise which might be required in constricted spaces takes two to four men depending on size and weight of ladder.

a hook at the tip of each beam, set in a spring-lock socket that permits rotation of the hooks. This permits them to be folded in the same plane as the rungs for easy storage. Used mainly for ventilating or working on peaked roofs, the hook ladder is laid flat on a roof with the hook extending over the ridge and digging into the opposite side of the roof for support. Hook ladders are also carried by fireboats for boarding other vessels. Many of these use permanently mounted hooks which cannot be folded. The position of the truss, if present, is no problem here since it will be positively determined by the position of the hooks.

Carrying and raising

Much has been written and diagrammed on the proper way of getting a portable ladder off an aerial truck and up against the side of the building. Evolutions vary from area to area and from training school to training school throughout the country. The important thing is that a standard for raising and carrying be established in a department and that this standard be used by all members at all times. Previous pages of this book offers one standard for raising and carrying ladders, but it must be remembered that other methods are accepted.

Even with the smaller sizes, carrying a raised ladder at a fire is at best a dangerous proposition. The man, or men, carrying it has to simultaneously keep his eyes to the ground for footing, and on the tip of the ladder to avoid wires or other obstructions. With larger ladders, three men carry the ladder—one on each beam and one on the rungs—with the fourth man guiding. However, the advantage gained by the guide is more than offset by the weight of the larger ladders, which require considerable strength and balancing to keep upright while being moved.

At fires there is considerable movement. Hose zips along the ground, apparatus jockey for position and heavy streams of water cut through the air. To carry a ladder upright in such an environment is not only difficult but extremely hazardous. Add to this wind and ice or snow on the ground overlaid by a film of water and you have an evolution that is almost suicidal.

It is therefore best, whenever possible, to leave the vertical carrying of ladders to the drill yard or outdoor company drill and to explore the alternatives. First, if a ladder is required at another location, take another one from the apparatus. Failing this, and if the distance is not too far, roll or slide the ladder across the face of the building. If the ladder is handled with reasonable care, it will receive little or no damage, and if a life is saved or a line stretched quickly to head off fire, the damage is not important. Finally, the ladder can be lowered to the ground, carried to the new position and raised again.

Hoisting ladders

When hoisting ladders to roofs with ropes, use the following guidelines: To determine where the rope should be placed on 10 to 20-foot ladders, divide by 5. The quotient denotes the rung from the tip under which the rope should be passed. Then tie the rope to the bottom rung. For example, with a 20-foot ladder, dividing by 5 gives 4. Pass the rope between the fourth and fifth rungs from the top and tie two half-hitches and a binder knot at the center of the bottom rung.

For 25, 30 and 35-foot ladders, divide by 5 and multiply by 2, then tie two half-hitches on each beam and make a bowline with a binder. Put on binding knot after bowline has been tied, and also make sure that the

Two clove hitches and a bowline are used as indicated to raise ladder to roof or other elevation.

bowline is midway between the beams. An example of the above calculation is as follows: 35-foot ladder divided by 5 gives 7 which, multiplied by 2, gives 14. The two half-hitches and bowline should be tied 14 rungs from the tip.

When hoisting a ladder, the hauling rope should be between the ladder and the building so that the tip will angle outward and clear windowsills, cornices and other projections. When lowering a ladder, the ladder should be between the rope and the building so that the butt will kick outward and clear any projections.

Climbing

Going up the side of a building on a ladder requires a lot of self-confidence, which some men initially lack but which can generally be developed by training and practice. Training officers are very aware of this and as a consequence, the novice fire fighter spends considerable time every day in just plain climbing ladders of all sizes and shapes. Many larger departments drill with the scaling ladder, which is probably the best training for acquiring confidence.

In climbing ladders as in climbing stairs, the legs do most of the work, with the arms and hands used for balancing. The climber should step off briskly but smoothly, stepping on the center of each rung with the ball of the foot, and holding himself at a loose arm's length from the plane of the ladder. The latter point is important as it tends to keep a man in the proper upright climbing position. Hugging the ladder in climbing may cause scraped shins. It can also lead to slipping and falling.

Whether a man grasps every rung or every other rung is a matter of personal preference, although the latter tends to make for smoother climbing. If the climber must carry a short ladder or a tool in one hand, he is then compelled to grasp the underside of a beam with the other, rather than make a one-hand grab for each rung. In this grasp, the climber makes a steady but somewhat loose contact with the beam to avoid possible splinters. The protection of gloves in this work is self-evident.

Occasionally, a fire fighter must stop at some point on a ladder and station himself for a period of time to perform work. If this period is long, it is best that he don a ladder or safety belt and hook on to the rung nearest his waist. For short periods of time, a man can lock himself on the ladder—leaving his hands free to work—by inserting one leg between two rungs, then back again between the next lower rungs, and getting a toe hold on a beam. He should lock in with the leg opposite the side on which he will be working. Again, whenever a man is on a ladder, either climbing or working, another man must butt the ladder.

Care and maintenance

Ground ladders used by the fire service are considerably more expensive than commercial ladders and if properly cared for will give years of safe service. Frequent and thorough inspection can add to this life, and efficient departments have regulations requiring that the ladder apparatus be stripped regularly, preferably outdoors and in good light. Each wooden ladder is carefully examined and then washed with a mild noncaustic soap. Beds used for carrying the ladders are also examined for defects and carefully washed free of dirt and grit. Before ladders are returned to these beds, they should be thoroughly dry. Wet spots on the surface of the bed can cause serious damage from rot to wooden ladders, many of which will be in service for years to come.

Brackets and locks that hold ladders flush to the sides of apparatus must also be gone over, not only because bending or warping can cause damage to the ladders, but because failure en route to a fire could have tragic consequences for the men on the side of a ladder truck.

Rub spots which remove varnish on wooden ladders are one of the most common defects found. Such spots bare the wood, permit moisture to penetrate the grain and, if unchecked, can cause blistering under large areas of the varnish with eventual rotting of the wood. Any such spot should be permitted to dry and then be carefully sanded and touched up with varnish. The same practice applies to minor splintering. Any major splintering or cracking calls for the attention of a skilled shop mechanic, as does large-scale blistering or chipping of varnish.

Ladders stored in heated quarters will naturally dry out. As this drying progresses, rungs tend to become loose, and the spacer blocks and parts of the beam on a truss ladder shrink away from each other. Weekly washing will aid in reducing this process, but occasionally adjustments will have to be made on the tie rods and on the bolts holding the beams.

Such adjustments should be made by an experienced man or a ladder mechanic.

In addition to regular inspections, ladders should be examined carefully after every working fire. A beam split along the grain can go unnoticed in a cursory examination and the ladder placed back on the apparatus to endanger the lives of men at subsequent alarms. Heel plates should receive particular attention after fires for loosening and chipping. Apparatus driven in rain or snow should be thoroughly dried on return to quarters.

Pawls on extension ladders should be kept free of rust and grit and lubricated to permit easy operation. The same applies to rollers, spring clamps and other appliances that hold or clamp ladders to the apparatus. The lubricant should be used sparingly to prevent its contact with the wood of the ladders.

Men on ladders

One serious cause for damage to ground ladders is overloading. Fire department ladders, both wooden and metal, have a wide margin of safety built into them, but it is better to be safe than sorry. On smaller ladders, 10 to 16 feet long, only one man should be permitted on a ladder. Two men are permitted on ladders from 20 to 30 feet long and on all larger sizes of ground ladders, three men are the preferred limit. Such recommended limits are for solid-beam and truss wood or aluminum ladders. Common sense dictates that, except for rescue work and when advancing hose lines, only one man is needed on a ladder to operate a line, break a window, etc. Any greater number is evidence of faulty training. It is better that additional men butt the ladder, steady a hose line or make themselves useful elsewhere.

Secondary uses

Ground ladders are among the most versatile of fire department tools and can be used for many purposes other than providing portable stairways to safety. Bridging is the first of these purposes that comes to mind. In bridging, a ladder is used as a horizontal exit—across alleys and narrow openings between buildings and, using smaller ladders, across light or air shafts between or within buildings. Bridging can also be used to carry hose lines over roadways or railroads to permit the continuance of traffic while fire fighters are operating. Still another form of bridging is to replace burnt-out stairs with a ladder.

Probably the most common use for a ladder is for ventilating the upper floors of a building. This operation can be performed quickly and efficiently by raising a ladder in front of the window to be ventilated and letting the tip drop into the building, smashing window and sash. Helmets, gloves and sturdy coats are a must here, and members controlling the ladder should stand to one side after the ladder is dropped to avoid falling glass, which has a tendency to slide down the beams. Held horizontally by several men, a ladder can also be used to clean out store windows and the partitioning behind them. Inserting a ladder through openings in a roof provides an excellent means of knocking down hanging ceilings such as are found in supermarkets. Short ladders taken up the inside of frame houses can be used to push out the roof to ventilate attic spaces.

Forcible entry

A ladder can be used to open the stoutest of doors. When so used, the beams of the ladder (preferably a 20-footer or better) are placed one above and one below the lock. A steady pressure is then exerted against the ladder—and the door—by several men. Since the men can stand well away from the door, they have much better protection against flame or back draft. If the door doesn't give readily, it is best not to use the ladder as a battering ram except in an emergency. Ladders have been damaged while being used as a ram in this situation and to no avail.

Fire fighters through the years have put ground ladders to many and unusual uses. A ladder can be made into a stretcher by laying planks or a door on the rungs. As a sling, it can lower the injured from upper stories or raise them from an excavation. Pushed out on ice, a wooden ladder makes an excellent tool for rescuing skaters or others who have fallen into ponds, rivers and the like.

In the area of salvage and overhaul, ladders can be combined with a tarpaulin to make a handy reservoir. As a barricade, the ladder can help keep the curious bystander away and permit fire fighters to work unhampered.

AERIAL LADDERS

The first successful mechanically raised turntable ladder was designed by Daniel D. Hayes, a New York City volunteer fireman who moved to San Francisco. There he took a job as a machinist for the San Francisco Fire Department, which accepted delivery in 1872 of the first "Hayes Hook and Ladder Truck and Fire Escape Combined." Local builders constructed the truck on license from Hayes.

The ladder on Hayes' truck was raised by a manually operated crank that turned a worm screw assembly. The turntable was basically the same as found in aerials today. Later aerials were elevated by compressed air in pistons. Then came the spring assist, followed by the completely spring-powered elevation piston types which prevailed until the introduction of the present hydraulically operated aerials.

In the beginning, aerial ladders were made strictly from wood and continued to be so right up until modern times. But it is interesting to note that as early as January 1888, a 90-foot, three-section, steel aerial was delivered to the City of St. Paul by E. B. Preston Co., apparatus builders in Chicago. In the same month they reported the sale of another steel aerial to Seattle, Territory of Washington.

Metal takes over

However, there is no further mention of metal aerials in apparatus history until the mid-30s, when the Seagrave Corporation introduced an all-steel aerial ladder and Peter Pirsch & Sons, an all-aluminum ladder. Pirsch had also pioneered, in 1931, hydraulically operated aerials that provided hydraulic elevation and mechanical extension and rotation. With modifications, such types of powered aerials, either aluminum or steel, are called for by today's specifications.

Metal aerial ladders all operate on the same principle. A power takeoff from the transmission drives a hydraulic pump which, in turn, transmits power to the various operating units of the ladder assembly through hydraulic tubing, swivels and swivel joints that carry a special mineral oil through the fifth wheel and turntable to a master control valve on the turntable.

Movement of an operating control lever sends oil under pressure to whatever working unit is selected. When all operating controls are in neutral, the oil is bypassed continuously to a reserve hydraulic tank and from there to the pump, completing an idling cycle.

Metal aerial ladders come in a variety of sizes, generally 85 to 100-foot, that can be mounted on a six-wheel chassis or on a semitrailer. All have an operating pedestal at the base of the ladder.

Invariably on this pedestal are three control handles or push buttons, used to raise or lower the bed, extend or retract the moving sections and rotate the entire assembly. In addition, there is a turntable lock which must be released before rotating the ladder and locked when the ladder is positioned.

Raising the bed

The control handle for raising the bed operates a valve which permits the flow of hydraulic fluid into the two elevating cylinders whose pistons actually raise the ladder. The more oil under pressure fed to the cylinders, the greater will be the distance the piston rods travel and hence

Three control handles and turntable lock operate valves and switches which direct hydraulic fluid under pressure to operate raising, rotating and hoisting mechanisms.

the greater the angle the ladder will achieve. When the desired angle is reached, the operator returns the control to neutral. This action stops the movement of the ladder and automatically locks it.

Moving the lever to the down position reverses the flow of oil and permits the ladder to return to the bed. Should any of the hydraulic lines fail, a safety device incorporated into the system permits a slow escape of oil from the two cylinders and prevents rapid descent of the ladder.

Elevation and sweep of ladder pipe make it an excellent tool for large-scale fires.

Basically, the same cycle of hydraulic flow and pressure applies to rotating the turntable. Moving the rotation lever on the control pedestal permits the entire assembly to revolve. In this operation the fluid, instead of activating a piston rod, drives a hydraulic motor which powers a gear train that rotates the table.

Again, returning the control lever to neutral will lock the turntable in whatever position selected. But as an added precaution, all manufacturers provide a hand-operated lock on, or adjacent to, the control pedestal.

Moving the ladder

Extending—and retracting—the moving sections of the ladder assembly is accomplished by a hydraulic motor and gear train which rotates a drum that carries the ladder cables. There is one ladder that has a hydraulic piston beneath the bed ladder for moving the fly cables.

Normally, the pressure in the retracting position is set to relieve at about 300 psi on most apparatus. This limits the retraction motor and is a safety feature designed to protect rungs and beams should a section be held firmly by a rung lock, an obstruction or ice.

To complete this unit, there is a manually operated valve which, in effect, eliminates the relief valve and permits delivery of full power (about 1000 psi) to the retraction motor. Improper use of this valve could lead to considerable damage to ladder pistons and even to the turntable. It should therefore be used only by a shop mechanic or, if there is none, by a man thoroughly familiar with the operation, design and construction of the ladder.

The hydraulic motors which provide power for the cable drum and for rotating the turntable are generally of the internal-external gear type, designed to operate in either direction by simply reversing the flow of

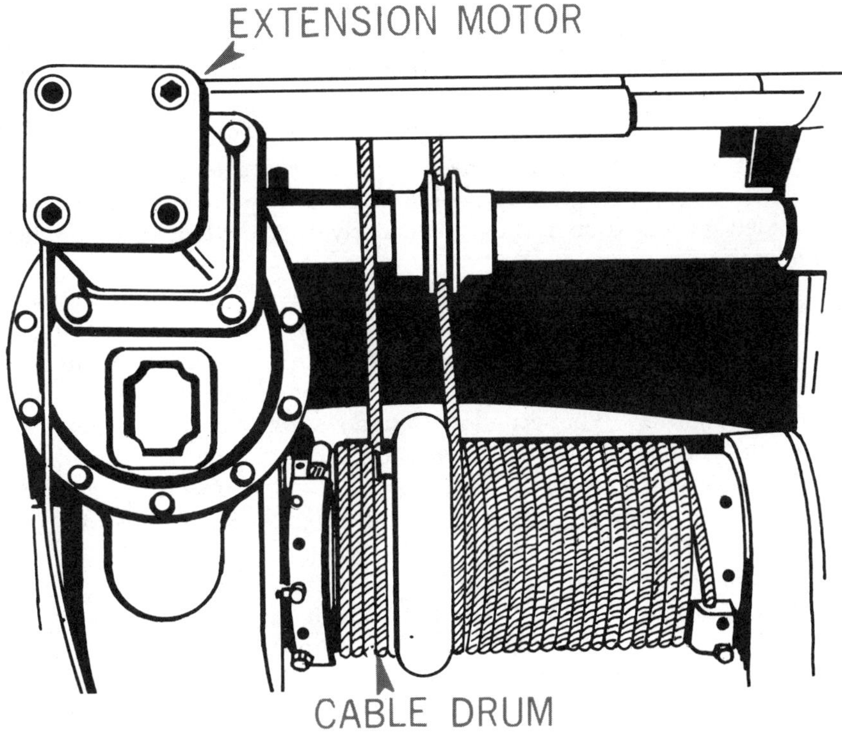

Hydraulic motor and gear train rotates drum that carries cables which move the ladder sections of aerial.

oil. Automatic limit stops are provided to halt both the bed and moving sections when they have reached the limit of travel. These stops function by automatically moving the control handle to neutral.

Finally, there is a ladder lock which holds the bed to the frame of the vehicle to prevent vibration and movement when the apparatus is traveling on the road.

All operations may be conducted manually by inserting a crank into the proper assembly. But in raising the bed, or extending the section, the rate of movement is such as to be almost imperceptible.

However, the turntable can be rotated quite easily by a crank and is the preferred method for rotation when the ladder pipe is in operation. With the power takeoff disengaged, the crank handle makes for much smoother rotation of the assembly when 600 to 1000 gpm are pushing out the pipe.

Rotating drum lifts ladders

On all metal aerials, the moving sections of the ladder are equipped with two cables, one for pulling up and one for pulling down. On all but one aerial, cables wind around, and are securely connected to, a drum which provides the motive power. On the other type, the cables are connected to a hydraulic piston beneath the bed ladder.

The need for the pull-up cable is obvious. But the need for the pull-down is not so obvious until one realizes that friction can prevent the extended sections from moving, particularly when the ladder is extended at a low angle.

The latest models of both 85 and 100-foot ladders have four sections, older models three, with rungs on both usually spaced 14 inches apart. When the control lever is engaged to extend a four-section ladder, the first sliding section (the one next to the bed ladder) moves one rung out of the bed ladder. The second section moves one rung out on the first. And the third, or fly, section moves one rung out on the second. A one-rung extension from the bed, therefore, will mean a three-rung extension of the ladder as a unit. Two rungs from the bed means six rungs as a unit and so on.

Such movement and spacing have a bearing on the rung locks which come two to a section. With a four-section ladder and rung spacing of 14 inches there is a distance of 42 inches of upper fly-section travel between locking points (three rungs times 14 inches). The difference in a three-section ladder is therefore 28 inches since there are only two sliding sections. Extension of ladders with different rung spacings are measured similarly.

 On occasion, and because of this 42-inch spread, a ladder may have

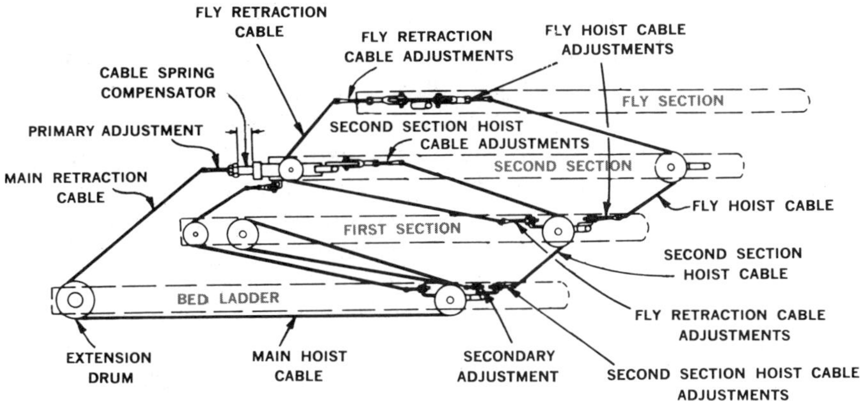

Typical arrangement of ladders on a four section aerial shows hoist and retracting cables with pulleys and cable adjustments.

to be operated without the ladder locks engaged, and with the sliding sections entirely supported by the cables. Hydraulic pressure will almost always lock the ladders in this position and hold them. But to be absolutely certain, once the ladder is positioned, the rung lock control should be placed in the on position. If the cable fails, the ladder will then drop only to the next locking position and not telescope all the way.

Stabilizing the tractor

Tormentors (also called jacks, stabilizers or outriggers) complete the parts necessary for the safe and efficient operation of the metal aerial. Originally, tormentors were designed only to firm up the turntable. They were positioned inside the wheels of the apparatus, with the wheels actually providing stability against tipping. But when metal aerials appeared, with their tremendous increase in weight, it was found that a wider foundation was needed. Tormentors were then designed to extend beyond the sides of the truck and constructed with much heavier components. Each apparatus comes equipped with at least two tormentors, one on each side, and sometimes two on each side.

Finally, there are stabilizing jacks. When a ladder is raised to a building, there is a considerable increase of weight over the wheel on the side to which it is raised. Unless supported, this weight causes the rear tractor springs to sag, throwing the tractor off level. To eliminate this action manufacturers have installed stabilizing jacks, one for each side, which provide a solid connection between the rear axle and frame of the apparatus, thus rendering the rear springs inoperative.

The greater the angle to the ground, the greater the strength and stability of the ladder, and the greater its vertical reach. A ladder must be brought to the angle recommended by the manufacturer before it is fully extended, whether or not it is supported at the tip.

To guide the operator there is an inclinometer on all metal aerials from which he can tell at a glance what angle the ladder has in relation to a horizontal plane. This inclinometer is invariably on the base of the bed ladder adjacent to the operating pedestal. On some apparatus it is coupled with a meter that indicates the extension of the ladder in feet. Some aerials have a load indicator in the form of a dial with a needle that indicates "safe" and "dangerous" zones. Manufacturers can provide other and more complex variations of this inclino-extension meter, but generally it is considered optional equipment.

However, some departments provide a do-it-yourself method for determining the extension of the ladder. It is inexpensive but still adequate. Spaced along the struts on the beam of the bed ladder are numerals painted on the surface of the strut that faces the operator at the pedestal. When the ladder is extended, a reading can be taken by lining up the lowest rung of the first sliding section with the marked strut on the bed ladder. The numerals are calibrated in feet for the maximum vertical extension of the ladder from the ground. To determine extension of the ladder only, subtract distance in feet from the turntable to the ground.

Practical placement

There are elaborate charts and diagrams to indicate the proper placement of apparatus from the fire building and the extension of the ladder. However, these charts are not very practical for the chauffeur of a ladder truck operating in a dark, possibly rainswept street in front of a fire building. A simple method calls for placing the center of the turntable preferably not more than 35 feet from the wall of a building. This method is almost foolproof. The wall acts as a barrier which prevents lowering and extending to a point where the stability of the ladder is threatened.

For ladder pipe operation, the recommended ladder angle is 70 degrees. At this angle, the ladder will have more than adequate stability when the pipe is operated at the maximum recommended height and extension. However, if the center of the turntable is positioned more than 35 feet from a building, the ladder can be retracted and lowered. The point to remember here is that in any ladder pipe operation, the tip of the ladder should be no more than 35 feet horizontally from the turntable.

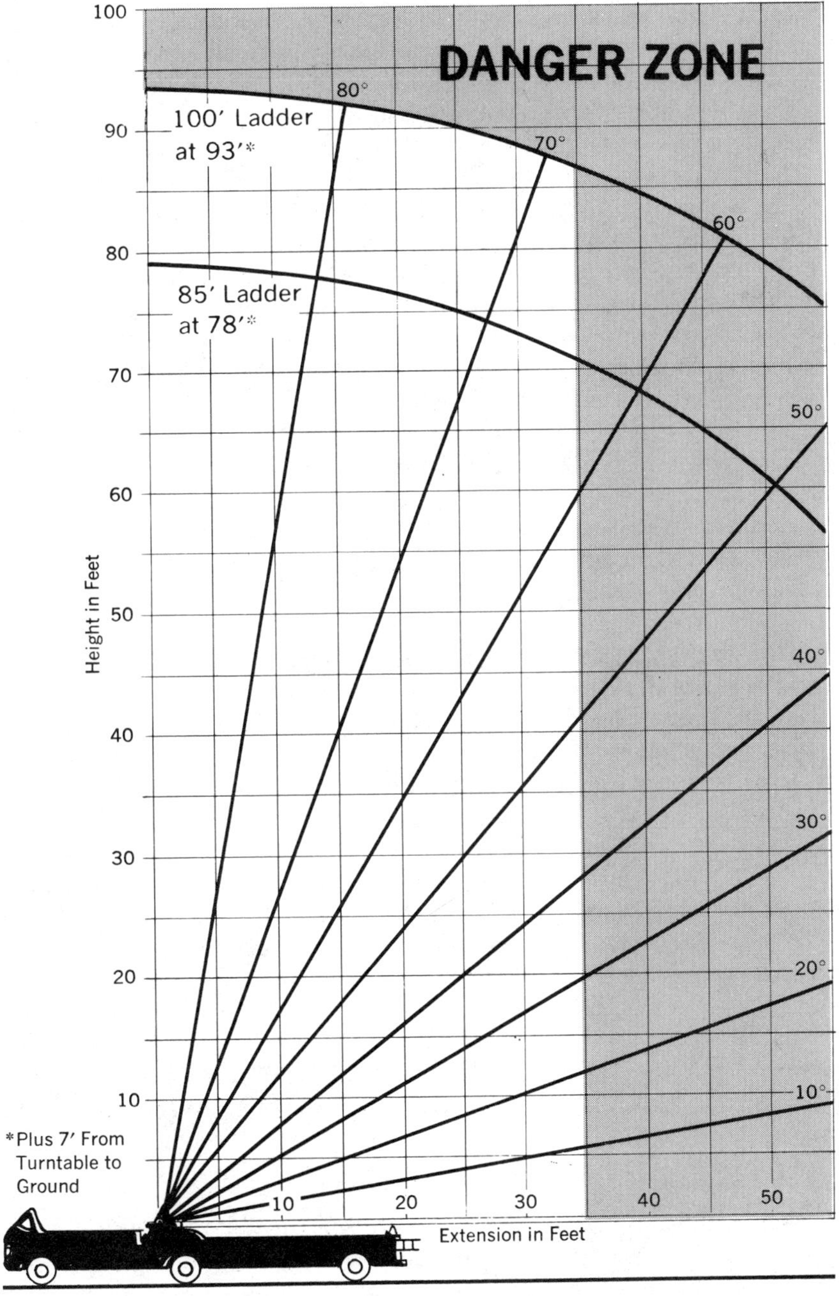
DANGER ZONE
100
90
80
70
60
50
40
30
20
10
Height in Feet
80°
70°
60°
50°
40°
30°
20°
10°
100′ Ladder
at 93′*
85′ Ladder
at 78′*
*Plus 7′ From
Turntable to
Ground
10
20
30
40
50
Extension in Feet

Operating manuals supplied by manufacturers always recommend that an aerial truck be jackknifed to provide maximum stability when ladders are raised. This should be done whenever possible. But in a downtown section of a city with cars parked on both sides of relatively narrow streets, this action is a practical impossibility. It would also have the effect of blocking off the street to other needed apparatus.

In a narrow street, therefore, chauffeurs should stop the truck parallel to the building, with the center of the turntable no more than 35 feet from the wall of a building and in line with the objective (window, roof, etc.). The next step is to put the transmission in neutral, apply parking and brake system lock (if provided), and set spring stabilizing control (if provided).

Final operations in the cab call for engaging the power takeoff, which is controlled by a cable connected to a rod that extends through the dashboard or the floor. Either way, depress the clutch pedal and pull out the control. Then release the clutch slowly. If the power takeoff does not readily engage, the gears are probably butting. Depress the clutch, return the control to its original position and repeat operation, which should generally prove successful. The power takeoff rod also automatically disengages the hold-down lock on the bed ladder of most manufacturers.

The next step in putting an aerial to work is to see to its stability. While this is the responsibility of the chauffeur and officer, it may be delegated simultaneously to other members of the company. The first thing in this phase of the operations is to chock the rear wheels of the tractor to guarantee immobility of the apparatus. Then set the tormentors. If footing pads are provided, place them under the base of the tormentors.

When the apparatus is not positioned on a firm roadway such as concrete, large planking—2 by 8 inches or better—should be placed under the tormentors or footing pads. Softening of an earth or cinder roadway can be anticipated, particularly from water if the ladder pipe is used.

Failure to properly set tormentors can also result in distortion and weakening of the trailer frame in the area of the fifth wheel. This action, in turn, can bind the turntable sufficiently enough to cause the relief valve to operate.

At the pedestal

When the apparatus is properly positioned and supported, the chauffeur mounts to the operating pedestal. The sequence of operation is to raise, rotate and extend. Preferably, each step should be performed

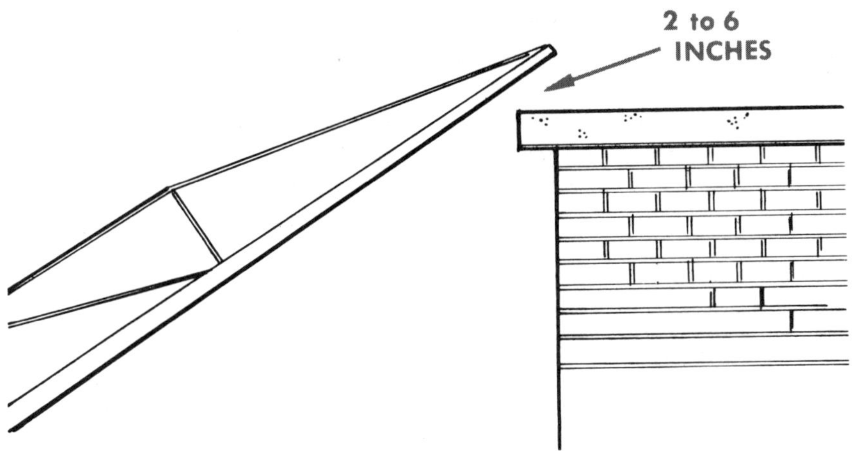

Final placement of ladder should be in cantilever position about 2 to 6 inches above roof or window sill.

separately. However, the ladder may be rotated and extended simultaneously, but no time is saved because the hydraulic power is divided between the two movements. Great care should be used to rotate the ladder smoothly since the stresses set up by jerking motions are most severe. Once at the pedestal, the chauffeur moves the raising lever to raise the ladder assembly from the bed. Occasionally the ladder will bow, indicating that power is being applied but the hold-down lock has not released. The chauffeur should then return the control handle to neutral and try again—almost always successfully unless the lock is defective.

The bed is then raised, stopped at an angle greater than the final desired angle, and rotated until the rungs are parallel to the wall of the fire building. In rotating, the chauffeur should be careful not to strike the side (beam) of the ladder against any obstruction. Metal ladders—in fact, all ladders—are least able to withstand a lateral force. Finally, the chauffeur aims the ladder at the objective, reducing the angle of the bed as necessary and extends the fly.

For example: Assume that his objective is the sill of a standard double-hung window on the fifth floor of a building. He sights along the beam of the ladder, much as one sights a rifle, aiming not for the sill, but for a point approximately halfway up the window. He then extends the fly to meet this point insofar as possible, considering his distance from the objective. Next, he lowers the ladder into the sill, making final adjustments as required to line up the locks and rungs. His efficiency in this operation will be greatly aided by the officer or other member standing adjacent to the wall of the fire building, beneath the tip of the ladder, and acting as guide—particularly in final adjustments. As stated previously, the ladder locks must be engaged or at least in the "on" position before the ladder is used.

Remember that when the ladder is finally placed, it should be in a cantilever position (unsupported) about 2 to 6 inches above the sill. This is done because when men mount a ladder, it will give with their weight and drift into the sill and rest lightly on it. In this way the ladder is under both tension and compression forces that are in reasonable equilibrium.

Remember, too, that the tips of both beams of the ladder should rest equally on the sill or other objective. If one tip is left unsupported, the other will carry all the force and the ladder will have a tendency to twist. As with lateral forces, the ladder is just not designed to withstand this type of stress.

To complete the raising operation, the chauffeur locks the turntable, and the bed-raising lock, if provided. Should he leave the turntable, or if the ladder will be in use for any length of time, the power takeoff must be disengaged for the sake of safety.

Bedding the ladder is simply the reverse of placing it, with the exception that the ladder is first brought out from the building before ladder locks are disengaged and the sections retracted.

Maintenance

Manufacturers provide an operating manual for each model aerial ladder they deliver. Given the proper care, aerials are relatively trouble free. Aside from technical data (provided for mechanics) these manuals give considerable information on the everyday operation of the aerial. Daily care and maintenance, minor repairs, how to shift gears, proper placement and angling, safe loading and many other subjects all come within the sphere of the manuals.

Metal aerial trucks require the same care as all other apparatus. But additional care is required for the moving parts that make up the ladder assembly. This care involves mostly lubrication and inspection and is the responsibility of both the chauffeur and the officer. Proper records should be kept of all such activities. Although many of the moving parts are self-lubricating, there are some that are not and the operating manuals provide diagrams and instructions for servicing grease fittings or oil holes.

Since the hydraulic fluid tank is the key to the whole operation, it should be checked frequently. The apparatus leaves the factory with this tank properly filled and if there is no unusual leakage, it should last for a year. However, if the supply drops below the figure recommended

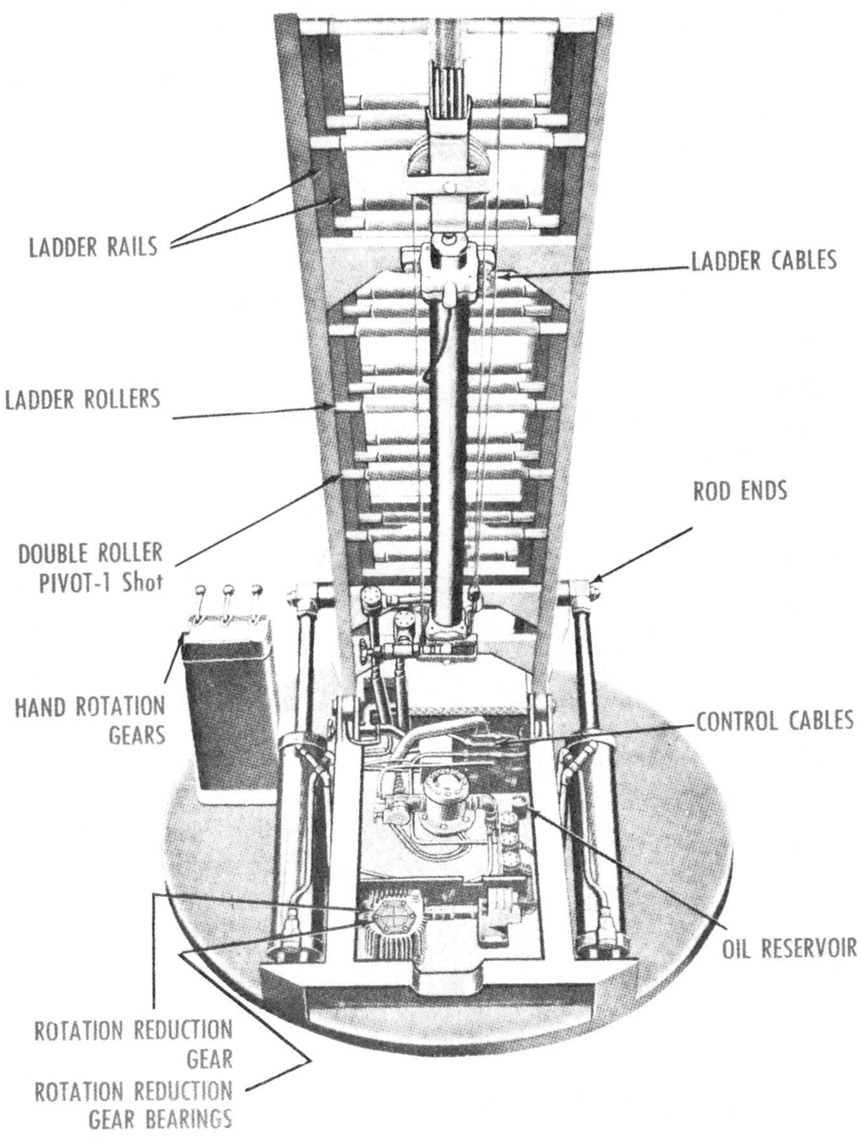

Lubrication points (arrows) cover the raising extending and rotating mechanisms on all makes of aerials, with little variation.

Ladder pipe can be placed in a window to provide heavy fog or solid stream that is manipulated from the street.

in the operating manual, it should be replenished. In any event, a complete change of fluid should be made at least yearly, but preferably every six months. A drain plug is provided in the bottom of the tank for this purpose. In refilling, only hydraulic fluid of the type recommended by the manufacturer should be used and the fluid kept absolutely clean. Minor leaks that develop in fittings can usually be stopped by tightening the connections.

The hydraulic system should be checked frequently and regularly, particularly in units where the ladder receives little use. This can be accomplished by taking the ladder out of quarters and raising it. But in inclement weather, if the ceiling of the apparatus quarters permits, the bed can be raised a few feet and the extensions run out. On some makes, there is a test valve, but the operation of this valve should be generally left to mechanics.

Both the turntable and the fifth wheel have grease fittings which require attention once or twice a year. The turntable should be rotated during the operation so that all parts of the ball race are lubricated. For the same reason, the truck should be jackknifed in both directions while greasing the fifth wheel. There are other grease fittings and oil holes on all makes, but these vary from manufacturer to manufacturer and can be determined only by consulting the appropriate manual.

Inspection

The ladder should be taken out of quarters frequently, raised, fully extended, and then carefully examined rung by rung. Ladder rollers can develop flat spots, generally from not turning because of lack of cleaning and lubrication. If unnoticed, such flattened rollers can cause serious damage to the affected section. Pulleys and cables should also be examined. If needed, the pulleys should be oiled and the cables greased, with only a light film left on the surface.

As required, but at least every six months, the ladder slides should be lubricated with a thin film of waterproof grease. Before this grease is applied, the ladder should be extended and the old grease and grime washed off with alcohol. During freezing weather, a more liberal application of grease should be applied to retard ice accumulation.

Bolts that hold the turntable to the platform present another and most critical inspection point. On some models, they have a tendency to work loose and must therefore be checked regularly and tightened if necessary. Ignored, they present the possibility of collapse, with destruction of the ladder and death or injury to fire fighters.

Operating procedures

In the field the greatest care should be taken to ensure stability of the apparatus. When placed for operation, the aerial should be on as level a surface as possible. If the truck must be positioned on a grade, compensation for this must be made in determining the angle of the ladder and permissible extension and loading.

Loading is always a problem. The question always comes up: How many men and how much equipment should be allowed on a ladder?

The many variables involved in the answer include the size of the ladder, the degree of elevation, amount of extension and whether the ladder is unsupported (in cantilever). And the answers can be found only in the manual for the make and model ladder in question.

With the ladder in cantilever within limitations of angle and extension, there generally may be one man at the top and one halfway up. At other times 12 men may be permitted on a supported ladder. It all depends on the design characteristics and will be stated in the operating manual.

Icing also presents a problem in loading. An accumulation of ice on a ladder can throw all calculations off and might render the ladder unusable. The added weight could be tremendous, particularly in a ladder pipe operation in bitter weather. However, icing presents its biggest problem when it comes time to bed the ladder and return to quarters.

Thawing a frozen aerial

A liberal layer of grease as mentioned above helps prevent ice from binding sections in the slides. But when this fails, other methods must be resorted to. Steam from a thawing apparatus is probably the best method of freeing a frozen ladder but this is a long, drawnout operation. Another method is to wash down the frozen parts with water from a hose. The water is, of course, above the freezing point and might melt the ice. However, this method will work only when the air temperature is just a few degrees below freezing and not in bitter weather. As a last resort, the ladder is bedded, if possible, with the sections still extended and the apparatus is driven back to quarters to thaw.

Some apparatus comes equipped with a deicing valve as mentioned before. Operation of this valve permits the working pressure to go as high as 1000 psi or more. It should be used with extreme caution.

Often, when sections are thought to be bound, the problem lies with frozen ladder locks. The ladder-lock control might be in the off position, but the locks themselves are still engaged because of ice. This situation can generally be relieved by having a man ascend the ladder, free the locks and tie them back with a piece of wire if they won't remain in position.

Another precaution to be taken involves the use of operating levers on the pedestal. These levers actually operate a switch, which in turn controls the throttle and the pressure in pounds per square inch that is transmitted to the moving part selected. There is occasionally a tendency on the part of chauffeurs to feather or baby the controls in an attempt to move the designated part more slowly. This should be avoided since it can result in burned-out switches.

Should the accelerating solenoid become inoperative for this or any other reason, set the hand throttle at 900 rpm to position the ladder, and when this is done, lower the rpm to idle. Chauffeurs should keep a constant eye on pressure and rpm and if either exceeds recommended readings, a mechanic should be called.

Personnel using metal aerials should always do so with extreme care. Pressures developed by the hydraulic machinery can snap a man's arm off or crush his body with the greatest of ease.

For this reason, no one is permitted on a metal aerial while it is being raised from the bed or while the sections are extending. Occasionally, conditions may warrant a man remaining on a ladder while it rotates, but the operator must make absolutely sure that the ladder locks are engaged. He must also disengage the power takeoff and rotate the turntable by the hand crank. As mentioned before, this prevents any possible jerking motions that would endanger the man on the ladder or possibly damage the ladder itself.

Additional safety recommendations, as well as other points of operation too numerous to elaborate on in a chapter of this scope, can be found in the manufacturers' manuals.

ELEVATING PLATFORMS

Elevating platforms made their first appearance in 1958 following experiments conducted by the Chicago Fire Department and the Pitman Manufacturing Company. The apparatus was of the articulating-boom type, which was the only type platform available until Mack Fire Apparatus, working closely with the New York Fire Department, developed a telescoping-boom elevating platform.

No matter what the type, elevating platforms are, like metal aerials, powered hydraulically, again with a power takeoff from the transmission that drives a hydraulic pump which, in turn, transmits power to the various operating units of the assembly. Again, like aerials, instrumentation on elevating platforms varies from manufacturer to manufacturer but is basically similar. On all such units there are two sets of controls, one on the platform and one at an operating station near the turntable. Ground controls override platform controls.

These controls resemble those on an aerial ladder and perform the same functions of raising, extending and rotating. Locking devices are provided so that the desired boom elevation and turntable position can be maintained indefinitely without dependence on engine power.

Leveling

All elevating platforms are equipped with a device which keeps the platform level in relation to the turntable. However, jacks, or outriggers, are provided on each unit both for stability of the entire unit when elevated and for some leveling. These jacks on the latest apparatus are hydraulically operated and are so designed that the raising and extending

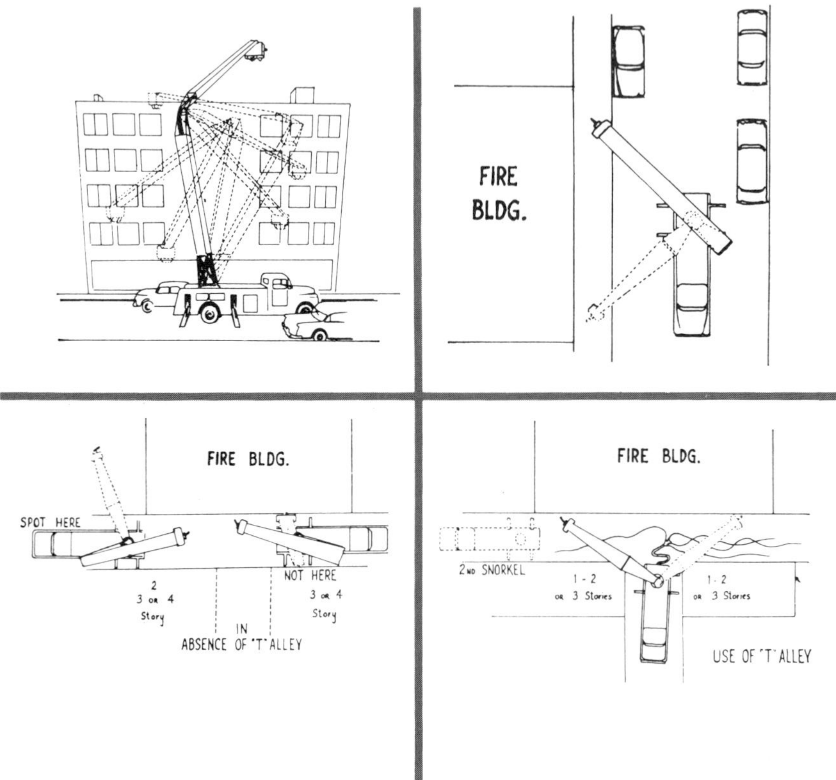

Placement of elevating platforms as recommended by the Chicago Fire Department. Operator should avoid need for later shifting.

mechanisms will not operate until the jacks are placed and locked.

To insure stability of the apparatus, brake-locking devices are provided at the driver's position for all axles. These are backed up by wheel chocks.

Water supply

Originally, regular large-diameter hose was threaded through the booms to supply a master stream nozzle. In the latest models, the hose has been replaced by fixed piping with flexible joints that can articulate with the booms. The piping is connected to a permanently installed turret nozzle on the platform. At ground level it is connected to three gated 2½-inch hose inlets. A pressure gage is also provided at this point.

Hydraulically operated jacks or outriggers are used on elevating platforms for stability of the entire unit when elevated and for some leveling.

Turret nozzles on the platform should have a capacity of at least 500 gpm, but some are equipped with nozzles that can give more than 1000 gpm in either the solid-stream or fog position. These nozzles have an advantage over aerial ladder pipes in that they can be rotated horizontally as well as vertically.

Basic operations

1. Position truck to provide maximum latitude for operation. Take advantage of terrain to provide maximum stability.
2. Set truck hand brake and other auxiliary brakes if provided.
3. Engage power takeoff. If truck is not equipped with automatic throttle, set hand throttle to run engine at speed recommended by manufacturer.
4. See that electric power and communications system to platform is turned on. Platform operators should enter platform and await "ready" signal from ground operator.
5. Ground operator extends outrigger jacks to make firm contact with ground. He places pads under jacks if ground is soft, or might become so from fire stream.

6. When "ready" signal is received, platform operator raises booms and rotates unit as required to attain desired position.

No matter what the function of an elevating platform, it is recommended that there be two operators in the platform and a man at the ground controls at all times. The fire fighters in the platform are closer to the scene of action and will under normal conditions direct its movement. However, the ground operator, with a broader view of the scene, can take over in an emergency which the platform operators may not notice or can't handle.

Considerable judgment must be exercised in placing an elevating platform at an emergency. Such placement will be determined by the desired function of the unit, whether it be as a water tower, mobile fire escape, derrick or any other. But no matter what its function, the apparatus should be placed to avoid any need to shift the piece afterward.

Operators must give due regard to overhead wires and obstructions, make sure that the street is sufficiently wide to take the span of the outriggers, and note the configuration of streets so that the job on hand can be accomplished more effectively.

If the platform is to be used as a water tower, operators should ascertain whether there are people, either civilians or fire fighters, in the building and avoid driving heat and gases against persons struggling down stairways and fire fighters struggling up. Solid streams are particularly dangerous, especially when under heavy pressure.

For the safety of the men on a platform, particularly in buildings that are heavily involved in fire, extinguishing operations should begin on the lower floors and then work upward. At fires in which a room just inside a window is involved, close application of a 90° fog can be used. The angle is, of course, reduced when greater penetration is desired.

For fires in unpierced attics and cocklofts, jackhammers or portable saws may be used off the platform to cut openings through which a fog stream can be operated.

Ventilation

With enough pressure and a solid stream, the elevating platform can be moved across the face of a building to break windows. If this does not suffice, fire fighters on the platform, using hooks, can be moved from window to window to clean them out. Great caution must be exercised in performing this latter evolution since flame can flash out at the operators and there is always the possibility of a back draft.

Using the platform, roof ventilation can be accomplished in several ways. It affords a quick avenue of escape to a man cutting an opening

Chicago fire fighters in Snorkel basket remove passengers from car involved in elevated train crash.

in a spongy roof. If necessary, the platform and the man can be tied together with a short section of ¾-inch rope that guarantees safety with reasonable mobility. Then a man working from a platform can, with a long hook or roof ladder, push down a top-floor ceiling once an opening is made and with relative safety.

Rescue operations

The elevating platform does not lend itself to as quick a mass evacuation from a single point of a building as an aerial ladder does. However, it is more effective than the aerial in incidents such as elevated railroad accidents. Here the platform can be used to lower the injured, the ambulatory, and particularly the litter cases, quickly and in comfort.

In other emergencies involving cave-ins, excavations and entrapments in tanks, the platform can be used as an overhead boom to support block and tackle or other equipment to remove trapped or injured persons.

In heavy storms, the platform can be used to facilitate either the se-

Latest type of aerial equipment, called the Squrt, is actually an articulating water tower mounted on a pumper.

curing or removing of signs that have torn loose, dangling limbs of trees, or any other high object that is in danger of falling.

The elevating platform also can be used as an elevator, raising hand lines, tools, short ladders, and any other objects that do not exceed its load capacity to a roof or higher floors of a building.

Finally, it can be used as a reconnaissance platform, giving a chief officer a high and wide look at the overall fire operation.

In the event of engine failure or loss of hydraulic pressure, an elevating platform can be safely lowered to the ground position. The turntable can be rotated manually by a crank that is provided with the apparatus. Lowering the booms can be accomplished by either bleeding the static hydraulic pressure in the hydraulic cylinders, or adjusting cylinder check valves, or both. In this way, the booms can be brought down at a controlled rate, once they have been aligned by the turntable. Controls for this operation vary according to manufacturer and are explained in the maintenance manual for the individual make and model. As with aerial ladders, the elevating platform requires the regular maintenance of other apparatus plus special maintenance for the moving parts which is best learned from the manual.

COMPARING THE AERIAL LADDER AND THE PLATFORM

Prior to the introduction of elevating platforms, fire departments relied on the aerial ladder to reach the upper floors of buildings. Down through the years, the ladder had also been increasingly used as a water tower. As a result, most cities abandoned their water towers when metal aerials with ladder pipes were developed.

But in so doing, chiefs then faced the possibility that fire in a high-value district could tie up most of their aerials when used as water towers. Should a simultaneous alarm occur in a building where aerial ladders would be required, they would not be available. To solve this problem, a new type of apparatus was developed—the mobile elevating or aerial platform.

Aerial platforms, however, brought new problems which are special to the fire service. The platform is somewhat unique in that it is one of the few pieces of equipment which was not developed initially to meet the needs of the fire service. Quite obviously in such a process the equipment has shortcomings and represents a compromise of what the fire service really needs and what it is able to obtain.

Tests have been made which included hospitals, apartment buildings, and schools. On buildings where a platform could not reach certain floors, neither could an aerial ladder. The setback of upper stories was too great to be reached by either type. In all cases, however, there was a service area at the rear of the buildings where either an aerial ladder or elevating platform could be used.

Other tests showed that on two apartment buildings and five hospitals, none could be reached from the front with any mobile platform manufactured at the time. The setback was approximately 60 feet from the curb line and this precluded any of the available elevating platforms reaching any part of the building. But all floors could be reached with a 100-foot aerial ladder.

When a city has enough aerial ladders to satisfy the grading schedule, then the elevating platform becomes a recommended choice for water tower use primarily and rescue use secondarily. The reasons for this are as follows:

1. Faster time to get into operation. All the piping from the inlet siamese on the truck to the turret is in place. It is necessary only to run hose lines from the pumper to inlets to put the platform nozzle in operation. The minutes thus saved in this operation spell the difference many times between a bad fire and one which is quickly knocked down. This is particularly true in church fires and others where a fast control is essential.

2. Greater water capacities with less friction loss and thus less pump pressure required for a given volume. Water capacities of 1000 gpm to 2000 gpm are practical and are being used for massive fog applications which have made some spectacular fire stops. Two-and one-half-inch outlets can be provided at the platform so that a ready-made source of water is available at the platform to extend lead lines from the platform into upper floors of the building.

3. Greater ease of control by fire fighters operating the nozzle. They have a wider latitude of operation, either lateral movement of the platform or the angular sweep of 45° right or left and 45° above horizontal to 45° below horizontal for nozzle discharge. Included is the ability to change the discharge pattern on the nozzle when required.

On the debit side, the elevating platform does not have all the rescue capabilities of an aerial ladder. First, it is limited by its reach which at medium and lower angles does not compare with an aerial ladder. Second, the load capacity of the platform has definite limitations because it always operates as a cantilever or unsupported structure at the outer end.

At medium and lower angles and supported at the outer end, the aerial ladder has a greater load potential. Because of this feature, it can be expected that more people can be evacuated in a given time from a given location by an aerial ladder than by an elevating platform.

Operating problems

During water tower operations by both an aerial ladder and elevating platform at a fire, with the atmospheric temperature near 0°F, the following observation was made: The turret operators on both types of equipment had to be relieved at intervals because of the extreme cold. Aerial ladder operation did not require a shutdown of water while operators were relieved. The elevating platform did and, in addition, the platform had to return to the ground to effect the exchange. During the period of shutdown the fire was observed to increase in intensity, and it took some time before extinguishment progressed to approximately the condition before shutdown.

Ice accumulation creates a weight problem. On an aerial ladder this can be serious. The elevating platform suffers the same problem of icing due to exposure to spray from nozzles. To prevent this ice accumulation, a 60,000-Btu gasoline-fired heater can be mounted inside the upper boom to heat the entire length, an advantage the aerial ladder doesn't have.

Elevating booms and platforms are much heavier than an aerial ladder of comparable vertical reach. Thus, having a concentrated load at the outer end, plus greater weight of the booms, a wider spread of ground jacks or outriggers is required. These outriggers are more massive than jacks on an aerial ladder and are therefore operated hydraulically.

Desirable features for elevating platforms are:

1. Low overall height to permit housing the apparatus in existing stations without altering the door height or ramp approach.

2. Low center of gravity to reduce roll on turns and provide a more stable feel to the driver. Also, it is felt this contributes to greater safety on wet streets, and particularly on ice and snow.

3. Reduced friction loss in the piping system so that a single 1000-gpm pumper can supply a 1000-gpm turret nozzle.

4. Maximum reach at the side, which is extremely important as it affects the vehicle's usefulness under many operating conditions.

The platform has established itself as a desirable and useful piece of fire service equipment. It, however, does not replace the aerial ladder. Each type of apparatus has a use in the fire service.

RIVATE PARKING
ECORD PLANT
P29
60281

CHAPTER FIFTEEN

Ladder company operations

Early in the history of fire fighting it was realized that there was more to the job than just squirting water on a fire. Frequently people were found hanging out of windows on upper floors, trapped by the flames behind them—ladders, of course, carried to the scene solved the problem. Buildings afire then as now were secured by locked windows and doors and so tools that were to be used for forcible entry were added to the truck that carried the ladders. Other tools such as the pike pole were added when the problem of hidden fire lurking in a ceiling or wall, or a pile of charred debris, became apparent.

For a long while the functions of rescue (including search), forcible entry and overhaul were all that the "hook and ladder companies" were charged with. But as the science of fire fighting became more sophisticated, the duties of the hook and ladder members were expanded to include ventilation (not deemed necessary until the turn of the century) and eventually salvage. Members of what are now called "ladder companies," not tied to hose lines, were also free to examine a building for fire extension and in effect became the reconnaissance "eyes" of the chief officer—a function that can often be carried on at the same time as search, rescue and ventilation. It must be remembered that ladder company operations have to be performed at all fires whether a ladder company is present or not. In some areas of this country there are just no ladder trucks responding to fires. When this lack occurs, some of the members responding with pumpers will have to double as laddermen to cover their required actions: rescue, search, ventilation, reconnaissance, overhaul and salvage.

RESCUE, SEARCH AND RECONNAISSANCE

Any officer responding to a fire and charged with ladder company operations must give his first thought on arrival to the safety of the occupants of the building. People at windows are the least of his problems, since they are readily apparent and can be taken down by ladder. Frequently and preferably they can be escorted down the interior stairs or a fire escape. We say preferably because a terror-stricken civilian on a ladder can be mighty dangerous to himself and his rescuer—particularly on an aerial ladder.

Not so apparent in a rescue situation is the invalid, the unconscious person, or a child trapped somewhere within the fire building. Here is where a thorough and determined search of every room and space within the building is called for. Rooms in the fire area or above or adjacent to it call for instant attention. But victims have been found remote from a fire area where they have succumbed to the products of combustion, notably carbon monoxide.

Surveying the situation

Reconnaissance can be simply defined as the surveying of a situation to gain information. At a fire this job is usually assigned to the ladder company or those charged with ladder company operations. It is probably the most important job undertaken at a fire and particularly in the initial stages.

"If you don't know where the fire is you can't put it out," is a favorite statement of many fire instructors. And in a smoke-filled building this knowledge is not always easy to come by. As will be explained in the next chapter, fire is a treacherous enemy that can spread stealthily through—even out of—a building unless steps are taken to track it down. The "trackers," of course, are the laddermen.

They are the ones who must make a quick survey to find out where the fire is and where it might be going. Ventilation aids considerably in this operation since it aids visibility. It is therefore really a part of reconnaissance.

Within the fire building walls and ceilings must be checked, and every vertical artery, including shafts and pipe recesses. Of some importance is the hanging ceiling or cockloft under the roof where many a fire has been "lost."

Then there are the adjoining buildings and, of course, any hazardous

Ventilation should begin at the top of a building and proceed downward floor by floor. Fire fighters here use roof ladders to maintain safe footing.

exposures. This is a big job sometimes, but one that must be done if the chief in charge of a fire is to operate efficiently.

VENTILATION

In discussing the behavior of fire within a building (in the First Edition of the Fire Chief's Handbook), Fred Shepperd likened the building to "an ordinary stove or furnace, with all doors closed and the damper shut.

"With the building closed, it acts as a gas producer . . . . the carbon monoxide produced by incomplete combustion, plus flammable vapors distilled from combustible materials are similar to commercial gases. Without ventilating at the top first, any opening of a window or door on a lower floor is about the same as putting on the draft in a furnace."

He went on to define ventilation as "the opening up of a building, in which fire is burning to relieve the structure of accumulated smoke, gases and heat." He cautioned that it be done in an orderly and systematic

Power saw provides quick and efficient ventilation at roof where one large hole is better than several small ones.

manner, and gave a list of the reasons why it is performed, including precautions to be taken, which are condensed as follows:

1. To save life by removing smoke and gases endangering occupants of the building who are trapped or unconscious.

2. To discover the exact location of the fire by allowing smoke to lift.

3. To permit fire fighters to enter and remain in the building to ex-

tinguish the fire and search for helpless occupants, as well as prevent extension of the fire. At most fires, the purpose of ventilation is to permit fire fighters to advance close to the blaze and extinguish it quickly with a minimum of damage. The danger of asphyxiation is reduced, discomfort lessened and visibility improved to make operations safer and more efficient.

4. To prevent backdrafts or smoke explosions. The backdraft is actually an explosion of carbon monoxide mixed with air. If a door is opened, sufficient air may enter and mix with the carbon monoxide, forming an explosive mixture. If there is sufficient heat to ignite this mixture, an explosion may result. This is a rare occurrence, but a dangerous one responsible for many deaths and injuries. Therefore, the possibilities must be considered. Proper ventilation may prevent it or lessen its harmful effects.

5. To control the spread of fire. Heat rises until it meets an obstruction such as a roof or ceiling. It then travels horizontally, seeking an opening where it may rise again. An opening made in the roof will "pull the fire" to that opening and allow it to vent upward into the atmosphere through that opening. Air currents are set up which cause the fire to move in that direction and tend to keep it from spreading elsewhere. Such an opening made directly over the fire will help to localize it, but an opening made at another spot not actually involved will draw the fire to that location.

Vent for smoke, gases and fumes

Ventilation should be performed at fires in buildings, ships or other enclosures where smoke is present; also where gases or fumes have accumulated from causes other than fire.

Ventilation should begin as soon as water is up to the nozzle, not before. Opening up a building permits more air to get to a fire and accelerates burning. A charged hose line must therefore be ready for action as soon as ventilation begins. There is an exception to this rule: a skylight, scuttle cover or door at the top of a stairway in a multistoried building may be opened to prevent mushrooming of heat and smoke banking up on the top floor when this would endanger life. This can be done without waiting for water.

Where to ventilate

1. At the roof: Heat and smoke rise, accumulate at the topmost point, then start banking down. An opening in the roof will permit smoke and heat to escape rapidly. When there are no natural openings in the roof, such as skylights, scuttles, etc., and conditions are not severe enough to

warrant cutting a hole, ventilation of the attic or top floor can suffice. Roof ventilation is often valuable even though the fire is in the lower floors or the basement. A hole may be cut in the roof when fire is in the cockloft or top floor. And sometimes when fire is elsewhere in the building and a heavy smoke condition prevails on the top floor that cannot be removed sufficiently by other means, the roof should be opened.

2. At windows: Windows should be opened on the floor where the fire is located and on all floors above that where smoke has accumulated. Usually there is no advantage in opening windows on floors below the fire.

3. At doorways: Doors should be opened to permit air circulation to remove smoke.

4. Any other covered or partly covered opening on a level with or higher than the fire should be opened.

When an entire building is to be ventilated, such work should begin at the top of the structure and proceed downward, floor by floor. If the lower part of the building is opened first, fire may break through the window openings there and make ventilation of upper floors impossible or endanger men who may be ventilating or performing other duties above the fire.

Roof openings

Fire fighters go to the roof and remove scuttle covers, skylights, etc., and sometimes cut holes in the roof surface. One large hole is better than several small ones. It should be cut directly over the fire, if possible, but not at a point that would endanger adjacent buildings.

Skylights may be removed by prying loose the coaming and lifting the skylight or by loosening the coaming on three sides, leaving the fourth for a hinge and folding the skylight back onto the roof. When removal is not feasible, individual glass panes may be removed without damage by prying up the metal divider strips and sliding the glass out. If no other means will work, the glass may be knocked out with an ax or any other tool.

Windows opened from inside

If conditions permit, windows should be opened by fire fighters working from the inside. Blinds and shades should be raised or removed and drapes or curtains pushed back or removed to permit smoke to escape. Screens should be removed and storm windows removed or broken out. Some fire officers believe that double-hung windows should be opened two-thirds of the way from the top and one-third from the bottom, but this is of little consequence. The main point is to get the window open at the top to let the smoke escape. Fresh air will find its way in to replace it. Good cross ventilation can be accomplished by opening windows on the leeward (away from wind) side of the building at the top, and those on the windward side from the bottom.

Casement and factory-type pivoting windows have to be opened according to their design. Many windows are difficult or impossible to open in the allotted time. If smoke conditions warrant, they should be broken. Glass is the cheapest part of most buildings and much valuable property has been destroyed by flames because fire fighters hesitated to break windows that couldn't be opened.

A quick way to break glass above the ground floor is to raise a ladder and let the top of it fall against the window. It can be moved from window to window, doing the job much quicker and more safely than can be done by a man working from the ladder.

Plate glass show windows in most stores usually have a lighter glass transom above the heavier glass. This is easily broken and often affords adequate ventilation, permitting the show window to remain intact. In extreme cases, the plate glass may be removed. In either situation, if there is a partition between the store and show window, it must be removed.

Venting basements

Basement or cellar fires present special ventilating problems. Windows, where present, and doors should be opened. Sometimes windows are recessed in enclosures covered with an iron grating at street level. This grating may be removed by breaking the concrete at the corners, or the bars may be spread and a pike pole inserted to break glass.

When deadlights are in the sidewalk over a basement, they may be knocked out with the back of an ax, a hammerhead pick, or a maul. In some stores, the removal of panels under the front show window gives direct access to the basement, affording good ventilation.

Where no other means is effective, a hole may be cut in the floor over the basement. This should be guarded by a charged hose line. Hot air heating registers in floors can be utilized by removing the grille and pushing down the hot air duct. This will have the same effect as cutting a hole in the floor and is quicker and less damaging.

In addition to ventilation by natural means, movement of smoke, gases and air can be forced by mechanical devices. Fans of varying size are employed by many fire departments; these usually range from 5000 to 15,000 cfm capacity.

Since the use of fans has become popular, there is a noticeable ten-

A hose stream directed into a window, doorway or other opening nullifies ventilation as if the opening were covered.

dency in some fire departments to neglect natural ventilation. In fact, many poorly trained fire departments depend almost entirely on mechanical ventilation and overlook the advantage of opening windows, etc., as previously described. Smoke ejectors are valuable when properly used, but they are best used as an adjunct to natural ventilation, or in cases where natural ventilation is ineffective.

If the results of natural ventilation are not satisfactory, a smoke ejector should be used. It must be remembered that if not properly employed, it can do more harm than good. An exhaust fan will draw the smoke and fire toward the fan; therefore, its location must be carefully selected.

This problem was exemplified at a fire in the attic of a one-story dwelling. The fire fighters were able to enter the ground floor with ease; only a slight amount of smoke was present there. They placed a blower fan in the front doorway and an exhaust fan in the rear doorway. In a moment, a large volume of smoke was drawn from the attic into the first floor and fire fighters were driven out of the building.

Fog nozzles have been used for ventilation for more than 80 years, yet today we find many fire departments using them only for extinguishing a fire. Common fog nozzles induce a great amount of air to follow the fog stream and can move from 10,000 to 30,000 cubic feet per minute, depending upon size, type, fog pattern and location of the nozzle.

To remove smoke with a fog nozzle, the nozzle is held inside a window or doorway and aimed toward the outside. Experiments in Wisconsin show that the wider the fog pattern, the greater the air movement, but the pattern should not cover the entire opening. Better results were obtained when the nozzle was a few feet from the opening than when it was close to it. The same precautions mentioned for the use of fans apply also to the use of fog nozzles for ventilation.

Precautions

It should be remembered that a hose stream aimed into a window, doorway, skylight, hole or other opening has the same effect of nullifying ventilation as if the opening had a cover placed over it. At the same time, openings should not be made where they may jeopardize nearby structures by extending the fire unless adequate protection by hose streams is at hand.

When holes for ventilation are cut in a floor, they should be near a window if possible. The relieved smoke will then go through the open window. If men with a protecting hose line are driven out of the building, upward extension of fire through the hole can be prevented by directing a stream from the outside through the window. It is not desirable to cut holes in the path of travel because fire fighters may step into them.

Whenever a hole is cut in a roof or floor, or a skylight or scuttle cover is removed, the opening should be probed with a tool or pike pole to find if there is any obstruction, such as a ceiling, below the hole. When such an obstruction is found, it should be opened or pushed down.

When breaking glass, make sure no one below will be struck by the falling debris. Warning should be given in ample time.

FORCIBLE ENTRY

Entry to burning buildings is usually the first step in combatting fire and is often accomplished by turning a knob. Frequently, however, entry is barred and the fire fighter must resort to tools. For years, he relied on the traditional hand tools such as the ax, claw and lock breaker, occasionally the hand saw, and rarely, the battering ram. These are still used, but for the heavier entry jobs today, the fire fighter turns to power tools.

Forcible entry covers a variety of fire department operations. It isn't easy to relate these different tasks to specific fire department tools and gear, or vice versa. Functionally, however, the various operations call for appliances which will perform one or more of the following: (a) cutting and chiseling; (b) striking, breaking, battering, breaching, punching; (c) boring, drilling, digging; (d) prying, ripping.

The kind and number of tools designed for entry varies with the preferences of the individual fire departments. There is no standard complement of such appliances, nor is there presently any universal method of employing them for specific operations. Even with the old standby, the ax, some departments prefer the flat-head type, while others can see no good in anything but the pick-head. Some departments have removed from their inventory the heavy battering ram and the pitchfork, claiming that both are relics of the horse-drawn apparatus era. Some fire forces teach their personnel to use a short ladder to force doors and a fireman's helmet to break in a glass window; others do not agree with these ideas.

Since most fires occur in dwellings, single or multiple, the following hand tools usually suffice for forcible entry:

Ax (flat-head)
Ax (pick-head)
Ax (Pry-Axe multipurpose)
Auger
Pry-bars (numerous types)
Battering ram
Chisels (including rivet cutter)
Claw tool (variety of types)
Cutters (bolt)
Cutters (wire)
Cutters (tin roof)
Hooks (plaster-ceiling)
Hooks (rubbish-cotton or plantation)
Jacks (various types)
Picks (hammerhead)
Pitchforks
Poles (pike)
Saws (various types, including floor)
Sledges (mauls)

 It is manifestly impossible to catalog all types and makes of tools used directly or indirectly for entry operations. This list includes the more important and universally used items.

In addition to these major tools, there are a number of what may be called minor instruments. These include hammers and hatchets of various types, small "jimmies" and wrecking bars, screwdrivers, etc.

Also included in the inventory of such facilities is light and power equipment, portable generators, lighting fixtures, etc. Power-generating equipment is essential for any of the listed major electrical forcible entry tools.

Power tools

Compressed air tools were used by fire departments as early as the 1920s. The first fire force to utilize them was the San Francisco Fire Department under Chief Charles J. Brennan. This unit also powered a number of special forcible entry tools. Air-operated tools are used today by many larger fire departments.

The introduction of the portable electric generator for lighting paved the way for many small motor-driven tools. Continual improvements in generators and the increasing interest in their use to mechanize certain manual operations removed most of the obstacles. The first portable generators were carried on fire department rescue and emergency units. Later, improved in compactness and capacity, they found their way onto ladder trucks and pumpers. Likewise, their application graduated from providing power for illumination to energizing mechanical tools and devices for both rescue and other operations, including forcible entry.

Portable power generators for normal fire department use range from 1500 to 3500-watt or more capacity. Alternating and direct current types have found acceptance, with the 110–115-volt, 60-cycle, alternating types preferred because of the possible application as a standby in the event of a utility power failure. Both 4-cycle and 2-cycle engine types are used by the fire service.

The three most versatile electric tools powered by these generators are saws, drills and hammers.

There are a number of electric saws now in use, including a powerful chain saw that will cut through almost anything. These saws also come in portable gasoline-engine units now more popularly used because of their complete portability (not tied to the cable and generator). The power saw performs most of the cutting tasks formerly done manually, laboriously, slowly and often painfully. Interchangeable blades permit the appliances to operate on wood, concrete, masonry or metal with equal facility.

There are several types of drills which will drill holes in a floor or roof,

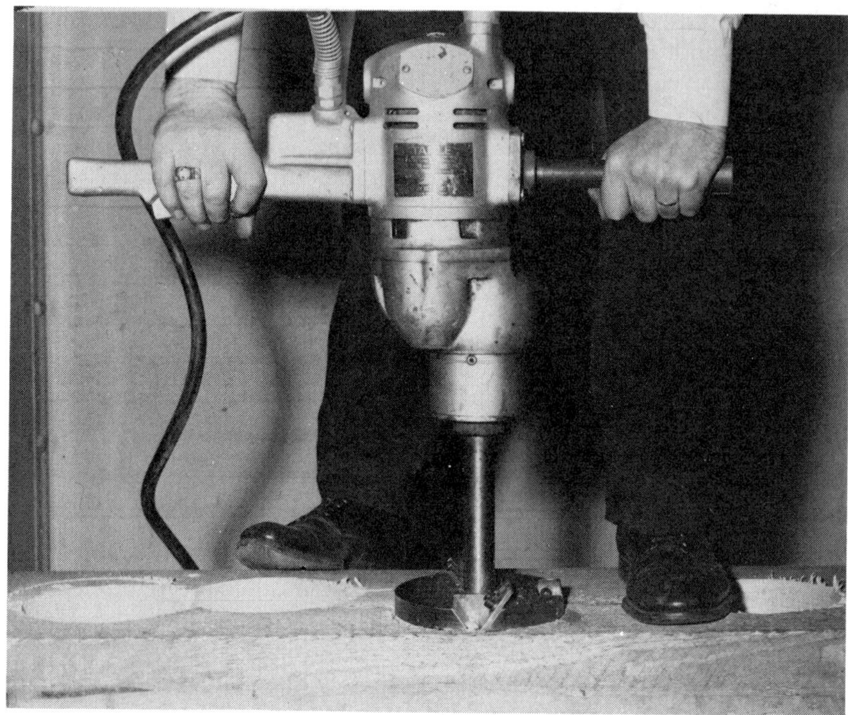

A variety of drills, including one shown above, can be used to cut holes in floors and roofs for ventilation and salvage.

for example, up to a size to permit the passage of a fire department distributor or fog nozzle, with one man operating the unit more quickly, easily and neatly than by any other means. These appliances cut through timber, masonry and metal with minimum damage to property and with less possibility of bringing about structural collapse than the slower, often tortuous, manual drilling.

The third power tool adaptable for forcible entry is the electric hammer. Like the drill or electric auger, as some prefer to call it, this device uses special bits to drive holes through almost any hard surface, such as cement, masonry, brick, tile, terra cotta, with minimum shattering effect on the structure and physical effort by the operator.

Hydraulic tools

Hydraulically operated machinery was used by industry a long time before its application to fire fighting. It is believed the first fire service hydraulic systems were used on aerial ladders. Certainly hydraulic power proved an innovation in the field. The most recent is the hydraulic rescue tool. Hydraulic tool kits are today becoming a chief reliance of scores of emergency and rescue units.

Gasoline-powered tools

Although a number of gasoline-powered tools have been produced in this country, only two, the chain saw and the circular saw, have received very wide acceptance in the fire service. Most departments carry them, and they have been used with excellent results in large-scale emergency operations, such as cave-ins, building collapses, etc.

Skills call for special training

Obviously, the introduction of mechanical equipment necessitates certain revisions of forcible entry methods. This does not mean the discarding of techniques taught over the years, which rely entirely upon hand tools and manual labor. It means readjusting forcible entry methods in line with the mechanized devices and systems now available to the fire fighter—and the developments that lie ahead.

For the most part, these tools must be operated with respect for their limitations. Just as a pump operator must be familiar with the capacity and other limitations of his apparatus, so the user of modern power devices must know how and where and under what conditions the respective types should be employed and what to expect and not to expect of them. The proper way to master the techniques of mechanized forcible entry is by actual practice. It calls for training by doing.

It should not be too difficult to secure the necessary instructors to acquaint fire fighters with the rudiments of mechanized forcible entry. Practically every fire department has personnel who are carpenters or "do-it-yourself addicts" and who can serve as instructors. The manufacturers of these appliances also are usually ready to provide instructors, as are local distributors and dealers in such equipment.

Using the hand tools

Before using a tool to gain entry, a fire fighter should be sure the door is locked. Frequently a door may appear locked when it is only stiff in operation. The first try is to open it by hand. If it does not respond, then appliances will have to be used.

Hinged doors (single): The first tool usually applied in this operation is the ax. Force the blade of it in between the jamb and the door, either just above or below the lock or latch. Pry the handle to one side

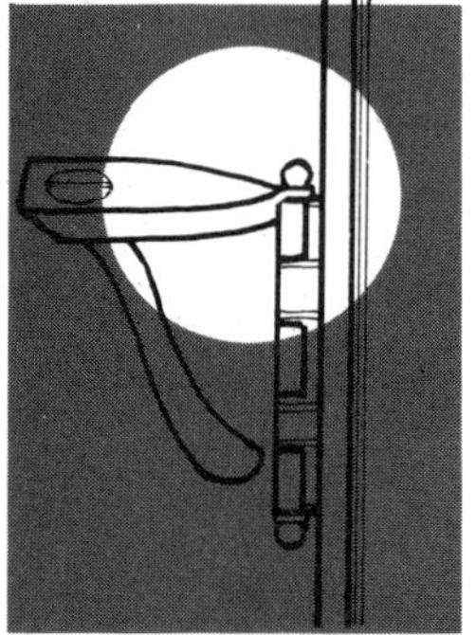

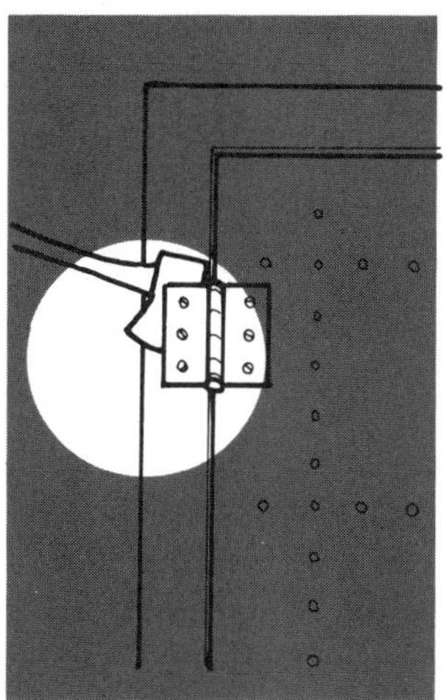

An ax can usually pry hinged, single door open (center). If this fails, hinge pins can be removed with ax or other sharp blade (left). When hinge pin cannot be removed, ax is used as a chisel (right) to cut screws holding hinge.

away from the door and thus spring it sufficiently to let the latch slip past the strike plate. The door then opens.

Better than the ax, on doors opening outward, are the lock breaker and similar tools. The blade is driven in between the door jam and the door, either just above or just below the lock. The handle is then pulled outward until the door springs clear of its fastenings and opens. If the door is bolted, or both bolted and locked, it is possible that none of the above methods will give results.

Two methods of opening the door still remain: First, drive out a panel or glass and reach the bolt on the inside. If the panels are thin, no more damage will be done by removing one of them than by removing the door, and there will be a saving of time. However, there is a possibility that the fire inside is so hot that a man cannot reach inside to get at the latch, or bolt. In this case, the removal of the door is probably necessary.

The second method for a door that opens outward calls for removing it at the hinged side. In some cases, the backs of the hinges are fully exposed on the outside. And many times all that is necessary is to drive out the pins joining the hinge halves, and the door can be quickly pried out with the blade of an ax.

If the hinges are not exposed, or if they are equipped with pins which cannot be removed, then the next best thing to do is to pry the door away from its hinges. Either the ax or the lock breaker can be used. The ax is driven between the hinge and the door (at each hinge), and the screws holding the hinges are either cut or drawn out. When the ax is driven

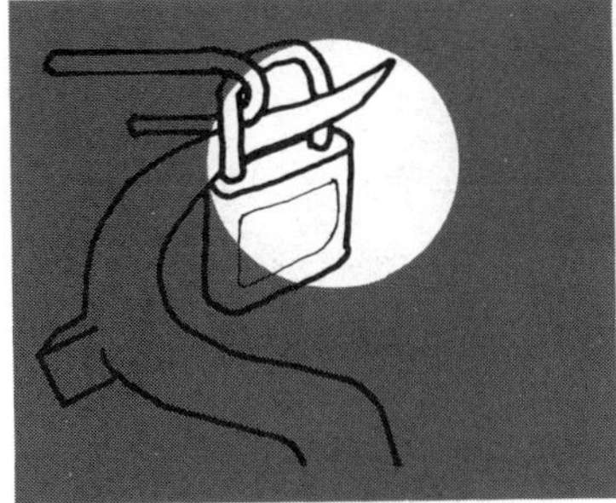

Padlock on outside of door can be twisted off with claw tool as shown at left and lower left. Padlock on inside of door required that staple be driven out with punch (below), showing outside front view and side view.

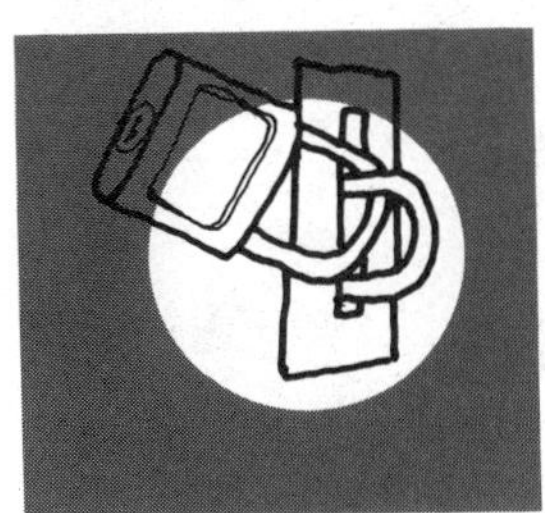

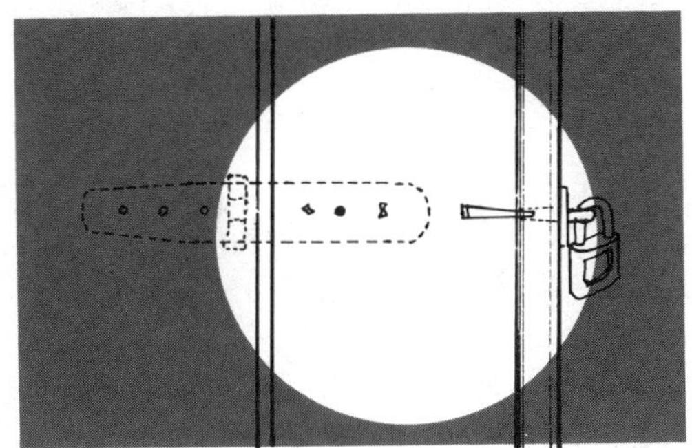

in at the last hinge, it is pushed to one side and the door is pried out. On these doors, it is pushed to one side and the door is pried out. On these doors, it is sometimes necessary to insert the ax only at one hinge, and the door can be pried free. The lock breaker can be used in removing doors from hinges in the same manner.

If the hinges are not visible, or it is not possible to drive an ax or lock breaker between them and the door, then the door will have to be pried free without first weakening the hold of the hinges. This means a little more damage, but it cannot be avoided. The ax, or lock breaker, is used exactly as described above, with the exception of its point of insertion. More force will have to be applied in prying the door free. Where a door is held closed by bolts, the hinged side is usually the weaker point and the attack should be centered there.

If the door opens inward and is locked or latched on the inside but not bolted, it will usually spring open after several heavy blows have been struck with the heel of an ax on the solid portion of the door beneath the lock.

But if the door is bolted, then it will have to be driven in at the hinged side. Direct the blows at points where hinges are likely to be located.

Double hinged doors can be forced easily with an ax or claw tool by inserting blade just above lock and prying outward.

If the door is a heavy one and too bulky to be handled with an ax, a battering ram will give quick results. Use the butt of the ram against the solid portion of the door and not against panels. Unless very securely bolted, the door can be opened with greater facility by directing the blows just beneath the lock instead of the hinged side. Ladders can similarly be used. More likely a power saw will be used to do the job more quickly and neatly.

Padlocked doors: If the padlock is on the outside, the problem is a simple one. The lock can either be twisted off with the claw tool by inserting the point of the tool in the bow of the lock, or in the staple, and swinging the handle of the tool around or by forcing the fork of the tool over the bow of the lock or the staple and twisting; or the lock can be broken or sprung by bracing the bow of the lock against the hasp or staple and striking the body of the lock with the back of an ax.

Where the padlock is on the inside of the door, the staple can be driven out by using the punch and back of the ax. First locate the points of the staple where they come through the door, and then drive the punch in directly between them. The point of the punch comes out of the door on the underside of the hasp and carries the hasp, with staple, away.

Hinged doors (double): These doors may, or may not, have window panes in them. If they have, care must be exercised not to break the panes unnecessarily. In either case, one door is likely to be bolted top and bottom, while the other door operates as a single hinged door and may be treated in precisely the same way.

First notice which way the doors swing. If they swing in, there will likely be a small weather strip attached to one of the doors on the outside, covering the crack between the two doors. This must be removed before the ax can be inserted to force the door.

Where the doors open outward, the strip may be on the inside, although with most doors which open outward, the strip is not on the bolted door, but on the door which is commonly used.

To open double doors, wedge the blade of an ax, or the blade of the lock breaker, between them and pry apart. The catch or lock will usually give without appreciable damage. If properly done, even glass panes will not be cracked.

Revolving doors: There are only three types of revolving doors insofar as the methods of keeping them apart are concerned:

1. A revolving door that has a ½-inch cable holding the doors apart; this is a panic-proof door. To close or collapse this door, it is necessary only to push or press on the doors or wings in opposite directions, or else hold one wing from moving and push on the next nearest wing.

2. A door with a solid arm passing through one of the doors. This is a drop-arm type. To close or collapse this type, a pawl will be found on the door through which the arm passes. Press this pawl to disengage it from the arm and push the door or wing to one side.

3. The third type of door is held in position by metal brace arms that resemble a gate hook with an eye. To close or collapse this type, lift the hook and fasten it back against the fixed door or wing. The hooks are on both sides of these doors. The pivots are in most cases cast iron and can be easily broken by forcing the door with a bar at the pivots.

Tempered glass doors: These doors possess several times the strength of ordinary plate glass of the same thickness and are able to resist much greater impact than plate glass. When they fracture, however, they practically disintegrate, and with almost explosive violence.

Whether fastened by locks at the top and bottom, or at the center, they are extremely difficult to force; and as they are costly to replace, other methods of gaining entrance to a building should be attempted before breaking them.

However, if they must be broken, this can be done by a sharp rap with a pointed tool, such as the point of a pick ax. Stand to one side when striking the door to miss the shower of glass fragments, as well as the heavy hardware.

Sliding doors (single): Single sliding doors are harder to open than double sliding doors, for their fastening is apt to be more secure. They are usually built heavier than double doors and are generally intended for heavier service.

The quickest way to open these doors is to remove a panel so that a man can get inside and open the fastening.

When found in industrial establishments, storehouses, etc., the single sliding door is nearly always locked on the outside by padlock and opening such a fastening is performed as previously described.

Sliding doors (double): These doors, when found locked in mercantile and industrial establishments, are fastened together by a catch hook, padlock and hasp, or by hasp and pin.

To open them, drive the blade of any ax in just below the fastening, and unlock, or break the fastening with another ax, a cutting tool, or maul, etc.

To open large sliding doors such as are found on freight sheds, shipping sheds, hay and grain warehouses, etc., first find out how they are fastened on the inside.

The fastening may be either of two types: hasp with padlock or hook and eye. To determine which fastening is employed, drive an ax between the doors and spring open far enough to see whether the fastener is round or flat. The round fastener is quite likely to be a hook while the flat fastener is almost invariably a hasp.

To unfasten the hook, drive an ax between the doors, beneath the hook, and drive upward with the back of another ax.

To open a hasp, locate the ends of the staple to the side of the crack (between doors) and drive a punch directly between the two points. This punch must go through the door directly under the lock, for it must strike the slit in the hasp. As it is then driven farther, it carries the hasp, lock and the staple with it. The punch which gives the best service is known as the combination punch and chisel. It has a punch on one end of an iron bar handle and a chisel on the other. As soon as the hasp is freed, the doors part readily.

Vertical doors (fire): There are numerous types of vertical fire doors, but when closed they are all opened in the same manner by lifting. Such doors are seldom locked; hence, if they appear fastened, try an ax to pry them up, for they may only be stuck.

 Vertical doors (rolling type): These doors, which are made of in-

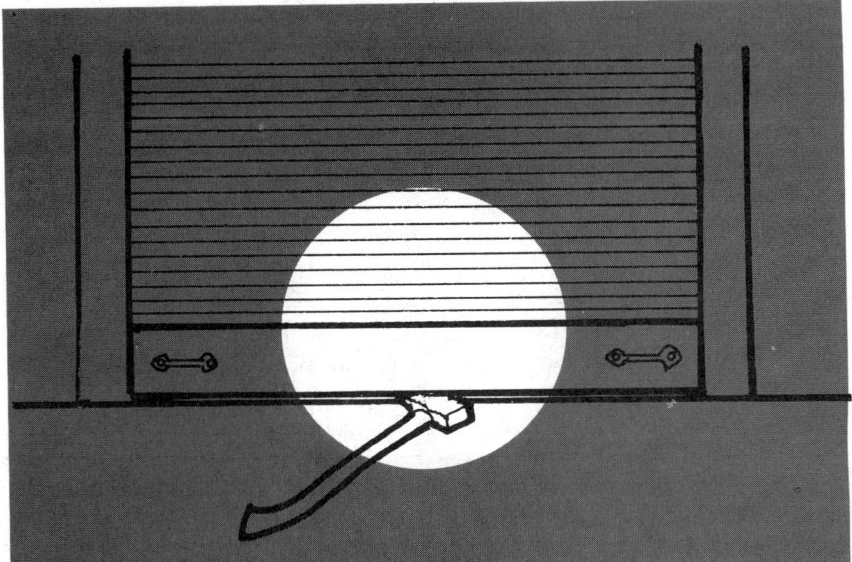

Vertical rolling doors. Force blade of ax or claw tool along under door until fastening is found. Then drive in ax with another ax until fastening yields.

terlocking strips of metal, are found on business houses and are drawn down at the close of business hours. The fastening, which in most instances is on the outside, may be found at the sidewalk. It generally consists of a ring or staple, or a hasp, on the door. An ordinary padlock secures the ring in the sidewalk to the fastening on the door.

The lock may be broken by a sharp blow with the back of an ax, as previously described, or it may be wrenched off with a claw tool or lock breaker. When the fastening is broken, the drop should be raised by lifting at the center, and not at the end. This prevents the door from jamming.

When vertical rolling iron doors are fastened on the inside, opening them is a more difficult operation. The usual method of accomplishing this is to drive the blade of an ax along the sill beneath the door until the fastening is met. At this point, the ax blade is driven in with the back of another ax and the fastening broken. The forked end of a claw tool, or spade end of a lock breaker, may be used instead of an ax for breaking the fastening as well as to spring the door sufficiently to make room for the other tool.

If the door is securely locked and does not yield to the above treatment, it may be necessary to chop a hole through it with an ax. The metal in the door is ordinarily of such thickness as to make it possible to cut through in reasonable time. If a powered circular saw is available, an opening can be made in much less time with this appliance.

Iron doors (swinging type): Where this type of door is found fastened on the inside, it is often possible to open it by lifting it off its hinges. This may be done by driving an ax blade beneath the door and prying up, or by using the forked end of a claw tool or lock breaker. The blade should be driven under the door at a point about one-third its width from the hinged side. The above applies particularly where the hinges are concealed or where they are on the inside.

If the hinges are on the outside and accessible, the pins may be removed with the blade of an ax. If this is not possible, the hinges can be broken with the back of an ax, or the screws or bolts holding them cut off with an ax, cutting tool or an oxyacetylene cutting torch.

To cut the fastenings of a hinge, either an ax or a cutting tool is used. With an ax, the blade is wedged down behind the hinge and then driven home with the back of another ax, cutting the screws or bolts. A cutting tool with sledge is much better for cutting bolts or screws, but it is frequently not available. The cutting tool is used in the same manner as an ax.

Iron shutters: These are found almost invariably fastened on the inside. Where handholes are provided for opening the shutters, there is no problem. But if the shutters are not provided with holes through which the latches can be reached, then one or more of the following methods must be employed.

First try striking the lower rivet of the fastening holding the catch with the back of an ax. The fastening for the catch is on the inside of the shutter, but the rivets project through. When the rivet is struck as directed, the latch may spring upward and out of the fastening, permitting the shutter to swing open. The ax blow should be at an upward angle.

If this does not bring results, an ax, a lock breaker or the forked end of a claw tool may be used for prying the shutter out to permit unfastening the catch. The tool should be inserted under the shutter near the latch and the shutter pried out so that the latch may be raised with a stick or the blade of another ax.

If neither of the above is successful, then force the blade of an ax under the shutter and pry it up. This will often raise the catch from its fastening and the shutter can then be opened.

If the shutter is raised sufficiently, it may be raised completely off its hinge. This is a good emergency method for opening a shutter, but great care must be exercised so that the shutter does not get away when raised off the hinges and go sailing down to the street. It is always good policy to warn those below to be on the alert when a shutter is to be opened by this method. Serious injury may result to fire fighters or bystanders below, for a shutter so freed may sail out quite a distance from the building.

Occasionally a 6-foot hook can be used effectively by men on a roof in removing iron shutters from top-floor windows. The shutters may thus be lifted clear of their fastenings. Here again, men on the street below should be warned.

Breaking hinges should be done only as a last resort, for it is slow and hard work. Cutting them, however, is an easy operation with a power saw.

Sidewalk doors: Metal sidewalk doors may be fastened in any of several different ways. They may be fastened near the center or front with a padlock and hasp, or the fastening may be through two eyes near the building. Occasionally doors are found fastened on the inside, though this is not the usual way of securing them.

When this condition is found, a chisel is used. First locate the master bolt where it projects through the door. This can usually be identified, for it stands by itself and is not as a rule, in a row of rivets. This bolt fastens, or supports, the catch on the inside of the door. Use the chisel and cut the top of this bolt off. It can then be driven out by using a punch, and the door can then be opened.

Where the door is fastened with a padlock and hasp on the outside, the lock is removed by either breaking it up by striking it with the back of an ax or by twisting the lock off with a lock breaker or claw tool.

Iron gratings: Iron gratings may be fastened in several different ways. They may be merely held in position by the friction of the grating against the sill or they may be set in masonry and locked in position with a padlock and hasp. In the first case, they are removed by using the blade of an ax and forcing it between the sill and grating and prying up.

When they are pivoted at the rear, the operation of opening is precisely the same, with the exception that the ax is inserted near the front of the grating so that on prying upward, the greatest leverage will be produced.

If the grating does not respond to the above method, then the proper thing to do is to drive an ax blade between the sill and the grating with the back of another ax so as to spring the grating free of the sill and then pry it out.

One precaution is necessary where sidewalk doors are opened or removed, or where gratings are taken out of the sidewalk in front of a

Gratings can usually be pried open with one ax (right). Two axes are used for tougher jobs as indicated (left).

building where the fire department is operating. It is this: Place doors or gratings removed in such a way as to protect men from walking into open holes.

Deadlights are opened in precisely the same manner as gratings. They are usually set in position and then sealed with tar or asphalt. Removing them requires appreciably more effort than removing gratings. The first ax must be driven in and then sprung to one side by striking it with the back of another ax before the deadlights will give sufficiently to be lifted.

Iron bars set in masonry: If haste is not necessary, bars may be cut with a cutting tool (cold chisel), hack saw, ax or pipe cutter. If a power saw is available, this can do the work quickly.

If, however, great speed is necessary and only hand tools are available, then any of the methods below may be used. In the case of bars set in masonry, each bar has a certain length, and when straight, reaches into the sockets in the masonry both top and bottom. But if it is bent, or bellied, by striking the center with a sledge or heavy ax, either or both ends will be drawn out of the sockets. This is one of the methods of opening the bars across windows.

Another method of freeing the bars is to strike the masonry sill with a heavy sledge or ax, cracking the stone or concrete.

Still another way of freeing a bar is to place the cutting tool alongside the bar and strike it with the back of an ax or a sledge. This breaks the masonry away from the bar and makes it possible to bend it out from the bottom.

If the bars are of small diameter, they can sometimes be pulled out one at a time by attaching a rope to the center of a bar and having a number of fire fighters pull on it or using the apparatus to pull.

Removing screens: Heavy wire screens sometimes found over windows may be fastened either by screws or may be set into woodwork. In the first case, they can easily be pried out by inserting the blade of an ax and prying the screen free from the wood. In the second case, where they are set in the framework, it may be necessary to chop away the framework with an ax before being able to get the screen out.

Once the woodwork has been chopped away, the screen can be pulled out with a 6-foot hook. If screens are on windows above the street, that is on the second or third floor, it will be necessary to operate from ladders.

The usual practice is to place a ladder on either side of the screen so that more than one man can work on the screen. If people are imprisoned behind screens, it may be necessary to protect them with streams of water until the screens have been removed. Screens on second or third floors can sometimes be opened from the street by using a ladder as a battering ram and driving the screens inward.

Iron gates: Frequently high iron picket gates are found in front of a business building. These gates are usually fastened by a rod which runs vertically to the lower sill, where it is attached by a padlock. It is sometimes impossible to get at this lock from the outside and a man should then be helped over the gate to work from the inside. He can usually find sufficient room there to use a claw tool or an ax to break the padlock.

Locked windows: Plate glass windows should be broken only as a last resort. If it is necessary to break windows the man should stand to one side (preferably the windward side) and hit the window with the flat side of an ax or with the side of a hook. The objection to performing this operation while standing in front of the window is the possibility of the glass sliding out on the ax or hook and catching the man on the hand or shattering and falling out on him.

In opening double-hung windows when they are fastened with a lock or catch at the center, the screws holding these catches or locks can be pulled out easily without shattering the glass. An ax blade is inserted between the center of the sash and the sill. The window can then be pried up. If the sash is fastened by spring pins set inside the framework, these will be bent and pulled out when the window is free to be lifted out.

With outward swinging windows, if they are suspended from the top, an ax must be inserted at the bottom to pry them open. Care should be

To break glass stand to one side and strike with flat side of ax or hook to drive glass inward (below). Standing in front of glass can have serious consequences as indicated (right).

taken to insert the ax blade near the center of the sash. If, on the other hand, they are swung by hinges on one side, then the ax is inserted near the middle of the central vertical sashes and pried so that one of the sashes will open either inward or outward as it is intended to open.

In opening double-swinging windows, the ax should be placed near the center of the vertical sash and pried so as to swing open the window which is not attached to the sill. Most windows which swing from hinges at the top open inward and, where such is the case, the ax is inserted at the base and pried so as to force the window inward.

Breaking Fox locks: It is indeed a difficult matter to spring a door open when fastened with a Fox or police lock, because it is necessary to spring or bend the bars of the lock sufficiently to clear the sockets in which they are set in each side of the door frame.

It usually takes three men to open a door of this sort. The first man uses an adz door opener, or similar tool, and forces the adz end between the door and the jamb. Then by catching the handle of the door opener and pulling outward, he is able to spring the door a trifle. Sometimes it requires two or even three men to spring the door sufficiently to get the second tool in position.

This second tool is a claw tool. It is placed just above the first tool used and is put in position when the crack is wide enough to permit its entrance.

As soon as the claw tool is in position, men on both tools begin pulling outward, that is, the man on the door opener and also the man on the claw tool. This springs the door sufficiently so that another man can place a 6-foot hook over the top of the door and beneath the upper frame.

Then the men on the three appliances pull together until the door springs the cross bar on the inside free from its sockets.

Cellar pipe openings: First determine a point at which the hole is to be put through the floor. In determining this point, the wooden flooring over concrete construction is not considered. The governing condition is the point in the concrete at which it is the easiest to make the hole.

The thinnest point of a concrete flooring, built in the usual arched manner, is the exact center of the arch. At this point, there is the least material to cut through, so it will be necessary to determine a point on the floor which is midway between floor beams. Locating this point on any floor can usually be done by observing the position of the beams on the ceiling above. The floor beams, in nearly all cases, run parallel and in line with the beams of the ceiling above. After the center point between floor beams has been determined, then the cutting operation may be started.

Using an ax, cut a hole of sufficient size in the wooden floor to allow plenty of room for cutting through the concrete flooring.

After the wood flooring has been chopped open, a rivet cutter and sledge are used for cutting through the concrete. Power tools, if they are available, reduce both time and labor. An air hammer is particularly useful for cutting concrete.

The hole should not be made any larger than absolutely necessary.

Breaching a brick wall: Before breaching a brick wall at a fire, be sure charged lines are right at hand. This is necessary, particularly where breaching is done between two buildings. There is a possibility of fire backing out through the hole in the wall and involving additional property.

The battering ram is used for breaching a brick wall. The first brick is taken out with a pick or other tool. When the brick has been removed, four men take the battering ram by the handles, with a fifth man on the end. The ram is swung upward and brick after brick is knocked out until the hole is big enough.

If an air compressor and air hammer are available, they can cut down the time needed to make a breaching and with far less labor.

Locked gates at the entrance to private residential districts may be opened with a ladder used as a battering ram or by pulling the gates open with a rope and a truck.

Chains across a private roadway may be broken by a rope and truck or bolt cutters.

An A-frame made of two ladders and fitted with a block and tackle is very effective in raising heavy objects, such as hatch covers, etc.

The hook roof ladder is very useful for operating over the side of a ship or dock in connection with forcible entry work.

Where time permits, men may frequently gain entrance to a residence through second-story windows and then unlock a street door from inside to save forcing the door.

Hot air registers in floors may sometimes be removed to operate cellar pipes, thus avoiding the necessity for cutting holes.

Screw and hydraulic jacks are effective appliances for moving sidewalk elevators and other heavy objects.

Bolt cutters provide a satisfactory means for opening heavy wire screens when they cannot be opened otherwise.

In many buildings, watchmen, janitors or superintendents who have keys to all rooms in the building may be found on duty.

Ordinary window glass is probably the cheapest construction material in a building. If entrance may be gained by breaking glass, do not hesitate to do so.

OVERHAUL

Before a chief officer can give the order "Take up. The fire is out," he must be certain beyond reasonable doubt that the fire is actually out. There must be no lingering spark that could bring him and his men back to the scene within two or three hours to face a fire that could be much worse than the one he had subdued and left. Of course, he could take the easy course of leaving a man or two behind with a watch line for hours. And this course is usually taken for large-scale fires. But for the smaller, but still serious fire, he can't justify this luxury. Instead, he must use the knowledge, skill and experience of himself and his men—usually laddermen—to seek out this lingering spark in a process called overhaul.

The overhaul is also used to pinpoint the origin and cause of a fire, if possible, with a wary eye kept open at all times for the possibility of arson.

The first objective of overhaul is, of course, to complete the extinguishment of fire with a minimum of additional damage to building or contents. The second is to leave the building in as safe and habitable condition as possible.

The task of overhaul at most serious fires is protracted and dangerous.

As a function of fire department operations it generally consumes more time than actual fire extinguishment. Many fires that are quickly controlled require extended overhaul before complete extinguishment is effected and all dangers of rekindle are removed.

Even though partial or complete extinguishment may be effected by the building occupants or by automatic sprinklers or other means, some checkup, and possibly overhaul, by the fire force is necessary.

Not only is overhaul considered the most tedious and distasteful task of fire suppression, but it is is oftimes dangerous. Many fire fighters have been killed or injured during overhaul.

Fire fighters doing overhaul are often exposed to toxic smoke and fumes, plus the dangers of storages such as chemicals, acids, flammable liquids and explosives. Infections due to cuts and scratches resulting from the handling of foreign matter are common.

Falling floors and walls have trapped and killed many firemen doing overhaul. Floors may become dangerously overloaded as absorbent contents pick up water from hose streams. Then floors need only the added weight of men or the shock of axes or other tools used in overhaul operations to give way. Attempts to get at concealed fire may bring down a false ceiling or stairway, or drop heavy elevator machinery. Overhaulers must use extreme caution in structures possibly seriously weakened by fire.

Teamwork necessary

Overhaul is closely related to fire extinguishment and salvage operations. It is not a separate or individual function to which certain men may be detailed, as in salvage operations. On the contrary, overhaul generally must be undertaken and shared by all hands in a fire department. The laddermen, perhaps, may have the major role, but hosemen and enginemen, and even rescue crews, may be part of the team.

The modern fire fighter is expected to be versed in all fire control and extinguishing operations. He is no longer exclusively a "water squirter" or a "ladder raiser," as in the old days. He may be a member of a ladder company today and detailed to an engine company tomorrow. He is expected to know the fundamentals of fire extinguishment and salvage. In this connection, he should be taught the importance of overhaul and its relation to all the other steps in the fire suppression cycle. What is also essential is the part each man and each company may be called upon to play in overhaul operations. Without that understanding and knowledge, and without the supervision and direction that is essential in serious fire operations, efficient overhaul is difficult, if not impossible.

Overhaul, like salvage, calls for teamwork above all. Laddermen and enginemen, or hosemen, should team up preferably, of course, under an officer's direction. But even without an officer, the operation can proceed smoothly if the men know their business.

Charged lines or other essential extinguishing agents should be available to quell any outbreak of fire. Normally, these should be manned by enginemen. The details of opening up concealed spaces, pulling ceilings, cutting walls or floors, and the like are usually left to laddermen. But in the modern overhaul team, hosemen do not stand idly by, nozzle in hand, waiting for their ladder company mates to complete their opening up before "giving it a dash." They take their turn with ax, claw tool and hook, just as laddermen may help them on the line.

In most departments, it has long been the custom for the first-arriving units to be the last to leave the fireground—in short, for them to conduct the final checkup and search in what we call overhaul.

There has been some difference of opinion over this practice, which apparently has been handed down from the horse-drawn apparatus era. Why, ask those who would revise the procedure, should the first-in fire fighters who usually take the most punishment, be assigned the arduous overhaul task after all others have returned to quarters?

The situation is further aggravated today by the almost universal shortage of personnel. It is not unusual to find the depleted first-arriving forces so exhausted, following their initial attack on the fire, that they are practically useless for overhaul and pickup. Since that is the case, authorities reason, why not return them to quarters first and leave the final phases of overhaul, as well as salvage, to the fresher forces that come later and take less punishment? Either that or, if conditions indicate, why not special-call fresh forces to perform the mopping up and picking up? Divide up the duties, they argue, by putting in fresh reserves on the overhaul team.

Of course, first-due companies are expected to know more about the occupancies and hazards in their districts and therefore, logically, should be better able to conduct overhaul efficiently. But proponents of the change in methods ask why it is necessary to keep an entire company or all first-due companies for overhaul. Why not leave a single man from those units—for example, the company inspector or some one else who knows the property—to serve as an adviser during overhaul?

The process of overhaul can be divided into two parts, chronologically: (1) operations while the fire is still burning, and (2) after the fire has been brought under control.

The extent to which overhaul, like salvage, can be carried on while fire fighting operations are under way depends upon several factors, the chief of which is manpower. With sufficient crews, overhaul can follow right along behind the attacking force. Major overhauling must of necessity follow the fire attack and not precede it.

Today, companies can return to service on the fireground after fires are under control and receive other alarms by radio—sometimes as promptly and efficiently as they would from their quarters. Obviously, companies stripped of equipment and manpower, must stay out of service while overhauling or performing salvage duty. But other companies engaged in overhaul can be placed in service, providing their personnel and equipment (or most of it) is available.

Fundamentals of overhauling

There is no universal pattern for overhaul, but there are certain fundamentals to be considered.

The fire fighters should be safeguarded from the possibility of injury; the structure and contents should be protected; all damaged areas and materials should be inspected and unnecessary physical exertion and hardship should be avoided.

Overhaul isn't all done with hands and tools; most of it has to be done with the head. Experienced men tackle their work systematically with no confusion or lost motion. Step by step, they thoroughly cover the ground.

In beginning overhaul, it is a general custom to clear away a space at each end of the floor to which overhauled materials are moved. If empty containers are available, they may come in handy, particularly if it is necessary to closely screen the material to locate valuables.

Overhaul usually begins at the top and works down. The men should be careful not to scatter or cover any material that retains fire. Care should be taken to see that materials not on fire are not knocked about with a fire stream or trampled on unnecessarily. If at all possible, the undamaged and less damaged goods should be set to one side. The damaged, in which fire may lurk, should not be washed with hose streams. Smoldering material can be dipped in a bucket or tub of water. Bathroom tubs or the kitchen sinks make good places for dunking these materials. However, a charged hose line should be kept handy.

Whenever possible, heavy material should be placed near walls or over supporting columns to lessen the danger of floor collapse.

Care should be taken against promiscuously throwing materials out the windows. Pieces of burned flooring, lath and plaster, burned and even unburned furniture and clothing, some of which might conceivably be salvageable, are often thrown out, mixed with dirty water, to make an unsightly pile. It is not uncommon to see this heap of debris rekindle, with the result that it must be overhauled again.

There will be times when, to facilitate overhaul, burned lumber, bits of tin and steel, ceiling material, glass, etc., must be removed from the floors of a burned building. But this can be done without littering the street or sidewalk. It is poor business to dump the damaged contents of a place of business out on the street. It not only looks bad, but it also means extra handling, with the possibility of injuries, and it conveys a bad impression to the building occupants and the public. It is also poor practice to dump debris in side or backyards, destroying costly shrubs.

Generally speaking, only nonsalvageable material, such as plaster, laths, paper, etc., should be removed from the fire building. If this material can be carried out in containers, such as large garbage cans, that is the best way to handle it.

Wet water aids overhaul

Until the advent of wet water, smoldering mattresses, overstuffed furniture and baled goods were usually removed from the building and then overhauled and wet down. Now, judicious use of wetting agents make most of this unnecessary, saving much overhaul and preventing the inevitable mess that follows the "disemboweling" of such articles (especially on a windy day).

Wetting agents have considerable value in the extinguishment of fire in cotton and other baled goods as well as in other materials. Every fire department, particularly those doing salvage work, should keep a wetting agent on hand for overhaul and salvage operations.

The use of wetting agents calls for judgment both as to its application and its possible effect on salvage covers and tarpaulins. Also, because it will not run off as does water, but will penetrate more deeply into some bales, it may have more of a tendency to increase the weight of the material than do other extinguishing agents. These and other details should be considered by all fire officers using the product.

It is well for all fire fighters to remember that all scorched or partially burned articles, sorted out from the debris, although they may have no salvage value, may prove helpful in preparing a loss inventory. Naturally, partially burned records and documents should be saved.

Losses can be reduced, also, by not opening any more containers, packages, bales and bundles of valuable material than is absolutely necessary to check for fire. By leaving them in their original packaging, losses can be materially reduced. In some cases, a package or bundle showing evidence of smoldering should be removed from the building, particularly if it is highly flammable. Opening such a package may spread the fire to other material or drive all hands out of the area. When removed, such materials should be collected as neatly as possible in a safe place. If necessary, as the packages are removed, they can be covered by water fog. Hitting them with a heavy stream will only scatter the material—and quite possibly the fire.

Too much emphasis cannot be placed on the importance of evaulating the possible effects of the extinguishing agent on large packages or bales, especially if of paper, wool, cotton, hay or the like. Not only may they become a weight hazard because the absorbed extinguishing agent may cause them to expand but they may produce much smoke. And frequently it is difficult to determine the exact location of the fire in such stocks. Furthermore, large quantities of water are usually required to control fires in such materials.

Remove baled materials

The wisest policy, whenever possible (if wet water is not available), is to remove bales from a building, taking out those from the center of the floor first to relieve the floor load. Pile the bales outside so that they are accessible in case of rekindling. Incidentally, care should be taken not to bury hose or other fire department equipment in this operation.

The removal of heavy, cumbersome bales, such as newsprint rolls, is always a problem and usually calls for extra manpower and equipment. Sometimes it may be necessary to breach a wall so that the material can more easily be removed. Power movers, such as fork lift trucks, may be called for in these operations, but at all times consideration should be given to the safety of operating personnel.

In overhauling premises where paper or rag stock is stored, it is not unusual to find that bales are piled to the ceiling and most of the floor is occupied. This makes floor operations difficult and accentuates the need to remove the bales from the structure. It is imperative to get the material out at the earliest possible moment to prevent further absorption of water.

Overhaul in this type of occupancy should start at the top floor, and an opening should be made from the windowsill to the floor level to permit throwing the bales to the ground. A passageway can be opened through the middle of the floor as this weakest point should be relieved first.

Where it is necessary to overhaul such material on floors below, it is better not to remove the wall below the windowsills in the same line, but to stagger the openings so as not to weaken the wall excessively.

As materials are removed to the street, a charged line should be available to wet down the bales or bundles as they are opened. Officers should make it a point to see that overhauled material is not washed into sewers, which might become clogged. Also, they should see that material placed in the street does not impede traffic.

Drugs and chemicals

Perhaps the second most hazardous overhaul undertaking is in drug stores, chemical warehouses, wholesale drug stores, paint shops, and other occupancies where toxic, explosive or corrosive substances are stored. Here, extreme care should be exercised not to pull any cans or bottles from shelves or knock such receptacles over because they may be broken or opened. If broken, bottles containing chemicals may cause explosions and spread fire. The solder on cans containing turpentine or other flammable material may have been melted by heat. If they should be dropped to the floor, serious complications may follow. If such containers must be removed from shelves, take them down one at a time.

It is a good plan to remove carboys or containers of sulfuric acid, calcium carbide, nitric acid and like acids, if they are not on fire. The safe practice in such removal is to carry them "heads up." And extreme care should be used to prevent spillage. If spilled, some acids can be absorbed with sand or dirt; others can be flushed away or diluted with large quantities of water. When water comes into contact with some acids, small explosions may occur and scatter the liquid. It is therefore a wise precaution to operate streams from a safe distance. Some departments make use of low-velocity fog applicators as protective screens in such operations.

Every fire fighter knows that certain chemicals produce violent reactions with other chemicals. Extreme care should be exercised by overhaulers in handling leaky or otherwise damaged chemical containers so as not to mix the contents.

This leads to another observation on overhaul. Where chemical hazards are believed to exist, breathing apparatus should be worn at all times. It is essential that hands and tools be thoroughly washed after overhauling operations around chemicals.

Beware of dusts

Overhaul also may be hazardous in structures housing wood-turning mills, coffee or spice houses, grain elevators, flour mills, and so on—in fact, any building in which considerable dust accumulates.

Most fire fighters are familiar with explosive dusts, but not so many realize that the careless use of streams in overhauling may scatter explosive mixtures to be ignited by a spark or flame.

Overhaul in any building where considerable dust has accumulated should include the inspection of all beams, rafters, ledges or other places where dust is likely to settle. As heat will ignite this dust, such examinations should be general in all parts of the premises. The dust will support fire in a smoldering condition and throw off very little smoke, so extreme care should be taken in the examination of overhead pulleys, belts, motors, and flat surfaces. Where considerable dust is present, and there is danger from a spark or open flame, special precautions should be taken not to dislodge such dust so as to diffuse it in the area and create a flammable mixture. Here again, water fog and wet water come in for consideration. Wherever high-pressure fog is used, care should be taken to see that entrained air does not scatter the dust, thereby adding to the hazard.

As a precautionary measure when overhauling in such occupancies, windows and doors should be opened to relieve the pressure (in the event of explosion) and all persons should be evacuated from the floors above. When it is necessary to overhaul bins that have contained dust or grain, it is considered well to treat such bins with applications of water to kill any spark or fire that may remain.

Overhauling dwelling fires

By far the largest number of building fires in this country occur in dwellings and one of the first essentials in overhauling a dwelling fire is to get everyone out of the house who hasn't a definite task to perform. This includes the police, extra fire fighters and occupants.

Although it may be true that municipal departments are short of men, the reverse may be true in volunteer departments, particularly at off-work hours. Under these conditions, it is not unusual to find many more fire fighters crowded inside the building than can possibly be used.

The use of canvas or heavy plastic runners will protect rugs and floors from dirt tracked into the building by fire fighters. These runners should be about 3×18 feet—wide enough to provide a usable passageway, long enough for most rooms in homes and yet small enough to be handled and stowed easily.

Hose lines and equipment no longer needed should be removed with the least possible disorder and confusion.

When fire fighters are overhauling rooms containing furniture upon which are jewelry, knickknacks, pocketbooks, and such, the proper thing to do is to open available drawers and place these articles inside. Fire fighters should not wait for salvage crews to do this. When ceilings, floors or walls are to be opened up for overhaul, the furnishings should be removed to locations where they will receive the least damage. If covers are available, so much the better, but it is difficult in some small, confined occupancies for salvage crews to team up and operate alongside the overhaul forces.

Make sure fire has not extended

Here are a few high spots concerning overhaul in this and similar occupancies:

When overhaul operations are started, only enough lath and plaster or metal ceilings should be removed to make sure that fire has not extended. Fire in concealed spaces can often be detected by (1) feeling with the sensitive part of the hand, (2) smell, (3) sight (discoloration of surfaces or blistering). Where it is necessary to remove curtains and drapes they should be taken down carefully and not yanked—pulling down the entire fixture. Much the same applies to the removal of paintings and pictures.

Burned clothes, cushions, etc., should be placed in a bathtub, sink, washtub or other receptacle and dipped in water if there is any evidence of fire. Cotton or kapok mattresses, excelsior, pillows or parts of overstuffed furniture should be removed to the outside unless only small portions are burned, in which case they can be pulled apart and placed in the washtub or bathtub. Of course, if wet water is available, it should be used on such materials. Before placing the materials in the bathtub or washtub, it is good practice to first place a salvage cover in the tub so that the finely divided fibers will not clog the drain. Beds can be taken down and removed to safe areas. But be careful! Many men have been burned handling hot metal articles after a fire.

General rules and recommendations

Careful, efficient overhaul furthers both extinguishment and salvage. This point should be kept in mind.

Be particularly alert for evidence of arson, especially in small retail occupancies. Preserve any evidence of incendiarism. Check the building, particularly during overhaul operations, for any evidence (windows and doors, etc.) that the structure may have been entered prior to the fire. Notify the officer in command of such evidence. Also check to see if there is any evidence of theft prior to or during the fire.

Officers should keep their men under personal supervision. Men should not be permitted to roam around the different floors. Company commanders should be held to account for actions of their men during overhaul.

Special care should be taken in handling all articles which appear to have great value to protect them from further damage. Each fire fighter should salvage every article he can by placing it where it will be safe.

Unnecessary water damage must be avoided by placing leaky nozzles in bathtubs, or pails, or out windows. Leaking hose connections should be tightened. Hose lines should be placed so that any sudden movement, such as the reaction to a nozzle being opened, will not damage anything.

While overhauling, do not allow unauthorized persons in the premises. Do not permit the removal of any stock records or books unless permission is granted by the chief in charge.

If the electric wiring has been exposed to fire or other damage, the system should be deenergized by pulling the main control switch. It may be advisable to have the electric service company cut the service lines to the building.

Much the same applies to gas lines. If piping and appliances have been exposed to damage, the service should be cut off at the street supply valve. Under no circumstances should such service be turned on again by the fire department.

If the building has automatic sprinklers, all fused heads should be replaced and the system restored to service if this can be done readily.

Relieve men frequently

Do not work men too long in an atmosphere where gaseous products of fire are present. Men should be relieved frequently and sent to the outer air to "get a blow." As previously mentioned, proper respiratory equipment should be worn by men overhauling in areas where they are, or may be, toxic fumes.

Overhaul crews should cover the complete area of the fire, paying special attention to its edges and possible extensions. Diligent search should be made for fire in concealed spaces and in channels through which fire can communicate to exposures.

As a general rule, confine all possible overhaul to the interior of the building. Remove to the outside only such material as is necessary to make way for thorough inside overhaul. Confine this material to the smallest possible area in neat piles.

Where possible, use debris carriers or containers to remove materials which may contain valuable articles.

It is essential that men doing overhauling should wear the proper fire clothing. Many departments insist that boots contain metal insoles. Some provide goggles and special face shields. It is a standard rule in many departments that men must wear gloves during this operation.

In some occupancies, fire fighters will encounter pails and other vessels marked "fire." Such containers are presumed to contain water. Care should be exercised in using such vessels, especially in occupancies where volatiles are used. It has sometimes happened that these containers have held gasoline or some other volatile mixture, and using them without first making an investigation may be dangerous.

In opening up baled cotton, paper, rags or other fibers, there is danger of the metal bands flying up and striking men in the face. The proper way to cut open bales for examination is to cut the end wires first and the center wires last. It is well to make sure no men are within range of the severed wires.

Care should be taken to see that men using axes or picks have room to swing them without endangering other persons, who should be instructed to remain at a safe distance. Fire fighters using hooks also should consider their teammates.

When removing doors, window frames, shutters or cornices, or cutting roofs, care should be taken not to let anything drop to the street, yard or roofs of neighboring structures unless it is absolutely necessary and then, only after warning those below.

In removing a cornice, every effort should be made to pull it back on the roof. If necessary to drop it to the street, it should be tied with a roof rope, then lowered after warning has been given.

A sharp lookout should be kept for glass skylights, floor openings, shafts, holes for cellar pipes, etc. Men should be warned to exercise care where such openings exist. Where possible, they should be covered or barricaded.

Before glass skylights or scuttles are broken, warning should be given to those who may be operating below. During overhaul, men should make it a point not to remain or work under such coverings any longer than is necessary.

SALVAGE

"Salvage enters into the way in which fire is fought as well as the condition in which the fire premises are left. It begins with the attack on the fire; the methods used, the points of approach, the ventilation secured, and the size and kind of streams all affect the total damage. Salvage has to do with the covering or removal of goods which may be damaged by fire or water. It includes the diversion and removal of excess water from floors and stairways, and includes the protection of property saved from fire. This may mean the temporary covering of roof and wall holes, cleaning out of debris after a fire, covering and protection of exposed furniture from the elements, and drying of polished furniture which may have been made wet by water or chemicals. At times it may even require heating and drying out the building.

"Salvage extends beyond the limits of fire fighting, and that instinctive regard for the property of others which is the hallmark of a good salvageman should also be found in every fireman."[1]

Damage caused by fire falls into two classifications: direct and indirect. Direct damage is caused by the actual burning. Indirect damage is that which is caused by factors relating to the fire and to its extinguishment. Indirect damage is caused by the products of combustion, such as heat and smoke, and by the products of extinguishment, the chief of which is water.

The prevention or the reduction of damage may call for many operations and actions, even to the removal of property immediately in the path of the fire or threatened by it.

With the disappearance of salvage companies (maintained by the insurance companies) some of the larger fire departments have established their own. Such units often operate as salvage-rescue companies and are not tied down exclusively to salvage. Fire departments in smaller cities and towns have equipped their apparatus with salvage covers and numerous other salvage appliances. This procedure provides some salvage protection for the entire municipality. It has proved to be efficient, economical and effective, as compared with the operation of a separate salvage company, which can render salvage service only within a limited district.

Salvage covers are carried on pumper and ladder units of such departments and one, preferably the latter, should in addition be equipped with salvage tools and equipment such as squeegees, brooms, shovels, sprinklers and sprinkler stops, tarpaper, sawdust, hammer and nails and such other salvage equipment as may be found necessary from actual experience.

Where a separate salvage company is established, in addition to response to first alarms within its immediate running district, it should also respond to all second alarms and special calls throughout the municipality.

If for any reason it is not possible to equip all major units of a fire department with salvage covers and other equipment, then provision should be made to provide such facilities in the quickest possible man-

[1]*Manual of Firemanship, Part 6a,* Her Majesty's Stationery Office, London, England.

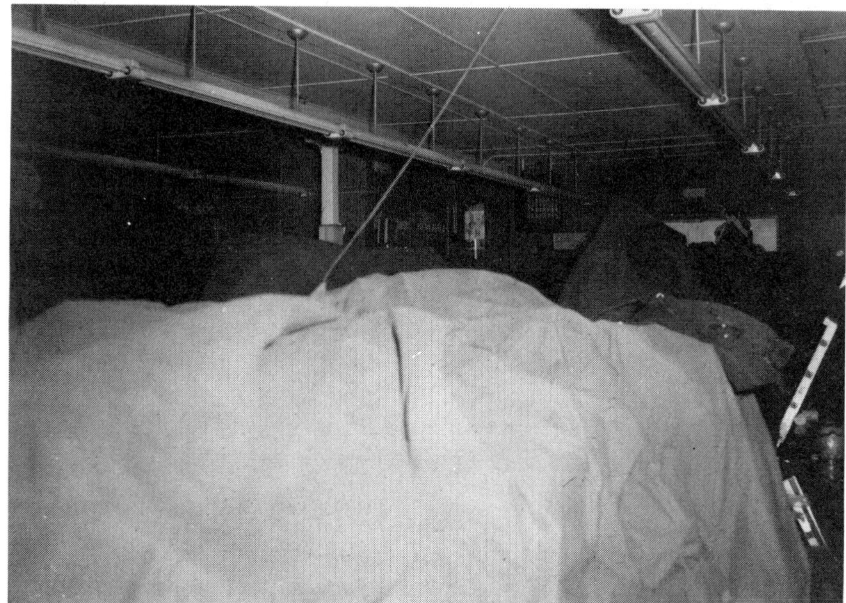

Major objective of salvage is to protect contents of a building against water damage. Salvage covers play important part in covering stock particularly below fire.

ner—even if it calls for the special response of regulation fire fighting equipment, which might carry some or all of the desired salvage equipment.

A practice adopted by a widening number of fire departments is to maintain a small utility or emergency truck carrying a stock of up to 20 or more covers, together with various essential salvage tools. This unit may normally be kept in reserve. But it can be quickly brought to the scene when needed, and it can be useful in post-fire operations, such as distributing and picking up covers, etc.

Such a piece of equipment should be fitted with, or have ready access to, portable generators, dewatering equipment, power tools, lighting equipment, deodorizing material and other special facilities.

All fire personnel, particularly officers, should be familiar with this salvage unit, its equipment, how it may be summoned, and the conditions under which it is operated.

Begin on the fire floor

Salvage operations, and we include dewatering, usually begin on the fire floor if possible and, if not, on the floor or floors below the fire, except, of course, where the fire is on the ground floor or below ground level. In any case, operations should begin as quickly as possible.

Basically, these operations have two major objectives: (1) to protect the contents against water and (2) to contain and discharge the water insofar as possible outside the premises to prevent further damage.

Salvage is performed below the fire floor by spreading and bagging covers. Containing the water on this floor may be difficult, depending upon the area of involvement, the availability of salvagemen and equipment, and the conditions (heat and smoke) under which men have to work.

It may be necessary to cut holes through flooring at the heaviest concentrations of water and to drain the discharge into chutes or funnels, thence out doors or down shafts. If the water can be bagged or dammed, it may be removed by mechanical means such as shallow-draft electric pumps, etc. Modern practice still relies heavily on sawdust to dam or divert water to where its exit will do the least harm.

The type of floor determines the speed with which water can penetrate it and reach areas below. So too will the number and kind of floor openings, pipe recesses, electrical fixtures and such. Stairways and fire towers may become natural waterways when the water volume permits their use. Where they are used, every effort should be made to block off doors and other openings so that the water will flow to the ground exit.

Where possible, the ideal practice is to chute or otherwise divert the water out the building via windows or other openings as nearly below the fire as possible, rather than to attempt to divert it down elevator shafts. Logically, the less water that is allowed to accumulate in the basement or on ground-floor levels, the less post-fire dewatering will have to be done. Sometimes basement windows are recessed, and water discharged from above into the open air will find its way back into the structure.

Possible ceiling collapse

Attention should be given to the ceiling below the fire floor because this is most likely to accumulate quantities of water and collapse on the heads of salvagemen or fire fighters. It may be advisable to puncture the ceiling and to drain the water into selected channels. Ceiling light fixtures may be a path of discharge to floors below and should be checked.

As soon as practicable, salvage units should enter the fire floor to begin dewatering and other salvage operations. If steps have been taken to direct water out of the building from the floor, or floors, below the fire

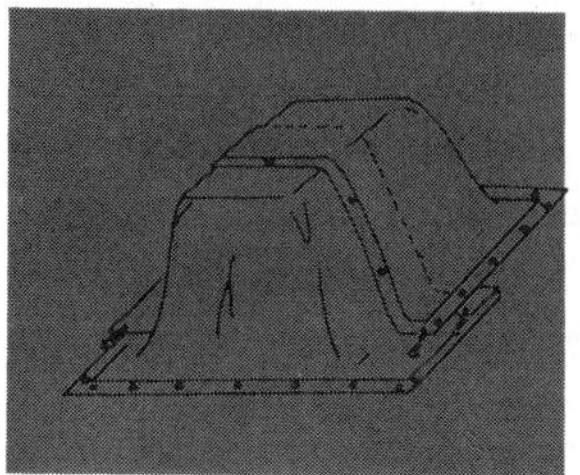 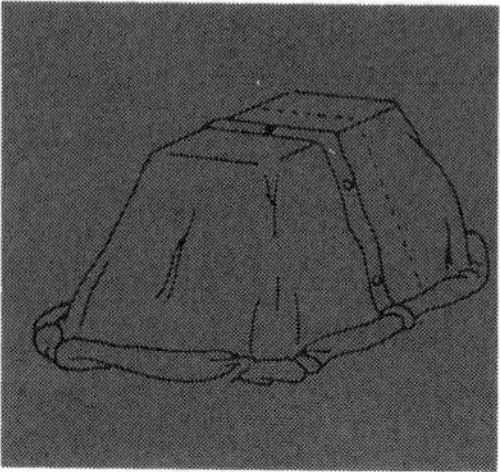 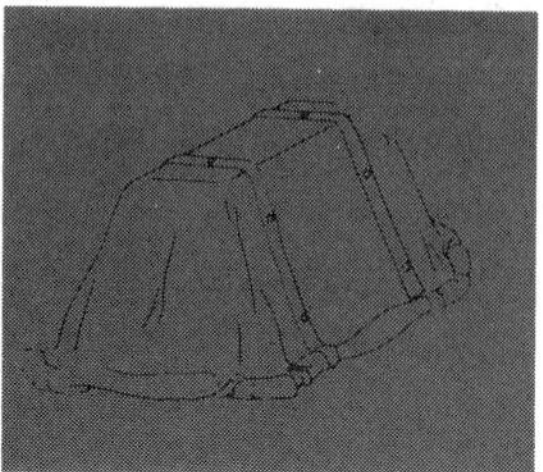

Covers should be spliced or overlapped when two or more are used on large areas of floor space or extensive piles of stock.

and the addition of water from the the fire floor will not overburden the dewatering facilities, it may be advisable to cut openings in the fire floor to direct the discharge to those facilities below. However, if water can be discharged directly out of the structure from the fire floor, this is preferable.

Rapid removal of trapped water on floors and from ceilings is important if for no other reason than to avert prolonged dripping, which will require leaving covers in place longer than necessary. Where little water is used in extinguishing small fires, such as in houses, the use of sponges, squeegees, mops and rags usually suffices to remove water.

Using covers

It may be necessary to use several salvage covers to protect large areas of floor space or extensive piles of stock. When this is done, some means of sealing the edges of the covers where they overlap must be used to prevent water from working its way underneath the covers.

Usually overlapping the covers a distance of 1 or 2 feet will provide sufficient protection, but if the water is cascading with considerable force, it may be necessary to splice or fasten the covers together by one of the methods described below.

A convenient method is shown. The first cover is thrown over the stock and the edge near the center of the stock is folded back a distance of about 1 foot. The second cover is then laid over the stock, lapping the first cover slightly. The edges on the floor are then rolled up to the bottom of the stock, locking in the overlap at the floor level.

Under normal conditions, this method will seal the splice sufficiently to prevent water seepage. Where the stock is of such size as to call for three covers, the same procedure is followed, with the covers on each end folded back and the third, or center cover, overlapping the others. The bottom edges of all three covers are then rolled to secure the overlap.

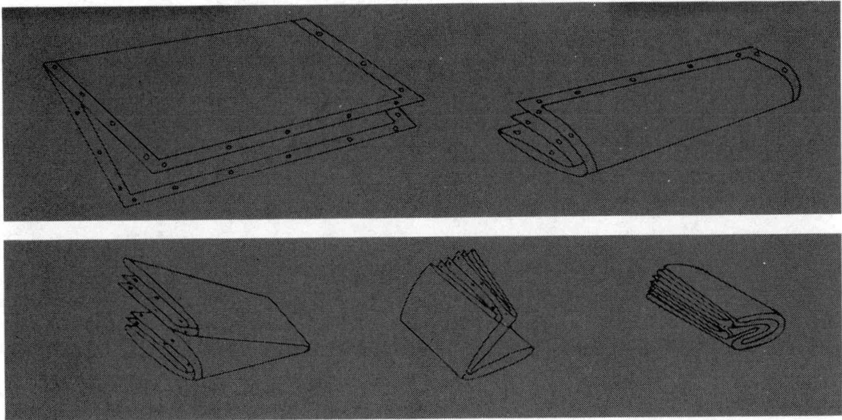

Underwriters or standard fold was designed for convenience in carrying covers and for storage on apparatus.

If water under considerable pressure is encountered, or an extensive floor area must be protected, a folded or rolled edge splice can be used effectively. Both methods use similar steps for preparation. The first cover is folded back about 2 feet from the edge to be spliced. The second cover is slid over the folded edge of the first until the edges are even. Both edges are then folded under about 1 foot.

A "roll splice" is made by making the overlap as before and then rolling both edges down into the fold.

Impounding the water

Catchalls or basins are used to impound water dripping from above. They are also useful as a drainage basin into which wet salvageable material may be deposited to prevent further damage. They are generally improvised on the spot from the material available, or they may be constructed with ladders and covers much in the same fashion as a suction basin would be prepared.

Water may be removed from a catchall by bailing with buckets, siphoning, or with wooden scoops. If metal scoops are used, it is necessary to use care to prevent tearing the cover.

A simple catchall can be prepared by laying a cover flat and folding the ends in about 24 inches. The edges are then folded in about 18 inches and all four corners are then turned in until the tips of the corners reach the intersections of the edges. Two narrow folds are then made on each edge to complete the catchall, or the edges can be rolled up. In making all the folds of the catchall, the edges should not be creased or

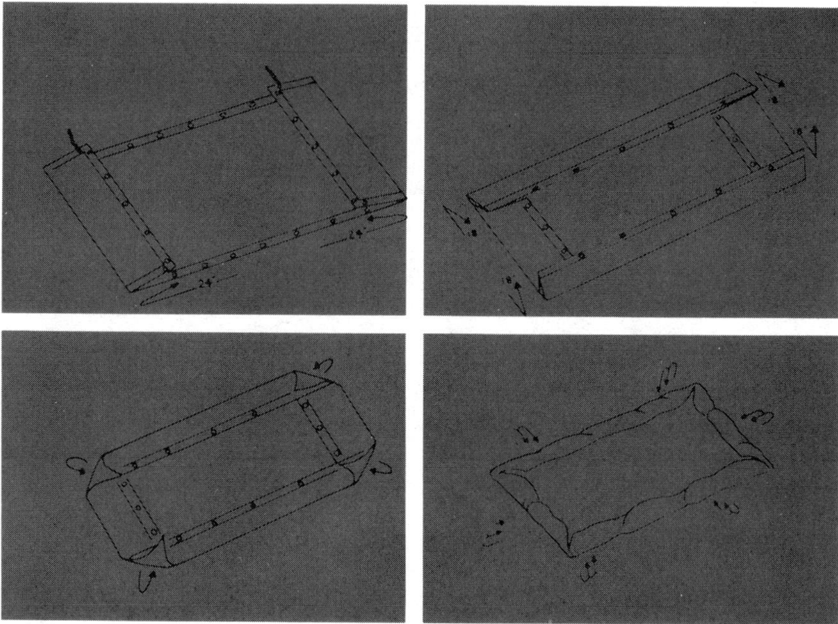

Improvised catchall or basin, made from a salvage cover is used to impound water dripping from above.

patted down flat. Some of the steps outlined incorporate a method of preparing covers known by salvagemen as "bagging."

Another method of making a simple catchall is to fold all edges of the cover in about 2 feet; sawdust is then banked up around the entire cover, forming a dike several inches in height. Then the edges are unfolded over the sawdust banks. As long as the edges are kept elevated, the cover will hold a considerable amount of water.

In another method of making a large catchall, chairs or any suitable objects are arranged to form a hollow square or circle. The cover is then spread over the supporting material and tucked down to form the basin. If considerable water must be handled, some salvagemen use two covers for greater strength.

Catchalls or basins should be placed where they will offer the least obstruction to movement in the area and so that, if necessary to handle overflow, they may be bagged and directed to the most convenient and safest exit.

There are five general methods of removing large quantities of water from upper floors. Some of these methods involve the use of salvage covers in one way or another.

1. By stairways
2. By elevator or other shafts
3. By openings made from floor to floor
4. By chutes to the outside of building
5. By building drains or scuppers and by breaching walls

Stairway chutes: Stairway chutes have a dual purpose: to serve as drains for the disposal of water and to protect stair coverings or finishings from damage caused by the passage of fire and salvage personnel during their work. They can be improvised on the spot, or covers can be prepared at the fire station and carried on the apparatus, made up and ready for immediate use.

When water is directed down stairways, covers should be opened to half their width and spread on the stairs with ample side elevation or roll, together with well-sealed or lapped connections where more than a single cover is used.

Window chutes: Where water is leaking from ceilings near windows a pike pole drain can be used.

First spread a salvage cover flat. Then lay two pike poles along opposite sides or ends with the handles extending past the cover. Then insert the points of the pike pole hooks through the top grommets and fold the edge of the cover down far enough to clear the hooks. If the grommets are too small for the point, tie with a rope. Lap the cover over the poles and roll the poles and cover toward the middle for the desired width. The chute is anchored in place at the top by putting the pole hooks over rungs of ladders, pipes, pieces of furniture, or by driving the points of the poles into the ceiling. The handle ends of the chute are placed over the windowsill so that the water flows outside.

For leaks some distance from a window, the ladder drain is popular. A straight ladder is placed to catch the water and elevated at some angle to speed the water out of the window. It may be placed on an improvised stepladder support or a high piece of furniture. Or the ladder tip can be jammed against the ceiling by fitting a pike pole head against the center of the top rung and wedging the end of the pole against the floor.

A salvage cover is placed on the latter, parallel with the rungs, and is then unfolded along the ladder, starting at the end extending out the window. The cover is secured to the ladder with salvage cord. If necessary, several covers may be used in the same manner and spliced by making overlap. Another cover can be hung from the ceiling to form a sort of catchall chute and spliced to the ladder chute to catch the water and direct it to the proper escape path.

It will be quickly noticeable that the accordion fold is ideal for constructing chutes in this manner due to the simple method of folding. The one-man throw fold can also be effectively used by merely opening the cover to the size desired. Some squads use the prepared floor chute for a ladder chute because it is necessary only to lay the chute on the ladder, unfold to the desired size and then unroll the sides to fit the width of the ladder.

Dikes: To control water flow, many squads build dikes with sawdust or salvage covers. Where much water is involved, sandbags may be used. It is difficult to predetermine the procedures that must be used because salvage operations vary widely with the construction of the building and the type of the contents.

Sawdust is usually sufficient for dikes on concrete floors. However, if a large amount of water is being directed to an opening, it may be best to use salvage covers banked with sawdust underneath at the edges. This will prevent any washing away of the sawdust. On wood floors, it is customary to use salvage covers as a trough with their edges laid over sawdust dikes.

A folded salvage cover may be used as a dam to prevent water from spreading through a doorway. The cover is jammed into the door opening at the floor and any seepage may be taken up by sawdust or by mopping.

Water in basements

At large fires, water may accumulate in basements faster than it can be removed. Then it is a foregone conclusion that dewatering will be a major operation.

When a fire has extended through an entire basement, or the basement becomes unsafe for personnel, salvage is generally confined to the control of water that may be penetrating through walls into adjoining basements. Covers may be used as blocks and runways to confine and direct the water to drains or other outlets. If this cannot be done, pumping or siphoning will be necessary.

Sometimes cellar walls can be breached where the water can be directed to drains or pumped out of the building. This method is particularly effective when the penetration of water through walls is taking place at a number of points.

However, as soon as conditions permit, entry should be made into the fire building to start removing water.

When fire is confined to a section of the basement and men can enter,

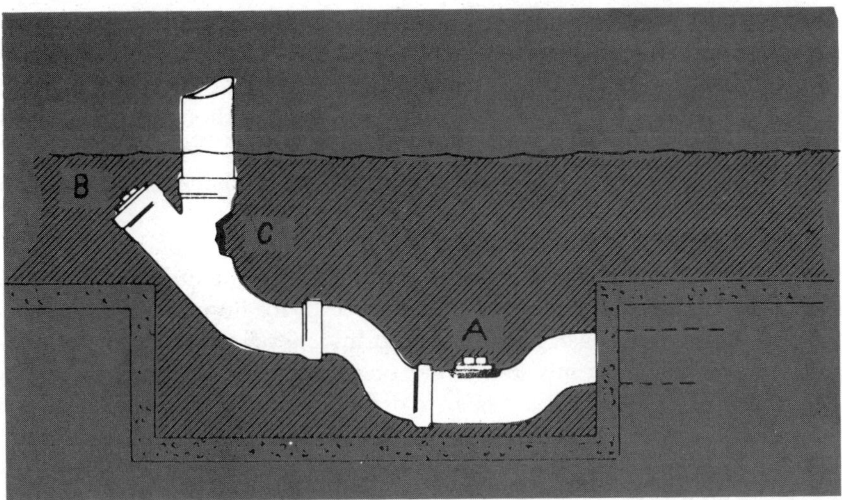

Sewer line offers quick path for removal of water in cellars: (A) preferable point, remove or break cap; (B) second choice, same; (C) break pipe.

the first action should be to hold the water to the smallest area possible by using covers as door blocks, and the water should be directed to available drainage, using covers as runways. Should the depth of water require it (and drainage facilities are inadequate), the removal of water should be expedited by pumping.

Few basements are without drains of some sort. Either that or they present the means for improvising drains, i.e., waste pipes, etc. The breaking of waste pipes may be necessary, even though the basement is equipped with floor drains and sump pumps are used.

Floor drains are often covered with stock, making them useless, or the holes in the drain pipes may be plugged with debris. Sump pumps are rarely big enough to keep pace with heavy water accumulations, and they eventually become clogged with debris.

When a large amount of runoff water must be handled in a basement, it is advisable to rupture waste pipelines. When this is done, strainers should be inserted in the openings so that debris will not clog the lines.

Where possible, efforts should be made to find pits for drafting. Locating them may be a tricky business and considerable care should be exercised in the search.

All water supply lines should be shut down to avoid prolonged discharge from broken pipes. Also, electrical equipment should be deenergized. Main switches, however, should not be pulled until the fire forces operating above are notified.

Removing water from basements is a serious and posssibly dangerous phase of salvage and should be given considerable thought. Basements are frequently the entrance point of the electrical power supply. If the power supply is interrupted, manufacturing and business activities may have to be shut down.

Basements also contain heating facilities which, if impaired, may have far-reaching effects on the uninterrupted use of the building. Lack of heat in cold weather makes the building unfit for human occupancy and results in the freezing of water pipes, sprinkler systems and storage tanks. It also can have an adverse effect on goods which cannot stand low temperatures. And lack of heat to dry out a building usually results in excessive warping and the possible formation of ice within the structure which later melts to cause unexpected damage.

Basement flooding also can affect refrigeration systems, particularly the motors and compressors. Salvage reports indicate that the interruption of refrigeration in certain occupancies has caused damage in excess of actual fire losses.

Mention has previously been made of elevator motors and equipment. The loss of transportation in a sizable building can not only seriously hamper fire fighters and salvagemen, but it can cause costly delays to the occupants.

Storage is indigenous with basements. Many below-surface areas in modern structures have large storage facilities, which can suffer extensive damage if water control is neglected.

A final detail is exposures. The fire forces may keep a fire from entering adjoining buildings above the street level, but if water is allowed to reach excessive heights in basements, it will penetrate walls and partitions and may severely damage the contents of adjoining occupancies.

Post-fire salvage

Restoring fire, water and smoke-damaged property as near its original condition as possible entails care and effort. Moreover, it calls for skill based on knowledge and experience.

Fire operations frequently necessitate cutting roofs, breaking out windows, ventilators and doors, and making other openings. Inasmuch as ventilation begins at the top, it is the roof that most often is damaged. Whether the fire or the fire fighters open roofs to the weather, it is poor practice for a department to salvage merchandise or household furnishings and leave them exposed to the elements.

The procedures for covering roof openings depend upon a number of factors such as the type and kind of roof, its supports, the extent of the openings, the weather and the available facilities for the salvage operations.

The modern salvage squad carries material for covering roofs and other openings. The important items for such tasks are waterproof covers, plastic sheeting, tar paper, a bundle of laths, nails, hammers, shingles, etc. Roofing ladders are needed for many roof operations.

Although special salvage units include such equipment on their apparatus, many fire departments are loath to carry it on vehicles which may already be loaded to capacity with essentials. Therefore, some departments maintain a small stock of such material at a fire station or the department shops. The procedure is generally acceptable because post-fire salvage of this nature is seldom of sufficient urgency to require having all salvage materials immediately available.

A small opening on a sloping or pitched roof can readily be protected by plastic sheeting or tar paper placed over a simple framework of boards. If more than one strip of sheeting or paper is required, the upper strip is lapped at least 6 inches over the one below. At the top of opening, the roofing material can be pried up and the tar paper or sheeting inserted underneath. Then the roofing is fastened down with nails. Wooden strips or laths are nailed over and around the edges of the temporary material to hold it fast against the wind. When the hole is near the ridge, carry the patch over to the other side of the roof.

Large openings

When closing up a flat roof, it is usually easier to fabricate the framework and put it firmly over the aperture. The framework serves to raise the covering above the roof line and thus facilitate the run-off of rain.

Where a large hole has been made in a roof, it may be necessary to use one or more salvage covers for protection. In this case, the procedure is the same as in covering with tar paper. On a gable roof, the covers are stretched over the ridge, with the upper covers lapping lower ones at least 6 inches. Some framework must be provided to support the covers. The edges of the covers should be held down with laths or wood strips, making sure that the nails go through the grommets and not the material of the covers.

Where holes are of considerable size in a flat roof, a somewhat different procedure is followed by many salvagemen. To keep out water, the roofing material is loosened around the hole and raised to a height of about 4 to 6 inches, where it is held in place by boards. A framework to hold the covers can then be erected over the hole. This is usually done by nailing short upright boards to the roof rafters at each end of the hole. These are connected with a crosspiece to form a temporary ridge pole.

Other boards are nailed from this ridge pole to the burned ends of the roof rafters and a cover is thrown over the hole. The edges of the cover are fastened down with boards nailed through the grommets, or are weighted with stones or debris.

Using the floor below

Where the burned section of the roof is too large to cover effectively, the roof drainage may be diverted to the floor below, which is well covered after being cleared of furnishings, etc. The covers (it usually requires more than one) should be raised above the floor to provide a runoff which may be directed through a window by means of a trough. If there is a possibility of any leak through the attic floor, covers may be placed over material on the floor below and bagged to catch all drip that may seep through.

Before attempting any extensive roof or other post-fire coverage, the officer in charge should survey all possible hazards to the salvage crews. Partially burned away roof members may weaken a roof which is to be covered. If the weakness is not apparent, salvagemen may be injured through the collapse of roof members or the entire roof structure. Frequently, the area around light shaft coverings and ventilators is burned away inside, leaving a serious structural weakness which may not be immediately apparent.

Another detail which may prevent injury to persons or covers is to clear the edges of windows, ventilators and shaft coverings of all glass or sharp metal.

Covering skylights, air shafts and other roof openings is generally accomplished by draping a tarpaulin around or over the framework of the opening and securing it by ropes, nailed laths or strips of wood. Tar paper or plastic sheeting may be used where possible. In covering shafts, remember that air currents in the shaft may damage the covering.

Plastic sheeting for windows

Window openings are usually closed with plastic sheeting or tar paper, except in the case of large store windows, big factory windows or picture windows in dwellings. In the latter cases, a tarpaulin may be more effective. However, if wooden crossmembers of a window offer nailing surfaces, it may be possible to use plastic sheeting or tar paper.

Plastic sheeting can be secured around openings in wood construction with a heavy-duty stapler.

Tar paper is secured to a window frame, starting at the top, with wooden laths and nails. The laths and paper are then nailed on each side of the window and a sufficient amount of paper is allowed to project over the sill before the bottom is secured with lath and nails. The projecting portion may help drain off any rain that falls before repairs are made. The lath acts as a cleat to help prevent the paper from tearing in windy weather. When nailing, drive the nails not over three-quarters of their length into the wood. This will facilitate their removal when permanent repairs are made. Some departments prefer scaffold nails, which have a double head.

Tar paper or plastic sheeting is usually fastened to the exterior of a window frame, although circumstances may make it necessary to fasten it on the interior, in which case care should be used to prevent needless damage to woodwork.

Covering openings exposing a building and contents to inclement weather is particularly important in the winter. This provides protection against the elements and enables heating units to be placed in operation sooner. If the contents require warmth, portable heaters and salamanders can be located advantageously (always under proper supervision).

Broken steam pipes or radiators should be checked and disconnected and the pipes capped to permit partial operation of the system. These precautions are especially important in occupancies such as wholesale markets, groceries and shopping centers, where the freezing of fruits, vegetables, and bottled and canned goods may cause heavy loss.

Attention should be given to sprinkler and other piping when there is any possibility of freezing and bursting pipes.

List of salvage equipment

Covers: 12 × 18 feet or 14 × 18 feet recommended.

Cover wedges: Small triangular wooden wedges, 6 to 8 inches long, for holding salvage covers in place between shelving and a wall. Also useful to hold doors open.

Floor runners: Heavy plastic or canvas, 3 × 18 feet.

Tar paper or plastic sheeting: Extremely useful in covering roof holes and other openings. One roll of cheapest quality usually suffices.

Heavy-duty stapler: To secure plastic sheeting to wood surfaces.

Laths: To hold patches of tar paper over openings exposed to the weather laths are necessary in addition to short nails as the covering is more tightly held over the opening and loosening by the wind is forestalled. Laths may also be used to hold down old tarpaulins with less nail holes and damage.

Sawdust: For use in making dams and channels to control the flow of excess water. Also a help in absorbing excess water from floors and out-of-the-way corners. One bag is usually sufficient for an average operation.

Squeegees and brooms: Used to remove surplus water from floors. The broom, particularly the wire broom, is also useful in cleaning up and removing plaster and other debris.

Scoops, wooden: Preferred to steel for removing excess water from floors and catchalls because they will not cut or scratch covers, rugs and flooring.

Shovels, steel: For cleaning up debris, digging into wreckage, etc. Sometimes used in removing shingles from roofs or siding, although a steel spade is better for this.

Sponges and chamois: Frequently used for drying furniture and polished surfaces. Sponges can also be used for removing water from corners and inaccessible places.

Mops and wringers: Useful in final cleanup and removal of moisture from floors.

Pickup bag (canvas carryall): Has many uses, primarily that of removing debris and facilitating sorting out of valuables.

Sash cord: Usually 50 feet in length. Useful for tiebacks, securing covers, guidelines, signal line for wearers of masks, etc. Many salvage corps carry a supply of short pieces of heavy cord or clothesline which can be fastened to grommets of covers for securing.

S-hooks: A plentiful supply of these should be carried for securing covers.

Hammer and nails and hatchet: For tacking down coverings, temporary chutes, tapping plugs, etc.

Pails: Have a multitude of uses besides removal of excess water. The 12-quart size is preferred.

Auger: Although not frequently used, the auger is valuable in providing emergency drainage openings to release surplus water and in making initial holes so that saws may be used to open up flooring. The 2-inch bit is the most widely used type. Some departments have power augers.

Punch and chisel: These tools, although seldom used, deserve a place in salvage equipment.

Sewer drain guard (strainer): In a fire of any duration, debris of various kinds is washed down to the floor drains. To facilitate the escape of water through drains, it is important that these be kept clear, and drain guards, or strainers, are a great help in permitting water to get to the sewer line.

Pipe plugs and caps: A box of assorted pipe plugs and caps may be useful in minimizing water damage due to ruptured water, steam, chemical or sewer pipes.

Sprinkler heads, stops and wrenches: Temporary stops are often necessary to shut off the flow of water from sprinkler heads until valves can be closed. There are many different kinds of stops, the most inexpensive and simple to make are wooden wedges. Wrenches and sprinkler heads are naturally used for replacing heads.

Bale hook (hay hook): Useful in moving baled and boxed goods, bundles, etc.

Water siphon ejector (eductor): Particularly valuable in dewatering basements which may be filled with dirty water. Can be used with hydrant streams when pressure is sufficient.

Portable electric generator: Invaluable for providing light and power for electric tools.

Floodlights: Essential in lighting up areas to be overhauled and facilitating salvage work.

Flashlights: The small hand type should be carried by every salvageman. There should also be a plentiful supply on the apparatus.

Hand lights (officers): A step above flashlights in range and life. There are many types, most of which can be used also as stationary lights.

Smoke ejectors: To remove smoke and fumes from an area and replace with fresh air. There are both electric and gasoline-powered models. Also used for drying.

Saws: May come in for miscellaneous uses in making openings, breaching, making salvage repairs, etc. Gasoline and electric power saws of various types are widely used.

Ladders: Short ladders are valuable in salvage work. Sometimes stepladders can be found in the occupancy but salvagemen should have their own. Short extension and folding ladders are particularly useful in reaching sprinkler heads, setting covers on high shelving, covering tops of piled storage, etc.

First-aid kits: An essential in salvage and overhaul as well as fire fighting operations.

Water vacuum: When water level has been reduced to the mop stage, an electric-powered vacuum device may be used to pick up remaining water. This device is carried on the back of the operator, who uses a wand with a squeegee-type opening at the end to pick up the water. Its tank holds between 5 and 6 gallons of water.

CHAPTER SIXTEEN

Basic fire fighting

Boiled down to its essentials, fire fighting consists first in locating a fire, second confining it and third extinguishing it. It is that simple. But very often the simplicity of fire fighting is ignored or forgotten in the excitement and sometimes the confusion that prevails on the fireground.

More often than not, the decisions made during the initial operations by the first-to-arrive officer determine the entire course of the fire. He might be the youngest and most inexperienced officer in his department. Yet, for the brief period that he is in charge until a superior officer arrives, he will be the one who may actually determine whether the fire will be an easy knockdown or a roaring conflagration.

Regularly we read newspaper stories of fires in which fire fighters quickly extinguished a blaze, let's say in a store, and then *suddenly discovered* that the fire was blazing merrily in a room upstairs or in a store next door or was perhaps roaring through a cockloft four floors above the store.

Actually, there was nothing sudden about the additional fire. It was there all the time that the fire fighters were putting out the flames in the store. It was there for anyone to see who had a knowledge of the basics of fire fighting and who had the judgment to ignore, or perhaps just hold, the visible fire—temporarily—and to head off the concealed fire which could eventually destroy other areas within the fire building and possibly other buildings.

So we can see that, no matter what his rank and experience, it is important for every fire fighter to know the basics of fire fighting—to know enough to hold his finger in the right hole in the dike until help arrives.

Any building can be likened to a box that has six internal sides and six external sides. Each of these sides must be considered by the first-to-arrive officer in relation to the path of travel a fire might take. In addition, the building encloses rooms, stairwells, shafts, partitions and a number of other spaces, all boxes that have six sides, inside and out, and all requiring attention.

For a simple illustration, take the box illustrated. This box, or rather this collection of boxes, represents a typical, brick and joist, three-story, store-and-dwelling occupancy, which can be found anywhere in this country and Canada.

Hold the cellar stairs

There are two stores on the first floor, a hardware store and a bar. Both are well stocked not only in the stores but in the cellar beneath them. The front entrance opens to a hallway, which has a door to the backyard and a stairway to the second and third-floor apartments. There is a ladder in the hall of the third floor that leads to a roof scuttle. The most threatening feature of this building is the inside cellar stair that leads to the first-floor hallway.

Even if he ignores pipe recesses, hidden spaces and possible shafts, the officer who arrives at a fire in this building has 12 boxes to consider, including the building itself and the cockloft. A total of 156 sides to which he must apply the basic principles of fire fighting: *locate, confine* and *extinguish.*

Now, let's assume that this first-to-arrive officer of a volunteer company pulls up to the front of this building in response to an alarm in the early afternoon. The fire whistle is still blowing and he has himself, four men and a fully equipped 1000-gpm pumper to work with. Experience tells him that he can expect another five men—no more—to arrive in their private autos.

We can see from the diagram that the fire started in the cellar of the hardware store, burned through the cellar ceiling, partially involved the store, and is threatening to burn through the wall to the liquor store and through the ceiling to the apartment above. What is even more threatening is that the fire has attacked the cellar stairs leading to the first-floor hallway and stairs.

Unhappily, the officer cannot see what we see. All he sees is a volume of smoke pouring out of the hardware store, a somewhat lighter volume

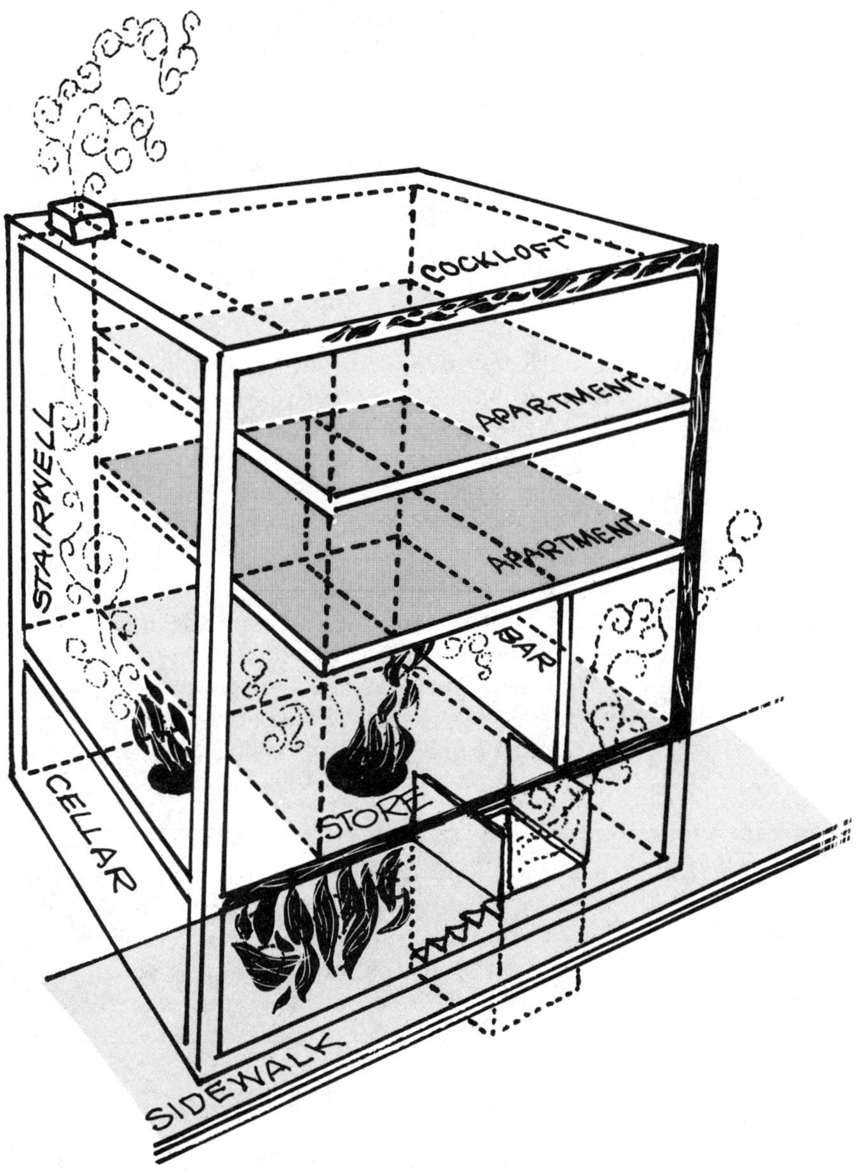

of smoke coming through the main doorway and a trickle pushing through cracks in the cellar door on the sidewalk in front of the building.

So, what is the first step he takes in *locating, confining* and *extinguishing* this fire? It is probably the easiest one that he will take at this fire and the most important.

He should call for more help immediately.

The potential of this fire is beyond the abilities of the manpower and equipment that he has. It is far better that any additional help be returned unused than additional help be called after the fire has fully developed.

Once this important call has been made, the officer can turn his attention to the boxes that represent his fire problem. And these boxes must be tended to in their *order of importance.*

It should be obvious to this first-to-arrive officer that he has immediately located his main body of fire: the hardware store and cellar. But fire is insidious, and what should concern him most is what is happening to the other boxes within the building and, of course, the building itself. He must therefore make a quick search of the building, using masks if necessary, to determine where the fire is traveling. (Lines may be stretched simultaneously.)

If heat and smoke are of such intensity that no search can be made, the officer can locate fire travel by deduction. Fire invariably *travels upward.* If its upward path is blocked, it will *travel horizontally* and, if both these paths are blocked, it will travel *downward.*

But no matter whether the fire is sought by inspection or deduction, remember that the boxes must be checked in the order of their importance.

Check escape paths

In any fire fighting operation, life hazard comes first. This makes the stairwell, which is the first path of escape for any occupants, the number one box (oblong and vertical) to check for fire. Referring to the diagram, we see that fire is traveling up the cellar stairs leading to the hallway.

The next box to be considered is the second-floor apartment directly above the hardware store. Fire could conceivably burn through the ceiling of the store to any one of four rooms.

The third box, or rather boxes, include the wall partitions that extend through the building to the cockloft.

The fourth would be the bar. Fire could burn through the wall that separates the two stores, or most likely come across the ceiling that is often common to both stores.

The officer who has located the fire either by inspection or deduction now must make the decision on how best to confine it. Remember that he has at the most nine men and a fully equipped 1000-gpm pumper.

There is a hydrant nearby and stretches will be short—three lengths to the front of the building. Remember, too, that he has sent for help which, for our purposes, will arrive in about 10 minutes. His major job is to confine the fire. And if he acts promptly and properly, he may be able to send the help back unused.

As stated above, the first and most important box to be tended to is the vertical oblong that is the stairway. It is an escape route for the occupants and a pathway to the upper floors for fire fighters. Every effort must be made to hold it no matter how fiercely the fire burns in other boxes within the structure.

The officer in this fire is fortunate to have nine men. His company therefore has the capability of ventilating the building (at least the stairwell) and stretching a line or lines at the same time.

Ventilation important

His first order should be for two men to go to the roof to open the scuttle over the stairwell. This releases any pent-up heat and smoke in the well and opens a path up or down. Two men should be sent on this most important assignment and, preferably, each should take a separate path (adjoining building, fire escape, extension ladder, even the stairway itself if conditions permit).

His second order, almost simultaneously, should be to stretch a line into the first-floor hallway and take it to the door leading into the cellar. The fire must be held there at all costs.

His third order would be for another line to be stretched and operated on the main body of the fire in the cellar via the sidewalk entrance. Or perhaps it could go into the hallway to back up the first line, which could then attempt to go down into the cellar via the interior stairs.

This, however, is about the most that could be expected from a single engine company, and if occupants had to be taken from the building, the company probably could not stretch the second line.

But the first line is a must in confining the fire, as is roof ventilation. *Hose streams and ventilation are as important in saving life as ladders.*

By the time the first-in company has placed itself in position to protect the most important boxes in our building, we can expect additional companies to have arrived.

A number of lines can now be stretched. But where?

Line placement

Surely one of the first should be taken to the apartment above the fire. And another into the bar next to the fire. In both these locations, walls, floors and ceilings can be opened and any hidden fire extinguished. Finally and perhaps simultaneously, lines can be taken into the cellar and hardware store to finish off the main body of the fire.

This, however, does not end the job. Check the box again and you will see that small channels of fire were traveling up the sidewalls. A dilligent search must be made to seek out and extinguish these tiny branches of the main fire else the fire may extend or a rekindle may occur. The last act at a fire, then, coincides with the first, which was to locate the fire.

So far, we haven't discussed in detail how the fire is to be extinguished. The building represented by our boxes will have a heavy fuel loading in both the store and the bar. And a heavy fuel loading calls for a considerable amount of water.

A hunter would not think of shooting an elephant with a BB gun, yet there are some fire departments that would make their initial attack on this fire with a 1½-inch line and even a booster line. Such small lines have the same effect on heavy fire as the BB pellet on the elephant. They are worse than nothing, since they will use up fire fighters' time and equipment without materially affecting the fire.

With this in mind, the officer makes his initial attack with a 2½-inch line or lines capped by a shutoff, or controlling nozzle. It is better to have some water damage in the cellar and stores than to have the entire building destroyed by a fire that gets away. The "blitz attack" is merely an extension of the military tactic: get there *first* with the *most*.

Fuel loading

According to Maddox [1], the average five-room dwelling contains approximately 8000 board feet of lumber, which weighs about 2½ pounds per board foot. Thus, the weight of such a home is about 20,000 pounds, or 10 tons.

If we figure this average house has at least 1000 square feet of floor area, with a contents load of about 4 pounds per square foot, then there is an additional 4000 pounds of fuel. Added to the weight for the house, this makes a total of 24,000 pounds of fuel.

When completely burned, wood produces about 8120 Btu per pound. Therefore the consumption by fire of our furnished average house will produce a quantity of heat equal to 8120 × 24,000 or 194,880,000 Btu. This quantity of heat could conceivably be liberated in one hour.

[1]Anthony J. Maddox, *500-GPM Minimum Flow Needed to Balance Fuel in 5-Room Home,* Fire Engineering, Vol. 121, No. 9.

As an extinguishing agent, water absorbs the Btu production and lowers the burning material's temperature below the point at which it gives off sufficient vapors to support combustion. One Btu will raise the temperature of 1 pound of water (at 60°F) 1°F. Since a gallon of water weighs 8.3 pounds, 8.3 Btu are needed to raise the temperature of 1 gallon of water 1°F.

If we assume that the average temperature of water in city mains is 55°F, raising the temperature of 1 gallon of water from 55°F to 212°F requires 1303 Btu. To convert this gallon of water to steam (to do its best extinguishing job) requires an additional 8053 Btu. Therefore, 1 gallon of water at 55°F when placed in a fire area can absorb 9356 Btu if all the water is converted to steam.

If 194,880,000 Btu (heat value of our average dwelling) can be produced by total destruction of our dwelling in one hour, we can assume an average burning rate per minute of 1/60 of the total Btu. This gives us an average of 3,248,000 Btu per minute. To control this quantity of heat production, we must apply water at a gallonage rate per minute that will absorb this quantity of heat. If we divide 3,248,000 by 9356, we find that 347 gpm of water are needed if the water application is 100 percent efficient and all the water is converted to steam.

Efficiency rate of 60 percent

Perfect efficiency is not probable in the fire service, so a more realistic efficiency rate is about 60 percent. The required 347 gpm then becomes about 580 gpm to control the burning.

To resolve the 580 gpm to fire service usefulness, divide 580 gpm by 250 gpm, the flow of a standard hose stream. This equals 2.3 standard hose streams. Rounding this to an even number, we arrive at two hose streams, or 500 gpm, as the minimum requirement for the average frame dwelling.

Understandably, there are few, if any, five-room houses that are ever completely consumed, and those that are consumed are gone before the arrival of the fire department. The point we are stressing here is the relationship between water application and fuel loading at a fire. Imagine the totals we would come up with if we applied the above figures to the 12 boxes represented in our illustration, or a supermarket, or a warehouse.

Just remember that a booster line operated into the blazing windows of a supermarket is a waste of time, equipment and manpower. So is a 2½-inch line operated into the living room of a private house. Somewhere in between these two extremes lies the proper action.

In any event, all of the foregoing basics can be applied to any structural fire as will be covered in the following pages. Just remember that, boiled down to its essentials, fire fighting means *to locate, to confine* and *to extinguish* an unfriendly fire.

SIZE-UP

There are seven basic fireground operations: (1) rescue, (2) protection of exposures, (3) confinement of fire, (4) extinguishment of fire, (5) overhaul, (6) ventilation, and (7) salvage. Five of these have already been mentioned or implied in our hypothetical fire above. The other two, salvage and overhaul, are treated in another chapter of this book. All, however, are part of the analysis of a fireground that has traditionally been called "size-up."

Size-up is actually a gathering of information—a survey, if you will—of the situation encountered on the arrival by a fire department at the scene of an alarm. From this survey an analysis is made, and from this analysis certain actions are taken.

Correct size-up is of tremendous importance, for upon it the initial plan of operations of the department is based. In addition, summoning of additional men and apparatus is determined by this survey.

The heaviest responsibility at a fire rests upon the first officer to arrive. He is expected to be familiar with buildings in his territory, the geographical features of the area, and the number of companies normally assigned to respond. He is responsible for making decisions upon which the success in handling the fire may depend.

Certain factors normally considered part of the size-up should be determined by planning. Pre-fire planning can be considered as the size-up (taken at leisure) of a fire that has not yet taken place. It is basically the same size-up, with few exceptions, taken at an actual fire on the points which follow:

Time of day

The hour of the day has a direct bearing on the life and fire hazards involved. Consider, for example, places of public assembly, schools, heavily populated factories, etc.

Time also has a direct bearing on speed of fire apparatus response. Traffic congestion at certain hours may all but paralyze apparatus movement. Delayed response, in turn, has a bearing on the apparatus needed to control a spreading fire.

If the fire occurs during hours of darkness, special lighting equipment may be needed. In addition, night operations may require augmenting fire fighting personnel.

The season of the year must also be taken into account. Christmas trade products, for example, may be under full production in some plants even during the night. Stores may be overstocked with Christmas goods. Housekeeping, both in factories and stores, may present serious hazards, for there is a tendency to permit the accumulation of combustible rubbish when establishments are faced with the holiday rush.

Weather

Weather is another factor that comes into play at a fire and it has many ramifications. Precipitation in the form of heavy snow or sleet or violent rain can delay response as much as traffic congestion. On the credit side, snow, and to a lesser degree rain, can eliminate or at least reduce the hazard of flying brands. Temperature, if it is very low, requires that a fire fighter "bundle up" before leaving quarters—another delay. And heavy clothing can hamper a fire fighter's movements and agility. Conversely, a hot humid day can so drain the energy from a fire fighter that it necessitates his relief in a short period and consequently requires more fire fighters on the scene. Heat and humidity can also cause a fire fighter to start peeling off garments designed to protect him from injury.

Finally, there is the wind. A high wind fans the flames (more oxygen) and increases the possibility of the fire jumping to exposures. It also inhibits operations on lee side of the fire. A low or nonexistent wind slows its ventilation which in turn slows the fire attack.

There are, of course, other factors that weather involves. A factory building may have its windows opened or closed depending on the time of the year—January or August. If opened, the windows assist in ventilation; if closed, they can hamper ventilation. But note, open windows can be a threat to exposed adjoining buildings, and particularly on the leeward side. We could go on and on about the weather and its effect on fire, but the point is that weather can have a powerful, and often unpredictable, influence on a fire. It must be considered early in a size-up.

The fire building

First among considerations given to a fire building in size-up is its location. A flaming barn standing out in the middle of a prairie doesn't present the problem in tactics and strategy to a fire chief that a fire in an aging woodworking factory does when the factory is nestled in a cluster of one and two-story dwellings. Exposures should usually be protected first, before the main fire is tackled. The only deviation from this occurs when life is in immediate danger.

We can see therefore that two types of exposures are commonly encountered, fire exposure and life exposure. By fire exposure is meant property exposed to the fire which is burning, such as property directly across alleys or alongside the fire building. Life exposures might include hazard to lives of occupants of buildings in line with the travel of dangerous fumes or gases thrown off by the fire, as well as as to occupants in a building which is seriously exposed by fire from the fire building.

As an example, fire may be burning in a wholesale chemical warehouse and dense, toxic fumes may be thrown off. If these fumes are carried into apartment houses, schools, or other occupied buildings, they may cause injury or death.

In his size-up of a building a chief will have to give early attention to the way he will move his forces in on the fire. Does an obstruction exist that makes it difficult to get heavy streams in position? Or does the construction or position of a building limit the placement of ladders, particularly aerial ladders or elevating platforms.

Finally, in relation to the building the chief making a size-up must look quickly to his water resources. Are there enough hydrants, well placed in relation to the fire, and are they adequately supplied by mains? Maybe there aren't enough—or any—hydrants and water will have to be hauled in, or drafted from a lake or a stream.

A building, of course, may have its own water supply, standpipe or sprinklers supplied by a roof tank or reservoir. It may even have its own yard hydrant and main system—all factors to be considered.

Occupancy

The occupancy of a building must be given early consideration as to its use. A fire in a theater at 3 a.m. has nowhere near the potential of one occurring during a standing-room-only performance at 8:30 p.m. An empty factory offers lesser hazards than one going at full blast.

Contents, aside from people, can certainly affect the actions of fire fighters. Taking the extreme example of a fireworks factory, we can readily see that fire fighters will act much differently in such a structure than in a light-hazard office building. Also, you can't treat a 100,000-gallon tank of fuel oil in the middle of a tank farm in the same fashion as a fire in a domestic oil burner. Suffice to say that the type use, contents and the number of persons occupying a building must have a heavy bearing on the size-up.

Construction

Construction of buildings varies all over the lot—a fact that anyone can vouch for just by taking a walk around his hometown. First to be considered is the type of construction—wood frame, brick and joist, concrete and steel, mill construction, or what have you. Knowledge of building construction and how fire will affect it is something that should be known by anyone who will have to make a size-up before he is called upon to make it.

The age of the building is another factor. Old buildings were constructed under old building codes and some have a tendency to collapse. On top of that, they usually have undergone multi-remodelings, all of which can create difficulty for operating firemen. Old buildings of any size should always be pre-fire planned if disaster is to be avoided.

Height and area of a building has a strong influence on size-up. Consider the high-rise hotel and a four-story apartment. Each is designed to house people. But what a difference in action is required under fire conditions.

Other factors to be aware of under this size-up heading of construction include the areas within a building—large and unbroken by fire stops or honeycombed with rooms as in a high-rise office building.

In his "construction" size-up a fire officer will check the paths or channels that fire can travel such as stairwells, shafts, ducts, pipe recesses and others. Windows which also offer a fire path—in or out—should also be checked to see if they have any protection.

The fire

Finally, there is the condition of the fire itself at the time the size-up is made. Where is it located within the building? What about the smoke and gases being generated? How large is it? What type of contents? Rags, flammable oils, plastics, etc.? Is there any actual or potential life hazard to the occupants or fire fighters?

These are but a few of the questions an officer in charge must ask and get answers to if he is going to have a successful operation.

Additional help

Then there is the question of additional help. This officer should consider the actual or potential need for respiratory equipment in excess of what's on hand, rescue equipment, emergency medical service, police assistance, wrecking equipment, public utility units and, of course, additional fire fighting manpower and equipment.

The quantity of additional manpower and equipment for fighting the fire will depend on the officer's judgment.

Occasionally too much apparatus is called by an inexperienced officer, but this is the exception rather than the rule. Analysis of a great number of fires which have resulted in the destruction of one or more buildings shows that the first-in officer did not appreciate the size of job that he had to handle with the result that he called insufficient apparatus. Usually it was upon the arrival of superior officers, who noted the rapidly extending fire, that additional apparatus was summoned.

Apparatus is maintained for one purpose alone, and that is for fighting fire. Unless the department is very much overworked, little harm will result in calling more apparatus than is needed, and great good may be accomplished. If more apparatus than is needed is called, it is a simple matter to dismiss the companies and have them return to their stations with very little loss of time. On the other hand, if too little apparatus is called, by the time additional apparatus is summoned and reaches the scene, the fire may have reached proportions which will necessitate the use of even a greater number of companies for a longer period of time.

EXPOSURE FIRES

To members engaged in fire service, an exposure fire is any blaze that has extended from the place of its origin either to another building or to an independent unit of the same building; the former being known as *external* exposure and the latter, *internal* exposure.

There are a number of causes which give rise to exposure fires. A blaze in an individual building may pass beyond the possibility of being localized at the place of its inception. Fire also may extend out through wall openings and roofs, or it may enter through them. Parts of a burning building, especially the walls, floors and roofs, may fall and scatter burning brands.

The presence or absence of outside open spaces, such as boulevards, parks and vacant lots, influences the spread of fire, as well as the direction and velocity of prevailing winds, general weather conditions, and the ability of neighboring construction to withstand the effect of heat waves or radiation, or flying brands.

Exterior exposures

External exposure hazard is the danger of one building becoming ignited by fire originating in an adjoining or neighboring building. When many structures, or a section of the city, are subject to the rapid spread of fire in this manner, a conflagration hazard exists.

Virtually any building is unable within itself to resist the intense heat developed by a fire in a neighboring building or group of buildings. Under such attack, windows may break or melt, and many floors simultaneously may be entered by fire and their contents destroyed.

 Radiated heat or flames may enter unprotected windows of a large building, ignite the contents, which in turn generates heated gases and flames that pass through the windows and re-enter the building above until the entire structure is ablaze.

This hazard stems from the buildings or combustible materials which may exist on adjoining or nearby properties. If they are poorly constructed or are used for the storage or manufacture of combustible materials, the possibility of exposure fires will always be present. Industrial plants and mercantile establishments may be classified under two general headings: those with incombustible walls such as brick, concrete, or terra cotta, and those with combustible walls. The degree of the hazard may be classified as severe, moderate or light.

Covering exposures consists of completely surrounding one fire so that it will be checked at every possible avenue of extension. The size-up usually determines at just what points the chief efforts have to be exerted. It may be unnecessary to operate on all sides of a building to cover exposures for some buildings, such as those having blind walls, which may be alongside similar buildings, creating a minor exposure hazard. In some cases where the building faces on a wide street with the wind blowing toward the fire, there is little chance of the fire extending across the street. In all cases, attention is given first to the most serious exposure hazards.

If endangered buildings have standpipes, companies can attach hose lines to them and extinguish burning window frames or stock near windows. By carefully wetting down material within the flame or heat radiation zone, the fire can be kept from extending. The same stream can be used to attack the main fire across a street or an alley.

Master streams used

At this point it might be mentioned that, unless a fire has reached considerable size, the exposure danger is usually not very serious. On the other hand where a fire has become very hot, then the hazard may be extreme. In view of this condition the use of large streams for covering exposures is doubly necessary. The exposed area will be seriously endangered, and will require streams with good range and plenty of volume to properly protect it (see master streams in Chapter 13).

One of the most effective means of covering exposures is by the use of turret guns, monitors or other heavy stream appliances. These can be placed at such a point as to reach either the fire building or the exposed building, and the stream can be quickly switched from side to side as necessity demands. It serves in extinguishing fire as well as wetting down the exposure and, in an emergency, can be used for providing back spray from the face of the building to cool the street so that the members may operate near the building and at close range. This is not as minor a point as might be supposed. There are on record a number of large fires where the narrow street in front of the fire building became so hot that men could not operate until such a spray was provided.

The ladder pipe, elevating platform and Squrt are very effective for use in operating into the high floors of a building. Due to the strength of the stream, the large volume of water discharged, and the elevation of the nozzle, such units are also particularly effective for covering high exposures. Heavy stream appliances, such as deluge sets, have also a use in this operation (see Chapter 13).

In narrow alleys, and particularly where the exposed buildings are not high, small streams may be effectively used, but they are limited in application. Their chief advantage is their ability to be moved and manipulated in close quarters.

It should be remembered in covering exposures that the leeward side is always the most dangerous, due to the fact that hot gases, heated air and even flames may be carried considerable distances by the wind. In addition to this, where volatile flammables are present, there is always a possibility of combustible gases traveling into adjoining buildings and igniting, thus carrying the fire to the structures.

The officer in charge, when planning to cover exposures, should take the leeward side first and note the conditions there. But if the fire has gone through the roof, the buildings which deserve first attention are those on either side, where they extend above the fire building. For last consideration in covering exposures on the outside, are the buildings across streets, particularly wide streets.

Once the positions have been chosen for operations in covering exposures, and turret pipes, street pipes, ladder pipes or elevated streams are in operation, the streams should be swept over the face of the exposed building, making sure to spray exposed windows. This process must be continued while the fire is at its height so that no window will heat up sufficiently to break or melt. Streams protecting buildings may also be directed on the fire to aid in reducing the heat. The very presence of the streams between the fire building and the exposed buildings will reduce the temperature of the air between these buildings and will retard the extension of fire by convection or radiation.

Covering external exposures of the fire building, when the fire is about to jump from a floor to the floor above by way of windows, involves the use of streams chiefly to extinguish the fire near the front of the building and thus prevent its vertical extension. While the windows and walls above may be wet down from the street, most effective work is done by getting streams in on the fire, near the windows.

Shafts

Where elevator or hoist shafts follow a line of windows at the front of a building, it is frequently possible to check the fire from extending through these inside vertical passageways by use of properly directed streams. Master streams driven through the window into the shaft will drench it sufficiently to prevent fire from passing as long as the streams are in operation. This is a very important point to remember in handling fires in old type commercial buildings where the elevator shaft is at the front or rear of the building, and where the shaft is provided with windows at each floor.

Interior exposures

Hand lines, due to their mobility, must be used to cover interior exposures. They should be used to cover vertical passageways through which fire may rise, such as dumbwaiter, elevator or hoist shafts, stairwells, pipe ducts, vent shafts, lightwells, etc. In most cases the lines are brought in on upper floors, usually the floor immediately above the fire, if it has not gained too much headway, and the stream directed into the shaft to kill the fire and to cool down the shaft. Sometimes lines are brought into the floors below the fire floor and operated into vertical shafts. Occasionally burning material drops to the bottom of such shafts and unless they are properly covered with streams, there is a chance of fire starting at the bottom.

A second method of covering exposures, not involving the use of streams, is to close windows and shutters in the fire building or exposed buildings. This is one of the first operations of ladder companies after ventilation and other immediately necessary duties have been accomplished. Closing windows and shutters will retard the spread of fire, and sometimes make it possible to confine the fire to a single building.

Other methods of covering exposures within the building or adjoining building include closing doors and other openings by which the fire may communicate from one building to another or from one part of a building to another. It is very necessary to see that all wall openings of adjoining buildings are properly closed, or covered by streams in the event that satisfactory doors are not provided. Moving combustible materials away from walls in adjoining buildings is also classed as covering exposures.

Partition fires

The partition fire rarely starts within a partition, but usually enters from some other source. However, the extinguishing of such fires will be considered only from the standpoint of the fire within the partition.

One of the simplest ways of locating a fire within a partition is to feel along the wall with the hand. The point behind which the fire is burning can readily be located by the heat transmitted. If fire has been burning for some time, wallpaper may be discolored or paint blistered. Either of the above indications will serve to locate the fire. When it is located, and a stream is ready for use, the partition should be opened near the baseboard with ax, claw tool, 6-foot hook, or whatever other suitable appliance is immediately available, and the stream put into play. For this work a very small stream will be satisfactory, and much more so if a bent tip is available. Fire burns upward, and by starting at the bottom it is a very quick operation to cover the entire fire. This applies where the fire is burning in one part of the partition only, between the studdings. On the other hand, if fire has risen in the partition at several points then it will have to be opened up as required at the different points in order to reach all of the fire.

A stream directed vertically in a partition strikes the partition, or braces, at points above and comes back in the form of a spray, which proves very effective in extinguishing the fire. A partition nozzle or piercing applicator with a fog head has been found particularly effective in control of such fires.

Attic fires

Attic fires may originate from defective chimneys, defective wiring, interior exposure fire from below, or exterior exposure fire.

Here again small streams are effective, if the fire has not involved too large an area. Such fires can usually be reached with greatest speed by stretching up the stairway to the top floor, and getting into the attic through a trap door, by attic stairway or ladder, or by opening up the bulkhead. Departments carrying 12-foot extension or folding ladders find them very effective for reaching attic fires from the inside. The dense smoke usually encountered at such fires may make it difficult to determine when the fire is completely extinguished. But any rekindling of the fire will be readily detectable so that while it takes some time to clear the attic, there is little danger of fire reigniting unnoticed. If the attic is provided with windows, these can be opened from the outside if they can't be reached from the inside, to provide ventilation.

Fog streams are very effective on attic fires, for they help to reduce the smoke concentration while extinguishing the fire. But, where the attic is completely ablaze, use solid streams such as those from 1-inch nozzles, or large fog streams.

In operating at attic fires, a ladder can be raised to the roof, a section of shingling pulled off, and a stream put into operation from the outside. If windows are available, they provide the most effective means of reaching the blaze. Just as soon as the fire has been brought under control, water should be shut off to avoid unnecessary water damage.

Chimney fires

Fire departments are often troubled with chimney fires, particularly in the fall when furnaces and fireplaces are used in the new heating season. Most of these fires are caused by ignition of tar-like deposits or soot in the chimney walls. Such deposits are generally caused by incomplete combustion. Usually chimney fires are of little consequence, but some departments have got into serious trouble by treating them lightly. Most authorities now agree that chimney fires should call for the same response of units as any other call from a building. In all too many cases, it has been found upon arrival that the fire has spread from cracks in the chimney near the roof or partitions and that a serious hidden structural fire is in progress. A mild chimney fire can be extinguished by knocking burning soot off the walls with homemade chain devices operated from the top of the chimney.

A more intense chimney fire should be handled with spray from a booster line. It is agreed that if a spray is used, there is no serious danger that the flue lining will be cracked. Before any water or even the chain treatment is given, the inside of the house should be carefully inspected to determine if there is an attic or partition fire in progress and to see if there are openings in the flue or fireplace from which sooty water and smoke can escape. Such openings must be protected. Many departments have made a most effective chimney pipe by attaching a garden hose nozzle in spray position at the end of a pipe bent to fit over the top of the chimney. This relieves the firemen of the unpleasant and dangerous job of climbing up to the top of a chimney from the roof. Some chimneys are entirely unsafe and may not support the weight of a fireman or ladder placed upon them. Chimney fires may throw showers of sparks that can ignite wooden roofs or roll into gutters to start hidden fires after the chimney fire itself has been forgotten.

Fire protection authorities believe that various chemical preparations for extinguishing chimney fires have a limited effectiveness. They recommend water as being most effective and readily available.

Basement fires

Basement fires, due to the fact that they are not so readily discovered, gain greater headway than do fires on other floors. Furthermore, the basement is usually the depository for a lot of material not commonly found in the upper floors of a building, such as old furniture, waste paper, fuel, etc., and once a fire gets a good start, a hot and smoky blaze results. While many of these fires can be handled with small streams, a great number call for heavy streams for control. There is an advantage here, however, in that less damage is likely to result from the use of water in the basement of a building than on the upper floors.

In operating on a basement fire that has gained considerable headway, it is just as important to make sure that the fire is not rising through partitions or other vertical passageways as it is to get a line into operation on the fire itself. A quick survey on the ground floor will determine whether or not fire is rising.

If a fire has gained little headway, the first line in can be stretched directly into the basement by way of stairway and operated on the fire. On the other hand, if the fire has assumed larger proportions, then it will probably be necessary to kill the bulk of it before entering. This may be done from windows leading into the basement, or by entering the stairway in front of the building, or the inside stairway. In some cases, however, entry may be impossible due to the advanced stage of the fire, in which case cellar pipes or distributors are put into operation by cutting holes through the floor. In order to ventilate the basement in this latter case, in addition to opening doors and windows, holes may be cut front and rear of the building near windows so that smoke and hot gases rising in the rooms will be quickly discharged to the atmosphere. Whenever such openings are made, lines must be available to cover exposures.

A technique in the control of basement fires which has been gaining in popularity involves the employment of water fog. A wide-angle fog stream advancing through the basement drives the smoke ahead while extinguishing the fire. But an opening ahead must be provided for the escape of the smoke and heated air. If not, there is danger of the flames flashing around the crew on the line and trapping them.

High expansion foam has also been used to combat cellar fires. Here again, there must be an opening ahead or above the fire to permit smoke and heat to escape.

Basement fires are probably the hardest of all fires of their size to combat, due to the lack of natural ventilation and the probable presence of dense smoke and heat.

Cockloft fires

Cocklofts in any flat-roofed buildings are between the top floor ceiling and the roof. They may be 2 or more feet high and are generally higher in the front of the building. Where dividing walls are built up to the roof

Cockloft fire: Wall (1) extending through loft forms parapet above roof that provides fire stop. However, adjoining loft (8) must be examined to check against possibility of radiant heat igniting stored material (5). Parapet (2) which reaches only to top floor ceiling permits rapid spread of fire to adjoining building at left. All roof coverings should be removed, holes cut as needed (6) and partitions opened in shafts (7) and (3). Pulling ceiling on top floor (4) and (9) gives quick access to fire, but charged lines must be at hand.

level (between units in a row of buildings) the cockloft does not present the dangerous condition that prevails where the wall reaches only to the hanging ceiling. In this last instance, the cockloft spans a row of houses without a break, permitting fire to spread rapidly over the entire row.

Having a large unbroken area to travel through, with everything in the construction being combustible, the fire will bank up against the underside of roof boards, and extend throughout the entire space rapidly. The cockloft is particularly dangerous when interior shaft partitions terminate at the hanging ceiling, as this is the point where the fire will mushroom.

Cocklofts should be promptly ventilated even though the fire has not extended to them, and they should be examined before leaving the premises.

The fact that smoke is seen coming from several cornices of a row of buildings does not indicate that they are all on fire. But it does show that there is either an absence of fire walls or stops, or ineffective fire stops, and it is a sign to take precautions to halt possible spread.

The officer of the first ladder company arriving at a cockloft fire should always go to the roof with a part of his company, as it may be necessary to open up a part of the roof to relieve the cockloft of heat and smoke. But in any case, this officer will prove of valuable assistance to the officer in charge of the fire by reporting promptly the conditions as he finds them. For example, if after having removed a scuttle cover and stripping the lath and plaster around it, he finds the fire traveling toward the adjoining building or that it has passed this point, his prompt report to the officer in charge will enable the latter to place the lines at points of vantage. The officer of the first ladder company being the first on the roof and having seen conditions, should be directed to finish his work, as he may have seen fire in a certain part of the roof and would be in a better position to attend to it than another officer coming later. After a fire in a cockloft, raise a ladder and examine it to make sure there is no fire hidden in crevices or nests. Clean wood or the presence of cobwebs are an indication that fire has not extended beyond.

Where the fire appears to be in the cockloft of one building, take the first line to the top floor. Second and third lines are taken to adjoining buildings as a precaution.

The first ladder company raises a ladder to the front of the building, sends part of the company to the top floor to ventilate and pull down lath and plaster ceilings or open up a section of sidewall, as may be necessary for the engine company to get water on the fire. The other part of the company goes to the roof to open up.

The second ladder company sends part of the company to the top floors of each of the adjoining buildings to open up ceilings or walls for engine companies. This company, when no longer needed in the adjoining buildings, may be ordered to assist the first ladder company.

DWELLING FIRES

A look at almost any fire department's annual statistics would probably show that about 95 percent of all fires are extinguished with one line or less. This look would also show that most fires occur in dwelling occupancies and most frequently are confined to one room. The greater

Dwelling fire: Partition (1) is opened to expose concealed fire and permit use of bent tip. Line to attic (2). Scuttle and ladder are often found in top floor closet. Stream from ladder (3) can be operated into attic. Openings are made in roof by man operating from ladder (4).

number of these one-room fires occur in kitchens, according to a National Fire Prevention and Control Administration survey. Living rooms came next and bedrooms run third.

So let's look at problems that fires in these rooms develop and the techniques used to extinguish them with the least amount of primary damage from flame and secondary damage from smoke and heat.

Good fire fighting requires the same basic strategy that makes successful generals—sufficient power in the initial attack to overcome the enemy (fire) and an adequate reserve capability to handle any unforeseen developments. That is why more than one line is stretched at every dwelling fire—even when one line should be able to complete extinguishment.

The use of preconnected 1½-inch lines—sometimes called live lines—is the quickest way to get water on a single-room fire in sufficient quantity for extinguishment without unnecessary water damage. Good practice incorporates the use of three 1½-inch lines. Generally, the first hits the fire, the second goes to the floor above to prevent extension of the fire and the third backs up the first line. Unusual circumstances will dictate differences in the use of these lines. For example, the first line may be needed to make a rescue. Then the second line might be the first to hit the main body of the fire.

In addition, a 2½-inch line is often stretched to an entrance to the building so that if the need arises, it can be put in operation immediately. In some departments, this is done as a standard operating procedure, while in other departments, the 2½-inch back-up line is laid only when the officer in charge thinks that the room fire is intensive enough to warrant the added precaution. At the very least, the second or third-due engine company should be prepared to stretch one or two 2½-inch lines if necessary.

By now, it should be standard procedure to use fog nozzles on all lines inside a building. The greater effectiveness of water fog over a straight stream in fighting interior fires is a well-proven fact.

Every fire fighter—not just the officer of the first-due company—should take a purposeful look at a burning house as his apparatus makes its approach. The exterior architectural design provides clues to the probable location of stairs and hallways, as well as the general layout of rooms. The configuration of the house around the built-in garage can be a tipoff to the fact that you are about to enter a split-level house, which is nice to know when you have to feel your way to the fire through the smoke-obscured interior.

Look at the exterior

A good look at the exterior also can identify a house as one of a type that is common in the community. Land developers often cover an extensive area with only two or three different architectural designs—which is often the only thing they do that aids the fire service. Once you have been inside one house of a specific type, you know your way around all others of the same type.

In areas where overhead wires are used, one of the most useful things to note as you arrive is the entrance of the electrical service to the house because the master switch will be in that section of the building. In some cases, the electrical service entrance will be in a garage, and the master switch will be located there instead of in the cellar or utility room. In any event, if you keep your eyes open while outside, you won't wander around looking for the switch on the inside when you wish to cut off the electrical power.

In most single-room fires electricity itself is not a problem. The electrical appliances, light fixtures, outlets and switches cause the difficulties, and when they are burning, overheated or smoking, they must be de-energized. When time is critical, pulling the main switch for the house will cut off power in the building. But if you have a minute or two to spare and the electrical circuits are identified, you can de-energize the troubled circuit by pulling the fuse or switching off the circuit breaker for that circuit.

This is the way to handle an overheated ballast in a fluorescent fixture, such as you find in some kitchens. Once the circuit is de-energized, you can then remove the fixture without damaging it and check the ceiling area for any burning or smoldering material.

Check electrical appliances

Kitchen fires often involve electrical appliances such as stoves, built-in wall ovens, dishwashers, washing machines and dryers. Sometimes they are installed as part of a work counter so that it is difficult to disconnect the plug from the electrical outlet. Major appliances will each be on a separate circuit, so it is easy to spot the right circuit breaker or fuse to cut off the power.

The involved appliance should be pulled out from the wall to check for hidden fire. When the appliance is built into a counter or wall, this should be done carefully to avoid doing physical damage to the surrounding area. A screwdriver is the most useful tool in most instances because the retaining material for the appliance is usually held in place with screws.

After overhaul has been completed, leave the power off on the circuit serving an appliance and then tell the householder to have an electrician check out the circuit and the appliance before restoring power. On fused circuits, leave the fuse on top of the fuse box to discourage immediate use of the circuit. This also should be done after shorts in electrical fixtures, outlets and switches.

In addition to electrical fires, minor kitchen fires include blazing grease on a stove and burning meat in an oven. If the fire has not extended beyond a small surface area from the stove, a portable extinguisher is usually all that is needed to put out the fire. Because stove fires are basically class B fires, you can use either a carbon dioxide or a dry chemical extinguisher.

When you have a choice, it is preferable to use a carbon dioxide extinguisher in a kitchen because this type leaves no cleanup problem for the housewife. And that makes for good public relations for the fire department. When you use a dry chemical extinguisher, you create a cleanup problem that is extensive beyond belief. The dry chemical will find its way into the most unlikely places and the housewife will be cleaning up traces of it days or even weeks after the fire when she opens a seldom-used drawer or cabinet.

The serious kitchen fire can reach the flashover stage and give you all the fire you ever want to see in a single room. These fires, and those of lesser volume that involve structural material and furnishings, require the full-scale attack with 1½-inch lines, just as in an other room. There may be enough fire to require the help of the backup line to darken down the kitchen. And of course, any flaming fire demands the positioning of a line over the fire to guard against extension of the fire to the floor above.

In overhauling, concealed spaces exposed to fire must be opened up for inspection. There is often a void space over kitchen cabinets where fire may smolder and finally burst into flame unless you open up the space. Also, the concealed wall area behind cabinets must be checked visually when fire has extended to the rear of the cabinets.

Exhaust system a danger

And don't forget the kitchen exhaust system. You will find exhaust ducts in some kitchens that outdo those in restaurants as far as a fire danger is concerned. For one thing, they have no extinguishing systems built into them and they are seldom properly cleaned. So it is easy for fire to get into a greasy duct and spread to another part of the home. Always check kitchen ducts before completing your overhaul.

A kitchen exhaust fan that is connected to a duct should never be used for ventilation during a fire because of the danger of drawing the fire into the duct. On the other hand, wall fans that vent directly to the outside can be used for ventilation if they are in a desirable location in the kitchen and the conditions are right. But don't use one just because it's there and draw fire across the room.

In kitchens that have gas stoves, the gas supply can be shut off by turning the gas cocks in the pipe beside the stove or the one at the meter. Turn the cock with the slot made for that purpose in traditional-style spanner wrenches. Closing the cock near the stove will give you a quicker shutdown because the distance to the stove is shorter. If bottled gas is used, the valve on the outside cylinder can be turned off.

Coordination of the operation of hose streams and ventilation makes for an effective attack on one-room fires that are larger than an upholstered chair or a pot of grease. When you attack a hot fire with a fog

Exhaust fans found in many kitchens can be used for immediate and effective ventilation. But they must not be used if there is a possibility of drawing fire across ceilings or through ducts.

stream, steam is generated in tremendous volume. Each cubic foot of water that is converted into steam produces about 1600 cubic feet of steam. The room doesn't increase in size, so the steam has to find space elsewhere. When no ventilation has been provided in a burning room, the steam will push through the doorway—right where you are holding the nozzle. At best, you will be mighty uncomfortable, and most likely you will have to retreat.

Fog streams affect ventilation

If a window in a blazing room is opened by the ladder company a couple of seconds before you start putting water fog into the room, the steam will vent to the outside and you will be able to think of advancing into the room instead of retreating. At the same time, the ventilation will provide an escape for smoke and heat. Some of the ventilation will be result of the expansion of the heated atmosphere in the room and the generation of large volumes of steam that has to have a place to go.

At the same time, fog streams initiate air currents that can become important factors in ventilation. In one-room fires, the window first opened for ventilation should be closest to the seat of the fire so that when fog streams push fire as well as hot gases out of the room to the outside, they will not contaminate and possibly spread fire in hitherto unburned sections of the building.

For one-room fire ladder company can provide ventilation through window just as engine company is ready to attack.

The intent is to utilize the pushing characteristics of fog streams to help push the fire gases back into the burned area and to the outside. This means that the attack must be made inside the building and ventilation must be coordinated with the advancement of the attack lines.

Walkie-talkies are a tremendous help in making it possible for ventilation to be accomplished just as a hose crew is ready to open up its line. This coordination eliminates venting before the hose crew is in position, which may let the fire make more headway than it should. Coordination also makes it unnecessary for a hose crew to take a beating while waiting in a hallway or on the stairs for the ladder company to ventilate.

In less serious room fires, it is often possible to ventilate by opening windows from inside the room. Naturally, you take advantage of this situation whenever it exists, but men assigned to ventilation should be prepared to operate on the outside of houses.

In large building fires, ventilation tactics are directed primarily at preventing extension of the fire and making it possible for hose crews to advance into the involved area by relieving heat and smoke conditions. Although these two objectives exist in the single-room fires that we are discussing, confinement of the fire and getting into the room often present little or no difficulty. But ventilation remains important for different primary reasons.

While concentration of smoke may be of minimum concern to the men extinguishing the fire, any smoke at all contributes to the total loss suffered by the householder. The smoke deposits on furniture, walls, rugs and draperies must be removed, and all traces of smoke odor must be eliminated before the home can be considered livable again.

Prevent smoke damage

Therefore, ventilation should be accomplished in these one-room fires as quickly as possible to prevent extension of smoke damage to other rooms. This is done even when the average fire fighter must consider the amount of smoke in the area inconsequential. For example, when an oil burning ignition failure has resulted in a moderate amount of smoke and fumes in the cellar of a house, the cellar should be ventilated by opening windows and using smoke ejectors. At the same time, the cellar door to the first floor should be kept closed. All this is done because we wish to avoid contaminating the upper floors with the odor of fuel oil fumes and increasing the residents' cleanup problem.

When you extinguish minor fires such as mattress or upholstery fires, a smoke ejector should be taken into the room right on the heels of the hose crew and put into operation as soon as possible. We are all familiar with the obnoxious odor of burning upholstery and mattress materials—especially foam rubber. Fortunately, most of us have had no experience living in a house with this odor after a fire has been extinguished. Rapid ventilation will minimize the extent of this problem for the occupants of a home.

Another reason for ventilation in relatively simple one-room fires is to make the working conditions more comfortable for your brother fire fighters. There isn't any point in working in an unnecessary amount of heat and smoke when you can do something about it. Associated with improved conditions is the ability to work more carefully and deliberately. With less heat and smoke present, men tend to use water more economically and effectively, and in searching for hidden fire, they become more careful to avoid excessive damage when opening up walls and ceilings—or even upholstered furniture.

So you see, in the one-room fire, ventilation actually extends into the area of salvage operations.

For the fires we are discussing, horizontal ventilation is generally preferred. It is the easiest and quickest to accomplish and results in no damage to the dwelling—other than a broken pane of glass now and then. Windows and doors are opened to provide the desired type of ventilation at the right time, and when available, exhaust fans in kitchens and bathrooms can be used to advantage.

Double-hung windows should be opened top and bottom. Theoretically, the upper sash should be lowered two-thirds of the way and the lower sash raised one-third of the way. The important thing is to arrange the sashes so that they just cover one another. This will provide the maximum window opening and therefore the maximum ventilation.

Any screen or full-length storm window should be removed to obtain the full effect of opening the window. Screens should be removed because the wire in them actually blocks a considerable percentage of the window opening and therefore reduces the effectiveness of ventilation. Screens also will be found on casement windows, which are not ordinarily fitted with storm windows.

Storm windows a problem

When the old-fashioned, full-length storm window cannot be removed, it at least should be swung open as much as possible. Inasmuch as they swing open from the bottom, raise the lower sash of double-hung windows as high as possible and leave the upper sash closed at the top.

The triple-track, aluminum frame storm window offers a similar problem inasmuch as it is not practical to try to remove the glass under ordinary one-room fire conditions. These windows are expensive and breaking them for ventilation at a minor fire comes under the heading of excessive damage. However, don't hesitate to break them when fire conditions make it vital to obtain every square foot of ventilation possible.

What you should normally do is to lower the upper glass to the bottom of an aluminum-frame storm window and lower the upper sash of the double-hung window as much as possible. This at least provides an opening at the level of the higher strata of temperatures in a room. These modern storm windows are designed to operate in so many different ways that fire fighters cannot be expected to figure out how to remove the glass in one piece in the limited time in which ventilation must be accomplished.

When we talk about utilizing as much of the maximum window opening as possible, we also must consider curtains and drapes. Both from a ventilation and a salvage viewpoint, they should be removed from a window. The easiest way to do this is to remove the rods with the curtains and drapes still on them. Sometimes, you have to take the drapes off separately. Then lay the curtains and drapes over a chair or bed so that they do not become soiled or wrinkled. This will gain you a few public relations points with housewives.

Burning mattresses and blankets create highly noxious atmospheres that make the use of self-contained breathing apparatus a must. Search and rescue, ventilation and fire fighting all can be done more effectively while breathing normally in a self-contained breathing apparatus. Without breathing apparatus in an irritating atmosphere, you begin to work hastily, and carelessness steps in as effectiveness departs.

If the fire is limited to a bed, relatively little water is needed to extinguish the flames. However, a 1½-inch line should be taken in because it provides the extinguishing power you may need if concealed fire has been overlooked in the size-up. In extinguishing fire in a mattress—or an upholstered chair—the full 50 to 100-gpm potential of the nozzle is not needed. So you open the shutoff only part way—just enough to provide the volume of water needed.

Once flames have been knocked down and glowing spots have been darkened, the best thing to do with mattresses and bedclothes is to get them out of a house. They often can be dropped out a window, but otherwise they must be carried to the outside. You should wear gloves when handling this smoldering material. Otherwise you may have to drop it before you get it to the outside.

Once mattresses and bed clothes are outside, they can be easily overhauled, although sometimes this takes extensive probing. As a matter of fire safety, no mattress that was burned should be returned to a house. Its next stop should be the dump.

Bedroom fires sometimes start in or get into closets. With the door closed, or nearly closed, the fire can build up a good deal of heat as it goes into the smoldering stage. Then you hit the closet with a fog stream and a tremendous volume of steam hisses back at you, threatening to scald you. After this has happened once or twice, you learn to keep your face and body out of the doorway. Using the partition for protection, reach into the closet with one hand directing the nozzle. Usually, one or two rotations of the nozzle in the closet are sufficient to knock down the fire. Then shut down the nozzle to permit inspection of the closet. Then perhaps all you need is another brief application of water before overhauling, but this second application will be made in a cooler atmosphere and the steam problem will be minimal.

Where bedroom fires have been extensive—beyond a single bed or chair—all drawers should be opened and checked for fire. Charred contents should be overhauled to search out glowing material and for salvage purposes.

Living room fires the largest

The third room fire we shall discuss is the living room fire, which can be expected to involve the greatest area in a dwelling. The initial attack does not vary in tactics from what we have described, although a higher

Concealed spaces, such as this void under stairs behind bookcase must be opened for inspection when there is reason to suspect hidden fire.

water application rate may be required for the larger living rooms. Now and then you will find in large homes a living room that is two stories in height. In fact, the ceiling may be at the roof, and when a living room of this type is seriously involved in fire, roof ventilation is your best bet for confining the fire. And that's when you may find good use for the 2½-inch backup line.

However, most living rooms, although the largest in the house are of reasonable size for 1½-inch lines and horizontal ventilation procedures.

Among the problems more commonly found in living rooms are paneling, thickly upholstered furniture, bookcases, television sets, rug pad or underlay, and fireplaces. These problems, of course, are not confined to living rooms.

When fire gets into paneling, there should be no hesitation about opening it up to search for any extension of fire. Some firemen hesitate to remove paneling because it is relatively expensive and its removal will add to the fire loss. What they don't realize is that once paneling has been in a house for a few years, it is practically impossible to match the old paneling with new boards or plywood sheets. Therefore, owners insist on replacing the entire wall, which means that you don't add to the dollar loss by ripping out enough paneling to make certain there is no hidden fire.

After the fire has been knocked down in a room, the walls should start to cool. When they don't, there should be no hesitation about opening up paneling, plaster or gypsum board. In the latter two materials, you can make small but adequate inspection holes that can easily be patched.

Television sets call for care

Fires in TV sets offer little trouble if they are discovered before fire has extended to the room. Pulling the plug for the TV set is the first thing to do. Many times, this is enough to cause the fire to go out by itself. However, there are two things to be cautious about—the high voltage that will remain in the chassis for some time after the plug has been pulled and an implosion of the picture tube. The voltage problem is taken care of by making certain you don't touch the set chassis.

The possibility of the picture tube imploding raises more complications. Sometimes it makes sense to take a TV set outside and then extinguish it. If you do this, drape an old salvage cover over the set so that it covers the sides. Then if the picture tube implodes, glass fragments will be kept inside the set. Because picture tubes have a vacuum, the glass fragments will move inward, or implode, when the tube breaks. Handle the set by the ends when you move it and work from the ends when you extinguish fire in a TV set.

A burning chair or sofa also sometimes can be moved outside for overhaul and final extinguishment. For one thing, having plenty of fresh air around immediately improves the working conditions and it eliminates additional smoke damage in the dwelling, The best thing to do with any upholstered chair or cushion that has been burning is to leave it in the backyard. If any smoldering material has escaped your notice, a rekindle will be limited to the article itself.

When the fire has extended to bookcases, all books must be removed and checked, and you also must inspect the backs of built-in bookcases. They sometimes cover void spaces in walls to which fire can extend. Again, if in doubt, open up.

Any fire that has burned into a rug calls for an inspection of the pad under the rug, which can be more flammable than the rug itself. Don't hesitate to rip the rug back far enough to be sure that there is no smoldering material under the rug.

A small line for fireplace

We mentioned fireplaces in connection with living room fires because the living room needs protection when a chimney fire is extinguished. Whether fog, chains or carbon-dioxide-producing flares are used to extinguish a chimney fire, sparks are likely to fly into the living room from the fireplace. The first thing to do is to stretch an old salvage cover, folded in half in front of the fireplace to protect the floor and rug from sparks. A small line or a water-type extinguisher can then be used to put out the fire in the fireplace. Then the chimney fire can be extinguished.

The wall area around the fireplace and along the chimney right up to the outside of the roof should be checked for excessive heat that might indicate an extension of the fire. Wherever necessary, the wall, ceiling or floor should be opened up just as in any room fire.

In discussing fires in kitchens, bedrooms and living rooms, we have seen that all three have common fire fighting problems and some of the same fire fighting tactics are used in each type of room. To our basic tactics, we add special techniques for handling the special problems that each type of room presents in a fire.

MULTIPLE DWELLINGS

Multiple dwellings have been defined in a variety of ways, depending on what code is used, from what city and even what section of the country. But for the purpose of this book, a multiple dwelling is a structure housing three or more families.

When people started to move into the cities in great numbers, the pressure for more housing increased. The cities, however, were limited in area, and plots were small and increasingly expensive. Economics dictated that dwellings go up and up, a process that has continued to this day, as witness the high-rise apartment.

A multiple dwelling then can be a two-story frame building completely non-fireproof, situated in a small town out on the Great Plains. Or it can be a 40-story, class 1 apartment house in Chicago, completely fire-resistant—except for the occupants and furnishings. In between we have a tremendous variety of sizes, shapes and number of apartment units all coming under the heading "multiple dwelling."

The original multiple dwellings, many of which are still in existence, were poorly constructed and had built-in life hazards that would not be permitted today. In general, they were of frame construction inside and out (later exteriors were made of brick), had an open stairwell that extended from the first floor to the roof, an open stairway that extended from the cellar to the first-floor hall, and one or more shafts that ran from the first floor to the roof. In addition, there were utility shafts or recesses (gas, water, plumbing, electricity) that extended from the cellar to the roof. Fire in any one of these vertical arteries permitted quick extension to the upper floors and often took a heavy toll of life.

This early type of multiple-dwelling construction had built-in hazards

Earliest multiple dwellings were of wood frame construction with wood exterior walls and ran from two to four stories high. They were built in rows with a common cockloft.

that brought on building codes that called for better protection.

The second generation of multiple dwellings had fire-retardant halls, and cellars that could be entered only from the outside began to appear. Later buildings had fire-protected light and dumbwaiter shafts. Still later, buildings appeared that had cutouts which supplanted the light and air shafts of previous years and in effect were open spaces around which the building was constructed.

It would be impossible to illustrate the variety of multiple dwellings that have been built in the United States and Canada. But it is possible to group them under three general headings: wood frame that was completely combustible; an intermediate type that was still wood frame but partially fire-resistive; and the modern, completely fire-resistive. All are still in existence—the oldest in increasingly lesser numbers.

Wood frame construction

The earliest multiple dwelling was of wood frame construction throughout and covered with wood exterior walls. Originally, these were built two stories high, but later went to three or four. A central open stairwell and halls divided the building in two, with apartments on each side of the stairs. Fortunately there were no other shafts in the building, but the framing for the walls was the balloon type. Balloon framing provides no fire stops between floors and fire on a lower floor can travel quickly upward via partitions to the upper floors and cockloft.

Another extremely bad feature of these buildings was that they were built in rows with a common cockloft that extended through a number of buildings. Fire in one building that reached the cockloft could then travel quickly down the row.

Builders later designed these buildings to include shafts to provide air for toilets but built them from combustible material, which only increased life and safety hazards. Buildings also went up, particularly in the northeast, with open porches and stairs attached to the rear wall. Later construction of this type included air shafts for interior rooms, again of non-fire-resistive material. Later still, brick supplanted wood for the exterior walls, but the rest of the structure remained the same.

The quick-burning characteristics of the first multiple dwellings led to stricter building codes. First codes generally called for structural features—fire-resistive—that retarded fire spread, particularly in hallways. Cellars, which were used for storage, also received attention. In the early 1900s, buildings went up in which cellar ceilings were fire-retardant and completely sealed off from the rest of the building. Access to the cellar could be gained only from outside the building.

Stairwells, hallways and interior shafts, while still not fire-resistive by today's standards, were covered with plaster instead of wooden wainscoting. Doors were metal-covered.

Most of these second-generation multiple dwellings—considerably altered—are still in existence. They now have fire escapes on either their front or rear, and sometimes both.

High-rise multiple dwellings

By the middle of the 1920s, multiple dwellings appeared that stretched anywhere from 10 to 20 stories. Codes required fire-resistive construction to separate all floors—not just between the cellar and the first floor. Egress was via fire-resistive stairs or fire towers separated from

San Francisco fire fighters begin operation at multiple dwelling fire that had involved two floors on arrival.

the hallways by fire doors and walls. And in general, all structural members and features were fire-resistive.

No matter how varied multiple dwellings may be, they have one common denominator: People—people gathered in greater numbers than usual, cooking, smoking, reading and perhaps drinking, all under one roof in any number of apartments. And it is to these people that fire fighters direct all initial fireground operations.

No matter what the construction or type of multiple dwelling, fire fighting begins with control of the means of egress, whether stairwell, fire escape or windows. Next comes control of interior shafts and recesses to check the spread of fire. Finally, and only when all occupants have been evacuated, the fire fighter goes after the main body of fire. These tactics presuppose a limited response of companies in the initial stages. However, with a heavy response, all actions can be taken simultaneously.

The older type multiple dwelling is a quick burner because of its completely combustible makeup and offers the greatest challenge to the first-to-arrive officer. In the illustration (page 457), fire originated in the living room of the first-floor apartment, extended to the kitchen and from there ate its way up the airshaft, from which it is threatening the second-floor apartment and the common cockloft which extends through several buildings. The illustration is greatly simplified to stress the major features of this type of fire. Actually, there could be anywhere from four to eight rooms in each apartment and two or three shafts leading from the cellar or first floor.

Positioning lines

Assume a response of two engines and a ladder company to this fire—all companies adequately manned. The first line should surely be taken into the hallway to check fire at the living room door, thereby protecting the stairwell. Men on this line would eventually move in on the fire.

A second line could then be stretched up the stairwell and in on the second floor. From this point, the nozzleman directs the stream into the shaft, and into openings made in the ceiling and walls by laddermen. This operation checks the fire at three major points.

If the main body of fire covers more than one room, the second line might have to back it up. A third line will then have to be stretched to the top floor, assuming there is adequate manpower.

If people are hanging out the front windows when the fire fighters arrive, they will naturally have to be taken down on ladders, portable or aerial. A good point to remember here is that in a fire severe enough to have people hanging out the front windows, there is a good possibility of them also hanging out the back windows, which must be checked immediately.

Laddermen will also have to get in on the floors to search for unconscious or panicky persons, particularly children who may have crawled under beds or into closets. They can gain entry to the various floors via fire escapes, ladders or inside stairwells if conditions permit.

Ventilation assists extinguishment

Adequate ventilation is another important function of the ladder company—a function that should be accomplished early in fire operations. Ventilation permits quick entry of hose lines and therefore quick extinguishment of fires. More important, ventilation is a life-saving measure. It relieves a structure of the pent-up heat and gases that threaten the lives of occupants and hinder search and rescue.

Removal of the skylights over the light shaft and hallway will immediately grant relief to occupants and fire fighters.

Once occupants have been removed, the officer in charge turns to the next most important job on the fireground: locating and extinguishing all the fire. If sufficient manpower is available, all jobs can be carried on simultaneously.

Even if fire did not burn through the light shaft or stairwell to the cockloft, it could still have reached the loft via the wall partitions. If this happens, or even if there is a suspicion of it happening, this most important blind spot must be checked.

The ladderman sent to the roof to ventilate can double as a scout, so to speak. Once he has the skylight or scuttle removed, he checks the cockloft not only of the fire building but in the buildings on each side. He can do this by checking for hot spots and smoke, or he can make an opening in the stairwell and shaft where they pass through the cockloft from the top-floor ceiling to the roof.

Fire in the cockloft calls for prompt action in any case, but it must be especially prompt and complete when several buildings connect via a common cockloft. The quickest way to get at such a fire is to pull ceilings on the top floor of the original fire building and the adjoining building or buildings. This is to be done with charged lines standing by.

The cellar fire in a six-story multiple dwelling is even more complicated as seen in the second diagram.

Shafts a problem

The second type of multiple dwelling brought on by stricter codes was better than the early frame building but by no means perfect. These

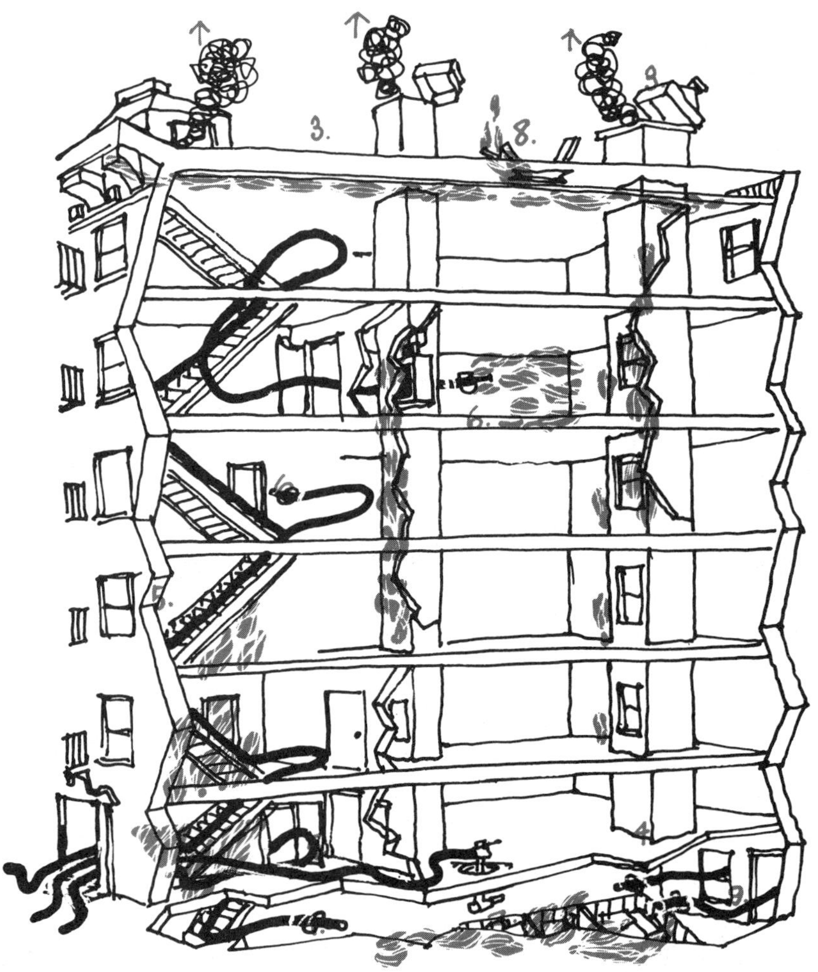

At cellar fire in multiple dwelling first line (1) should be taken to interior stairs to hold fire, and then down to cellar. Cellar pipe (2) and hand line through window (9) may also be used, but not when (1) is operating. Lines must also be stretched to control stairwell (5), and then to head off fire in shafts at (6) and (4). Quick ventilation over stairwell and at (8) and (3) is necessary.

buildings ran from four to six stories with walls that extended through the roof in row construction, thus eliminating the common cockloft, and the cellar was sealed off from the first floor by a fire-retardant ceiling. Entrance to the cellar could be gained only from outside the building, which eliminated a fire threat to the stairwell. The buildings were also larger in area.

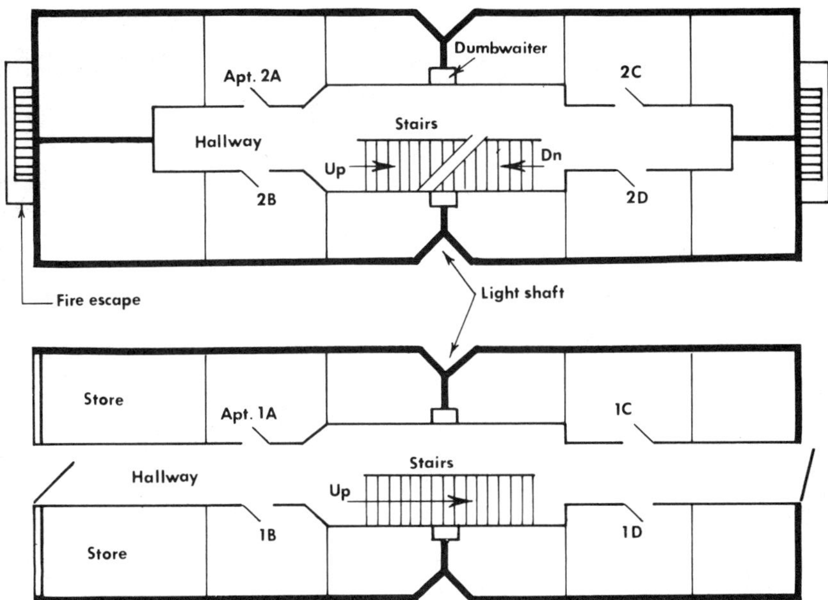

Second-generation multiple dwelling was still of wood frame construction but with brick walls. Common cockloft was eliminated and in later models cellar was sealed off from rest of building by fire-resistive ceiling.

Unhappily some shafts (dumbwaiter, plumbing) still went from the cellar just up to the roof and occasionally were stopped at the top-floor ceiling to make things worse. Narrow courts that were notched out between buildings now made their appearance. So did large shafts that were centered between the front and back walls, either in the center of a building or between two buildings. These courts and shafts had windows opening on bedrooms and baths that could permit fire to spread from one building to another.

In this second type of building, fire fighting tactics remained basically the same; interior fire fighting with hose streams to control the stairwell and quick ventilation.

The interior courts and large shafts did complicate matters, but lines could be stretched through the adjacent building to protect this exposure.

Larger area buildings also made for larger cocklofts, and these still had to be tended to as in the frame multiple dwellings. Even though the walls extended above the roof, adjoining cocklofts still had to be checked—there was always the possibility of a fault in the wall that could permit fire spread.

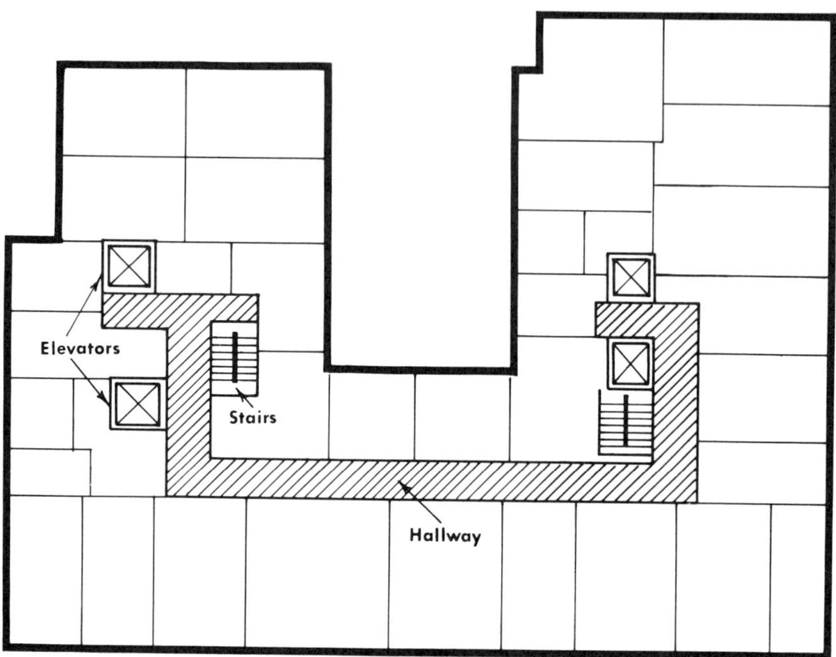

Latest multiple dwelling is completely fire-resistive throughout. This typical floor plan shows required stairways (two remote from each other) and the complex of apartments fire fighter must face.

It would be hard to establish the year, but sometime around 1910, buildings began to appear that were called apartment houses. They were large, often H-shaped, ran from four to six stories high and housed anywhere from 20 to 60 families. As in its immediate predecessor, the cellar was sealed off from the first floor. Stairs, however, were completely enclosed, and there were no shafts running through the building except for pipe recesses. Structural members (other than the stairwell), however, still were frame but fire-stopped at each floor.

But the pressure for city housing still existed, and multiple dwellings started reaching for the sky. Once they went above six stories, they had to be fire-resistive throughout. The fire fighters' problem was considerably reduced, as witness the low losses of both life and property in these well-constructed buildings.

However, fires do occur in these buildings and fire fighters have to take care of them. Fire fighters can stretch lines up the fire stairs in relative comfort until they reach the fire floor. From there down the hall to an apartment can be a punishing walk (or crawl) but it must be done.

Probably the biggest problem met is the ventilation of upper floors and stairwells (there are almost invariably two) when a severe fire occurs in an apartment. The floor above the fire floor can become heavily charged with heat and smoke, and this calls for search and possibly rescue.

On higher floors, beyond the reach of ladders, apartment fires are difficult to ventilate and often can be ventilated only from above by special appliances, such as a ball and chain to break windows below.

Persons trapped in an apartment in a modern building can usually be rescued only under cover of hose lines (there is rarely a second entrance) but a scaling ladder and occasionally a man on a rope has been used.

Persons on floors above the fire should be left where they are unless they are subject to heat and smoke. If this is the case, they should be removed via the stairway most remote from the fire.

We can see now that fires in multiple dwellings—old and new—call for similar actions: interior fire fighting with aggressive nozzlemen, ventilation, search and rescue, all depending on a knowledge of the building construction.

Multiple dwellings, as stated before, come in an almost infinite variety of shapes and sizes. They can only be covered generally in this small space. But it would be well for all fire fighters to have full knowledge of the shapes and sizes of the multiple dwellings in their communities.

CHAPTER SEVENTEEN

Advanced fire fighting

The types of fires described in the following pages are different from the run-of-the-mill fires described in the previous chapter in that they are larger or unique. They require more men and equipment to extinguish and with oil fires some specialized equipment and techniques. The basic strategy, however, to locate, confine and extinguish the fire, remains the same. So do the tactics, spelled out in previous chapters, such as engine company operations.

Unquestionably the biggest difference between a dwelling fire and such a major fire as can be found in an oil storage yard is that for most departments the big oil fire is one that comes once in a lifetime, if ever. As a consequence no experience in such fires is ever acquired by the average fire department. But still, there are small oil depots scattered around in every hamlet and town in this country. They can and frequently do make a pretty big fire. It is best then that every fire department know how to handle them—at least in theory.

In these larger fires, too, more attention must be paid to the size-up. Wind will, of course, have a greater effect on a lumber yard than on a 1½-story dwelling, as will the weather—rainy or hot and dry. Two hundred occupants in a factory will require greater consideration and effort than in this same dwelling. Height and construction are points in the size-up that carry considerable weight when applied to a high-rise building, and particularly one with a central core.

Finally, to make up for a lack of experience and a reliance on theory, a small fire department can substitute the technique called pre-fire planning. "Pre-fire planning will identify major problems, prescribe what is needed to meet them, and provide for meeting such needs."[1]

In a town, let's say, with two theaters, a few large factory buildings or lofts and a shopping center, the fire department should be able to pre-fire plan these target hazards.

Following are the more common type buildings and installations that should be pre-fire planned:

THEATERS

The stage of a theater represents one of those few instances where effort has been made to start the business of fire fighting as soon as the fire starts. In modern theaters the skylight over the stage is arranged to open by the cutting or burning of a hemp cord or rope. The fire curtain is designed to drop down and cover completely the proscenium opening. The action of these devices is to prevent fire, heat and smoke from going out into the auditorium, and to draw them up and out of the theater.

With few exceptions, the modern theater of either legitimate or movie type is of fire-resistive construction and is provided with sufficient means of egress. In spite of the superior construction of such places, however, the legitimate theater presents a problem to the fire extinguishing force because it contains a wood stage, combustible scenery, draperies and decorations, as well as property rooms, dressing rooms, musicians' rooms and a carpenter shop, all with materials of flammable nature.

Fire always possible

In such theaters—during performances—you have more or less a human hazard in and around the stage due to the fact that members of the cast, as well as workmen or stagehands, are constantly up and down between stage floor, cellar and various rooms, and the fly galleries. Because of the human tendency to be careless, or to smoke, there is always the possibility of fire. Most cities require that the proscenium wall opening be provided with a fire-resistive curtain capable of withstanding 1700°F for 45 minutes, separating the stage from the auditorium. In the event of fire, the cutting or burning of ropes at the side of the stage will cause the releasing device to operate and allow the curtain to drop into position to separate the stage from the rest of the theater.

[1]Clark, William E., *Fire Fighting Principles and Practices,* Dun-Donnelley Publishing Corporation, New York, N. Y., 1973.

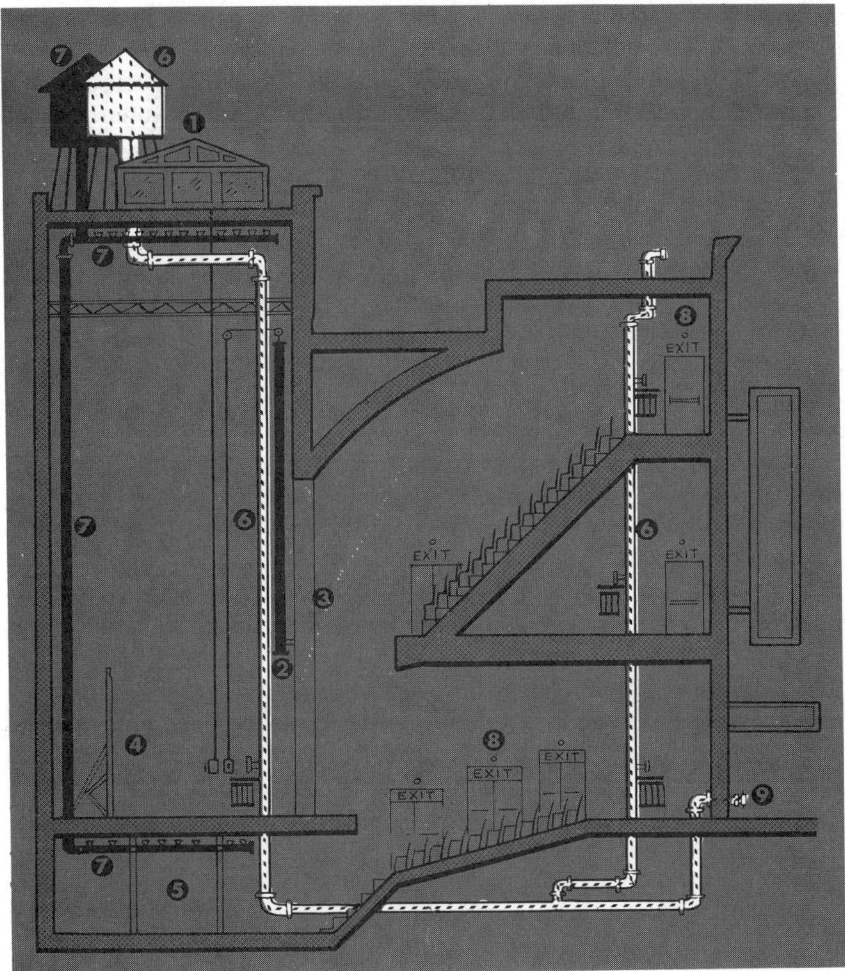

Theater: Sprinkler system (7), standpipe system (6) with fire department connection (9) protect stage (4) and rooms beneath (5). Skylight (1) over stage opens automatically from heat of fire. Fire curtain (2) drops to cover proscenium (3) to protect audience leaving auditorium at exits (8).

Another requirement of most cities is that automatic vents be provided over the stage. They may be as much as one-eighth that of the stage in area, and be so arranged as to open instantly once the fusible link holding them in place is melted by the heat of the fire.

A standpipe system and a wet automatic sprinkler system with heads to cover the stage space and with additional heads over the proscenium opening are also usually required.

The out-and-out moving picture theater has no stage—just a screen upon which motion pictures are projected. Sound equipment will be found behind the screen.

Quiet response needed

In the event of an alarm for fire being received from a special building box in a theater during a performance, fire companies should respond to the scene with as little noise as possible from sirens and bells.

Assume that a fire has occurred on the stage of a legitimate theater during a performance. The first officer arriving finds the audience leaving the building by the various exits. His first action should be to see that the protective curtain in the proscenium wall is lowered to provide a stop against the passage of fire, heat or smoke into the auditorium. His next step is to make sure that the ventilators over the stage are open and, to make doubly sure of this, ladders should be raised to the stage roof.

The placing of lines depends upon conditions. If the protective curtain has been operated properly, the fire will be confined to the stage. But if it has not fallen into its position, the first lines should be taken into the auditorium for the purpose of checking the spread of fire. Because of the high ceiling of the auditorium and the stage, nozzle pressures above the ordinary inside working pressures are necessary in order to reach the fire and enable the streams to do effective work. After these lines have been placed in position, other lines should be taken to the rear to operate through the stage doors.

Members of ladder companies should assist persons from the premises and make a search to ascertain whether any person may require removal or assistance. Other members should be sent to the roof of the stage to check danger to exposures, while the remainder raise ladders to fire-escape balconies to assist the movement of people and to force open exit doors from the outside if necessary.

Whether or not additional hose lines should be connected to siamese connections for the standpipe and sprinkler systems depends upon the judgment of the officer, who should estimate the intensity of the fire and whether sprinkler delivery would be more effective than a nozzle stream. But where fire involves the stage, it is absolutely necessary to connect one or more hose lines to the sprinkler siamese connection.

While people are leaving the theater, hose lines should be stretched in such a manner that the line of travel will not be interrupted or any confusion created. Let police efforts be concentrated particularly on getting cars away from exits and hydrants, so that companies arriving on additional alarms, if necessary, may get to work quickly.

Cover vertical openings

Fires may originate in places other than on the stage, such as in the auditorium, balcony, gallery, property room, carpenter shop, under the stage or in one of the many dressing rooms. The action taken by the fire fighting force on the scene must necessarily be governed by the location of the fire and the extent to which it may endanger the audience.

In some modern large theaters, there are sections of the stage which can be moved up and down from cellar to stage level. If these sections happen to be down at the time of any understage fire, the vertical opening created must be covered by lines without delay.

Fires in carpenter shops, property rooms and dressing rooms should be held there by allowing the sprinklers to operate and by keeping the fireproof doors closed until lines are in position.

PLACES OF PUBLIC ASSEMBLY

In addition to theaters, places of public assembly include nightclubs, cabarets, dance halls, lecture halls, music halls, indoor arenas, hotel ballrooms, etc.

In general, the procedures in handling fires in such establishments include: prompt evacuation of persons, covering their safe exit with fire streams, ventilation of building or fire area, maintaining unobstructed egress facilities and extinguishment of the fire.

The first officer arriving at a fire in such places occupied by the public must see that all exits are thrown open immediately.

Occasionally, when fire has been started by defective electrical equipment, the place will be thrown into darkness. In such case, portable lighting equipment will prove invaluable in checking panic and speeding up evacuation.

The great danger in dance halls is that of a fast-burning fire in decorations consisting of streamers, festoons and other forms of flammable draperies.

Most to be feared here is panic. Even while lines are being stretched, the first officer to arrive should see that every window and fire-escape balcony is "covered" with a ladder to assist in emptying the building quickly. As in theater fires, his men must be sent in to seek out those who have fainted or who have been injured and extend their search to washrooms, dressing rooms and other portions of the premises. Nightclubs have a bad record as far as fatalities are concerned. Overcrowding,

Typical lumber yard fire: Roadways (6) lead to front of every pile or shed. Line (3) protects exposed shed (5). Line (1) can hit shed and main fire. Line stretched from other street hits fire (2) between piles. Men on line (4) lower distributor between piles.

lack of sufficient exits, locked exits and obstruction of fire exits all have contributed to the loss of life. Where they occupy basements, the hazard is increased.

Here the fire department must exert every effort to keep paths of exit free, using fire streams if necessary to hold back the fire until life saving operations have been completed.

Hotel ballrooms are found on various floors. Some of the larger hotels have two or three ballrooms and it frequently happens that all will be occupied at the same time. They may be situated on different floors and many are not provided with separate and distinct exits as required of balconies and galleries in theaters, but depend upon inadequate interior stairs and whatever help elevators can give. These ballrooms present a serious life hazard. They have temporary wooden stages on which nightclub acts are given without any of the fire protection required in a regular theater—no ventilation over the stage, no automatic sprinklers, and no proscenium wall or curtain. Combine that situation with the fact that upward of 2000 people may sometimes be crowded into such rooms, on separate chairs with profuse decorations of a flammable nature and with totally inadequate exits, and the serious situation it presents can be appreciated.

Motion picture exhibitions are commonly given in ballrooms—which means that they are in darkness while filled with crowds of people. A small fire or excitement of any kind during such a performance may create a very dangerous situation through panic and the inability of people to get out.

If the ballroom is situated on the street floor of the hotel, the first officer to respond would not be handicapped as severely as he would be if the ballroom were on an upper floor. His first efforts, while stretching lines, must be concentrated on the life hazard and in securing as much ventilation as possible. If on an upper floor, he should use elevators remote from the immediate vicinity of the ballroom to get his men and equipment to the scene. Above the fourth floor he will have to depend upon standpipes and again he must use judgment in stretching from outlets away from the ballroom in order not to interfere with the safe exit of people. That means that extra hose must be taken up. If such ballrooms are facing the street, he must be quick to raise ladders to windows and use them, not only for removing persons, but for stretching lines since stairways might be blocked with people.

LUMBER YARDS

In the average lumber yard, roadways lead to the front of each and every pile of lumber or shed contained within its area, along which trucks may be driven for loading or unloading purposes. These arteries of travel are very useful not only in facilitating fire extinguishing operations but in many instances, because of their width, they prevent fire from communicating to lumber piled on the opposite side.

Two methods are employed in piling lumber: The space-pile method, where circulation of air is wanted within piles, and the solid method. With the first method, the wood is layered by being placed on furring strips. Fire readily travels through the horizontal spaces created between the different layers by such strips.

The greatest fire hazard in piled lumber, from the standpoint of fire extension, is on the sides and rear of piles because of the small spaces separating one from the other. When boards are not of the same length, a veritable hedge of board ends project horizontally at the rear of piles, providing means for the fast spread of fire. The smooth face on the front of all piles is less dangerous to a fire's extension. If a pile is straight in front, the flames will go along and just lick up the front and char the face of it. They will not have as much chance to get in between the boards.

Upon arriving at a lumber yard fire, it is good practice to pay no attention to the pile on fire for the time being, but wet down the adjoining piles and work in on the burning pile or shed.

The extension of the fire along the top layer of any pile is of minor importance and it can be easily controlled. What an officer should be alert to guard against is the fire communicating to the interior of the pile. Lines should be used to the best advantage in wetting down the ends and sides of piles with a view to preventing interior communication. An occasional sweep of the line on the tops of piles is also necessary.

In preventing an extension from pile to pile along the rear, a distributor or fog nozzle may be used to good advantage if there is insufficient space to use hand lines. These appliances can be lowered on the end of a line between piles and will insure a better distribution of water with more effective results than can be obtained from a straight stream. They can be easily raised, lowered or shifted from pile to pile. A few of these appliances skillfully and promptly used would, because of the manner in which the water is distributed, create an effective barrier against a fire's extension from pile to pile.

Fighting from leeward

In covering exposed lumber piles, it must be remembered that the leeward side is the most dangerous because hot gases, heated air and even flame may be carried a considerable distance by the wind and draft created by the fire. First consideration should be given to the fire on that side. The very presence of the stream between the fire and the exposed lumber piles will reduce the temperature of the air and retard the extension of the fire by radiation.

Where intense heat, smoke and flames make it impossible to operate on the leeward side, make a flank attack upon the fire with heavy streams. Effective work can be accomplished in this manner. Operating on the windward side is ineffective and dangerous.

Avoid having companies work from opposite ends of driveways. Move them in from one direction so they will not be driving smoke and fire against each other.

Where there is a strong wind blowing, and the fire has gotten a hold in the lumber yard, heavy stream appliances are vital. The use of big streams, particularly from a height, such as from a ladder pipe or elevating platform, gives large coverage and aids materially in checking the advance of the fire.

CHURCHES

The average church is a high one-story building. The smaller ones are usually of frame construction, while others have brick or other form of masonry enclosing walls, and usually a slate roof on wooden sheathing supported on timber trusses. There is generally a steeple, an organ loft, and an altar. The floor above the cellar is wood, and wood is generally used in pews and benches, the interior trim and wainscoting. A wooden balcony is not uncommon, and there is often a wooden choir loft. To make the interior attractive, the walls, recesses and pipe channels are sometimes furred out to make a smooth interior, leaving in some places concealed spaces of over a foot in depth.

Large concealed areas are found in attic or roof spaces and in the organ loft. The attic space is most important because of its inaccessibility for locating and controlling the fire that may be spreading through it.

Construction aids fire

Church construction, in brief, favors the fast spread of fire. A typical church fire, starting in the basement, spreads through the concealed spaces, such as heating pipe openings, into the main auditorium, as well as to the rooms in the rear of the pipe organ, and even to the organ gallery itself. It rises to the blind attic or overhanging ceiling through partitions or hidden spaces, where it spreads in all directions, building up heat and gases and charging the structure with heavy smoke. Back drafts are not uncommon, as the large windows are broken. Strong air currents develop to intensify the fire.

As a rule, fire involving the blind attic attacks the roof trusses and beams and after a short time the roof falls, carrying the ceiling and fixtures with it. In some cases the supporting trusses, upon collapsing, force some of the masonry work outward to bring down walls and endanger fire fighters. Once the fire has progressed into the steeple, it is almost impossible to save that structural detail.

The average church roof has large, unbroken areas and is sharply

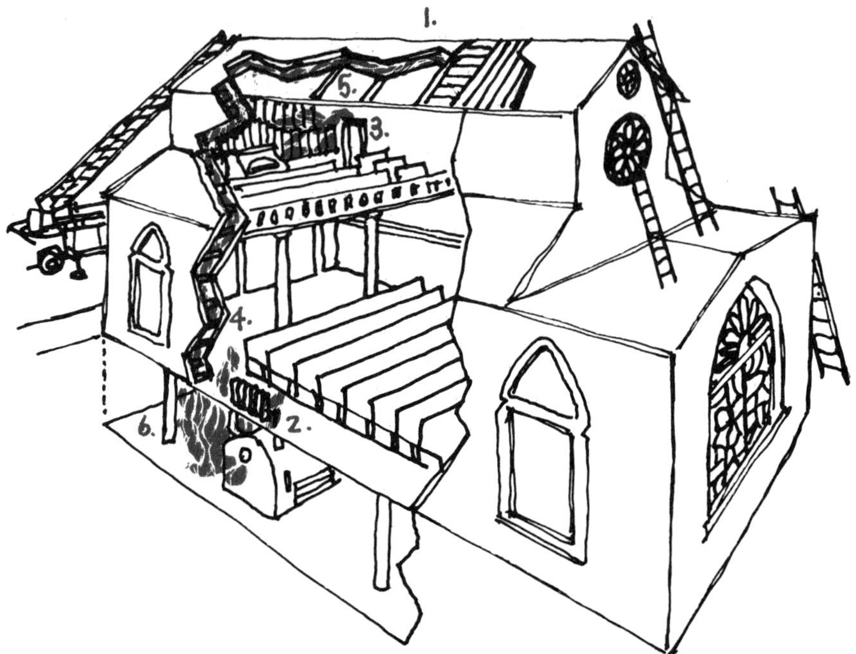

Fire in a church can spread rapidly from cellar (6) via walls (4) to organ loft (3) and then to hanging ceiling (5). Ventilation at roof (1) is difficult and dangerous and can only be accomplished with ladders. Danger of falling ceiling rules out use of hand lines in main body of church (2).

peaked. Of late years, slate and composition materials have replaced the old flammable wood shingles, reducing the exposed hazard but adding to fire fighters' troubles. Falling slate is dangerous.

It is not uncommon to attach the parish house, or hall, and the rectory to the church proper, with connecting passageways and openings. In such cases, fire, if not soon checked, will communicate to the connecting structures.

The church heating plant is usually located in the cellar or basement and as a rule is not cut off by fire-resistant construction, either horizontally or vertically, from the rest of the church. In the past, the common type of heating was by means of gravity-type hot air systems.

The organ loft is one of the most vulnerable features in the church structure. Almost wholly of wood with many concealed spaces and vertical vents, it permits fire to travel freely.

With the blind attic, or hanging ceiling, fully involved, it is extremely hazardous for the men to operate within the auditorium of the church due to the possibility of the roof, ceiling and fixtures falling. In view of these conditions, it is a common and necessary practice to operate entirely from the outside of the building once fire has secured a hold on the structure. This naturally slows up work and results in marked ineffectiveness in controlling the fire. However, it is a question of safety to men rather than hazarding their lives in an endeavor to save property.

Where the fire is limited to the basement or organ loft on arrival of the fire department, fast work in locating and covering lanes of possible fire travel may prevent extension.

When a church of any size is heavily involved with fire, large streams are absolutely necessary. The high ceiling, large open areas of the auditorium and intense heat require the use of streams of great range and volume. Even if such large streams cannot penetrate the blind attic or other concealed spaces, they can kill the fire in the main auditorium of the church and leave the work of controlling the attic fire to outside lines operated from aerial ladders or adjoining structures. This latter operation depends somewhat upon the type and construction of the roof and the ability of fire fighters to open it effectively and safely.

Fire control may be complicated by the desire to prevent needless damage to costly stained glass windows, interior decorations and religious furnishings. In some cases, windows can be swung open to provide ventilation and permit the application of hose streams in the effort to cut off and confine the fire to one section of the structure. In others, master streams may be directed into the church through front or rear windows. Where heavy streams are available, they may be operated from doorways or archways where men are afforded some protection from falling debris. They cannot hold these positions, though, if ventilation is not effected.

Church fires call for ample manpower, rapid mobilization of fire forces and advancement of hose lines. In the case of volunteer forces, particularly where long stretches and possibly relaying operations may be involved, prompt summoning of aid is imperative.

The records indicate also the wisdom of painstaking overhauling after church fires. Not a few such fires which were believed extinguished rekindled with consequent complete destruction of structures.

BRUSH FIRES

Brush fires are of three types: the surface fire which involves dry grass, young trees and leaves on the ground; the ground or peat bog fire which starts from a surface fire and burrows into soft spongy ground; and the crown fire which starts as a brush or surface fire and then travels through the tops of trees.

In operating on a surface fire, it should be remembered that fires do not gain much headway against the wind. Therefore it is a good policy to start operations on the lee side. Try heading the fire toward a road, a creek, clearing or other natural breaks. By that means, the crew will work toward the front, leaving stumps of trees and other fallen timber in the interior of the burnt section until the fire is under control. The crew can work much faster by going down on the side until they get to the front.

At times it may be necessary to go to the front. For example, at a large fire in a meadow or field it may be judicious to get ahead of the fire to extinguish sparks or embers that may be carried by the wind, or to set up in an open space, a crossroad or creek where a stand can be made with the aid of a backfire. In other words, start another fire on the lee side so that when the main fire reaches that spot it will die out for lack of fuel.

Backfiring

A backfire is a fire made purposely in front of a fire to burn back toward it, but care must be taken by the person starting a backfire to see that it burns against the wind. It should be done only as a last resort and involve only a small section at a time, or there may be two fires to extinguish. Keep the men away from the center. When the two fires meet, intense heat is generated and any man caught between them has small chance of escape.

Backfiring may be done by first clearing a path some distance ahead of the fire and then starting the fire on the fire side of the clearing, road or creek, having men with brooms ready to extinguish any fires that may start from heat or sparks on the lee side of the clearing. When the main fire gets that far, it will burn itself out.

Bog fire

A ground or bog fire is one involving earth composed of decayed vegetable matter. The bog may be many feet deep, and sufficiently dry to support combustion. A fire in a bog generally starts from burning brush and burns slowly underground. Such a fire may burn for weeks, always underground.

Water under good pressure is essential in operating on bog fires. Nozzles are equipped with piercing applicators. When ready for operation, an applicator is pushed into the ground. When a particular section has been flooded, pick up the nozzle, advance the line 5 or 10 feet and stick it down in the ground again. When the nozzle is opened, the immediate underground area is flooded, and a bog fire can be put out much quicker than if tons of water were thrown on top of the ground.

Crown fire

A crown fire generally starts as a surface fire in heavy brush, is carried along by a strong wind and heat waves, and reaches the tops of trees. From here the fire takes off in a manner similar to a grass fire.

A fire on the side of a slope or hill presents a special problem. Here will be found heavy brush, briers, leaves and young trees. The strong draft of heated air arising from the fire carries up an immense quantity of sparks in advance of the main fire. In addition to natural air currents, a fire creates its own draft when underway. It is usually advisable to get up on top of the hill at once. Generally on top there will be a roadway or path. Send the company to that road and have them ready to hit the fire. Do not permit men to get in between the fire and the top of the hill. Heat waves may be found anywhere from 100 to 150 feet in advance of the main fire and men may be caught in between.

Use 1½-inch hose and meet the fire as it comes up by throwing water over the top.

In fighting a fire of any size, it is wise to study the ground, direction of the wind, location of roads, creeks or clearings.

Fighting grass and brush fires

The methods of fighting grass and brush fires vary widely due to the variety of fire protection facilities available. For example, where a brush fire is burning outside the city limits beyond the reach of fire hydrants, the methods employed will be entirely different. In any event, only small quantities of water are required. The usual method of extinguishing brush fires is with brooms, knapsack or other tanks which hold 5 gallons of water. These tanks are usually fitted with hand pumps. They will throw a stream 25 or 30 feet.

Shovels are needed to smother fire with dirt. Water for the back-pack tanks may be obtained from a creek or a well, or may be carried on the apparatus to fires. One tank of water used sparingly, followed by a man with a broom, will extinguish considerable fire. The man with the back-pack pump goes along the edge of the fire and uses his water sparingly, while the man with the broom follows him and sweeps any remaining fire back into the burn.

PIERS

Any city with an extensive waterfront which is developed for transportation, with docks, piers and warehouses, has need for fireboats for protection from spread of a fire from pier to pier, or to shipping. Land apparatus can prevent the spread inland but cannot be counted upon for controlling the waterfront fire.

The officers and men stationed in the harbor district must possess, besides the fire fighting knowledge common to all in the department, a special intimacy with the shoreline and everything built upon it. They should know the architecture of ships of all kinds in order that they may know how and where to attack a blaze most effectively. Finally, they must know the peculiarities of cargoes which are found in pier sheds.

The hazards found on piers and wharves result largely from these cargoes, and may include such stores as sisal, jute, rags, paints, oils, cotton and lumber.

Another waterfront hazard is oil that forms a coating under piers and represents a ready means of spreading fires. Fuel oil, in the form of a viscous, tarry mass, spreads over the surface and is carried by the action of tide and wind and deposited where it forms a coating on piling and other pier and wharf structural members. This coating will extend from the low water to high water marks.

Underpier fires

As usual in all fires, the first effort at a pier fire is to confine it to the point of origin. This is difficult where there is a heavy deck above the fire which is shielded below by girders and beams that impede the fire streams.

To confine a fire of this type, if the pier is not equipped with sprinklers beneath, fireboats should be brought to each side of the pier or against the bulkhead, and rafts or small boats lowered. From these, lines can be operated. Bear in mind that the object is to cut off and prevent spread of fire. Sometimes it is possible to get a stream—solid or fog—on the fire under a pier by use of a short ladder. A man equipped with a life belt is let down the ladder, from which position he can operate a line at the water level with great effectiveness. The ladder is suspended down the side of the fireboat. In many instances, lines have been operated from the portholes on fireboats onto a substructure fire. Another technique is to use scuba divers with floating monitors.

At the same time, the pier deck above the fire should be opened up in the center between the points where the fireboat lines are operating and where the fireboat streams cannot reach. In the case of a concrete

At pier fires, lines from fireboat (1) can supply floating monitor (4) maneuvered by scuba-equipped fire fighters, and man on ladder (2). Hand lines (3) can be taken in from land end of pier to supply nozzles or cellar pipes. Monitor (5) on fireboat is shut down when man is on ladder. Hand lines can also be used from punts.

pier deck, if power cutters are not available, local utilities or other city departments should be called for the use of their pneumatic tools to open it quickly. The extent of the fire beneath the deck and the smoke and fire conditions determine the procedure to be followed. If conditions are bad enough to drive men away from the pier side, and boats have to direct streams from a distance, their effectiveness is much reduced.

As at other fires, officers should not delay in sending for additional help as indicated by the size-up. It may mean saving the entire pier. When vessels are exposed at the side of the pier, they should be removed promptly since the heat can set fire to their cargoes. Removal of ships will also provide greater convenience and facility in handling the fireboats in extinguishing the fire.

When attacked by fire, unprotected pier structures of steel, wood and corrugated iron collapse quickly, enveloping the contents. Because of the difficulty of access from the shore end, the extinguishment of pier fires is extremely difficult except by fireboats and sprinklers.

Officers on fireboats when responding to a pier fire and observing that it has control of the outer or water end of the pier, should bring their boats into the slip and get between the fire and the land end of the pier, using all available pipes to prevent the further spread of fire toward the land end. This is necessary because of the tremendous area, combustible contents and rapidity of spread of this type of fire.

SHIPS

Fires on vessels severely expose piers, and prompt stretching of lines to the various cargo doors and to the roof of the pier shed is necessary to prevent extension of the fire to the pier. The fireboats can take care of the water side and stretch lines to extinguish the fire aboard the vessel. Crews of land companies can be placed aboard the fireboats to cover adjacent piers with lines to prevent ignition from sparks or heat radiation.

The first duty of the fire department officer in charge of a fire on a ship is to get in touch with the captain or officer in charge, and ascertain from him the location and extent of the fire and character of the cargo carried. He should ask for the cargo map and diagram of the ship. The cargo map will show the kind of cargo, where stored, etc. The diagram will show the construction of the ship.

Most ships are divided into compartments, each having watertight bulkheads in the lower hold. Some ships have watertight bulkheads in the 'tweendecks with watertight doors. In passenger ships these doors can be closed from the deck or engine room. It is very important that the watertight doors be closed on each side of the hold on fire. If they are not, the water pumped into the hold will flow into adjoining compartments and do a great deal of unnecessary damage.

Some vessels have fire alarm systems or smoke detectors in the form of pipes running from the various parts of the ship and terminating in the charthouse. In the event of smoke arising from a pipe, the location of the fire can be determined.

Ships may be equipped with a dry sprinkler system, carbon dioxide fire system, steam fire fighting equipment, fire pumps, standpipes, hose, nozzles, hooks, axes and pails.

Ventilators are present in practically every ship and are used to ventilate the spaces below and to prevent dangerous gases from collecting. Smoke from the ventilators shows where the fire is; the diagram of the ship shows the location of the ventilators.

Fire in the hold

Among the most common types of fires encountered on the waterfront is the blaze which involves the cargo in a vessel's hold, where it must be fought through ventilators and hatches—a kind of cellar blaze aboard ship. Few fires are more difficult to handle. They occur from a variety of causes. Many serious blazes, preceded by vapor explosions, have occurred in port while repairs were being made to leaky bunker tanks aboard oil-burning ships.

The fighting of fires aboard ships at wharves or in harbors is largely determined by the cargo, whether the vessel is partly or wholly laden, and how great a start the fire may have gained before the arrival of fire equipment. It is assumed that the fire must be fought almost wholly from the hatchways or from holes cut in the deck. On arrival, locate the fire, find what the cargo consists of, and how it is stowed. If the ship's officers are unable to give this information, the fire officer must be guided by the volume of smoke arising from the ventilators and the heat on adjacent parts. By these signs a shrewd guess can be made, but it is only a guess and he may be mistaken. Remove the covers of one or more hatches as deemed necessary and turn the streams into the holds. In dealing with certain goods and chemicals that generate noxious fumes and gases, it would be impossible for men to enter holds without using self-contained breathing apparatus.

Men not on the lines should not crowd passageways or hatches where other men are working, but should keep in the open air as much as possible.

If the ship is loaded to the top of the hatches, it is sometimes necessary to flood the hold to the point of the fire. In many cases there is little or no chance to remove the cargo and get at the actual seat of the fire, and it can be subdued only by flooding.

When a general mixed cargo is on fire, it should be removed, if possible, to a safe place on deck or on shore. Charged lines should be led to the

A ship fire may originate in engine room, center, or cargo holds (5) and (6) from which it is separated by bulkheads (1). Fire can also be found in 'tweendecks (2) or cabin (7). Watertight doors (3) that separate sections of ship should be closed during fire operations. Smoke from ventilators (4) often indicates location of fire. Handlines can be stretched as indicated. Fire in bilge (8) is most difficult to get at.

place of landing so as to wet down cargo being removed if it shows sign of fire. Charged lines should also be led into the hold to the location of fire, if at all possible, to confine it.

Where fire is burning in a compartment, water fog should be applied, if practicable, to all surrounding bulkheads, to the overhead in the compartment below, and to the deck of the compartment above. The fire fighter is aware of the fact that a fire in a compartment means that he has a fire in a metal box that is sending out heat in all directions.

Cooling the bulkheads and decks of a compartment on fire has two purposes—to prevent the spread of the fire to combustibles in adjacent compartments and to prevent the heat from weakening and distorting the steel.

The quantity of water necessary to extinguish some marine fires may be sufficient to cause the ship to list, threatening or actually resulting in the ship capsizing or sinking.

Danger of fuel oil

The use of oil as fuel adds another danger, for oil fires in any location are usually quick and vigorous. They spread rapidly and cannot be controlled by solid streams. Oil floats on water because it is lighter than water. Any attempt to extinguish burning oil confined in a tank, hold or fire room by use of solid streams can have but one result—the water sinks to the bottom, the flaming oil rises as more water is pumped in, and the flaming liquid may overflow, spreading the flames. Fog streams, if they can be applied promptly, may bring the fire under control. Foam is effective if the surface of the burning oil can be reached.

Many fires occur in boatswain's stores, hemp rope, oakum, canvas, brooms, mops, etc. Paint lockers are also a fire hazard aboard ship. These stores are usually kept in separate compartments forward. Large volumes of smoke can issue from a few mops or a small amount of oakum stored in these compartments. At such fires, hand extinguishers or a small line should be put to work and breathing apparatus should be used when necessary, with men working in relays.

Fire in passenger quarters

Fires in passengers' quarters can give considerable trouble and take a long time to extinguish. Fire may be located two or three decks down that have innumerable passages which have to be traversed before the seat of the fire can be reached. Usually it is a case of working down to it with breathing apparatus.

There are many times when the fire can be reached from both ends of the ship. This is possible if both the fire and the point of ventilation are in the center, but if the ventilation is at either end, there is danger of one company driving the fire toward the other. In any case, ventilate, and the men can then get near the fire and do more effective work.

Before proceeding to flood a compartment, see that all watertight doors as well as port lights are closed.

OIL STORAGE AND OIL FIRES

Fire departments with oil refineries or storage yards in their cities face many serious problems in fire fighting. The possibility of a conflagration always exists with an oil fire. If an explosion occurs, the burning oil is apt to be scattered over other tanks or adjoining buildings and cause further fires. If a tank boils over, the burning fluid, if not restrained by dikes, is apt to involve surrounding tanks or stills.

Fires in oil refineries, storage stations and other places where petroleum products are handled require a strict application of the first principles of fire fighting, namely, isolating the fire and confining it to as small an area as possible. All agencies available for the controlling or extinguishing of oil fires must be brought into play.

Fires originate generally in tanks, stills and filling and storage buildings, and are caused by lightning, static electricity, flashing of vapors, leakage in equipment, carelessness of employees, etc. The most serious hazard develops when a large oil tank is involved with fire because the fire may spread to adjoining tanks or structures by radiated heat or burning oil flowing through a rupture in the tank.

Handling oil tank fires

Assume a tank is involved in fire. Its sides are intact, only the top having been ruptured by an interior explosion. Employees are using foam and are drawing oil from the tank and piping it to other tanks. Hose streams are brought into action by the fire department, which should use them only in cooling down the side plates on the tank below the fire line or in wetting down adjacent tanks to prevent ignition by radiated heat. Skillful direction of the stream is necessary so that none of the water enters the involved tank, as it may displace the burning liquid and cause it to flow out of the tank. Or the water may be converted into steam and bring about the same result by expansion.

Where a tank has a rupture in its side and burning oil is pouring out, an entirely different action by the fire department is required. A sufficient number of streams should be used to check and divert the flow of the burning oil to directions that will not endanger other tanks or structures.

Where large quantities of oil are burning and it is necessary to restrict its flow, sand bags, loose sand or earth should be used to form a dam.

Under no circumstances should water streams be directed on a still, as the hazard may be increased by rupturing the metal and releasing the burning product. Filling houses, where cans are filled and sealed, also present a serious hazard, and the fire department should endeavor to prevent the fire from extending out of the structure. Such fires are best controlled by placing hose streams around the involved structure and using them to wet down exposures and prevent any flow of burning liquid from the building.

Flammable liquid in an unopened container offers only a moderate hazard by itself. It is when a considerable number of drums are exposed to fire that they become especially dangerous. Then heat may cause the containers to burst, adding to the intensity of the fire. Partly emptied drums also offer an explosion hazard.

Where large quantities of flammable oil are stored in tight containers or drums, it is absolutely necessary, if they are exposed to fire, that a liberal supply of water be directed on them to keep them cool. Water fog is more effective than the same volume of water in a solid stream. Coating a tank with foam will help insulate it from outside heat.

Where oil is stored in large tanks, the value of earth or concrete dikes in a fire is beyond question. Some city ordinances require that levees shall be built around oil storage tanks and shall be capable of containing the contents of the tanks.

Tanks are constructed generally of iron or steel throughout, except in some instances where the tops or covers are of wood. Where the tops are of iron and steel, their construction is sometimes much weaker than that of the lower plates of the tanks. This is done to instantly vent through the top any unusual force generated inside the tank by explosion, etc., thereby preventing any side rupture which would allow burning oil to flow out of the tank.

Find out what's burning

In gasoline fires, extra precautions should be taken. The gases arising from a burning gasoline tank, if confined, are apt to cause an explosion, endangering men nearby. While gasoline is a highly flammable liquid, its explosive properties do not appear until its vapor becomes mixed with air. For this reason, a tank completely filled with gasoline is less dangerous from an explosive point of view than one recently emptied.

Always get in touch with the men in charge of the plant that is afire. Obtain from them all information possible as to the kind of oil that is burning and what is being done to extinguish the fire. Also, be sure that there are several lines of retreat open in case of a spill of oil.

Three methods may be followed in extinguishing an oil fire: first, reducing the temperature of the burning mass to a point below that necessary to sustain combustion; second, smothering or shutting off the supply of oxygen and third, shutting off the supply of fuel.

In the case of highly volatile oils, there is enough vapor given off at ordinary temperatures to support combustion; and at many oil fires the flames are so far from the oil itself that the fire may be regarded as a vapor or gas fire. The form in which such fires are usually encountered is a stream of vapor burning at the vent of a tank or other container.

Telltale color of flame

The explosion possibility of a vapor-air mixture burning at an outlet can be fairly well estimated from the color of the flame. The flame from a rich mixture is yellow, smoky and luminous, whereas the flame from an explosive mixture is blue, nonluminous, and contains little smoke. Extinguishment of vent fires is best accomplished by either cutting off the fuel supply or shutting off the air supply from the vapor. Dry chemical extinguishers can usually effect extinguishment.

When rich vapor is burning at a tank vent, the supply of fuel can be stopped, or materially reduced, by cooling the tank with water streams and extinguishing outside fires that may be heating the tank. A reduction of the vapor pressure in the tank will decrease the fuel flow through the vent. Any method of shutting off the supply of vapor will be effective in extinguishing a fire of this character. For example, if the opening can be closed by means of a hatch cover, flow is halted. If the fire is not great, carbon dioxide or dry chemical may accomplish extinguishment.

Oil fires are really vapor fires above the surface that are fed by evaporation from the oil's surface. The heat of the fire greatly accelerates evaporation. To extinguish an oil fire by cooling, the surface temperature must be reduced below the flash point of the oil.

Fog lines

The use of water fog for extinguishing oil fires depends to a large extent on the nature of the oil on fire. As already mentioned, to extinguish an oil fire by cooling, the surface temperature must be reduced below the flash point. In the case of nonviscous oils, this means that the entire body of the oil might have to be cooled, for if there were hotter oil beneath the cooled surface, it would rise and furnish vapor to continue the fire. In viscous oils, water spray on the oil may not only cool the surface below its flash point, but will cover the surface of the oil with an emulsion that will extinguish the fire by smothering. The droplet size of the fog is a major factor in its effectiveness.

Oils which froth, such as asphalt, crude, fuel and lubricating oils, can be extinguished with fog by producing an emulsion on the surface. This insulates the oil and stops the formation of vapor essential to the burning of an oil, thus starving the fire.

Refined distillates with low flash points, and having little tendency to froth, can sometimes be extinguished with water, but only by applying a fine spray.

There is a rule of thumb that water fog is incapable of extinguishing flammable liquids with a flash point below 100°F. To extinguish these liquids, foam, dry chemical or carbon dioxide must be used.

Fire extinguishment by foam

In fighting oil storage fires, foams have proved most successful. In installed systems, two-solution chemical foam was first used, then came chemical powder foam and finally mechanical foam, which today predominates.

Where foam is to be applied to the surface of the burning oil, it must be delivered so that it covers the surface gently.

Unless the foam-mixing chambers of a tank are undamaged, a portable foam tower should be erected and foam supplied by this means. If sufficient foam can be supplied for two towers, the second one should be erected as far as possible from the first one. As soon as flames have subsided so that men can work from the rim of the tank, a foam hose stream should be operated from the top of a ladder to knock out spot fires.

When neither fixed nor portable foam towers are available, fires in light oils can be extinguished with foam hose streams by directing the streams across the tank. The inside of the shell on the opposite side will serve as a baffle to deflect the stream so that the foam will slide over the oil.

Another method of extinguishing fuel oil is the subsurface injection of foam. This is accomplished by the cooling of the burning oil layer by replacement with cold fuel "lifted" with the foam from the base of the tank. A foam blanket must be built on the liquid surface to effect complete extinguishment.

Basically, the subsurface injection method supplies a cooling agent in the form of water to a burning hydrocarbon at the point where this cooling agent can accomplish the most efficient action. In cases of hydrocarbons which involve downward propagation of heat and the formation of a heat wave, the highest temperature encountered is in the order of 500°F. Temperatures above the burning surface, where vapor mixes with the requisite amounts of oxygen for complete combustion, will exceed 2000°F under ordinary conditions.

A basic characteristic of the extinguishment mechanism of fires in oils which produce heat waves concerns the fact that when water impinges on this hot oil, a frothing or oil-foam emulsion takes place, due to the expansion of the water into steam. If this frothing occurs close to the top edge of the tank, it comes over the sides, forming a slop-over. This may be extremely dangerous to exposed fire fighting personnel, but is actually beneficial to extinguishing the fire, since it removes a great deal of the heated oil. Obviously, the higher the viscosity of the hot oil, the more stable will be such a mixture of oil and steam bubbles. If the oil is not viscous at the water boiling point temperature, this foam or froth production is very temporary and no appreciable expansion of heated oil layer occurs.

If the contents of burning tanks can be stirred or agitated, the distribution of heat can be made more uniform, and the extent of the ignition-temperature oil layer will be decreased, making extinguishment less difficult. In the subsurface foam injection process, a considerable amount of agitation is achieved through the displacement of oil by foam.

Extinguishment by agitation

A method of fighting oil tank fires was developed by the Mobil Oil Company, utilizing air or other gas injection to induce upward flow from the colder subsurface body of the oil layer and thereby cool the surface of the burning liquid. This cooling is sufficient to extinguish fires of high flash point oils and to reduce the severity of fires of low flash point oils so that they can be readily extinguished by conventional means.

The method is applicable to contained fires of any petroleum liquid having a Reid vapor pressure of 13 pounds or less. Complete extinguishment can be obtained of contained fires in kerosine, diesel oil, fuel oils, transformer oils, lubricating oils, and distillates, and under special circumstances, asphalt and high flash point crude oils. The intensity of fires of gasoline, naphtha and low flash point crude oils can be reduced to the point where they can be readily extinguished by other means.

In fighting crude oil tank fires with this method, care must be taken to avoid a slop-over of the oil. Slop-over can be caused by the contact of water with the heat wave which forms in burning crude oil. Water may be stirred up from the bottom of the tank by too rapid air agitation. A heat wave forms in burning crude oil because of the wide boiling range of its constituents. This heat wave travels into the body of most crude oils at 12 to 18 inches per hour.

Controlled burning of explosive hydrocarbons

Refineries are producing flammable volatile substances such as butadiene that water as now applied cannot extinguished. It has been found practical to dispose of the flaming escaping substances by controlled burning. Even if such substances were extinguished, the escaping vapors could form explosive mixtures capable of doing greater damage than the fire.

For controlled burning, fog and foam have proven both effective and practical. Fog streams are used to maintain a covering film of water over surfaces of tanks, pipes, structures and equipment exposed to the heat of volatile liquid fires. This fine-droplet spray prevents serious distortion and buckling while the escaped liquids and vapors are permitted to burn. Where such volatile materials are stored under pressure in tanks, these sprays are able to limit heat transfer to the product inside the tank to a degree at which the safety vents can take care of the increased vaporization without danger of explosion.

Foam sprayed over the surface of a tank provides an insulating coating which has proven effective in protecting the exposed tank.

LP AND NATURAL GAS FIRES

Propane and butane fuels are petroleum products somewhat lighter in weight and much more readily gasified than gasoline. Such a fuel is called liquefied petroleum gas, or LP gas. At ordinary atmospheric temperatures and pressures the fuel exists as a gas, but when subjected to pressure it liquefies readily. This convenient characteristic makes possible its use as an easily burnable gas and its storage and transportation in concentrated form as a liquid under pressure. Liquefied petroleum gas is sold under many trade names.

Propane is somewhat lighter, gasifies at a lower temperature, and has less heat value (Btu) per cubic foot than butane.

Ordinary commercial LP gas may be essentially propane or butane, or it may be a mixture of these gases. Usually, minor amounts of other similar products are also present.

The only facilities for transporting LP gas used to be Interstate Commerce Commission-approved cylinders, often termed "bottled gas" cylinders. Such cylinders, ranging in size from 20 to 300 pounds capacity of gas, are still in use for some types of service, particularly home use. The development of high-pressure tank cars and trucks made possible the location of bulk distributing and bottling plants near areas of large consumption and reduced the long haul of comparatively heavy cylinders. The usual practice today is to make bulk shipments of LP gas in 8000 to 12,000-gallon railroad cars or 3000 to 8500-gallon truck and trailer units from points of production to points of distribution. These distributing bulk plants may have one or several storage tanks ranging in size from approximately 15,000 to 30,000 gallons. Here ICC cylinders may be filled for delivery to customers, or the LP gas may be distributed in tank trucks of 550 to 5000 gallons capacity to fill customers' on-the-premises storage tanks of 150 to 1000 gallons capacity. Pipelines are also used to transport LP gas from producing areas to large bulk storage farms.

There are three principal methods that can be used to transfer the liquid from the delivery container to the storage tank: (1) gravity, (2) pump, and (3) vapor compressor.

The gravity method may be used if the truck is at a higher level than the tank and a pipeline connects the vapor spaces of each. However, the gravity method is usually slow and rather undesirable. Most trucks delivering to general consumers' storage tanks are equipped to pump the liquid from the the truck. Sometimes pumps are installed at storage tanks. An equalizing vapor line connection from truck to tank should be used.

The vapor-compressor method is often used. Instead of pumping the liquid into the receiving storage tank, vapor from the storage tank is pumped into the tank car, raising its pressure. This forces the liquid from the tank car through the connecting liquid line into the storage tank. The equipment is arranged so that the compressor may also pump vapor in the opposite direction. After the liquid is transferred to the storage tank, considerable remaining vapor in the tank car can then be pumped back to the storage tank. LP gas as an engine fuel is also used in the trucking field.

Fire hazards

In fighting large-scale propane fires where liquid propane is escaping under pressure, the use of the straight stream position on the dual-stream dry chemical nozzle is the most effective as it carries the dry chemical into the heart of the fire while the operator is some distance back.

There are two general methods of extinguishing propane fires. The first is to employ the "blast" or "snap-out" technique. Using this technique, it is essential that fire fighters wear heavy protective clothing against the radiant heat of the propane fire.

The men walk toward the fire until they are quite close to the point at which the propane is escaping, and then all simultaneously open their nozzles with the dry chemical streams directed at the point of the leak. The advantage of this method is that a heavy concentration of dry chemical is shot into the point of combustion of the propane. Using this method, it is possible to extinguish large propane fires quickly.

The second method is the use of the "wave" technique. Using this method, the fire fighters open their dry chemical streams at a comfortable distance from the fire. The dry chemical is first directed to the top of the propane jet and then slowly dropped to the base of the fire and back to the top of the fire again. This slow vertical sweeping motion provides a heat shield for the operators as they advance closer to the fire. It is essential if more than one stream is used that all streams move up and down in unison.

This provides a solid dry chemical wall, which carries into the fire, greatly diminishing the intensity of the flames. If the dry chemical cloud set up by the stream is large enough to cover the entire flame area and is of sufficient concentration, the flames will ordinarily be extinguished upon contact with one of the dry chemical "waves." This method will ordinarily take more dry chemical extinguishing equipment and will usually take longer to extinguish the flames, but it has the advantage that fire fighters in ordinary clothing may approach fires that give out intense radiant heat by using the heat-shielding effect of the dry chemical cloud.

Natural gas fires

The control of high-pressure natural gas fires has always imposed a severe task on the fire fighting forces. The escaping gas from a high-pressure gas main, for instance, if ignited may constitute a severe threat to adjacent property. The methods employed for controlling such fires, outside of closing valves on supply lines, have varied. Prior to the general use of dry chemical on high-pressure natural gas fires, extensive tests were conducted at Longview, Tex.

The tests, conducted on a 24-inch gas transmission line, with a volume of gas available at a pressure of about 850 psi, were the largest and most comprehensive conducted up to that time with dry chemical.

In all, some 191 individual tests were made. The maximum rate of flow for one test was 2610 cubic feet per second (equivalent to 225,504,000 cubic feet per day).

Throughout the entire process, at producing wells, in the transmission lines, and at the utilities or industries which store or use the gas at high pressures, all of the elements necessary for fire or explosion exist in close proximity. Under such conditions, fires occur despite the careful engineering and safety precautions of producers, transmission line operators and users.

There have been a number of fires involving high-pressure natural gas but no consolidation of information regarding the methods of fighting them or the ability of any agent to extinguish them. The objectives of the tests referred to above, in addition to determining the suitability of dry chemical fire extinguishing equipment on natural gas fires, were: (1)

to select the proper size and type equipment for compressor stations and (2) to determine the limiting volumes and conditions under which burning gas can be extinguished by various size dry chemical units.

At the Longview tests, approximately 500 feet of 6-inch pipe were laid from the large main to an open test site. The end of this pipe was anchored to a large block of concrete for safety. A meter run was provided in the 6-inch pipe where the flow of gas could be measured accurately. Fittings were provided so that the gas could be discharged vertically or horizontally and so that the 6-inch line could be reduced to ½, 1, 1½, 2 or 4-inch pipe. A tap was provided near the end of the 6-inch pipe so that the pressure at this point could be recorded.

Types of tests

The tests were set up to duplicate as closely as possible conditions that might be encountered in actual practice. These include the following:

1. Vertical jet with 6-foot stack on outlet
2. Low-level vertical jet
3. Horizontal jet
4. Horizontal jet impinging against earthen bank
5. Horizontal jet impinging against steel plate
6. Downward impingement
7. Pit fire with gas discharging from slit in bottom of pipe

The tests indicated that dry chemical fire equipment is suitable for use on natural gas fires involving pressures up to 850 psi.

Dry chemical is used in pipe installations as well as in portable and set installations. In the pipe installation the mixture of dry chemical and gas is blown through pipes to the locations of hazardous operations much the same as foam installations or sprinkler installations.

It required but six 150-pound wheeled units to put out a well fire that had raged unchecked for five days in a Venezuelan oil field. The extinguishing time was approximately 50 seconds. For controlling high-pressure natural gas fires, such as occasionally occur when high-pressure lines open up, dry chemical has proven itself highly effective.

COTTON MILLS

Fires are more frequent in cotton mills than in any other industry, due to the highly combustible nature of cotton fiber and the ease with which it is ignited, even by small ignition sources such as mechanical or electrical sparks or machine friction. Surface fires in cotton spread rapidly. This is followed by persistent burning or smoldering which produces disagreeable smoke, making fire fighting difficult. Surface fires are usually not difficult to control, although the speed of flame travel requires extinguishers having rapid, broad area coverage rather than highly concentrated extinguishing power.

Extinguishers most suitable for cotton fires are also suitable for fires in rayon or blends of cotton with other fibers. Viscose rayon has the same chemical composition as cotton and when in similar physical form, has an almost identical fire hazard. Acetate rayon is slower burning than viscose.

Dry chemical gas-actuated extinguishers backed up with water spray provide the most effective combination of first-aid fire equipment for quick control and extinguishment of cotton process fires.

With dry chemical extinguishers, a most valuable feature is the speed with which an operator can cover an extensive area with a single extinguisher, enabling quick control of flash fires in cotton fibers. This minimizes the number of sprinklers likely to open and decreases the need for large amounts of water by fire fighters, an important factor in reducing damage to stock and equipment.

The extinguishing effect is due, first and most important, to the fire-retardant powder coating on the fibers. A light deposit prevents rapid flame spread and enables quick control of the surface fire.

Dry chemical is best applied by area flooding. The operator should approach within about 8 to 10 feet of the fire. First, discharge the powder about 3 to 4 feet above the flame, laying down a protective blanket over the flame and the surrounding area. Next apply the powder discharge directly to the burning material. This can then be done without danger of spreading the fire by burning particles.

After the surface fire has been extinguished by dry chemical, slow residual smoldering may persist where lint or cotton stock has depth. For this reason, it is necessary to have water in some form, preferably spray, for mopping-up purposes.

Water spray is an effective extinguishing medium for cotton lint fires and has been used in opener and picker rooms for many years. Solid hose streams are not suitable on loose burning cotton; the force of the stream may scatter the burning fibers, starting new fires.

Low-velocity water spray applicators of approved type on ¾-inch or 1-inch-diameter hose are especially suited for locations where the path of fire may extend to a higher level such as the harness and pattern cards of jacquard looms. The fine water spray minimizes water damage to stock and equipment. A 6-foot applicator is sufficient.

One and one-half-inch hose is desirable where there are large amounts of loose cotton, as in larger opener rooms, sizable stock bins and waste houses, and at opener-picker rooms processing lower-grade stock. The 1½-inch fabric rubber-lined hose can be laid faster than similar size unlined hose and is free from weepage.

LOFT BUILDINGS

The term "loft building" is an old one and one generally applied to buildings that were constructed before the advent of the modern "fireproof" building. The term today is applied to a building usually constructed of brick and joist and one in which fire can travel through unprotected openings: elevators, stairs, air shafts and a variety of pipe recesses. They run from four to six stories high and cover an area of about 50 × 100 feet. Some, however, are much larger.

Originally most of them were occupied by a single tenant engaged in the manufacture of related products. But as time wore on the buildings were broken up into multiple occupancies with a separate tenant on each floor and frequently more than one tenant to a floor. So, what originally had been a building that presented a simple problem to pre-fire planning such as a shoe manufacturer is now a building that has become almost a nightmare of mixed processes and products. Almost anything from flammable volatiles, to rags, to death-dealing plastics can be found in them. And some of them can have anywhere from five to ten tenants.

Unfortunately, these lofts are found in the older sections of cities and towns where they are surrounded by similar type buildings, not all necessarily lofts, but all of non-fire-resistive construction. When one of them goes up in flames they present a severe problem to a fire department. The loft building alone can produce an intense, fast-burning fire—building and contents—that can not only destroy the building but any exposed buildings.

Heavy streams needed

In severe loft building fires it is usually necessary to cover the building with heavy streams from the outside while hand lines are getting into position. As with any fire, the outside streams must be shut down or diverted when the interior lines are in operation. This is to prevent the men working with such lines from being driven out of the building.

Hand lines within a loft building should throw at least 250 gpm and preferably 300 gpm, not only because of the contents but to provide as much reach as possible. If a building were 150 feet deep, no one hand line could reach every extremity on a floor. This failure can be counteracted by stretching lines up another stairway or a fire escape on the rear of a building from which points all parts of a floor can be covered. The use of streams in this situation should be coordinated so that opposing lines do not drive heat and smoke at each other. Every attempt should be made, however, to advance the lines, which is the best method to overcome lack of reach.

Ventilation

Ladder company members should begin at the roof, opening skylights, bulkheads and scuttles. Before beginning, great care must be taken to make sure that the roof is safe. When this job is finished, the men work their way down through the building opening windows on each floor. A fire escape, usually present, can facilitate this job.

At severe cellar fires, quick ventilation is imperative. It may be necessary to break windows on the first floor to ventilate this floor at least to the point that cellar pipes can be used. This also permits any vertical openings to be covered with lines. A cellar fire, incidentally, is indicated when smoke is issuing from windows of several floors, or smoke appears on several floors with no flame showing.

In opening the windows and shutters on a building involved by fire, first open the ones farthest away from the point of safety, and work back toward the more secure position. Open the roof so that the wind will blow smoke away from the men at work. When opening windows in an areaway, first open the one farthest away from a ladder.

Avoid opening up a fire floor beneath a company before sufficient warning is given to them to back down. Avoid cutting holes in passageways or breaking deadlights in front of doorways. When this is unavoidable, see that the openings are guarded to protect the men from injury.

When partitions are found inside a floor, break them down and enter the floor under cover of a stream and open windows as quickly as possible.

The first-due truck company, at the earliest possible moment, ventilates the fire floor to permit the engine company to advance lines and extinguish the fire.

Open up, ventilate and examine the floors above the fire as soon as possible after arrival at the fire. Use aerials or platforms if necessary.

General precautions

At fires in buildings which have been closed for some time, there is a danger of a back draft when opening up. This can be expected when the building is heavily charged with heat, smoke and gases of combustion.

When the building cannot be ventilated quickly by roof openings, it is advisable to break the window glass with a master stream, being careful to cause as little water damage as possible by throwing the stream up over the roof as soon as the glass is broken.

When buildings are stocked with rags, paper or vegetable fiber, and the fire has involved more than one floor, a large quantity of water is, of necessity, thrown on the fire. When this occurs, it is advisable to back companies out and operate with exterior streams until a survey can be made of the building to determine its stability. Vegetable fiber can absorb several times its weight in water. It should be remembered that the discharge from one ordinary 2½-inch fire stream represents a considerable quantity of water. If the discharge is 250 gpm, then a ton of water per minute is being discharged on the fire. Five such streams would mean 5 tons per minute, or 300 tons per hour. The added weight may cause floors to collapse.

At a fire in an old loft building, where more than two floors are involved, it is good practice to keep the companies out of the building and work from outside vantage points.

WAREHOUSES

Probably the most difficult fire to control is that encountered in a warehouse, and particularly, a furniture warehouse. In the first place, either the windows have iron shutters or there are no windows, making entrance by the fire department very difficult. Secondly, each floor is divided into relatively small compartments by combustible partitions and these partitions possess openings through which fire may pass.

However, the partitions frequently do not reach the ceiling, so that it is possible to get water into them if the fire has not advanced so far that the passageways are untenable.

If passageways are impassable, the fire can be reached only by streams operating through windows, and the opening of shutters may be a time-consuming operation. The fire can then be reached only from fire escapes or ladders.

The extension of the fire throughout the floor is almost a certainty if it has secured a good hold, and extension to floors above is possible.

Because of the necessity of close work if fire control is to be accomplished, prompt ventilation is vital. Opening up over elevator shafts and stairwell must be done at once, as well as opening windows to provide cross ventilation.

In the initial attack on a fire in a furniture warehouse, it will be necessary to work from passageways. If the fire cannot be struck with a direct stream, the nozzle should be directed so that the stream strikes the ceiling over the compartment, or compartments, involved, letting water come down into them. Use a stream, or streams, into passageways to check the spread of fire across them.

Fog streams can aid materially in clearing out smoke as well as extinguishing fire.

Where fire has gained headway, it may be necessary to breach walls to get streams to the base of it. This should be done, if practical.

If fire has gotten control of a floor, or threatens to get control, use ladder pipes, deck guns and water tower streams from elevating platforms to prevent extension to floors above and bring the blaze under control.

Should fire start in the cellar, ventilate promptly by opening up skylights, the enclosure over the elevator shaft and the bulkhead door and scuttles. This will aid in keeping the fire from mushrooming while lines are placed in operation, and the entry into the cellar will be made easier.

CHAPTER EIGHTEEN

Sprinklers and standpipes

Standpipe and hose systems and automatic sprinkler systems are frequently referred to as the "first line of defense" against the spread of fire. Sprinklers provide an early means of notification plus an efficient method of extinguishing or holding a fire in check. In the comparatively few cases of initial fire spread, they provide protection for exposures and thus prevent further fire extension.

It is essential for all fire fighting personnel to be familiar with the various types of installations, their components, how they operate, and what to do in various fire or emergency situations.

While the two extinguishing systems are totally different in operation, there are certain similarities incorporated in their installation. As a rule, each receives its primary source of water from a large roof or tower tank. Since this supply is limited, both systems have their water supply and pressure augmented by lines stretched from fire department pumpers to siamese connections located outside the building or area protected.

Care must be exercised when hooking up to a siamese to make sure that it is the proper connection for the intended usage, since the piping for both systems is completely independent. In appearance, the siamese connections are alike, but their purpose should be clearly indicated on the connection itself or nearby. If only part of the building or area is so protected, this fact should also be indicated.

Next to an automatic sprinkler system, a standpipe system offers the best means of applying water on fires within buildings, particularly those

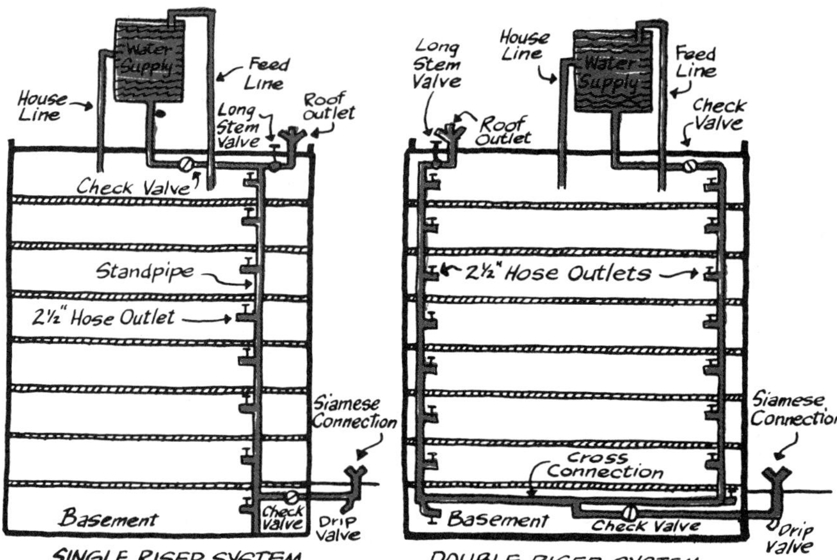

Single and double riser standpipe systems. Water supply can come from tank at roof or outside fire department siamese connection.

at considerable height or of extensive area. Each protective medium provides its own specialized service of which the other is incapable and in the main, they may be said to complement each other.

Classifications and uses

Standpipe systems are most commonly installed in tall buildings and those of large floor areas—also in hotels, schools, theaters, factories, high-hazard occupancies, places of public assembly where large numbers of people congregate, and similar occupancies. Standpipe systems are classified as:

1. Wet systems with the supply valve open and water pressure maintained at all times.
2. Systems so arranged through use of approved devices as to admit water to the system automatically by opening a hose valve.
3. Systems so arranged as to admit water to the system through manual operation of appproved remote control devices located at each hose station.
4. Dry standpipes for which water is supplied through fire department pumper connections (siameses).

Standpipe systems may be efficiently used by building occupants (employees, watchmen, etc.) to control or extinguish small fires pending the arrrival of the fire department. Utilizing the standpipe system eliminates the necessity of an exhausting and time-consuming stretch by fire personnel, who carry several rolled or folded lengths of hose to the fire floor or the floor below, and attach their hose to the standpipe outlet valve.

Standpipe systems can be efficiently used to prevent an exposure fire from entering a building. In some cases, standpipe lines from the upper floors of a noninvolved building may be the only means of directly hitting a fire in an adjacent fire building. Fog nozzles on standpipe lines may be used to advantage from points above the fire to cool the atmosphere where men are working under particularly adverse and hot conditions in the street below. These fog streams are directed downward to provide relief.

Under unusual fire conditions (hydrants too far distant or public water supply failing) the standpipe water supply in one building may be used to fight a fire in another building by stretching lines from the ground floor outlet to the intake side of pumpers. These then discharge directly on the fire or through the outside siamese for extinguishment of fire in the adjacent building.

Standpipe risers

The size of standpipe risers is governed by the size and number of fire streams that may be needed simultaneously and by the distance of the floor outlets from the source of water supply. Both of these factors will be reflected in friction loss in the piping. The number of standpipe risers and arrangement or distribution of equipment for proper protection are governed by local conditions such as occupancy, character and construction of the building, exterior exposures and accessibility.

The number of risers (single or multiple system) as well as their location is further dictated by the fact that all portions of each story must be within reach of a stream from a nozzle attached to not over 100 feet of hose. Standpipes for small hose should be located so that all portions can be reached by a stream from not over 75 feet of hose.

The outlets (hose stations) on risers are located near or in stairway enclosures or near fire escapes for ready availability to fire fighters.

Control valves needed

Valves, known also as indicating, stop, outside stem and yoke (OS&Y) or gate valves, are installed throughout the system to meet emergency and other conditions such as repairs, breaks in the standpipe lines, and for testing purposes. Globe valves are used at the hose outlets off the

Control valve, also known as post indicator valve (PIV): Condition of valve (open or closed) shows on telltale opening. Some valves are locked in position with either a padlock or iron strap that must be removed.

riser on each floor and also at the roof manifold. In the case of a multiple-riser system, sufficient controls should be provided so that one riser may be cut off without interrupting the supply to other risers from the same source of supply. Sections of risers may also be similarly isolated.

Check valves are installed at various locations to prevent the flow of water past a check point in a standpipe or sprinkler system. The check valve near the siamese connection is normally kept on its seat (closed position) by the pressure of the water in the riser above it. This valve is unseated and permits water to be fed into the system when pressure on the pumper side exceeds that on the riser side. A drip valve is installed between the check valve and the siamese connection to prevent an accumulation of water which may seep past the check valve in the line between these two points.

The check valve in the line beneath the roof tank is normally in the open position (off its seat) to allow the flow of water. It is closed when flowing pressure on the pumper side exceeds the pressure on the tank side of the valve. This prevents the water supply from below from entering and overflowing the roof tank. Therefore, the roof tank cannot be refilled by this means.

In case the tank supply runs low and the automatic fill pump is inoperative, water may be fed into the tank through its inspection hatch by supplying water through the street siamese and taking a line off the roof manifold.

These manifolds are installed to connect hose lines for roof operation. No house line is ordinarily found connected to this manifold. Since this part of the standpipe system is subject to freezing, it is normally maintained dry and water is supplied to it from the roof tank by operation of a long-stem valve reaching down to the top-floor piping. Because of the limited elevation of the tank, pressures at the manifold are often insufficient for effective streams and should be built up from another source.

Individual control of the pressure in each line off the manifold is exercised by manual operation of the shutoff handle. Lines from the roof manifold may be used to advantage in fighting roof fires, for stream application on an adjacent building, or to cover exposures. The threads on the outlets are protected by a cap on a chain.

Outlets on each floor

The number of siamese connections found on a building depends on the size and number of risers, as well as the street frontage of the building. More than one such connection may be installed on the same street and additional connections may be found at the sides or rear of the building, if it has street frontage there. One type has a sill cock for connecting a garden hose to flush sidewalks. The wye type of siamese connection resembles a siamese on a pumper or deluge set. The free-standing type is generally found in a wall recess.

Before connecting a line to it, the inlets of the siamese should be checked for the presence of gaskets. It is recommended that the left inlet be supplied first and that the reverse procedure be followed when disconnecting the line.

Hose outlets are taken off the standpipe riser at each floor and are provided with sufficient linen hose to reach distant points on the floor for stream application. For fire department operations, the house line is removed and the stronger fire department hose substituted. The house line may be either 2½ or 1½-inch, depending on the occupancy. In the latter case, a reducer (2½-inch × 1½-inch) will have to be removed before connecting fire department 2½-inch hose.

To guard against wetting and resultant deterioration in the linen hose used on house lines, a drip connection is often provided between the control valve and the first hose coupling. If the drip valve is of the pet cock type, it should be closed before opening the control valve. Nozzles provided are usually of the open type.

Hose outlets for sprinkler system are taken off each standpipe riser on each floor. Sufficient hose must be available to cover all points on floor with an adequate stream.

To guard against excessive pressures, a pressure reducer is often installed between the valve outlet and the hose coupling. One common method of obtaining the pressure reduction is by use of an orifice disk.

Where hydrostatic pressure at any outlet for small hose exceeds 100 psi, an approved device is installed at the outlet to reduce the pressure so that the nozzle pressure will be approximately 80 psi. Where hydrostatic pressure on any outlet for 2½-inch hose exceeds 55 psi, and 2½-inch hose is provided for use by building occupants, a pressure-reducing device should be installed.

The pressure-reducing device should be removed before connecting a fire department hose line and the pressure should be controlled by a member who remains at the control valve.

Standpipe water sypply

The quantity of the water supply for a standpipe system is dependent on the size and number of streams likely to be required and the length of time such streams may have to be operated. This standpipe supply is calculated over and above that required for the simultaneous operation of automatic sprinklers. In some installations, it will be found that both types of systems are supplied from the same source, e.g., a gravity tank with a total capacity equal to the needs of both a standpipe and a sprinkler system.

In buildings in the course of construction and in other occasional in-

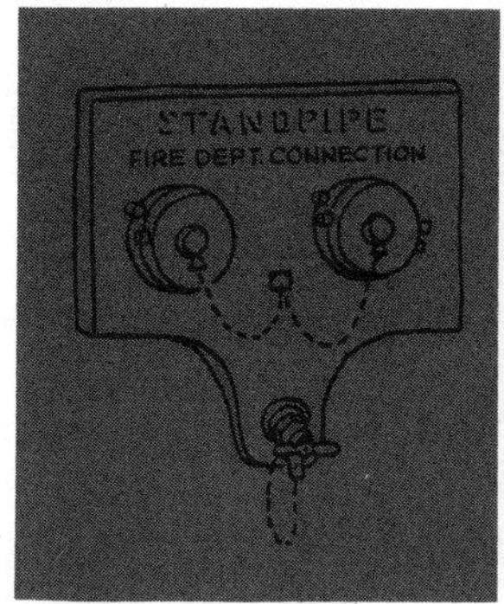

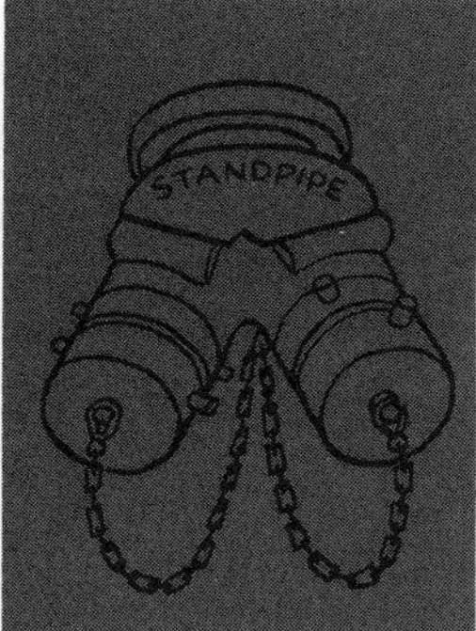

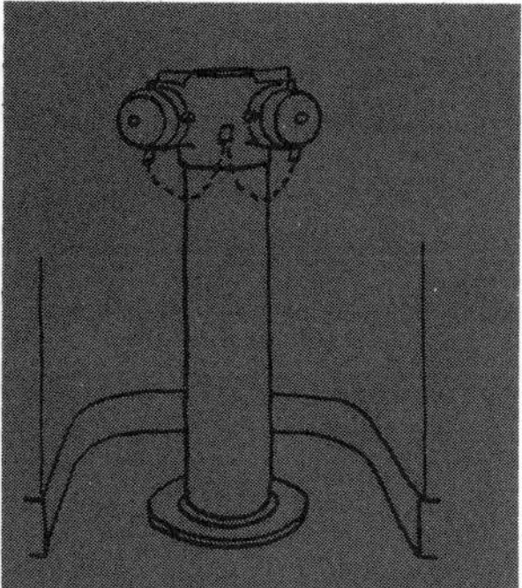

Siamese connections. Flush type (left) has sill cock for garden hose. Wye type (center) resembles standard siamese used in stretching hose. Free standing type (right) is generally placed in recess.

stances where standpipes are installed exclusively for fire department use, the standpipes are normally dry and the only means of supply is through a fire department connection (siamese).

The sources of water supply for a standpipe system may be: (a) gravity tanks, (b) pressure tanks, (c) automatic fire pumps, (d) city or town water works systems, where domestic pressure is adequate, (e) manually controlled fire pumps with pressure tanks, (f) manually controlled fire pumps operated by remote control devices at each hose station, (g) siamese connections which are supplied by lines from a fire department pumper.

In buildings of unusual height, standpipes are often supplied by means of a series of fire pumps and tanks, usually about 20 stories apart.

Two independent sources of water supply are desirable. The primary source should be capable of supplying the streams first operated until the secondary source can be brought into action. The secondary supply should enable the streams to be kept in operation for a long time. To promote efficiency, the layout, controls and sources of water supply for each installation in the company district should be studied, mapped and carried on the apparatus.

Gravity tanks, with a minimum recommended capacity of 5000 gallons for standpipe supply, are located on the roof or as a separate water tower at least 20 to 25 feet above the highest house outlet or top line of sprinklers to provide pressure by gravity.

If the tank is not located in a heated enclosure, special precautions are necessary to prevent freezing in the tank or its piping, unless the tank water is also used for domestic purposes and there is a continuous flow.

Freezing is prevented by the installation of a tank heater, which should be started before cold weather sets in. The temperature of the water should never be permitted to fall below 40°F.

The frostproof casing around the riser leading from the gravity tank prevents heat loss. And care should be taken to see that the casing remains intact.

Access ladders to the inspection hatch are provided and may be used by fire department personnel on their inspection visits. Proper safety precautions should be observed on these inspections and the integrity of the ladder established before it is mounted by a member.

At times it may be advisable to drain the tank by means of the emergency drain valve. This condition could result if the tank supports were weakened by fire, or if the heating unit failed.

The tank water is maintained at the proper level by the action of a ball float, which is connected to the controls of a fill pump, generally located in the basement. If the fill pump is not automatic, an audible alarm is sounded when the water level in the tank drops below normal. Although it is connected to a street main, the capacity of this fill pump (usually about 65 gpm) is not enough to replace the drain of a fire hose line, and so other sources of supply must be brought into action when the tank supply is depleted.

In some installations, standpipe or sprinkler supply may come from a tank filled with air and water under pressure in a ratio of 1:2. The minimum recommended capacity of these tanks for standpipe supply is 4500 gallons, although for light-hazard occupancies only, the tank may have a minimum capacity of 3000 gallons. Tank capacity is considered as the total contents, both air and water. These tanks are normally located on the top floor or in a heated enclosure on the roof.

Water level is maintained by the action of an automatic fill pump; air is maintained at the proper pressure (at least 75 psi) by air compressor equipment with suitable automatic controls. Audible alarms are sounded when either the water or air varies from normal levels or pressures.

A sight water gage and an air pressure gage are installed so that the operative condition of the tank may be determined during a fire or maintenance inspection.

Standpipe risers may be supplied by a fire pump, which is commonly installed in a pump room at or below ground level. This pump should be capable of delivering a satisfactory water supply (250 gpm minimum) and pressures at the highest hose outlet. The same fire pump or pumps which supply the standpipe system may be used for sprinkler supply, provided their capacity is adequate for both systems and relief valves are installed to prevent pressure in excess of the safe operating pressure for the sprinkler system.

The fire pump may be fed by any of the following arrangements:

1. By piping connected to two public water mains, each fed two ways, and with control valves provided on inlet and outlet sides of the pumps.

2. From one main, provided a suction tank (or tanks) is installed with sufficient capacity to furnish each pump with at least one-half hour of water supply at the rated capacity of the pump. A bypass is also provided so so that the pump is fed directly from the public water main in case of failure of the suction tank.

3. By a connection to either a public water main or a suction tank capable of supplying the pump at its rated capacity for 15 minutes. In conjunction with this arrangement, the fire pump supply may also be from one or more siamese connections reserved exclusively for fire department use and with this purpose clearly stated.

Standpipe procedures at fires

It is considered good practice for all engine companies that respond to buildings equipped with standpipes to carry on the apparatus at least two lengths of 2½-inch hose, folded or rolled, and separate from other hose or appliances.

Beyond the immediate need to accurately locate the fire, no hard and fast rule can be established as to when the standpipe system should or should not be used. This decision must be based on existing fire and other conditions. If the fire is located above the fourth floor, connect a pumper to the street siamese and stretch from the riser at the upper floors.

Carry at least two lengths of hose (more if sufficient personnel is at hand), folded or rolled, and a shutoff nozzle up the stairway *to the floor below the fire.* Elevators may be used for this purpose if they are not endangered by the fire.

If the building is of fireproof construction, it may be more efficient to operate from outlets in the enclosed stairways or fire towers on the fire floors. Forcible entry tools are also required.

On arrival at the selected outlet, detach the house line, as well as any pressure reducer or the reducing connection if the house line is 1½-inch hose. The lengths of fire department hose are then coupled and attached to the hose outlet. The nozzle is put on and the hose is stretched up the stairway to the fire floor.

Surplus hose should be laid neatly down the stairway toward the floor below the outlet, or toward the floor above the fire if working from a fire tower. The hose should be free of kinks so that air may readily escape and a good stream be promptly assured at the nozzle when the door of the fire floor is opened. A fire fighter should remain at the control valve to regulate pressure on the hose line.

In high buildings where fire pumps are directly connected to the standpipe system, the officer in charge of the fire should immediately send orders to the building engineer to start the pumps and maintain sufficient pump pressures to provide effective nozzle streams. Necessary changes in pumper or fire pump pressures can be relayed by messenger, walkie-talkie radio or standpipe telephone system, if one is installed.

If a second company is ordered to stretch from the standpipe, the officer in charge of this unit should consider the point from which his unit is to operate so that enough hose can be brought up.

If the officer in command orders a second company to operate from a fire escape, the company officer should order two extra lengths of 2½-inch hose to be carried into the building in addition to the usual pair of roll-ups.

The reason for this order may be noted from the following: The first-due company has connected to the outlet on the floor below the fire. The second-due company will, therefore, probably have to connect on the second floor below the fire. It will probably require two lengths of hose to reach from this outlet to the rear or side of the building on that floor, and two additional lengths will be needed to make the stretch up the fire stairs and into the fire floor.

In taking-up operations, the hose outlet control valve should be closed solidly, the drip pet cock opened, and the building line reconnected. To prevent unnecessary water damage, the line should be emptied by discharging the nozzle out of a window or down a stairway at a point lower than the outlet.

In hotels, office buildings, and other light occupancies, 1½-inch hose is often found on standpipes and may under certain fire conditions be replaced with the same size hose by fire departments. However, in standpipe operations where riser water supply comes from a gravity tank or a weak water main, it is inadvisable to use 1½-inch lines on floors immediately below the roof. Here, the pressure at the riser outlet will not be sufficient to overcome friction losses in the small hose.

Supplying a riser through hose outlet valve inside the building

Occasionally the outside siamese may be inoperable in a system that is otherwise serviceable. In such instances, and also where the check valve below the siamese connection is inoperative, the following procedure should be followed:

Stretch a line from the pumper to the gated outlet on the first floor. The house line, with reducing connection and pressure reducer, must be removed and the pumper line connected, using a double female coupling. If the supply line is 3-inch, a reducer (3 × 2½-inch) must be placed on the male before attaching it to the double female coupling. When the water is started in the supply line, the outlet valve is opened fully to allow water to flow into the riser. If necessary, additional lines line can be similarly stretched to hose outlets on other floors.

Where the hose outlet extends at a right angle from the riser, the weight of the hose and fittings should be supported by a short length of rope. Tie a clove hitch and binder around the riser above the outlet valve. With the other end of the rope, tie a clove hitch and binder around the butt of the hose and double female connection. Push the clove hitch upward on the riser until the rope is taut.

Engine pressures for standpipe supply

The use of pencil and paper, and relatively long, drawn-out hydraulic formulas, has little place at an actual fire operation. From a practical standpoint, rule-of-thumb methods, giving approximate figures, will prove satisfactory.

Excessive pressure on the pumper may burst standpipe lines or hose lines, possibly losing the fire and endangering or injuring men in the building. Too little pressure may give unsatisfactory streams and have the same results. The average requirements call for a range of 150-200 psi on the pumper. If the engine pressure is excessive, surplus pressure on a fire line can be compensated for by partially closing the standpipe outlet valve.

The following information will serve as a guide in determining supply pumper pressures to provide effective streams:

It requires 0.434 psi to push up water 1 foot vertically, or 43.4 pounds per 100 feet. Assuming that the average height of a story is 12 feet, it will require 12 × 0.434, or about 5 pounds per story to overcome back pressure.

A standard figure of 25 pounds is taken to cover the friction losses in the riser, siamese connection and hose outlet valve.

A nozzle pressure of about 30 to 35 pounds is usually adequate for reach and maneuverability of inside lines.

The proper size nozzle to be used depends on the policy of the department or the judgment of the officer in charge, but usually a 1, 1⅛, or 1¼-inch tip is used. Approximate friction loss allowances equally applicable to a ground level stretch, may be used for the hose line from the standpipe outlet to the nozzle. With 35 pounds on a 1⅛-inch nozzle, about 220 gpm is discharged. For a flow of 220 gpm, there is a friction loss of about 12 psi per 100 feet of 2½-inch hose. The same nozzle pressure on the 1 and 1¼-inch nozzles gives a friction loss per 100 feet of about 8 and 18 pounds respectively.

The friction loss from the engine to the siamese connection will depend on the number of lengths and the size of the hose. In the first stretch (35 pounds on a 1⅛-inch nozzle), the loss will be 5 psi (4.6) per 100 feet, if a single supply line of 3-inch hose is used. From these explanations and figures, the required engine pressure in a typical case can readily be determined.

Assume a fire occurs in a building 10 floors above street level, and the company is to operate from the standpipe:

10 floors at 5 psi back pressure per floor	50
35 psi at the 1⅛-inch nozzle plus nearly 15 pounds friction loss in 100 feet of 2½-inch hose from outlet	50
Friction loss for standpipe, siamese and outlet valve	25
200 feet, or 4 lengths, from engine to siamese (single line of 3-inch hose used)	10
Total (required engine pressure)	135 pounds

From the above, an officer or pump operator should be able to estimate the pump pressure necessary to give the proper nozzle pressure and volume on the fire floor. If an additional similar line is stretched from the standpipe riser to the fire floor, the original nozzle pressure and engine pressure will drop as the second nozzle is opened. Engine pressure must, therefore, be increased slightly to allow for the increased friction loss in the supply line, or lines, to the siamese. Friction losses in each hose line off the riser outlet, the required nozzle pressures and the back pressure would remain the same. The standard allowance of 25 pounds would still apply to cover the friction losses in the standpipe riser as well as the losses which exist at the siamese connection and the hose outlet valve.

Where the volume of fire requires an additional line or lines from a standpipe system, it is good policy to connect another pumper and feed another siamese in the system or an outlet valve on the ground floor.

Additional lines

On arriving at the fire building, the pumper operator should not wait for orders before stretching into the standpipe siamese, regardless of apparent fire conditions. One 3-inch line—and if fire conditions warrant it, a second one—should be stretched immediately to the siamese, but water should not be started until the order to do so is received. If only

2½-inch is available, two lines should be initially laid to the siamese connection.

Many authorities consider it good practice to stretch two lines of hose to the fire department connection even if one line can supply the required volume. If one line bursts, the other can continue the supply. Where men are in a dangerous position in the building, the failure of a single supply line can place their lives in jeopardy.

Where a pumper is using its full power to supply a standpipe and a number of streams are in operation, a second pumper should be connected to the system at another siamese, or connected to the same siamese by placing two portable siamese connections on the two branches of the standpipe siamese. This will permit four lines to be connected to the same street siamese.

In making a stretch from a pumper to a standpipe connection, the hose should be laid along the curb on the fire side of the street, if the pumper is on the same side. Otherwise, it should be stretched on the pumper side of the street to a point opposite the siamese connection and then carried across the street. This will reduce the crossing of hose lines by fire apparatus. When placing lines to a standpipe system, care should be taken not to obstruct entrances or interfere with the placement of ladders.

Occasions may arise when it is necessary to play a heavy stream from a standpipe in one building to another building involved in fire. When it is necessary to throw water in large volume a considerable distance, siamese lines by taking the supply from the standpipe outlets on two different floors or from two outlets on the same floor. But when the volume and pressure secured by a "two-to-one" connection is insufficient, additional connections may be used.

If a building with standpipes is exposed to fire, the services of members of ladder companies should be utilized to enter the building, stretch lines from standpipes and extinguish any incipient fire. By carefully wetting down material within the flame or heat radiation zone, they can prevent the fire from extending. These units can further help by closing all windows on the exposure side and removing portable stock near them.

Care in stretching lines

At fires in theaters and other places of amusement which are equipped with standpipe systems, special precautions should be taken when stretching lines. Hose should be stretched from the standpipe on the side of the theater in which the fire occurs. For example, if a fire occurs in the smoking room on the west side of a theater, the proper stretch from the standpipe is from the outlet on that side—not the east side. This avoids laying a line of hose across the rear of the auditorium and obstructing front entrances and exits.

Inspecting the system

All portions of a standpipe system should be periodically examined by building maintenance men and fire department inspectors. A check should be made to see that gravity and pressure tanks are filled to the proper level and that at least 75 psi is maintained constantly in the pressure tanks. If the source of water supply is automatic, the control valves should be opened at all times.

Valves at the hose stations should be examined frequently for tightness. Leakage may be detected by inspecting the drip valves. Care should be taken to see that they are not clogged. If the system is normally dry, make sure that all hose valves are operable and closed.

Fire hose should be in good condition and properly positioned on the racks. Periodically, new gaskets should be installed in the couplings, at hose valves, and at the nozzles. More frequently, nozzles should be removed and examined for foreign objects which might adversely affect a hose stream.

Unlined linen hose should not be tested because it is difficult to dry thoroughly. It should, however, be carefully examined for cuts, loose couplings and deterioration, which may readily result from a leaky hose valve or from long standing in a damp atmosphere.

The outside siamese connection should be checked to see that its threads are compatible with those of the fire department, its usage is properly indicated, the couplings are not out of round, and the swing check valves and washers are present.

SPRINKLERS AND SPRINKLER SYSTEMS

Basically, an automatic sprinkler system consists of a series of pipes at or near the ceiling of each story of a building, filled with water or compressed air, and equipped with automatic devices to release water for fire fighting. Fitted at intervals in the pipework, there are sprinkler heads that embody a mechanism whereby a rise in temperature to a predetermined heat causes the head to open and discharge water in the form of spray. The heads are staggered on the piping so that, if more than one head opens, the area sprayed by each overlaps that of the adjacent one.

Sprinkler systems are required by law in various occupancies, or they may be installed voluntarily by the owner or occupant to protect a building, its contents, its occupants, or to obtain a reduction in insurance premiums.

This form of protection may be found in the following types of occupancies: schools, institutions, theaters, factories, hospitals, hotels, flammables stored or used, oil cloth or linoleum manufacturing, garages, pyroxylin plastics stored or used, large undivided floor areas, rooming houses, and many others. Except for chemicals which react violently with water, or where water might cause a boilover in an oil tank, there are few fires in which water cannot be used from a sprinkler head.

The installation of sprinklers has a pronounced effect in reducing fire losses. A study of the most recent records shows that sprinklers either extinguished or held in check 96 percent of the fires in which they were involved. The 4 percent failure was due to a variety of causes, such as explosions that ruptured the piping, closed supply valves, freeze-ups, and failure of the water supply.

Water supplies for sprinkler systems

The methods used to supply water to sprinkler systems are the same as those for standpipe systems. Sprinklers may be supplied from one or a combination of sources, such as public mains, gravity tanks, pressure tanks, fire pumps, reservoirs, rivers, lakes, wells, etc.

Theoretically, a single water supply would appear to be all that is necessary for satisfactory sprinkler protection, provided the volume and pressure are sufficient. However, a single supply may be temporarily out of service; it may be disabled at the time of the fire or before the fire is extinguished; or the pressure or capacity may fall below normal during an emergency. Adequate secondary or additional water supplies may therefore be advisable or necessary, depending on the strength and reliability of the primary supply, the value and importance of the property, the height, area and construction of the building, its occupancy and the exposures, or legal requirements.

But despite the added insurance of reliability when two independent water supplies are provided, it is recognized that a single supply of adequate volume and pressure can give satisfactory protection.

City water connections from large mains, fed two ways, or connections from two mains on a gridiron system with adequate pressure may provide an excellent and completely satisfactory supply for sprinklers.

When a sprinkler system is supplied from a public water main, the entire system may be closed down by operating a control valve between the building and the water main. This shutoff valve is frequently located in a box which is recessed in the sidewalk, with its location designated by a sign on a building or post nearby reading “Shutoff for Sprinkler

Two lines into siamese provide a margin of safety in the event one should burst.

System Located 6 Feet From This Sign," or similar instructions. A special key may be required to operate this valve.

The control valve for the building may also be attached to an upright post, known as a post indicator valve (PIV). The building or section of the building controlled by the valve is generally indicated on the post. The condition of this valve (open or closed) is shown through a telltale opening in the post. On some posts, a padlock must first be opened or forced to release the operating wrench. On others, an iron strap must first be released by cutting a riveted leather section.

The water main supply for sprinklers may also be controlled by valves of the OS&Y type which are found just inside the building wall on the main riser, or outside in protected pits. Fire fighters can tell at a glance if the valve is open or shut because the stem is all the way out when the valve is open and all the way in when it is closed.

Additional valves of this type may be used to control the supply for individual floors, and separate valves may be installed to shut off certain sections of a floor. In many cases, parts of a system subject to freezing are isolated in cold weather by closing the OS&Y valve and draining the pipes.

Siamese connections for fire department use

Although normally a sprinkler system is connected to an automatic source of water supply, engine companies responding to a sprinklered occupancy should stretch one of their first lines to the siamese connection of the building.

It is the policy of most departments to supply the standpipe system first, if one is present, and then stretch one or more lines to the sprinkler siamese. Care should be taken to see that the proper siamese is selected for the needs of the operation, as those for standpipe systems, sprinkler systems, transformer vaults and other installations are alike in appearance. The exact purpose of each should be indicated nearby or on the siamese itself. Some building codes require that siamese supplying different systems be painted a different color, such as red for standpipes and green for sprinklers.

On wet-pipe systems having a single riser, the siamese connection to the system is made on the system side of the controlling gate valve. On dry-pipe systems having a single riser, the connection to the system is made between the gate valve and the dry-pipe valve. This makes it possible to pump water into the system even if the gate valve is closed.

If there are two or more sprinkler risers connected to a public main, each system should have its own fire department connection attached to the supply side of the gate valve, so that with any one riser shut off, the supply from the pumper will feed the other risers.

Types of sprinkler systems and equipment

In addition to the wide variety of sprinkler heads as manufactured for different kinds of occupancies (light, ordinary, extra hazardous), sprinkler systems are classed as follows:

1. **Automatic wet-pipe systems:** The piping is always full of water under pressure, so that if for any reason the fusible link in the sprinkler head is relased, water will instantly flow from the open head. This type is installed in heated buildings.

2. **Automatic dry-pipe systems:** This is installed where a wet-pipe system cannot be properly heated and there is danger of freezing. The pipes are filled with air, the release of which when a sprinker head opens permits the water pressure to open a valve known as a "dry-pipe valve." Water then flows into the piping and out the opened head. In some cases, a separate dry system is installed in an unheated area of a building in which the rest of the system is wet.

3. **Nonautomatic systems:** In this type, all pipes are normally dry and water is supplied, when necessary, by pumping into the siamese connection. At times some of these systems are supplied by manual operation of a control valve. Nonautomatic systems include: (a) Perforated pipe systems consisting of single lines of pipe drilled at intervals

for water discharge, and intended to protect basements or other areas which are difficult to reach in fire fighting operations; (b) Open fixed-spray nozzles or distributor systems for transformer vaults and similarly hazardous areas; (c) Exterior exposure sprinklers (or window sprinklers), using open-type sprinkler heads to form an external water curtain on the walls of a building; and (d) foam supply systems for the protection of special hazardous occupancies into which a foam mixture is pumped, or into which water is supplied to augment that required by foam-mixing apparatus inside the yard or building.

Dry-pipe sprinkler valves

Manual control of the water to a sprinkler system is provided by post indicator and OS&Y valves. Automatic systems also contain two special types of dry and wet-pipe valves, each with specific purposes. Dry-pipe systems are quite similar to wet-pipe systems with the exception that, in the former, the lines are maintained full of air until a head opens.

When this occurs, the dry-pipe valve is "tripped" (unseated), charging the system with water which pushes the escaping air ahead of it. This action also sounds a local alarm, and in some cases transmits the alarm to a supervisory service which notifies the fire department. In certain occupancies where life hazard is very high (schools, hospitals, etc.), the alarm is directly transmitted to the fire department.

When fire conditions indicate the system should be shut down, the supply may be closed off at the individual OS&Y valve for the floor or area, or at the main valve. After the main valve is closed, the drain valve should be opened so that the remaining water in the system beyond the dry-pipe valve will not have to be discharged and possibly cause additional damage in the fire area.

Before the main supply valve is again opened, the drain valve must be closed, the dry-pipe valve reset, air pressure again built up in the system by the compressor, and the alarm system drained and once more placed in its normal position ready to operate.

The dry-pipe valve is designed so that in the normal position the air pressure on the top side of the valve will hold a pivoting counterweighted clapper down over the water supply inlet. A latch holds the clapper in the open position, once the valve trips.

The design is based on the area differential between the air seat and the water seat of the clapper, enabling the air pressure to hold back water pressure which may be six times as great. Some ratios are greater to allow lower air pressures to be used. The latch release is used when resetting the valve.

Excessive air pressure in the system is undesirable, as it delays action

Demonstrator sprinkler valve assembly at New York Training Academy. O.S.&Y. (outside stem and yoke) valve (center) is open when stem is all the way out; closed, all the way in.

at the dry-pipe valve. A pressure of 15 to 20 psi over the normal tripping pressure of the valve has been found to be the maximum necessary in most cases.

According to fire statistics, more sprinkler heads operate on the average with dry-pipe than with wet-pipe systems, which tends to indicate that fire control is not as prompt with the former due to the loss of time between the opening of the sprinkler head and the issuance of water—an interval made necessary to allow the escape of the compressed air in the sprinkler pipes. This problem can be overcome by the installation of quick-opening devices on the valve of the system.

Such quick-opening devices are of two types: accelerators and exhausters. In the first type, when a sprinkler opens and air pressure drops 1 or 2 psi, a diaphragm is unbalanced and by its movement opens an auxiliary valve to admit sprinkler system air pressure to an intermediate chamber beneath the air clapper of the dry-pipe valve. This balances the closing force and allows the water valve to be opened by the water pressure. In the exhauster type, movement of the diaphragm causes an auxiliary valve to open, which discharges system air pressure to the atmosphere, permitting water under pressure to unseat the dry-pipe valve and quickly fill the piping.

Special types of sprinkler systems

There are several special types of automatic sprinkler systems among which may be found any of the following, or a combination of two or more, in an occupancy:

1. **Deluge systems:** These may be described as a system of open heads, or a combination of open and closed sprinklers, controlled by a quick-opening mechanical or hydraulic valve known as the deluge valve. This valve may be operated by automatic heat-responsive devices or by manual control upon receipt of a fire alarm. This type of system is installed when it is desirable to immediately wet down an entire area in which a fire may occur. It is done by admitting water to the open heads, rather than by using a system in which the automatic sprinklers open independently as the fire gains headway.

Such systems are commonly actuated by the rate of rise of heat within a given space and are used in rooms of very dangerous occupancy, such as explosives and manufacturing, film manufacturing, film cutting and packing, lacquer mixing and coating operations. They are also installed in airplane hangars and assembly plants where ceilings are unusually high and ordinary sprinklers would not open due to high drafts.

2. **Preaction systems:** These systems also operate on a rate-of-rise type detection system and differ from deluge systems in one main respect: All heads have fusible links and the alarm is given before the heat has risen enough to melt the links and permit the flow of water.

Preaction systems are designed to protect properties where there is danger of serious water damage which could result from premature or accidental operation of a sprinkler or a break in the piping system. Here the action of the heat-responsive device, or thermostat, releases the preaction valve, water fills the piping system, and an alarm operates in advance of the fusing of the sprinkler heads.

3. **Antifreeze sprinkler systems:** These are installed in areas subject to low temperatures, such as cold storage rooms, truck-loading docks, etc. Sprinkler piping is normally filled with an antifreeze solution such as calcium chloride. At times, these systems are small extensions from wet-pipe systems, arranged with check valves and a trap so that the system water does not mix with the antifreeze solution. When a head opens, the solution is lost and must therefore be replaced when the system is again placed in operation.

4. **Combined dry-pipe and preaction systems:** These were originally developed for the protection of long, unheated structures such as

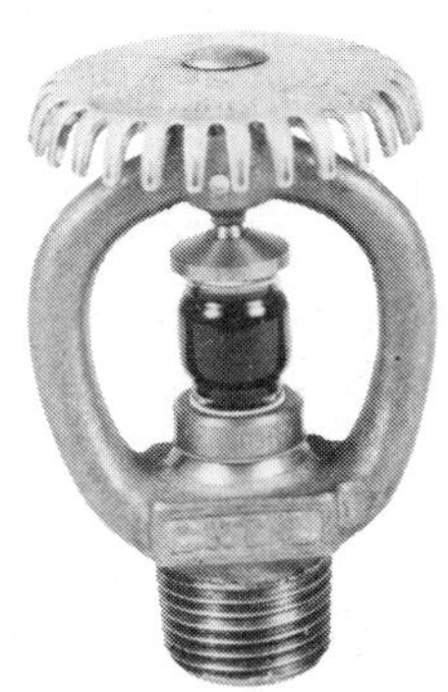

Typical sprinkler heads: Fusible link (left), solid type (center) and glass bulb (right).

the superstructures of piers. Their main advantage is that two dry-pipe valves can be controlled in parallel and supply a system that is larger than would be permitted for a single valve. These valves are located in a normally heated area or in an area where heating equipment can easily be installed. They incorporate the rate-of-rise tripping features of a preaction system, including the sounding of an alarm before sprinklers operate. The two dry-pipe valves are connected so that the tripping of one will cause the other to trip immediately, thereby flooding the entire system from a city water main.

5. Junior sprinkler systems: This inexpensive system is used in basements of dwellings and similar locations where not more than three or four sprinklers are likely to operate. The system is directly connected to the service water supply pipe where it enters the building. The shutoff valve is commonly found at this connection.

A smaller orifice sprinkler is used, usually 3/8-inch, discharging about one-half as much water as the standard sprinkler, but designed to cover about the same amount of floor area. This difference must be borne in mind when replacing heads after a fire.

Sprinkler heads vary

Sprinkler heads are made of metal, are screwed into the piping at standard intervals, and generally have a 1/2-inch opening. The disk or seat is held in place (preventing the escape of water) by a strut or two levers inserted between the seat and the top of the yoke. Most frequently, the strut is of metal, consisting of two or more pieces held together with solder. Many types, however, use as a strut a quartz bulb which expands and breaks under heat, or a solid chemical held in a cylinder which disintegrates by heat action.

When constructed, the struts or levers are set in place under compression and are released when the fusible device operates from the heat of the fire. The disk is released from the opening and water flows out under pressure. The force of the water against the deflector creates a heavy spray which is directed outward and downward.

The latest type of sprinkler head is called the "cycling sprinkler," which cycles water on and off depending on the temperature. This action is made possible by a pilot valve, permanently installed and held closed by a snap disk. When the disk reaches a temperature of 165°F, the valve opens, permitting water to flow. When the disk temperature cools to 100°F, the valve closes to shut off the water.

The sprinkler head is designed to withstand at least 500 psi without injury or leakage. If properly installed, there is little danger of the sprinkler breaking apart unless it is damaged.

Care must be taken to make certain that no part of an automatic sprinkler head is covered when the piping is painted or whitewashed. Such a coating may interfere with the free movement of parts and delay its opening, or render it inoperative. During the painting of piping or nearby areas, the heads should be protected by covering them with paper bags that are removed immediately on completion of the job.

Sprinkler heads of specific types are used for special purposes and in certain locations. When they fuse, care should be taken that their replacements are exact duplicates. In installing wax-coated sprinklers (used in corrosive atmospheres), precautions should be observed to avoid damaging the coating. Other types of corrosion-resistant coatings should not be applied to the heads except by, or on the recommendation of, the sprinkler manufacturer.

Spray pattern changed

In 1952-53, a radical change was made in the pattern of the water discharge from a sprinkler head which improved its effectiveness considerably. This new design was for a time called the "spray sprinkler," but is now designated as the "standard sprinkler." Both new and old-type heads are similar in appearance, but seemingly minor differences in deflector designs brought about major differences in discharge characteristics. This change might be referred to as the adoption of the reverse-spray sprinkler. This move has resulted in improved efficiency in the control and extinguishment of fire.

Formerly research and developments in this area had been concerned with attaining a reasonably uniform distribution of water by a single head and also with wetting the ceiling on the assumption that this was essential for efficient fire extinguishment.

Extensive investigation, however, showed that more effective extinguishment and a larger area of coverage could be secured by directing all the water downward and horizontally. It was further shown that this pattern was very effective in controlling fires on the ceiling above the sprinklers, owing to the improved cooling effect of the spray and a better high-level water distribution. There was decreased exposure to the ceiling because of a more effective direct discharge of water on the burning materials.

Because of the new design of the deflector, the solid stream of water issuing from a sprinkler is broken up to form an umbrella-shaped spray, with a pattern roughly that of a half sphere. At a distance of 4 feet below the deflector, the spray covers a circular area having a diameter of approximately 16 feet when the sprinkler is discharging 15 gpm.

These new heads are made for upright or pendant installations. They permit sprinklers to be placed farther apart and allow flow rates to be appreciably decreased with the same protection as the old-type sprinkler. More effective utilization of water flow is reflected in a reduction of water damage, a factor which often outweighs the actual fire damage.

Temperature ratings of heads

Automatic sprinkler heads have various temperature ratings which approximate the temperatures at which they will operate. The temperature rating of all solder-type automatic sprinklers is stamped on the soldered link. For other heat-sensitive units, the temperature rating is stamped on one of the releasing parts. The temperature ratings of various heads are also indicated by different colors.

Where high temperature prevails, such as over boilers, ovens and in drying rooms, a higher degree head must be used than in ordinary occupancy. If high-degree heads are used where not required, i.e., in an ordinary atmosphere, the value of the sprinkler protection is materially reduced.

While sprinkler systems are an excellent means of controlling fires, they can add to the loss if they are not shut down at the proper time. However, no control valve of the system should be closed except on orders of the fire officer in charge, who must decide when the fire is under control.

In many instances, considerable time elapses before the proper control valve can be located. This problem can be anticipated when a company visits a premises on an inspection. A small sketch of the sprinkler system, including the location of the control valves should be made and kept

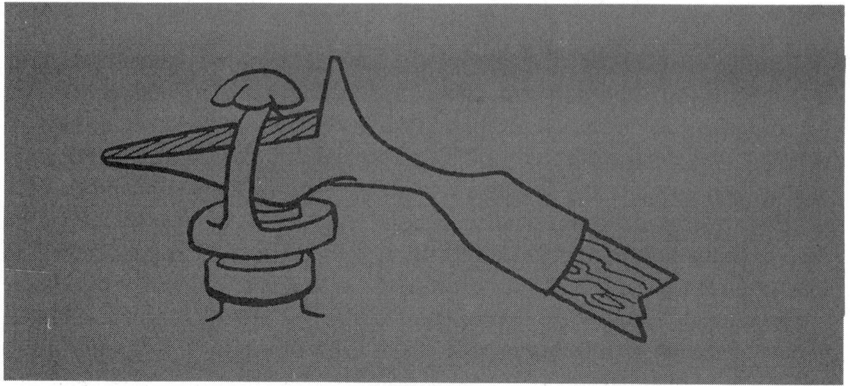

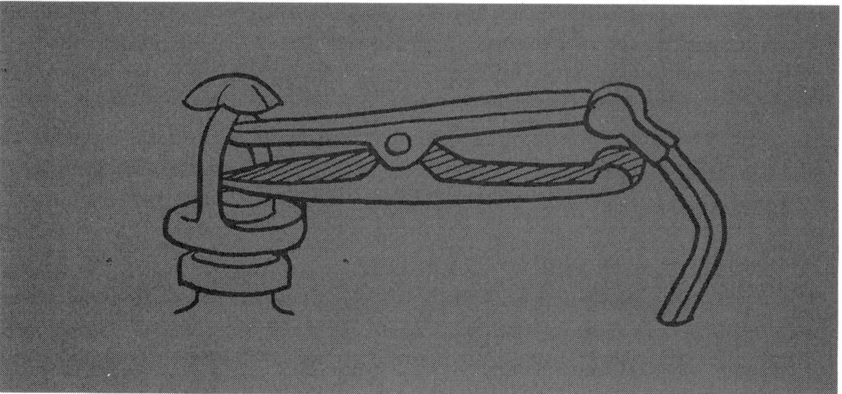

Pole shutoffs, tongs and even wooden wedges are used to quickly shut off sprinklers until valves supplying them are located.

in a file on the apparatus. This information is invaluable at a fire because many times it will be found that the control valve is actually located at some remote point in the building or in another wing or adjoining building.

Generally speaking, the location of the control valve for a particular area of a building may be found by tracing the pipes on which the heads are mounted. It will be found that the diameter of the pipe increases as it approaches the source of supply.

Shutting off heads

If the fused heads are few in number, they may be closed by using a pole shutoff, sprinkler tongs, or a wooden wedge inserted in the ruptured head. The pole shutoff has the advantage of being operated from a distance, enabling fire fighters to stay out of the main discharge of water from the sprinkler head while stopping the flow. Poles on this type of sprinkler stopper vary from 6 to 20 feet in length. The tong-type sprinkler stopper is first inserted in the ruptured head in the closed position and held between the strut and the seat of the sprinkler head with one hand. The tongs are then opened by releasing the control lever with the other hand.

Sprinkler discharges and head pressures

The exact amount of water being discharged from a system depends on the number of heads open, the type of head, and the pressure maintained at the orifice. Seven to 8 psi of working or flowing pressure is generally considered a minimum for the proper action of sprinklers having a nominal ½-inch opening. At this pressure, a sprinkler will discharge about 15 gpm and cover an area of approximately 100 square feet, or more if the newer heads are used.

Discharges, of course, increase as pressures at the orifices increase. For most systems, approximate discharges may be calculated by the following method:

Discharge in gpm equals ½ psi at the head plus 15.

Where the fire involves a large area and sprinkler needs are high, more than one pumper should be connected to the system to augment the supply. At a discharge of 20 gpm per head, a 750-gpm pumper can supply only about 35 heads and a 1000-gpm pumper about 50. Generally, a 750-gpm pumper will need more than two lines if located more than 200 feet from the connection and a 1000-gpm pumper will need more than three lines of hose. Fire departments will therefore have to use siamese connections on the building's sprinkler connection to provide additional lines.

Engine pressure for sprinkler operations

Exact computations of engine pressures are impractical on the fireground due to required information on such factors as the number and types of heads opened, and the number, length and size of the supply lines to the building siamese. Where the pumper is stationed near the fire building, most authorities recommend that a pump pressure of 100 psi or more be maintained. On the older systems, consideration must be given to the possibiity of the system bursting should the pumper build up excessive pressures. This recommendation is made in spite of the fact that piping in all systems is originally tested at pressures far in excess of those normally required at fire operations.

Naturally, higher pressures may be safely maintained on new installations. Such pressures may be necessary if the flow is considerable, the supply lines to the siamese long, or the fire located many stories above the street.

If only a few heads open, and the fire is at or near ground level, the losses will be minimal. In such cases, engine pressures approximate nozzle pressures.

Miscellaneous information

If the volume and pressure of the water on the fire is adequate, it makes little difference from a practical standpoint whether the source of standpipe or sprinkler supply is a fire department pumper or another source, such as a gravity or pressure tank, fire pump, or public water main. If the riser is already filled with water from a gravity or pressure tank on the roof, it will be necessary for engine pressure to be sufficient to overcome the head pressure of this column for the pumper to be the actual source of supply. In other words, it will have to unseat the check valve in the basement and close the check valve under the gravity or pressure tank.

This point of information is more than of academic interest, as the pumper may be damaged if it pumps continuously against a closed basement check valve. If no water is discharged from the pumper, the action of the pump will tend to heat up the water considerably, even to the point of creating steam. This hot water may adversely affect the packing or other parts of the pump and is unsuitable for auxiliary cooling purposes. Whether it is directly or indirectly used, it can raise the temperature of the engine coolant. This may then prove inadequate to absorb heat from the engine cylinders and may allow the oil to heat up, thin out or vaporize, and reach a point at which the cylinders may crack or the motor seize up.

These possibilities can be minimized by "cracking" a bleeder valve on a discharge gate, thereby insuring a continuous discharge to the ground and preventing an undesirable increase in the water temperature in the pump.

Whether or not the check valve beyond the siamese connection is actually open in a standpipe or sprinkler system may readily be determined as follows:

Working with caution, partially or completely close the discharge gate(s) of the pumper supplying the siamese. If the check valve is open, i.e., the pumper is actually supplying the water, the engine pressure will rise until the relief valve opens or the pressure governor operates and slows down the engine.

In addition, if the water output is considerable, the pumper intake gage will show an increase in pressure during the closing of the discharge gate(s).

If the pump is not putting water into the system, i.e., the check valve is closed, there will be no change in pump pressure or motor speed upon closing the gate(s).

This same condition and solution would apply if pressure from a building fire pump or city main held the check valve on its seat or if two pumpers were supplying the same system—one pumping into a siamese against the face of a closed check valve, the other keeping the valve on its seat by pressure at its rear, supplied through another siamese or an inside hose outlet.

Sprinkler system suggestions

Studies of large-loss fires in sprinkler-protected buildings show that fire departments should follow the suggestions of the Engineering Department of the American Insurance Association to use sprinkler systems most effectively:

1. Each fire department should have a list of all sprinkler-protected buildings in its area. Each officer should be familiar with at least those buildings in his first-alarm district.
2. Sketches should be prepared showing the locations of alarm valves, control valves and fire department connections. Officers should be familiar with this data on buildings in their district.
3. Fire departments should have information on the available water supply, such as: How many pumpers can be used in addition to those supplying the fire department sprinkler connections; is there a water supply separate from that supplying the sprinkler system that can be used; is there a nearby static water supply, such as a pond, from which pumpers can draft?
4. Fire department connections for sprinkler and standpipe systems should be inspected at regular intervals by the fire department to assure that caps can be readily removed, that threads are in good condition amd match those of the fire department, and that the connection is otherwise ready for use.
5. One of the first-alarm engine companies responding to a fire in a sprinkler-protected building should lay two 2½-inch lines (or a 3-inch line) to the fire department connection.

FD
FIRE DEPT
DANGER
ACETONE

CHAPTER NINETEEN

Fire prevention

A very large percentage of the people in this world go through life without ever experiencing an unfriendly fire, even in the United States which leads the world in fire losses. As a consequence, they tend to ignore the dangers of fire and pay little more than lip service to the fire prevention message. Fire departments, however, "realize that their full measure of service to the citizens requires as much attention to preventing fires as to putting them out."[1] Getting the citizen and the fire departments together, therefore, is the function of this chapter.

"Fire Safety and Control" is the blanket heading in the Grading Schedule that covers all facets of what is commonly called fire prevention. The opening paragraph under this heading states that "a reasonable degree of safety to life and protection of property from fire can be provided by state and municipal control of hazards. Control can best be accomplished by the adoption and enforcement of appropriate codes and standards for the manufacture, storage and use of hazardous materials and for building construction."

In general, this reasonable degree of safety has been provided in places given over to the manufacture of flammable gases and liquids and special hazards that involve dangerous plastics, fireworks and similar products. Reasonable safety has also been provided for factories—places where people work at manufacturing any product.

---

[1]*Special Interest Bulletin No. 5, The Value and Purpose of Fire Department Inspections,* American Insurance Association, New York, N. Y.

Unfortunately, the average citizen seems to be confident that the state legislature or city hall or the fire department has provided a reasonable degree of safety in all occupancies. As a consequence of this belief, he will blithely place himself in extreme peril. This peril can frequently be found in places of public assembly, which include nightclubs and dance halls among others and the "light hazard" office building (high-rise) which have contributed to a few holocausts in recent years.

A citizen out for a night on the town or at work in an office building should not have to think of obstructions to exits, inadequate or defective fire alarm or fire extinguishing systems, or conditions within a building that create a severe fire hazard potential.

This citizen is out of his normal element and there is usually nothing in his background that would enable him to evaluate his surroundings.

Some people do have a background (limited) in fire prevention and fire prevention education which they have acquired on their own, or from the local fire department. Most of this education has centered around how not to start a fire, how to extinguish a fire, and how to exit from one's burning home. But if fire prevention educators would expand their efforts to include "how to get out of a blazing office building or nightclub" or "why one should not go into them in the first place," the fire toll in deaths and injuries would drop.

Fire prevention, therefore, consists of three elements: codes and code enforcement, fire prevention inspections and fire prevention education.

Fire inspections

According to the American Insurance Association, "Careful, systematic and intelligent fire inspections are the background of effective fire prevention work and subsequently a powerful factor in the reduction of loss of life and property. Good inspections not only prevent fires, but by observation present opportunities to study and plan for more efficient and intelligent extinguishment of fires."[2]

The AIA also notes that the average businessman or property owner is not trained to recognize fire hazards and does not have a practical knowledge of fire fighting and the factors influencing the spread of a fire. The association lists the value and purpose of fire department inspections under the seven headings which follow:

To obtain proper life safety conditions: In carrying out this responsibility, it will greatly assist fire departments to know in advance

[2]*Ibid.*

where and under what conditions people live, work, and assemble and how they may escape or be rescued. Life safety inspections call for attention to the adequacy of exits, obstructions to rapid and orderly egress at time of fire, the adequacy of building evacuation plans and the determination of the number of occupants permitted in a place of public assembly.

To keep fires from starting: Persons who work among materials or situations which are hazardous often become negligent of their own safety, just as long periods without a fire produce overconfidence and underestimation of the fire danger. Fire inspectors, being constantly in contact with actual fires are able to more accurately judge a fire hazard and can point out hazardous conditions and explain their seriousness (fire prevention education).

To keep fires from spreading: Most people have little appreciation of the value that structural features (stair and elevator enclosures, fire doors and fire partitions) have in preventing the spread of fire. Inspectors should stress this value to owners and occupants to secure proper maintenance of such structural members and when possible and practical have additional features installed.

To determine adequacy and maintenance of fire protection equipment: Private fire protection equipment such as extinguishers, standpipes, hose systems, automatic sprinkler systems, private water supplies and alarm systems are installed to alert and protect building occupants, to aid fire department operations and to extinguish fires automatically. Under normal conditions this equipment is seldom used. Frequent inspections therefore are necessary to insure that the equipment will always be in good working order.

To pre-plan fire fighting procedures: It is difficult for a fire department to attack a fire intelligently without first knowing the building and its occupancy. And it is too late to plan procedure and the attack after the fire has started. The pre-fire plan of a particular building calls for a knowledge of the building's fire hazards, fire protection equipment, construction features affecting the spread of fire, exposures and exit facilities. This plan is necessary for the protection of the fire fighters as well as the occupants and aids in efficient extinguishment.

To stimulate cooperation between the fire department and owners and occupants: The interest of the fire department not only in preventing fires but in being better prepared to handle them when they occur will be appreciated. Fire prevention inspectors should inform the owners and occupants of a building that the fire department is rendering a service in the prevention and control of fires, and it is to their advantage to call it immediately in case of fire.

The inspectors should give advice on problems of fire protection and prevention. Such advice tends to bring about closer cooperation between the public and the department. It also serves to increase the standing of the department within the community.

To assure compliance with fire codes, laws and regulations: Some or all of these matters may be under the jurisdiction of the fire department. But whether specifically so or not, an inspector should be able to recognize violations and report them to the proper authorities.

Dwelling inspections

According to figures released by the National Fire Prevention and Control Administration, fire in the home is the second most frequent cause of accidental death in the United States. Roughly two-thirds of the fire deaths occur in the victims' own homes. In fact, only a small fraction of fire deaths are in commercial or institutional occupancies. We should not, of course, permit these statistics to get us complacent about fire in public places. But residences can usually be inspected quickly and easily and should play a large part in a department's fire prevention program.

Most fire departments today have some form of regular dwelling inspections in which all members on duty take part. The introduction of two-way radio made this possible since companies can remain "on the air" and available for instant response while making their inspections. But for those departments who are just starting, the initiation of a program of dwelling inspections requires careful preparation because its success depends on the cooperation of the residents.

Fire Prevention Week or Spring Clean-up Week are good times to start such work. Cooperation of the local chamber of commerce through its fire prevention committee or a committee specially created for the purpose can be used to good advantage. Newspaper publicity and announcements over local radio and television stations are a great help. Through these facilities the citizens can be prepared for the inspection, and by articles summarizing the conditions found and the amount of rubbish removed, any opposition on the part of the public can usually be overcome. The wide use of posters and stickers provides further good publicity. The interest of the children and of women's clubs and commercial clubs in this work is of decided value.

After the residents have become accustomed to having fire fighters inspect the basements of their houses, much of the explanation and publicity needed at first can be dispensed with, but initially considerable attention to this phase of work is essential.

In addition to proper publicity, the success of the program requires careful instruction of the fire fighters who are to make the inspections. They should be instructed in what to look for, the character of suggestions to be made, and how to make a tactful courteous approach. The fact that the inspections are being made on the basis of courtesy and not law should always be remembered.

Special arrangements will usually have to be made regarding the disposal of the large amounts of refuse, discarded furniture and the like that will be cleaned out of basements and attics as a result of the inspection program.

In the actual work of inspection, fire fighters should always appear in uniform, working in pairs on the inspection and usually confining the inspection to the daytime hours. The inspectors ask permission to make an inspection of the basement, explaining the purpose of the inspection program and asking the housewife to accompany them if she has time.

Cities which make such inspections have found it worthwhile to repeat the inspection program annually. They find that after the first year the benefits are such as to command the support of the whole community.

The inspection of any building should begin with a look at the building's exterior surroundings. Hazards are often found here and frequently are an indication of the building's interior. Note:

Condition of roof. Roofing that is old and warped collects sparks and flying brands.

Condition of chimneys. Chimneys supported on wood posts or brackets are apt to crack from settlement and allow hot flue gases to set fire to the woodwork. Loose bricks, open joints and cracks indicate that similar defects may exist in other parts where they might start a fire. In such cases, a thorough investigation should be made.

Condition of yard. Dry grass, leaves, papers, boards, branches of trees and other combustible waste materials in yards and under porches and houses are readily ignited and are a fire danger to buildings.

Condition of garages and sheds. Cleanliness and good maintenance are important precautions against fire that apply to sheds and garages as well as other buildings.

Materials of special hazard. Oil and kerosine containers or tanks must be substantial and of such a type that the contents will not spill. Preferably they should be provided with a pump. Gasoline, benzine and naphtha, except in very small quantities and in suitable containers, should not be kept in dwellings. Such materials should never be used for home dry cleaning.

After the dwelling exterior, the basement becomes the next target of the inspector. It usually contains the furnace and frequently a considerable amount of unnecessary combustible material. Hazards are:

Accumulations of waste and discarded material. Waste papers and discarded furniture constitute a wholly unnecessary fire hazard which householders would frequently be glad to be rid of. A suggestion from a fire fighter may provide just the necessary impetus to get such accumulations removed. Oily rags are especially hazardous because of the danger of spontaneous ignition. Occasionally other waste materials found in basements are subject to the same hazard.

Disorderly arrangement of fuel. Firewood should be neatly piled or placed in a bin and kept separate from all waste papers and rags. Papers and rags if contaminated with vegetable oils may start spontaneous heating.

Ashes in contact with wood. The practice of putting hot ashes in wooden boxes or barrels or piling against wooden partitions is a dangerous one, responsible for many fires. Metal containers are the only safe kind to use.

Furnaces, stoves or smoke pipes close to combustible ceilings or partitions. Fire fighters should be familiar with local regulations governing such installations, and see that they are complied with. Charring of wood and blistering of paint indicate exposure to excessive temperature. During operation of the furnace, wood that is too hot to touch may be considered subject to excessive temperature.

Condition of smoke pipes. Poorly supported and corroded smoke pipes present a fire hazard.

Gas appliances. Corroded piping and rubber tubing may result in gas leaks. Automatic gas devices without thermostatic provisions for cutting off a supply when the pilot flame is extinguished may produce an explosion.

Oil burner installations. Oil burners, supply tanks and piping need to be properly installed to avoid danger of fire.

Chimney defects and clearances. Wood beams extending into chimney walls have started many fires. Unused chimney openings should be sealed with brick or with tight-fitting metal stops.

Clean-out door at base of chimney. These are needed in cleaning out the soot, which is necessary to avoid chimney fires.

Workrooms. Removal of shavings from workbenches and the orderly storage of paints, varnishes, oils and turpentine are features to be commented upon.

Exits. Fire fighters should note, for their own convenience in fighting fires, location of exits from basements.

Electrical appliances. The condition of electrical appliances, including cords, sockets, plugs which are often improperly used or in bad shape should be noted.

Inspecting the mercantile building

Accumulations of waste materials present an easily recognized fire hazard. In addition to checking up on ordinary rubbish conditions, the kind and location of receptacles for ashes, and the method of storing and handling waste paper, rags, empty packing cases and excelsior should be investigated. Rags containing paint or vegetable oils are especially hazardous because of the danger of spontaneous heating and ignition.

Chimneys should be examined for defects which might cause fires, the more obvious of which are cracks in the chimney, and stovepipe openings which are not properly closed. These may allow hot gases to escape into the building and thus cause the ignition of combustible materials. Other important items bearing on the fire hazard are the construction of the chimney, its height above the roof, and the clearance of wood beams, joists and lathing from the chimney. These should be checked up as far as practicable.

The principal source of fire in connection with heating equipment comes from insufficient clearance from combustible materials. Heating appliances, smoke pipes, gas appliance vents, range hoods, warm air ducts and registers, and steam and hot water pipes should be examined for their clearance from combustible materials. The mounting of heating appliances and the construction and protection of warm air ducts and range hoods should also be checked.

Check electrical equipment

Electric wiring and equipment should be examined for the more prominent defects which may cause fires. This includes wiring that is insecurely supported or unduly subjected to injury, loose or broken fixtures, wires with damaged insulation, fuses bridged or too large for the circuit they protect, outlet, fuse or switch box covers open or missing, improper use of flexible cord, and highly flammable materials in contact with light bulbs. If a large number of defects is found or the wiring appears to be in a hazardous condition, the situation should be called to the attention of the local authority governing electrical installations.

With regard to gas piping and equipment, the principal things to look for are: conditions which may allow gas leaks, clearances of gas appliances from combustible material, and proper venting of gas appliances to the outer air.

The storage and handling of flammable liquids should be carefully investigated. The more commonly found are gasoline, kerosine, alcohol, ether, turpentine, benzine, linseed oil and fuel oil. The principal features in regard to their safe handling and storage are the type and construction of storage containers, the quantities stored in the building, methods and devices used for drawing liquids from the containers, and proximity of open flames or other sources of ignition.

Special hazards

Among the many other hazardous substances which may be found in mercantile buildings are: matches; explosives; small arms ammunition; pyroxylin plastic materials (called by such names as celluloid, parylin, viscoloid and others); calcium, carbide, nitrates, nitrites, chlorates and other oxidizing materials; nitric sulfuric, hydrochloric, and other strong acids; and compressed gases such as oxygen, acetylene, hydrogen, chlorine, bottled gas (butane and propane) and others.

Inspections should be made to determine whether all fire hazards are properly safeguarded, also to acquaint the members of the fire department with the hazards which exist in the buildings where they may at any time be called to fight a fire. The fire department should know the locations where flammable liquids or hazardous chemicals are kept, and approximately how much. They should know the location of the main gas shutoff valve and the electric service switch. They should also know what gas the refrigerating system contains and what to do in case the gas becomes released.

Careful attention should be given to the type of fire extinguishers. The number and location should be checked to see that they are properly distributed for quick and effective action on a fire in any part of the building, and their accessibility noted to see that none is out of easy reach or blocked by piles of stock.

The maintenance of extinguishers should be checked and the date of recharging or weighing noted. Nozzles of extinguishers should be examined for clogging.

Standpipe and sprinkler inspections

Larger mercantile buildings have standpipes, some with small hose intended for use by occupants of the building, and others with 2½-inch hose for use principally by the fire department. Conditions should be noted as to whether hose stations are freely accessible, and the hose, valve and nozzle should be examined for condition. The hose should be attached to the outlet, neatly arranged on rack or reel, with nozzle attached ready for instant use. The hose valve must be tight and provided with a drain.

The water pressure at the top of the standpipe should be noted, and valves controlling water supplies to the system should be examined to see that they are open. Fire department connections should be examined to see that they are not obstructed with foreign material, and that caps are in place. Tanks and pumps furnishing supplies to standpipes should be inspected to see that they are in order, with water in tanks at proper level, air in pressure tanks at proper pressure, and fire pumps in operable condition.

Where an automatic sprinkler system is provided, the inspection should also include a general checkup of the system to see that it is properly maintained.

Building fire alarm boxes should be checked to see that they are freely accessible and plainly marked as to what they are and how to use. Also that they are sufficiently conspicuous to be easily discovered in the excitement of a fire. The name and location of the person responsible for the protective equipment, or who should be notified in case of a fire, should be placarded in the engine room, office, or other suitable place and also recorded by the inspector.

Check for exits

One of the primary considerations in mercantile building inspections is the matter of exit facilities for use in time of fire. The number, location and accessibility of exits should be noted, as well as the width of stairways and passages, to see that all are adequate to permit the complete emptying of the building in reasonably quick time. Consideration should be given to the exit arrangements available when any one exit, especially the main exit, is blocked as from a fire. Exits from upper floors and those not ordinarily used but considered as fire exits should be noted to see that they are plainly marked. Obstructions preventing the free access to, or use of, exits should always be watched for. Exits should be looked at with particular regard to their usability and safety in time of fire. Stairways serving admirably as exits under ordinary circumstances may be the first part of the building to be filled with smoke, and thus rendered useless in the early stages of a fire.

With respect to types and materials of construction, there are three elements of a building which are of outstanding importance to the fire department. These are: the type of wall construction (both exterior and division), the type of floor construction, and the type of roof construction. The construction used for these three elements determines the general classification of the building with respect to fire resistance and has an important bearing on how the fire should be fought, on the problem of removing occupants in a fire, and on the dangers to men.

The height and area of a building and the location of windows, doors, stairways, and partitions are other features to be noted that have a decided bearing on the fire fighting problems.

The inspector should note all features which tend to let a fire spread. The greatest factors in this connection are stairways and elevators. Channels in walls, pipe openings through floors, absence of fire stops in furred or joisted walls, dumbwaiters and ventilating or heating ducts also permit ready spread of fire and should be noted in an inspection. Other features permitting rapid spread are open cocklofts extending over several buildings, windows exposed by other windows in the same or a nearby building, or exposed by a roof or skylight on a lower building.

Where people congregate

There is just not enough space in this chapter to cover all the different occupancies that a fire department might have to inspect. But for any occupancy, the seven purposes of fire department inspections (given at the beginning of this chapter) apply. The principles given for dwelling and mercantile inspections also apply to all occupancies. However, there are two other types of occupancies that require a lot of attention and for obvious reasons. These are hotels and schools that hold large numbers of persons and which can be found in every city and town.

In hotels, as in other occupancies, order and cleanliness are important and should be noted, especially in storage and workrooms. Electrical fixtures and wiring should be observed, as far as possible, as to maintenance and conditions. Common defects to watch for are unsafe use of flexible cord, improper fuses and improperly made extensions to the wiring system. The heating equipment should be examined for defects and faults of installation which may cause fires, chiefly, improper clearance between combustible material and hot surfaces of all kinds, including steam and hot water pipes, warm air pipes, furnaces and boilers, and smoke pipes.

Where a mechanical ventilating or air-conditioning system is found, the extent to which the system provides communications (through the air ducts) from one room to another should be investigated. The location of outside air intakes should be noted to see whether combustible materials are stored at a point where, should they become ignited, they would feed fire and smoke into the system, and whether under such conditions the necessary automatic protection against such exposure is provided. The location of fan shutoffs should be noted so that the fire department may know how to shut down the system in time of fire.

Kitchens of hotels are one of the common sources of fire. The setting and location of cooking ranges should be examined to see that if on a wood floor they are sufficiently insulated and are properly separated or insulated from any combustible partitions. The flues or vents to which the hoods of ranges and kettles are connected should be checked to see that they are safely constructed and sufficiently separated from all combustible material and lead to a lined chimney or a stack running above the roof. The construction must be such as to allow for a safe, complete burn-out of the grease which collects in such vents.

In connection with refrigeration for food storage or air conditioning, the fire department needs to know the character of the refrigerant used and the provisions for handling a leak of refrigerant gas.

In larger hotels, various kinds of accessory and repair shops are frequently found, such as carpenter, plumbing and electrical, and sometimes furniture-repair, mattress-renovating and paint shops. Other shops commonly found are tailor shops and laundries. The possibility of fire spreading from these shops to the other parts of the hotel should be studied. Any heat-producing devices in them should be examined to see that their use is properly safeguarded. Notice should be taken of the promptness and care with which all combustible wastes are disposed of, safety of methods used for the storage of combustible stocks, and adequacy of fire extinguishing and fire-detecting equipment.

The importance of proper exits to the safety of persons in a hotel is obvious. Fire department inspectors should therefore give particular attention to hotel exits. In all events, the fire department should be made acquainted with the exit facilities for its own benefit.

Of the common structural defects, the unprotected floor opening is probably the one most responsible for serious hotel fires and loss of life. All such openings should be carefully noted and it should be seen that doors to stairs, elevator and dumbwaiter enclosures, especially those in the basement, are kept closed.

Fire protection equipment in hotels is similar to that in ordinary mercantile buildings and needs the same kind of careful maintenance and inspection. Of first importance is the fire alarm system and the arrangement made by the management for promptly sounding an alarm in the building and notifying the fire department. Where a sprinkler system is provided to make up in part for serious defects or weaknesses in construction, maintenance becomes extremely important to insure its operation.

Inspecting a school

It is recommended that inspection be made each month by a representative of the local fire department accompanied by the school custodian and a member of the teaching staff.

Good housekeeping is of prime importance in the prevention of school fires. The method of handling and disposing of waste paper should be investigated, and all areas, especially under and near stairways, searched for accumulations of waste or discarded material. In manual training and all such workrooms, the presence of the necessary self-closing metal waste cans should be checked.

Heating equipment, the cause of a large portion of school fires, should be given careful attention. The clearances between combustible material and furnaces, smoke pipes and all other hot surfaces should be examined to see that they are adequate. Electric wiring should be checked for improperly made extensions, hazardous use of flexible cord, and broken fixtures, and fuses checked to see that they are not oversize.

The extent to which ventilating ducts provide ready means for the spread of fire through the building should be considered; also the need for protective devices such as fire dampers in the ducts and automatic shutoff for fans, to guard against such occurrences.

Of great importance in all schools are exit drills. The inspector should check on the frequency of drills and the time taken to vacate the building, and occasionally witness the conduct of a drill. The building fire alarm system should be examined to see that the alarm can be heard in all parts and that it can be sounded from each floor. The arrangements for promptly notifying the fire department should also be investigated.

The inspector should examine all fire extinguishers to see that they are well maintained, sufficient in number and properly spaced. Standpipe systems should be checked for the location and accessibility of hose stations and to see that hose is in good condition with the nozzle properly attached. Where a sprinkler system is provided, it should receive frequent checkups. Water supplies for sprinkler and standpipe systems should be noted.

Fire-resistive stair enclosures serve a two-fold purpose in the school building. Such exit facilities, if properly maintained, assure a safe exit of the occupants in time of emergency and retard the rapid spread of fire from one floor to another. The inspector should examine all doors to stairway enclosures to see that they are in good condition and are not blocked open.

Evacuating a school

Exit facilities of school buildings need careful study, particularly from the standpoint of their usefulness in time of fire. Attention should be given to each of the following basic requirements:

1. That each large assembly room and each floor have at least two

means of egress, and more if needed, for quick evacuation of the building,

2. That all exit doors open outward and have only panic bolts for locks (if other locks are necessary, they should never be locked while the building is in use), and

3. That stairways, corridors and fire escapes are kept free from obstruction.

Consideration should be given to the other exits available should any one exit be blocked by fire, as well as the probability of exits being so blocked. With outside iron fire escapes, fire issuing from windows frequently blocks their use. To guard against this, windows near fire escapes should be of wired glass in metal frames. Heating plants not properly cut off by partitions and fire doors from the corridors may also be the cause of exits being blocked.

(Editor's note: Further information on inspections, ranging from churches to grain-handling, can be found in the Special Interest Bulletins of the American Insurance Association's Engineering and Safety Service.)

FIRE PREVENTION EDUCATION

The average person has little knowledge of fires, fire causes or fire prevention. For most, fire is an isolated occurrence seen in passing or an item of news in the daily paper to be soon forgotten. As a consequence of this attitude, the public's interest in fire prevention must be stimulated by fire departments and other agencies. But unfortunately much fire prevention literature is full of statistics that, according to the American Insurance Association, "is meaningful to the professionals but meaningless to most laymen."[3]

Better than the statistical approach, the association claims, is "alerting the public, in its own language to the dangers of fire. Of these dangers, the peril to life and body is, of course, outstanding."

It is necessary therefore to install in the minds of the people the thought that the fire department gladly lends its aid in preventing fire and in suggesting changes and additions that will lessen the effects of fire. A fire department therefore must sell this idea to the citizens it is sworn to protect. This can be done with the aid and cooperation of the various media, schools, institutions and service organizations. Public speaking courses for members of a fire department help. And some departments have used outside speaker and writers. But to be most

[3]*Special Interest Bulletin No. 25, Fire Department Activities—Public's Interest in Fire Prevention Work,* American Insurance Association, New York, N. Y.

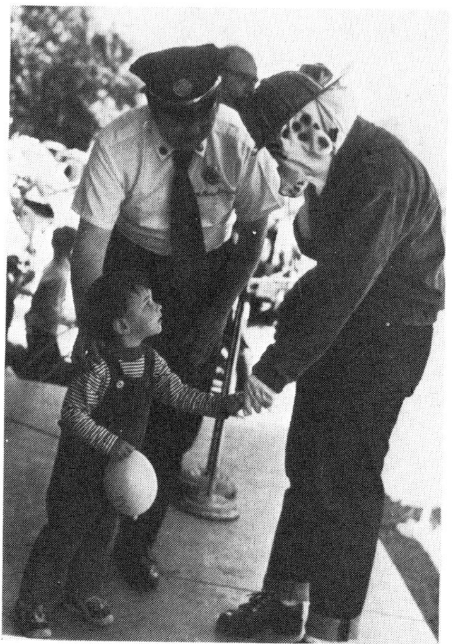

Grade school children should be a prime target for fire prevention education.

effective, the functions of a fire prevention campaign should be performed by the uniformed members of a department.

Newspapers, radio and television are of prime importance in spreading the fire prevention word. Where possible, news releases should be handled by men of the department and it helps if those men familiarize themselves with the media formats. Personal contact with the local news editors also helps. Timing of releases is also important. A headline noting a loss of life by fire in a kitchen should be followed the next day by a fire department release on the hazards of a kitchen—and how to avoid them. Timeliness and impact is lost if the department waits until the next Fire Prevention Week to send out its message.

Demonstrations important

Demonstrations of fire hazards and of fire extinguishing equipment offer another way to get the fire prevention message across. A fire prevention bureau can assemble miniature houses, or special processes, or other features that demonstrate proper and improper fire practices. Beyond this, there are collections of pictures and other exhibits that can be shown in store windows. Many departments annually put on extensive shows open to the public in which the work of a fire fighter is shown, both at fires and in training. The show, of course, is a front for the fire prevention education that accompanies it.

As mentioned earlier, two-thirds of all fire deaths in the United States occur in the home, either in a dwelling or an apartment house. Each home fire prevention insepction should therefore be part inspectional and part educational. Good houskeeping should be stressed. The accumulation of unused materials in basements, attics, closets and garages should be regularly cleaned out and particularly old newspapers. Another accumulation to be guarded against by the home dweller is grease in a kitchen oven or hood.

Smoking, of course, is the leader in fire causes and its dangers should be pointed out.

Another leading cause of fire is defective electrical equipment. The dangers of overloaded circuits and worn or defective wiring and wiring assemblies should receive great emphasis in the inspection and education of a tenant.

Gasoline stored for a lawnmower and kerosine used for cooking often bring tragedy to a home. A tenant should be instructed in their safe handling and that they and others are volatile liquids whose vapors can readily ignite from a spark, an open flame of any kind and a cigarette.

These volatiles, including cleaning fluids, should be stored outside the house, safe from the hands of mischievous children.

Exit drills

Most fire departments by now are familiar with Operation EDITH —Exit Drills In The Home, which is published by the American Mutual Insurance Alliance. When taught, or perhaps supervised by a fire department that is inspecting a home, it can be a telling factor in reducing the loss of life and injuries caused by fire.

Briefly, there are five steps in this plan. In the first step occupants determine two means of escape from each bedroom, one of which is the normal exit from the home and the other a window. Second-floor windows call for a ladder.

Another step calls for a floor plan to be drawn up that shows windows, doors, stairs and rooftops that can be used for escape. A personal escape for each member of the family should be indicated and these escape routes, as with any exit, should be kept free of obstructions.

EDITH also calls for an early warning device to alert residents to the presence of fire (see below), and for a selection of a meeting place outdoors for all members of a family to check in to ensure that they are all accounted for. Regular practice of the plan is recommended.

In addition to the plan, Operation EDITH gives some instructions,

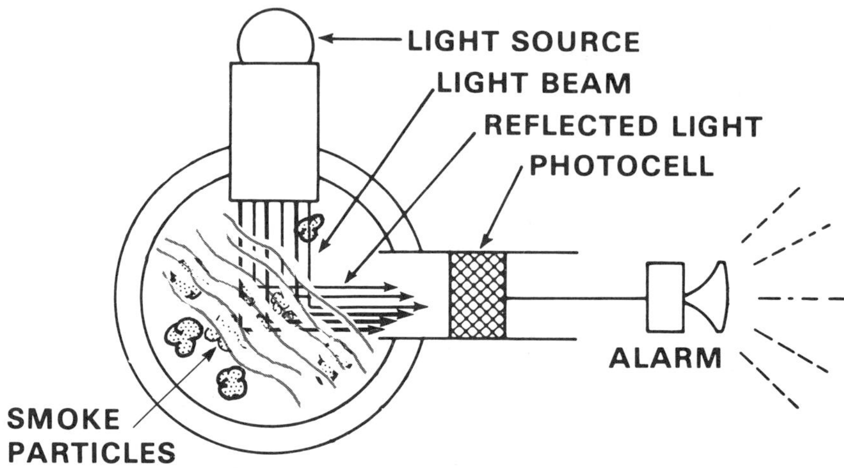

Photoelectric smoke detector houses a light source and a light-sensitive cell in a darkened chamber. The detector goes into alarm when smoke enters the chamber and reflects a light beam into the cell.

familiar to fire fighters, as to how one should act when fire strikes the home—"close doors," "feel doors for heat" and "crawl in smoke," among others. Unquestionably, this booklet should be in every fire department's fire prevention kit.

Smoke detectors important

As mentioned above, Operation EDITH calls for a warning device to alert occupants of the presence of fire—usually a smoke detector. However, in purchasing and installing such a device, a home owner will need some reasonably expert advice and instruction. And logically, he will turn to his local fire department to get this advice. It was for this reason that the National Fire Prevention and Control Administration prepared a series of smoke detector public education manuals to teach the fire prevention community the basics about home smoke detectors. Additionally, the administration has encouraged the installation of smoke detectors in all the nation's homes, feeling that the detectors have the potential of reducing home fire deaths by over 40 percent.

The home fire detector can also help the fire fighter in two very important ways: It can warn of fire while the fire is still small, making extinguishment easier. And when occupants escape from a burning home because of early warning, there is no need to attempt unnecessary rescue.

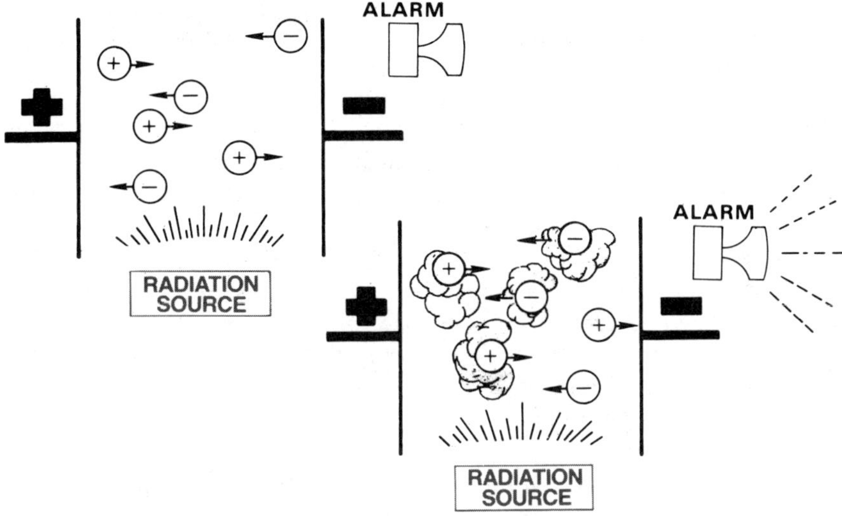

Ionization smoke detector uses a radioactive material to make the air within a sensing chamber conduct electricity as indicated.

There are two types of home detectors in current use: the photoelectric smoke detector and the ionization detector. The photoelectric detector uses a light source and a light-sensitive cell in a darkened chamber. The light source produces a light beam. The photoelectric detector goes into alarm when smoke enters the darkened chamber and reflects the light beam into the light-sensitive cell.

The ionization detector uses a radioactive material to make the air within the sensing chamber conduct electricity. The alarm sounds when smoke interferes with the flow of electrical current in the ionization chamber. According to the National Fire Prevention and Control Administration, the radiation source in this type detector "presents no health hazard to a home's occupants."[4]

Which of the above two detectors is best is a question that is frequently asked. The ionization detectors "best sense the fires that produce very small or invisible particles."[5] Photoelectric detectors "sense smoky smouldering fires best—those that produce larger smoke particles."[6]

However, both detectors alarm quickly. And since most home fires produce both visible and invisible smoke particles, the National Bureau

[4]*Smoke Detector Training,* United States Department of Commerce, National Fire Prevention and Control Administration, Washington, D. C.

[5]*Ibid.*

[6]*Ibid.*

of Standards has concluded that properly installed photoelectric or ionization detectors are both adequate in homes for lifesaving potential.

Powering the unit

Smoke detectors are powered in a variety of ways, the most common being battery-operated. When properly maintained, battery-operated units will give round-the-clock protection. All Underwriters Laboratories-listed units are designed so that the batteries will last one year if operated according to manufacturers' instructions. The batteries, of course, will eventually weaken and need replacement. When this happens, a warning sound (similar to a chirp or a beep) occurs at least once a minute for a minimum of seven days. Some units have a red flag (plastic) that is mounted within the unit and which displays to signal a weak battery.

There are some electric-powered detectors that are equipped with a cord that plugs into an electric outlet in the same manner as an appliance or a lamp. When using these plug-in units, owners should be sure that the outlets used cannot be turned off by a wall switch. In addition, the outlet selected should not be on the same circuit as heavy-duty electrical appliances that may malfunction and blow a fuse.

Some electrically-powered detectors may be wired directly into a home's electrical system. This will usually require the services of a licensed electrician. Electrically-powered units are also available with a back-up battery. The battery, however, must be properly maintained and replaced when necessary. But it will keep the detector operating if electric power fails.

Maintenance and testing

Most smoke detectors require little maintenance. Any failure can usually be attributed to human failure—failing to replace batteries and burned-out incandescent bulbs which are supplied with some units. Other maintenance requires that the detector be vacuumed or dusted periodically.

Some detectors have a test button that will activate the alarm, others have a power on signal (light) only. The NFPCA recommends that all smoke detectors be tested at least once a month—with smoke. And be tested weekly according to the manufacturer's instructions.

Placement of detectors

The hallway outside of a home's sleeping area is the most important location for a smoke detector. And in homes with more than one group

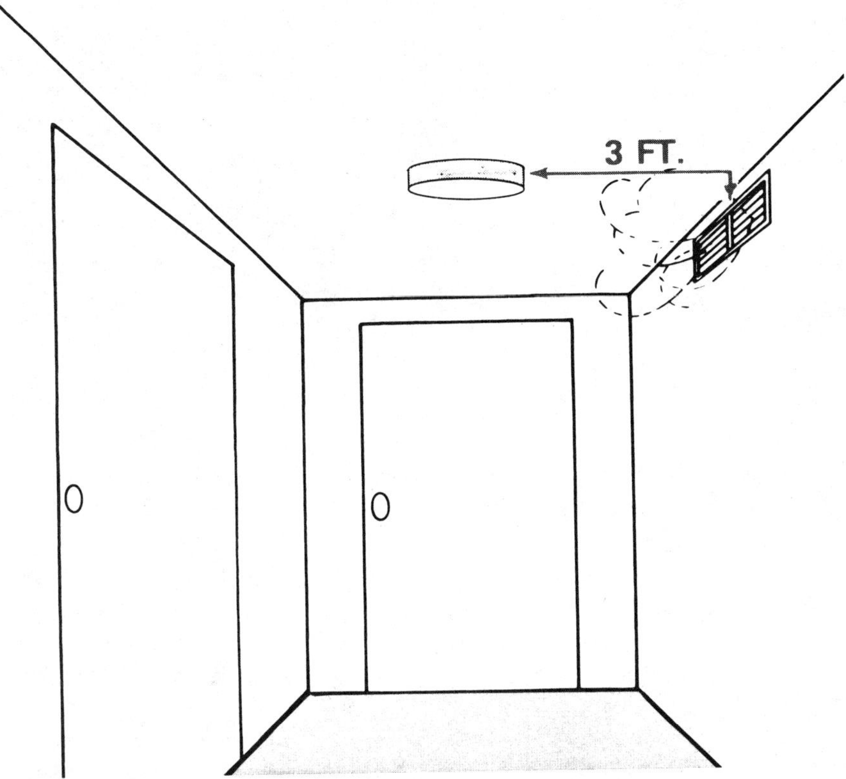

Detector's efficiency can be reduced unless placed at least 3 feet from air register.

of bedrooms, there should be a detector for each sleeping area. In addition, homes with more than one level should have a detector installed for each level. Finally, a detector installed in each bedroom considerably increases a family's protection.

Once the area has been selected for a smoke detector, care must be taken in selecting the spot where it is to be installed. Dead air spaces at the top edge of a room (where the ceiling and wall meet) should be avoided. Here, air flow patterns can prevent smoke particles from reaching the corners in the early stages of a fire.

Do not install a smoke detector on a poorly insulated wall or ceiling, such as are found in mobile homes or light wood frame construction. Extreme exterior temperatures can cause a thermal barrier (heat or cold)

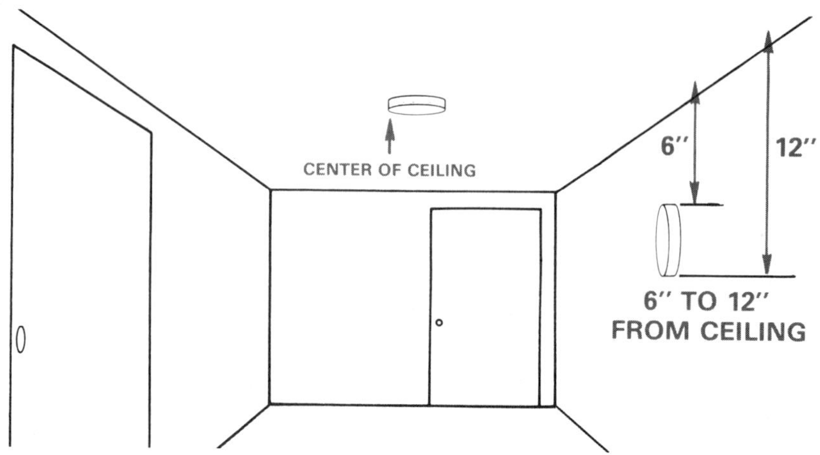

Smoke detectors should be placed on ceiling or high on wall. Dead air spaces at top edge of room (where ceiling and wall meet) should be avoided.

on the inside which prevents smoke from reaching detectors mounted on a poorly insulated surface. If poor insulation is suspected, the detector should be mounted on an interior wall 6 to 12 inches from the ceiling.

Installers should avoid placing a detector within 3 feet of an air supply register or return. Failure to do this could result in smoke being pushed or pulled away from the detector by air flow.

To minimize false alarms, detectors should not be placed in a position where they would be exposed to cooking or furnace fumes, fireplace smoke or dust.

Editor's note: Further information can be found in the following volumes that are published by the United States Department of Commerce, National Fire Prevention and Control Administration, Public Education Office, National Fire Academy. They are for sale by the Superintendent of Documents, U. S. Government Printing Office, Washington, D. C. 20402.

Volume I: The Smoke Detector Resource Catalog. A fact sheet on smoke detectors, guides to finding smoke detector materials, case histories of successful programs, a legislative overview, and evaluation techniques.

Volume II: Smoke Detectors: Moving the Public. A two-part manual on generating support through community organizations and the media.

Volume III: Smoke Detector Technology. A detailed description of how smoke detectors work, including comparisons of ionization and photoelectric detectors.

Volume IV: Smoke Detectors and Legislation. An in-depth review of the current status of state and local smoke detector legislation.

Volume V: Smoke Detector Training. A suggested curriculum for training members of the fire prevention community to present smoke detector education to the public.

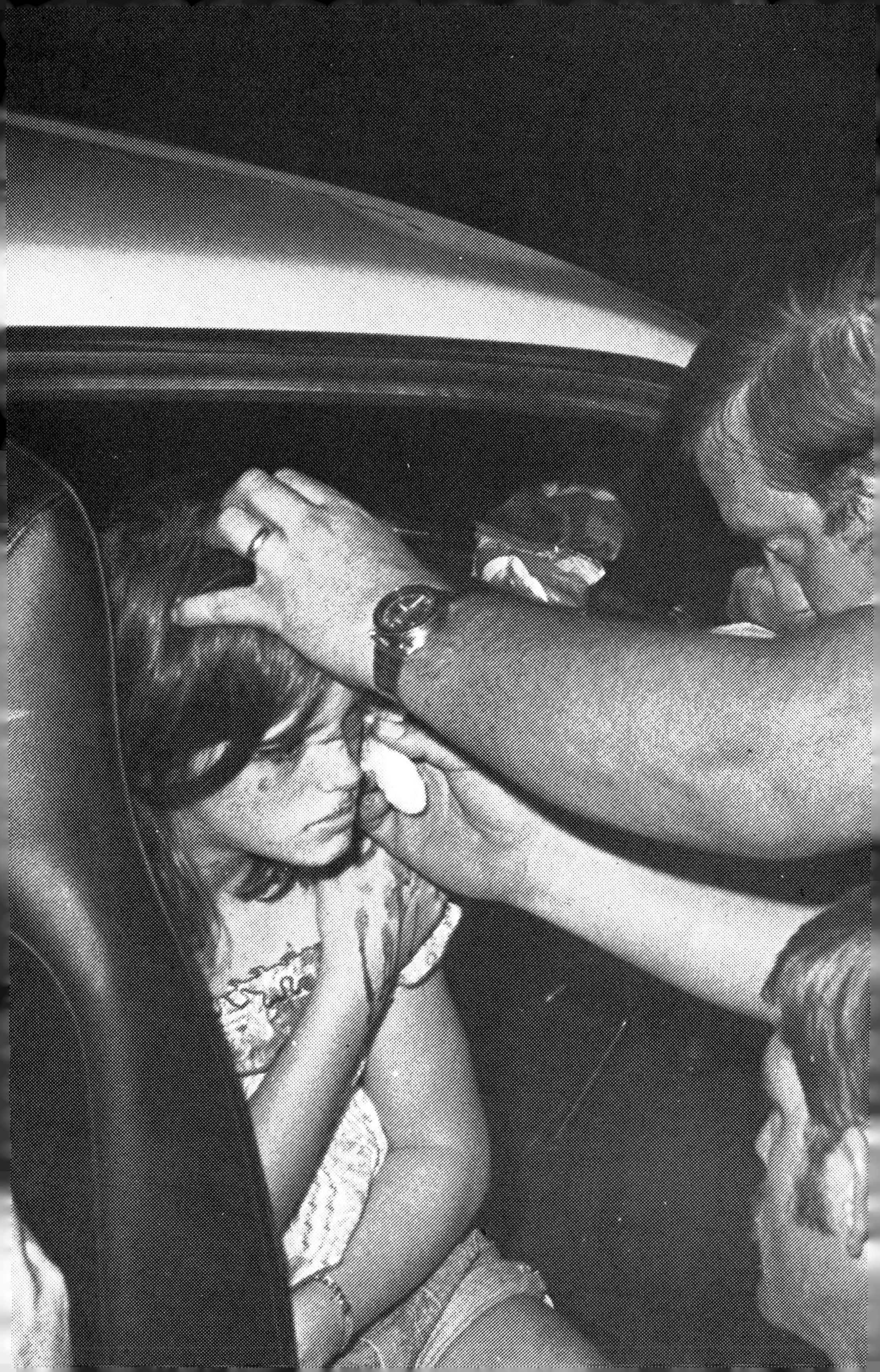

CHAPTER TWENTY

Emergency medical service

"The obligation to render this humanitarian service rests upon the city and the county authorities," according to a Chicago citizen's council report on ambulance service made in 1944. The council also felt that the fire department seemed to be the most logical place to put the ambulance service. One reason was that the public "has confidence in its fire department." Another was the department's fast and efficient dispatching system. This was pretty good reasoning more than a quarter of a century ago, and it still holds. At that time, the average citizen had little awareness of the ambulance service now called the emergency medical service. But that unawareness doesn't hold today. Back in 1970, the National Academy of Sciences jolted the public (and Congress) with a widely publicized report that called for more and better emergency medical service while labeling accidental death and injury as "the neglected disease of modern society."

The biggest boost, however, that EMS got was the passage by Congress in 1973 of the Emergency Medical Services Systems Act. This act, which provided a national focus on the neglected disease emphasized the need to integrate proposed emergency medical services projects with existing state, regional or local programs and facilities. The act also provided grants for feasibility studies and planning of emergency services systems for their establishment and initial operation—and for expansion and improvement. As a consequence, hundreds, perhaps thousands, of fire departments have instituted emergency medical services.

But many fire departments had been involved in emergency medical services well before 1973. Back in 1967, Fire Engineering reported on the "cardiograph radio transceiver" pioneered for use in vehicles of the City of Miami Fire Department. Miami was "the first in the nation to operate routinely a portable radio device which records the heart action of a stricken person at the scene and transmits it to a hospital." At that time the word telemetry and the acronyms EMS and EMT were relatively unknown in the fire service.

It is significant that in the article describing Miami's new transceiver mention was made that "the equipment has already attracted the attention of the United States Department of Transportation and the Emergency Medical Services, United States Public Health Service." That attention turned into an abiding interest that has radically changed the design of the ambulance and its associated equipment and upgraded the skills of the ambulance attendant, EMT, to the highest degree.

Starting up

Once a community has decided to institute an emergency medical service organization, the first problem that arises is money. For the affluent there is no problem. They will do it on their own. But for those who cannot do it on their own there is help on hand from the federal government through the act mentioned above and from the Department of Transportation, Division of Highway Safety.

In 1973, the Sarasota, Fla., Fire Department got into emergency medical service almost overnight when the local ambulance operator notified the city that his services would cease (because a subsidy was withdrawn). At that time the existing fire department rescue van was modified to carry patients. The department was also able to rent two new van-type ambulances from a local firm. Fortunately, the department had the full cooperation of the Division of Highway Safety and a grant request was prepared and hurriedly submitted—with sufficient justification. The result was a grant of $195,000 which went for the purchase of four completely equipped ambulances. In addition to the vehicles, Sarasota acquired telemetry and radio units as well as other rescue and emergency equipment. Such assistance is, of course, available to all fire departments in the United States.

Manpower and training

Equipment is important, but equipment without manpower—properly trained manpower—is next to useless. The training of the EMTs, however, takes time. Their selection is usually quite quick. In Birmingham, Ala., the "rescue" personnel are called fire medics. They are

Cave-in rescue is one of many types of emergencies to which Birmingham's dual unit responds.

fire fighters first, as in many departments, and medics second. They are selected by the chief's staff from a list of volunteers. Attitude, aptitude, education and the ability to adapt to the position are considered.

A problem that occurs in many fire departments was no problem in Birmingham. All personnel assigned to the new "rescue" units were replaced in their line companies by additional men hired for the fire fighting division. The same held true for Sarasota. Sarasota also had a fringe benefit in establishing its EMS. The department went from a Class 5 fire department to a Class 3. The change was partially the result of adding personnel because of the ambulance service.

Basic EMS equipment

A-B-C—airway, breathing, then circulation. These are the three steps in cardiopulmonary resuscitation, according to a 1973 joint statement by the American Heart Association, National Academy of Sciences and National Research Council. Breathing comes first, although the equipment technology is somewhat less complex than that of cardiac monitoring.

But here, too, the EMS technician encounters a bewildering variety

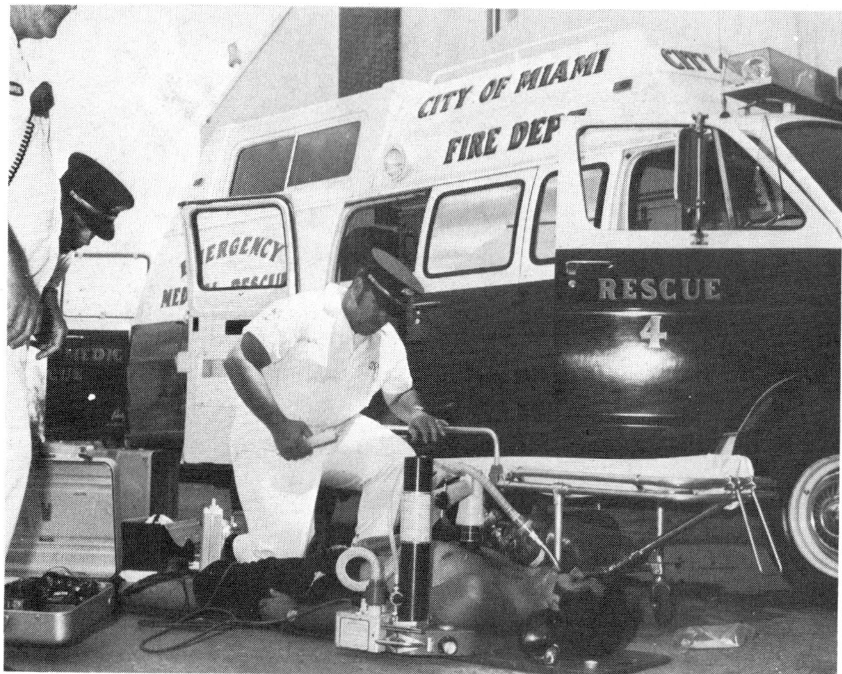

Miami EMS vehicles carry the usual extrication tools, masks and are equipped with built in scope, telemetry, oxygen and suction systems.

of apparently similar devices. What are the basic functions of each? What standards apply? What lies ahead?

Resuscitation methods go back hundreds, if not thousands, of years. A primitive bellows was used to ventilate nonbreathing patients more than four centuries ago. In this century, in the wake of the gas mask developments of World War I, fire departments began to use devices which evolved over generations into the resuscitators of today.

For many years, rescue breathing apparatus generally provided a constant flow of air or oxygen, usable by breathing patients. This usually did little good unless artificial respiration methods got breathing started.

Today, there are three common types of portable resucitators for EMS use. One is the intermittent positive pressure (IPPB) type with optional high flow capability. In the one version, the maximum pressure is selected by the operator, who manually triggers oxygen flow which stops automatically when the selected back pressure is reached in the patient's lungs.

The high flow feature, initiated manually by the operator through a lever or button on the face mask valve, will supply the 100 to 150 liters per minute of oxygen needed in treatment of cardiac arrest. Physicians at one time felt that 60 liters per minute was enough, but today's higher valves are intended to allow for face mask leakage.

The second type of resuscitator is the positive/negative pressure device, which uses a factory-set value of positive pressure (typically 10 centimeters of water, or about ½ psi) not variable in the field. When the lung back pressure reaches that figure, the valve automatically switches to its negative pressure mode and "exhales" for the patient. Again, a manual high flow option is available.

The third type of resuscitator has a demand valve with a high flow override. The demand valve is similar to that on self-contained breathing apparatus with which most fire fighters are familiar.

Once the patient is breathing on his own, the slight negative pressure created by his inspiratory effort triggers the valve from a non-flow state to a flowing state. When the inspiratory effort stops, the flow stops. Exhaling opens the valve chamber from the mask to the atmosphere, to eliminate rebreathing exhaled gases. Such valves were first developed for bail-out breathing equipment needed by World War II fliers.

Resuscitator valves are complex mechanisms. The latest types generally have two basic functions in common:

First, an oxygen-powered pressure ventilation cycle is controlled by the patient's own lung pressure. Oxygen is supplied to the mask in accordance with the lung's ability to absorb the flow.

Second, the manual override control allows the operator to directly pressurize the lungs of a nonbreathing patient up to the limit of probable safety, usually about 50 centimeters of water column. By operating the high flow override cyclically, the operator "can breathe for the patient," timing the flow cycles to fit in with such other rescue efforts as cardiac compression.

Resuscitators thus equipped have been available for about a decade. Demand valves were available years earlier, but they lacked a market because of the absence of trained EMS personnel to use such equipment.

Choosing the device

In choosing these devices, there is no substitute for (1) the opinion of the medical staff with which the EMS group is training or working, and (2) the reputation of the device manufacturer, the extent of his field experience and his acceptance in the medical community.

With the advent of paramedics, and the general high level of EMS training in today's fire-rescue service, the rescuer tends to exercise more control, more feel for patient response, more on-the-spot judgment. There is less strict reliance on automatic mechanical devices with preset operating characteristics that may not fit all emergency situations.

Again, what is acceptable to the physician must govern what is used.

What standards apply to resuscitation equipment? So far, almost none. But in June 1976, the medical device amendments to the Food, Drug and Cosmetic Act became effective, requiring national standards to be written. Groups such as the General Hospital Panel of the Food and Drug Administration are expected to oversee development of standards under contract by outside research firms.

Devices may be classified into one of three groups. For example, Class I, which will probably cover bag mask equipment, requires only that "good manufacturing practice" be monitored by quality assurance procedures to yield a good product. Other types of resuscitators may fall into Class III, requiring "pre-market clearance," performance standards and clinical data proving efficacy.

How long it will take to get the standards will depend on the priority assigned, but could take years. In the medical device field more than 2000 separate standards are expected eventually, but they won't be completed overnight.

Meantime, there is the performance standard developed by the May 1973 National Conference on Cardiopulmonary Resuscitation. This was later published as a February 1974 supplement to the Journal of the American Medical Association and reprints of it should be available from local Heart Association offices. Here are some brief quotations:

"Conventional pressure-cycled automatic resuscitators (IPPB respirators, positive-negative pressure resuscitators, resuscitators-inhalators) should not be used in conjunction with external cardiac compression because effective . . . compression prematurely triggers termination of the inflation cycle so inadequate ventilation results. . . Manually triggered (time cycled) devices are easier to use effectively. They have high instantaneous flow rates that allow them to be used for artificial ventilation alone. The devices also allow breaths to be interposed between compressions during CPR. Most will function as inhalators, too, for patients who are breathing spontaneously but require oxygen.

"Manually triggered, oxygen-powered resuscitators should be able to provide instantaneous flow rates of 100 liters/minute or more. . ."

Are there any radically new wrinkles in resuscitation equipment to be expected?

 Says one manufacturer of several types: "There is only so much you

Birmingham's rescue unit is fully equipped for EMS and rescue work, but does not transport patients.

can do to a lung. We have some difficulty in finding consensus among doctors on such matters as the proper oxygen flow rates... Valve design depends on flow and pressures to be used, and what do you do if you find 20 percent of the market wanting one set of numbers, another 20 percent something different, and so on? We work closely with medical groups, especially in anaesthesiology, and we do field testing, and changes in approved techniques are going to continue to arise. But nothing drastically new in valve design seems likely."

Although changes in both function and electronics are reducing the size and weight of cardiac monitoring equipment, such change seems unlikely for resuscitators. The limitation, as with demand mask equipment, is in the air/oxygen cylinders. A basic change in these must come about to significantly cut resuscitator weight from the 40-pound package typical today.

Portable monitoring

Literally the "heart" of today's emergency medical service is the portable cardiac monitor/defibrillator, product of a fast-growing technology only a few years old.

Although electrocardiography is not a new science, only recently was equipment made for portable use by technicians in the field. The first battery-operated portable defibrillator came on the market prior to 1969—except there was no market. Too few EMS programs existed to support its manufacture. Many hospitals, physicians, and fire and police services developed their own systems using equipment often custom-made for their requirements. In August 1971, an international conference on engineering in medicine-biotelemetry was held in New Hampshire. An emergency vehicle workshop there concluded that such vehicles would require telemetered biosignals, including the electrical activity of a patient's heart.

Physicians described early telemetering (radio transmission of data rather than conversation) then in use. The problems then were short battery life of portable gear, difficulty of getting maintenance and radio interference.

Since the '60s, progress has been rapid. In 1970, the practice of emergency medicine became a recognized medical specialty. In 1973, the newly formed American College of Emergency Physicians (ACEP) held its first national meeting in Washington, D. C.

In addition, a sizable number of paramedic operations have sprung up around the country, largely within the fire service, compiling an outstanding performance record with portable equipment. Programs in Los Angeles County, Seattle, Miami, and Jacksonville are well known. But there are many others in Texas, Maryland, Connecticut, Alabama and Minnesota. One EMS system in northern Illinois began with nine communities in 1973. It now serves 13 and similar systems operate nearby.

Technicians develop ideas

From this wide experience, the technicians involved, their instructors, and the physicians with whom they work have developed many ideas on what features their portable equipment should have. Such people are represented in meetings like the Puerto Rico EMS workshop. Manufacturers attend also to benefit from user feedback.

Naturally, it's hard to find universal agreement because local operating conditions vary. But certain recommendations tend to crop up over and over in discussions with paramedics and physicians.

What features are desirable for the monitor/defibrillator? The first answer is "simplicity, light weight, and ruggedness."

Said one paramedic instructor, "Some of these things weigh more than 40 pounds. You get tired lugging that up three flights of stairs. They get dropped. The paddles in some designs are hard to get at when you want them, yet when you're running across the street with the unit, the paddles fall out and hit the curb."

Exposed knobs and controls can be damaged when paramedics crawl into confined spaces or strike the unit against other objects. Some monitors have a cowling or projecting frame below which the controls are recessed for protection—a good feature to look for.

Some units are quickly separable. The technician can stay at the patient's head with the defibrillator portion during transport while the monitor section is placed at the patient's feet, where it can easily be watched. (This separability was recommended by the Puerto Rico workshop.) Since the crew must carry drug boxes and communications gear when leaving the vehicle, such a unit is preferable to one having the defibrillator and monitor in two separate packages that can't be combined.

Almost all monitors use an oscilloscope screen for visual display of the patient's heart activity. There are several options here. The most popular—and recommended by the ACEP workshop—is the "no fade" scope. The trace persists on the screen for a short while rather than fading out immediately. This allows the viewer to see it as a whole so hasty judgment isn't necessary.

Somewhat lower in cost and lighter, because electronics is less complex, is the bouncing ball display. This shows a moving spot of light with little or no background line trace, requiring close observation to get the picture.

A third option, not favored by most of the technicians and physicians questioned, is the freeze-trace scope. This allows the pattern displayed to be "frozen" on the screen, or changed from a moving to a still picture which can be studied at leisure.

Paper printout important

Besides the oscilloscope display, an important feature of today's monitor is the electrocardiogram paper printout. The ACEP workshop favored the heat stylus type. The paper used is heat-sensitive, and a heated metal tracing point, activated by heart function signals, "burns" a display line on the paper passing through the printer. Two drawbacks are that the paper is sensitive to extraneous marking through careless handling and battery power drain is high.

A second printout method uses voltage-sensitive, or ionic transfer, paper marked by the passage of tiny electrical currents through the paper. This takes only one-sixth as much power, and the paper is less sensitive. The trace, however, isn't always as clear.

The defibrillator itself has fewer variations. The important question here is whether it will deliver its rated output. Some designs rated at 400 joules or watt-seconds of cardioversion energy may actually deliver much less. Another useful feature available with some units is the ability to transmit an EKG directly through the paddles, saving the time to connect normal patient electrodes.

Said one technician, "This is important if the patient has no pulse and isn't breathing. You need to ascertain the heart condition fast."

The battery supply is vital, of course, to the operation of any of the equipment. Some units can be operated from an AC power line or a 12-volt vehicle battery, but the most common power source is nickel-cadmium rechargeable batteries. Long battery life is desirable, but more important is the ease of replacement. The unit should have a test switch to check battery condition daily. Batteries typically deliver anywhere from 50 to 500 defibrillations plus as much as 1½ hours of EKG printout from one charge.

For more detailed comparative ratings of monitoring equipment offered by various suppliers, publications of the Emergency Care Research Institute (ECRI) may be useful. The subscription service through which hospitals can receive this information is relatively expensive, however, and not all hospitals use it.

Growth of telemetry

Basic to all fire service EMS programs is the concept that the technician in the field functions as a remote arm of the hospital physician, hence the growth of telemetering. There are half a dozen equipment manufacturers, but there is less variation in product function than with monitors. Normally, technicians have radio equipment in the vehicle using five pairs of UHF (450–470 mHz) frequencies set aside in 1972 for EKG use. The three basic radio links are simplex, in which a single EKG (or voice) pattern can be sent in one direction at any one time; duplex, in which transmission and reception of voice and EKG can occur at the same time via two separate frequencies; and multiplex, giving the same effect with single frequency. The more heavily oriented the EMS system is toward control and decision-making at the hospital, the more useful the duplex or multiplex arrangement becomes.

When leaving their vehicle, technicians carry walkie-talkies which relay signals back to the vehicle, where a repeater steps up the power and retransmits the signals to the base. There are also telephone attachments available to permit sending EKG or voice signals via land line. This comes in handy in areas where radio transmission may be blocked by structures or terrain.

Some units on the market combine monitor, defibrillator and telemetry in a single package. But most systems keep the telemetry separate. This is a changing field and new developments in one area (such as telemetry) can obsolete the whole package if everything is combined.

Unlike monitors, newer telemetry packages tend to be heavier than formerly—up from about 20 pounds to as much as 28. This results from capacity for multiplex plus transmission from more patient leads.

Choice of telemetry will depend on the terrain, too. If radio communication is difficult, the paramedics may have to be more on their

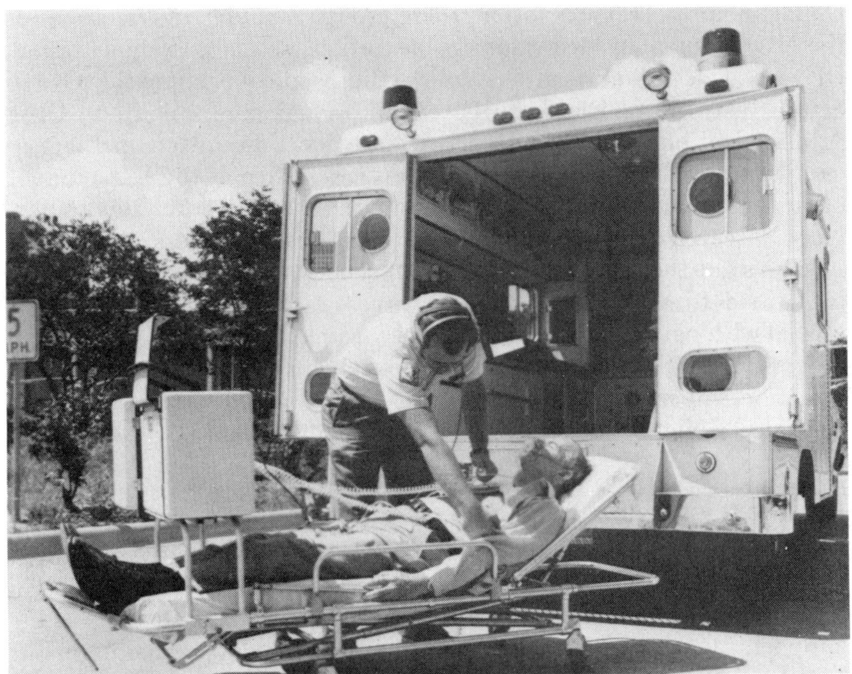

Telemetry equipment wired to patient sends EKG to hospital without disrupting voice communication.

own—true, in Anchorage, Alaska, for example, because of mountains in the area. Therefore, extensive testing of all communications equipment is advisable in the actual EMS system environment to see if any bugs develop. Just getting good equipment isn't enough.

Last, but not least, a factor in choosing equipment is phrased this way in the report of the ACEP Puerto Rico workshop: "A view toward compatability with existing hardware, spare parts, supplies, etc. At the time of the original purchase, the long-term expansion plan must be considered."

This means also a consideration of what's being done in other communities which may some day form part of the EMS system.

As noted, some of the features described are recommended by medical groups. Are there any overall governing standards like those concerning hose threads or the NFPA standards on fire apparatus and pumps? Unfortunately not yet, but they are on the way.

One difficulty has been the almost bewildering variety of groups and agencies involved in EMS. Besides the ACEP and the United States

Department of Transportation, these groups include: Association for the Advancement of Medical Instrumentation, Veterans Administration, Office of Telecommunications Policy, Bio-Medical Engineering Group of the Institute of Electrical Electronics Engineers, Food and Drug Administration, American Heart Association Committee on Electrocardiography, Emergency Medical Services Office of the Department of Health Education and Welfare, and National Center for Health Services Research and Development. The list seems endless.

Who's got the ball? Right now, everybody and nobody. Specs for monitor-defibrillator design fall in three categories. The first is concerned with patient and operator safety from electrocution, mechanical defects, etc. The second deals with survival of the equipment under vibration, impact, moisture, heat, etc. A third category is the functional spec, describing basic features the equipment needs to do the medical job.

Emergency service training

The term emergency medical technician was introduced, or at least popularized, back in 1966 when the United States Department of Transportation issued the first course for teaching basic skills in life support. It is now the course used by most fire departments in the country. But it was basic, and with the introduction of telemetry and other sophisticated equipment and techniques, the concept of the EMT was expanded and training increased.

Originally there was no uniform testing and certification program for EMTs and most communities did their own with varying results. But in the early '70s a national EMT registry was established that provides examination and certification for EMTs throughout the nation. Some states, however, have created their own standards for EMT training, testing and certification, feeling perhaps that local needs differ from other regions. The basic 81-hour EMT training program has had few changes since its inception but curriculums can vary considerably from state to state, and even regionally within a state. Since the DOT basic course came out, most states have gone beyond basic EMT training to some form of advanced EMT or paramedic. The hours and the scope of training for paramedics again vary from state to state.

To overcome these variances, Dunlap and Associates under a contract from DOT developed an advanced EMT training outline that requires 480 hours for completion. And in Florida, an EMT-II curriculum was created by the Miami Dade Community College on a grant from Florida Regional Medical Programs Inc. Rather than hours of training this curriculum emphasizes training units or modules.

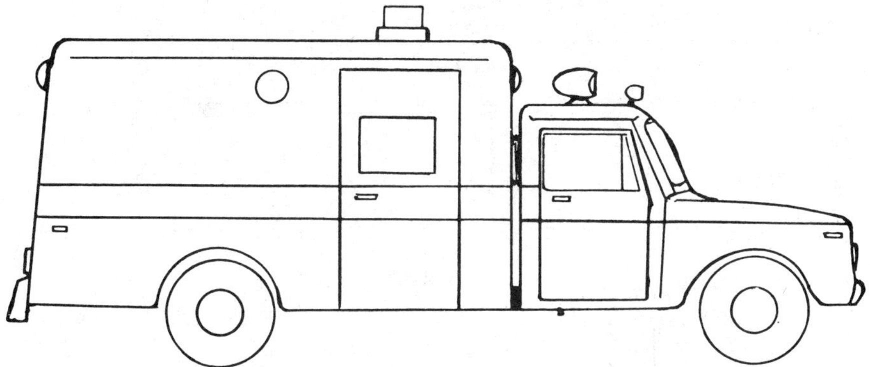

Type I Ambulance (per federal specification) is conventional cab-chassis with modular ambulance body.

As an example of how states vary in EMS practice, we can take the Glynn County, Ga., Fire Department and that of Birmingham, Ala. In Georgia, EMTs are required to pass a 125-hour state course and EMT-As receive an additional 40 hours in cardiology and 30 hours in IV therapy plus many hours of in-hospital training that covers the use of IM (intramuscular) and IV medications. There is also an advanced cardiac life support course that requires a minimum of 40 hours.

Turning to Birmingham, we find EMT-I, the basic course, intermediate EMT-II and advanced EMT-III. The courses include 500 hours in physician's assistant training, plus work in the emergency rooms of local hospitals. But no matter what the hours or the modules used, the training in all areas of emergency medical service is designed to teach the student to:

1. Communicate with a hospital from the field,
2. Monitor, interpret and transmit electrocardiograms,
3. Defibrillate patients,
4. Administer necessary drugs and fluids, and
5. Minister to victims of a variety of injuries stemming from auto accidents, drownings, electrocutions and many others.

Selecting the vehicle

"There is nothing magic about the size and shape of any form of vehicle if it is committed solely to transporting properly trained life support personnel to the scene of a medical emergency."[1]

Accordingly, any vehicle can be used and many fire departments have

---

[1] Page, James O., *Emergency Medical Services,* National Fire Protection Association, Boston, Mass.

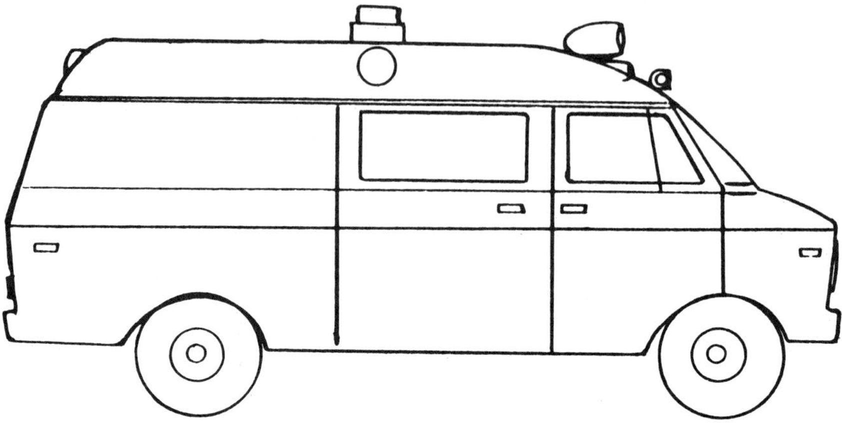

Type II ambulance is a standard van, integral cab-body vehicle.

entered the emergency medical service using the apparatus on hand, including pumpers, ladder trucks and rescue vehicles to get men and life-saving equipment to the scene. Actually the type vehicle selected will depend on the sophistication of the EMS that a fire department wishes to provide, and whether or not the vehicle will double as a rescue unit. Taking the City of Miami Fire Department (mentioned above), we find that the vehicles used for its paramedic service are fully equipped with the usual extrication tools, air masks, etc., in addition to a built-in scope, telemetry units, oxygen system, suction devices and others used for life support and treatment. Birmingham's fire medics also serve in a dual role as their title indicates. It is interesting to note that in both these departments the paramedic unit is called a "rescue" company. And that the Miami department units have the capability of transporting while the Birmingham do not. Miami, however, provides transport via contract ambulance, using their own vehicles in less than 2 percent of alarms.

Many other departments operate under the rescue-EMS concept, but just as many more separate these two functions, using only an ambulance equipped for emergency medical service and transport and the standard heavy-duty rescue unit.

Classes of vehicles

Ambulance design used to vary all over the drawing board, but in recent years the Division of Highway Safety of the Department of Transportation and the Department of Health Education and Welfare

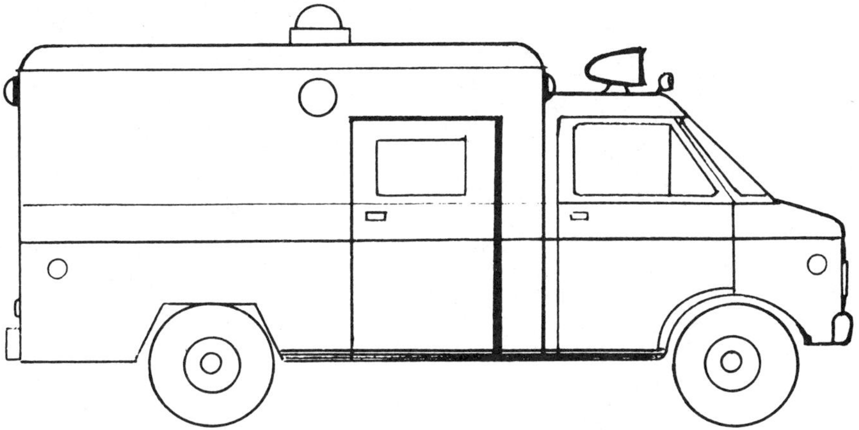

Type III is called a specialty van with integral cab-body ambulance.

have exerted considerable influence on ambulance design. Both departments provide funding for EMS equipment and those communities seeking this support will have to comply with the regulations of the departments. Among these regulations is that vehicles must comply with federal specifications for ambulance and emergency medical care vehicles. Manufacturers of vehicles adhere quite closely to these specs and as a consequence EMS has available to it what is basically a standard vehicle. And any vehicle built in compliance with the federal specification is considered to be a "standard ambulance." The specification covers everything from rustproofing to windshield wipers and is too lengthy for this chapter. One section, however, is of importance and is worth mentioning:

"Intended use. The vehicles covered by this specification are intended for on and off the road emergency medical services. The ambulance is designed with a driver compartment or cab, a patient compartment accommodating one medical technician and two litter patients. The ambulance (properly equipped and supplied) is intended to provide optimal emergency care, light extrication work at the scene of an emergency, and intensive life support for a least one patient during transit."

These specifications do not include all the varieties of ambulances which are commercially available. They cover only the ambulances generally purchased, or used to provide service under contract, or approved for funding by the federal government. The ambulances are specified under three types as indicated by the illustrations.

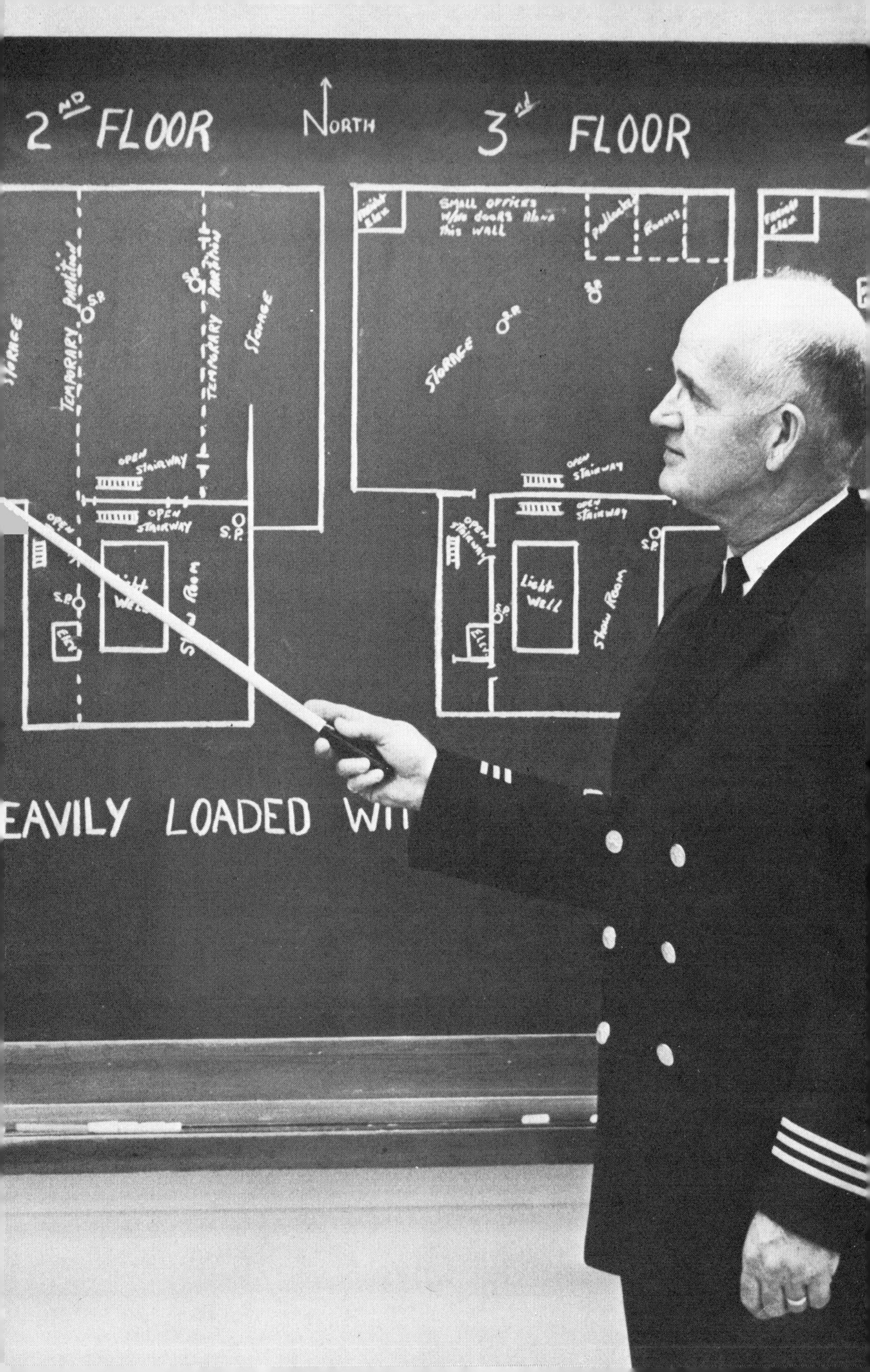

2ND FLOOR
NORTH
3rd FLOOR
TEMPORARY PARTITION
S.P.
STORAGE
OPEN STAIRWAY
LIGHT WELL
SHOW ROOM
SMALL OFFICES WITH DOORS ALONG THIS WALL
EAVILY LOADED WI

CHAPTER TWENTY-ONE

Teaching and training

In its simplest definition, training is learning. But the learning process requires an instructor and, therefore, training can also be called teaching. Actually, training is a combination of learning and teaching—which still sounds fairly simple. From here on, however, things get more and more complex as we move into the theory of learning, and eventually the principles and techniques of teaching.

So let us start with the word "learning." One definition of the word is: "the act or process of acquiring knowledge or skill." Another defines learning as: "knowledge acquired by systematic study in any field." Both, of course, take in the things that the learner could not do before, or perhaps not do well. The first refers to the manner or the means we use to learn, and the second to the results attained. The latter, however, depend on the knowledge or skill retained or memorized.

If a student or fire fighter is taught something one day and can't perform it a week later, he has learned nothing. What happened to him in that week? By an "act or process," he did insert something into the computer that we call a brain but he couldn't retrieve it—get a readout. Now, let's suppose the student did acquire some knowledge that he had used for a year. And then he had stopped using it for a year. Chances are that when he tried to again use or remember this knowledge, it had become at least blunted and possibly buried irretrievably in his computer. Why this happens can be explained by the psychologists with three words: **intensity, frequency and recency.**

Intensity refers to the initial impression or impressions that are planted in a student's mind. Intensity is best exemplified by the child who burns his hand on a stove. He has learned something, an association between hot stove and pain that he will never forget. This is, of course, memorizing the hard way but the principle here is that learning and remembering come easier if the initial impressions are meaningful, intense.

Frequency, of course, refers to drilling. And this is probably best exemplified by the neophyte typist who runs through a series of carefully designed lessons over and over again. At some point, his fingers and his mind will have memorized the keyboard to such a degree that he will unerringly strike the right key every time.

Recency can be defined as review. We all know that skills can be lost or impaired. The only way to hold them (once learned) is to exercise them at whatever intervals of time are deemed necessary to retain them. The golfer, who puts away his clubs in the fall after a final round of 85, often finds that on returning to the course in the spring he will shoot a 95 or worse. His skills have diminished from lack of practice.

Frequency and recency are easy to achieve in the disciplined atmosphere of a fire department. But intensity, in the learning or memorizing process, requires considerably more doing, particularly by the instructor.

How and what to teach

As mentioned before, in addition to learning, training is also teaching—what to teach and how to teach. The subjects to be taught derive from an analysis of a fire fighter's occupation, the essential information about his trade or occupation. This analysis provides an inventory of the various jobs that a fire fighter (in all ranks) must perform. The jobs are then arranged in a logical order and grouped in divisions of what a fire fighter does, what he should know, his sources of information and methods of instruction. While the purpose of analysis is to inventory the job knowledge and information, it also arranges this subject matter in an orderly and systematic outline—a chart to steer by.

Now, some might say, "Why bother with this analysis? It has already been made and published by many fire departments. All you have to do is get a copy and start in." This, of course, is a lazy man's attitude and, admittedly, it can work. But a good instructor and particularly the chief instructor, will derive much satisfaction, knowledge and value from making his own analysis of his own fire department and its jobs. After all, no two fire departments are exactly alike and some can vary considerably from region to region.

Cable TV hookup provides an electronic classroom in Rockford, Ill. fire station. Fire fighters use response units on table.

Knowing what to teach, however, is still only part of an instructor's job. Knowing how to teach comes next, and it is much more difficult than making an analysis of a fire fighter's occupation to establish a training program.

One idea leads to another

Knowing how to teach requires first a knowledge of how people learn, which brings us back to step 1: "the act or process of acquiring knowledge or skill." Starting from birth, people learn through the association of ideas. "One idea leads to another" is an expression that we are all familiar with and one that's as old as the hills.

The association of ideas, then, is a linking of past experiences with new conditions and experiences. This association can be compared to the *construction of a building.* The builder starts with a hole in the ground and fills it with a concrete footing—a foundation. Next he builds a frame that is supported by the footing and to this frame he attaches a siding and a roof. Beyond this, he finishes interior walls, installs plumbing and heating and what have you. Note that the roof is actually part of an interlocking chain that goes all the way back to a foundation.

So it is with the structure of learning, which is basically a linking process of one's own experiences. A person uses his own thinking apparatus, his brain—the computer—to achieve this linking process. This computer, of course, can't do anything without input. And the input is carried by the five bodily senses of touching, tasting, smelling, hearing and seeing. The stronger the message delivered to the brain, the better the learning. And a message that employs five senses instead of one or two will be the most effective. Which brings us back to the word *intensity* and the effect it has on the learning process.

Recall the child who burned his hand on the stove. Only one sense—touch—was involved here, but the initial impression that was sent to his brain-computer was so intense—meaningful—that it became instantly retrievable and for the rest of his life. An instructor can develop somewhat the same meaningfulness by taking a group of probationary fire fighters into a roomful of hot smoke for a brief period. This would, of course, be for the first time. Later when the men enter this room wearing masks, they will appreciate the comfort and safety that the mask provides. The combination of learning experiences is meaningful. For the same reason, the group could be taught to climb a ladder dressed in full protective equipment and with a hose stream hissing past them and splattering against the wall in front of them. Such teaching would involve at least three senses and again provide an intensity to the impressions entering the mind.

The fire service instructor

So far we have discussed how to teach from the learning viewpoint of the student. What about the teacher whom we call an instructor in the fire service? Teaching is at the same time an art and a science. The ability to teach depends on previous training, experience, disposition and intelligence. No matter how good a natural born teacher a man is, a systematic study of this other occupation—teaching—will make for better instruction and unquestionably a better fire department.

The first step in the teaching process is to prepare the mind of the learner for the new ideas to be presented. And you teach by using the techniques of demonstration, illustration and lecture on the new material. The student is then given the opportunity to apply the new ideas. As he develops in practice under actual test conditions and gains ability of performance, the lesson becomes a part of his experience that can be retrieved from this computer-brain at will.

According to Granito[1], there are six principles of learning that a teacher must know in order to teach properly. These principles in

---

[1] Granito, Anthony R., *Fire Instructor's Training Guide*, Dun-Donnelly Publishing Corporation, New York, N. Y.

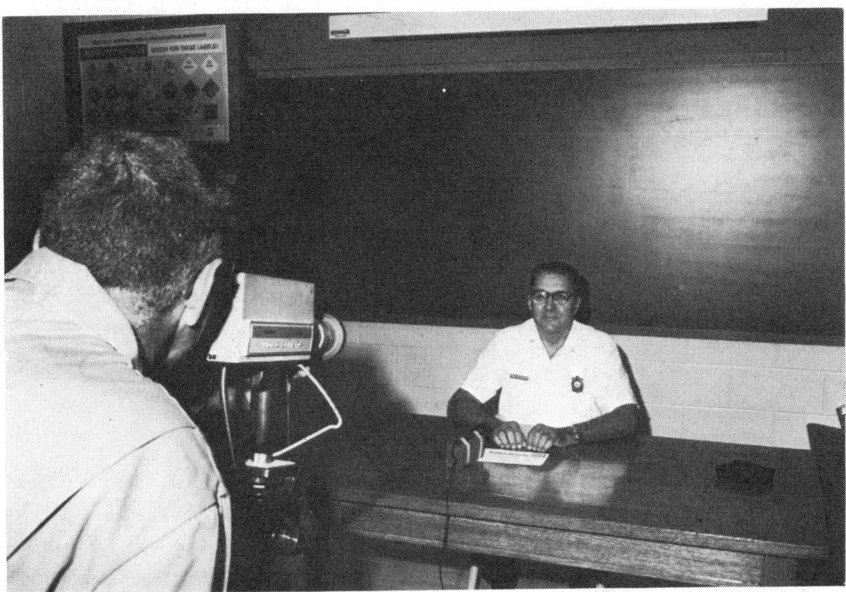

Video tapes are produced by the Rockford Fire Academy for viewing by fire fighters.

general describe the conditions under which learning takes place. They serve as guides to the instructor in his selection and use of teaching methods, devices and techniques. The principles are mutually supporting and all apply to each period of instruction:

1. Motivation. Learning is more efficient when the student is motivated properly—when he is mentally and physically ready to learn because he knows the reason why he should learn.

2. Objective. Learning is more efficient when the student knows exactly what he is to learn and what is expected of him.

3. Doing. One of the most efficient ways of learning is by doing.

4. Realism. The more realistic the learning situations, the more efficient the learning.

5. Background. A student acquires learning only by building upon what he already knows.

6. Appreciation. The learning process is not complete until the learner has acquired the attitudes, appreciations, interests, ideals, and habits of conduct which cause him to apply his knowledge in the desired direction to accomplish his fire service goal.

To use the techniques of *demonstration, illustration* and *lecture,* an instructor must take the by now traditional steps. These steps are: (1)

preparation, (2) presentation, (3) application, and (4) test. These four steps that the instructors use do not necessarily guarantee good teaching. They do, however, represent a form of imparting information (ideas) in a systematic manner and in keeping with the principles of learning.

Using the lecture technique as an example, let's see what steps a speaker takes to deliver an address, which are the same steps that an isntructor takes in preparing a lesson. He has a general arrangement, a scheme, a system or a form for presenting his message. He starts with an introduction (preparation), then gives the body of his speech (presentation), draws a few conclusions, and makes a summary (application) and the audience goes home to carry out his advice (test).

Lecture least effective

Of the three basic techniques—demonstration, illustration and lecture—the straight lecture is no doubt the least effective teaching method. Few people remember what they hear in a sermon or speech. There is limited carryover, mostly because with this technique the learner uses only his ears. Also, he has little chance to use his reasoning powers, since most of this has been done beforehand by the speaker. It is best, therefore, for a fire instructor to stick to the *demonstration* and *illustration* techniques, particularly when teaching the "hands-on" manipulative skills.

There are other techniques used in teaching, but they are really offshoots of the three basic techniques that have already been covered. One of them is the *discussion* which everyone has experienced many times in his life. In the discussion technique, three or four people stand around and argue or discuss a subject. This can be a very effective teaching method when one of the people is a trained instructor who can guide the discussion into the right channels.

A second technique that is frequently used by instructors is the *question and answer* method. This might appear to be the easiest method of all to use, but the ability to ask effective questions requires considerable skill, preparation and a thorough knowledge of the subject. Questions are used primarily to check on what the learner has learned. They can also be used to suggest a line of thought or to clarify information that a group has already received. Some questions are used to create interest.

Finally, there is the *experimental* method which has been called trial and error. A teen-age boy who fools around with his father's automobile can frequently become a proficient, if amateur auto mechanic. But while trial and error has certain advantages such as limited drain on an in-

Classroom lab at New York Fire Academy is equipped for demonstrations on physics and chemistry.

structor's time, it is not recommended. It is wasteful of the student's time and energy and hard on equipment. It is method of training that the fire service discarded 40 years ago.

In summary, the instructor must first prepare himself to be a teacher. And when he has done this, he must teach in such a way that the input to his student's brain-computer is intense and meaningful; something the student can effectively retrieve next week, next month, next year, aided, of course, by some recency and frequency.

Armed with the knowledge of the learning and teaching processes and an inventory of the fire fighter's occupation, a training instructor—and particularly the chief instructor—will still have to break his training program into the needs of the groups that it is designed to inform.

Needs of the group

The first training need in the fire service is to train the new man, beginning on the day he walks into the department. And the first thing to be done is to train him how to take care of himself—at a fire he has yet to fight. A fire fighter who steps into a hole in a roof and winds up in a hospital does nobody any good—including himself. A fire fighter who smashes his foot with an ax comes into the same category. So does the man who exceeds the limit of his mask.

Training in personal safety for the new man is therefore the first need for training. Careless, often stupid, actions must be eliminated else the cost in pain, anguish and money will be high.

Personal safety should be included in the basic training in which the fire service instructor strives to (1) impart information, (2) change attitudes, (3) improve working skills. Individual or group training can be used to attain any one of these three goals.

A fire department must, of necessity, go in for group training and fortunately, changes of attitude—concerning safety for instance—are more likely to result from such group training. However, the most important part of basic, or probationary, training is to teach and then improve working skills. This refers to the sensory-motor coordination needed for the performance of work.

As in other occupations, a fire service skill consists of three parts: technical knowledge, sensory observations and muscular coordination. Practically anything a fire fighter does has some of these three elements in it.

The fire prevention inspector has a skill which is largely one of knowledge. The pump operator has a skill which is largely a sensory development. And the nozzleman operating off a ladder has a skill which plays up muscular coordination. However, one can see where each task also has elements of the other two.

When a probationary fire fighter walks into a fire station or a training ground, he may not know the difference between a nozzle and a gas pipe. And as for knots, he can tie his shoelaces and maybe a package—but that's it. He needs the basic, repetitive training in the multitude of skills which he will eventually assemble into an efficient whole to be a fire fighter.

Every fire fighter should be able to put on a self-contained mask with his eyes closed. He should be able to tie a bowline-on-bight with his hands behind his back. He should be able to hold a nozzle so that it will never be wrested from his hands by a sudden pressure surge.

This is basic training. This is what the new man needs. Training instructors must tell him, show him, have him do it and, finally, check on how well he has done it. After he knows how to do it, he must do it over and over until he reaches a point where he'll never forget—the frequency that we mentioned previously.

Teamwork needed

Once the new man has acquired the basic skills, he must be trained in the big picture—the entirety of fire fighting. It is not enough for him to know how to screw a nozzle on a hose butt and how to manipulate the control handle. He must be then shown how to stretch the hose, told

Live-fire training under realistic conditions provides fire fighters with the confidence and skills needed in the field.

when to call for water and then how and where to direct the stream. And preferably, he should direct the stream on an actual fire on the drill ground.

Even when the new fire fighter knows how to don a mask, swing an ax, play a nozzle, climb a ladder, he is still like a rough-cut diamond which has little value until it is polished. He doesn't know much about the art of fire fighting. Here is where the second need for training enters. The new man must be taught to operate with a group—two groups actually. One is the company to which he is assigned and in which he will work with four or five men, for instance, on the relatively uncomplicated action of stretching a line into a hallway of a burning building. The other is the big group—his fire department—in which he and his company will have to work with other companies in the cohesive action called teamwork.

In the latter he will have to stop concentrating on the simple basic skill, which by now should be an almost reflex action, and turn his attention to what is happening around him. It is in this phase of training that he

Multi-unit drills simulating what takes place in the field provide training in teamwork.

will start to use his judgment. The instructor will point out that one doesn't clutter up the street in front of a fire building with apparatus that is not being used. That one doesn't fill up the street with 20 lengths of hose when eight will do the job. That one doesn't direct a master stream into a floor until he is sure that there are no firemen operating on this floor. That one doesn't direct a ladder pipe stream into a hole in a roof that has been cut for ventilation, and thereby ensure that no ventilation will take place. These and many more are the higher skills that a fireman must acquire, but they are still only on a little higher plane than the basics.

From here the fire fighter goes on to learn tactics—the third need for training. And it is with tactics that he finally enters the field of higher education in fire fighting. In this phase of training, instructors concentrate on the placement of manpower and equipment at a fire. Nothing looks more ridiculous than a group of enginemen, with the wind at their backs, chasing a fire across a meadow, or from one pile of lumber to another in a fiercely burning lumberyard. It's just as ridiculous for truckmen, also with the wind at their backs, to open a skylight on a roof only to have the fire leap hungrily out of the fire building and into the windows of an adjoining building.

Such happenings, such poor tactics, should not occur in a well-trained department. On his way up the ladder of training, which becomes more complex with each step, the new man must be taught tactics. He must be told that the weather affects tactics. Is it raining? How strong is the wind, and from what direction is it coming? Is it a hot day that will cause windows to be open in exposed buildings?

He must also be told that the construction of a building affects tactics. Is the stairway of such fireproof construction that it will permit him to take his line in reasonably safety to the fire floor? Would it be better not to ventilate in certain situations? Is it better to take the first line to the floor above rather than directly in on the fire floor? Or is it even better to take the first line into the adjoining building rather than into the fire building?

Another condition that affects tactics is the occupancy of a building. A crowded apartment house calls for a thorough laddering of the face of the building. A one-story warehouse might call for just one ladder to the roof for ventilation.

Company officer decisions

These are just a few of the factors that affect tactics and come under a heading that is called size-up. This size-up is tremendously important to know and be skilled in. Decisions made in the first minutes of a fire often determine whether there will be a building with relatively light fire damage or a building destroyed. These decisions are generally made by company officers first on the scene and not the chief.

Eventually the new fire fighter, if he has been instructed properly, will become skilled not only in the basics but in the more sophisticated skills—tactics. By this time he has acquired some experience in fighting actual fires. He is now ready to become an officer. This leads to the fourth need for training, which is the need for training in leadership, or management.

Someone once said that leaders are born not made. But if the fire service waits for someone—a whole lot of someones—to be born, the fire losses will continue to rise.

The fire service, in the person of the chief of department and his training instructors, therefore must train men in leadership-management as it does in other skills. But before a chief can train a man in leadership, he must search for those in his group who seem most capable of becoming leaders. This search should be an organized and continuing effort. The principal searching devices are observation, study of personal history, aptitude testing and rating by supervisors.

In most departments, the burden falls on the fire chief. And the persons who can assist in the development of fire officers—the leader

A full variety of audio-visual aids are required for maximum teaching efficiency.

managers—are principally the *man himself,* his immediate supervisor and the fire chief and his assistants, who constitute the top management of a fire department.

There are various management training devices which all organizations have used successfully and which are designed to improve a man's knowledge (what he should know about his job), his activities (what he does—his actual performance), and his personal traits (what he is, how he gets along with other people).

In addition to these somewhat general development devices of management, there are certain specifics which can be applied to the entire fire service or to individual fire departments where geography, economics and size dictate differently. There are libraries filled with information on the subject of management training, and it is here that the training officer must take over. It is much too broad a subject to cover in a short chapter. The point to remember is that any organization is about as good as its leaders and a fire department is no different.

The fifth need for training is tied in with the leadership mentioned above and the tactics discussed previously. This fifth need concerns strategy, which lies mainly in the realm of the chief of department and his higher-echelon assistants, but which occasionally depends on a junior officer.

In the long run, it is strategy that will determine whether a fire will be confined to one building or one block. Strategy determines whether a fire station will be built on one side of the railroad tracks or the other; and whether that newly developing section in the north end of town will need a new fire station in three or in five years.

Strategy involves the making of command decisions. And it is a rare department that can satisfy solely from within its own ranks the training in the making of command decisions.

The chief who wants to find out how to make command decisions must not only look to his own experience but also look beyond. He should read widely in his field. He should subscribe to the professional journals of the fire service to keep informed about the latest developments. He should attend various state and national fire schools and conferences, and he should be a member of the various associations. It is only through association with his peers, by reading their papers, or at the various meetings and conferences, that he can acquire the enlargement of experience that is called knowledge.

CHAPTER TWENTY-TWO

Chemistry and physics of combustion

Because of the fact that all combustion and fire involves chemical reactions and many of the effects of fire that can be easily observed involve the physics of heat phenomena, the professional fire fighter must know something about these two branches of science—chemistry, which concerns itself with the properties and interactions of matter and materials; and physics, which measures various purely physical characteristics and shows the relationship of types of energy.

The study of these subjects need not be complicated nor difficult to meet most of the needs of the fire service. This chapter covers the basic and important facts about combustion which can be used to explain what happens in ordinary fires. With this knowledge the fire fighter can attack everyday, common problems with a feeling of mastery instead of mystery.

Fire is chemical combustion or oxidation

When a burnable substance unites with oxygen in a rapid manner, heat—and usually bright light—is given off, and the substance is said to "burn." Burning is then, a rapid *oxidation*. The oxygen provided for most fires comes from the air surrounding the combustible. Air always consists of approximately 21 percent (or one-fifth) oxygen gas and approximately 79 percent (or four-fifths) nitrogen gas. The nitrogen part of air acts as a diluent to the oxygen to slow up burning reactions. If it were not present, all fires would proceed very rapidly and attempts to halt them would be very difficult indeed. On the other hand, if there were more nitrogen in ordinary air, burning or oxidation of burnable substances would proceed very slowly and the fire fighter's job would be very simple. The only difficulty here is that our bodies too need oxygen for the "process of life." This sustainment of life is also a "burning" or oxidation reaction and we must have oxygen continually supplied at almost the exact ratio of 21 percent to 79 percent nitrogen or our "combustion" of food would either go too fast or too slow and illness or death would follow.

Burning or combustion can be represented like this:

Paper (burnable substance) + Oxygen (in air)
= Paper Oxide (ash) and Heat (and Light)

Now, if we make this into a chemical equation (both sides of the = sign are equal), and if we designate pure carbon as the burnable substance, we have:

$$C + O_2 = CO_2 + \text{Heat (and Light)}$$

Notice that we designate oxygen gas as a diatomic element and, of course, the union of carbon and oxygen, carbon dioxide, is a gaseous substance which, although it is "carbon ash," will disappear as a gas.

All kinds and types of combustion and burning can be represented in this way, i.e., as chemical oxidation reactions.

Flame or visible light is usually produced during chemical combustion or fire. It is important to know that all flames consist of burning gases or vapors. When combustible substances "catch fire," we really mean that the substance has been heated to its *ignition temperature* in some way and it will then continue to burn by decomposing to give off combustible gases or by vaporizing (if it is a liquid) into a gaseous form. Since the oxygen in air is a gas, it can mix and unite vigorously with combustible substances to give a flame only when the combustible is in gaseous form.

Chemical formulas and some basic definitions

The modern profession of fire protection has become complicated because of the great progressive strides of recent science and technology. New hazards have arisen and new chemical compounds are being produced which the intelligent fire fighter must know about if he is going to be capable of combating the fire and the threat to life safety which these new materials present. Chemical formulas and a knowledge of various important basic properties of substances are important to understanding what can and does happen in a fire.

A *chemical formula* is a type of "shorthand" which shows the number of atoms of elements which combine in that ratio to give a molecule of a compound with definite properties or characteristics. The symbols which denote the various elements are in Table 1, which gives only the common elements.

The *atomic* weight of an element indicates the weight of its atom as compared with the weight of an atom of oxygen, which has been arbitrarily assigned as 16.000. Example: an atom of hydrogen, H, atomic weight 1.008, weighs about 1/16th the weight of an atom of oxygen, atomic weight 16.000. Atomic weights of the more common elements are given in Table 1.

The *molecular* weight of a compound is the sum of the weights of all atoms in its molecule. Subscripts after an element's symbol indicate the number of atoms of that element present. For instance, water H_2O, is a compound having molecules consisting of two atoms of hydrogen and one atom of oxygen and is formed according to the reaction: $2H_2 + O_2 = 2H_2O$. The molecular weight of water is $2(1.008) + 1(16.000) = 18.016$.

An *oxidizing agent* is a material that is capable of reacting with a combustible material in a combustion type of reaction similar to the way that oxygen of the air reacts with combustibles. Heat is generated by this union. Certain oxidizing agents will start this reaction without any external application of heat or ignition by flame. Sometimes, the reaction proceeds so fast that it is called an explosion. Common hydrogen peroxide, oxygen and ozone, and the nitrates, chlorates, perchlorates and peroxides are in the class of oxidizing agents.

A *reducing agent* is a material which will react with an oxidizing agent in a combustion type of reaction. All combustible fuels which contain carbon and hydrogen are reducing agents. Combustible metals, such as magnesium and sodium, are also reducing agents.

The *specific gravity* of a substance is the ratio of the weight of the substance to the weight of the same volume of another substance. Specific gravity, as commonly used, refers to the ratio of the weight of a solid or liquid substance to the weight of an equal volume of water.

Vapor density is the relative density of a vapor or gas (with no air present) as compared with air. A figure less than 1 indicates a vapor is lighter than air, and a figure greater than 1 that a vapor is heavier than air.

To calculate the vapor density of a compound, the following formula may be used.

$$\text{Vapor density of a compound} = \frac{\text{Molecular weight of a compound}}{29}$$

In the formula, 29 is the composite molecular weight of air. This formula gives reasonably accurate estimates of vapor density only when there is no disassociation of molecules at the time of vaporization.

Vapor pressure and boiling point

Because molecules of a liquid are always in motion with the amount of motion depending on the temperature of the liquid, they are continually escaping from the liquid to the space above.

If the liquid is in an open container, the molecules of the liquid substance tend to escape from the surface or move away from above the liquid, and the liquid is vaporizing or is said to evaporate. On the other hand, if the liquid is in a closed container, the motion of the escaping molecules is confined to any vapor space above. As an increasing number escape only to re-enter the liquid, a point of equilibrium is eventually reached when the rate of escape of molecules from the liquid equals the rate of their return to the liquid. The pressure exerted by the escaping vapor at this point of equilibrium is called the vapor pressure of the liquid. Vapor pressures are measured in pounds per square inch, absolute (psia) or millimeters of mercury (mm).

In order to fully understand the workings of atmospheric pressure and its variation by means of suction pumps and other pressure changing situations, it is convenient to picture that we live on the earth at the bottom of a sea of air. Just as in the bottom of the ocean, the pressure of the water is greater the farther you are below the water's surface, so it is at the bottom of our sea of air which we call our atmosphere. We live and breathe under an almost constant air pressure of 14.7 pounds per square inch.

Remembering what was said about vapor pressures of liquids in an earlier paragraph, it is now easy to see that when the temperature of a liquid is raised to the point at which the pressure of the molecules (the vapor) escaping from the surface is equal to the atmospheric pressure, the vapor comes off the liquid at a fast rate and huge vapor bubbles will form in the liquid and come to the surface. The liquid is then said to be boiling and this temperature is the *boiling point* of the liquid.

Table I The Common Chemical Elements

Element	Symbol	Atomic Wt.
Aluminum	Al	26.98
Antimony	Sb	121.76
Argon	A	39.944
Arsenic	As	74.91
Barium	Ba	137.36
Beryllium	Be	9.013
Bismuth	Bi	209.00
Boron	B	10.82
Bromine	Br	79.916
Cadmium	Cd	112.41
Calcium	Ca	40.08
Carbon	C	12.011
Chlorine	Cl	35.457
Chromium	Cr	52.01
Cobalt	Co	58.94
Copper	Cu	63.54
Fluorine	F	19.00
Gold	Au	197.0
Helium	He	4.003
Hydrogen	H	1.0080
Iodine	I	126.91
Iron	Fe	55.85
Krypton	Kr	83.8
Lead	Pb	207.21
Lithium	Li	6.940
Magnesium	Mg	24.32
Manganese	Mn	54.94
Mercury	Hg	200.61
Molybdenum	Mo	95.95
Neon	Ne	20.183
Nickel	Ni	58.71
Nitrogen	N	14.008
Oxygen	O	16.000
Phosphorus	P	30.975
Platinum	Pt	195.09
Potassium	K	39.100
Radium	Ra	226.05
Rubidium	Rb	85.48
Silicon	Si	28.09
Silver	Ag	107.880
Sodium	Na	22.991
Strontium	Sr	87.63
Sulfur	S	32.066
Tantalum	Ta	180.95
Tin	Sn	118.70
Titanium	Ti	47.90
Tungsten	W	183.86
Uranium	U	238.07
Vanadium	V	50.95
Xenon	Xe	131.30
Zinc	Zn	65.38
Zirconium	Zr	91.22

Flammable liquids give off vapors from their surface which are capable of burning in air. However, sustained burning or *flame propagation* (spreading) cannot occur in the space above such liquids unless enough vapor is present in proportion to the air (and vice versa, enough air in proportion to the flammable vapor) to sustain the ignition of a continuous flame.

Flammable or explosive limits

In the case of gases or vapors which form flammable mixtures with air or oxygen, there is a minimum concentration of vapor in air or oxygen below which propagation of flame does not occur on contact with a source of ignition. There is also a maximum proportion of vapor or gas in air *above which* propagation of flame does *not* occur. These boundary-line mixtures of vapor or gas with air, which if ignited will just propagate flame, are shown as the "lower and upper flammable or explosive limits," and are usually expressed in terms of percentage by volume of gas or vapor in air.

In everyday terms, a mixture of flammable vapor in air below the lower flammable limit is too lean to burn or explode, and a mixture above the upper flammable limit is too rich to burn or explode.

The flammable limit figures of combustible vapors or bases are based upon normal atmospheric temperatures and pressures, unless otherwise indicated. There may be considerable variation in flammable limits at pressures or temperatures above or below normal. Increases in temperature always increase the distance between flammable limits. Increases in pressure above atmospheric may or may not affect the flammable limits, depending upon the nature of the vapor involved, but substantial decreases in pressure most always tend to narrow the distance between flammable limits.

No attempt is made here to differentiate between the terms "flammable" and "explosive" as applied to the lower and upper limits of flammability. The range of combustible vapor or gas-air mixtures between the upper and lower flammable limits is known as the "flammable range"; also it is often referred to as the "explosive range." For example, the *lower* limit of flammability of the chemical liquid acrylonitrile at ordinary ambient temperatures is approximately 3 percent vapor in air by volume, while its *upper* limit of flammability is about 17 percent. All concentrations by volume of acrylonitrile vapor in air falling between 3 percent and 17 percent are in the flammable or explosive range.

The *flash point* of a liquid is the lowest temperature of the liquid at which it gives off vapor sufficient to form an ignitible mixture with the air near the surface of the liquid or within the vessel used. By "ignitible mixture" is meant a mixture within the flammable range (between upper and lower limits) that is capable of the propagation of flame away from the source of ignition when ignited. Combustion is not continuous at the flash point. Some evaporation takes place below the flash point when vapor does not go off freely enough to meet flash point classification requirements. This term applies mostly to flammable liquids, although there are certain solids such as camphor and naphthalene, that slowly sublime (change from a solid to a vapor) at ordinary room temperature and therefore have flash points while still in the solid state.

Fire point is the lowest temperature of a liquid in an open container at which vapors are evolved fast enough to support a continuous combustion. The fire point is usually a few degrees above the flash point.

The *ignition temperature* of a substance, whether it is a solid, liquid, or gas (or vapor), is that minimum temperature to which the substance must be heated in order to cause it to burn or cause it to propagate combustion in a self-sustained manner. In general, ignition temperatures should be regarded as only approximations because of the fact that small changes in conditions surrounding the ignition can cause large changes in the observed ignition temperature or point at which the substance propagates (spreads) flame without further application of the igniting source (match flame, spark or heated point). In the case of solid substances like wood, the ignition temperature means that point at which the wood fiber begins to decompose sufficiently to give off combustible gases which are evolved continuously so that their combustion can give off heat to make more wood fiber decompose. The process must continue without further application of heat or flame from an external source. It can be easily seen that the conditions surrounding the wood, such as the air flow over the material and the speed of its heating can vitally influence the temperature at which the self-sustained combustion takes place.

Basic properties of materials that influence combustion

Because of the fact that all of the world around us consists of *matter* and chemical *materials* with many different properties, combustion and fire proceed in different ways in different materials and with varying speed or severity. The temperature surrounding combustible materials also causes combustion to take place in different ways.

Temperature, of course, is closely related to *heat,* which always accompanies burning or an oxidation (combustion) reaction. The extent or amount of heat that is evolved and what happens to it during a fire are of critical importance and will be dealt with in detail later.

One of the most important factors influencing the combustion and propagation of flame and the severity of fire fighting problems is the extent to which a combustible substance has been subdivided or the average state of size of single particles. Since combustible fuels of all types must be fully mixed with, or their surfaces fully exposed to, oxygen or an oxidizing agent of any kind before combustion can take place, the smaller the size of the fuel subdivision (and thus the greater proportion of surface exposed), the more quickly can this mixing and exposure take place. In the case of solid materials, powders and thin sections, or even threads or "fluffed-up" surfaces, burn easily and rapidly, whereas large solid pieces will resist burning until their exposed surfaces can be raised in temperature. In the case of flammable liquids, an aerosol composed of a very fine spray or droplets of the liquid will burn easily and quickly. The vapor from flammable liquids will burn even more quickly because vapors have similar physical properties to gases. Obviously, combustible gases are the most easily burned of all substances because they mix in all proportions with the oxygen gas in air. Burning of combustible gases when they are properly mixed with air proceeds with explosive rates and violence.

Chemical stability of molecules

Substances "burn" in a variety of ways. The particular manner in which oxygen unites with combustible materials is largely dependent on the *chemical stability* of the molecules in the compounds that make up the substance. Unstable chemical compounds change their characteristics easily when exposed to heat and oxygen. Ordinary oil-base paint, for instance, when spread in thin films for decorating purposes, begins to slowly unite with oxygen, reacting within its own composition, and develops hardness and changes its character to a smooth surface-protecting coating. When heat is applied to such a coating, the molecules in the paint film change their properties and begin to give off combustible gases and decompose to other substances which quickly oxidize, violently burning and blistering and exposing the surface beneath them.

This same unstable oil in paints is responsible for the occurrence of *spontaneous ignition* in many cases. This type of burning is characterized by slow oxidation of a substance like linseed oil (or any vegetable *drying oil*) within an enclosure of some type containing air which holds in the heat of the reaction of the union of oxygen with the oil. When an insulated space becomes the enclosure for this slow oxidation, the temperature of the oil goes up and any combustible material with which the oil is in contact (such as rags, etc.) begins to rise in temperature also and soon active burning takes place. In general, chemical reactions double in their speed or rate with each 18°F rise in temperature so that the ignition temperature of the mixture of oil-soaked rags is reached relatively rapidly when heat cannot be dissipated as it is produced, however small or minute it was in the beginning.

Mineral oils of all types are stable substances and do not oxidize in air at ordinary temperatures, consequently they cannot slowly generate heat. Almost all vegetable oils are "drying" (oxidizable) oils containing unstable or unsaturated chemical compounds and can cause spontaneous combustion under the correct conditions of oxygen exposure and heat confinement.

Rate of oxygen supplied

Another important factor that influences combustion processes to a very great extent involves the *rate* at which *oxygen* is supplied to the site where combustion occurs. When a combustible substance burns, it produces materials which are noncombustible. In fact, most burning reactions produce inert gases like water vapor and carbon dioxide which, if they were confined to the same area where the burning took place, would be capable of smothering the fire and would cause self-extinguishment of the fire. The slowly decreasing burning of a candle in a closed glass jar, ending in flame extinction, illustrates this type of extinguishment through its own products of combustion.

The converse of the above reaction can be shown by the way in which the burning of combustible materials of all types can be accelerated by forcing air (containing its 21 percent oxygen) into the burning zone of a fire. When the velocity of the air supplied to a fire is increased, it acts to more quickly remove the inert gases of burning from the burning zone, blowing away any solid ash produced in the combustion and making oxygen more available to complete the combustion process. When a smoldering fire in a fireplace is blown up with bellows or with the breath, the action brings more oxygen to the glowing embers, raising their *rate* of combustion and causing nearby combustibles to heat up and enflame.

It is impossible to list all the chemical and physical properties of the many thousands of hazardous materials and compounds which the fire protection expert might encounter in his experience with fires. There are many important reference tables which may be used for this purpose. These tables and compilations contain information such as flash points, ignition temperatures, vapor densities or specific gravities and water solubilities and other characteristics of vital importance to the knowledgeable fire fighter.

The dynamic processes of ignition and combustion

Progress has been made over the past few years by science and technology in learning more about what goes on in the combustion and burning process of fire and in the chemistry of controlling fire. Although a great deal more remains to be discovered about this complex phenomenon, there are many new bits of valuable knowledge which the modern fire expert can employ to help him to better understand and combat this complicated and evasive enemy. Knowledge is power, and the onward march of civilization complicates the fire fighters' task each year with new, more hazardous materials and fire fighting problems, each of which requires the generation of new information.

Oxidation or combustion processes of fire are dynamic, continuously reacting, processes. They are unbalanced and unsatisfied systems containing energy seeking an equilibrium between the molecules of the reactants of the system to a lower, less active level of energy. In the course of this procedure they give off heat energy in the form of fire and flame. These processes are initiated by a small input of activation energy (spark) to start the reaction, after which propagation (flame spread) continues as long as there is a supply of energy (combustible) and a reactant (oxygen) for consummation of a union to a more satisfied, lower level of energy (ash).

The reactions which occur during combustion and burning are *chain reactions* which branch off or fragment into very active chemical species called *free radicals.* These free radicals are very reactive, unstable combinations of atoms which are only temporarily present and immediately link up with other atoms to form more stable molecular compounds.

Research has shown that extinguishment procedures that utilize actual chemical reactivity for halting the process of the fire, attack these free radical fragments, rendering them incapable of furthering or extending the combustion chain reaction. This is more extensively treated in a succeeding section on the fire triangle picturization.

Fire fighting personnel who have witnessed large, difficultly controlled fires can quickly understand that combustion is a steadily increasing, time-rate oxidation reaction involving many vigorous chemical (and physical) reactions. The fire "supports itself" and the rate at which it continues depends upon a host of factors, not the least of which concerns the type of material burning and the chemistry of such fuel. In most cases, unwanted fires consist of *diffusion flames,* that is, the fuel mixes (or diffuses) with the air or oxygen as the fire proceeds to make combustible vapors available. The graphic picturization shown in Figure

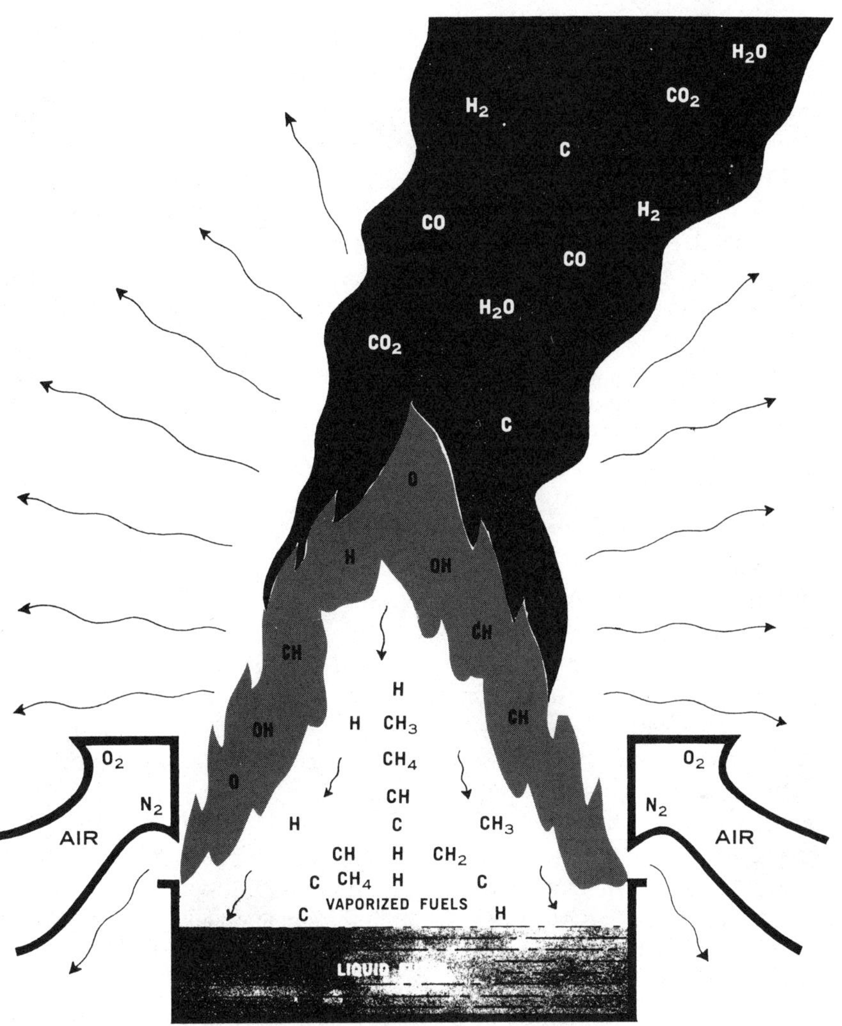

THE ANATOMY OF FIRE

Figure 1.

1 depicts the many free radicals and the chemical entities produced in a typical fire. Similar reasoning can be used to show what occurs in fires where almost any fuel is concerned. Obviously, chemical reasoning is an important factor in explaining the phenomena of unplanned combustion, which situation will continue to exist as long as mankind uses

combustible materials in his life at the bottom of a sea of air containing one-fifth oxygen.

HEAT AND ITS METHODS OF TRANSFER

The most important and most easily observed characteristic of fires and oxidation reactions is their evolution of heat. Fortunately, this property is quickly and easily detected by the human senses and the professional fire fighter must be constantly aware of the extent of the heat evolution of his fire at all times so that he may judge its effect and take appropriate actions from every point of view, with the objective of achieving successful control of the combustion process. This chapter is concerned with a survey and study of the physical factor of heat in fires and its companion phenomena, temperature elevation and light evolution.

What is heat and how is it measured?

Basically, heat is a *form* of *energy* which is produced when a substance undergoes a change from a *higher* state of energy to a *lower* one. In the oxidation process of combustibles, an "active" and reactive material like gasoline vapor unites with oxygen in the air, producing heat, bright flames, and infrared radiation, and under the right conditions violent explosions, to end up as an inert, nonreactive gas, carbon dioxide, along with water vapor, a relatively inactive material. The heat given off during the process is transferred to its surroundings, where it causes an increase in the "state of the activity" of the molecules of matter in this surrounding area. The intensity of this increase is shown by a *temperature rise* in the matter making up the surroundings, whatever they might be. The *amount* of heat which has been evolved and transferred may be measured in terms of calories or Btu (British thermal units).

The technically accurate description of the evolution of heat from burning combustible material is considerably more involved than is indicated in the above paragraph and requires a more lengthy consideration of *entropy, thermodynamics* and energy levels of *light* and *electromagnetic radiation.*

The following definitions are important in the understanding of heat and its detection and measurement.

The *temperature* of a material is the measurement of the heat "condition" of a material which indicates whether it can take up heat from its surroundings or give it out to its surroundings. It is a purely relative measurement and has been standardized in terms of the melting of ice and the boiling of pure water as follows:

Fahrenheit degrees denote the melting point of ice as 32 degrees and the boiling point of water as 212 degrees. The difference between these points is divided equally into 180 divisions (or degrees). Temperatures above and below this range maintain the same increment of measurement.

Celsius degrees denote the melting point of ice as zero degrees and the boiling point of water as 100 degrees. The difference between these points is divided equally into 100 divisions.

To convert Celsius to Fahrenheit, multiple the °C by $9/5$ and add 32. To find °C, subtract 32 from the °F and multiple the result by $5/9$.

Remember, the above additions and subtractions must be done algebraically below zero according to sign. It is also convenient to remember that -40°C equals -40°F.

A *British thermal unit (Btu)* is defined basically as that quantity of heat required to raise the temperature of 1 pound of water 1 degree Fahrenheit. It is a heat quantity unit of measurement that may go in either direction, *to* a body (when fire causes heat to raise the temperature of its surroundings) or *from* a body (when a combustible burns, releasing heat from the burning process undergone by the combustible body).

A *calorie* is defined as that amount of heat required to raise the temperature of 1 gram of water, 1 degree Celsius. (Note that this unit of measurement is similar to the Btu, but on a decimal C.G.S. system.)

The *heat capacity* of a substance, or its *thermal capacity,* is that property of a material for absorbing heat with a consequent temperature rise per unit weight. It is measured in terms of heat units necessary to raise the temperature of the substance 1 degree, i.e. the number of Btu required to raise the temperature of 1 pound of a substance 1 degree Fahrenheit; or the number of calories required to raise the temperature of 1 gram of a substance 1 degree Celsius. Heat capacity should not be confused with the term *heat content,* which involves many other factors not necessary to cover here such as the thermodynamic term of *enthalpy,* which is complicated by considerations of volume and pressure.

The *specific heat* of a substance is the ratio of the heat capacity of the substance to the heat capacity of water at 60°F (15°C). This value is 1.00 Btu per pound (or 1.00 calories per gram). It can be seen that specific heat, heat capacity and thermal capacity are synonymous terms in this sense.

The specific heats of various substances vary over a considerable range. This can be seen by Table 2.

The table shows that if it takes 1000 Btu of heat from a fire to raise the temperature of 1000 pounds of water 1 degree Fahrenheit, it only requires a heat input of 694 Btu from a fire to raise the temperature

Table 2 Specific Heats of Some Common Materials

Substance	Specific Heat	Substance	Specific Heat
Water	1.00	Zinc	0.093
Ice	0.502	Iron	0.109
Paraffin	0.694	Platinum	0.032
Copper	0.093	Mercury	0.033

of 1000 pounds of paraffin 1°F and only 109 Btu to raise the temperature of 1000 pounds of iron 1°F. Conversely, the same relationship holds in lowering the temperatures of these substances 1°F by removing heat or subtracting Btu in order to cool them to safe temperatures.

One reason for the effectiveness of water as a heat removing and fire extinguishing agent can be seen in its high specific heat.

Heat is absorbed by a substance when it is converted from a solid to a liquid, and from a liquid to a gas. Conversely, heat is released during conversion of a gas to a liquid or a liquid to a solid.

Latent heat is the quantity of heat absorbed or given off by a substance in passing between liquid and gaseous phases (latent heat of vaporization) or between solid and liquid phases (latent heat of fusion). Latent heats are measured in Btu or calories per unit weight. The latent heat of water (normal atmospheric pressure) at the freezing or melting point of ice (32°F) is 143.4 Btu per pound; the latent heat of water at the boiling point (212°F) is 970.3 Btu per pound. The high heat of vaporization of water is another reason for the effectiveness of water as an extinguishing agent. The latent heats of most other common substances are substantially less than that of water. Table 3 contains examples of latent and specific heats.

Thermal expansion of all substances occurs when they are heated. In no service is the phenomena of expansion by heating so frequently applied as in the fire service. Thermostats and fire-detecting alarms represent useful applications of it, while the expansion of steel girders at a fire is an example of a manner in which it proves damaging. Solids expand in every direction when heated and contract when cooled. But all solids do not contract nor expand the same amount when cooled or heated to the same extent, nor do liquids. On the contrary, all gases expand very nearly alike at atmospheric pressure when heated in like amounts.

There are three kinds of expansion which a body may undergo: linear expansion, superficial expansion and cubical expansion. Linear expansion is the increase in length; superficial expansion is the increase in area; cubical expansion is the increase in volume.

Table 3 Examples of Latent and Specific Heats

	Latent Heat of Fusion at Melting Point		Latent Heat of Vaporization at Boiling Point		Specific Heat at Listed Temperature	
	Cal/ gram	Melting Point °C	Cal/ gram	Boiling Point °C	Cal/ gram	At Temp °C
Acetone	23.4	−95.5	124.5	56.1	0.506	0
n-Butane	19.2	−138.3	92.1	−0.5	0.549	0
Carbon Tetrachloride	41.6	−22.8	46.42	76.8	0.198	0
Ethyl Alcohol	25.8	−114.4	204.26	78.3	0.680	0
Water	79.8	0.0	539.6	100.0	1.008 1.000	0 15

The coefficient of linear expansion is the fraction of its length a body expands when heated from 0 to 1 degree Celsius.

The coefficient of superficial expansion is the fraction of its area a body expands when heated from 0 to 1 degree Celsius.

The coefficient of cubical expansion is the fraction of its volume a body expands when heated from 0 to 1 degree Celsius.

In the fire service, the buckling of hot girders when struck by water, the crackling of cast iron ornaments and building fronts when in a heated condition and struck by cold streams, and the bulging of walls due to elongation of girders are common examples of expansion and contraction.

The methods of transfer of heat

Transfer of heat is responsible for the start and extinguishment of most fires. Heat is transferred by one or more of three basic mechanisms or methods: (1) *conduction,* (2) *radiation,* or (3) *convection.*

Heat is transferred by *conduction* from one body to another by direct contact or through an intervening solid, liquids, or gas heat-conducting medium, as through a teaspoon removed from hot coffee to the hand. Thus, a steam pipe in contact with wood transfers its heat to the wood by actual contact. In this example, the pipe is the *conductor.* The amount of heat transferred by conduction depends upon the thermal conductivity of the materials through which the heat is passing and the area and thickness of the conducting path.

The *rate* of heat transfer through any material is in direct proportion to the temperature differential between the points of entrance and departure of the heat. There is no conduction transfer through a perfect vacuum. In the normal pressure range, solids are better heat conductors than gases, so that the best commercial heat insulators consist of fine particles or fibers of solid substances with the spaces between the particles filled with air.

The transmission of heat cannot be completely stopped by any "heat-insulating" material. In this respect the flow of heat is unlike the flow of water, which can be stopped by a solid barrier. Heat-insulating materials have a low heat conductivity; heat flows through them slowly, but no amount of insulating material can actually *stop* the flow. This fact should be remembered in devising protection against stoves, hot pipes or other sources of heat which might ignite nearby woodwork. Filling the space between the source of heat and the combustible material solidly with insulation may not be sufficient to prevent ignition, no matter how thick the insulation. If the rate of heat conduction through the insulation material is greater than the rate of dissipation of heat from the combustible material, the temperature of the combustible material may increase to the point of ignition.

If the heat continues for a sufficient length of time to flow through the insulation, and if it does not escape somewhere, it will eventually build up the temperature on the wood. For this reason, there should always be an air space or some way of carrying the heat away by convection rather than relying solely on heat insulation material to protect exposed woodwork. Fires have occurred by transmission of heat over a long period through as much as a 2-foot thickness of solid concrete.

The transmission of heat by conduction is demonstrated to the greatest extent by metals, but other solids also will conduct heat in varying degrees. Table 4 shows some comparisons of these materials.

Heat may be transferred by *radiation* from one body to another by heat rays through intervening space, much the same as light is transferred by light rays. Thus, heat comes to us from the sun. The heat from the steam pipe mentioned in a previous example can be transferred to some extent to the wood construction by radiation even though there is an air space between the two.

Radiated heat passes freely through a vacuum and through gases with symmetrical molecules such as hydrogen, oxygen, and nitrogen. Since air is primarily a mixture of oxygen and nitrogen, there is no absorption of radiated heat by the air except as it may contain water vapor, carbon monoxide, carbon dioxide, sulfur dioxide, hydrocarbons, or other contaminants. Like light, radiated heat travels through space in a straight

Table 4 Thermal Conductivity of Some Common Materials

In this table the conductivity is given in number of calories transmitted per second through a 1 centimeter cube of material ($^{13}/_{32}$ inch^3) when the temperature change is 1°C.

Material	Conductivity	Material	Conductivity
Aluminum	0.504	Asbestos	0.0004
Brass	0.260	Brick	0.0015
Copper	0.918	Concrete	0.0022
Gold	0.700	Glass	0.0025
Cast Iron	0.109	Paraffin	0.0006
Lead	0.083	Wood	0.0003
Magnesium	0.0519	Alcohol	0.0004
Silver	1.006	Glycerin	0.0007
Zinc	0.265	Gasoline	0.0003

line until it encounters an opaque object, where it is absorbed and proceeds through the object by conduction. Like light, radiated heat is reflected from bright surfaces and will pass through glass.

Heat radiation is a two-way process. Heat radiates from a stove to a wall, and the wall, in turn, radiates heat in all directions when heated above the temperature of other objects in the room. The rays from a heat source spread out in all directions. Thus, the farther an exposed object from the source of heat, the less is the concentration that will reach it. However, where the area of the heat source is very large in relation to the distance, as in the case of a large burning building exposing another building across a narrow alley or in the case of a large individual oven a few inches from a wooden wall, small variations in distance have little or no practical effect on the severity of exposure. Other factors affecting heat transfer by radiation are the composition, color and smoothness of surfaces. Rough, dark surfaces usually radiate and absorb heat more readily than light polished surfaces. One exception to this rule is white vitreous enamel which has almost the same radiation capability as a surface coated with lampblack.

Heat radiation is largely in the red and infrared light range, and is generally similar to sunlight. Since heat is stopped by any opaque body, a thin sheet of metal or even paper will furnish temporary protection against radiated heat, but ordinary glass does not stop heat radiation. Water has almost the same absorptivity as glass, so if a water film on glass is equal in thickness to the glass, the amount of heat absorbed will be doubled. (In any event, a film of water alone on glass will not stop radiation.)

When heat is transferred by *convection,* it uses a circulating medium—either a gas or a liquid. Thus, heat generated in a stove is distributed throughout a room by heating the air by conduction; the *circulation* of heated air through the room to distant objects is heat transfer by *convection.* Heat is thus transferred from the air to the objects by *conduction.* Heated air expands and rises, and for this change in density reason, heat transfer by convection occurs naturally in an upward direction though forced air currents can be made to carry heat by convection in any direction.

Where all conditions are known, quantitative calculations may be made of heat transmission by conduction, convection and radiation, but in actual fires there are so many unknown factors that exact calculations are impossible. However, the above characteristics should be remembered for estimating conditions that occur during fires.

Common sources of heat

There are three principal and common sources of heat and heat energy. These are: *chemical oxidation* heat reactions; *electrical* heat energy sources; and *mechanical* heat energy sources. Nuclear heat energy is, of course, another source of heat, but some very special requirements are needed in its consideration and the fire officer is referred to special texts and manuals for this information.

Chemical oxidation heat energy reactions are responsible for most of the burning of fires and their effects, which are encountered in normal operations. Much of this subject is covered under "Fire is chemical combustion or oxidation" and will not be repeated here.

In order for an oxidation reaction to take place, both a combustible (or oxidizable) material and an oxidizing agent (oxygen in air) must be present. There are innumerable materials or fuels that are capable of being oxidized or burned. In general, the most common fuels are those which contain large amounts of carbon and hydrogen in their composition. A detailed knowledge of chemistry and the properties of materials would be needed to determine the capability of a substance to burn without actually igniting it in air.

It is important to realize that most substances oxidize to some extent upon exposure to air. In most cases of such very slow oxidation, the heat that is given off during this process is so very little and at such a slow rate that it cannot be called *burning.* However, just as iron rusts, it is continually giving off some heat of oxidation.

The *heat of combustion* of a substance is the amount of heat released during its complete oxidation (combustion). Heat of combustion, commonly referred to as *calorific* or fuel value, depends upon the kinds and numbers of atoms in the molecule and also upon their arrangement. Calorific values of representative materials are given in standard ref-

Table 5 Standard Heats of Combustion

Compound	Formula	State (Phase)	Heat of Combustion Btu/lb.
Carbon	C	Solid	14,100
Hydrogen	H_2	Vapor	51,520
Methane	CH_4	Vapor	21,540
Propane	C_3H_8	Vapor	19,960
Benzene	C_6H_6	Vapor	17,490
Ethyl Alcohol	C_2H_5OH	Liquid	11,910
Coal, Anthr.		Solid	13,800
#6 Fuel Oil		Liquid	17,500
Natural Gas	83% CH_4	Gas	19,600

erence handbooks. They are commonly expressed in Btu per pound but are sometimes reported in gram calories per gram (1 gram calorie per gram = 1.8 Btu per pound). In the case of fuel gases, calorific values are usually reported in Btu per cubic foot. Calorific values are used in calculating fire loading but they do not necessarily indicate the relative fire *intensity* capacity of materials since intensity is dependent on *rate of burning* as well as on total amount of heat produced. Table 5 lists the heats of combustion or calorific values of some common fuels.

Electrical heat energy sources consist of several important types. Heat may be generated from the resistance of metallic conductors to the flow of electricity; it may also be generated by electrical arcs, discharging across gaps between conductors; electrical sparks and lightning discharges also generate heat by initiating combustion through several different mechanisms.

Resistance heating is the most common form of generation of heat from electricity. It is employed in a useful sense in electrical space heating equipment where a metallic alloy of the nichrome type having high resistance to the flow of electricity is connected to the electrical mains. Properly designed and engineered devices must be used for this purpose.

The type of resistance heating that leads to unwanted fires is concerned with the use of electrical conductors such as copper wire and switch components, etc., which are small in cross section but are used for carrying large quantities of electrical current or load. All metal electrical conductors (including copper wire) have some internal resistance to the flow of electricity. This resistance causes only very slight heating effects when electrical current of the correct and normal amount flows through the conductor. However, when too large a current is used with metal wires and conducting parts of an electrical system which is too small, heat is generated which is proportional to the square of the current or load in the circuit. This heat will quickly cause insulation on the wires to melt and burn (depending on the composition of the insulation covering) and arcs or short circuits leading to concealed fires in nearby combustibles can then take place. Obviously, correctly sized electrical wires and outlet connections, etc., must be used to prevent such combustion.

When a loaded electrical circuit is broken by disconnection of some type ("pulling" a switch, pulling a male electrical plug, unscrewing a screwplug, defusing a fuse plug, etc.), an *electrical arc* in the air gap thus exposed between the conductors will occur. Arcs of this type evolve large quantities of heat in a very short time and, unless the action of disconnecting the circuit is continued to make a wide air gap, across which the arc cannot continue, enough heat will be developed to bring nearby combustible materials to the ignition point. Sustained electrical arcs cause metals to melt very quickly (the principle used in electrical arc welding) and the resulting hot globules of metal can fall to even distant areas containing combustible materials.

Electrical energy generated by friction or static electricity can accumulate on the surfaces of various materials to the point that a considerable amount of energy is released when discharge in the form of a spark to a grounded conductor takes place. The heat energy released by such frictional sparks is small but is fully capable of providing the activation of energy for ignition of gaseous mixtures of combustible vapors and air.

Lightning discharges are high-capacity sparks containing great amounts of electrical energy. When this energy discharge takes place on or near combustible materials, the materials in the path of the spark take up the energy in the form of heat. This heat may easily be sufficient to reach the ignition point of wood construction materials.

Mechanical heat energy is responsible for a significant number of fires each year. *Frictional heat* is responsible for most of these fires and there are a few notable examples of combustible ignition by the mechanical heat energy released by compression.

Frictional heat is developed when mechanical energy is used up during the process of overcoming the resistance to friction. Any friction generates heat. The danger depends upon the amount of mechanical energy transformed into heat, and the *rate* at which the heat is generated and dissipated. The heat caused by friction of a slipping belt against a pulley, and the hot metal particles (sparks) thrown off when a piece of foreign metal enters a grinding mill are examples of frictional heat.

Aircraft wheels often become dangerously hot when the landing process requires extensive braking to slow down the ship.

Heat of compression is the heat released when a gas is quickly compressed. The fact that the temperature of a gas increases when compressed has found practical application in the diesel engine, where heat of compression eliminates the need for a spark ignition system. Air is first compressed in the cylinder of a diesel engine, after which an oil spray is injected into the compressed air. Heat released when the air is compressed is sufficient to ignite the oil spray.

Methods of heat detection and temperature measurement

Fire protection experts learn early in their careers that the detection of heat and the temperature rise in materials are of fundamental importance in dealing with combustion phenomena and the control of fires. The senses of touch and sight and skin sensations of warmth when areas of the body are exposed to radiation are ever-present instruments for detecting the effects of heat and flame. Even the sense of hearing is sometimes employed to judge the progress of heating or burning when one listens for the "roar" of flames or uses the "hiss" of his saliva on a hot surface to judge the relative temperature of the surface.

However, there are situations where more accurate methods of measurement of the temperatures of surfaces or spaces might be needed in order to determine many useful facts about fire propagation and the cooling or extinguishing process. The science of fire fighting and the technology of arson investigation must have adequate instruments and tools to accomplish their similar goals of detecting and measuring paths of temperature development in fires. The following elementary description of instruments and temperature measurement methods are given to alert fire officers of these techniques.

The *bimetallic strip thermometer* encased in a metal housing with its protected dial is perhaps one of the most useful and durable types of temperature indicating devices available for general use. It may be used to indicate air and liquid temperatures and in the case of materials such as cotton bales, etc., it may be used to carefully pierce the material and thus determine temperatures in depth.

Thermocouple devices with their millivoltmeters and associated readout equipment are obtainable in many different types. One is a portable hand type which may be used in a variety of situations where measurement of irregular surfaces of solids are concerned. Similar instruments are available with special flat circular, thermocouple tips provided for determining the surface temperatures of flat bodies.

The modern *resistance thermometer* or *thermistor* is a very useful

Table 6 Approximate Color Scales of High Temperatures

Visible Color	Temperature (°F)	Range (°C)
Very dull red (can be seen only in dark)	932 to 1022	500 to 550
Dark red	1200 to 1380	650 to 750
Bright red	1560 to 1740	850 to 950
Yellowish red	1920 to 2100	1050 to 1150
Whitish yellow	2280 to 2460	1250 to 1350
Brilliant white	2640 to 2820	1450 to 1550

device for determining temperature. Its readout device is connected to one or more probes for measuring temperature. These probes are designed according to the work required of them—surface temperature probes, deep immersion probes and gas diffusion probes.

Temperature indicating crayons are available for quickly approximating the progress of heat in various situations requiring such estimations. These crayons are applied to the surface being heated and when the temperature of the surface reaches the melting point of the crayon used, it changes to show a wet, melting and dripping surface. These crayons are available in a range covering temperatures from 113°F to 2500°F.

The estimation of high temperatures by the *color of hot radiating bodies* is sometimes very useful, but it must be remembered that this is only an approximation. The above table may be used where it becomes necessary or advisable to judge high temperatures by the color of hot iron or glowing ceramic materials, etc.

BASIC METHODS OF EXTINGUISHING FIRES

The professional fire fighter and fire officer are called upon for many types of duty. They are asked to be experts in everything from climbing vertical walls of buildings to being emergency physicians in the saving of human lives and alleviation of suffering. Some fire fighters come close to being just such experts in many diverse tasks, others are not able to do so many things expertly. However, the one field in which the professional fire fighter must excel concerns the actual extinguishment of fire and control of combustion.

This section begins the specialized information which the fire fighter must have at his finger tips at all times concerning the important mechanisms and methods of extinguishment of fire and flame.

Many years ago when it became evident that modern civilization was producing an increasingly large number of fire hazards, each of which required some special consideration to control fires in that hazard, it was decided to categorize and put these hazards into similar *classes* according to *fuels* in order to make the fire fighter's job easier.

The following classifications are recognized nationally in the United States:

Class A fires are defined as fires in ordinary combustible materials such as wood, cloth, paper, rubber, and many plastics.

Class B fires are defined as fires in flammable petroleum products or other similar flammable liquids, gases and greases.

Class C fires are defined as fires involving energized electrical equipment where the electrical nonconductivity of the stream of extinguishing media is of importance.

Class D fires are defined as fires in combustible metals, such as magnesium, titanium, sodium and potassium.

Since the above classification is given in terms of *fuel* hazards, it is natural that one thinks in terms of "Class A fuels" or "Class D fuels," etc. However, it must be remembered that some fires in some fuels are really mixtures of several classes of fires. For instance, Class C fires in electrical equipment quickly become Class A fires as soon as all the electrical equipment is shut off and all that remains are fires in burning rubber, cloth and/or plastic insulation. Similarly, fires in large oil-filled transformers become Class B fires when no electrical current is flowing in the system. Extinguishing methods appropriate to these classes of fire must be used to efficiently combat them.

The most important usefulness of the A-B-C-D classification of fires is concerned with the applicability of various extinguishing agents and portable extinguishers for general fire extinguishment and combustion control. By using classes of fires, we can quickly team up the best extinguishing agents for combatting them.

Basic fire extinguishment mechanisms

It would seem that with the multitude of combustible fuels that exist today and the large number of fire extinguishing methods and materials that are available, we should have a large number of basic mechanisms by which fires are halted. This is not the case. There are only *four* fundamental methods or mechanisms, physical and chemical, by which fire is extinguished. These are:

1. Reduction of heat (cooling)
2. Reduction (replacing) or exclusion of oxygen or air (smothering)
3. Removal of fuel (starving)
4. Chemical free radical quenching or suppression (inhibition of chain reactions of combustion)

To be sure, there are modifications of the above basic mechanisms which sometimes include several methods simultaneously. However, every fire extinguishment can be analyzed and its *principal* extinguishing method found and denoted in one of the listed mechanisms.

Reduction of heat

The *reduction of heat* or *cooling* method of extinguishment is the most familiar when water is mentioned as the principal agent used to put out a fire. Remembering what was said in the previous section about the high *specific heat* of water and the low specific heats of almost all other substances, it is easy to see that water is our best heat remover and can reduce temperatures in other materials at a rapid rate. When water is applied to hot materials at or above the boiling point (100°C, 212°F), we also take advantage of the enormously high *latent heat of vaporization* of water, taking away heat and lowering temperatures at high rates per quantity of cooling water.

Water is not the only useful cooling agent for fire fighting purposes; in fact, *any* external agent added to a fire acts to first cool it, and, if sufficient amounts of *any* cooling agent are added rapidly, the temperature of the combustible will be reduced to below its temperature of continuation of flame propagation (ignition temperature). Cool oil circulated from the bottom of a full fuel oil tank (not gasoline or flammable liquids with flash points below ambient temperatures) to the burning top layer of the oil will extinguish the flames.

Reduction of oxygen

The *reduction, replacement* or *exclusion* of oxygen or air is also an easily understood and common method of flame control and fire extinguishment. In a fundamental sense, there are two ways of accomplishing the reduction of oxygen to a fire: (1) The fire may be completely surrounded by an envelope which does not allow gas and air transfer or circulation to the burning surface (i.e. putting a lid on a burning pot of cooking oil); (2) The air above the burning surface may be replaced with an inert gas which does not support combustion (i.e. causing carbon dioxide gas to flood across the burning surface, thus *displacing* the air).

In the first example above, the *smothering* action occurs by causing the fire to produce its own exhausting of air needed to continue combustion. There are many simple examples of this. The alert fire fighter realizes, however, that this action also produces some combustible gas or vapor mixture inside the envelope during the process of combustion cessation. If a building is tightly closed during a fire, an explosion of combustible gases may ensue should a door be opened or oxygen enter before *all* flames or ignition points cease to exist.

Fire fighting *foams* also act to cut off a fuel from its supply of oxygen. When foam is flowed over a combustible liquid or solid material, it forms a continuous layer of bubble films which restrict the access of oxygen to the burning surface. Because of their high water content, foams also *cool* the combustibles on which they are applied. This is a very necessary action in fighting fires in flammable liquids with high boiling points, such as crude oil or heavy fuel oil, where heat penetrates *downward* through the oil as the fire progresses.

It is interesting to note that the newer, high expansion, "dry" foams that are generated in copious amounts by the action of streams of air (usually from a forced-draft fan) across foam-soaked porous nets or screens, control fires and finally extinguish them by a basic action of surrounding the fire with a continuous envelope of foam which restricts air circulation to the fire. When the fire cannot receive fresh air and oxygen for the burning process, because of the large volume foam plug or wall which has been interposed on it, the fire actually extinguishes itself.

Removal of fuel

The process of *removal of fuel* for fire extinguishment is quite obvious as a generally recommended action where it is possible. The problem to the fire fighter is that very seldom can he accomplish fuel removal for controlling a large fire. Large solid combustibles require power, either horsepower or manpower, to remove them from the burning zone. Buildings and walls can be dynamited to halt fire progression and fire lanes can be plowed around brush fires to remove combustible fuels. Under certain conditions, a carefully supervised backfire may be completed to remove combustibles from the path of flames, but this is not easily accomplished. Wetting down operations near a fire also prevent combustibles from being burned.

The pumping down of flammable liquid storages during the progress of a fire in them, or near such storages, is an acknowledged procedure for halting fire destruction. This requires the full cooperation of other operating personnel of the fuel storage area or tank installation which is burning.

The dramatic extinguishment of oil and gas well fires by a sudden, powerful but very *temporary* separation of fuel from flame through the use of an explosion wave generated by carefully placing explosives is an example of fuel removal for *very* short times. Such a temporary isolation of flame from fuel may be sufficient to halt the fire if *no* ignition points, such as hot derrick steel or sparks, continue to exist immediately following the detonation with its sudden flame separation from fuel.

Chemical free radical quenching

The methods of fire extinguishment through *chemical free radical quenching* or suppression is a new concept, old in actual use, but only recently determined and explained by the chemist and the physicist.

For many years past, the superior fire extinguishing action of certain chemical materials could not be satisfactorily explained or accounted for. Carbon tetrachloride, one of our oldest chemical agents, has always demonstrated extinguishing action at a higher level of efficiency than would be expected, when its cooling effects or inerting capabilities are carefully considered. Similarly, sodium bicarbonate (and its new counterpart, potassium bicarbonate) dry chemical powders are capable of extinguishing more fire in an efficient manner than can be explained from a knowledge of the heat-removing capacity and carbon dioxide production of these chemicals in fires. In the past, the mysterious and beneficial effect of these chemicals (and some others) was called "negative catalysis" in fires, for want of a better explanation of their efficient flame-quenching actions.

The modern study of the chain reaction of combustion and its control has led to the important discovery of the formation in the fire of the unstable and temporary, but very reactive, chemical fragments which are called "free radicals." In the first section of this chapter these chemical species and how they exist in flames are described.

Modern chemistry has shown that when chemical extinguishing agents are heated in the reactive zone of a flame some other completely different free radical fragments are produced. These latter chemicals react quickly with the free radicals produced by the combustion and "tie them up" securely, halting further progress of the propagation of the fire.

A little "chemical shorthand" will explain this more clearly:

Taking the simple chain combustion (branched type) of hydrogen gas in oxygen gas as an example of chemical oxidation:

$$2H_2 + O_2 + \text{Spark} \begin{Bmatrix} \text{activation} \\ \text{energy} \end{Bmatrix} \rightarrow 4 \underset{\begin{Bmatrix} \text{active} \\ \text{atom} \end{Bmatrix}}{\boxed{H}} + 20$$

And then this reaction takes place:

$$4 \boxed{H} + O_2 \rightarrow \underset{\begin{Bmatrix} \text{active free} \\ \text{radical} \end{Bmatrix}}{\boxed{OH}} + O$$

Also this reaction takes place:

$$2O + H_2 \rightarrow \underset{\text{active free radical}}{\{OH\}} + H$$

Now, taking up the reactions which occur when an extinguishing agent like carbon tetrachloride is directed into the same flame zone matrix where the hydrogen gas is uniting with oxygen:

First, the heat decomposes the vapor of the carbon tetrachloride like this:

$$CCl_4 + \text{Heat} \rightarrow C + 4\underset{\text{active atom}}{\{Cl\}}$$

Reactions then occur with the *active fragments* of the hydrogen combustion shown above to finally produce *inactive* water vapor:

$$4\{Cl\} + 4\{H\} + 4\{OH\} \rightarrow 4H_2O + 4Cl$$

Similarly, when potassium bicarbonate dry chemical extinguishing agent is directed into the flame zone matrix of the burning hydrogen:

First, the heat decomposes the bicarbonate:

$$2KHCO_3 + \text{Heat} \rightarrow 2CO_2 + K_2O$$

Then water vapor (from the combustion) unites with the K_2O:

$$K_2O + H_2O \rightarrow 2\{KOH\}$$

Then a union takes place.

$$2\{KOH\} + \{H\} + \{OH\} \rightarrow 2H_2O + K_2O$$

When *water molecules* are produced, as in the above reactions, the chemical reactivity of the components in the combustion is halted and sudden "quenching" takes place which halts further reaction or burning. This chemical suppression is a very efficient one, operating in terms of *molecules* of agent instead of gallons or pounds, such as we usually think of when water is used to put out fires or cool combustibles below their ignition temperature.

In general, this chemical free radical quenching mechanism is principally demonstrated in Class B fires where flame propagation occurs in the gaseous phase in conjunction with fuel *vaporization*, rather than fuel *decomposition*. The action must take place in the flame zone and not in the fuel itself.

It is essential that the fire protection expert have a well-founded knowledge of the correct extinguishing agent for every class and type of fire or fuel. Appropriate national test standards have been set up by which the fire extinguishing equipment in portable sizes are *rated* in terms of the amount of fire which may be extinguished by their use. These standards utilize fuels or conditions in every case which are typical of each class of fire. Complete familiarity with these standard tests, coupled with a knowledge of the agents rated by their use, makes the problem of linking up the extinguisher with the type of fire and fuel an easily remembered task.

Standard Tests for Class A extinguishers and agents

Class A fire extinguishers, under conditions of continuous discharge, shall be capable of extinguishing wood-crib, wood-panel, and excelsior test fires as designated in the following requirements for a given classification and rating and the type of extinguisher and/or agent. A test fire shall be considered to be extinguished if it reaches a state which will not be subject to self-reignition or continued smoldering under the conditions of the test.

It has been determined that the extinguishment of test fires for Class A water, soda-acid, and foam extinguishers is primarily a function of the amount of extinguishing agent and the duration and range of its discharge. Extinguishers up to and including 33-gallon capacity and otherwise conforming with the appropriate requirements for discharge capacity, duration, and range may be eligible for rating without fire testing. In such cases the classification and rating may be applied in accordance with Table 7.

Other extinguishing agents or water-type extinguishers utilizing improved application methods, which may develop greater Class A extinguishing potential than would be anticipated by the proportionate ratings provided for in Table 7, may be subjected to comparative fire tests as the basis for determining the Class A rating.

Standard tests for Class B extinguishers and agents

Class B fire extinguishers under conditions of continuous discharge, shall be capable of extinguishing flammable liquid test fires as designated in the following requirements for a given classification and rating. A test fire shall be considered to be extinguished if it reaches a state which will not be subject to self-reignition under the test conditions.

Standard tests for Class C extinguishers and agents

The discharge of an agent from an extinguisher toward a grounding plate, during a test for electrical conductivity, shall not increase the electrical conductivity, as measured by a milliammeter, through a 10-inch air gap established between an electrically insulated extinguisher and

Table 7 Classification Based on Capacity

Extinguisher Capacity United States' Gallons	Classification and Rating
1¾	1-A
2½	2-A
4	3-A
5	4-A
10	6-A
17	10-A
33	20-A

a grounding plate at a potential of 100,000 volts, 60 cycles, alternating current.

The Class C classification is given to an extinguisher only in conjunction with a rating previously established under the requirements for Class A or Class B, or both.

No tests for the fire extinguishing ability of a Class C extinguisher on incipient electrical fires are to be conducted. There are to be, therefore,

Table 8 Flammable Liquid Pan Materials and Arrangement

Classification and Rating		Pan Size, Square Feet	Minimum Effective Discharge Time, Seconds	Naphtha Used,* U.S. Gallons (Approximate)
1-B	Indoor Tests	2½	8	3¼
2-B		5	8	6¼
4-B		10	8	12½
6-B		15	8	19
8-B		20	8	25
10-B		25	8	31
12-B		30	8	38
16-B		40	8	50
20-B		50	8	65
30-B	Outdoor Tests	75	11	95
40-B		100	13	125
60-B		150	17	190
80-B		200	20	250
120-B		300	26	375
160-B		400	31	500
240-B		600	40	750
320-B		800	48	1000
480-B		1200	63	1500
640-B		1600	75	2000

* The amount of naphtha to be used in each test is to be determined by the actual depth as measured in the pan and not by the gallons indicated.

TYPICAL MARKINGS

1. SODA-ACID EXTINGUISHER 2. CARBON DIOXIDE EXTINGUISHER

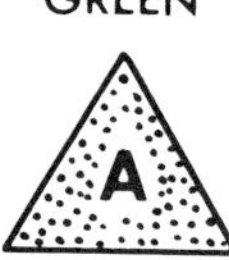

3. MULTI-PURPOSE DRY CHEMICAL EXTINGUISHER

4. EXTINGUISHER FOR METAL FIRES

Figure 2.

no numerical components for Class C ratings as only the nonconducting characteristics of the agent as discharged are significant.

Standard tests for Class D extinguishers and agents

Class D fire extinguishers, or an extinguishing agent arranged for manual handling, shall be capable of extinguishing combustible metal test fires as designated for a given metal in the following, and of preventing the scattering of burning metal beyond the test bed area during the test. An extinguished test fire shall be in that state which will not be subject to reignition under the test conditions and shall contain sufficient unburned combustible metal to show extinguishment by the agent prior to burnout.

There are to be no numerical components for Class D ratings. The type of combustible metal for which the extinguisher or an agent is applicable and the area, depth and other characteristics of the fires which may be controlled and extinguished are to be as stated in any published advices and as described in the manufacturer's recommendations for use.

Fire tests are generally conducted to include the tests designed for the combustible metals specified. Other tests may be required if it is desired to cover other fire conditions, where such conditions are different in nature than those suggested by the specific programs.

Area fire tests are intended to represent fires occurring in magnesium chips and dust, both in the dry state and mixed with cutting oils, as accumulated over an area and at a reasonable depth.

Significance of extinguisher markings

The foregoing sections on extinguisher testing methods provide the fire officer with information showing the how and why of the markings on commercially obtainable modern portable fire extinguishers. The standard letter markers similar to Figure 2 have also been recently adopted to make the choice of extinguisher and agent a simple task for even the unpracticed person confronted with a sudden fire fighting problem.

THE MODERN FIRE TRIANGLE

It is a well-known fact that the process of learning and remembering important facts is greatly assisted by picturization. Graphic aids, such as designs or drawings, which dramatize and explain important technical facts are much easier to understand and retain than a table of Arabic numerals or a paragraph of technical language. For this reason, the fire fighting specialist or fire officer, who must continually teach and educate and inform, should have suitable graphic material at his command to make the presentation of technical points a simple and effective task. This section discusses several methods by which the picturization and explanation of modern methods of fire extinguishment may be accomplished.

The "simple" fire triangle

In the early years of the fire fighting profession the mechanism of chemical oxidation and combustion and the countermechanism of

Figure 3.

halting combustion was quite simply and easily pictured with the now well-known fire triangle.

This device is very useful because it explains so clearly in a two-dimentional diagram the important fundamentals of the combustion process. When all sides of the fire triangle of Figure 3 are present and joined together, *fire can proceed.* If any *one* of the sides is removed or taken away by any method whatsoever, the triangle is opened and *fire is halted.*

Before the advent of modern knowledge about *chemical* fire extinguishment, there were only three methods of fire extinguishment, each of which is aligned very nicely with each leg of the triangle. *Cooling* the fire with water removed the *heat* leg; *excluding oxygen* from the fire with foam, etc., removed the *oxygen* leg; and *separating* the *fuel* from the fire by removal of fuel in some mechanical manner removed the *fuel* leg of the triangle.

When science began to try to answer the puzzle about the very high efficiency of chemical extinguishing agents, it was evident that fire extinguishment needed an additional piece of information which could explain this phenomenon. The free radical quenching process of com-

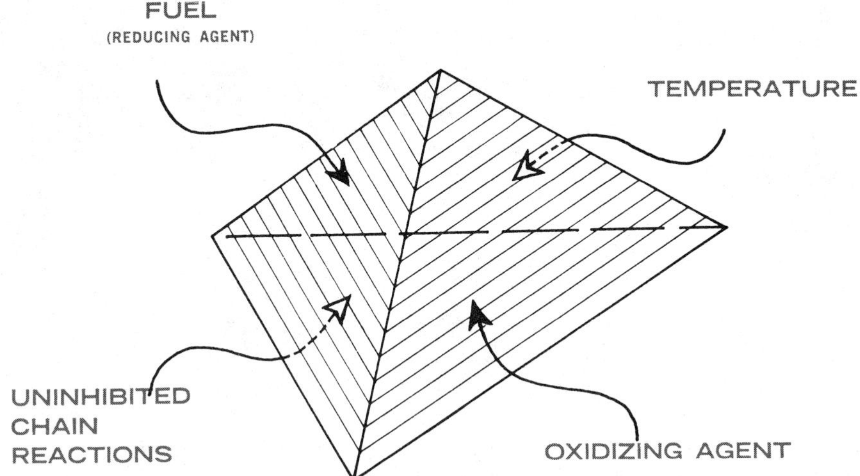

THE TETRAHEDRON OF FIRE

Figure 4.

bustion chain breaking was the result of these studies. It is fully explained in a previous section of this chapter.

The "tetrahedron" of fire

With this new knowledge about a *fourth* method of fire extinguishment we are now confronted with a *fourth side* to the old fire triangle if we are to use this excellent design device to picture extinguishment and combustion. This can be done geometrically by adding the dimension of depth to the fire triangle so that it becomes a solid pyramidal form with *four* triangular surfaces.

Figure 4 pictures a solid triangle of the tetrahedral form. Each of the triangular *surfaces* of this solid are necessary for continuation of combustion and if any surface is removed by a fire-extinguishing action of the four types outlined in the section on the basic methods of extinguishing fire, the structure is incomplete and the combustion process is halted. It is somewhat difficult, however, to exhibit a picture of a form having depth as well as length and width on a paper or blackboard where only length and width can be clearly shown.

Modernizing the fire triangle

One of the principal shortcomings of the old "simple" fire triangle is concerned with the fact that it omits the important *dynamic* consider-

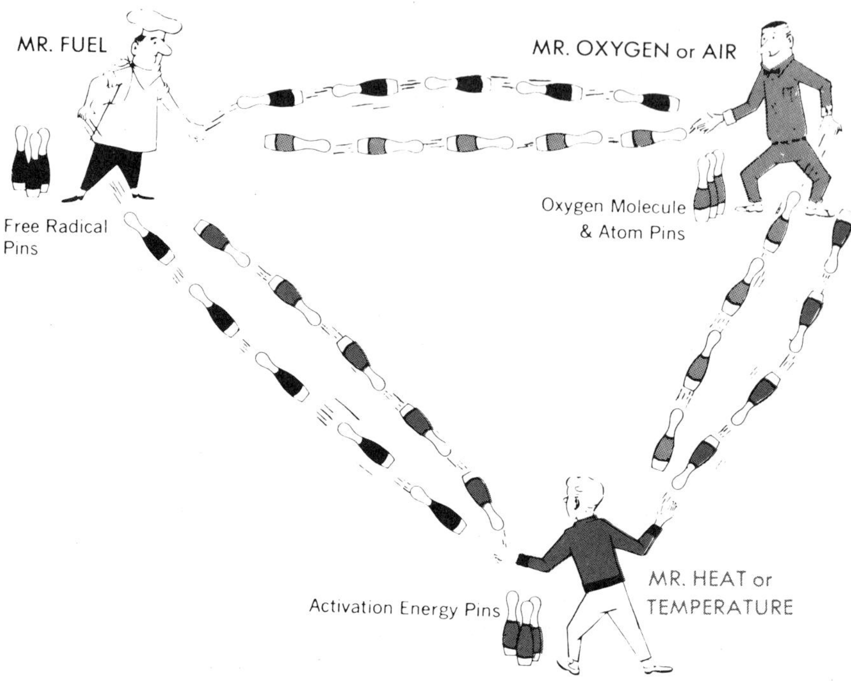

Figure 5.

ations of fire and combustion. The propagation of flame and continuation of combustion is a continuous chemical reaction, constantly changing due to external conditions. Fire is not a static state as pictured by simply naming three legs of a triangle. It must be pictured as a *phenomenon of exchange.*

It is a distinct advantage to retain the simplicity of a two-dimensional triangle in explaining combustion and this can be done if we place each of the three necessary components for fire in the *corners* of the triangle. By conferring names and personifications to them, we get a "cartoon" like Figure 5.

In this picturization we have three skilled jugglers who pass reactants back and forth to each other in the form of the familiar juggler's Indian clubs. Each important factor of fire in each corner then has a supply of important particles that we have correctly named for each player, which he trades around, and the fire proceeds. The intensity (speed of propagation) of the fire then is governed by the number of "active particle" Indian clubs which are put into the game by each of the players.

Figure 6.

Figure 7.

Figure 8.

This modern fire triangle is capable of some interesting graphical effects when picturization of extinguishment methods is made. Figure 6 shows the effect in halting combustion when cooling water is applied to a fire. The *activation energy* Indian clubs of Mr. Heat have been diminished in number by the cooling action and dissolved by the water. At the same time, the production of *free radicals* by the fuel diminishes and the *atomic* or *active* oxygen particles have less and less to unite with at the slower rate at which they are produced by the diminished (or cooled) source of heat. The fire slows down and finally halts.

Figure 7 dramatizes the process of halting flammable liquid fires using foam blankets on the fuel. The removal of a fuel by preventing its access to oxygen is easily shown by this means.

An outstanding advantage of this type of modern fire triangle is the picturization of the complicated free radical quenching process of extinguishment shown in Figure 8.

The invisible shield between Mr. Oxygen and Mr. Fuel, with its consequent interruption of dynamic exchange of *activated oxygen atom* clubs and *free radical* Indian clubs from the fuel, vividly portrays the quenching action of materials like potassium and sodium bicarbonate type dry chemicals or vaporizing liquid agents which depend on chemical exchange and reaction for their extinguishing action. This picture shows the temporary quality of such chemical extinguishment. When the "visible shield" is removed, the game—and the fire—proceeds again, unless Mr. Heat has lost all his interest.

There are many areas of application of the modern fire triangle, and study of its use in conjunction with other chemical and extinguishment information given in preceding sections of this chapter will enable the progressive fire officer to enlarge the capabilities of his instruction material and clarify the important tasks of normal fire fighting practices in the light of the latest technical advances.

EXTINGUISHING AGENTS AND THEIR EQUIPMENT

Ever since man first observed the flame-quelling action of drops of rain on his cooking fire, water in some form has been our most important and useful fire extinguishing agent.

Modern technology, however, has given us new petroleum fuels for our fires and with them has had to come a new chemistry of fire extinguishing agents. Scientific research has produced some improvements in the use of water for halting fires, and evolved some entirely new chemical materials for dealing with combustible hazards that hardly existed a generation ago.

In this section we will discuss the various extinguishing agents of basic importance to the fire officer and describe their characteristics. Because some of these agents require special equipment for applying them to the fire, the design of the devices necessary for easily and efficiently employing them will be dealt with to a limited extent.

Water and wetting agents

The basic physical characteristics of water, its almost universal availability, combined with cheapness, make it our most important extinguishing agent for many fire protection purposes.

Water absorbs heat to a far greater extent than any other easily available material. When 1 pound (or about a pint) of water is raised in temperature from its melting point (32°F, 0°C, its freezing point) to its boiling point (212°F, 100°C), it absorbs 180 Btu. If it is then vaporized into steam, an additional huge amount of 970.3 Btu will be suddenly absorbed. No other easily transported, cheap, pumpable, inert, nontoxic liquid exists which can accomplish this high cooling capability.

The formation of steam by water which has been applied to burning

P
P-PROJECTION IN FEET
100 LBS. P.S.I.
W-PATTERN DIAMETER
IN FEET
W

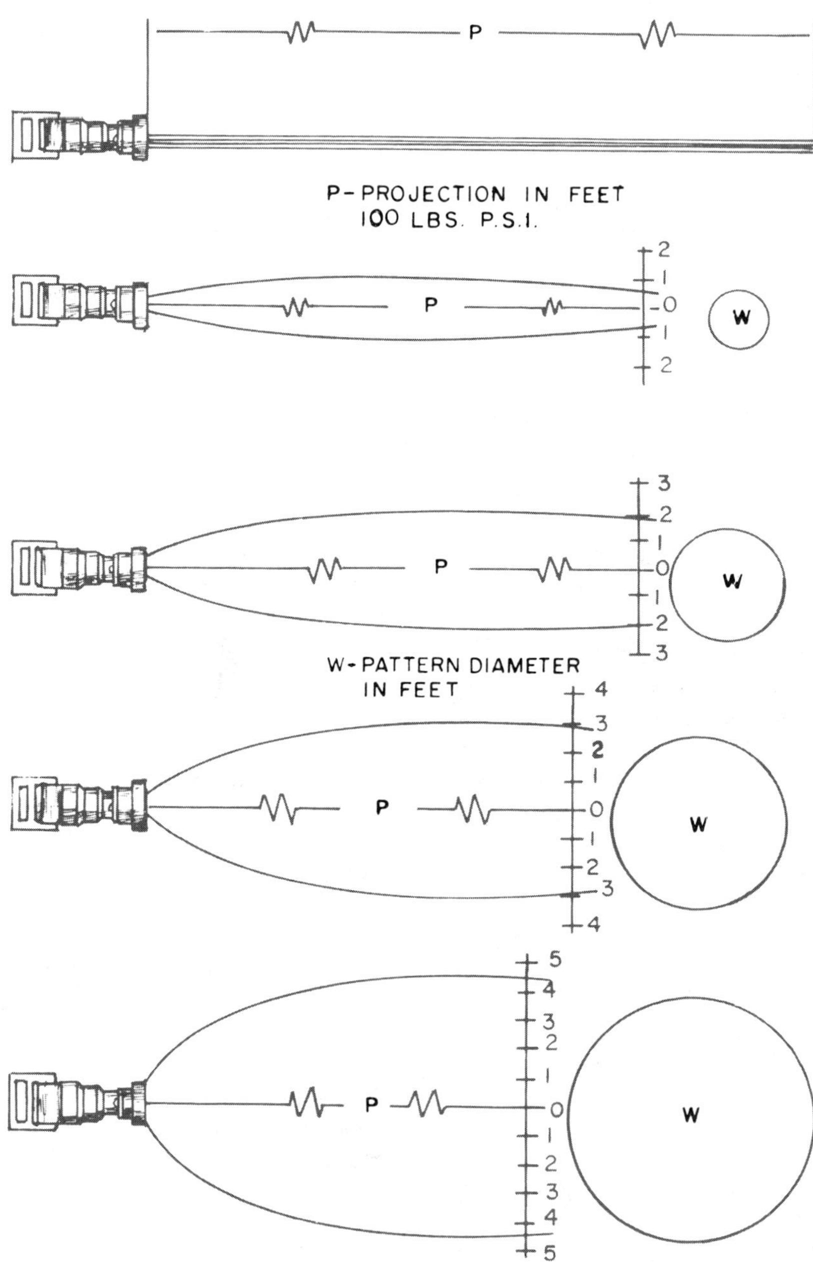

Figure 9.

combustibles generates a temporarily inert zone of gaseous water or steam in and near the burning zone. This aids the extinguishment action of the water. If steam can be continually produced at an equal rate to its condensation in nearby cool air or cool surfaces, the oxygen feeding the flames will be displaced and the fire will accordingly diminish due to this factor. This is sometimes difficult to achieve in actual fire fighting practice.

Since water is noncombustible, there are occasions where it may be used to dilute a water-solvent combustible liquid, such as alcohol, to a point where it cannot continue to burn. This requires a large amount of water—up to 90 percent of the volume of burning liquid, depending on the condition of the burning.

There is one interesting case of a common, non-water-soluble, combustible liquid which is *heavier* than water and when fires occur in this liquid it is necessary only to "float" water over its burning surface to extinguish it. Carbon disulfide liquid burns quickly if its vapor is ignited, but water gently applied over its surface will cut off its access to oxygen and fully extinguish it.

The application of cooling water in solid streams to the base of a fire is a centuries-old method of application. However, in many modern fire fighting problems, it is very desirable to cause rapid heat absorption over large areas, using a minimum rate of application of water. Less water damage is caused and greater economy of water (and pumping equipment, etc.) can be achieved thereby. The application of water in spray or droplet form from suitably designed spray nozzles greatly increases the rate of heat transfer to the water because of the proportionality which exists between this rate and the free surface of the small, spherical water droplet.

There are many advantages to the use of water spray nozzles or fog nozzles as they are commonly called. This dispersed pattern of the water acts as a heat shield for the nozzleman, permitting him to approach closer to the fire. The spray also acts to bring in fresh cool air to the man at the nozzle. In some cases, such as burning kerosine and fuel oil, water through a fog nozzle will extinguish these fires because of the wide and simultaneous cooling action of the fog pattern.

There are a large number of commercially available spray or fog nozzles. Figure 9 illustrates the adjustable water spray patterns of one type of nozzle. Figure 10 shows the all-purpose type of nozzle with its varied capability of forms of delivery of water.

Portable water-type fire extinguishers are available in a large number of different forms. They are designed for operation by air pressure, hand pumping or by chemical reaction and can be supplied for storage in areas

1½" DIA.
2½"
12' APPLICATOR
90°
1" DIA.
10' APPLICATOR
90°
1½"
1" DIA.
4' APPLICATOR
STRAIGHT STREAM
FOG
SHUT
HIGH VELOCITY FOG
FOG
4' APPLICATOR 60° ANGLE
LOW VELOCITY FOG
FOG
LOW VELOCITY FOG
10' APPLICATOR 90° ANGLE

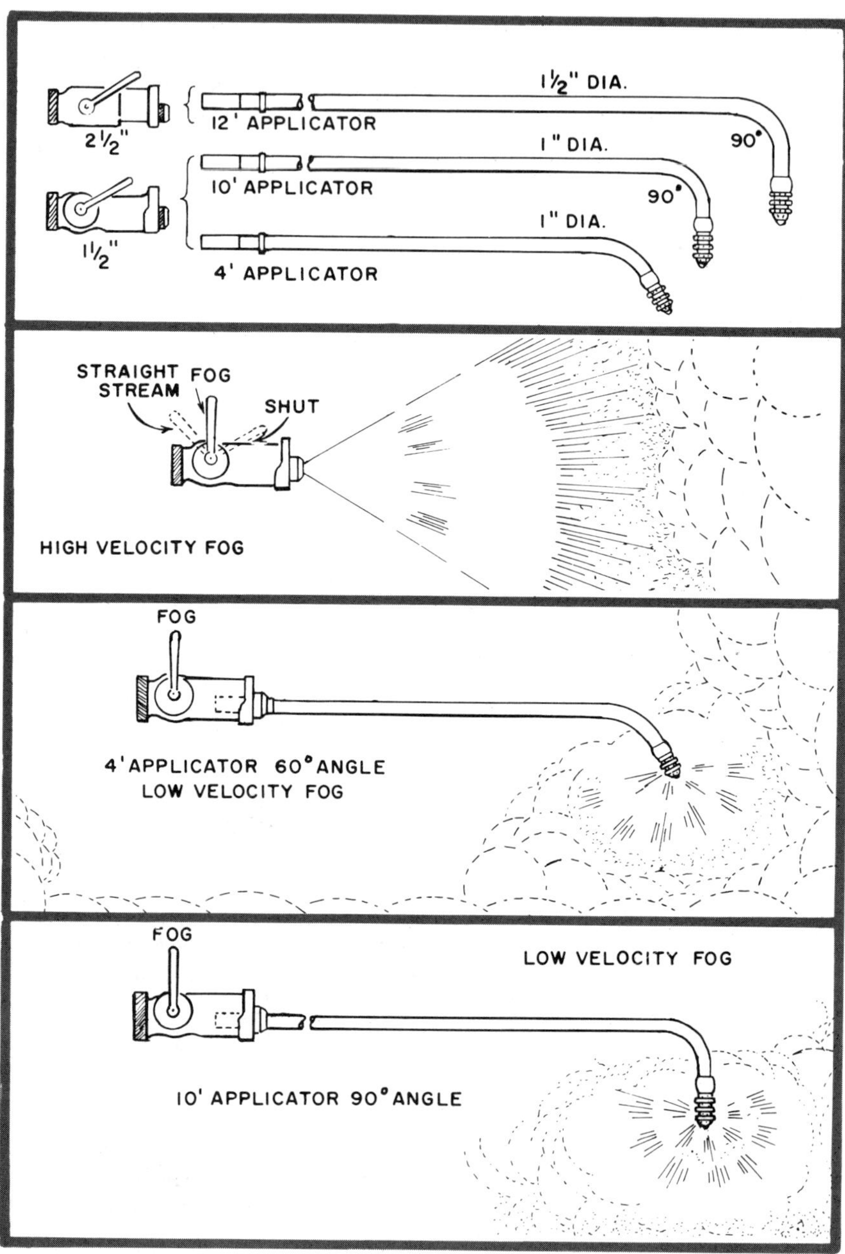

Figure 10.

not protected from freezing, as well as for normal temperature conditions. It is advisable that the National Fire Codes be consulted for detailed information on these extinguishers.

Water which has been treated by the addition of various types of chemical compounds called *wetting agents* retains all of its basic qualities with the addition of a capability for wetting, spreading and penetrating more quickly into materials such as upholstery or cotton mattresses. This action is related to a decrease in surface tension of the original water caused by the wetting agent. Ordinary water exhibits a "skin" on its surface. This skin is responsible for forming a stable droplet of water. Wetting agents decrease the strength of the skin of water and smaller drops can be formed more easily and the water solution can soak into substances more rapidly by capillarity, thus reaching deep-seated or hidden fires.

Wet-water solutions foam very easily and the very temporary foam thus formed shows better capabilities for controlling and extinguishing Class B fires than does ordinary water. The fire and flame resistance of this type of foam is very poor, however, and it is not a fully effective agent for flammable fuel fires. In general, wet water is used in similar equipment and for the same purpose as those for which water is employed.

Fire fighting foams

Foams used for extinguishing fires are masses of air or carbon dioxide gas bubbles dispersed throughout water. Before introducing the gas phase into the liquid phase, it is necessary to add a "foaming stabilizing" agent to the water. This agent helps entrap the gas and gives the resulting foam *stability,* enabling it to resist the attack of heat and fuel vapors and to persist for an appreciable time.

Practically all flammable liquids are lighter than water so they have a specific gravity (or density) of less than 1. These include all the petroleum products like gasoline, kerosine, jet fuel, diesel oil, lubricating oils, fuel oil, and benzene. Water, when applied to these burning liquids, sinks uselessly to the bottom and the fire continues to burn. Foam applied to such a fire forms a continuous floating blanket over the oil surface, and two mechanisms operate to extinguish the fire: first, the foam seals off the fuel vapors from reaching oxygen in the air, and second, the water in the foam provides an appreciable amount of cooling of the fuel, thus cutting down the generation of more flammable vapors. Foam may be thought of as a way to make water light enough to float on top of fuels.

There have been two kinds of foam in use for many years. One is named *chemical foam* because it utilizes a chemical reaction to form carbon dioxide gas, which is then trapped by a dissolved stabilizing, or foaming, agent in the water to form a thick, stable, foamy mass. Because of numerous problems with low temperatures and handling large amounts of dry, foam-making materials, chemical foam has been almost completely replaced by a different type of foam called *air foam* or *mechanical foam.* This name comes from the fact that the bubbles are filled with air instead of carbon dioxide gas, and the foam is formed by a mechanical beating action of water containing the foaming or foam-stabilizing agent.

Mixing air with water will not create a foam unless there is also present in the water a foaming agent or some type of foam bubble stabilizer. The material used in making fire fighting foams is called *foam concentrate.* Although there are several types available commercially, the kind most commonly used at refineries, chemical plants and airports is a dark brown liquid derived from chemically processing protein-containing products such as horn and hoof meal, or chicken feather meal. The concentrate is mixed into water to form a dilute foaming solution as it is consumed at the scene of the fire.

Foam concentrates are made in several types in order to fit special applications. The original concentrates were made to be used as 6 percent solutions in water, and these are still used by military forces and other government activities. Later, more concentrated products were developed to be used in a 3 percent concentration in water, and these have been widely adopted by industrial users. Alcohols and many other solvents break down foams before they can act to extinguish the fire. Therefore, special foam concentrates which produce alcohol-resistant air foams must be used on solvents. These are commercially available and are known as "alcohol foams." Where conditions exist requiring foam concentrates to be stored in unheated structures, low-temperature concentrates, usable at -20°F, can be obtained.

A federal specification has been prepared for all government purchases of ordinary foam concentrates for use in a 6 percent solution and this document sets forth the requirements a good concentrate should have. Unusually low-priced bargains of these concentrates are to be avoided and only the fresh products of reputable manufacturers should be considered.

For use, the foam concentrate is added to a water stream in just the correct amount by the use of a flow-proportioning device. An inline venturi in a hose line will educt concentrate to supply a foam-making nozzle, or the nozzle itself may have a built-in pickup tube, which is dipped into the 5-gallon cans. In larger installations of foam-making

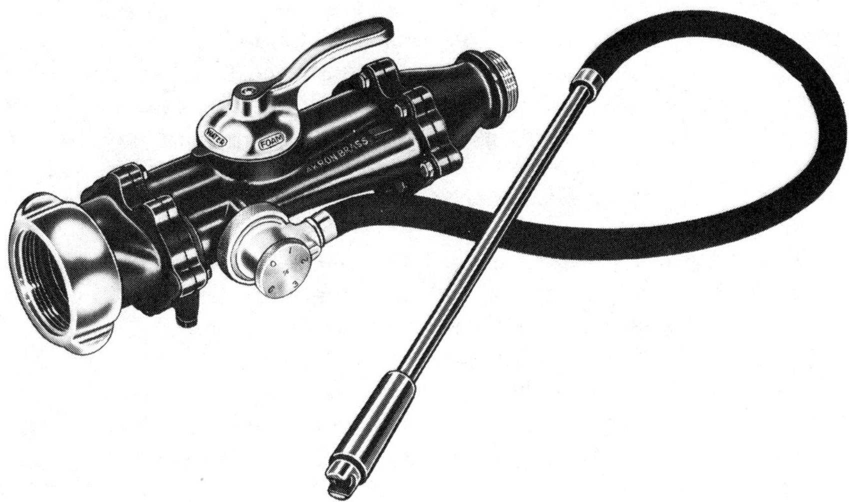

Figure 11.

equipment, the proportioning system may be quite complex, involving special pumps, flow meters, automatic valves and pressure gages and drawing foam from large storage tanks. For fire department use there are several types of proportioners available which are employed at the pumper pressure outlets. Figure 11 shows one of the types of proportioners useful for educting foam concentrate into lines to generate fire fighting foam.

Foam-making devices

There are many different devices useful for making and applying fire fighting foam from the solution of foam concentrate produced by the foam proportioners described above. All of these foam appliances depend on the basic principle of turbulent mixing of air and foam solution under conditions of velocity and pressure. Discharge pattern characteristics of the formed foam may be influenced by the construction of the outlet end of the appliance. In some cases there are adjustable stream-shaping deflectors or outlet nozzles that can produce widely divergent patterns of foam discharge or narrow, solid-stream jets for maximum reach.

Foam hand lines, of course, are limited to their capacity for combatting large flammable fuel fire areas. Large oil storage tanks have foam makers, permanently mounted near the top of the tank. In case of fire, foam solution is supplied to the foam makers through pipe lines leading back to a safe distance where heat will not prevent necessary operations. Portable foam towers also provide a means of applying foam to a large tank. A high-capacity foam maker is connected to a long riser pipe terminating in a gooseneck outlet which can be hung over the explosion-opened top of the burning tank. Specialized equipment, like the foam towers, and large stocks of foam concentrates are normally provided by the refinery or operator of the fuel storage facility and not the municipality involved.

Ordinary water sprinkler heads have been modified for foam use by adding a short barrel-shaped attachment over the discharge jet. These are known as foam-water sprinklers and are installed in the manner of a sprinkler system in buildings where there are Class B fire hazards. In the event of exhaustion of the foam concentrate supply to the foam-water sprinkler system, they operate like regular sprinklers with water and will do well at protecting the exposures even though they may not be capable of extinguishing the burning Class B fire. Aircraft hangars are one place where these foam makers may be used. A similar device, the foam spray-fixed nozzle, is used where more Class B extinguishing capability is required. This device makes a better foam but it does not provide the degree of coverage that a sprinkler head does and, therefore, its exposure protection capability is lessened.

A few foam applications involving critical conditions sometimes require foams of certain characteristics which cannot be obtained with the ordinary air-aspirating type of foam-making device. In these instances, positive displacement rotary pumps are used in order to add precisely the desired amount of foam solution and air and then accomplish the desired high degree of mixing under pressure. This type of foam making may also be achieved by using foam solution from centrifugal pumps and adding compressed air to it. With either of these systems it is possible to generate the foam under pressure and conduct it through long pipelines or into the bottom of oil tanks. Such devices are also employed at airports to deal with large aircraft fires, where foaming capacities and requirements are critical to the saving of lives.

Foam characteristics

There are three physical properties of foams which are often used to describe foams as they are made by different foam makers or used for special applications. One property is foam expansion. It relates to the relative amounts of air and foam solution (water) contained in a foam. When 9 gallons of air are mixed into 1 gallon of foam solution to create 10 gallons of foam, the ratio of foam volume to solution volume is 10/1 (or 10 to 1) and the foam expansion is said to be 10. The higher the expansion value, the lighter the weight of a given volume of foam. (The expansion of a foam sample may be found by weighing a known volume.)

The degree to which the air and foam solution mixture is agitated determines the *stability* or *quality* of the foam applied to a fire. As more work or mechanical mixing energy is put into the foam through high pressure, high turbulence or other methods, the bubbles become much smaller and more uniformly distributed throughout the mass. The liquid drains very slowly from a well-made foam mass and thus it is said to be *stable*. It is by virtue of the water in the foam that it resists heat and flame and retains proper fluidity. After the water has dropped out of the foam, it is left dry and rigid and with a minimum of fire fighting capability. A standardized method is used to determine this property. A foam sample is collected and the rate at which the water comes to the bottom is measured. The time in minutes required for 25 percent of the total water contained to drain out is called the *drainage time* of the foam; the higher the drainage time, the higher is the foam's *stability*.

Percentage of foam concentrate

The third important property of foam concerns the percentage of foam concentrate in the water supply to the foam-maker. Measuring this concentration is necessary to check on the operation of the proportioning system. Too low a concentration of the foam concentrate will result in weak, poor-quality foams, while too rich a concentration will be wasteful of a limited available supply—as well as uneconomical.

In today's petroleum fuel-oriented society, air foam has become an important tool of modern fire protection. The increasing frequency of fire emergencies involving flammable liquids has made it imperative that the up-to-date fire officer have foam fire fighting facilities at his command.

Air foam is acknowledged to be the only *permanent* fire extinguishing agent for flammable liquid fires. It allows the fire fighter to work his fire line forward, consolidating his gains and finally dealing with fuel spreads which can't be permanently extinguished by any other material—and this includes water spray or fog.

Foam may be used for other purposes than extinguishing flammable liquid fires. Its whiteness and its capability of adhering to vertical surfaces make it an exposure-protecting agent with some lasting qualities. It may be used to *protect* flammable liquids from igniting by spreading it over the surface *before* vapor ignition has occurred. At airports it may be used as a water carrier to spread a film of foam-water over an aircraft landing runway so that sparks cannot be struck from metal parts of an aircraft landing on it with its wheels up in the fuselage.

Air foam is easily removed from surfaces and materials over which it has been spread. Unlike the old chemical foam, it leaves very little residue. (when completely dry, air foam "skeleton bubble masses" may be blown off with an air current.) It may easily be washed off with water sprays and even though its odor is not particularly pleasant, foam does not damage most materials or react with them.

Aqueous film-forming foam

This class of foam concentrates for generating air foams is comparatively new. It was discovered by the author and his associates in 1962 while searching for new, more efficient foaming agents. Water solutions of fluorinated compounds of the following type chemical structure possess unique surface and interfacial characteristics when they are properly spread over flammable fuels:

$$[C_8F_{17}SO_2NH(CH_2)_3N(CH_3)_3]I$$

Even though these water solutions of fluorochemicals are heavier in density than flammable fuels, they will float in very thin layers over the exposed surface, restricting the evolution of a flammable concentration of vapors from materials such as gasoline. This occurs because of the capability of these compounds to "line up" or "orient" in water at the interface with a fuel where the "surface skin forces" of the fuel are in action. (A similar action occurs in the familiar floating of a thin steel razor blade on water. The "skin" of the water at the interface with the metal supports the area of the heavier razor blade.)

When air foam is generated with these chemical compounds in a water solution, the foam first acts in the same water-spreading and vapor-excluding fashion as other foams. But any water that drains from the foam bubbles or that results from foam breakdown, slides out from the foam mass, and quickly spreads over the flammable fuel. It aids in the extinguishing process, and is not wasted by sinking below the burning or freshly extinguished fuel surface. Fire fighting efficiencies of two to four times that of other foams are achieved with this "floating water" action on fuels. Of course, as long as a reservoir of foam exists on the fuel surface, water drains out and continues to vaporproof the flammable fuel.

The formation of aqueous film-forming foam concentrates is somewhat complex but in general these concentrates are water solutions of:

1. Active fluorochemicals which exhibit the necessary surface tension

lowering and orienting characteristics in conjunction with good foaming properties.

2. Foam bubble stabilizers which consist of water "thickeners," or agents which give longer life to the foam bubble wall.

In operating on Class B fires, the aqueous film-forming foams are our fastest and most efficient foam fire fighting agents, judged on a basis of the gallons of solution necessary to extinguish a number of square feet of burning fuel surface. These foams are comparatively short-lived, however, in contrast to the much thicker and more viscous protein foams or the very tenacious and stiff chemical foams. The film of vapor-suppressing water solution which they spread on the surface of extinguished fuel is very thin but will "heal" itself when disturbed mechanically. It is the only foaming agent which exhibits this property.

The fuel fire extinguishing efficiencies of aqueous film-forming foams do not seem to be critically dependent on the expansion of the foams as in the case with other foaming agents. This operates in favor of poorly designed foam-making devices or substandard performance of equipment in a fire emergency.

The storage of the concentrates of this class of foaming agents is similar to that of the synthetic foam concentrates. Because all constituents in the formulation of aqueous film-forming concentrates are finished synthetic compounds which do not decompose or change with time, the shelf life of the liquid is practically indefinite.

An important factor to keep in mind is the fact that they are basically detergent in action and are powerful wetting agents. This means that they are capable of removing protective coatings of grease or oil from iron surfaces, promoting the rusting type of corrosion.

Dry chemicals

Nontoxic, efficient, flame-quenching chemicals are difficult to find. Because of the similarity of the process of burning combustibles to the process of sustaining human life by breathing and using oxygen, most fire extinguishing chemicals that will halt burning will also damage the human body to some extent. Dry chemical extinguishing agents are a class of materials which are contradictions of this principle. They are noninjurious in ordinary fire use amounts, but yet they are our most effective and powerful chemical extinguishants for flames of all types.

There are three principal classes of dry chemical fire extinguishing agents. These are somewhat subdivided and their uses are shown in Table 9.

Dry chemicals are essentially free-flowing powders consisting of dry crystals suitably ground to a very small particle size and treated with

Table 9 Classes of Dry Chemical Extinguishing Agents

Type and Chemical Material	Fire Class Use
Ordinary sodium bicarbonate (plus 50, etc.)	B, C
Compatible sodium bicarbonate (CDC, etc.)	B (with foam), C
Ordinary potassium bicarbonate (Purple-K,etc.)	B, C
Compatible potassium bicarbonate (Purple-K)	B (with foam), C
Multipurpose monammonium phosphate (Foray, etc.)	A, B (with foam), C

certain materials to make them resist moisture or caking. The added materials also confer properties for sliding past each particle of the powder so that the dry crystals flow through pipes and out of the containers similar to the way water does.

The fine powders are dispensed from an extinguisher by dispersing them in a turbulent current of gas, such as carbon dioxide or dry air or nitrogen. There are two ways of accomplishing this. In the cartridge-type dry chemical extinguisher, a separate gas bottle or cartridge of carbon dioxide is secured to the side of the dry chemical container. This gas bottle is closed with a puncturable disk and may be removed for inspection and weighing to assure full contents and freedom from leakage. When operation of the device is desired, a piercing shaft is thrown and the gas is directed into the dry chemical container. Opening the hose valve nozzle then directs the dry chemical (with some pressurizing gas) at the base of the flames. Figure 12 illustrates this type of extinguisher.

In the *pressurized* (or *prepressurized*) type of dry chemical extinguisher, dry gas is pumped into the main dry chemical container to set a pressure (120 psi, and in some designs, 300 psi). The extinguisher is then ready for use. Any gas leakage during storage is shown by a drop

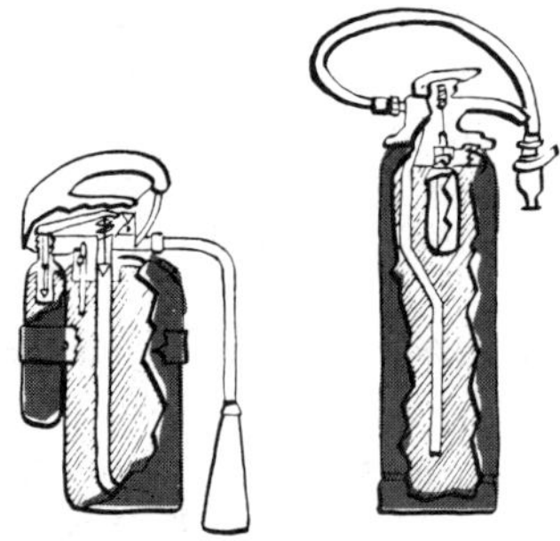

Figure 12. Dry chemical extinguisher with pressurized gas cartridge at side of cylinder.

Figure 13. Pressurized type of dry chemical extinguisher.

in pressure reading on the gage. Figure 13 illustrates this type of dry chemical extinguisher design.

Dry chemical extinguishing equipment is commercially obtainable in sizes from 2½ to 4000 pounds. Dry chemicals have found their most useful employment in the extinguishment of flammable liquid fires, high-pressure combustible gas and liquefied petroleum gas fires. Here their action in suddenly quelling flames and halting flame propagation is immediately evident. However, since they are good extinguishers of all types of flame, they may be used for surface flame fires on all combustibles. Multipurpose monoammonium phosphate dry chemical is especially useful for fires on the surface of Class A combustibles, such as wood and paper.

Complete suppression required

Since dry chemicals are basically flame-quenching agents in function, they do not achieve permanent fire extinguishment unless they have attained complete suppression of all reignition sources by virtue of almost simultaneous surface flame coverage. This is not difficult to do in many fire situations, since the powder issues in large clouds and spreads over large areas quickly upon discharge from the nozzle. In the case of the multipurpose type of dry chemical used on ordinary Class A combustibles, a glassy coating of decomposed frothy phosphate compound is left on the extinguished wood or paper. This coating resists reignition and an increased extinguishing efficiency on Class A materials is thereby gained. It must be remembered that deep-seated fires in Class A combustibles are not extinguished by multipurpose phosphate powders since no cooling or penetrating qualities are shown by the powder.

A very detrimental reaction occurs when multipurpose ammonium phosphate powder is mixed with bicarbonate powders. Free ammonia is produced, and a solid cake or crystalline material will be formed in the container by this mixing.

The fire extinguishing mechanism of the bicarbonate powders has been explained in the section "Basic Methods of Extinguishing Fires," where the *chemical free radical quenching* mechanism is explained in some detail. Potassium bicarbonate accomplishes this chemical fire extinguishment with twice the efficiency of equal weights of sodium bicarbonate because of its lower temperature of decomposition and quicker reactivity to yield inert water vapor, thus halting the combustion process. Small quantities of nonluminous flame-producing potassium bicarbonate powder quickly halt the propagation of flames of hydrogen gas, a material that requires huge, high-velocity discharges of bicarbonate for fire control, during which large yellow clouds of flame blind the fire fighter.

Dry chemicals leave a residue where they have been used. Since this residue becomes electrically conductive by absorption of water vapor, the powder can cause a serious breakdown of electrical or electronic equipment. It should be used only as a last resort for fires in such areas.

The residues of dry chemicals can be easily washed away with water or, in some cases, vacuum cleaning will remove them quite well.

Carbon dioxide

Carbon dioxide (chemical formula CO_2) is normally encountered as a colorless, tasteless, odorless gas. It is also commonly seen as a solid material called "dry ice" in blocks, or "snow" when in flake form. The foamy head on a glass of beer and the bubbles in soft drinks or champagne are all carbon dioxide gas in action.

The fire extinguishing action of carbon dioxide is dependent on its ability to displace and temporarily dilute the oxygen-containing air around a burning material and thus starve or suffocate the fire. This action is also described as blanketing or smothering. It can be readily understood that the successful surrounding of a fire by a cloud of oxygen-excluding gas depends a great deal on the combustion conditions. When carbon dioxide is discharged from an extinguisher, a certain amount of snow forms in the discharge cloud. As the snow turns to gas, it causes some cooling by heat absorption exactly in the manner of water turning to steam. The cooling action also contributes to a small degree to the extinguishing action.

Carbon dioxide is not a very efficient fire extinguishing agent because it takes more pounds of material than other Class B fire extinguishing agents. However, it remains in usage because of many desirable properties. It is gaseous, leaves no residue, is low in cost, nontoxic, easily compressed into small containers, is a nonconductor of electricity, and is noncorrosive. It has an uncommon property which allows it to go directly from a solid to a gas and never exist as a liquid. It does not contaminate and can do no damage to materials. These properties make it ideal for use on delicate machinery, moving mechanisms and electronic or electrical equipment. One caution is suggested, however: carbon dioxide discharge will chill electronic components and may cause water condensation (sweating) which must be removed in some manner.

Carbon dioxide's largest application is probably for Class C fires where electrical voltage is present. It is capable of extinguishing Class B fires, but here the more efficient dry chemical agents have replaced CO_2 as first choice, except where the dry chemical residue cannot be tolerated. Carbon dioxide is not effective on Class A fires, except in enclosures where inert atmospheres may be produced. It is not effective on Class D combustible metal fires and vigorous reactions may occur in some cases, so it should not be used on such fires.

Carbon dioxide is not toxic or poisonous in the normal sense of the word, but it does cause human suffocation at high concentrations (9 percent upward). Discharge of portable extinguishers will rarely build up such concentration except in closed areas. The biggest hazard to life is found in large-capacity CO_2 systems for total flooding of rooms or vaults.

Carbon dioxide is applied from a wide variety of devices ranging from 2-pound-capacity portable extinguishers up to units which have capacities of several tons. Sizes up to 20 pounds are portable; 50, 75 and 100-pound sizes are mounted on wheels. Pressures of 900 psi are usual inside cylinders. Hydrostatic pressure tests must be made on the containers at least every 12 years. Routine maintenance requires weighing semiannually to determine if any gas leakage has occurred.

Large-capacity fixed CO_2 systems are used to protect industrial hazards either by direct application or by total flooding of confined spaces. In the latter, no attempt is made to apply the CO_2 to the burning area. Sufficient CO_2 is discharged into the enclosure to inert it completely, thus extinguishing the fire wherever it may be. Low-pressure carbon dioxide systems are used for large installed units. The CO_2 is kept in mechanically refrigerated storage tanks, which permits lower storage pressure and simplified discharge piping. Low-pressure units are also mounted on vehicles to serve as aircraft fire fighting and rescue trucks at airports.

Carbon dioxide extinguishers should have inspection laboratories' approval or meet federal government specifications for portables and for wheeled units.

Combustible metal fire extinguishers

The combustible metals such as magnesium, sodium, etc., form the newest class of fires, Class D. They have been given this separate classification because these fires are very difficult to extinguish and require special materials for doing the job. Unlike other classes of fires, no one Class D agent will extinguish all types of metal fires and the Class D agents are restricted almost to use for one type of metal fire. In the following paragraphs the most common agents and their particular uses will be discussed.

Met-L-X is the trade name for a powder composed of common salt

(NaCl) with additives to promote easy flow, moisture resistance and high-temperature fusing. Application is made from extinguishers which appear and are operated like regular dry chemical extinguishers. However, the method of application to a fire is entirely different. In order to be effective, thick layers of the agent must be built up over the burning metal to cut off the supply of oxygen from the air. If the fire is approached using the typical high-velocity discharge of the dry chemical extinguisher, there is great danger of blasting molten metal and sparks around the vicinity, thus intensifying the fire. Throttling the powder nozzle by only partially opening it and causing a gentle stream of the powdered agent to drop onto the fire area avoids this blasting effect. As long as the metal remains hot, there exists the possibility of reignition and the fire-agent pile of residue must be carefully monitored until it is known to be thoroughly cooled down. It should be realized that a material such as this is really a first-aid agent and suitable only when the fire is small enough to be approached closely and treated intensively. Also, if the fire is burning on a vertical surface or above the ground, it becomes impossible to bury the fire in agent and its usefulness is limited. Met-L-X is approved by the Underwriters' Laboratories for fires of the following metals: magnesium, sodium, potassium, mixtures of sodium and potassium, zirconium, uranium, aluminum and titanium.

G-1 is a trade name for another powdered Class D fire fighting agent. It is a mixture of graphite and an organic phosphate which like Met-L-X is inert and can be used to cover a burning metal fire. This material is not applied from extinguishers, but instead is poured on the surface of the fire by a shovel or scoop or from a tube. It is subject to the same application limitations as Met-L-X. It has been approved for use on dry magnesium materials. It has also been found to be effective on the following metal fires: sodium, potassium, lithium, titanium, thorium, hafnium, uranium, and plutonium.

Lith-X is a trade name for a graphite-base powder suitable for discharge from a dry chemical type extinguisher. As the name implies, it is especially suitable for lithium fires. It is also satisfactory on magnesium, zirconium, and sodium.

Metal fire extinguishing agents which are liquids can overcome some of the application problems of the powders and have been found satisfactory in many fire cases. TMB (trimethoxyboroxine), developed by the United States Navy, is a liquid agent for magnesium metal fires. It is carried on aircraft fire fighting and rescue vehicles at all U. S. Navy air activities. The liquid TMB stream discharge from a 2½-gallon extinguisher makes it possible to reach otherwise inaccessible burning magnesium areas and parts such as in aircraft engine compartments. The material also has the property of inerting the burning of magnesium vapor at the metal (characterized by the intense white light) so it can be cooled with water without causing explosions. Being able to use water to cool the mass of metal greatly extends the effectiveness of the small amounts of agent available from portable extinguishers. TMB liquid is flammable and burns with a quiet green flame when first applied to a fire but is self-extinguishing. This property makes some precaution necessary in handling the liquid but causes no problems in extinguishing metal fires. TMB is also used successfully on magnesium and titanium fires.

Water on some combustible metals

Water, when properly used, can be an extinguishing agent for some combustible metals, but with others it should never be used. Magnesium is one metal on which water can be properly used, but the fire chief can never be certain before he applies the water to a magnesium fire whether it is going to be a case of proper usage. If the fire goes out, it was proper, but if the fire only gets worse, then it will be said to have not been properly used. In general, the degree of success of water on magnesium fires depends on the ratio of amount of water to amount of burning metal. A large amount of water quickly applied can cool and subdue the metal with but perhaps a single burst of "fireworks." An amount of water below a critical, but unknown beforehand, value will only intensify the fire and explosions may spread the fire over a big area, creating an even greater hazard to fire fighters and exposures. Any application of water to burning magnesium fires of any appreciable size should be made with the expectation that some kind of violent reaction is going to occur.

Water should not ordinarily be applied to fires in titanium, zirconium, or uranium. If the fire is small, however, and burning in small pieces or chips which can be carried in a shovel, they may be dumped and successfully drowned in a large volume of water. Personnel must wear protective clothing for this operation.

Water must never be used directly on fires involving the alkali metal group: lithium, sodium and potassium. To do so will only aggravate the fire situation without accomplishing any benefits.

CREDITS FOR ILLUSTRATIONS

Page 6—William Clark, Insurance Services Office
Page 9—William Clark, Insurance Services Office
Page 13—William Clark, Insurance Services Office
Page 19—William Clark, Insurance Services Office
Page 28—Miami, Fla., Fire Department
Page 31—Contra Costa County, Calif., Fire Department
Page 32—Racine, Wis., Fire Department
Page 34—Joseph R. Guyther, Jr.
Page 36—Birmingham, Ala., Fire Department
Page 40—Cincinnati, Ohio, Fire Department
Page 66—Charlotte, N.C. Fire Department
Page 68—New Haven, Conn., Fire Department
Page 70—Corning, N.Y. Fire Department
Page 71—Corning, N.Y. Fire Department
Page 73—Koster and Associates Architects
Page 74—New Haven, Conn., Fire Department
Page 75—Los Angeles County Fire Department
Page 77—New Haven, Conn., Fire Department
Page 78—Schaardt & Fullan, Architects
Page 80—Ogden, Utah, Fire Department
Page 83—Richard P. Sylvia
Page 84—Richard P. Sylvia
Page 85—Richard P. Sylvia
Page 86—Richard P. Sylvia
Page 88—Mine Safety Appliances Company
Page 89—Richard P. Sylvia
Page 91—New York Fire Department Photo Unit
Page 92—Richard P. Sylvia
Page 93—Richard P. Sylvia
Page 94—Richard P. Sylvia
Page 95—Richard P. Sylvia
Page 96—Richard P. Sylvia
Page 98—Los Angeles City Fire Department
Page 99—Gamewell Company (left)
Page 99—Norelco Division, North American Phillips (right)
Page 105—San Jose, Calif., Fire Department
Page 106—James F. Casey
Page 108—Motorola Communications & Electronics Inc.
Page 110—Gamewell Company
Page 112—Darien, Conn., Fire Department
Page 113—New York Fire Department Communications Bureau
Page 114—Richard P. Sylvia
Page 116—Milwaukee, Wis., Fire Department
Page 118—Tucson, Airz., Fire Department
Page 120—Tucson, Ariz., Fire Department
Page 121—Tucson, Ariz., Fire Department
Page 123—San Diego, Calif., Fire Department
Page 125—Richard P. Sylvia
Page 127—Richard P. Sylvia
Page 131—Richard P. Sylvia
Page 138—Richard P. Sylvia
Page 141—Richard P. Sylvia
Page 145—Richard P. Sylvia
Page 154—Richard P. Sylvia
Page 158—Joseph R. Guyther, Jr.
Page 164—The Mueller Company
Page 184—National Fire Hose Company
Page 187—National Fire Hose Company
Page 189—National Fire Hose Company
Page 191—Akron Brass Company
Page 193—NASA
Page 202—Fire Protection Training Division, Texas A&M University
Page 204—Cliff Dektar
Page 207—Hale Fire Pump Company
Page 208—Waterous Fire Pump Company
Page 210—Hale Fire Pump Company
Page 213—Waterous Fire Pump Company
Page 222—San Jose, Calif., Mercury
Page 224—New York Fire Department Photo Unit
Page 226—San Jose, Calif., Mercury
Page 232—Fire Protection Training Division, Texas A&M University
Page 233—Fire Protection Training Division, Texas A&M University
Page 234—Fire Protection Training Division, Texas A&M University
Page 235—Fire Protection Training Division, Texas A&M University
Page 237—David W. Hirsch
Page 242—David W. Hirsch
Page 244—James F. Casey
Page 247—Consolidated Edison Company
Page 248—Consolidated Edison Company
Page 250—James F. Casey
Page 254—James F. Casey
Page 260—Consolidated Edison Company
Page 263—Consolidated Edison Company
Page 264—Consolidated Edison Company
Page 271—Robert T. Burns
Page 272—Robert T. Burns
Page 273—Robert T. Burns
Page 274—Chet Born, San Francisco, Calif., Fire Department
Page 284—New York Fire Department Photo Unit
Page 286—Milwaukee, Wis., Fire Department
Page 288—Colin A. Campbell
Page 289—Colin A. Campbell
Page 290—Collingswood, N.J., Fire Department
Page 292—Toronto, Ont., Fire Department
Page 295—Colin A. Campbell
Page 296—James F. Casey
Page 302—Mike Meadows

Page 320—Akron Brass Company
Page 321—Elkhart Brass Company
Page 327—Richard P. Sylvia
Page 330—Robert C. Bartosz
Page 331—Richard P. Sylvia
Page 332—Richard P. Sylvia
Page 337—Chet Born, San Francisco, Calif., Fire Department
Page 339—David W. Hirsch
Page 341—David W. Hirsch
Page 342—David W. Hirsch
Page 344—David W. Hirsch
Page 349—American LaFrance Fire Apparatus Company
Page 350—New Orleans, La., Fire Department
Page 355—New York Fire Department
Page 357—David W. Hirsch
Page 359—Maxim Motor Division
Page 360—Milwaukee, Wis., Fire Department
Page 364—Chicago, Ill., Fire Department
Page 365—Chicago, Ill., Fire Department Photo Unit
Page 367—Chicago, Ill., Fire Department Photo Unit
Page 368—Andrew Urban
Page 372—Mike Meadows
Page 375—San Clemente, Calif., Fire Department
Page 376—Mike Meadows
Page 380—Milwaukee, Wis., Fire Department
Page 384—Boston, Mass., Fire Department
Page 412—District of Columbia Fire Department
Page 413—Los Angeles City Fire Department
Page 414—District of Columbia Fire Department
Page 417—George Post (formerly of New York Fire Patrol)
Page 424—Harvey Eisner
Page 442—David W. Hirsch
Page 445—David W. Hirsch
Page 449—Gordon Draper
Page 450—Gordon Draper
Page 454—Gordon Draper
Page 457—Gordon Draper
Page 459—Chet Born, San Francisco, Calif., Fire Department
Page 466—Los Angeles County Fire Department
Page 469—David W. Hirsch
Page 472—David W. Hirsch
Page 476—David W. Hirsch
Page 481—David W. Hirsch
Page 484—David W. Hirsch
Page 500—Factory Mutual Engineering
Page 502—David W. Hirsch
Page 504—James F. Casey
Page 506—Elkhart Brass Company
Page 507—David W. Hirsch
Page 516—David W. Hirsch
Page 519—James F. Casey
Page 521—Factory Mutual Engineering
Page 524—David W. Hirsch
Page 528—Automatic Electric Company
Page 542—Dan McCarthy
Page 544—Public Education Office, National Fire Prevention & Control Administration
Page 545—Public Education Office, National Fire Prevention & Control Administration
Page 547—Public Education Office, National Fire Prevention & Control Administration
Page 548—Public Education Office, National Fire Prevention & Control Administration
Page 550—Glynn County, Ga., Fire Department
Page 553—Birmingham, Ala., Fire Department
Page 554—Miami, Fla., Fire Department
Page 557—Birmingham, Ala., Fire Department
Page 561—Houston, Texas, Fire Department
Page 566—Miami, Fla., Fire Department
Page 569—Michigan State University
Page 571—Mike Sheridan
Page 573—James F. Casey
Page 575—San Clemente, Calif., Fire Department
Page 576—San Clemente, Calif., Fire Department
Page 578—Richard P. Sylvia
Page 580—Los Angeles City Fire Department
Page 591—Walter M. Haessler, The Fyr-Fyter Co.
Page 613—Walter M. Haessler, The Fyr-Fyter Co.
Page 624—Akron Brass Company

Acknowledgement is made of the help of Gordon Draper, presentation editor of Fire Engineering, in preparing the many pieces of art used in this edition.

INDEX